Under the editorship of
WAYNE C. MINNICK
The Florida State University

Methods of Research in Communication

Edited by

PHILIP EMMERT
Case Western Reserve University

and

WILLIAM D. BROOKS
Purdue University

HOUGHTON MIFFLIN COMPANY · BOSTON
New York · Atlanta · Geneva, Ill. · Dallas · Palo Alto

11716

Contents

Part Three

RESEARCH TECHNOLOGIES

Preface

This is an age of science, an age of inquiry into man's behavior and his relationship with his environment. Though earlier civilizations used the scientific method to study the natural order, only recently has it been used to study the social order and human behavior. As Zajonc has pointed out, "Social Psychology is almost entirely the product of this century and of this generation. Social psychologists credited with the crucial developments in the field are still alive. More than ninety percent of all social psychological research has been carried out during the last twenty years, and most of it during the last ten."[1] The same is true of experimental research in communication. From a period of trial-and-error exploration, the study of human communication has steadily grown in precision and sophistication. This book was written to facilitate that development.

One purpose of this book is to help students acquire the knowledge and skills to design and conduct experimental research. Information especially relevant to communication research is needed in at least three major areas: (1) research designs and settings, (2) research methodologies and instruments, and (3) research technologies. Accordingly, the book is organized around these three topics.

Another purpose is to acquaint potential researchers with the various methods and instruments available. Most researchers in communication are competent only in the methods they habitually use; if they are not familiar with an instrument, they tend to ignore it or to construct a new one. Cattell, discussing the limitation of researchers' knowledge, has observed that "few psychologists move much beyond their graduate education."[2] The statement is no less true of many doing research in communication. But the researcher who would make careful comparisons with previous research and develop sound strategies of his own needs to be aware of the tools of the trade. Consequently, this book brings together selected instruments, methodologies, and technologies that have, or promise to have, wide use and validity in communication research. Each is fully explained, its strengths and weaknesses identified, and its applications noted.

Still another purpose of this book is to suggest new areas of research. Each contributor identifies problems to be studied or new modes of studying problems already identified but yet to be solved. New procedures, technologies, and instruments have reciprocal and positive effects on each

[1] R. B. Zajonc, *Social psychology: An experimental approach* (Belmont, Cal.: Wadsworth, 1966), pp. 2–3.
[2] R. B. Cattell (Ed.), *Handbook of multivariate experimental psychology* (Chicago: Rand McNally, 1966), p. 3.

other. Today's scientific quest is, in fact, a search for procedures and instruments that will allow new explanatory concepts, principles, and theories to be tested.

The chapters in *Methods of Research in Communication* differ in range and level of difficulty. Even so, we have attempted to give the book unity and to prevent it from becoming a collection of unrelated articles. We have tried to integrate chapters and insert cross-references, and to arrange the sections and chapters in a logical sequence.

Part One, Research Design and Setting, includes four chapters. Chapter 1 is concerned with the basic design considerations and common requirements for any experimental study. The concepts and principles presented are related to the bivariate methods frequently used in communication research today. Chapter 2 introduces multivariate research design, identifies its fundamental characteristics, and shows its application to the study of communication. The nature of interacting phenomena, the fallibility of the theory of unitary causality, and the danger of manipulation contaminating the phenomena under study make it necessary that communication researchers become sophisticated in the use of multivariate research methods. Chapters 3 and 4 are concerned with two research settings: the laboratory and the field. The laboratory environment is conducive to better manipulatory control, and the field makes possible the study of behavior in its natural setting.

The chapters in Part Two, Research Methods and Instruments, describe a number of methodologies for communication research, including Q-sort technique, content analysis, rating scales, nonverbal analysis, and interaction analysis. These methods of measurement are not simply theories but guides to the direction research can take in any given study. It should be pointed out that although we commonly think of a methodology as a measuring *instrument,* it is not. Semantic differentiation, for example, is a *method* of constructing an instrument; it is not a tool of measurement. The same can be said of attitude scales. The emphasis, then, in Part Two is on methodologies that can be used to develop measuring instruments for use in communication research.

Part Three, Research Technologies, includes chapters on the techniques of psychophysiological measurement, the place of computers in communication research, and methods of information storage and retrieval. This section of the book deals with the more technical aspects of measurement and discusses a great deal of the new technology which has grown out of the physical and biological sciences.

The contributors were selected because of their special competence in the areas covered by the chapters. In most instances, it would have been difficult to find a better authority in communication research to write the chapter. In every case, the contributor was the first and only person invited to do the job. The willingness with which all of them accepted the task indicates their concern for improving research in communication.

Preparing this book has been a long and arduous task, but the editors and authors will consider the effort worthwhile if it results in increasingly rigorous research into communication phenomena. We hope this book will give students the background they need to conduct original research and to evaluate critically research already completed. If our hopes seem great, so does the challenge at hand.

PHILIP EMMERT
WILLIAM D. BROOKS

Methods of Research
in Communication

Part One

RESEARCH DESIGN
AND SETTING

Perspectives on
Communication Research

WILLIAM D. BROOKS

Man is continually asking questions and seeking answers to them. One way of seeking answers is the scientific method, at the heart of which is observation. An incidental observation motivates the scientist to ask questions about a phenomenon, and then he must make further observations to find answers. A physicist observes the physical properties, changes, and reactions of matter to solve his problem; a behavioral scientist, whether psychologist or communication researcher, observes behavior — what organisms do and say.

The behavioral researcher studying communication works like any other scientist. He gathers facts about communication behavior, verifies his data, and subjects his interpretations to rigorous tests. The business of the behavioral scientist in communication is to predict and explain human communicative behavior. The broad, major questions he seeks to answer are these: Why do people communicate as they do? How can certain results of communicative events be explained? How can the behavioral scientist help individuals communicate more effectively? How can one modify communicative behavior by training? To gain insight into these questions, the communication scientist, like any other scientist, has to make observations. He observes casually bits of communicative behavior as they occur about him, and he observes purposively communicative behavior in the laboratory with refined instruments under highly controlled conditions.

Not only does the behavioral scientist make observations; he also makes statements about the objects and events he observes — *protocol statements* as they are called. He must be able to make unambiguous statements and to distinguish between the language of scientists and the less precise language of common daily use.

The language of scientists aims at a goal of high intra- and inter-subjective consistency: that the same objects or events should be described in the same way by different scientists and by the same scientists at different times. Highly consistent interexperimenter language must be used in describing, analyzing, and classifying communicative behavior. One method of reducing vagueness and inconsistency is defining particular terms operationally — specifying the rules that govern their use and identifying the nonverbal behaviors (operations) that accompany them. By stating its operations, the scientist attempts to communicate the "meaning" of a term while at the same time providing a means of determining interscientist reliability — *i.e.,* he observes the resulting nonverbal behavior to find out whether or not the physical conditions accompanying the prescribed use of the term are there. The behavior that precedes an operational definition must be the same as the behavior the statement elicits in a replicating scientist. Operational definitions are discussed more fully in Chapter 1 (pp. 30–41).

THE ROLE OF THEORY IN SCIENCE

What is theory? Where do theories come from? Why is theory important to behavioral research? Theory is important to the behavioral scientist because it directs him to the right questions to ask and methods to use to acquire data which will answer his questions. He cannot observe the entire world; he must select phenomena to be observed. Behind the intelligent selection of phenomena lies a theory.

Theory is also important to the scientist because it integrates data which otherwise would remain mere collections of facts. Thus, scientific study depends directly on the quality of theory or conceptualization that gives it direction and focus. Von Bertalanffy (1962) has expressed clearly the important relationship between theory and experiment:

> Theoretical and experimental science are necessary complements of one another. A systematic science can only be constructed by their mutual cooperation. . . . The ideal of science without hypothesis is quite justified if it means the rejection of superfluous speculations, but it is a mere phantom if it intends to suggest that any science is possible without a framework of theoretical concepts [p. 26].

Another characteristic and function of scientific theory is that it establishes certain expectations; the theory's set of assumptions *directs* one to perform particular acts and to be ready to observe particular consequences of these acts. This anticipatory function of theory is often labeled *prediction*. Predictions can be made only in terms of given relationships and occurrences of specified events. Therefore, theory *instructs, i.e.,* it specifies the conditions under which the prediction can be hypothesized. When the scientist tests a theory and the predicted consequence does not occur, he may doubt the theory or wonder whether he has adequately applied the theory's instructions and definitions. If he has, he must then revise the theory.

THE NATURE OF AN EXPERIMENT

The relationship between theory and experimentation has already been explained. Now an explanation of what an experiment is seems in order as grounding for other chapters of this book. Some researchers, trained in classical, bivariate, dependent-independent variable methods, hesitate to call anything an experiment which takes place outside the laboratory. Some researchers say that manipulative control is the identifying characteristic of an experiment, but as Cattell (1966) has pointed out, such a definition ignores astronomy as an experimental science. Cattell suggests a definition of "experiment" that is more accurate and useful: "An experiment is a recording of observations, quantitative or qualitative, made by defined and recorded operations and in defined conditions, followed by examination of the data by appropriate statistical and mathematical rules, for the existence of significant relationships [p. 20]." "Experiment" so defined includes observation and measurement of naturally occurring events as well as manipulated events in laboratories. This definition is rapidly gaining acceptance over the rigid and restrictive "brass instrument/laboratory" definition.

The Cattell definition allows for considerable difference among experiments. Six of the ways experiments may vary follow:

(1) *Number of observed variables.* The number of variables may range from two (bivariate) to any number (multivariate).

(2) *Presence or absence of manipulation.* The experimenter may or may not produce changes in the value of one or more variables and observe the subsequent changes in values for another variable or variables.

(3) *Degree of control of unmeasured variables.* Control of unmeasured variables may range from holding them constant to allowing their values to change as they will.

(4) *Choice of variables.* Variables may be selected to be studied or the research design may be trying to catch as many variables as possible.

(5) *Representativeness of distribution population.* Sometimes the samples are selected from extremes in the population; at other times a random sample representative of all the subjects in a population may be drawn.

(6) *Presence or absence of a known time sequence between measurements.* The value of one variable may be measured later than that of another variable, or variables may be measured simultaneously.

EXPERIMENTER EFFECT

Although the results of studies on experimenter effect indicate that there are important implications in how one conducts research, most of the literature reporting experimental research in communication shows an alarming absence of attention to this source of error. When one realizes that almost all of what the behavioral scientists have learned about human communication has been learned within the context of experimenter-subject interaction, it is clear that experimenter effect is a problem of great concern. The results of several experiments in the past few years clearly show that different experimenters obtain from comparable subjects significantly different responses (see Rosenthal [1966] for a comprehensive review of this research).

Experimenter effects are of two different types: (1) effects influencing subjects' behavior in the experiment and (2) effects on the data that are caused by the experimenter's behavior alone.

The *biosocial characteristics* of experimenters are one source of influence on subjects. Researchers have noted the effect of the experimenter's sex, age, and race on subjects in an experiment.

A second source of experimenter influence is *psychosocial attributes:* the anxiety level of the experimenter, the experimenter's need for approval, and the experimenter's hostility, authoritarianism, dominance, and warmth.

A third general source of experimenter effects is *situational factors.* Researchers have found that acquaintanceship between experimenter and subjects affects subjects' responses. The degree of experience or expertise the experimenter shows in conducting the experiment also seems to be influential.

Experimenter modeling, a fourth type of experimenter effect, is defined as the experimenter demonstrating the task he sets for his subjects. This kind of experimenter effect has been studied in the interviewing situation and in laboratory experiments.

A final experimenter effect on subjects' responses is *experimenter expectancy.* Of course any experiment reflects certain experimenter expectancies. The experimenter chooses dependent and independent variables, experimental design, and procedures on the basis of expected relationships. However, experimenter expectancy becomes dangerous when it affects the responses of subjects; when the subject knows what the experimenter wants, naturally he will try to please him. Expectancy effects have been noted in survey research, clinical psychology, experimental psychology, and, of course, in experiments specifically designed to test the hypothesis that experimenter expectancies affect research results.

The second general type of experimenter effect is errors wholly within the behavior of the experimenter. One source of influence in experimental studies is *experimenter error in observation.* Several researchers have documented and described its history in communication research. Moreover, they have revealed that experimenter error in observation, although unintentional, is not random. The discovery and subsequent verifying observation of "*N* rays" by famous scientists was later shown to be a colossal compounded observer error; further, as the error became generally known, "*N* rays" were no longer observed! Observers have made errors in counting blood cells, reading dials, noting interactions in psychotherapy sessions, transcribing data, and performing other observations. Obviously, observer bias and error can significantly influence the outcomes of experimental studies.

A second kind of experimenter effect not related to subjects' responses is *incorrect interpretation of the data.* Different experimenters often interpret identical observations differently. Some data are more easily interpreted in several ways than others. For example, data produced by observing and counting large objects can be interpreted with more confidence than data related to psychological states. And there seems to be another subtler cause of interpretation error; a given theoretical framework from which the experimenter operates may affect his perceptual process so that he interprets his observations to be consistent with his theory.

A third type of experimenter error is *intentionally fabricating data*. This probably happens rarely, but it must be included in the listing of possible experimenter effects.

There are ways of controlling experimenter effects. One is simple *awareness* that experimenter effects are likely. *Mechanical apprehenders and recorders* may be used to reduce errors in observation. Errors in interpreting data are less dangerous when the *data is public* than when it is not. Errors in interpretation are most serious when an investigator keeps data or the correct interpretation of data out of public scrutiny. In the case of intentional error control is extremely difficult, but when such error is discovered the sanctions are severe. Generally, frauds are neither overlooked nor quickly forgiven.

Among the possible strategies that may be used to control all types of experimenter effects are: (1) increasing the number of experimenters in order to randomize expectancies, increase generality of results, and permit statistical correlation of expectancy effects; (2) observing the behavior of experimenters in order to standardize it; (3) analyzing experiments for order effects; (4) developing selection and training procedures in order to predict expectancy effects; (5) maintaining blind contact by avoiding feedback from the principal investigator or from the subjects; (6) minimizing experimenter-subject contact by issuing instructions to subjects that are written, tape-recorded, filmed, or televised; (7) employing expectancy control groups. (See Chapters 19, 20, 21, 22, and 23 of Rosenthal [1966] for detailed discussions of these control techniques.)

The communication researcher obviously should bear in mind these tools and strategies for controlling experimenter effects in every phase of his work, from his first casual observation to formulating his theory and forming and testing his hypothesis. It is easy to see how excitement and fervor about a project can dull awareness of experimenter effect. But it is also easy to see that it must not be allowed to, if the results of an experiment are to be valid, reliable — and scientific.

References and Selected Readings

Benney, M., Riesman, D., and Star, S. A. Age and sex in the interview. *American Journal of Sociology*, 1956, **62**, 143–152.

von Bertalanffy, L. *Modern theories of development*. New York: Harper & Bros., 1962.

Cattell, R. B. (Ed.) *Handbook of multivariate experimental psychology.* Chicago: Rand McNally, 1966.

Cleveland, S. The relationship between examiner anxiety and subjects' Rorschach scores. *Microfilm Abstracts,* 1951, **11,** 415–416.

Crowne, D. P., and Marlowe, D. *The approval motive.* New York: John Wiley, 1964.

Erhlich, J. S., and Riesman, D. Age and authority in the interview. *Public Opinion Quarterly,* 1961, **25,** 39–56.

Heller, K., and Goldstein, A. P. Client dependency and therapist expectancy as relationship maintaining variables in psychotherapy. *Journal of Consulting Psychology,* 1961, **25,** 371–375.

Hyman, H. H., Cobb, W. J., Feldman, J. J., Hart, C. W., and Stember, C. H. *Interviewing in social research.* Chicago: University of Chicago Press, 1954.

Kanfer, F. H., and Karas, S. C. Prior experimenter-subject interaction and verbal conditioning. *Psychological Reports,* 1959, **5,** 345–353.

Marcia, J. Hypothesis-making, need for social approval, and their effects on unconscious experimenter bias. Unpublished Master's thesis, Ohio State University, 1961.

Robinson, J., and Cohen, L. Individual bias in psychological reports. *Journal of Clinical Psychology,* 1954, **10,** 333–336.

Rosenthal, R. Experimenter modeling effects as determinants of subjects' responses. *Journal of Projective Techniques and Personality Assessment,* 1963, **27,** 467–471.

Rosenthal, R. *Experimenter effects in behavioral research.* New York: Appleton-Century-Crofts, 1966.

Rostand, J. *Error and deception in science.* New York: Basic Books, 1960.

Saranson, I. G., and Harmatz, N. G. Test anxiety and experimental conditions. *Journal of Personality and Social Psychology,* 1965, **1,** 499–505.

Saranson, S. B. The psychologist's behavior as an area of research. *Journal of Consulting Psychology,* 1951, **15,** 278–280.

Stanton, F., and Baker, K. H. Interviewer bias and the recall of incompletely learned materials. *Sociometry,* 1942, **5,** 123–134.

Stevenson, H. W., and Allen, S. Adult performance as a function of sex of experimenter and sex of subject. *Journal of Abnormal and Social Psychology,* 1964, **68,** 214–216.

Summers, G. F., and Hammonds, A. D. Toward a paradigm of respondent bias in survey research. Unpublished paper, University of Wisconsin, 1965.

Williams, J. A. Interviewer-respondent interaction: A study of bias in the information interview. *Sociometry,* 1964, **27,** 338–352.

Wilson, E. B. *An introduction to scientific research.* New York: McGraw-Hill, 1962.

Winkel, G. H., and Saranson, I. G. Subject, experimenter, and situational variables in research on anxiety. *Journal of Abnormal and Social Psychology,* 1964, **68,** 601–608.

Wyatt, D. F., and Campbell, D. T. A study of interviewer bias as related to interviewers' expectations and own opinions. *International Journal of Opinion and Attitude Research,* 1950, **4,** 77–83.

1

Basic Communication
Research Considerations

ROBERT J. KIBLER

The introduction to Part One initiated the notion of scientific research. Subsequent chapters will deal with various aspects and details of design and research methodologies in the scientific study of communication. This chapter is intended to bridge a number of the ideas presented in the introduction and some of the more comprehensive methodological treatments appearing in following chapters. The purpose of this chapter is twofold: (1) to provide an overview of the scientific investigation process in the study of communication and (2) to introduce selected key concepts, terms, and procedures in this process.

Obviously, this brief introductory chapter cannot be a comprehensive encyclopedia of all the terms, procedures, and particulars necessary for understanding scientific inquiry in communication. Moreover, it is unlikely that the brief treatment possible here will contribute measurably to many fields of study pertinent to scientific inquiry in communication which have been treated competently elsewhere, such as sampling procedures and problems (Stephan and McCarthy, 1958; Cochran, 1963), simple and complex experimental designs (Edwards, 1954; Federer, 1955; Cochran and Cox, 1957; Sidman, 1960; Campbell and Stanley, 1963; Kerlinger,

1964; Cattell, 1966; Peng, 1967; Cochran, 1968; Kirk, 1968), and statistical analyses (Lindquist, 1953; Siegel, 1956; Winer, 1962; Hays, 1963; Ferguson, 1966), to mention a few. In addition, this chapter is not intended to be a "cookbook" detailing step-by-step procedures for conducting scientific communication research. Such an effort would be pretentious, at best, in the space available here. Where a topic critical to scientific investigation in communication necessarily has been either omitted or considered briefly, interested readers are directed to appropriate detailed references and supplementary sources.

SCIENTIFIC INVESTIGATION

The so-called scientific method, discussed in detail in the previous essay, is a set of logical rules for determining the validity of assertions about observable events. Kerlinger (1964) has defined scientific research formally and completely as follows: *"Scientific research is systematic, controlled, empirical, and critical investigation of hypothetical propositions about the presumed relations among natural phenomena* [p. 13]." Those who study human communication use the scientific method, among other methods, in an effort to describe and explain man's observable communicative behavior, toward the end of compiling a reliable body of knowledge about human communicative behavior.

Scientific Method

The scientific method may be viewed as a "thinking tool"; it is a special systematic form of reflective thinking involving reason and observation. Facts are gathered purposefully and systematically through the scientific approach. Moreover, hypotheses are tested by systematically examining and assessing the observable evidence. As will be noted later (see Hypothetico-Deductive Method, pp. 12–13), the scientist moves back and forth between inductive and deductive processes when using the scientific approach.

The following discussion is based on Dewey's (1933) analysis of the stages involved in the problem-solving act, but it has been modified to include the scientific structure emphasized throughout this volume. First, the scientist will typically encounter some *obstacle,* barrier, or doubt which puzzles him. For example, he may observe an event which he does not understand and be curious about it.

Second, the scientist tries to locate and define his "felt difficulty" — he moves from an essentially "emotional" encounter with the obstacle to an "intellectual" encounter. During a period of perplexity, the scientist asks questions, reflects on previous experiences and information, makes observations, and gathers facts in order to formulate a precise *statement of the problem.* A statement of the problem is necessary for the scientist to continue his inquiry.

Next, the scientist formulates *hypotheses* to explain the facts he thinks are related to the difficulty. Hypotheses (discussed in detail on pp. 25–30) are conjectural statements which predict the relation of dependency between two or more variables. But clearly an hypothesis must propose a logical explanation for the specific problem under examination; otherwise, it is eliminated from further consideration.

Then the scientist deduces the *consequences* of his hypothesis, reasoning that if his hypothesis is true, certain consequences should follow. Previous information and experience may cause him to modify his original hypothesis or even the problem. For that matter, he may altogether abandon his original hypothesis.

The logically deduced consequences should be *observable* if the hypothesis is to be assessed empirically (see Hypothetico-Deductive Method, pp. 12–13). Accordingly, the scientist conducts appropriate empirical tests to determine whether the relation(s) predicted in the hypothesis occurs. Obviously, this step in the research process usually comes only after the scientist has recognized his problem and tried to state and explain it; otherwise, he is likely to be doing "something" without really knowing what or why. Such undirected and random activity cannot be labeled fairly as scientific investigation.

Subsequently, but not finally, the scientist draws a conclusion: he confirms or disconfirms his hypothesis on the basis of the empirical evidence of his research. This conclusion is an *inductive inference*. In the scientific approach to inquiry, hypotheses are established only as *tested probabilities* (*i.e.,* they possess a degree of probability), not assumed truth. Clearly, the cogency of the logic connecting each of the above phases in the process is of great importance in reasoning outcomes from the enterprise. Van Dalen (1966) summarized this concern as follows:

> The deduced consequences must be logically implied by the hypothesis, the test situations must adequately represent the essential factors expressed in the consequence, and the conclusions must be based on the factual evidence collected in the empirical tests [p. 157].

Finally — if anything is ever final in the inquiry process — the information resulting from the whole process is related or fed back to the initial problem, and the problem is modified or not according to the evidence produced.

Some additional comments on the scientific approach are in order. This sequence of phases in scientific inquiry is not an inflexible pattern imposed on all practicing scientists and beginning researchers. Dewey himself observed that the reflective thinking sequence was not necessarily fixed and inflexible. The sequence varies from individual to individual and problem to problem. A given phase is not always completed before the next is started. Moreover, the phases or steps may be undertaken out of order or even simultaneously. There may be a major emphasis on one phase of the process and limited interest in another phase. Dewey also recognized that some steps may be eliminated and others may need to be added for different types of problems. It is a process; the parts or phases are inter-dependent.

One should leave this section with the idea that the scientific method is a systematically reflective and reasoned approach to inquiry. Chapter 3 discusses applications of the scientific approach in the experimental, in-vestigational, and mixed model paradigms, so no additional comments on such applications are made here. The following remarks focus on the hypothetico-deductive method of the scientific approach and its importance in theory construction.

Hypothetico-Deductive Method

A consideration of the scientific approach is linked inevitably with what has been described as the *hypothetico-deductive method* of theory construc-tion. Bachrach (1965) identifies this system appropriately as a formal theoretical method of constructing theory with hypotheses. In this method scientists begin with an hypothesis and deduce from it consequences that can be observed in an experiment or in a natural setting. Marx and Hillix (1963) have emphasized that such hypotheses should be connected ade-quately in a logical system to permit their consequences to be deduced. Theorists relate the deductions to specified empirical observations which are to be made under the particular conditions stated for a given theorem. Through an experiment or observation in nature the validity of the empirical statements is determined. If the predicted observation is verified, the hypothesis is retained; if the predicted observation is not verified, the hypothesis is rejected or perhaps modified for subsequent consideration. Boring (1957) has indicated that verifying a predicted observation pro-duces these results: (1) the predicted observation is verified, and (2) the given hypothesis is strengthened. For a comprehensive theory of behavior constructed in a hypothetico-deductive framework, see Hull (1943, 1951). Readers interested in a more detailed examination of this method should examine the work of Tatsuoka and Tiedeman (1963) and Cattell (1966).

Some critics of the standard textbook treatment of the hypothetico-deductive method say justifiably that it misrepresents the scientific process of inquiry. Cattell (1966) has observed that this treatment overemphasizes the testing of a single isolated hypothesis, whereas the method actually in-volves a *process* — "what is truly a chain, or more exactly, a spiral [p. 14]" of hypotheses. Each link in the chain is checked against facts, and other properties are deduced and checked again, resulting in interrelated, well structured hypotheses. Cattell, among others (Boring, 1957; Marx and Hillix, 1963; Van Dalen, 1966; Wise, Nordberg, and Reitz, 1967), has noted that the research process probably begins with a "hunch" or a "guess"; this is the informal, creative, intuitive stage of the research effort. Ultimately, based on a logical system and through rigorous deduction, the scientist develops his guess into an hypothesis linked to observable consequences and subsequently tested experimentally; these activities are the formal stages of the hypothetico-deductive method.

Marx and Hillix (1963) distinguish similarly between *public* and *private* hypotheses. Private hypotheses are those the researcher is thinking about but has not expressed publicly. Public hypotheses are those stated by the researcher formally and publicly, typically in some published form. The formal, public hypotheses usually represent only the few reasonably formulated hypotheses of the many the investigator may be considering privately. When a researcher publishes an hypothesis (and perhaps concurrently or subsequently tests it experimentally), it is open to the public scrutiny of the scientific community. The public expression of an hypothesis permits other researchers to examine it critically and test it empirically. Obviously, the investigator offering the hypothesis may continue to reflect, both privately and publicly, about the formally expressed hypothesis.

Cattell (1966) has emphasized the process nature of scientific efforts in his description of scientific investigation as an *inductive-hypothetico-deductive-experimental-inductive* cycle. Those familiar with scientific investigation will know that there is substantial interplay among the various phases of the cycle. Clearly, it is important for communication researchers to understand the nature of the hypothetico-deductive method, but it is just as important that they understand that much intellectual, creative activity comes before and after this phase in the total process of scientific investigation. Among others, Bakan (1967), Aronson and Carlsmith (1968), and Polanyi (1968) have argued cogently for the systematic place of the investigator's insights, experience, and creativity in the scientific research enterprise.

The first part of this chapter summarized the scientific approach to inquiry. The next few sections will zero in on specific terms and ideas necessary for a general understanding of the process of scientific investigation.

CONCEPTS AND CONSTRUCTS

The word *concept* is currently fashionable and is used in a variety of ways by different people. To a layman, "concept" usually designates an idea or a thought, that is, the object of meaning when thinking. Obviously, such an explanation is vague and not very useful to scientists when conducting research. Those interested in communication research should develop a fundamental understanding of how some scholars have characterized the term and the role of concepts in the research process.

Concepts in Science

Brodbeck (1963) suggests that the use of words in typical speech behavior corresponds to the use of concepts in science, an observation at least partially accurate. At present, discussions of concepts in the social sciences appear to focus on the choice and definitions of terms (Gould and Kolb, 1964). English and English (1958) have defined the term "concept" as "anything one can think about that can be distinguished from other 'things' [p. 104]." In this definition, concepts are used to classify experiences, albeit grossly and imperfectly. For example, all researchers in speech communication may not agree on who is and who is not an "effective speaker," but undoubtedly, more researchers than not would agree to include in this class some speakers rather than others.

In psychology, a concept refers to a classification of stimuli having common characteristics. Typically, a concept is given a name or label, like "message" or "speaker." Bain (1964) asserts this position rather absolutely: "Nothing can be observed as a datum for science that cannot be named or categorized; hence all observations require symbols and concepts . . . [p. 77]." Objects or events may be among the stimuli so categorized. However, identifying a given stimulus or experiencing a given event does not necessarily result in the formulation of a concept; one *forms a concept* when one classifies persons, objects, events, or the like having common characteristics extending beyond the single person, object, or event. For example, the concept of "boulevard" is formed when one thinks of boulevard*s* one has observed, not when one thinks of only a single boulevard. Moreover, all stimuli are not concepts: a particular stimulus, such as a given message or a given boulevard, obviously is not a class of stimuli. DeCecco (1968) has noted that concepts can be differentiated by their distinguishing features (attributes), the particular variations in an attribute (attribute values), the number of attributes, and the dominance of attributes. Readers who want a detailed discussion of general types of concepts (*e.g.*, conjunctive, disjunctive, and rational) and how such classifications are learned should examine the work of Vinacke (1952), Bruner, Goodnow, and Austin (1956), or Guilford (1967).

Several years ago, Brodbeck (1957), among others, noted the observation of some critics of behavioral science that "definition, operational or otherwise, deprives science of the rich halo of meanings surrounding ordinary use [pp. 428–429]." These critics identified major differences between everyday concepts and those used by behavioral researchers in communication and other social sciences. Though physical objects like boulevards, tables, or cows may be conceptualized by listing the observable attributes of these objects (*e.g.*, shape, color, etc.), science takes the meaning of physical object concepts for granted. Scientific conceptualizing focuses rather on more abstract properties of physical objects and the terms which identify them. For example, we can observe a boulevard, a table, or a cow and judge what each is with minimal difficulty. This is not so easy to do for terms like "anxiety," "intelligence," and "learning." Scientists have relied on operationism (see pp. 31–33) for defining such terms. Scientific terms are not defined in isolation, as in a dictionary; they are defined by specifying the observable conditions under which a statement containing the term is true or false (Brodbeck, 1957). Some representative examples of scientific definition in different types of communication research may be found in the work of J. W. Bowers (1964), Miller and Hewgill (1966), Feather (1967), Liberman, Cooper, Shankwiler, and Studdert-Kennedy (1967), Barker, Kibler, and Geter (1968), and Sassenrath and Yonge (1968).

Behavioral scientists may formulate concepts to describe facts, events, relationships, and other particulars they observe. A concept in this sense represents "an abstraction formed by generalization from particulars [Kerlinger, 1964, p. 31]." This definition is valuable to the behavioral researcher in communication for several reasons. First, it emphasizes the logical process by which concepts are formed in science. For example, the term "imitation," a concept which concerns behavioral scientists, generalizes an abstraction from observing certain actions which copy other actions with reasonable precision.

A second reason for the importance of viewing a concept as an inductive generalization is the relationship the concept-forming process has to other logical operations associated with theory construction.[1] A set of concepts which are interrelated by theoretical and hypothetical propositions forms a *conceptual scheme*. When a scholar analyzes, specifies, clarifies, and interrelates key concepts he is engaged in a phase of constructing theory; but the simple analysis of concepts does not constitute theory as such, even though it may contribute information to a theoretic system. Merton (1957) has summarized the role of key concepts in theory building as follows:

> It is only when such concepts are interrelated in the form of a scheme that a theory begins to emerge. Concepts, then, constitute the definitions (or prescriptions) of what is to be observed; they are the variables between which empirical relationships are to be sought. When propositions are logically interrelated, a theory has been instituted [p. 89].

Kibler and Barker (1969) have pointed out that one of the high priority tasks facing communication scholars is defining the outlines of speech communication theories. Defining key concepts, as Merton and others (Brodbeck, 1957, 1963; Kaplan, 1964; Kerlinger, 1964; Rudner, 1966) suggest, will play an important role in the effort.

Kerlinger's definition of a concept is valuable to the behavioral researcher in communication for a third reason. It is a constant reminder that all concepts are formulated by man. Therefore some will be fallacious, and all may or may not be related to reality. A concept is nothing more than it appears to be.

Constructs

Different researchers define the meaning of *construct* in various ways. At a very basic level, one may say that constructs are universal terms char-

---

[1] The term *construct* (see pp. 15–17) may be more accurate here than *concept*. Some writers use the two terms interchangeably.

acterizing properties and relations (Mandler and Kessen, 1959). In this very general sense, a construct is formed when one ascribes a scientifically observed *property* (*e.g.,* common characteristic or quality) to two or more objects. Furthermore, a construct describes and summarizes *relationships* among events, objects, and the like. Following Margenau (1950) and Torgerson (1958), constructs in a satisfactory theory must be defined in terms of other constructs in the set; though all constructs may not necessarily possess direct operational definition (see pp. 33–35), an adequate number in any theoretical system should. Constructs that do not possess operational definition directly must at least be linked indirectly with observable data by other constructs possessing operational definition.[2]

One source of potential confusion is the relationship between a concept and a construct. *A construct is a concept expressing relationships among events or objects and other constructs which has been intentionally created or adopted for a particular scientific aim and for which empirical support is available.* Kerlinger (1964) suggests that constructs "might more accurately be called 'constructed types' or 'constructed classes,' classes or sets of objects or events bound together by the possession of common characteristics, characteristics defined by the scientist [p. 4]."

English and English (1958) note that a fully scientific concept is also a construct; the primary distinction between the two terms appears to be the degree to which a researcher creates or adopts a given term for a special scientific purpose. A construct, then, may also be considered as a purposefully designed model; as such, the relations between model and empirical data are explicated. For example, "imitation," defined earlier as a concept, may be used as a scientific construct in a particular, intentional, and systematic fashion. "Imitation" may be related to and defined in terms of numerous other constructs, like "motivation" and "reinforcement"; it also may be defined in terms of observable data (Bandura and Walters, 1963).

HYPOTHETICAL CONSTRUCTS

Sometimes behavioral scientists use constructs to refer to an entity or process inferred as actually existing (though not completely observable at present), containing some empirical support, and giving rise to measurable phenomena (phenomena other than the observables that led to postulating the construct). "Attitude" is an example of such a construct (Scott, 1968); others of interest to behavioral scientists are "belief," "fear," and "anger." These are called *hypothetical constructs:* they express an abstraction of empirical relationships that introduces at least one phenomenon or process which is not observable (McGinnis, 1964). Sometimes the term "hypothetical construct" has been restricted to the type of construct which is inferred from data based on observation, is presumed to exist, and will probably be disclosed later by experience. (The similarities between hypo-

---

[2] For a more complete account of this view see Margenau (1950), Torgerson (1958), and Kerlinger (1964).

thetical constructs and intervening variables are discussed on pp. 23–24. For the present, communication researchers are well advised to remember that the value of hypothetical constructs ultimately is contingent on the extent to which they lead to variables having predictive power.)

VARIABLES

Variable, like "concept" and "construct," is a specialized term behavioral scientists use to impose some order on what they study. Behavioral scientists unconstrainedly identify the constructs they examine as variables. R. V. Bowers (1964) has observed that the term "variable" is being used increasingly in the social sciences to identify any element in an empirical study. Used this way, "variable" may be employed in a *theoretical* frame of reference as well as in an *empirical* frame of reference. A variable has also been identified rather loosely as anything that can change (English and English, 1958), or anything that may appear in changed amount or quality, such as an attribute or a characteristic (Cook, 1965). In this sense, anything that can be conceived of or perceived as distinguishable from other things, events, and the like may be called a variable. But these gross definitions are not particularly helpful in the scientific study of communication.

The term "variable" is used in different contexts of empirical inquiry. An understanding of some key types of variables and labels typically assigned to them is necessary to consider efficiently the empirical research process discussed throughout this volume. Variables are distinguished and classified below by several key functions they serve in experimental design.

A Notion of Variables

In a very general sense, a variable is used to identify a class of objects or events, or their properties, for empirical investigations; thus, it is a term applied to a factor or condition conceptualized for scientific investigations (Marx and Hillix, 1963). "Variable" so defined is not appreciably different from "construct"; in fact, some researchers use the two terms interchangeably. By identifying a variable as a set of objects or events (or their properties) which may fluctuate according to an adequately defined scheme of classification, one emphasizes that it is subject to change — that it varies. In a narrower sense, *a variable may be a symbol expressing a thoroughly defined category classifying a given phenomenon according to how its characteristics vary.*

Similarly, Williams (1968) has used the term "variable" to refer to the varying characteristics of a phenomenon. The general and the narrower ways of characterizing variables differ slightly in that the emphasis in the broader is on classifying the varying characteristics of phenome*na*, while the focus in the narrower is more operationally oriented, with an emphasis on classifying the fluctuating characteristics of a particular phenomeno*n*.

A variable, particularly in the narrower sense, is said to assume or to take on different values. Among the variables of interest to communication researchers are intelligence, achievement, sex, fear, credibility, persuasibility, and language intensity.

A variable may be used fruitfully by behavioral scientists to identify a given category of fluctuating characteristics of a particular phenomenon in empirical studies. Researchers select variables for scientific study that theory and previous research indicate might be related, and name them. "Reinforcement," for example, might identify a variable to predict whether a given stimulus-response (S-R) tendency will increase when the S-R sequence occurs and is followed immediately by a specific reinforcing stimulus situation. In order to identify the class of events and their properties related to the variable called "reinforcement," one might wish to specify the types, strength, and schedule of the reinforcers, to determine the "attractiveness" of the stimulus situation and related characteristics (Perkins, 1968). The characteristics of the variable labeled "reinforcement" probably would be classified in substantial detail to study the predicted relationship. Moreover, the characteristics of reinforcement might be classified according to how they are subject to change. This all-too-brief and oversimplified example suggests that substantial thought should be given to identifying and classifying the characteristics of a variable. One may conceptualize considerably beyond the mere observation of a single event. Conditions, objects, events, and the like that vary in observable degrees or amounts and that differ from one another in degrees or amounts undoubtedly would be considered in the scheme for classifying a given variable.

Variables and Constructs

Some scientists use "variable" and "construct" indiscriminately, but here we shall distinguish between them, using them at different investigational levels. One may say that a scientist operates on two levels (Kerlinger, 1964). When scientists are operating on the *theoretical* level, they are concerned primarily with such matters as identifying constructs, developing theory, and formulating hypotheses. These efforts are never entirely divorced from observation, but the primary focus is on the use of constructs and the formulation of rational statements at the theoretical level. The second basic level of operation for scientists is *observation*, the level at which they collect data and test hypotheses. Scientists frequently vacillate between these two levels. The two levels are connected by operational definitions (rules of correspondence) defining at least partially particular constructs in terms of observable data (Torgerson, 1958). The scientist operates with variables at all levels; the use of constructs is appropriate particularly when the *relations* between variables are under consideration.

These two general levels at which the scientist operates provide a recognizably crude and imperfect basis for distinguishing between using a construct or using a variable; but perhaps the distinction made here for using the two terms will aid the investigator in clarifying the level at which he is operating. When operating at the theoretical level he probably will be dealing with constructs; as such, the constructs are not observable, although they are supported empirically. When operating at the observational level the scientist probably will be dealing with variables; when a variable has been operationally defined it is observable. One way of understanding the distinction suggested here is to imagine an observational-theoretical continuum with theory and corresponding theoretic terms at one end, and observation and corresponding observational terms at the opposite end. Though recognizing that the scientist vacillates between the two operational levels at the ends of the continuum, constructs generally would be used on the theory side of the continuum when relations between variables were being examined, and variables typically would be used on the observation side of the continuum.

Variables as Quantities

If a variable may take on or assume any justifiable set of values, numerical values may be assigned to it varying in *quantity* or *magnitude*. From a mathematical perspective, a variable is "a quantity which may take any one of a specified set of values [Kendall and Buckland, 1960, p. 310]." In this view, a variable is an abstraction of quantity. For example, "comprehension" (a symbol) may be considered a variable when the fluctuations of observable characteristics have been specified in a given, thoroughly defined, classification scheme. The variable "comprehension" mathematically defined may take on any justifiable set of values; one may assign to this variable a set of numerical values (abstractions) obtained by designated procedures, the scores from a given comprehension test ranging, say, from 0 to 100. Any given observation is called a *value* of the variable and the value determines the class to which a variable is to be assigned. As Edwards (1968) and others have noted, such classes are mutually exclusive; thus any particular observation may be classified into only one of the classes.

Variables have been classified in other ways which are related to quantification and measurement. Some of these will be mentioned here, but readers are referred to Chapters 2, 3, and 4 in this volume, and to other sources (Weinberg and Schumaker, 1962; Hays, 1963; R. V. Bowers, 1964; Kerlinger, 1964; Guilford, 1965; Edwards, 1967, 1968; Popham, 1967) for a more detailed treatment.

QUANTITATIVE AND QUALITATIVE VARIABLES

Suppose one views a *qualitative* measure as representing two extreme levels of a particular variable (*e.g.*, its presence or absence), and views a *quantitative* measure as simply a more precise distinction within the classification expressing the degree of the variable's presence. The position taken here is that this distinction between qualitative and quantitative variables is probably overemphasized and overrated for classifying variables functionally. However, a discussion of some distinctions between qualitative and quantitative variables is included here because those being introduced to scientific research will encounter them often and should understand them to avoid confusion.

Qualitative variables may be described as those differing in sort or kind, rather than degree — that possess no inherent ordering system. Some examples of qualitative variables are political party, color of eyes, and social class. Any ordering of these variables is said to be arbitrary. Kerlinger (1964) has noted that "qualitative variable" has been used unwisely to describe dichotomies (entities distinguished by a property which is either present or absent); he contends that if it is not quantifiable, then it is not a variable.

When the possible values for a variable differ in degree, amount, or frequency it may be described as a *quantitative variable*. Quantitative variables are ordered; that is, their different observed values can be ordered on a continuum. Scores on an examination, numbers of students entering a college course, and frequencies of speeches given are examples of quantitative variables.

CONTINUOUS AND DISCRETE VARIABLES

Continuous variables and discrete variables are two types of quantitative variables. When one may either find or postulate an intermediate value between two values of a particular variable, it may be described as a *continuous variable*. Regardless of the accuracy of the measure, one is nearly always uncertain about the recorded and/or observed value of a continuous variable; thus, the values are not exact. Distance, age, and time are examples of continuous variables. When values change by distinct steps or jumps between which it is not possible to place another value of a particular variable, it may be described as a *discontinuous* or *discrete variable*. The values of a discrete variable are said to be exact. A population and the number of correct responses in five trials are examples of discrete variables. Many times, usually for practical reasons, researchers assume that most variables (even discrete variables) are theoretically capable of representing continuous values.

Independent, Dependent, and Intervening Variables

It is possible to classify variables by their relationships to one another. The introduction to Part One made the point that the investigator in an experiment attempts to control or manipulate particular variables. He is interested in finding relationships between variables, in classifying them according to their *use* in empirical studies rather than fixed categories of *kind*.

In terms of relationship and use, variables may be classified as dependent or independent. The classifications of stimulus, organismic, and response variables also are described below briefly, particularly in terms of their relationship to independent and dependent variables. Because intervening variables serve an important function in theory building, analytical considerations, and interpreting empirical research, they are considered also.

INDEPENDENT VARIABLES

Variables manipulated by an experimenter typically have been called *independent variables*. Other terms sometimes used to identify this type of variable (under certain conditions) are "antecedent," "experimental," "treatment," "predictor," or "casual." The experimenter manipulates variables when he varies the experimental conditions and/or selects subjects with particular characteristics for the experiment. (Miller gives detailed examples of each of these manipulations in Chapter 3.) The independent variable is manipulated toward the end of establishing its relationship to an observed phenomenon. As Kerlinger (1964) has observed, in an experimental study the independent variable is the presumed cause (the antecedent) of the dependent variable, which is the presumed effect (consequent). The independent variable is thus the variable an investigator *predicts from,* while the dependent variable is the one he *predicts to.* Independent variables, then, are associated with lawful changes in the dependent variable. For example, an independent variable is manipulated in an experiment to determine what effect, if any, changes in that variable produce in the variable dependent on it. Moreover, in a problem in which a regression analysis is used, an estimation or prediction may be based on the independent variable. As the foregoing comments imply, the "independence" affirmed is not really absolute, because absolutely independent variables are not identifiable (English and English, 1958).

Some examples of independent variables in experimental investigations may help to clarify the concept. One study (Kibler and Barker, 1968) investigated the effect of mispronunciation in a message. The investigators manipulated mispronunciation, the independent variable in the study, by using different degrees or levels of mispronunciation in the stimulus message. Another study (Barker, Kibler, and Hunter, 1968) examined the effect of different evaluation conditions imposed on students rating speeches. The evaluation condition, the independent variable, was manipulated by using different evaluative conditions. Independent variables are used sometimes in nonexperimental research. For example, when Kibler, Kelly, Gibson, and Gruner (1968) investigated the relationship between selected language characteristics (predicted from) and grades (predicted to) in a speech class, the independent variable was the selected language characteristics.

Another point, often presumed and sometimes neglected in experimental research, should be made about the independent variable. The experimenter must exercise some procedure to ascertain on either a formal or an informal basis the level of the independent variable in each of the experimental conditions he uses. That is, as Scott and Wertheimer (1962) note, the investigator must determine "what level of the variable is represented by each of his experimental conditions [p. 101]." This procedure is referred to here as *assessing the stimulus conditions or experimental conditions*. The procedure is designed to determine on empirical grounds the level of the independent variable represented by each experimental condition. The experimenter hopes the level(s) of the independent variable will represent what he presumes they represent. If not, conducting these procedures will at least clarify the nature of the independent variable represented by each of the experimental conditions. Miller (1969) has presented a particularly valuable treatment of this topic, but the execution of such procedures is long overdue in communication research.

DEPENDENT VARIABLES

The comments above have suggested the nature and functions of dependent variables. A *dependent variable* has been identified rather loosely as that which is going to be measured in an experiment. More precisely, the dependent variable is one whose changes are presumed to be consequent on modifications in the one or more other variables referred to collectively as the independent variable. The dependent variable, then, is the presumed effect, the variable being assessed; it is that which an investigator measures in an experiment and treats as being influenced by, or varying concomitantly with, modifications in the independent variable. Typically, the dependent variable is the condition the experimenter is trying to explain. Some other terms which have been used to identify the dependent variable are "consequent," "resultant," or "effect." When using a regression technique, a dependent variable would be the variable whose value is being estimated from that of the one or more other variables labeled collectively as the independent variable and to which it is related (Good, 1959). (Kelly discusses applications to this type of dependent variable in Chapter 2.)

In the Kibler and Barker (1968) study of the relation between mispronunciation and comprehension, mispronunciation was the independent variable and comprehension was the dependent variable. When the relationship between evaluation conditions and (a) comprehension and (b) rating of speech effectiveness was investigated in another previously noted study (Barker, Kibler, and Hunter, 1968), the evaluation condition was the independent variable; the dependent variables were (a) comprehension and (b) rating of speech effectiveness. Other examples of dependent variables used sometimes in communication research are voting behavior, speaker credibility, achievement, time to complete given tasks, attitude change, and donation of money. (Under certain conditions, of course, the variables listed here might serve as independent variables.)

STIMULUS, ORGANISMIC, AND RESPONSE VARIABLES

Experimental psychologists, among others, frequently classify variables as stimulus variables, response variables, or organismic variables (the latter also are referred to as intervening variables). *Stimulus variables* (physical or social environmental conditions which produce a response in the organism) or *organismic variables* (characteristics of a person or organism) may serve as independent variables in experimental investigations (English and English, 1958). For example, differences in the conditions of stimulation which the investigator alters in an experiment may be referred to as differences in the *treatment* or *experimental variable* (*i.e.,* the independent variable). A *response variable* (that which changes as a function of changes in stimulus or organismic variables) refers to a response or action of an organism. Response variables (sometimes called behavioral variables [Edwards, 1968]) are said to be dependent variables in psychological investigations. The relationship between these variables may be stated thus: response variables are functions of organismic variables and stimulus variables. Obviously, this classification of variables is similar to the classification specified above for independent and dependent variables. Readers are referred to Travers (1964) and Edwards (1968) for a more complete explanation of these variables.

INTERVENING VARIABLES

Most behavioral scientists today recognize that a science of behavior must be built on something more substantive than simply examining the relationship of stimulus variables to response variables. For example, it is necessary to account for the different responses of subjects exposed to the same stimulus (Travers, 1964, 1967). In an effort to explain such concerns, behavioral scientists have postulated certain internal conditions (intraorganismic functions) to account for psychological processes presumed to influence particular observed behavior. Some time ago Tolman (1938) suggested the use of the term *intervening variable* for those theoretical constructs assumed to intervene between the independent environmental variables and dependent response variables. "Motive," "aptitude," "drive," and "hunger" are examples of intervening variables. As McGinnis (1964) notes, such constructs "are used because of scientific dissatisfaction with the explanatory power of purely functional descriptions of relations [p. 351]."

Intervening variables are not observable directly; behavioral scientists create and use them to account for observable relations between stimulus and response in a given learning paradigm. An intervening variable then expresses an *abstraction of a set of empirical operations* which are preferably, though not necessarily, experimental in nature; assumptions about the existence of entities which presently are unobservable are not required for these variables (McGinnis, 1964).

Chaplin and Krawiec (1960) note that although intervening variables sometimes may be assumed to have "real" existence, the "reality" of intervening variables appears unnecessary and unwarranted. This position is assumed here. Any "reality" associated with an intervening variable is only a postulated reality. An intraorganismic function which abstracts the relationship between antecedent (stimulus) and consequent (response) conditions does not suggest meaning beyond the specified relationship (Marx and Hillix, 1963). However, although intervening variables cannot be observed or measured directly, it is possible to infer them and investigate relationships among them by empirical studies designed to reveal their effects behavioristically. In addition, intervening variables may become important links in developing theoretical structures or systems (Chaplin and Krawiec, 1960). Spence (1951) discusses how various learning theorists have conceived and used intervening variables in developing their theoretic systems. Brown (1963) and Suchman (1967) have emphasized the role of intervening variables in constructing theory in other areas of inquiry.

There is a great deal of similarity between *theoretical constructs* and *intervening variables.* Many behavioral scientists do not differentiate appreciably between the two, and some not at all. Therefore, readers will note considerable similarity between some of the remarks made here and those stated previously about hypothetical constructs. MacCorquodale and Meehl (1948) tried to distinguish clearly between the two concepts, but other scientists offered considerable objection. To oversimplify the distinction, they indicated that a hypothetical construct included meaning beyond that attributed to an intervening variable; intervening variables abstract merely empirical relationships while hypothetical constructs include the supposition of entities or processes that are not observed. However, the authors did note that hypothetical constructs' "actual existence should be compatible with general knowledge and particularly with whatever relevant knowledge exists at the next lower level in the explanatory hierarchy [p. 107]." The meaning of a hypothetical construct includes more than the relationship between the antecedent and consequent conditions which it represents, making it a higher order of abstraction. The insertion of at least one phenomenon or process which is not observable is included in the expression of an abstraction of empirical relationships identified as a hypothetical construct; assumptions about the existence of a presently unobservable phenomenon or process are not required for an intervening variable (McGinnis, 1964). Because of this distinction, the hypothetical construct is less operationally valid than the intervening variable. Underwood (1957) has related his five levels of concepts (particularly Levels 3 and 4) to the distinctions made by MacCorquodale and Meehl. The distinctions made between intervening variables and hypothetical constructs may prove useful as the science of behavior progresses, but at present their usefulness is limited.

HYPOTHESES

In his general effort to acquire reliable or dependable knowledge, man uses the scientific method; he tries to determine the relations among variables. The experimental method is probably the most powerful device for assessing the relations among variables, and the hypothesis is one of the most important components of the method. Previous sections of this chapter (pp. 11, 12–13) have suggested generally what an hypothesis is and how it is used in scientific investigation. Additional comments are now in order. Unfortunately, because of limited space, some important topics related to hypotheses have been omitted or seriously neglected — such as significance level, one- and two-tailed tests, Type I and Type II errors in hypothesis testing, and the detailed inferential limitations and implications associated with confirming or disconfirming an hypothesis.

The following section focuses on two major types of hypotheses, the nature and essential characteristics of research hypotheses, and some limited implications in testing them. For a more detailed discussion of the logic of hypothesis formulation and testing, readers are referred to Churchman (1948), Poincaré (1952), Braithwaite (1955), Cohen (1956), Bergmann (1957), Selltiz, Jahoda, Deutsch, and Cook (1959), Weinberg and Schumaker (1962), Kerlinger (1964), Travers (1964), Guilford (1965), Van Dalen (1966), and Aronson and Carlsmith (1968).

Before proceeding to a discussion of hypotheses, it will be advantageous to consider briefly a few points pertinent to the research problem. In order to define the problem, the scientist first expresses it as a *question* about the relation existing between two or more phenomena or variables. However, the question per se cannot be answered scientifically; even though the potential for empirical testing is implicit in it, the problem stated as a broad question is not directly testable. So the scientist tries to base his problem on theory and experience so that scientific techniques can be used to examine it. He reduces it to an *hypothesis* postulating the relationships between the variables and then designs research to test the relationships.

Research and Statistical Hypotheses

It is necessary at the outset of this discussion to distinguish between two types of hypotheses, the research hypothesis and the statistical hypothesis. The *research hypothesis,* sometimes referred to as a "theoretic," "empirical," "experimental" (Marx and Hillix, 1963), or "test" hypothesis (Kaplan, 1964), is the particular prediction of a relation between two or more variables the investigator wants to test, a statement of expected outcomes of the experiment based on theory and previous research. It is sometimes characterized as an *explanation;* but as Brown (1963) has observed, one must be cautious in making such an assertion.

As noted previously, one cannot test the research hypothesis directly. Researchers frequently assess a research hypothesis by testing a statistical hypothesis. A *statistical hypothesis* is a conjectural statement expressing the statistical relations deduced from the relations specified in the research hypothesis (Kerlinger, 1964). As the label implies, a statistical hypothesis is stated in statistical and quantitative terms. Suppose the research hypothesis was that girls would score higher than boys on a particular reading test. Where the Ms stand for population means and the subscripts $_b$ and $_g$ stand for boys and girls respectively, the statistical hypothesis would be expressed as $M_g > M_b$.

Like the research hypothesis, a statistical hypothesis is not tested directly; it is necessary to test it against an alternative hypothesis. For the example given above, one might specify several logical alternatives, such as $M_g < M_b$; $M_g = M_b$; the alternative typically selected is the null hypothesis (*e.g.*, $M_g = M_b$). The *null hypothesis* states that no relationship other than chance expectation exists between the variables for which a relationship is predicted in the statistical or research hypothesis, *i.e.*, that the observed relation is a function of chance.[3]

The null hypothesis is used to test obtained data against chance expectation; it is the hypothesis which frequently is subjected to statistical test. The investigator's prediction of the outcome of an experiment is not necessarily included in a null hypothesis. In fact, the relation between variables stated in the null hypothesis typically is diametrically opposed to that stated in the statistical or research hypothesis; even though the null hypothesis is assumed to be true until disconfirmed, an investigator usually expects it to be rejected or disconfirmed (by finding it to be relatively improbable at a level of significance specified prior to conducting the study). Then the investigator, usually by logical implication, finds support for (confirms) the alternative, stated, statistical hypothesis.

Another matter should be mentioned here in passing. Sometimes the researcher applies inferential statistics to data to determine whether the performances of two groups are significantly different. In so doing, it may appear that the concern has been lost for examining the *relationship* stated between variables in the statistical or research hypothesis; such is not the case. Even when using a "difference test," one may be concerned with the relation between variables. Popham (1967) has clarified this potential

---

[3] Some authors do not differentiate between research, statistical, and null hypotheses. Sometimes research and statistical hypotheses taken together are referred to as the research or substantive hypothesis because of their similarity. Other authors, particularly the writers of statistical textbooks, frequently identify the statistical hypothesis and the null hypothesis by other names; for example, what is called the null hypothesis here might be labelled — independently, or collectively with other types of alternative, quantitatively expressed hypotheses — the statistical hypothesis. Readers should certainly be aware of the different uses of terms among authors and textbooks, but for purposes of simplicity in the discussion here, an effort has been made to distinguish operationally among the hypotheses used in scientific research procedures.

source of confusion: "When a researcher tests for group differences on a particular measure, he is in reality assessing the nature of the relationship between (a) the variable represented by the measure and (b) the variable represented by the groups [p. 48]." In effect, by using inferential statistics an investigator tests a research hypothesis by testing a statistical hypothesis. He uses inferential statistics to aid him in making decisions between alternative hypotheses.

Hypotheses are stated explicitly or implicitly in a variety of forms in published research related to communication. Sometimes the researcher may state only the problem in a declarative or an interrogative form. Other times only the objective or purpose of the study is stated in very general terms. Still other times the research hypothesis or the null hypothesis or both are reported in published research. Whatever the form in which the investigator reports his prediction, one ultimate task of the critical reader is to try to determine the research hypothesis of the study. Naturally, he does not have to guess at it if it is stated, but when an investigator reports only a vague problem statement, a general question, or a set of objectives as the basis for guiding his research, the reader is forced to infer the research hypothesis from the operational procedures used in the study. Clearly, the published form of the research hypothesis should be a precise statement of the relations between variables being tested and should result in minimal guesswork for the reader.

The investigator also may wish to publish the null hypothesis, but this does not seem to be "fashionable" or necessary in many of the social sciences today. Williams (1968) gives the rationale for this current custom: "In practice, the null hypothesis is frequently implied rather than stated. In fact, if there is nothing special about the null hypothesis — that is, it is clearly implied by the research hypothesis — a statement of the null explanation is apt to be redundant [p. 61]." Even though the research hypothesis is generally the best one to include in published reports, readers will find that most authors of statistical textbooks encourage the use of null hypotheses for statistical purposes. However, it is beyond the scope of this chapter to elaborate on the rationale for using null hypotheses. For treatments of this topic interested readers are referred to such sources as Weinberg and Schumaker (1962), Hays (1963), Kerlinger (1964), Guilford (1965), Edwards (1967), Lehmann (1968), and Williams (1968).

The Research Hypothesis

Because of the importance of the research hypothesis, additional discussion will concentrate on it and its characteristics. An hypothesis has been described very generally as a tentative, unproven "guess" explaining particular, natural phenomena. In this sense it is little more than a statement to guide thinking, which may initiate and guide observation, stimulate the quest for relevant data, and predict particular results or consequences

(Good, 1959). More precisely, a *research hypothesis in scientific investigation is a conjectural statement specifying the relation of dependency between two or more variables.* In this sense an hypothesis is a prediction. For example, a scientist may be interested in predicting that changes in a particular variable will produce changes in, or will be accompanied by, changes in another variable. A research hypothesis so perceived may be said to consist of two parts. First, an *antecedent* clause specifies the condition that will produce a particular result or given conclusion. Such antecedent clauses are introduced frequently by "if" or some equivalent term. Second, a *consequent* states the given occurrence or conclusion. When the hypothesis is stated "If A occurs (antecedent) then B will occur also (consequent)," the dependency relation between the variables is explicit: "B depends (at least in part) on A." Moreover, if a scientist then varies A and observes that B varies concomitantly, the hypothesis is said to be confirmed. (Kelly discusses concomitant variation in relation to regression techniques in Chapter 2.)

It is appropriate now to return briefly to independent and dependent variables (see pp. 21–22) for the purpose of examining their relations in an hypothesis. Following Kerlinger (1964), the independent variable is the presumed cause (antecedent) of the dependent variable, which is the presumed effect (consequent); thus the independent variable is the one an investigator predicts from while the dependent variable is the one he predicts to. Although Kibler and Barker (1968), in their study of the relation between mispronunciation and comprehension, published their hypothesis in the null form, the research hypothesis was easily perceived as: If the degree of mispronunciation in a message presented by a speaker increases (antecedent), then the receivers' comprehension (*i.e.*, immediate and delayed recall) will decrease (consequent). The degree or level of mispronunciation in the message was manipulated (independent variable) and changes in comprehension (dependent variable) were presumed to be consequent on modifications in the degrees of mispronunciation presented to subjects. This research hypothesis states the relation between the independent and dependent variable in the "If . . . then . . ." form; the independent variable is in the antecedent clause and the dependent variable is in the consequent.

SELECTED CHARACTERISTICS OF RESEARCH HYPOTHESES

Certain other observations concerning research hypotheses should be emphasized. First, as noted before, hypotheses are conjectural statements about the relations between variables. These statements should be expressed in the simplest terms possible to make their meaning clear to others; vague terms or constructs should be avoided. The "principle of parsimony" should be followed, the avoidance of unnecessary complication. However, this does not mean complexity should always be abandoned for the sake of simplicity. When a complex hypothesis is required, it should be formulated, if there is enough theory or empirical evidence to support it. (Miller provides some examples of more complex hypotheses in Chapter 3 when he discusses three types of design paradigms.)

Second, research hypotheses specify how the particular variables are related (if *A*, then *B*) and therefore direct the researcher in his investigation. Kaplan (1964) has noted that when test hypotheses (conjectures or surmises concerning the solution to the problem) emerge in inquiry, "we then organize the inquiry so as to facilitate the decision on whether the conjecture is correct [p. 88]." Moreover, because the researcher states in an hypothesis how the variables are related, he predicts and commits himself to the direction the relations between variables will take. Then he subjects the relations between the variables to empirical test. Some contend that this ordering of the process gives powerful evidence of the specified relations between variables. It is probably a more important matter that hypotheses specifying how variables are related impose on the investigator a more rigorous, more objective set of rules for governing the nature of his inquiry. If an experiment is conducted to test a hypothesis, one outcome must be specified from among the alternatives. Kerlinger (1964) likens the hypothesis and its use to a betting game.

> The scientist makes a bet that *x* leads to *y*. If, in an experiment, *x* does lead to *y*, then he collects his money. He has won the bet. He cannot just enter the game at any point and pick a perhaps fortuitous common occurrence of *x* and *y*. Games are not played this way (at least in our culture). He must play according to the rules, and the rules in science are made to minimize error and man's fallibility. Hypotheses are part of the rules of the game [p. 28].

When an investigator fails to specify in his hypothesis how the variables are related, it is difficult to assess the effects of the independent (antecedent) variable. The investigator also may be accused of using post hoc explanations to support the original hypothesis and/or its rationale (Kibler and Barker, 1969).

A third point has been implied throughout this discussion but it should be made explicit. If it is not possible to determine in the research hypothesis how variables will be measured, it is even more difficult to imagine how to test the relations between the stated variables. Perhaps another way of saying this is that the variables identified must be capable of being defined operationally (see pp. 21–22). The implications for measuring the variables and testing the relations between them must be reasonably clear in the hypothesis. Because of this characteristic, hypotheses typically state the relations between *observable* phenomena or variables; however, *unobservable* variables also are included in such relational statements in communication research (*e.g.,* as in the case of intervening variables; see pp. 23–24).

Fourth, just as the problem question must be stated so it can be solved empirically, the relations between variables in hypotheses must be stated precisely enough so they can be either confirmed (shown to be probably true) or disconfirmed (shown to be probably false) empirically; the hypothesis must be "testable." Statements that are too general to be disconfirmed or to predict effectively are of limited value as hypotheses and are not scientifically useful.

This continual effort of the investigator to confirm or disconfirm hypotheses points up another concern relevant to theory construction. Hypotheses, by their nature as tentative propositions, are never final. They help investigators confirm or disconfirm theory; if the empirical evidence supports them, confidence will probably grow in their validity and, eventually, they may become part of an established theory (Bergmann, 1957). When an hypothesis is widely accepted and its implications are observed to obtain without fail, it may eventually become a scientific law, an honored hypothesis (Kaplan, 1964). Unfortunately, communication theories are not replete with honored hypotheses. But it is the task of those engaged in communication research to devote their efforts to this end: formulating and establishing lawful statements and theory concerning man's communicative behaviors. The discussion here should not be construed to imply that when an hypothesis is not confirmed nothing has been learned. Negative findings may suggest avenues for the development of other, more scientifically viable hypotheses; they also may reduce superstition and/or lack of knowledge in a field of inquiry. One of Kerlinger's cogent observations is a fitting closing comment: *"But the scientist cannot tell positive from negative evidence unless he uses hypotheses* [p. 28]."

OPERATIONAL DEFINITIONS[4]

This section is devoted to a discussion of operational definitions and their uses in scientific investigation. It may be useful to begin this discussion, following Kerlinger (1964), by differentiating between two general types of definitions in common usage.[5] The first is simply a *dictionary* or *literary* type of definition in which one defines a word or phrase with other words or phrases. Boring (1945) has called such definitions "statements of synonyms [p. 245]." For example, one might define "comprehension" as "the ability to know," "the capacity to grasp ideas," or "understanding." These are commonsense language definitions. As noted in the discussion of concepts, the commonsense meaning of a term may be defined, among other ways, by listing its observable characteristics (*e.g.*, size, shape). In effect,

---

[4] The author has been influenced considerably by Margenau (1950), Torgerson (1958), and Kerlinger (1964) and has tried to credit them throughout this section for the excellent distinctions and discussions that are substantially theirs.

[5] Clearly, there are ways of defining words or concepts other than those mentioned here; the two types of definitions discussed here were chosen merely for illustrative purposes. They each have characteristics which should be helpful in understanding how scientific terms are defined and used in scientific inquiry.

one defines the term with synonymous concepts or related expressions instead of explaining its meaning.

Another way of defining a word in common usage is by describing or showing the particular *behaviors* or acts which, through implication, reveal its meaning. For example, to define "comprehension," one might stipulate the behaviors required of individuals who "comprehend" and those who do "not comprehend" the instructions for a given task. The behavior required for comprehension of specific instructions for going from a starting point to a given restaurant might be accurately restating the instructions to another person, or it might be actually going to the restaurant via the specified route. If the person does not perform the required behavior correctly, then one might say the person does not comprehend. Behavioral definition may be based on the observation or description of given behaviors.

As noted earlier (pp. 14–15), communication researchers concentrate on concepts which name the more observable aspects of experience. Moreover, scientists use precise definitions adapted specially from common use for scientific inquiry. Scientific definitions differ from those in common use in that they identify features of the discernible only under special conditions. The words themselves do not have meaning; they are given meaning through their use in particular investigations and their meaning is so specified in the investigations.

Operationism

This chapter has implied that the effective communication researcher possesses a critical attitude; he is cautious and systematic in selecting problems for research, formulating hypotheses, planning investigations, employing procedures, analyzing data, and interpreting findings. Predictably, colleagues evaluate the acceptability of the results of an investigator's study partly on the validity of the operations used in arriving at the results. The principle affirming that the validity of a scientific finding or a given theoretical construct is contingent on the validity of the operations used to arrive at that finding or construct has been identified as *operationism* (Chaplin and Krawiec, 1960). This principle, interpreted strictly, asserts that an experiment's results and conclusions cannot transcend its methodology.[6]

Early "pure" forms of operationism and empiricism, which appear to be still accepted by some, required that all constructs possess direct operational definitions (Bridgman, 1927; Stevens, 1935; Verplanck, 1957; English and English, 1958). That is, a given construct in a scientific investigation was to be defined in terms of physical referents — the physical operations per-

[6] Some scholars do not share this view as conclusively as it is stated here. For a discussion of a number of criticisms and objections raised about operationism and the use of operational definitions see Stevens (1939), Israel and Goldstein (1944), Pratt (1945), Benjamin (1955), Bachrach (1965), Nebergall (1965), and Scriven (1968).

formed. Bridgman's (1927) work stressed the value of placing rigorous requirements on the definition of physical concepts in modern science, an emphasis also appropriate to certain experimental research in communication. For example, concerning the concept of length he wrote:

> The concept of length is therefore fixed when the operations by which length is measured are fixed: that is, the concept of length involves as much as and nothing more than a set of operations; *the concept is synonymous with the corresponding set of operations* [p. 5].

Bridgman's efforts were designed to make the meaning of scientific concepts more explicit (*e.g.*, through a written report) to another investigator and to the user through eliminating unmeaningful connotations of terms from definitions — by defining a concept synonymously with its corresponding set of operations. The type of definition Bridgman advocated is typically referred to as *operational definition*.

Through the years there has been a movement away from the earlier operationism orthodoxy (frequently derived from Bridgman's [1927] work). Bridgman himself appears to have indicated, particularly in some of his later writings (1950, 1952), that there are other aspects of meaning than the operational.[7] Based on an examination of Bridgman's writings, Benjamin (1955) has identified two distinct meanings of *operation*: (1) a reasonably narrow and specific meaning restricted to physical operations and under certain conditions to metrical operations; (2) a more general meaning permitting verbal, mental, and paper-and-pencil operations. Although Bridgman (1952) appears to accept the use of concepts with operations that, for the present, do not correspond to physical operations, he also notes that if a concept is to be useful scientifically it must be reduced ultimately to performable operations.

Margenau (1950, 1954) takes a position closely associated with the position held today by many behavioral scientists conducting communication research. Margenau (1954) views operationism as an attitude emphasizing the need to resort to instrumental procedures when establishing meanings wherever feasible. This chapter supports this view. Skinner (1945) recognized the worth of the *operational attitude,* despite its deficiencies, in any science. He emphasized its special value in psychology "because of the

---

[7] It is of particular importance to investigators in communication that Bridgman notes the value of somewhat more abstract concepts. Unlike some of the well developed sciences, much research in communication, like that in other social and behavioral sciences, reveals a serious deficiency of important theoretical and/or empirical connections between some pertinent constructs. Many theoretical concepts in certain current communication research are deficient in empirical meaning; corresponding empirical concepts may be deficient in theoretical value. As was noted previously, a scientifically useful concept must possess both types of support (Margenau, 1950; Torgerson, 1958).

presence there of a vast vocabulary of ancient and nonscientific origin [p. 271]." Communication researchers also have recognized the presence of an archaic vocabulary in their area of inquiry. Moreover, most would concur that the principle of operationism formulates the rules to be followed at some phase in the development of the scientific study of communication — if scientific activity concerning communication is to be evaluated, if defining scientific concepts is to be made more precise, and if the science of communication is to produce a communicable knowledge. Participants in a recent speech communication conference urged researchers to devote attention to just such matters (Kibler and Barker, 1969).

Constitutive and Operational Definitions

Torgerson (1958) has noted that a model is formed by a given set of constructs and their accompanying formal connections, and that the model becomes a theory capable of being tested empirically only when particular constructs are linked to the empirical world by rules of correspondence (also called rules of interpretation or operational definitions).[8] Following Margenau (1950), he further indicates that an adequate theory has a set of constructs characterized by two distinguishable types of definitions roughly paralleling the two common-usage definitions designated in the opening paragraphs of this section.[9]

CONSTITUTIVE DEFINITIONS

The first type, a *constitutive definition,* is used when one defines a construct in terms of other constructs (one or preferably more) in the set of constructs in a theory. Constructs possessing constitutive meaning deal with the more covert aspects of a theory. One might express the connections between constructs in a theory verbally as, for example, "A student's achievement in a particular area is a function of his self-concept, his motivation, and his aptitude." One also might express connections between constructs by a formal equation in which two or more constructs are interrelated. Cronkhite (1964) has provided an interesting and rare equational example. A formal equation which expresses the interrelations of two or more constructs defines any one of the concepts relative to the others. As noted earlier, if constructs are to be scientifically useful they must possess *constitutive meaning* (Margenau, 1950, p. 236) — that is, they must be capable of contributing to the formulation of theory.

---

[8] The discussion on pp. 15–17 underscored the importance of constructs and their relationship to one another and to theory construction. For more detailed remarks on constructs and operational definition readers are referred to Margenau (1950), Hempel (1952), Torgerson (1958), and Kerlinger (1964).

[9] The distinction presented here between constitutive and operational definitions was made earlier by Margenau (1950) and subsequently discussed by Torgerson (1958) and Kerlinger (1964). The discussion which follows relies considerably on the distinction made by Margenau and Torgerson.

In the section on variables it was noted that constructs having primarily constitutive meaning are used by investigators principally on the "theory" end of the imaginary theoretical-operational continuum. Though to some degree empirically based, such constructs are not observable. It was suggested earlier that researchers may find useful, although oversimplified, the distinction between constructs (which possess primarily constitutive meaning and are not defined operationally) and variables (which also possess constitutive meaning but are defined operationally).

OPERATIONAL DEFINITIONS

This chapter has emphasized that an adequate scientific theory contains enough operationally defined constructs. All concepts in a scientific theory need not be directly defined operationally; but those constructs which are not directly defined operationally (*i.e.*, those possessing only constitutive meaning) must at least be connected with observable data through other constructs which are defined operationally. (Those possessing *direct operational definition* were referred to earlier as variables.)

As the reader undoubtedly has guessed from previous comments, *those constructs which are defined in terms of observed data or specified procedures to reproduce the phenomenon or object being described are said to be defined operationally.* Operational definitions (sometimes called "epistemic" definitions) serve as a bridge between theoretically defined constructs possessing constitutive meaning and observable data. Sometimes operational definitions are called "rules of correspondence" or "rules of interpretation," because they define, or at least partially define, certain theoretical constructs by connecting or linking them to observable data or operations. When one operationally defines a construct he includes (a) the observations made by the investigator and (b) the conditions under which they were made. Rapoport (1952) states the point well when he says that an operational definition specifies *what one must do* to experience the thing defined; the investigator defines a term by specifying *what to observe* and *how to observe it.* Operational definitions as viewed here thus serve as a basic means of control in empirical inquiry (Underwood, 1957; Bachrach, 1965).

Over the years numerous criteria for operational definition have been formulated and summarized. Communication researchers will find valuable a full issue of *Psychological Review* (1945, Vol. 52, No. 5) devoted to an excellent symposium on operationism and the role of operational definitions in scientific inquiry. In one of the papers in this symposium, Feigl (1945) summarized a set of criteria for operations defining a scientifically useful concept. Bachrach (1965) later modified Feigl's criteria as listed below:

1. They [operational definitions] should be logically consistent, that is, derived logically one from the other and be related to other operational definitions.
2. They should be definite, preferably quantitative.
3. They should be empirically based, linked to the observable.

4. They should be technically possible, subject to experimental manipulation.
5. They should be intersubjective and repeatable, demonstrable in different species and repeatable by different experimenters.
6. They should aim at the creation of concepts which will allow for laws or theories of greater predictiveness [p. 82].

While the investigator struggles with all the obvious problems apparent in defining operations in language (which may preclude complete operationism), he attempts to reduce the ambiguity of the commonsense language — the common-usage meanings of vague terms — which may impede effective communication. The probability is increased that both the investigator and his audience will understand what he means by terms when he specifies the operations he followed in making observations. Underwood (1957) and Bachrach (1965), among others, have stressed that operational definitions begin with observation. As Bachrach notes, "The observer records and reports facts and tries to communicate these in a manner that will give maximal clarity [pp. 75–76]." Recording and clearly reporting facts are two of the major tasks of the scientific researcher. But where does definition in science stop? Brodbeck (1963) has provided a reasonably clear answer to this question:

> In general, definition in science stops when all descriptive terms in the definition refer either to physical objects, or to some directly observable properties and relations of and among them. To say the same thing differently, definition ends when the defining words are all part of the basic vocabulary of science. In social science, the "physical objects" are people and the characters, among others, their observed behavior. When this basis has been reached, anyone understanding the basic vocabulary can determine whether any sentence containing defined terms is true or false. The longer the chain of definition before this basis is reached, the more "abstract" is the concept being defined [p. 51].

Periodically scholars have attempted to classify the types of operational definitions useful to inquiry concerning human behavior. For instance, Underwood (1957) has insightfully identified and discussed six types of operational definitions of behavioral phenomena. Beginning researchers in communication will find Underwood's discussion of operational definitions thorough, provocative, and useful, but comments concerning Underwood's classification system and others similarly complex are beyond the scope of this introduction to operational definitions. Kerlinger (1964) has classified operational definitions into two kinds, *measured* and *experimental*. The following discussion is based on his distinction.

Measured operational definitions. A measured operational definition stipulates what one must do to measure a given variable. To oversimplify, information presented in measured operational definitions may be classified into two types: (1) statements about operations naming, constructing, and assessing the instrument(s) used to do the actual measuring of a variable and (2) statements about the operations the investigator follows in obtaining and measuring the actual data from subjects. The second type might be appropriately labeled *management* or *administrative* operational definitions of a variable.[10]

As for the first type, suppose an investigator defined "listening" as what listening test *X* measures and referred the reader to sources supporting the adequacy of the test. If the adequacy of the listening test has been determined previously (*e.g.*, by operations determining reliability and validity), then one may under certain conditions be willing to accept the measured results. But for such instruments as speech performance rating scales, questionnaires to determine attitudes, various attitude scales, and investigator-constructed instruments to assess comprehension and retention, it is necessary to include in the definition statements about the operations performed in constructing them and assessing their adequacy for measuring a particular variable. If possible, the instrument should be reproduced in research reports with appropriate "construction operations" specified. If this is not possible, examples of items used should be specified and the investigator should offer to make available to other interested researchers the instrument and a report on the operations performed to develop and assess it. Clearly, in addition to including sample items in published research reports, investigators should also report appropriate reliability and validity results when investigator-constructed or other little known instruments are used for measuring variables.

Administrative and management operations — which cannot always be distinguished from the first type — are used to take or produce the measure once the instrument has been constructed and assessed. The focus in this type of definition is on *how to obtain* the measures for a particular variable from, on, or about subjects, once the instrument has been developed and its adequacy determined. These definitions answer the questions: Given an adequately developed instrument for the purpose intended, what must one do — step by step — to obtain data from, on, or concerning subjects? Given the data obtained from or about subjects, what step-by-step operations does one perform with these data (*e.g.*, transformation, discrepancy computations, etc.) prior to submitting them for data analysis? Such "little" operations in measured operational definitions frequently are major concerns in experimental investigations.

A few examples of measured operational definitions used in communication research follow. The reader should make an effort to determine

---

[10] Some researchers might group administrative or management operations under *experimental* operational definitions. How one classifies this type of operational definition is not so important as understanding that such operations exist and that they should be specified among the operational definitions in research reports.

whether the two types of measured operational definitions and minimal information required for them are included in the examples.[11]

A rating scale is often used in communication research to define operationally such variables as the "effectiveness" of speech performance, particular attitudes, or attitude change. Becker (1962), for example, defined "speaking performance" by having three instructors rate each of 442 students' speech performance from 1 through 7 on each of 11 scales. Becker further clarified his definition by reporting the 11 scales and the explanations for them actually used on the rating form in the study. Haines and McKeachie (1967) used ratings, among other measures, when they investigated the use of discussion methods in teaching psychology. "Satisfaction" was one variable in the study and was defined as follows:

> The following items of the student post-session questionnaire comprised the measure of satisfaction: (a) "I preferred this technique to the other one"; (b) "This technique made me doubt my own abilities and lowered my self-assurance"; and (c) "I would enjoy being taught by this technique" [p. 388].

The authors also reported that they used a Likert-type scale ranging from "Strongly Agree" (+3) to "Strongly Disagree" (−3) to assess these items. Powell and Miller (1967) included "attitude change" as a variable, defining it as follows:

> *Attitude change.* In order to test the hypotheses of the study, measures were obtained of subjects' attitudes toward the two positions dealt with in the "interviews": donating blood to the Red Cross versus selling one's blood for profit. Twenty attitude statements were used for this purpose, ten statements dealing with blood donations to the Red Cross and ten parallel statements dealing with the sale of blood for profit. Illustrative attitude statements are: "The Red Cross blood-donor program definitely should have everyone's full support," and "It is not at all immoral to sell one's blood if one needs money." Subjects responded to each statement on a seven-interval scale, ranging from "Strongly Agree" to "Strongly Disagree." Each subject's summed attitude scores with respect to the two positions was the attitude change measure employed in the data analyses which follow [p. 155].

Measured operational definitions are often used to define dependent variables. However, sometimes (and probably not often enough in communication research) an investigator may wish to assess the level of the

---

[11] It should be remembered that the following examples are just that — examples, and brief ones, at that. No effort has been made to detail every operational definition of a given variable that was originally included in the cited research report; rather, selected operational definition statements focused primarily on a particular variable or related matters are presented, in order to provide a reasonable variety and quantity of examples. Readers interested in the complete operational definitions of the variables in the examples are referred to the original research reports.

independent variable in each of the experimental conditions of his study. (This point was discussed earlier and in much greater detail on pp. 21–22.) For example, in the research just mentioned, Powell and Miller defined the measure to determine whether their anxiety manipulations were successful:

> *Felt anxiety.* To measure the success of the anxiety manipulation, subjects were asked to respond to a series of five statements designed to tap the amount of anxiety they felt while listening to the tape-recorded "interviews." "I was bored while listening to the interview," is illustrative of the five statements used for this purpose. Subjects responded to each statement on a seven-interval scale ranging from "Strongly Agree" to "Strongly Disagree." The sum of a subject's responses to the five statements was taken as a measure of his anxiety while listening to the communication [p. 155].

This is a measured operational definition stating how the independent variable will be measured. It should not be confused with the experimental operational definition, which specifies the particulars or operations used by the investigator in manipulating a given variable (see pp. 39–41).

Comprehension and retention are examples of variables used in investigations dealing with communication. For example, Frandsen (1963) used recall in one of his studies and defined the variable simply "as a fifteen-item constructed response test of immediate recall (p. 102)" given as soon as the stimulus message was presented. Gerard and Fleischer (1967) defined recall as used in their study in somewhat greater detail:

> The first recall measure asked the subject to write down the title of each story, the names of the characters, and as much detail about the plot as he could remember. The second measure presented the names of P, O, and X in the three pairs P-O, P-X, and O-X for each story and asked the subject to circle one of the three words "likes," "dislikes," or "don't know" for each pair. This latter measure did not discriminate at all since once reminded of the characters' names most subjects recalled all the relationships perfectly [p. 333].[12]

The last example of a measured operational definition is the definition of "autonomic arousal" in Cronkhite's (1966) imaginative study:

Autonomic Arousal

> Heart rate and skin conductance were chosen as the measures of autonomic arousal. Both were recorded by means of a Gilson two-channel polygraph, consisting of an ink-writing recorder and amplifiers combined in one unit, with appropriate electrodes and pream-

[12] The following statement in Gerard and Fleischer's report clarifies the meaning of P, O, and X in this definition: "The stories were very simple descriptions of a main character (P) and another character (O) in a real-life situation in which P's attitudes toward O and toward a third person, object, or event (X) are revealed [p. 333]."

plifiers picking up and transmitting the signals. Heart rate was computed in beats per minute. In quantifying the skin conductance records, the experimenter counted the individual, transient changes in conductance level and expressed the results in responses per minute [p. 395].

The measured operational definitions noted above demonstrate to some degree the variety of variables and operational definitions specified for them in communication research. Interested readers may wish to consult the references cited for the complete operational definitions.

Experimental operational definitions. The second major type of definition identified by Kerlinger (1964) is an experimental operational definition, which stipulates the operations or specific procedures followed by the investigator when manipulating a variable. When an investigator specifies the operations executed to construct the levels of the independent variable expressed by each of the experimental conditions in the investigation, he is stating experimental operational definitions. Examples of experimental operational definitions reported in communication literature follow.

J. W. Bowers (1963) studied the relations among intensity of stimulus, degree of self-esteem, attitude change, and other selected variables. He used one of the variables, "language intensity," as the specific means of varying the stimulus, and defined intensity as *"the quality of language which indicates the degree to which the speaker's attitude toward a concept deviates from neutrality.* High intensity, thus, is characterized by emotionalism and extremity [p. 345]." Bowers subsequently proceeded to define the variable operationally by describing the specific, procedural operations he followed to construct speeches of varying intensity levels. Frase (1968) investigated the effect on retention of a passage when an orienting question is asked which requires processing a reasonably large or small amount of information in the given passage:

A very simple, highly structured, paragraph of 36 words was constructed which described two attributes about each of four individuals. The paragraph follows.

Jim is a pilot. He was born in 1921. John is a policeman. He was born in 1930. Jack is a butcher. He was born in 1926. Jeff is an engineer. He was born in 1934 [p. 198].

Brooks and Scheidel (1968) investigated changes in the evaluative responses of an audience to a speaker during his speech. The researchers defined the "stimulus speech" used and its construction for the study's purpose in this statement:

Stimulus speech. The stimulus speech for this study was a tape-recorded 25-minute address to a predominantly white, college audience by Malcolm Little (Malcolm X), the late spokesman for the

Black Muslims.[5] He spoke in support of the proposition that American Negroes should separate from white society. The tape recording was edited by splicing seven silent periods into the speech and attaching an eighth silent period immediately after Malcolm's closing words. Each silent period had a duration of thirty seconds. Each was positioned at what seemed a "natural" division of the speech: the first silent period came at thirty seconds into the address, following a brief introductory prayer by the speaker; the remaining silent periods were spaced at intervals from three and one-half to five minutes apart, with an average interval of four minutes, usually at the conclusions of the main themes of the speech. Our major concern in positioning the silent periods was to avoid disturbing the continuity of the speech while approximating equal spacing. The silent periods provided eight intervals during which evaluative responses toward the speaker were measured [p. 2].

[5] The data for this study were collected at San Diego State College, prior to Malcolm's ouster from the Black Muslims and before his assassination. The speech originally was given before students at Cornell University in March 1962.

A study conducted by Sereno and Hawkins (1967) investigated the relationship between the quantity of speaker nonfluencies and the amount of attitude shift toward the speech topic. The authors defined nonfluencies as follows:

Nonfluencies were operationally defined as consisting of five categories and were based upon those reported by Mahl.[6] They were the following:

1. *"Ah."* The sound /ʌ/ or /ə/ inserted between two words of the speech. For example, "The Muslim 'ah' movement is the best example. . . ."
2. *Sentence correction.* A correction in the choice of a word or words while the sentence content remained basically unchanged. For example, "The Black Muslims benefit the Negro by insisting on high morality . . . moral standards."
3. *Stutter.* The serial, superfluous repetition of sounds. For example, "Martin Luther King, the first Negro to win the N-N-Nobel Peace Prize. . . ."
4. *Repetition.* The serial, superfluous repetition of a word. For example, "To him all . . . all Negroes were only. . . ."
5. *Tongue-slip correction.* A correction of an unintended sound. For example, "We shall realize that the Black Mos . . . Muslim Movement . . . [p. 59]."[7]

[6] George F. Mahl, "Exploring Emotional States by Content Analysis," in *Trends in Content Analysis*, ed. I. Pool (Urbana, 1959), p. 111.

[7] Mahl, through content analysis, discovered eight categories of speaker nonfluency. Only those categories that could be inserted readily into the original message text without altering basic content were used in this investigation.

The last example of an experimental operational definition is taken from a study by Williams and Tolch (1965). They conducted research to test the generality of dimensions of recognizing facial expression in both decoding and encoding. In their study they defined "encoding" in the following statement:

> Encoding took place under controlled conditions where a performer was handed a typed card containing one of the above five messages and was told to photograph himself when he felt that he had best exhibited the message by means of a facial expression. Head and shoulder color slides were taken in a separate testing room where a camera and lighting arrangement were mounted in a fixed position and equipped with extension-type shutter release to be operated by the encoder as he stood before the camera. The experimenters were not present during the photographing nor did the encoder have any means for feedback. Slides of each performer expressing the five messages were obtained in random sequence to avoid possible order effects [p. 23].

Obviously, other types and varieties of operational definitions used in communication research might be included here, but those presented should provide the beginning researcher with some idea of what operational definitions are and how they are reported in communication literature. Some definitions presented above are more complete and clear than others; but this is typical throughout the literature. The amount of useful information included in operational definitions by investigators varies considerably from study to study, but more often than not, too little information is presented. Conversely, it is important to recognize that an operational definition can usually express only a limited portion of the total meaning of a variable; it is unlikely that an operational definition can express all the meaning. No one should be aware of such matters more than those who focus their inquiry on symbols, language, messages, and the like.

INTERNAL AND EXTERNAL VALIDITY OF DESIGNS

In order to add to some of the comments made about the scientific approach to inquiry in this chapter and the previous essay, and to provide a basis for comprehending the aspects of communication research design, method, and measurement examined in the next three chapters, it is pertinent to consider now the general problem of the validity of research designs — particularly of the quasi-experimental designs so frequent in communication research. Considerable attention has been devoted to validity by Lindquist (1953), Campbell and Stanley (1963), Hays (1963), Kerlinger (1964), Cattell (1966), Ferguson (1966), Aronson and Carlsmith (1968), and Campbell (1968), so the discussion here will be brief and incomplete. There is, however, some merit in at least introducing beginning researchers in communication to the general notions of internal and external validity.

As noted in the introductory essay to Part One, an experiment is that part of the research process where an investigator manipulates one or more (independent) variables and observes their effects on one or more other (dependent) variables. The well developed research design is a kind of blueprint which includes structure and strategies for controlling the experiment in order to obtain dependable answers to research questions. By implication, a primary purpose of experimental research design is aiding the investigator in acquiring dependable answers to research questions; but as Kerlinger (1964) and others have argued, the research design also aids the experimenter in controlling the experimental, extraneous, and error variances peculiar to the problem being investigated.[13] Through research design, controlled constraints are placed on the observation of phenomena under investigation. The investigator must plan designs that adequately satisfy such general criteria as answering the research questions or testing the research hypotheses, controlling extraneous variables, controlling the independent variable, etc. (Selltiz *et al.,* 1959; Kerlinger, 1964; Travers, 1964).

There are two classes of criteria, however, which have not received until recent years the attention merited by their particular pertinence to some designs for inquiry in communication research — external and internal validity. The discussion of internal and external validity presented below closely follows the work of Campbell (1957, 1968) and Campbell and Stanley (1963).

Internal Validity

Suppose an investigator posed this question about a study: Did the experimental manipulation or treatment (independent variable X) really produce a significant difference in this particular experimental study? The investigator has raised the question of *internal validity*. When one or more extraneous variables are not controlled in an experimental design and it is possible to mistake their effects for the effect of the experimental treatment, the design is not internally valid. Before stating that the experimental treatment really made a difference in a given experiment, an investigator must make every effort to determine that extraneous or uncontrolled variables did not, in fact, produce the observed results. It is fair to say that internal validity is the least criterion required for interpreting any experiment; as Campbell and Stanley (1963) indicate, without it any given experiment is uninterpretable. Campbell and Stanley have identified eight classes of variables relevant to internal validity, which, if not controlled, produce effects that could be confounded with the experimental treatment's effect. Beginning researchers in communication will benefit from reading Campbell and Stanley's comprehensive and insightful analysis of the conditions under

[13] Interested readers are referred to Kerlinger's (1964) excellent discussion of the nature and functions of research designs, and the control of experimental, extraneous, and error variance (pp. 275–289).

which these eight classes of variables threaten the internal validity of various quasi-experimental and experimental designs.

External Validity

External validity refers to the representativeness or generalizability of the experimental findings. What are the populations, situations, experimental variables, and measurement variables to which this particular effect can be generalized? Nebergall's (1965) treatment of such concerns and numerous pertinent observations made at a recent speech communication conference (Kibler and Barker, 1969) should prove a valuable introduction for beginning researchers to external validity in communication research. Campbell and Stanley (1963) have identified four classes of variables relevant to external validity and have provided an extremely useful analysis concerning the conditions under which each may jeopardize the external validity of various quasi-experimental and experimental designs.

Summary

This chapter has presented an overview of the process of scientific investigation in communication research and selected key concepts involved in it. In the first section of the chapter, the nature of scientific investigation was reviewed with an emphasis on the logical basis of such inquiry in communication research. Selected procedures and concepts important to an understanding of communication research were presented in the second section with an emphasis on the interrelated functions served by each in the scientific research enterprise. Among the concepts and procedures introduced were concepts and constructs, variables, hypotheses, operational definitions, and internal and external validity of designs.

The explanations of scientific investigation and related key concepts developed here necessarily have been introductory and sometimes oversimplified in an attempt to present ideas meaningfully to beginning communication researchers and to provide a basis for comprehending some of the concepts, procedures, and methodologies examined in subsequent chapters of this volume. But more important, an understanding of the ideas presented here should serve as a starting point for students to acquire greater insight into the nature of scientific research in communication. This chapter is merely an initial step, not a terminal effort, for those seriously interested in communication research. With this in mind, considerable effort has been made to refer readers to books and studies which expand in greater detail the concepts and procedures reviewed. After the nature and methods used in scientific research are understood clearly, then students will be confronted with the ultimate test of their understanding — engaging in the production, hard work, and enjoyment of scientific communication research.

References and Selected Readings

Aronson, E., and Carlsmith, J. M. Experimentation in social psychology. In G. Lindzey and E. Aronson (Ed.), *Handbook of social psychology.* (2nd ed.) Vol. 2. Reading, Mass.: Addison-Wesley, 1968. Pp. 1–79.

Bachrach, A. J. *Psychological research.* New York: Random House, 1965.

Bain, R. Category. In J. Gould and W. L. Kolb (Eds.), *A dictionary of the social sciences.* New York: The Free Press of Glencoe, 1964. P. 77.

Bakan, D. *On method.* San Francisco: Jossey-Bass, 1967.

Bandura, A., and Walters, R. H. *Social learning and personality development.* New York: Holt, Rinehart & Winston, 1963.

Barker, L. L., Kibler, R. J., and Geter, R. W. Two investigations of the relationship among selected ratings of speech effectiveness and comprehension. *Speech Monographs,* 1968, **35,** 400–406.

Barker, L. L., Kibler, R. J., and Hunter, E. C. An empirical study of overlap rating effects. *The Speech Teacher,* 1968, **17,** 160–166.

Becker, S. L. The rating of speeches: Scale independence. *Speech Monographs,* 1962, **29,** 38–44.

Benjamin, A. C. *Operationism.* Springfield, Ill.: Charles C Thomas, 1955.

Bergmann, G. *Philosophy of science.* Madison: University of Wisconsin Press, 1957.

Boring, E. G. The use of operational definitions in science. *Psychological Review,* 1945, **52,** 243–245.

Boring, E. G. *A history of experimental psychology.* (2nd ed.) New York: Appleton-Century-Crofts, 1957.

Bowers, J. W. Language intensity, social introversion, and attitude change. *Speech Monographs,* 1963, **30,** 345–352.

Bowers, J. W. Some correlates of language intensity. *Quarterly Journal of Speech,* 1964, **50,** 415–420.

Bowers, R. V. Variable. In J. Gould and W. L. Kolb (Eds.), *A dictionary of the social sciences.* New York: The Free Press of Glencoe, 1964. Pp. 746–748.

Braithwaite, R. *Scientific explanation.* Cambridge, Eng.: Cambridge University Press, 1955.

Bridgman, P. W. *The logic of modern physics.* New York: Macmillan, 1927.

Bridgman, P. W. The nature of some of our physical concepts. *British Journal for the Philosophy of Science,* 1950, **1,** 257.

Bridgman, P. W. *The nature of some of our physical concepts.* New York: Philosophical Library, 1952.

Brodbeck, M. The philosophy of science and educational research. *Review of Educational Research,* 1957, **27,** 427–440.

Brodbeck, M. Logic and scientific method in research on teaching. In N. L. Gage (Ed.), *Handbook of research on teaching.* Chicago: Rand McNally, 1963. Pp. 44–93.

Brooks, R. D., and Scheidel, T. M. Speech as process: A case study. *Speech Monographs,* 1968, **35**, 1–7.

Brown, R. *Explanation in social science.* Chicago: Aldine, 1963.

Bruner, J. S., Goodnow, J. J., and Austin, G. A. *A study of thinking.* New York: John Wiley, 1956.

Campbell, D. T. Factors relevant to the validity of experiments in social settings. *Psychological Bulletin,* 1957, **54**, 297–312.

Campbell, D. T. From description to experimentation: Interpreting trends as quasi-experiments. In C. W. Harris (Ed.), *Problems in measuring change.* Madison: University of Wisconsin Press, 1963. Pp. 212–242.

Campbell, D. T. Quasi-experimental design. In D. L. Sills (Ed.), *International encyclopedia of the social sciences.* New York: Macmillan and The Free Press, 1968. Pp. 259–262.

Campbell, D. T., and Clayton, K. N. Avoiding regression effects in panel studies of communication impact. *Studies in Public Communication,* No. 3. Chicago: Department of Sociology, University of Chicago, 1961. Pp. 99–118.

Campbell, D. T., and Stanley, J. C. Experimental and quasi-experimental designs for research on teaching. In N. L. Gage (Ed.), *Handbook of research on teaching.* Chicago: Rand McNally, 1963. Pp. 171–246.

Cattell, R. B. (Ed.) *Handbook of multivariate experimental psychology.* Chicago: Rand McNally, 1966.

Chaplin, J. P., and Krawiec, T. S. *Systems and theories of psychology.* New York: Holt, Rinehart & Winston, 1960.

Churchman, C. W. *Theory of experimental inference.* New York: Macmillan, 1948.

Cochran, W. G. *Sampling techniques.* (2nd ed.) New York: John Wiley, 1963.

Cochran, W. G. Experimental design: I. The design of experiments. In D. L. Sills (Ed.), *International encyclopedia of the social sciences.* Vol. 5. New York: Macmillan and The Free Press, 1968. Pp. 245–254.

Cochran, W. G., and Cox, G. M. *Experimental designs.* (2nd ed.) New York: John Wiley, 1957.

Cohen, M. *A preface to logic.* New York: Meridian Press, 1956.

Cook, D. R. *A guide to educational research.* Boston: Allyn & Bacon, 1965.

Cronkhite, G. L. Logic, emotion, and the paradigm of persuasion. *Quarterly Journal of Speech,* 1964, **50**, 13–18.

Cronkhite, G. L. Autonomic correlates of dissonance and attitude change. *Speech Monographs,* 1966, **33**, 392–399.

DeCecco, J. P. *The psychology of learning and instruction: Educational psychology.* Englewood Cliffs, N. J.: Prentice-Hall, 1968.

Dewey, J. *How we think.* Boston: D. C. Heath, 1933.

Edwards, A. L. Experiments: Their planning and execution. In G. Lindzey (Ed.), *Handbook of social psychology.* Vol. 1. Cambridge, Mass.: Addison-Wesley, 1954. Pp. 259–288.

Edwards, A. L. *Statistical methods.* New York: Holt, Rinehart & Winston, 1967.

Edwards, A. L. *Experimental design in psychological research.* New York: Holt, Rinehart & Winston, 1968.

English, H. B., and English, A. C. *A comprehensive dictionary of psychoanalytical terms.* New York: David McKay, 1958.

Feather, N. T. An expectancy-value model of information-seeking behavior. *Psychological Review,* 1967, **74,** 342–360.

Federer, W. T. *Experimental design.* New York: Macmillan, 1955.

Feigl, H. Operationism and scientific method. *Psychological Review,* 1945, **52,** 250–259.

Ferguson, G. A. *Statistical analysis in psychology and education.* (2nd ed.) New York: McGraw-Hill, 1966.

Frandsen, K. D. Effects of threat appeals and media of transmission. *Speech Monographs,* 1963, **30,** 101–104.

Frase, L. T. Some unpredicted effects of different questions upon learning from connected discourse. *Journal of Educational Psychology,* 1968, **59,** 197–201.

Gerard, H. B., and Fleischer, L. Recall and pleasantness of balanced and unbalanced cognitive structures. *Journal of Personality and Social Psychology,* 1967, **7,** 332–337.

Good, C. V. (Ed.) *Dictionary of education.* (2nd ed.) New York: McGraw-Hill, 1959.

Gould, J., and Kolb, W. L. (Eds.) *A dictionary of the social sciences.* New York: The Free Press of Glencoe, 1964.

Guilford, J. P. *Fundamental statistics in psychology and education.* New York: McGraw-Hill, 1965.

Guilford, J. P. *The nature of human intelligence.* New York: McGraw-Hill, 1967.

Haines, D. B., and McKeachie, W. J. Cooperative versus competitive discussion methods in teaching introductory psychology. *Journal of Educational Psychology,* 1967, **58,** 386–390.

Hays, W. L. *Statistics for psychologists.* New York: Holt, Rinehart, & Winston, 1963.

Hempel, C. G. Fundamentals of concept formation in empirical science. In *International encyclopedia of unified science.* Chicago: University of Chicago Press, 1952. P. 43.

Hull, C. L. *Principles of behavior.* New York: Appleton-Century-Crofts, 1943.

Hull, C. L. *Essentials of behavior.* New Haven, Conn.: Yale University Press, 1951.

Israel, H. E., and Goldstein, B. Operationism in psychology. *Psychological Review,* 1944, **51,** 177–188.

Kaplan, A. *The conduct of inquiry.* San Francisco: Chandler, 1964.

Kendall, M. G., and Buckland, W. R. *A dictionary of statistical terms.* New York: Hafner, 1960.

Kerlinger, F. N. *Foundations of behavioral research.* New York: Holt, Rinehart & Winston, 1964.

Kibler, R. J., and Barker, L. L. An experimental study to assess the effects of three levels of mispronunciation on comprehension for three different populations. *Speech Monographs*, 1968, **35**, 26–38.

Kibler, R. J., and Barker, L. L. (Eds.) *Conceptual frontiers in speech-communication*. New York: Speech Association of America, 1969.

Kibler, R. J., Kelly, F. J., Gibson, J. W., and Gruner, C. R. Predicting speech grades from selected spoken language variables. *Southern Speech Journal*, 1968, **34**, 94–99.

Kirk, R. E. *Experimental design: Procedures for the behavioral sciences*. Belmont, Cal.: Brooks/Cole, 1968

Lehmann, E. L. Hypothesis testing. In D. L. Sills (Ed.), *International encyclopedia of the social sciences*. Vol. 7. New York: Macmillan and The Free Press, 1968. Pp. 40–47.

Liberman, A. M., Cooper, F. S., Shankwiler, D. P., and Studdert-Kennedy, M. Perception of the speech code. *Psychological Review*, 1967, **74**, 431–461.

Lindquist, E. F. *Design and analysis of experiments in psychology and education*. Boston: Houghton Mifflin, 1953.

MacCorquodale, L., and Meehl, P. E. On a distinction between hypothetical constructs and intervening variables. *Psychological Review*, 1948, **55**, 95–107.

Mandler, G., and Kesson, W. *The language of psychology*. New York: John Wiley, 1959.

Margenau, H. *The nature of physical reality*. New York: McGraw-Hill, 1950.

Margenau, H. On interpretations and misinterpretations of operationalism. *Scientific Monthly*, 1954, **69**, 209.

Marx, M. H., and Hillix, W. A. *Systems and theories in psychology*. New York: McGraw-Hill, 1963.

McDonald, F. J. *Educational psychology*. Belmont, Cal.: Wadsworth, 1965.

McGinnis, R. Intervening variable. In J. Gould and W. L. Kolb (Eds.), *A dictionary of the social sciences*. New York: The Free Press of Glencoe, 1964. Pp. 351–352.

Merton, R. K. *Social theory and social structure*. Glencoe, Ill.: The Free Press, 1957.

Miller, G. R. Human information processing: Some research guidelines. In R. J. Kibler and L. L. Barker (Eds.), *Conceptual frontiers in speech-communication*. New York: Speech Association of America, 1969.

Miller, G. R., and Hewgill, M. A. Some recent research on fear-arousing message appeals. *Speech Monographs*, 1966, **33**, 377–391.

Nebergall, R. E. A critique of experimental design in communication research. *Central States Speech Journal*, 1965, **16**, 13–16.

Peng, K. C. *The design and analysis of scientific experiments*. Reading, Mass.: Addison-Wesley, 1967.

Perkins, C. C., Jr. An analysis of the concept of reinforcement. *Psychological Review*, 1968, **75**, 155–172.

Poincaré, H. *Science and hypothesis*. New York: Dover, 1952.

Polanyi, M. Logic and psychology. *American Psychologist,* 1968, **23,** 27–43.

Popham, W. J. *Educational statistics.* New York: Harper & Row, 1967.

Powell, F. A., and Miller, G. R. Social approval and disapproval cues in anxiety-arousing communications. *Speech Monographs,* 1967, **34,** 152–159.

Pratt, C. C. Operationism in psychology. *Psychological Review,* 1945, **52,** 262–269.

Rapoport, A. What is semantics? *The American Scientist,* 1952, **40,** 123–135

Rudner, R. S. *Philosophy of social sciences.* Englewood Cliffs, N. J.: Prentice-Hall, 1966.

Sassenrath, J. M., and Yonge, G. D. Delayed information feedback, feedback cues, retention set, and delayed retention. *Journal of Educational Psychology,* 1968, **59,** 69–73.

Scott, W. A. Attitude measurement. In G. Lindzey and E. Aronson (Eds.), *The handbook of social psychology.* (2nd ed.) Vol. 2. Reading, Mass.: Addison-Wesley, 1968. Pp. 204–273.

Scott, W. A., and Wertheimer, M. *Introduction to psychological research.* New York: John Wiley, 1962.

Scriven, M. The philosophy of science. In D. L. Sills (Ed.), *International encyclopedia of the social sciences.* New York: Macmillan and The Free Press, 1968. Pp. 83–90.

Selltiz, C., Jahoda, M., Deutseh, M., and Cook, S. W. *Research methods in social relations.* New York: Holt, Rinehart & Winston, 1959.

Sereno, K. K., and Hawkins, G. J. The effects of variations in speakers' non-fluency upon audience ratings of attitude toward the speech topic and speakers' credibility. *Speech Monographs,* 1967, **34,** 58–64.

Sidman, M. *Tactics of scientific research.* New York: Basic Books, 1960.

Siegel, S. *Nonparametric statistics for the behavioral sciences.* New York: McGraw-Hill, 1956.

Skinner, B. F. The operational analysis of psychological terms. *Psychological Review,* 1945, **52,** 270–277.

Skinner, B. F. *Cumulative record.* New York: Appleton-Century-Crofts, 1961.

Spence, K. W. Theoretical interpretations of learning. In S. S. Stevens (Ed.), *Handbook of experimental psychology.* New York: John Wiley, 1951. Pp. 690–729.

Stephan, F. F., and McCarthy, P. J. *Sampling opinions.* New York: John Wiley, 1958.

Stevens, S. S. The operational basis of psychology. *American Journal of Psychology,* 1935, **47,** 323–330.

Stevens, S. S. Psychology and the science of science. *Psychological Bulletin,* 1939, **36,** 221–263.

Suchman, E. A. *Evaluative research.* New York: Russell Sage Foundation, 1967.

Tatsuoka, M. M., and Tiedeman, D. V. Statistics as an aspect of scientific method in research on teaching. In N. L. Gage (Ed.), *Handbook of research on teaching.* Chicago: Rand McNally, 1963. Pp. 142–246.

Tolman, E. C. The determiners of behavior at a choice point. *Psychological Review,* 1938, **45,** 1–41.

Torgerson, W. S. *Theory and methods of scaling.* New York: John Wiley, 1958.

Townsend, J. C. *Introduction to experimental method.* New York: McGraw-Hill, 1953.

Travers, R. M. W. *An introduction to educational research.* (2nd ed.) New York: Macmillan, 1964.

Travers, R. M. W. *Essentials of learning.* New York: Macmillan, 1967.

Underwood, B. J. *Psychological research.* New York: Appleton-Century-Crofts, 1957.

Van Dalen, D. B. *Understanding educational research.* New York: McGraw-Hill, 1966.

Verplanck, W. S. A glossary of some terms used in the objective science of behavior. *Psychological Review,* 1957, **64** (Monogr. Suppl. 2), 23.

Vinacke, W. E. *The psychology of thinking.* New York: McGraw-Hill, 1952.

Weinberg, G. H., and Schumaker, J. A. *Statistics an intuitive approach.* Belmont, Cal.: Wadsworth, 1962.

Williams, F. *Reasoning with statistics.* New York: Holt, Rinehart & Winston, 1968.

Williams, F., and Tolch, J. Communication by facial expression. *Journal of Communication,* 1965, **15,** 17–27.

Winer, B. J. *Statistical principles in experimental design.* New York: McGraw-Hill, 1962.

Wise, J. E., Nordberg, R. B., and Reitz, D. J. *Methods of research in education.* Boston: D. C. Heath, 1967.

2

Multivariate
Design Considerations

Francis J. Kelly

The preceding chapter presented design considerations fundamental to communication research in a *univariate* context — that is, one or two independent (predictor) variables were investigated to determine their relationship to some dependent (criterion) variable. The intent of this chapter is to introduce the reader to *multivariate* design, which compares a number of predictor and/or criterion variables simultaneously. Since these designs are more complex than univariate studies, the novice in communication research may find the concepts and writing style a bit difficult. Some of the difficulty will be reduced if he recognizes that this chapter provides only an introduction to the field of multivariate design. Before attempting to investigate a complex theory of communication, he should consult the references at the end of the chapter for the detailed explanation of the processes and mathematical models essential to fruitful research.

Rather than confusing the reader with several multivariate approaches to communication research, this chapter will attempt to show how one —

multiple linear regression analysis — can statistically reflect the complexities of the newer communication theories. A review of the several relevant variables that constitute communication behavior is presented first. The basic linear statistical model is discussed, and a number of expansions on the basic model are developed to account for interaction and curvilinear functions.[1] One possible predictive study is given to show the power of the general regression approach; since the complex use of multiple regression analysis is a relatively recent development, no actual communication study using it seems to be available. A series of regression models is cast to illustrate how the technique might provide answers to the research questions. A brief discussion regarding other multivariate techniques is also presented. A number of sources, both theoretical and practical, are provided for the investigator who might want to use the general regression procedure in future research.

THEORETICAL BACKGROUND

Modern communication theory and other modern behavioral theories are based on complex models of human behavior. These models (*e.g.,* Osgood, 1957; Berlo, 1960; McGuire, 1961; Wiseman and Barker, 1967) indicate that a broad number of variables influence the response of the decoder. A simplified presentation of these variables is this:

> The *sender* encodes a message using some channel(s) and the *receiver* decodes the message impinging on him. Upon decoding the message, some mediation (interpretation) and encoding takes place before the receiver responds (the evidence that some message was received).

For purposes of analysis, we can express these variables in a quasi-mathematical model:

$$R = f(R_c, S_c)$$

where

R = the response of the receiver
S_c = stimulus characteristics or factors impinging on the receiver
R_c = receiver characteristics

---

[1] The basic *linear* statistical model refers to those statistical analyses and tests designed to measure the value of variables (independent and dependent) assumed to be related in a constant, unchanging way, *i.e.,* in one way. It rests on the assumption that differences between measures on the dependent variable are directly caused by the independent variable. If one plotted a line on a graph having two axes, one for the dependent variable and one for the independent variable, the line would be a single, straight line.

This quasi equation should read: The response of the receiver is a function of within-receiver characteristics and stimulus characteristics.

Furthermore, on the basis of empirical data we can expand the equation to reflect a number of *known* within-receiver characteristics and stimulus characteristics which the research investigator may consider relevant to a particular communication behavior.

RECEIVER CHARACTERISTICS

A   *Ability* of the receiver. This might include: divergent thinking ability, convergent thinking ability, listening ability, etc.

E   *Expectations* of the receiver regarding the credibility, significance, etc., of the message source (some call this "attitude").

M   *Motivation* of the receiver regarding the importance (value) of the message received.

S   *Sex* of the receiver. Social interaction and sex-typed expectancies are imposed on males and females, so they may be expected to respond differently to a particular message.

L   *Learnings* of the receiver relevant to decoding and interpreting the message (*e.g.,* a message transmitted regarding a physical event may be coded so as to communicate only to a knowledgeable physicist).

STIMULUS CHARACTERISTICS

Cm   *Channel mode:* Visual, visual-auditory, auditory, etc.

Cx   *Context* of message transmission which might differentially influence the receiver (*e.g.,* classroom, beer hall, locker room, church).

St   *Structure* of the message: The particular ordering of the stimuli for differential impact.

No   *Noise* accompanying message (*e.g.,* irrelevant stimuli, rambling presentation, etc.).

Sc   *Source characteristics* (*e.g.,* dress, sex, etc.) of the message source which influence the receiver's judgment of the credibility of the source.

These several variables illustrate *only* the complexities relevant to a specific study of human communication behavior. If we cast these variables into an expanded quasi-mathematical equation, we get:

$$R = f[(A, E, M, S, L), (Cm, Cx, St, No, Sc)], X$$

where $X =$ unknown factors (residual or error).

For any particular study, the tasks of the investigator are to (1) select the variables which theoretically are related to the criterion behavior —

the behavior that will be measured as the dependent variable — and (2) explicate the functional relationships among the several relevant independent variables and the criterion behavior. Once he has selected the relevant variables, the investigator must specify research questions and cast statistical models which test the functional relationships. He may ask: "Are the several predictor variables interacting (a multiplicative function)?" "Are these variables curvilinearly related to the criterion (a quadratic function)?" He may specify other functional relations (on the basis of theory) reflecting complex relations among within-receiver variables, stimulus characteristics, and the behavior under investigation.

CONVENTIONAL STATISTICAL MODELS

If, indeed, the newer models of communication behavior more closely reflect the existing state of affairs, then how adequate are the conventional *statistical* models to test the *theoretical* models?

Consider the investigator who wishes to study the influence of a visual presentation versus a nonvisual presentation on student learning. He may collect a group of college freshmen, randomly assign the students (receivers) into two groups, and give one group a presentation with visuals and the other group a presentation without visuals. He may give a post-test to determine the effects of the presentation and a *t* test to determine whether observed group mean differences were due to sampling error. Of course, if the investigator is a bit more sophisticated, he may give a pre-test, subdivide the groups by sex, and calculate a 2×2 analysis of covariance.[2] Such an analysis can provide information about differential treatment effects on the two sexes and control for pre-test differences between groups, but it does not reflect the real complexities which the newer theoretical models express. Post-test differences due to receiver ability, expectations, motivations, etc., are all assumed to be randomized and, therefore, not likely to bias post-test group differences. But if the complex theoretical models more closely reflect the vagaries of human behavior, then the error variance may be unreasonably large because of the random effects of nonrandom variables.

For example, in the 2×2 covariance problem given above, if some *nontested* variable, such as listening ability, interacts with sex so that (1) males

[2] A 2×2 analysis of covariance is a statistical analysis in which two degrees of one variable (in this case sex) and two degrees of a second variable (mode of presentation of material, visual or nonvisual) are tested to determine what effect changing one variable has on the effect produced by either of the degrees of the other variable *on the dependent* variable, *i.e.,* student learning, with adjustments for pre-test group differences. We are asking: "If the sex varies, will the effect of a nonvisual presentation on learning be the same as if the sex were not varied?" Both main effects and interaction effects of the two independent variables on the dependent variable can be tested. If there were three types of presentations, then the analysis would be a 2×3.

with low listening ability score better with the visual presentation and (2) males with a high listening ability score better with the nonvisual presentation, then a conclusion might be drawn that the two treatments are equally effective for males. Apparently we need to use statistical models which will discriminate more clearly and allow us to express a research question more completely.

MULTIPLE REGRESSION ANALYSIS

A number of multivariate designs have been invented and used to reflect complexities in economics and agriculture. Factor analysis, as a multivariate technique, has been widely used in communication and psychological research and is discussed elsewhere in this book (see Chapter 11, p. 319). On the other hand, multiple regression analysis, the simplest and one of the oldest multivariate techniques, has had little use in behavioral research. Furthermore, when multiple regression analysis has been used, the applications failed to take advantage of the full power of the model. Bottenberg and Ward (1963) have resurrected multiple regression analysis, and their exposition can be adapted to explicate and test many of the functional relationships suggested by modern communication theory.

Basics in Multiple Regression Analysis

Before discussing complex regression models, a brief review of the simple linear model might be appropriate. In the case where a perfect linear relationship exists between X and Y, the formula for a straight line holds:

Equation 1 $\quad Y_1 = a + bX_1$

where $\quad a =$ the "Y-intercept" of the line (the point on the Y axis where the line on the graph would intersect, if extended)

$b =$ regression weight, the amount of increase on Y_1 for each unit increase in X_1 (the "slope" of the line)

Of course, when the relationship between X_1 and Y_1 is not perfect, no two weights, a and b, can be found to make the equation $Y_1 = a + bX_1$ true. Linear regression analysis does calculate the weights for a and b so that the sum of the squared differences between the predicted score and the observed score is minimal [$\Sigma(Y_1 - \tilde{Y}_1)^2$, where $\tilde{Y}_1 =$ the predicted score]. Statisticians often refer to this equation for simple linear regression as "the least-squares solution to a line of best fit."

To test the significance of the linear relationship, an R^2 can be calculated using the equation:

Equation 2 $\tilde{Y}_1 = a + bX_1$

The R^2_f (R^2 full) gives the percentage of variance in Y_1 that is associated with X_1.

A second R^2_r (R^2 restricted) can be calculated deleting the knowledge of the X_1 variable (essentially setting the weight of $b = 0$). The model would be

Equation 3 $\tilde{Y}_1 = a.$

In this case the mean of the Y_1 variable would be the a weight, and a horizontal line would be cast (the R^2 would be 0). An F test can be calculated to test the significance of the predicted variance associated with the full model using the formula:

Formula 1 $$F = \frac{(R^2_f - R^2_r) \,/\, df_1}{(1 - R^2_f) \,/\, df_2}$$

where R^2_f = the percentage of variance accounted for in the full model

R^2_r = the percentage of variance accounted for in the restricted model

df_1 = the number of unknown weights in the full model minus the number of unknown weights calculated in the restricted model [in the example, two weights are calculated in the full model — (a) and (b) — and one for the restricted model — (a). Therefore $df_1 = 1$.]

df_2 = the total number of subjects (N) minus the number of unknown weights in the full model (in the example, $df_2 = N - 2$)

The expression $R^2_f - R^2_r$ in the numerator gives the percentage of common variance between X_1 and Y_1 (percentage of among-group variance).

The expression $1 - R^2_f$ in the denominator gives the percentages of variance in Y_1 not associated with X_1 (percentage of within-group variance or "error" variance).

The typical multiple regression problem (by definition including more than one predictor) might be:

Equation 4 $\tilde{Y}_1 = a + b_1X_1 + b_2X_2 \ldots b_kX_k$

One can test the additive independent contribution of any predictor using Formula 1 by casting two equations: (1) with the predictor variable included in the equation (which yields R^2_f), and (2) an equation without the predictor variable (which yields R^2_r). In general, we can test the difference between a complex regression equation and an equation which is simplified by means of deleting some predictor variable(s) and using the generalized F formula.

Interaction in Regression

The preceding discussion summarizes the typical use of regression analysis where all predictors and the criterion are assumed to be additively related — *i.e.,* the effect of one is simply added to the effect of the second, and of the third. However, the situation may be that *new interactions* produce effects greater than that of the sum of their individual effects on the dependent variable. The well-known interactive case in typical analysis of variance is seldom used in regression. Consider the case where two treatments might be expected to interact with a continuous predictor, such as listening ability, on some criterion.

We can define four vectors (variables):

$X_1 = 1$ if the score on the criterion comes from a person who had Treatment I; zero otherwise

$X_2 = 1$ if the score on the criterion comes from a person who had Treatment II; zero otherwise

$X_3 =$ a continuous vector whose elements are made up of STEP Listening scores

$Y_1 =$ score on some criterion

An additive linear equation (*e.g.,* $\tilde{Y}_1 = a + b_1X_1 + b_2X_2 + b_3X_3$) will *not* reflect an interacting state since the weight (b_3) associated with X_3 (the listening test) is common for both groups. Figure 1 (p. 58) shows a possible set of predicted lines using the above equation and where $b_3 \neq 0$ and b_1 is larger than b_2.

Interaction means that two or more vectors are multiplicatively related to the criterion. We can use the following linear equation to reflect interaction:

Equation 5 $\qquad \tilde{Y}_1 = a + b_1X_1 + b_2X_2 + b_4(X_1X_3) + b_5(X_2X_3)$

Note that in Equation 5 the last two vectors are products of X_3 with X_1 and X_2. Since X_1 is composed of ones and zeros and X_3 contains STEP Listening scores, (X_1X_3) gives a vector of STEP Listening scores if the

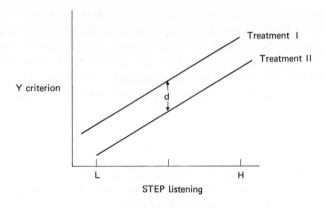

FIGURE 1

Theoretical lines of best fit for two groups using the equation $\tilde{Y}_1 = a + b_1X_1 + b_2X_2 + b_3X_3$ and where the weight associated with Treatment I is larger than Treatment II and where "d" represents a constant difference.

store on the criterion comes from a person who had Treatment I; zero otherwise. Likewise, the (X_2X_3) vector will contain the listening scores for Treatment II subjects. Figure 2 shows a hypothetical X_1X_3 vector.

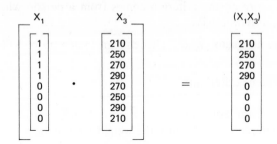

FIGURE 2

The (X_1X_3) vector shows the product of the combined elements in X_1 and X_3.

Equation 5 *allows* the slopes for each treatment across X_3 to be different since each treatment has a separate weight (b_4 and b_5) associated with the X_3 variable.

Figure 3 shows a possible case where interaction between treatment and STEP Listening exists.

An R^2_f can be calculated using Equation 5. One may hypothesize *no* interaction and, therefore, impose the restriction that $b_4 = b_5 = b_3$, a com-

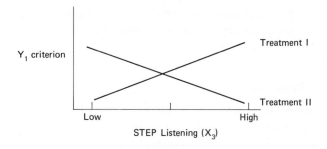

Y₁ criterion — Treatment I — Treatment II — Low — High — STEP Listening (X₃)

FIGURE 3

A case where near perfect interaction exists between treatment conditions and listening scores.

mon weight. The R^2_r can be calculated with the equation $\tilde{Y}_1 = a + b_1X_1 + b_2X_2 + b_3X_3$. An F test can be made using Formula 1. If the R^2_r is significantly smaller than the R^2_f, one may then assume interaction and may wish to plot the relationships using the partial regression weights. As was mentioned earlier, these partial regression weights are calculated to minimize the sum of the squared differences between the observed score (Y) and the predicted score ($\tilde{Y}$). If two regression weights (one for each group) significantly reduce the value $\Sigma(Y - \tilde{Y})^2$ when compared with a single regression weight (one for both groups), then the two weights cannot be said to be equal. Further detail regarding the calculation of partial regression weights at this time is not central to the present discussion and would only make this chapter more complex. The interested reader may pursue the matter of regression weights in Cattell (1966).

You may note in the example given that dichotomous vectors (variables) and continuous vectors were used in the predictor set.[3] In some ways multiple regression analysis has an advantage over conventional analysis of variance since continuous data do *not* need to be categorized into two or three levels.

Interaction essentially means that the relationship between a criterion and a predictor depends on some other variable. The predictors might both be continuous (*e.g.*, an intelligence measure and an anxiety measure). The interaction of intelligence scores (X_1) with anxiety (X_2) to predict some performance measure (Y_1) can be simply cast:

Equation 6 $\tilde{Y}_1 = a + b_1X_1 + b_2X_2 + b_3X_1X_2$

where X_1X_2 contains the product of each pair of elements in the X_1 and X_2 variables. The test would restrict Equation 6 so that $b_3 = 0$. If the F value

[3] A dichotomous variable is one having only two classes or categories, while a continuous variable has an infinite number of values.

is significant, then interaction undoubtedly exists. Higher order interactions can be tested using the appropriate number and combination of interacting variables.

Curvilinear Regression

Many studies using measures of anxiety as predictors reveal curvilinear relationships between anxiety level and performance. Multiple regression analysis need *not* be limited to rectilinear forms; if quadratic functions are expected, one can cast a regression equation to reflect the relationship. One simply adds to the rectilinear equation ($Y_1 = a + bX_1$), where X_1 might be a vector of anxiety scores, another vector whose elements are the square of the elements in X_1. The equation would be:

Equation 7 $\qquad \tilde{Y}_1 = a + b_1X_1 + b_2X_1^2$

The R^2_f derived using Equation 7 can be compared with an R^2_r calculated using a model without the vector with squared X_1 elements (X_1^2). Formula 1 will provide the appropriate F test. If the weight b_2 is nonzero, then a power function exists. A plotting of predicted scores may look like Figure 4.

Interaction and curvilinearity can be combined to reflect curvilinear interaction. Equation 5 can be expanded to provide two new vectors representing the square of the elements in (X_1X_3) and (X_2X_3):

Equation 8 $\qquad \tilde{Y}_1 = a + b_1X_1 + b_2X_2 + b_4(X_1X_3) + b_5(X_2X_3) +$
$b_6(X_1X_3)^2 + b_7(X_2X_3)^2$

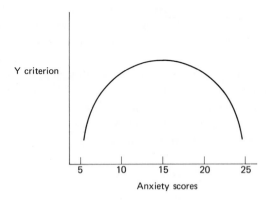

FIGURE 4

A possible line of best fit using the equation: $\tilde{Y}_1 = a + b_1X_1 + b_2X_1^2$.

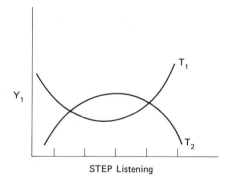

FIGURE 5

A case of curvilinear interaction using the equation: $\tilde{Y} = a + b_1X_1 + b_2X_2 + b_4X_1X_3 + b_5X_2X_3 + b_6(X_1X_3)^2 + b_7(X_2X_3)^2$

Figure 5 shows a possible plot of points which might be derived using Equation 8. A restricted model might be Equation 5, which specifies a *recti*linear interacting state.

Regression Model Construction

The equations specified here only illustrate the flexibility which the linear regression analysis provides the research investigator. Essentially, once the research question is asked, the statistical model can be cast to reflect the hypothesized state of affairs. Then restrictions are imposed to test the tenability of the hypothesized model.

Applications of Multiple Regression Analysis

Since the complex use of multiple regression analysis is a relatively recent development, few exemplary models are available in the literature. This writer knows of no complex use of regression analysis in empirical communication studies, although an experimental study conducted by Barker, Kibler, and Kelly (1968) used the approach with relatively simple regression models.

A series of studies by Whiteside (1964) perhaps best illustrates the power of complex regression analysis. Whiteside was concerned with predicting high school grades using ninth-grade information. On the basis of a comprehensive model of behavior (McGuire, 1961), Whiteside selected a number of variables which, according to some theorists, were definitely related to success in school.

In a preliminary analysis using one of four subsamples (representing one of four communities), Whiteside selected eight within-subject characteristics as relevant to high school success:

Ability:

STEP Listening
California Test of Mental Maturity (CTMM)
Mutilated words
Seeing problems

Peer Expectations:

Nomination as an academic model

Motivation:

Scholastic motivation
Cooperative Youth Study (CYS) personal maladjustment

Sex:

Categorization by male and female

Note that no context variables were selected in this analysis. Whiteside tested each variable for rectilinearity and also tested interaction effect among several ability measures. Table 1 shows the variables and the functions which best predicted observed high school grades.

The regression equation shown in Table 1 accounted for 70 per cent of the observed high school grade (GPA) variance (R squared). The expectation that STEP Listening would interact with CTMM was based on the assumption that listening ability would moderate the effects of mental maturity. The curved interaction represented by vector X_5 is a result of testing the assumption of rectilinearity rather than a result of theoretical expectations.

The equation expressed in Table 1 has two limitations: (1) the number of predictors is large and thus likely to yield great shrinkage in cross-validation; and (2) the predictor set does *not* include expectations of teachers (this is significant since GPA reflects an evaluation, by the teacher, of student performance). In order to investigate the practical educational use of these data and to overcome the two limitations, Whiteside conducted another series of analyses. First, using students in the previous analysis, he added ninth-grade GPA and ninth-grade GPA squared to the full model reported in Table 1. The ninth-grade GPA was included as an estimate of teacher expectancy. Second, he arbitrarily selected the five strongest predictors in the set. The R squared (RSQ) derived from the analysis with an N of 130 was .78. Table 2 (p. 64) shows the equation and partial regression weights.

You will note that the CTMM times STEP Listening variable remains but not the curvilinear interaction. Likewise, the squared ninth-grade GPA stands without the original GPA which allows for a simple power function.

TABLE 1

The Complete Regression Model
Reflecting the Empirically Tested Functional Relationships
in Whiteside's Preliminary Study

$$Y = a_0U + a_1X_1 + a_2X_2 + a_3X_3 + \ldots + a_{13}X_{13} + E$$

where

Y = the criterion, high school grade point average (GPA) in standard score form

$a_0, a_1, a_2 \ldots a_{13}$ = regression weights

U = the unit vector (a "1" for each subject)

Impulsivity $\quad X_1$ = STEP Listening

Convergent thinking
$\begin{cases} X_2 = \text{CTMM mental function} \\ X_3 = (\text{CTMM})^2 \end{cases}$

Catalysts
$\begin{cases} X_4 = (\text{STEP Listening}) \times (\text{CTMM}) \\ X_5 = (\text{STEP Listening}) \times (\text{CTMM})^2 \end{cases}$

Divergent thinking
$\begin{cases} X_6 = \text{Seeing problems} \\ X_7 = (\text{Seeing problems})^2 \end{cases}$

Symbol aptitude $\quad X_8$ = Mutilated words

Elements of
  motivation
$\begin{cases} X_9 = \text{Scholastic motivation} \\ X_{10} = \text{CYS personal maladjustment} \end{cases}$

Peer expectancies
$\begin{cases} X_{11} = \text{Nom: academic model} \\ X_{12} = (\text{Nom: academic model})^2 \end{cases}$

Sex role $\quad X_{13}$ = 1 if subject is female, 0 if male

E = Error $(Y - \tilde{Y})$

Constructed by the author from data of R. Whiteside (1964), by permission.

Regression weights and RSQs were calculated for the other three communities using the same set of predictor variables. The RSQs were: Community B $(N = 106)$ .71; Community C $(N = 176)$ .80; and Community D $(N = 246)$ .69. Twelve cross-validations were made where the weights derived from each of the communities were applied to the other three. Using raw score predictors rather than derived scores, the lowest cross-validated RSQ was .66 and the highest .79.

Apparently the comprehensive model and multivariate regression technique has some practical value since these cross-validated RSQs over four different communities are about twice as large as are those reported in similar studies. Of course, one must bear in mind that a number of

TABLE 2

The Model Using the Five Best Predictors for Community A

$$\tilde{Y} = -2.574 + .028\ (X_1) + .120\ (X_2) + .019\ (X_3) + .011\ (X_4) + .011\ (X_5)$$

where $\tilde{Y}$ = predicted high school GPA
X_1 = score on Mutilated Words
X_2 = score on Nomination: Academic Model
X_3 = 1 if subject were female; zero if male
X_4 = CTMM score times STEP Listening score divided by 100
X_5 = ninth-grade GPA squared

truncations of the original ninth-grade subject pool were observed due to moving, etc. Nevertheless, if we wish to upset predicted failure, Whiteside's models may well provide a basis for selecting Ss for intervention procedures.

A POSSIBLE COMMUNICATION APPLICATION

Whiteside's studies illustrate the power of the multiple regression approach for prediction purposes, but we can easily invent a study more closely related to communication research to illustrate experimental use of the approach.

A recent development on the political scene has been the emergence of the "pretty boy" politician (PB). One might wish to investigate the influence of *this* source characteristic on the relative probability that the listener might vote for the PB candidate when opposed by another candidate whom, for the purposes of our study, we shall call "mature" and "somewhat distinguished" (MD).

In view of the theoretical model presented earlier, one might wish to consider a number of possibly relevant *receiver characteristics* and *stimulus characteristics*.

POSSIBLE RELEVANT RECEIVER CHARACTERISTICS

(1) *Sex:* the "pretty boy" may attract women

(2) *Age:* young people may identify with the "pretty boy," older people with the "mature, distinguished" candidate

(3) *Age × sex interactions:* females may like the "pretty boy" under audio-visual (AV) conditions; older males under AV conditions may be less likely than younger males to be attracted to the "flashy young punk"

(4) *Educational level:* the educated might moderate judgments and be less influenced by the AV-PB treatment

POSSIBLE RELEVANT STIMULUS CHARACTERISTICS

(1) *Source:* (a) "pretty boy" (PB); (b) "mature, distinguished" (MD)

(2) *Context:* control and provide all conditions in similar contexts

(3) *Structure of message:* use identical messages or replicate the study using several structural approaches

(4) *Noise:* minimize noise in message

(5) *Channel mode:* (a) with audio-visual (AV) presentation, *i.e.,* video tape; (b) with audio (A) only. Expect "pretty boy" will be no more attractive than "mature, distinguished" with audio only.

Of course, the usual care in selecting a control passage, defining source characteristics, etc., should be taken. The speakers might be introduced as candidates for Congress with party affiliations not designated. The sample subjects will supposedly reflect the population to which the investigator wishes to generalize. Before the message is transmitted, the subject characteristics can be determined, and after the message is completed, the subjects can be asked to indicate on some scale the degree to which they are favorably impressed with the candidate. Subjects should be assigned to one of four treatments: (1) "pretty boy" audio-visual (PB-AV); (2) "pretty boy" audio (PB-A); (3) "mature, distinguished" audio-visual (MD-AV); or (4) "mature, distinguished" audio (MD-A). The sex, age, and educational level of the subjects in each subsample should be roughly the same.

The research question may take many forms. For example, one may hypothesize the following expected outcomes:

(1) Less well educated subjects given treatment PB-AV will rate the candidate higher than those with more education.

(2) The influence of source characteristics on judgments among subjects exposed to audio only is not relevant.

(3) A sex × age interaction on judgment will exist between source characteristics under audio-visual conditions for subjects exposed to PB.

Table 3 (p. 66) shows the full regression model which reflects the possible outcomes necessary for testing the hypothesized relationships. The equation takes into account source and stimulus characteristics and treatments.

The first eight vectors represent each treatment condition by sex, and Vectors 9–16 provides a sex × treatment × age interactions. These 16 vectors provide the basis for testing Expected Outcomes 2 and 3. Vectors 17 and 18 represent education for the two groups (PB-AV Male, PB-AV Female) in which education is expected to moderate the subjects' judgments about the two candidates.

TABLE 3

*The Unrestricted Model Which Reflects
the Possible Hypothesized State of Affairs*

$$Y_1 = a_0 U + a_1 X_1 + a_2 X_2 + a_3 X_3 \ldots + a_{18} X_{18} + E_1$$

where

Y_1 = criterion score, candidate favorability

U = a unit vector, which when multiplied by a_0 yields the regression constant

X_1 = 1 if score on Y comes from a subject who had treatment PB-AV and is male; zero otherwise

X_2 = 1 if score on Y comes from a subject who had treatment PB-AV and is female; zero otherwise

X_3 = 1 if score on Y comes from a subject who had treatment MD-AV and is male; zero otherwise

X_4 = 1 if score on Y comes from a subject who had treatment MD-AV and is female; zero otherwise

X_5 = 1 if score on Y comes from a subject who had treatment PB-A and is male; zero otherwise

X_6 = 1 if score on Y comes from a subject who had treatment PB-A and is female; zero otherwise

X_7 = 1 if score on Y comes from a subject who had treatment MD-A and is male; zero otherwise

X_8 = 1 if score on Y comes from a subject who had treatment MD-A and is female; zero otherwise

$X_9 = X_1 \times$ Age (therefore, this vector will contain the age of the subject if the score on the criterion comes from a member of PB-AV treatment and is male; zero otherwise)

$X_{10} = X_2 \times$ Age

$X_{11} = X_3 \times$ Age

$X_{12} = X_4 \times$ Age

$X_{13} = X_5 \times$ Age

$X_{14} = X_6 \times$ Age

$X_{15} = X_7 \times$ Age

$X_{16} = X_8 \times$ Age

$X_{17} = X_1 \times$ Educational level in years

$X_{18} = X_2 \times$ Educational level in years

E_1 = the difference between observed score and predicted and where $a_1, a_2 \ldots a_{18}$ are partial regression weights derived to minimize the square of the elements in E_1

Expected Outcome 1. In order to test Expected Outcome 1, which indicates that educational level will moderate the judgments of the subjects exposed to PB under AV conditions, the restriction $a_{17} = a_{18} = 0$, where a_{17} refers to the partial regression weight associated with variable X_{17} and a_{18} refers to the partial regression weight associated with the variable X_{18}, is imposed on the unrestricted model. The equation means that differences in education between the two groups have no relationship to PB-AV differences between the two. The restriction effectively eliminates knowledge of educational level from the linear equation. The RSQ calculated using the unrestricted model can be compared with the RSQ calculated with the restricted model in an F test:

$$F = \frac{(\text{RSQ unrest.} - \text{RSQ rest.}) \,/\, (18-16)}{(1 - \text{RSQ unrest.}) \,/\, (N-18)}$$

If the obtained F exceeds the table F at the specified alpha level (a specified probability that differences between measures occur by chance), then the restriction $a_{17} = a_{18} = 0$ is *not* tenable; and one may accept the expected outcome that educational level *does* moderate judgment under condition PB-AV. Figure 6 shows the possible outcome for the relevant groups.

The reported lines show that women with more education rate PB lower at all age levels than less educated women and that males with more education rate PB higher than less educated males (the lines as drawn reflect

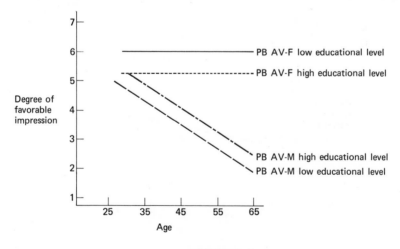

FIGURE 6

The possible outcome where educational level moderates subject evaluation of PB under AV conditions.

the sex × age interaction, Expected Outcome 3, which we shall discuss shortly). The influence of education across age is constant since the full model does not include a sex × age × education interaction. This triple-order interaction could be easily tested; however, for introductory purposes, the present model already approaches overcomplexity. The reader should note that education level is a continuous variable; for descriptive purposes one can plot lines for two levels that are sufficiently disparate to graph the differences. If Expected Outcome 1 were rejected, the two lines for females would be superimposed and the two lines for males would also be super-imposed. These lines would represent the fact that educational level is unrelated to judgment for the PB-AV condition.

Expected Outcome 2. This outcome suggests that without the visual distinguishing source characteristics, the judgments regarding the two sources will be the same, although sex and age might still influence subject judgment. The restrictions necessary to test this expected outcome would be: $a_5 = a_7$; $a_{13} = a_{15}$; and $a_6 = a_8$; $a_{14} = a_{16}$. If you look back to Table 3, you should note that setting the weights $a_5 = a_7$ combines males given audio conditions and eliminates information regarding the source (PB and MD); likewise, setting $a_{13} = a_{15}$ eliminates source information for males × age under audio conditions. The second set of restrictions ($a_6 = a_8$ and $a_{14} = a_{16}$) carries out the same operation for females. The F test can be used comparing the RSQ unrestricted with the new RSQ restricted. If the F value exceeds the alpha level, then the stated expectation is *not* tenable (we hypothesized no difference). Figure 7 shows a possible outcome where the expectation *was* confirmed.

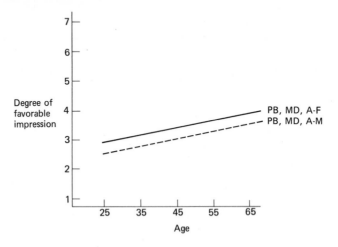

FIGURE 7

A possible outcome where source characteristics is not relevant to subject judgment.

As shown in Figure 7, judgments of females exposed to either PB or MD under audio conditions are *not* different. Likewise, source characteristics are not relevant among males given the audio treatment. As depicted, females rate the candidates higher than males, and older subjects tend to rate the candidates higher than younger subjects. If the state of affairs expressed in Figure 7 existed, the investigator could test the sex and age differences to determine the likelihood that these were chance differences, but again this procedure will not be discussed for sake of brevity.

Expected Outcome 3. If the age × sex outcome for PB-AV is observed, the results might look like Figure 8.

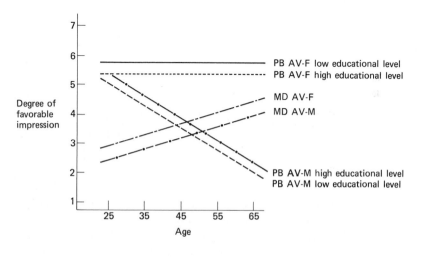

FIGURE 8

The outcome where age and sex interact with source characteristics under audio-visual conditions in subject judgment.

You should note that Figure 8 includes the four lines given in Figure 6 plus two lines representing the judgments of males and females of candidate MD. The test for Expected Outcome 1 indicated education was relevant for those exposed to PB-AV (Figure 6). The test for Expected Outcome 2 indicates that source characteristics do not interact with age and sex under audio conditions. For Expected Outcome 3, the four groups exposed to AV conditions should yield different slopes across age group by sex (this assumes $a_1 \neq a_3$; $a_9 \neq a_{11}$; and $a_2 \neq a_4$; $a_{10} \neq a_{12}$). To test the expectation, a_1 is set equal to a_3 and $a_9 = a_{11}$, etc. If the comparison of the RSQ associated with the unrestricted model is significantly larger than the RSQ associated with the restricted model, then the different-slopes expectation is supported, as shown in Figure 8.

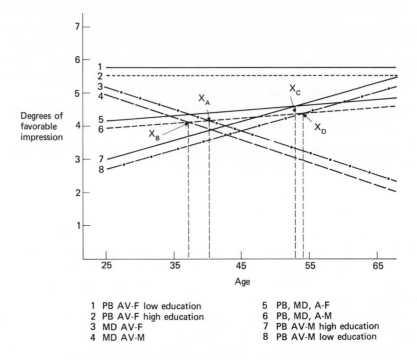

1	PB AV-F low education	5	PB, MD, A-F	
2	PB AV-F high education	6	PB, MD, A-M	
3	MD AV-F	7	PB AV-M high education	
4	MD AV-M	8	PB AV-M low education	

FIGURE 9

The several lines cast in Figures 6, 7, and 8 placed into one summarizing figure. Since Expected Outcome 2 indicated $a_5 = a_7$; $a_{13} = a_{15}$ and $a_6 = a_8$; $a_{14} = a_{16}$, the most efficient equation to reflect these lines is:

$$Y_1 = a_0 u + a_1 X_1 + a_2 X_2 + a_3 X_3 + a_4 X_4 + a_{19}(X_5 + X_7) + a_{20}(X_6 + X_8) + a_9 X_9 + a_{10} X_{10} + a_{11} X_{11} + a_{12} X_{12} + a_{21}(X_{13} + X_{15}) + a_{22}(X_{14} + X_{16}) + E_2$$

where a_{19}, a_{20}, a_{21}, and a_{22} are new weights which apply to the several combined vectors.

From the information derived from the three figures a composite figure can be cast (Figure 9). A number of conclusions can be drawn and recommendations made to maximize a candidate's favorability rating (FR — vote-getting potential):

(1) If the candidate is a pretty boy *and* the audience is female, FR can be maximized using an audio-visual channel mode regardless of receiver age. Educational level does not make too much difference (lines 1 and 2).

(2) If the candidate is a pretty boy and the audience is male, FR can be maximized using an audio-visual channel mode if the male audience is under 40, but if the male audience

is over 40, audio only maximizes FR. This can be seen where lines 3 and 4 intercept line 6. For both lines 3 and 4 a rapid decrease in favorability is associated with increasing age with the AV mode. With the audio mode, etc., only (line 6), a slight increase in favorability is noted with age. Lines 3 and 4 represent the two educational levels, and the different intercepts of line 6 (X_B and X_A) are only four years apart (38–42). One would assume the tested relationships are not precise enough to discriminate at such a fine age level.

(3) If the candidate is a mature, distinguished person, he can maximize FR using the audio only channel mode for both sexes up to audience age about 52 and AV for older audiences. Lines 5 and 6 represent the audio channel and lines 7 and 8 represent the AV channel mode. Lines 7 and 5 (female subjects) cross at about age 52 and lines 8 and 6 also cross at about age 52.

From these fictitious outcomes the pretty boy is a shoo-in if he uses the correct channel mode. If the majority of the voters were males over 40, "pretty boy" would likely lose if he used audio-visual presentations.

Analyzing the several within-subject characteristics and their relation to stimulus characteristics at first glance looks complex. If the investigator knows his data, the relationships expressed will seem less complex once he becomes familiar with the multiple regression technique. In the example given, age and educational levels were assumed to be rectilinearly related to the criterion. A simple expansion of the equation adding 10 new vectors (one representing the squared elements in vectors 9 through 18) could reflect a possible curvilinearly interacting state of affairs. If these 10 new vectors accounted for a significant increase in the predictive variance, then curvilinearity exists somewhere in the set, and a series of tests could determine the specific curved relationships.

Special Considerations Regarding Multiple Regression Analysis

At the outset we stated that the multiple regression analysis is a statistical tool which might permit the investigator a means of reflecting and testing the complexities underlying communication behavior. A few points should be made about research, some specifically related to the regression approach and some general in nature.

First, statistical tests are only tools for decision making. A variable or set of variables might be significantly (statistically) related to the criterion, but it may be of no practical value. In the fictitious study just presented, educational level was a significant moderator of judgment; however, when cast into the decision making recommendation, knowledge of educational level provided little information. Since a new statistical tool is often hailed as a panacea, it is well to remember that regression analysis and all other analyses are only tools in service of the theoretical model with its epistemological structure. Regression analysis as presented here has one saving grace: one cannot build a multiple regression model without first stating a research question.

In all research the character of the criterion is a central problem. As much psychometric care should go into selecting the criterion as into selecting the predictor set.

The size of the sample merits a comment. In complex designs, care should be exercised not to overfit the line. Given a set of predictors equal to the number of subjects, no inference can be made because no degrees of freedom remain. Horst (1966) suggests that when one is using multivariate procedures, the larger the sample size the better. Of course, the economics of data collection must always be considered. If one had the funds, he could measure the population and describe the reality, and no inferences would be necessary. Since no rule exists, the present author recommends that the investigator use special intuitive rules based on his knowledge of his data. For example, in the fictitious study there were eight groups across an age range. For each group a number of observations should be made within age ranges in order to have confidence in the generality of the results. In the study the ages given were from 25 to 65. If these were conceptually grouped into five-year blocks (*e.g.,* 25–29.9, 30–34.9, etc.), one might wish to have at least five subjects for each group. This means about 40 subjects for each treatment; therefore, an N of 320 might be desirable. (Note that the regression models developed do not demand equality or proportionality in groups. The general notion is to have enough observations at each point on the concomitant variable [age, in this instance] to merit a generalizable statement.)

When subjects for a particular level are not available (*e.g.,* subjects in the age continuum between 30 and 35) and one's theory does not expect this group to differ from the overall trend, then one can interpolate scores for this missing level using the partial regression weights obtained with information of the other levels.

OTHER MULTIVARIATE TECHNIQUES

Multiple regression analysis was introduced here as the simplest form of multivariate analysis. Fisher has reserved the term "multivariate" for analyses with multiple dependent (criteria) variables. Cattell (1966), on the other hand, calls multiple regression analysis a "multivariate technique" since multiple predictor variables are used. If one has a low tolerance for ambiguity, he may wish to call multiple regression analysis a "multivariable technique" and thus hedge on the word-magic game.

Multiple Discriminant Analysis

If one is concerned with discriminating between two groups from a set of predictor variables, multiple regression analysis can be used. The criterion can be a dichotomous vector with a "1" in the vector to indicate Group A and a "0" to indicate Group B. Models can be cast and restrictions made using any of the procedures described earlier. If the RSQ in one's full model is significantly larger than the RSQ obtained from the restricted model, then the predictor(s) deleted from the full model bears some relationship to group membership. One can say the predictor discriminates between groups. One set of weights is used to discriminate the two groups.

When the investigator wishes to discriminate among three or more groups, the regression model is not appropriate unless the groups can be logically expressed as interval data.[4] If the three or more groups are instead "really" nominal (*e.g.,* Latin, Anglo, Negro, etc.), multiple discriminant analysis can be used to separate the groups. Multiple discriminant analysis provides a number of independent discriminant functions each with its own set of weights which permits separation of groups along more than one dimension. The maximum number of discriminant functions necessary to represent group differences will be the smaller of two numbers: the number of groups minus one, or the number of predictor variables. Tests of significance for overall dispersion as well as for each discriminant function are available (Veldman, 1967).

McNeil (1967) used this procedure to investigate the separation of four subcultural groups on six connotative dimensions using the semantic differential. Of the three possible discriminant functions, two were significant. Figure 10 (p. 74) shows the group centroids of the four groups in the two-dimensional discriminant space. Discriminant Function I tended to separate the two Anglo groups from the Latin and Negro groups, and the second function tended to separate the Negroes from the Caucasians.

Although multiple discriminant analysis provides a procedure for testing hypotheses, the flexibility for testing higher order functions among the predictor sets (*e.g.,* interaction and higher order functions) has *not* been developed. This limitation should be removed in the near future.

Canonical Correlation

When the investigator has a set of criterion variables and a set of predictor variables, canonical correlation can provide an analysis of how each set of variables is related to the other. Such a problem might involve a

---

[4] Interval data represent measurement of a variable in which the units represent *equal amounts* or *equal intervals*. Nominal data represent unique, unordered subclasses such as blue, green, or brown eyes.

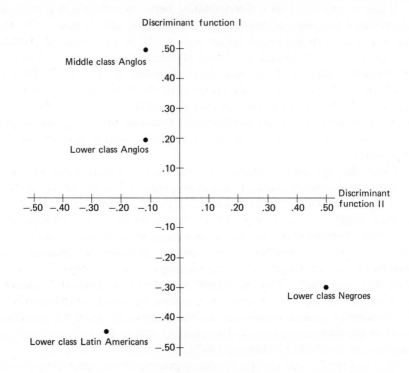

FIGURE 10

*Graphic Representation of Group Centroids Found
for the Four Subcultural Groups in McNeil's Study*

Constructed by the author from data of K. McNeil (1967), by permission.

situation where multiple desirable outcomes of a presentation are investigated. For example, several factors in presentation of information might be manipulated and one might want to maximize: (1) amount of information gained; (2) a positive attitude toward the content; and (3) a positive attitude toward the source. In order to handle this type of problem, the canonical correlation model finds two sets of weighting coefficients, rather than just one set as in the linear model. Since there is not just one criterion variable, the procedure must find weighting coefficients so as to maximally predict a composite criterion score. The function minimized in multiple linear regression is the error sum of squares between the predicted criterion and the actual criterion. The function minimized in the canonical model is the error sum of squares between a predicted score (predicted from the one set of variables) and another predicted score (predicted from the other set of variables).

If one were to submit the two sets of predicted scores to the Pearson Product correlational model, one would obtain the numerical value of the canonical correlation (R_C). Thus, the canonical correlation is nothing more than the bivariate correlation between two predicted scores. The square of the R_C can be interpreted as the amount of variance in the one composite score accounted for by the other composite score.

To gain an insight into what these composite scores are measuring, we can look at the bivariate correlations of the original variables with the new composite scores. Variables which are highly correlated with the new composite scores are measuring somewhat the same construct, and variables lowly correlated with the composite score are not measuring the same construct.

As in discriminant analysis, the one canonical correlation will probably not account for all the variance in the data. Additional canonical correlations are computed with the restriction that the subsequent composite scores be uncorrelated with the previous composite scores. It is entirely possible that the two sets of variables are significantly related in two (or more) ways. If this is the state of affairs, the investigator should be aware of the situation and incorporate the fact into his theory.

Tests of significance exist for each canonical correlation and for the total amount of variance accounted for in the two sets of variables. These newer multivariate techniques do allow the investigator to reflect the functional relationships among the several sets of relevancies included in the newer behavioral models, but few tests are available for comparing subsets of functional relationships. Because of these present limitations, the author has directed the major part of this chapter to multiple linear regression analysis, which does permit tests of subsets of functional relationships.

Summary

This chapter has attempted to show how complex theories of communication might be tested using simple multivariate techniques. A number of illustrations were presented to show the construction of multiple regression equations which reflect the functional relationships expected from modern communication theory. Essentially, the hypothesized functional relationships among several variables can be expressed and then restrictions can be imposed on subsets of these variables to test the tenability of the hypothesized relationships.

More complex multivariate techniques (*e.g.,* canonical correlation and multiple discriminant analysis) were discussed in relation to general overall tests of hypothesized relevancies. At the present time, however, these techniques seem to have limited value for the theoretician since tests for comparing subsets of functional relationships are not yet available. This lack may indeed be a blessing for the present-day behavioral scientist because our experience with even the simplest multivariate procedures (*e.g.,* multiple regression analysis) is severely limited. At the moment multiple regression analysis can reflect the complexities underlying most of the problems we wish to investigate. By the time appropriate tests are developed for the more complex multivariate techniques, perhaps we shall be familiar enough with tested multivariate behavioral theories to use the new tests fruitfully.

References and Selected Readings

Barker, L. L., Kibler, R. J., and Kelly, F. J. Effect of perceived mispronunciation on speech effectiveness ratings and retention. *Quarterly Journal of Speech,* 1968, **54,** 47–58.

Berlo, D. K. *The process of communication.* New York: Holt, Rinehart & Winston, 1960.

Bottenberg, R. A., and Ward, J. H., Jr. Applied multiple linear regression. *Technical Documentary Report,* No. PRL-TDR-63-6. Lackland Air Force Base, Texas: 6570th Personnel Research Laboratory, 1963.

Cattell, R. B. (Ed.) *Handbook of multivariate experimental psychology.* Chicago: Rand McNally, 1966.

Horst, P. *An overview of the essentials of multivariate analysis methods in Cattell.* Chicago: Rand McNally, 1966.

Kelly, F. J., Beggs, D., McNeil, K., Lyon, J., and Eichelberger, R. *Research design: A multiple variable approach.* Carbondale: Southern Illinois University Press, 1969.

McGuire, C. The prediction of talented behavior in the Junior High School Invitational Conference on testing problems. Princeton, N.J.: Educational Testing Service, 1961. Pp. 46–73.

McNeil, K. Multivariate relationship between the semantic space of various sub-cultures and selected personality variables. Unpublished doctoral dissertation, University of Texas, 1967.

Osgood, C. E. A behavioristic analysis of perception and language as cognitive phenomena. In D. Ausubel (Ed.), *Contemporary approaches to cognition.* Cambridge, Mass.: Harvard University Press, 1957. Pp. 75–118.

Veldman, D. J. *FORTRAN programming for the behavioral sciences.* New York: Holt, Rinehart & Winston, 1967.

Whiteside, R. Dimensions of teacher evaluation of academic achievement. Unpublished doctoral dissertation, University of Texas, 1964.

Wiseman, G., and Barker, L. L. *Speech — Interpersonal communication.* San Francisco: Chandler, 1967.

3

Research Setting:

Laboratory Studies

GERALD R. MILLER

CHARACTERISTICS OF LABORATORY RESEARCH SETTINGS

How can one differentiate between laboratory and field research settings for a field of inquiry like communication? In this chapter, the quest for a neat, concise definition of a *laboratory research setting* has been abandoned; rather, it appears that the setting of any research undertaking must be placed at some point on a continuum ranging from relatively "pure" field research, on the one hand, to relatively "pure" laboratory research on the other. In certain cases, most observers will agree that a study should be placed at one of the extremes. For example, if a researcher had college undergraduates report individually to a specially designed room in a psychology research building, systematically manipulated the amount of alcohol introduced into each student's bloodstream, and then recorded the number of trials necessary to learn sets of tachistoscopically presented paired-associate word lists, there should be general agreement that the research took place in a laboratory setting. Conversely, if an investigator drew a national probability sample, went to the homes of the sample's

77

members, asked them a series of questions about their television viewing preferences, and then compiled a descriptive summary of their responses, there should be general agreement that the study was conducted in a field setting.

Unfortunately, all communication studies do not divide this neatly into scientific fish or fowl. Therefore, in attempting to arrive at some means for distinguishing between the laboratory and the field, it seems reasonable to stress differences in degree, rather than kind. Given this approach, three salient characteristics of communication research conducted in laboratory settings will be discussed.

Investigator Structured Environment

One distinguishing characteristic of laboratory research settings is the extent to which the investigator structures the environment in which the research takes place. It is tempting to assert broadly that in laboratory research the subjects report to the investigator's environment, while in field research the investigator reports to the subject's environment. As we shall see, this deceptively straightforward generalization is an oversimplification; even so, the extent to which the investigator is free to structure the environment does offer one useful means for distinguishing the laboratory from the field setting.

Investigator prerogatives are not limited to physical features; they extend also to human inputs. Thus, in the previous example dealing with the effects of alcohol intake on paired-associate learning, the researcher is not only relatively free to arrange the experimental room as he wishes, to control the length of tachistoscopic exposure of the word lists, and to make other similar decisions about physical dimensions of the environment. In addition, given certain other data parameters, he can also determine to some extent the kinds of subjects used in the study. For example, he may choose to use only subjects who are high in manifest anxiety (as measured by some scale such as the Taylor Manifest Anxiety Scale), subjects with IQs of 130 or higher (as measured by some standard intelligence test), or subjects with common backgrounds of drinking behavior (as measured by subject reports of frequency and quantity of alcohol consumption). Each of these choices represents an attempt by the investigator to structure the physical and human environment being studied.

Moreover, further examples of the investigator's influence on the environment are evident in other types of studies interesting to communication researchers. Consider the studies of Leavitt (1951) and Shaw (1954, 1955) dealing with the effects of various group communication networks on group productivity and morale. Here the investigators structured at least two dimensions of the communication environment: the content of communication behaviors was largely determined by the task assigned to the group, and the availability of communication channels was fixed by the kind of communication network in which the subjects were placed. In fact, most small group studies commonly thought to exemplify laboratory settings are distinguished by investigator structuring of communication inputs, usually through the use of a bogus, tape-recorded discussion engaged in by confederates. Thus, in their study dealing with the effects of severity of initiation on group attractiveness, Aronson and Mills (1959) required that all subjects listen to the same dull and banal bogus discussion, regardless of whether they had undergone a severe or a mild initiation. Though the subjects were told that they were listening to the last discussion of an ongoing group which they were to join, the investigator was actually structuring the communication environment so that it would be constant for all subjects.

Contrast the procedures of Aronson and Mills with those of Festinger, Riecken, and Schachter (1956) in a classic small group study conducted in a field setting. Festinger *et al.* were interested in studying the behaviors of a group who had predicted that the world would end on a certain date. To accomplish this objective, a research assistant managed to infiltrate the group by professing to accept its prediction. Once he had achieved group membership, the assistant observed and recorded the content and pattern of the group members' communication behaviors. But the crucial point to note is that the observer made no attempt to structure or control the communication environment; in fact, the study's success hung largely on his ability to avoid exercising influence on the group's proceedings. In a real sense, the Aronson and Mills study is an instance of the subject coming to the investigator's environment (laboratory setting), while the Festinger, Riecken, and Schachter study is a case of the investigator conducting his inquiry within the environment of the subjects (field setting).

Rigorous Control of Variables

A second characteristic of communication studies conducted in laboratory settings is the relatively rigorous control that the investigator exercises over variables likely to influence research outcomes. One could argue that this distinguishing feature is a corollary of the investigator structured environment characteristic, for this structuring process makes tighter controls possible. For instance, Aronson and Mills were able to control the content of the communication their subjects heard by structuring the situation so that all subjects heard the same bogus discussion. Differences in ratings of group attractiveness (the dependent variable of interest in the study) could therefore be attributed with some confidence to differences in the severity of initiation (the independent variable of interest in the study).[1]

[1] Typically, an *independent variable* has been defined as a variable the researcher manipulates, while a *dependent variable* has been defined as one the researcher measures. Later, in discussing certain research paradigms (particularly the investigation), it will become apparent that some independent variables are not established by manipulation. With this fact in mind, the author prefers Kerlinger's (1964) approach: for him, the independent variable is the variable the researcher predicts *from,* and the dependent variable is the variable the researcher predicts *to.* (See Chapter 1, pp. 21–22.)

Suppose, however, that Aronson and Mills had followed somewhat different procedures. Rather than having subjects undergo either a severe or mild initiation and then asking them to listen to the same dull bogus discussion, Aronson and Mills could have selected two existing organizations, one that required new members to undergo a severe initiation and one that had relatively mild initiation rites. Given that the investigators could have identified a group of new members in each organization (*e.g.,* individuals who had joined two weeks earlier), they could have obtained ratings of group attractiveness and compared the ratings of new members in the severe initiation organization with those of new members in the mild initiation organization. How would this change in procedures influence the degree of control exercised over potentially relevant variables and the subsequent interpretation of research findings?

Using these procedures, it would be difficult to ascertain whether any observed differences in group attractiveness ratings resulted from variations in the severity of initiation or from other aspects of the interactions between new group members and the old hands of the organization. Perhaps the old hands in one organization are generally more friendly to new members; perhaps one organization elevates new members to positions of leadership more rapidly; perhaps members of one organization have more opportunities to interact apart from formal organizational meetings. The list of such possibilities is almost endless. Moreover, even if group attractiveness ratings could be obtained immediately following initiation into the organizations, each new member would have had numerous preinitiation experiences with the organization, and these experiences might differ drastically from one organization to the other. In short, though it would be possible to conclude that members of the two organizations differed in their ratings of group attractiveness, it would be difficult to ascertain that the differences resulted from variations in the initiation procedures of the two groups.

Since the preceding hypothetical set of procedures provides minimal control of potentially relevant antecedent variables and since the hypothetical study would, therefore, fall in the field setting portion of the proposed continuum, some readers may feel that field research is uncontrolled, or even worse, that field research is a second-class scientific undertaking. No such implication is intended. Research conducted in a field setting does seek to control the conditions under which measurement occurs, *i.e.,* the field researcher structures the environment in which dependent variables are measured. For example, in the television viewing study presented earlier as an example of "pure" field research, the investigator would assess viewing preferences by using a standard interview protocol or a written questionnaire. Moreover, he would establish some reliable, standardized method for coding viewers' responses. Such procedures would ensure comparable data for all subjects; the procedures would provide measurement controls.

It is in the domain of independent variables that the field researcher ceases to structure and control the environment. Though he may compile an accurate description of viewers' television preferences, he will have no confident means for determining the variables that led to the particular preferences expressed. To be sure, he may demonstrate correlations between viewing preferences and other dependent variables (socioeconomic status, intelligence, education, age, etc.), but these obtained correlations do not permit unambiguous statements of chronological relationships. For example, is high intelligence antecedent to certain viewing preferences, are certain viewing preferences antecedent to high intelligence, or most probably, is some other set of genetic and/or environmental variables antecedent to both high intelligence and particular viewing preferences? Such relational mysteries can be solved only by controlling and manipulating certain independent variables prior to the measurement of viewing preferences.

Concerning the notion that research carried out in field settings may be inferior to laboratory undertakings, it should be stressed that these two approaches to scientific inquiry often have different purposes. Specifically, and consistent with the preceding discussion, research in laboratory settings usually aims at *explanation,* while research in field settings usually aims at *description.*[2] More will be said about the explanatory function of laboratory research as this chapter progresses.

A final point is in order. Taken together, the two characteristics of laboratory research settings thus far discussed often lead to ambiguous criticisms about the "artificial" nature of laboratory research settings, and to disjunctive statements contrasting the "real" world and the "unreal" laboratory. Though the intent of such criticisms may have scientific import, their semantic form obscures the significant issues. Whether in laboratory or field setting, the communication scientist's basic datum is always human behavior. Viewed in this light, it is meaningless to speak of one set of behaviors as real and another set as unreal: *all behavior is real, or stated differently, behavior is behavior.* As Homans (1961) has so aptly said, "The laws of human behavior are not repealed when a man leaves the field and enters the laboratory [p. 15]."

What the critics of laboratory research settings are attempting to say may perhaps be summarized as follows: The communication researcher's structuring of the environment and his control of potentially relevant variables results in a laboratory setting that is extremely less complex than the daily communication situations in which people find themselves. If scientific findings in communication are to have social importance, explanation and prediction must be extended beyond the simplified confines of the laboratory setting. As yet, the communication scientist has been only minimally successful in demonstrating that bridging from laboratory to field is possible.[3]

[2] Later it will be emphasized that some types of laboratory studies have limited explanatory power; therefore, use of the qualifier "usually" is more than a cautious hedge.

[3] Brunswik (1947) has used the term *ecological validity* to describe this bridging process. A laboratory study has ecological validity to the extent that its results can be appropriately generalized to the field.

When viewed in this way, it must be admitted that continued inability to demonstrate the ecological validity of laboratory research in communication would impose serious limitations on its scientific and social utility. It should be emphasized, however, that it is still early in the game, and that it is probably premature to expect a level of knowledge needed to predict accurately in the complex world in which communication transactions occur. Contrary to the popular stereotype, scientific advancement is a slow, painstaking process, and the social fruits of laboratory research in communication may not be fully ripened for many years.

Restricted Parent Populations

A final characteristic of communication research conducted in laboratory settings is a general reliance on samples drawn from rather limited, restricted parent populations. Though the use of such samples is not an inherent dimension of laboratory research, practical and economic limitations ensure that such sampling procedures will be the rule, rather than the exception. These procedures, in turn, give rise to numerous thorny questions about the extent to which findings obtained in laboratory studies can be generalized beyond the parent population from which subjects were drawn.

Suppose, for instance, that a communication researcher becomes interested in this question: Will a communication that contains testimonial evidence attributed to a high credible source result in more attitude change than a message attributing the same evidence to a low credible source? In order to be as certain as possible that any differences in attitude change result from variations in the credibility of the evidential source, the researcher devises a set of procedures aimed at keeping the situation constant, save for the individual to whom the evidential statements are attributed — *i.e.,* he uses the laboratory research principles of environmental structuring and rigorous control of variables discussed earlier.

Once procedures are formulated, it is necessary to decide on subjects: who will listen to or read the prepared messages. Although a random sample of individuals living in a wide geographical area would be desirable, getting one may be practically impossible: the subjects may not be willing to participate unless they are paid (and there are not sufficient financial resources to pay them); it may be impossible to assemble the subjects at a common time and place; other commitments may limit the time available for conducting the study, and so forth. Readily available to the researcher, however, are the students in his undergraduate course in communication theory. Students enrolled in the course can be easily contacted; they can be quickly assembled at a common time and place, and certain features of the situation ensure that most of them will agree to participate. For these reasons, the researcher elects to use communication students as subjects in the study.

Subsequent analysis of the data reveals that the group exposed to the communication containing testimonial evidence attributed to a high credible source demonstrated significantly greater favorable attitude change than the group exposed to the message in which a low credible evidential source was used. Thus, the study demonstrates a positive relationship between an evidential source's credibility and the amount of favorable attitude change resulting from a persuasive communication. But for what population of message receivers does this relationship hold? Someone is likely to ask this question; furthermore, if he is skeptical, he will probably suggest that the relationship holds only for college undergraduate students. In short, some people will probably doubt that the finding can be generalized beyond the particular population from which the sample was drawn.

Note that this question does not deal with generalizing from laboratory setting to field setting, the ecological validity issue raised earlier; rather, it relates to the validity of generalizing laboratory findings obtained with one sample of subjects to identical laboratory settings in which subjects from other parent populations are used. In other words, if a second sample of subjects were drawn from employees at a local industrial plant and if these subjects were exposed to identical experimental conditions, would the same relationship between evidential credibility and attitude change be observed? Note also that if some of these employees, some local business-men, and some members of various local churches, to mention but a few, had been included in the first sample, it would have been unequivocally possible to justify generalization to a broader parent population. Many field studies draw such area probability samples.

How is the perplexing question of generalizability to be handled? Unfortunately, there are no easy answers to the problem. One unsatisfactory and essentially unscientific dodge is for the communication researcher to include a disclaimer stating that his findings are applicable only to this particular audience, for this specific topic, at this one time. Since one of the major goals of science is to generate empirical statements having truth value in situations other than those in which the statements were originally tested, this evasion of responsibility is totally unsatisfactory. After all, the physical scientist is not primarily interested in demonstrating that at standard pressure, this particular sample of water will boil at 212 degrees Fahrenheit on this one occasion. Instead, the physical scientist seeks to develop generalizations about the behavior of any sample of water placed in this particular physical environment. By the same token, the communication researcher studying the relationship between credibility of an evidential source and magnitude of attitude change seeks generalizations that extend beyond the confines of the particular subjects used in the study. If he is not willing to make a case for generalizing beyond this group, his results may be of anecdotal interest, but they are almost by definition scientifically trivial.

On the other hand, it is usually unsatisfactory to hold either implicitly or explicitly that findings obtained for subjects drawn from one limited parent population can be generalized safely to numerous other populations. Because of this fact, the best solution to the generalizability dilemma is for the researcher to examine the context of his study carefully and to make commonsense judgments about potential limiting features of his results. It is particularly important to consider relevant characteristics of the independent and dependent variables used in the study. If these variables relate most closely to cognitive or intellectual skills, it is indeed likely that results obtained with a sample drawn from a population of graduate students cannot be generalized confidently to a sample of elementary school dropouts. Conversely, although rules of thumb are always dangerous, if the variables relate primarily to affective or emotional states, the chances for generalization to members of other parent populations are usually good. For example, most persons in our society probably experience anxiety when faced with cues indicating that others are reacting negatively to them, and in turn, the presence of such anxiety probably leads to certain uniformities of behavior. If a relationship between anxiety and subsequent behavior can be demonstrated for a group of college students, it can likely be extended to individuals drawn from other parent populations.

To be more specific, reconsider the preceding hypothetical study dealing with the relationship between evidential source credibility and amount of favorable attitude change. Relevant theory, empirical findings, everyday observation, and common sense dictate that the major finding could probably be generalized to members of other parent populations. In other words, employees of a local industrial plant should also report greater favorable attitude change if they are exposed to a communication containing evidence attributed to a high rather than a low credible source. If an identical study is conducted using employee subjects and if the original finding is not replicated, the researcher would not initially be likely to doubt the generality of the originally obtained relationship between evidential source credibility and amount of attitude change. Rather, he would first assess his manipulation of the variables used in the study: sources perceived as highly credible by college students may not be perceived as highly credible by plant employees, or college students and plant employees may differ in their perceptions of what constitutes effective testimonial evidence. It is important to note that these potential differences between the two populations do not cast doubt on the general validity of the originally obtained relationship; instead, they emphasize the fact that variables often have to be manipulated differently for subjects drawn from different parent populations.

Obviously, much more could be said about the generalizability problem. The preceding remarks have stressed the general tendency for laboratory researchers to sample from narrowly restricted parent populations. This tendency requires the laboratory researcher to assess the meaning of his findings for members of other parent populations. Though the same problem occurs in many field settings, field studies usually sample from a larger parent population, thus assuring that findings can be generalized more broadly.

LABORATORY SETTINGS AND COMMUNICATION INQUIRY

Research Paradigms

How can the frontiers of communication knowledge be extended through research conducted in laboratory settings? Or, stated more specifically, what are the various types of research paradigms used in laboratory settings, and with what kinds of hypotheses and/or laws does each deal?

EXPERIMENTAL PARADIGM

Perhaps because of their perceived prestige value, the terms *experiment* and *experimental* have been used rather loosely by some proponents of scientific research in communication. At one time, departments of speech found it fashionable to seek new faculty who were experimental researchers. This phrase, *experimental researcher,* apparently alluded to anyone interested in studying oral communication from a behavioral science vantage point. For after all, the experiment is only one of several methods for answering scientific questions about communication processes. Not only do other methods exist; they may often be more functional. In fact, one recent discourse on method (Bakan, 1967) has argued persuasively that indiscriminate and unimaginative use of the experimental paradigm has impeded rather than accelerated progress in behavioral areas such as communication.

What are the defining features of the experimental paradigm? To illustrate them, consider a laboratory study by Miller and Hewgill (1964) dealing with the effect of nonfluencies on audience ratings of communicator credibility. Specifically, Miller and Hewgill hypothesized: (1) that as the number of nonfluencies presented by a source increases, receiver ratings of his credibility will decrease; and (2) that this hypothesized effect will be greater for a repetition nonfluency (a nonfluency in which a word is partially stated and then repeated) than for a vocalized pause nonfluency.

Students enrolled in an introductory undergraduate speech course were randomly assigned to one of ten treatment conditions. Table 1 (p. 86) describes the experimental design of the study. All 160 subjects heard a tape-recorded version of a speech presented by an unidentified source arguing that college athletic scholarships should be abolished. The nine versions of the speech differed only in the quantity and type of nonfluency they con-

---

[4] Both the 0-nonfluency and the 0-repetition conditions heard the same speech. The two groups were used to provide an independent replication of the control procedures. Ratings of subjects in the two conditions were almost identical for all three dimensions of credibility.

tained.[4] In order to minimize other differences in delivery, all versions were recorded by a person with extensive training in both speaking and acting.

TABLE 1

Design of the Miller and Hewgill Experiment

Type of Nonfluency	Quantity of Nonfluency				
	0	25	50	75	100
Vocalized pause	$n = 16$	$n = 16$	$n = 16$	$n = 16$	$n = 16$
Repetition	$n = 16$	$n = 16$	$n = 16$	$n = 16$	$n = 16$

Immediately after hearing the appropriate version of the speech, subjects in the ten conditions rated the source on three dimensions of credibility: competence, trustworthiness, and dynamism. Subsequent analyses of these ratings produced support for both hypotheses, at least for the competence and dynamism dimensions. Subjects who heard speeches containing a large number of nonfluencies rated the source as significantly less credible than subjects who heard the 0-nonfluency speech (Hypothesis 1), and this effect was more pronounced in the repetition conditions (Hypothesis 2).

What features of this laboratory study led to its selection as an example of the experimental paradigm? First, all the subjects were drawn from the same parent population: students enrolled in introductory undergraduate speech courses. These subjects were then randomly assigned to the ten treatment conditions used in the study. Here, randomization is used as a control, for it is assumed that the many extraneous variables which could influence performance on the experimental task are distributed across all conditions. Thus, suppose a critic of the study argues that the lower credibility ratings in the 100-repetition condition should not be attributed to the large number of nonfluencies, but rather to the fact that this group contained an unusually high percentage of suspicious subjects. The rebuttal to this argument is obvious: sound procedures for randomization negate the possibility that most of the suspicious subjects will end up in one or two of the 10 groups. Rather, when the sample is large enough, it is more likely that each condition will contain approximately the same number of suspicious individuals.

Having randomly assigned the subjects to treatment groups, Miller and Hewgill attempted to structure the environment so that only two of its features, quantity and type of nonfluency, were systematically varied across the 10 conditions. This systematic manipulation of the stimuli to which subjects are exposed is a second characteristic of the experimental paradigm. As indicated earlier, precise specification of the nature of these stimulus conditions depends not only on effective manipulation of the variables of interest — here, quantity and type of nonfluency — but also on holding all other relevant variables constant. Thus, the same trained actor and speaker recording all versions of the speech served to equalize, as much as possible, other delivery variables. Had the necessary electronic equipment been available, even greater stimulus control could have been achieved by recording the 0-nonfluency speech and then dubbing in the nonfluencies for the other eight versions. By contrast, if a different person had recorded each of the versions, the numerous uncontrolled delivery variables would have made it difficult to interpret any differences in credibility ratings among the 10 groups.

Finally, after exposure to the appropriate stimulus conditions, all subjects' responses were measured to ascertain whether or not systematic variations in the independent variables would produce the hypothesized differences in subsequent behavior. Here the response of interest was the subjects' ratings of communicator credibility. Of course, other responses, such as attitudes toward the message proposal or retention of message content, could also have been measured. The important point is that a particular response was specified and measured. Failure to stipulate the particular response and/or the measurement procedures to be used would make it difficult to assess the effects of the independent variables. In certain cases, it could also lead to the charge that the researcher is providing post hoc interpretations supporting his original reasoning and hypotheses. Thus, if Miller and Hewgill had observed no differences in credibility ratings but had argued that the nonfluencies adversely affected credibility because more subjects were sneering and laughing in the 100-vocalized pause and 100-repetition conditions, a critic could justifiably accuse them of creating post hoc circumlocutions to buttress shaky hypotheses.

The preceding discussion has underscored the important features of the experimental paradigm. Figure 1 (p. 88) provides a shorthand description of these features. The value of the experimental approach to communication inquiry lies in its potential *explanatory power.* For if sound control procedures are used, differences in measured communication responses can be attributed to variations in particular antecedent variables. In other words, the experimental paradigm not only permits the researcher to identify response differences, it also enables him to pinpoint the particular *circumstances that led to these differences.*

Stated differently, the experimental paradigm contributes to the development of what Spence (1944) has labeled *S-R* laws. These laws stipulate that some response variable is functionally related to variations in antecedent stimulus variables: symbolically, $R = f(S)$. If the relevant S variables can be ascertained, then explanation and prediction are, in principle, possible.[5]

---

[5] Some philosophers of science treat *explanation* and *prediction* as equivalent terms. The author likes to distinguish between them, for he can conceive of situations in which one has predictive but not explanatory power. The converse, of course, would not occur: if one can explain an event, he could have predicted it.

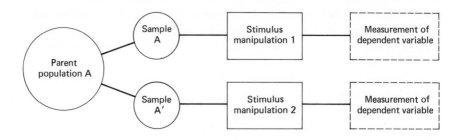

FIGURE 1

Basic Characteristics of the Experimental Paradigm

Thus, in the illustrative study discussed above, Miller and Hewgill could *explain* differences in communicator credibility ratings on the basis of variations in the quantity and type of nonfluency presented by the source. Moreover, they could *predict* that future variations in these variables would lead to similar differences in receiver perceptions of credibility. The general *S-R* law concerning the relationship between nonfluency and ratings of credibility would permit predictive statements for any instance of that particular *S-R* relationship: in a nutshell, *it would foster conditions that satisfy the requirements for scientific explanation.*[6] As will be indicated shortly, these requirements are not satisfied to the same extent by certain other paradigms often used in laboratory settings.

INVESTIGATIONAL PARADIGM

Let us turn to a second approach to communication inquiry frequently associated with the laboratory. After Norton (1959), the writer labels this paradigm the *investigation*. As with the experiment, the defining features of the investigational paradigm will be illustrated by a recent study, this one by Miller and Bacon (1967).

This study began with the assumption that certain theoretical distinctions between open- and closed-minded persons (Rokeach, 1960) might lead to differences in the amount of time taken by the two types to identify the humor of a visual stimulus. Specifically, the following major hypothesis was investigated: When the humor of a visual stimulus stems from the introduction of information which conflicts with existing beliefs, closed-minded individuals will require more time than open-minded individuals to recognize the humor of the stimulus.

Fifty-six students enrolled in undergraduate courses in communication and business were assigned to open- or closed-minded groups on the basis of a median split of their scores on an abridged, 20-item version of the

---

[6] That is, the occurrence of a particular event could be deduced from a more general law. In the classical sense, this is *scientific explanation.*

Rokeach Dogmatism Scale (Troldahl and Powell, 1965). Because of the content of the humorous stimulus, a sex split was also used. Table 2 summarizes the study design.

TABLE 2

Design of the Miller and Bacon Investigation

	Sex	
Mindedness	*Male*	*Female*
Open	$n = 18$	$n = 10$
Closed	$n = 17$	$n = 11$

A centerfold picture from the 1966 *Harvard Lampoon Parody of Playboy* was used as a humorous stimulus. The picture showed a nude woman reclining on a beach towel. The picture's humor was in the woman's reversed tanning pattern, *i.e.,* she was tanned where one would normally expect her to be untanned, and vice versa. Since most persons have well established beliefs about tanning patterns, the informational locus of the picture's humor conflicted with existing beliefs.

Subjects reported individually to the study. Conditions for presentation of the stimulus were constant: each subject was given a standard set of instructions about the task and seated in a chair. The researcher then dropped a screen approximately four feet in front of the subject and projected on it the visual stimulus. At the same time, the researcher activated a stop watch, and timing continued until the subject correctly identified the picture's humor.

Analysis of the time measures provided support for the major hypothesis, particularly among males. Closed-minded males took significantly more time than open-minded males to identify the picture's humor. While the difference for open- and closed-minded females was not significant, it was substantial and in the predicted direction. The findings supported the assumption that certain initial differences between open- and closed-minded subjects resulted in the latter group experiencing greater difficulty in identifying the humor of the visual stimulus.

What features of this study led to its selection as an example of the investigational paradigm, and how do these features differ from those of the experimental paradigm discussed earlier? Figure 2 (p. 90) presents the distinguishing characteristics of the investigation. Note first that unlike the subjects in the experiment, subjects in an investigation are drawn from two or more parent populations. Moreover, the various groups used in the investigation consist of samples drawn from these differing populations. Thus, Miller and Bacon used two groups of open-minded and two groups of

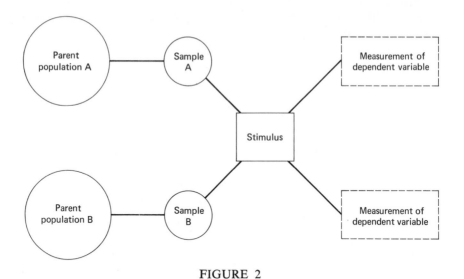

FIGURE 2

Basic Characteristics of the Investigational Paradigm

closed-minded subjects. The researchers did not assign subjects to these groups; rather, the subjects assigned themselves by their responses to the dogmatism scale items.

Second, there is no manipulation of stimulus variables in the investigation. Instead, all subjects are exposed to essentially the same stimuli. In the Miller and Bacon study, all four groups were given the same task instructions and viewed the humorous picture under identical circumstances. Contrast this procedure with the earlier discussed Miller and Hewgill experiment, in which each treatment group was exposed to a different set of stimulus conditions.

Finally, after all subjects in an investigation have been exposed to a common stimulus, a particular response is measured to determine if, as predicted, subjects drawn from various parent populations will respond differently. Thus, Miller and Bacon confirmed the hypothesis that a sample of subjects drawn from a closed-minded parent population would respond differently to a particular visual stimulus than would a sample drawn from an open-minded parent population. In so doing, they verified the existence of initial differences between subjects drawn from the two populations.

In short, the logic of the investigational paradigm differs fundamentally from that of the experiment. In the experiment, the researcher manipulates stimulus variables in order to ascertain whether these stimulus variations are systematically related to response differences. In the investigation, the researcher holds the stimulus variables constant in order to ascertain whether subjects drawn from two or more parent populations will respond differently.

This distinction is crucial, for it emphasizes that the investigational paradigm lacks explanatory power. Since it is assumed that the various populations differ initially, it is impossible to specify the variables that led to these differences. To be sure, the investigator may invoke such notions as *prior learning histories, schedules of reinforcement, cultural norms,* or *reference groups;* but when used in this manner, the explanatory value of these amorphous constructs is negligible.[7]

To further underscore the previous distinction, consider the following two statements: "The differences in ratings of credibility resulted from variations in the quantity and type of source nonfluency" (referring to the Miller and Hewgill experiment); "The differences in time spent identifying the picture's humor resulted from variations in scores on the abridged dogmatism scale" (referring to the Miller and Bacon investigation). While the first statement intuitively makes sense, the latter seems absurd. It seems more sensible to argue that differences in humor identification responses and differences in dogmatism scale marking responses *both* resulted from variations in certain antecedent stimulus variables to which open- and closed-minded persons have been earlier exposed.

The previous sentence pinpoints the type of law that results from the use of investigational procedures; Spence (1944) has labeled it an *R-R* law. Such laws stipulate relationships between two different responses: symbolically, $R_1 = f(R_2)$. An *R-R* law does not allow for control or manipulation of relevant behavior-producing stimulus variables; thus it does not allow for explanation. Given prior knowledge of one set of responses (R_2), *R-R* laws do possess some *predictive* power, for they enable us to predict performance on a second set of responses (R_1) with greater than chance success. Because of this predictive function, *R-R* laws dealing with communication behaviors have scientific utility; however, they are not as scientifically valuable as the previously discussed *S-R* law.

MIXED MODEL PARADIGM

By combining features of the experimental and the investigational paradigms, a mixed model can be developed for laboratory research in communication. Again, as with the experimental and investigational paradigms, the features of the mixed model will be illustrated by describing a recent study.

Miller and Lobe (1967) were interested in determining the relative persuasive efficacy of nonopinionated and opinionated language, given a highly credible communicator. Nonopinionated language (Rokeach, 1960) conveys information relating solely to the communicator's attitude toward a particular issue, *e.g.,* "I believe that Red China should be admitted to

---

[7] In fact, to invoke such constructs may represent little more than a resort to what Scriven (1964) has labeled the *translation trick.* One falls prey to the belief that he has explained an event, when in fact all he has accomplished is placing the problem in different verbal garments.

the United Nations." By contrast, opinionated language conveys two kinds of information about the communicator: it indicates his attitude toward a particular issue *and* his attitude toward those who agree or disagree with him, *e.g.,* "Only a stupid fool would oppose admission of Red China to the United Nations" (*opinionated rejection* statement) or "Any intelligent person knows that we should admit Red China to the United Nations" (*opinionated acceptance* statement).

The relative persuasive effectiveness of these two types of statements could have been tested experimentally. Miller and Lobe could have prepared two messages, one containing only nonopinionated statements and the other containing some opinionated statements. Both messages could then have been attributed to the same high credible communicator and presented to two randomly assigned groups of subjects drawn from the same parent population. By obtaining measures of attitude change, the persuasive efficacy of each message could have been assessed.

Certain considerations led Miller and Lobe to assume, however, that differences between receivers' open- and closed-mindedness would result in variations in the effectiveness of the two messages. Therefore, they not only chose to manipulate the language type variable, they also had subjects assign themselves to open- or closed-minded groups, a procedure consistent with the investigational paradigm. The resultant mixed experimental-investigational design, summarized in Table 3, enabled them to test the following interaction hypothesis:

> When presented by a highly credible source, a message containing opinionated language will result in greater favorable attitude change on the part of closed-minded receivers, but conversely, a message containing nonopinionated language will result in greater favorable attitude change on the part of open-minded receivers.

TABLE 3

Design of the Miller and Lobe Mixed Model

| | Type of Language | |
Mindedness	*Opinionated*	*Nonopinionated*
Open	$n = 20$	$n = 20$
Closed	$n = 20$	$n = 20$

Further description of the study is superfluous to this discussion; the interested reader is directed to the original report. Suffice it to say that the interaction hypothesis was not confirmed; instead, the opinionated language message was more persuasive for both open-and closed-minded subjects. The important point is that the study incorporated features of both

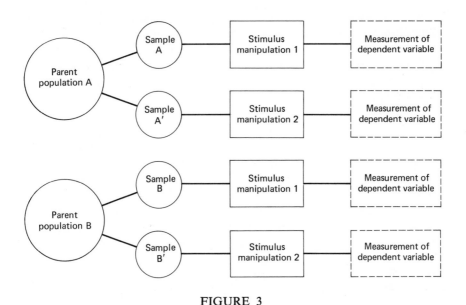

FIGURE 3

Basic Characteristics of the Mixed Model Paradigm

the experiment and the investigation. The reason for this melding can be found in the original assumption that the functional relationship between a stimulus variable (language type) and a response variable (attitude change) would be mediated by the effects of an organismic variable (relative open- or closed-mindedness). To test this assumption, a mixed model was necessary. The distinguishing features of this model are depicted in Figure 3.

Thus, the mixed model paradigm incorporates both environmental stimulus variables and organismic variables which reflect individual subject differences. As such, it results in the development of what can be labeled *S-O-R* laws: symbolically, $R = f(S, O)$. Though the mixed model provides partial explanatory power by the systematic manipulation of stimulus variables, it also creates explanatory ambiguity by using treatment conditions containing subjects drawn from differing parent populations.

Even though this ambiguity exists, the mixed model paradigm is an important tool for communication researchers. The development of complex laws that will enable explanation and prediction of communication behaviors rests on a concern for both stimulus and organismic variables. The mixed model provides a means for examining relationships between these two classes of variables.

Special Problems

This particular section has posed more difficulties than any other, for many problems of laboratory research are personally inviting. For instance, a section on the logic of hypothesis testing originally seemed appropriate. In particular, it appears that some researchers do not understand the inferential limitations associated with failure to demonstrate significant differences between treatment groups. It is especially distressing to encounter studies using the statistical hypothesis of no difference (null hypothesis) as the theoretic hypothesis (anticipation statement), and then proceed to test the null with such error-laden, inadequate procedures that an outcome of no significant differences is a foregone conclusion. In such cases, the only thing more mystifying than the researcher's misunderstanding of the logic of hypothesis testing is the fact that the study managed to withstand editorial scrutiny and gain page space in a professional journal.[8]

Likewise, some studies reflect misunderstanding of the process of establishing a confidence level. Setting a confidence level logically precedes conducting a study. The researcher should decide this level on a priori grounds, state his decision, and then label all differences as either *significant* or *not significant,* depending on whether or not they exceed the required level of confidence. Norton (1959) has commented cogently on the confusion inherent in the frequently used alternative of reporting the exact level of confidence for each comparison conducted in the study. Not only is such an approach potentially misleading to scientifically naïve readers, it logically implies that the researcher had previously defined that particular level of confidence as the dividing line between significant and nonsignificant results. In the case of 0.001 and 0.0001 confidence levels, such an implication is obviously at odds with the realities of most scientific research in communication.

Even though problems like the previous two are both important and intriguing, they will not be pursued further: first, because they are relatively common in both laboratory and field settings, and second, because they are dealt with in other chapters of this volume. Instead, the next remarks will focus on two special problems that are inextricably bound to an investigator structured environment and the rigorous control of variables, two characteristics associated with communication research in laboratory settings. For purposes of shorthand identification these problems will be labeled the *elusive variable problem* and the *deception problem.*

ELUSIVE VARIABLES

Laboratory research in communication involves some form of controlled interaction between a researcher and a number of subjects; these are the human elements of the structured laboratory environment. Since both the researcher and the subjects bring with them rich and varied backgrounds of social learning, it is reasonable to view any laboratory setting as a social situation and in turn to raise questions about the role expectations of the

---

[8] The writer has deliberately refrained from naming names or, what would amount to the same thing, giving examples. His purpose is not to criticize particular researchers, but rather to underscore a general problem.

persons placed in the setting. For instance, what are the subjects' expectations? In an essay of relatively ancient vintage, Pierce (1908) speculated on this question:

> It is to the highest degree probable that the subject['s] . . . general attitude of mind is that of ready complacency and cheerful willingness to assist the investigator in every possible way by reporting to him those very things which he is most eager to find, and that the very questions of the experimenter . . . suggest the shade of reply expected. . . . Indeed . . . it seems too often as if the subject were regarded as a stupid automaton [p. 264].

More recently, Orne (1959, 1962) has investigated the effects of the demand characteristics of psychological experimentation on subjects' behavior. The term *demand characteristics* refers to "the totality of cues which convey an experimental hypothesis to the subject [and which] become significant determinants of the subjects' behavior [1962, p. 779]." In general, Orne holds that subjects will strive to be "good research participants," that they will seek to behave consistently with the investigator's hypothesis. If the demand characteristics are sufficient to provide the subjects with a working knowledge of the theoretic hypothesis, its subsequent verification may result not from differences in supposedly relevant experimental variables, but rather from the subjects' desires to conform with the researcher's predictions.

A recent study (Amato and Ostermeier, 1967) illustrates how the demand characteristics of an experiment may confound the interpretation of research findings. These researchers were interested in the effects of various kinds of audience feedback on speaker encoding behavior. Specifically, they hypothesized that unfavorable feedback would have adverse effects on such delivery variables as eye contact, nervousness, bodily movement, and fluency.

An audience of 22 students was used, *both to manipulate the independent variable and to provide ratings of the speaker's delivery.* Each audience member used four-by-six index cards to present feedback during a speaker's presentation. The audience was instructed to assume a predetermined response role for each speaker. In one condition, the audience responded favorably by holding up white index cards; in a second condition, they held up red cards to indicate unfavorable feedback; and in a third, they held up green cards to indicate neutral feedback. Prior to their presentations, the speakers were told how to interpret the variously colored cards.

At the conclusion of each speech, the audience rated the speaker on six delivery variables. A second round of speeches was then presented, with the audience instructed to respond either unfavorably or neutrally, but not favorably. Again, post-communication speaker ratings were obtained from all audience members.

Subsequent analyses indicated a significant between-treatments effect on four of the six delivery variables. As a result, the researchers concluded that negative feedback not only leads to a disruption of encoding behavior but also produces a deterioration in delivery.

Consider a second interpretation suggested by the demand characteristics of Amato and Ostermeier's study. If an experimenter instructs a subject to present repeatedly a favorable response to a speaker and then asks him to rate that speaker, the subject is provided with numerous cues concerning the probable hypothesis of experimental interest. Moreover, if he plays the role of "good subject," he will respond consistent with the experimenter's wishes; that is, he will report lower ratings of speaker delivery in the unfavorable feedback condition than in the favorable feedback condition. Thus, no way exists to determine whether Amato and Ostermeier's findings are a function of type of feedback (the experimental variable of interest) or another set of variables associated with subjects' perceptions of the demand characteristics of the situation.

To test the possibility that the latter interpretation may hold, Combs and Miller (1968) replicated the Amato and Ostermeier study with certain modifications. The principal modification was in the assignment of feedback roles: one-third of the audience listening to any particular speech performed each of the roles. Thus, for any speech, differences in ratings could not possibly result from variations in the quality of presentation, for the entire audience was hearing the same presentation. The only systematic variation introduced was the way subjects were instructed to respond to the speech.

Subjects rated the speaker on four characteristics: delivery, content and analysis, language, and overall effectiveness. Obviously, if one assumes that quality of presentation is the only determinant of ratings, there should be no significant differences between the post-communication ratings of subjects assigned to varying feedback roles. Conversely, the demand interpretation implies that ratings should be consistent with the experimentally prescribed role.

Combs and Miller's results support the latter interpretation: there were large, significant differences in ratings for each of the four variables. Subjects assigned to the favorable feedback condition rated the speaker highest; ratings of subjects in the neutral condition fell between, and subjects in the unfavorable condition rated the speaker lowest. These findings suggest that the behavior of the speaker was irrelevant to the ratings reported by the subjects; rather, the subjects were responding entirely on the basis of the role assigned by the experimenter.

The preceding remarks are not intended to be unduly critical of a particular study but are instead meant to illustrate a general problem in much laboratory communication research. For instance, the typical pre-test / message stimulus / post-test approach to laboratory research in persuasion is often laden with cues for the perceptive subject. As Orne (1962) has stated, "If a test is given twice with some intervening treatment, even the dullest college student is aware that some change is expected, particularly if the test is in some obvious way related to the treatment [p. 779]." In fact, in his more candid moments, the researcher will probably admit that his scientific success is frequently contingent on staying one step ahead in the guessing game between experimenter and subject.

Thus far, we have considered only half the human dimension of the laboratory environment: the subject. But the experimenter may also contribute to the elusive variable problem, as Chapter 1 pointed out. Rosenthal (1966), whose extensive and ingenious research efforts provide the foundation for an understanding of the importance of experimenter effects in behavioral research, has written:

> When the experimenter serves as observer of the subject's behavior, when he records the data, summarizes, analyzes, and interprets the data, he may err in significant ways but not by directly affecting the subject's response.
>
> However when the experimenter interacts with the subject, his more enduring attributes, his attitudes, and his expectancies may prove to be significant determinants of the subject's behavior in the experiment [p. xiii].

Note that Rosenthal does not stress intentional experimenter bias (*e.g.*, deliberate and conscious distortion of data, outright dishonesty, etc.). Rather, he is primarily concerned with instances in which cues are unintentionally communicated to the subject, cues that may in turn cause the subject's behavior to conform to experimental expectations. Nor are trained experimenters immune to such biasing behaviors; in fact, Rosenthal's research indicates that they may be even more likely to exercise unintentional influence. Many variables, as identified in Chapter 1, can contribute to such unintended experimenter effects.

For the individual interested in conducting laboratory studies in communication, the problem can be summarized as follows: Interaction between a researcher and a group of subjects is an essential ingredient of almost any laboratory situation. Both the researcher and the subjects bring to the social setting of the laboratory prior attitudes, knowledge, and role expectations which influence their relationships with each other. To the extent that these influences produce behavior consistent with research predictions, it is difficult to determine whether confirmation of an hypothesis resulted from differences in relevant experimental variables, or whether it is an artifact of the social psychology of the laboratory itself.

How is the elusive variable problem to be resolved? Unfortunately, there is no easy answer to this question. One step is to be found in continued study of experimenter, subject, and situational variables that may affect behavior in laboratory settings. If these variables can be identified, it may be possible to devise means for controlling their effects, or at least to construct behavioral generalizations which number such variables among specified relevant antecedent conditions.[9]

In addition, more energy should be devoted to identifying instances in which experimental outcomes are influenced by demand features of the experiment. Extensive debriefing of subjects could provide clues concerning the extent of their awareness of the purposes of a given study. The importance of such information is underscored by Orne's (1959) finding that a particular experimental effect was present only for those subjects who were able to verbalize the experimenter's hypothesis. Unless results can be obtained without the subject's awareness of the experimenter's purpose, it is hard to place confidence in an interpretation that stresses the importance of manipulated experimental variables.

Finally, it is likely that communication researchers will continue to use deception in their attempts to minimize subject awareness of experimental purposes. The use of deception, however, creates numerous problems, and it is to these problems that we now turn.

DECEPTION

In order to minimize demand characteristics of a study or to pave the way for use of certain methodological procedures, a laboratory researcher may practice various kinds of deception with a subject. The following list, though not exhaustive, summarizes commonly used deceptions.

(1) Simple misrepresentation of a study's purpose. Often, the researcher assumes that knowledge of the true purpose of a study will influence the behavior of subjects. To guard against this possibility, the researcher may misrepresent the study's purpose to the subjects. For instance, while the genuine objective may be to study the effects of various kinds of feedback on encoding behaviors, the researcher may tell the subjects that the study deals with an individual's ability to plan and present an oral communication with minimal preparation time. This type of deception is practiced frequently; in fact, the true purpose of a laboratory study in communication is seldom divulged until the data have been gathered.

(2) Misrepresentation of a study's purpose to facilitate manipulation of a variable. Sometimes, manipulation of a variable may depend on successfully misrepresenting the study's purpose. Suppose, for instance, that a researcher wished to study the effects of task success or failure on subsequent persuasibility. The subject could be told that the study aims at establishing norms for performance of a particular task. After completing the task, the subject could be given bogus information indicating that he has

---

[9] To argue that experimenter and subject variables influence experimental outcomes in no way suggests a philosophy of indeterminism. Rather, the argument implies that the relevant antecedent variables which determine behavior may be others than those manipulated in the experiment.

performed extremely well or extremely poorly. All subjects could then be exposed to a persuasive message, and the amount of attitude change for the success and failure groups could be compared. In this instance, manipulation depends on deception, and the skullduggery is more elaborate than simply misrepresenting a study's purpose.

(*3*) *Misrepresentation of the relationship between researcher and subject.* This form of deception can be thought of as a special instance of misrepresentation to facilitate manipulation of a variable. For example, a researcher may cause a subject to believe that he is serving as a confederate in the study, when actually the subject's behavior is being observed and measured. In other words, the subject is still performing the role of subject.

(*4*) *Misrepresentation of the rewards to be gained from participating in a study.* This form of deception also relates to the manipulation of variables. The subject may be given, or told that he will be given, a substantial cash reward or an attractive gift for participating in the study. After the study is completed, he is asked to return the rewards or is told that they will not be forthcoming. Economic limitations are intimately related to this deceptive practice, for researchers would probably let subjects keep their cash or gifts if they had sufficient funds to go around.

Use of at least one of these types of deception in a study is almost routine. Speaking of the use of deception in social psychological research, Kelman (1967) has asserted:

> The use of deception has become more and more extensive, and it is now a commonplace and almost standard feature of social psychological experiments. Deception has been turned into a game, often played with great skill and virtuosity. A considerable amount of the creativity and ingenuity of social psychologists is invested in the development of increasingly elaborate deception situations. Within a single experiment, deception may be built upon deception in a delicately complex structure. The literature now contains a fair number of studies in which second- or even third-order deception was employed [p. 2].

Subterfuge is often a valuable ally to the researcher attempting to disguise the demand characteristics of a study or to manipulate variables effectively. Moreover, it is necessary for communication researchers to continue to use deception intelligently. But excessive, routine use of deception creates a number of important ethical, methodological, and theoretical problems for the laboratory researcher in communication.

The absolutist may, of course, argue that it is never ethical to deceive a subject. The moderate would probably counter with the argument that for any particular case, one must weigh the negative aspects of temporary deceit against the positive values associated with the discovery of new communication knowledge. As Kelman has stated:

> If we regard the acquisition of scientific knowledge about human behavior as a positive value, and if an experiment using deception constitutes a significant contribution to such knowledge which could not very well be achieved by other means, then we cannot unequivocally rule out this experiment. The question for us is not simply whether it does or does not use deception, but whether the amount and type of deception are justified by the significance of the study and the unavailability of alternative (that is, deception-free) procedures [p. 2].

What is ethically worrisome is the possibility that communication researchers will make no effort to find alternatives to deception, that they will come to accept deception as an intrinsic feature of laboratory research methodology. Such an unqualified endorsement of deceit has profound ethical implications for the relationship between researcher and subject. Not only is the element of trust removed from the interaction, but in addition, the subject is likely to perceive the researcher in particular, and communication research in general, as ethically repugnant. As Ring (1967) queries, "What is the perceptive student to think, finally, of a field where the most renowned researchers apparently get their kicks from practicing sometimes unnecessary and frequently crass deceptions on their unsuspecting subjects [p. 118]?" In a society that has traditionally emphasized honesty in carrying out social and professional relationships, scientific effort cannot flourish on a norm of deliberate subterfuge.

There is another bothersome ethical question associated with deception, namely: In terms of the subject's psychological welfare, what are the long-range emotional, behavioral, and attitudinal effects of certain deceptive procedures? Suppose, for example, that in order to induce a feeling of social failure, we cause subjects to believe that they are socially insensitive and incapable of relating to others. Can the self-esteem of these subjects be restored to its original level through a post-experimental debriefing which emphasizes that the information was fictional?

Most researchers have optimistically assumed that a debriefing does, indeed, erase the negative effects of deceptive manipulations; however, recent research by Walster, Berscheid, Abrahams, and Aronson (1967) casts doubt on this assumption. These researchers studied the effectiveness of debriefing after an experimental manipulation in which some subjects were falsely informed that they were not very sociable and that they lacked self-insight into their own shortcomings. Walster *et al.* summarize their findings as follows:

> . . . it is disturbing that . . . even after a very lengthy and thorough debriefing (probably atypical in thoroughness) subjects still behaved to some extent as though the debriefing had not taken place. Subjects behaved in this manner even though they had voiced . . . their understanding that the manipulation was false, their understanding

of the true purpose of the experiment, and even though . . . the experimenter had been satisfied that they did indeed understand the nature of the deception.

Even more disturbing is the evidence that the after effects of debriefing might be complex, unpredictable, and may depend in part upon the personality traits of the subjects [p. 380].

In short, debriefing may not provide a magic formula for erasing the negative emotional or attitudinal effects of a threatening manipulation. Given this possibility, does the communication researcher have the prerogative of adding to the many anxieties that most subjects are already experiencing? A strong ethical case can be made for a negative answer to this query.

Deception need not be examined solely from a moral perspective, for its excessive use also poses potential methodological difficulties. When viewed from the researcher's vantage point, excessive reliance on trickery may eventually contribute to a gamesmanlike attitude that pictures behavioral communication research as little more than a contest of wits. Ring (1967) has argued that social psychology has already arrived at this stage:

Experimental social psychology today seems dominated by values that suggest the following slogan: "Social psychology ought to be and is a lot of fun." The fun comes not from the learning, but from the doing. Clever experimentation on exotic topics with a zany manipulation seems to be the guaranteed formula for success which, in turn, appears to be defined as being able to effect a *tour de force*. One sometimes gets the impression that an evergrowing coterie of social psychologists is playing (largely for one another's benefit) a game of "can you top this?" Whoever can conduct the most contrived, flamboyant, and mirth-producing experiments receives the highest score on the kudometer. There is, in short, a distinctly exhibitionistic flavor to much current experimentation, while the experimenters themselves often seem to equate notoriety with achievement [pp. 116–117].

Whether or not one agrees with Ring's assessment, preoccupation with deceit is one factor that can eventually result in such methodological license. We can only hope that laboratory research in communication will not degenerate to the level of scientific fun and games.

From the subject's vantage point, excessive deception creates methodological barriers which are closely related to the previously discussed elusive variable problem. It has already been stated that subjects enter the laboratory with expectations about the researcher's purposes, and that in turn, these expectations affect the subjects' behavior. If one of the shared prior assumptions of subjects is that experimental tomfoolery is inevitable, it becomes even more doubtful that they will perceive the situation in the way the researcher had hoped. Kelman (1967) has underscored this methodological dilemma forcefully, stating "that deception increases the subject's tendency to operate in terms of his private definition of the situation, differing (in random or systematic fashion) from the definition the experimenter is trying to impose; moreover, it makes it more difficult to evaluate or minimize the effects of this tendency [p. 7]."

Finally, excessive deception imposes severe theoretical limitations on the communication researcher. Obviously, as emphasized throughout this chapter, the goal of scientific research in communication is the development of a comprehensive set of generalizations that will enable us to explain and predict human communication behavior. If these generalizations are tested with subjects drawn entirely from a population of suspicious persons, the domain of explanation is limited to that population; *in a sense, we have developed a theory of communication that deals only with suspicious people.* Since much daily communication occurs within a psychological atmosphere of trust and good will, our theory is irrelevant to numerous interesting and important communication phenomena.

How can the laboratory researcher in communication come to grips with the deception problem? A good beginning rule of thumb is: Never employ deception when deception-free methods will work as effectively. In other words, deception should be viewed as a last resort rather than as a prerequisite for a good laboratory study. Moreover, some of the effort and ingenuity that frequently go into devising deceptions could profitably be directed to the task of developing new deception-free research procedures. For example, both Kelman (1967) and Ring (1967) have pointed out the research potential in role-playing.

More research dealing with the effects of deception on experimental outcomes is also desirable. As yet, we know very little about this issue. It would indeed be ironic if we discovered that elaborate duplicity is often superfluous, that subjects behave in much the same way if they are told the true purpose of the study. While this possibility may seem far-fetched, it deserves more attention than it has received.

The best immediate approach to the deception problem can be captured in two words: *awareness* and *moderation*. The laboratory communication researcher should be constantly aware of the possible contaminating or confounding influences of deception; furthermore, in his own research undertakings, he should practice deception with studied moderation.

Conclusion

This chapter has sought to identify the fundamental characteristics and the basic logic of the laboratory research setting. As indicated earlier, this setting lends itself to various approaches to inquiry: the experiment, the investigation, or the mixed model. For this reason, no single study discussed here "exemplifies" laboratory research; rather, the studies used to illustrate each research paradigm should underscore the diverseness of the process that we label *laboratory research.* The criteria for evaluating a laboratory study are similar to those for judging any scientific endeavor, or, for that matter, any rational approach to inquiry: they involve such considerations as the significance of the problem, the clarity with which the problem is formulated, the adequacy of methods used to investigate the problem, and the soundness with which data derived from these methods are interpreted.

Two points merit a final restatement. It is imperative that the laboratory researcher in communication understand the basic logic of his chosen method of inquiry and that he constantly seek to become more sensitive to the special problems associated with the method. While a "cookbook" approach may enable an individual to conduct laboratory studies, it will not allow him to become a *good* laboratory researcher. Understanding involves more than knowledge of a few research designs and a handful of statistical techniques for analyzing data. Theory, method, and attitudes operate conjunctively to produce research competency.

The attitudinal dimension of research competency motivates this final comment: laboratory researchers in communication should maintain a posture of moderation toward their chosen method of inquiry. No method is sovereign; instead, each contributes to the scientific goal of explaining and predicting human communication behavior. The field and the laboratory are not exclusive domains, but rather parts of a common scientific puzzle. The important consideration is not *what kind* of research it is, but rather *how much* scientific importance and social utility can be attached to it. No esoteric arguments about the relative merits of various approaches to inquiry can salvage the results of a poorly conducted laboratory study.

References and Selected Readings

Amato, P., and Ostermeier, T. The effect of audience feedback on the beginning public speaker. *The Speech Teacher,* 1967, **16,** 56–60.

Aronson, E., and Mills, J. The effect of severity of initiation on liking for a group. *Journal of Abnormal and Social Psychology,* 1959, **59,** 177–181.

Bakan, D. *On method: Toward a reconstruction of psychological investigation.* San Francisco: Jossey-Bass, 1967.

Brunswik, E. *Systematic and representative design of psychological experiments with results in physical and social perception.* Berkeley: University of California Press, 1947.

Combs, W., and Miller, G. R. The effect of audience feedback on the beginning public speaker: A counterview. *The Speech Teacher,* 1968, **17,** 229–231.

Festinger, L., Riecken, H., and Schachter, S. *When prophecy fails.* Minneapolis: University of Minnesota Press, 1956.

Homans, G. *Social behavior: Its elementary forms.* New York: Harcourt, Brace & World, 1961.

Kelman, H. Human use of human subjects: The problem of deception in social psychological experiments. *Psychological Bulletin,* 1967, **67,** 1–11.

Kerlinger, F. *Foundations of behavioral research.* New York: Holt, Rinehart & Winston, 1964.

Leavitt, H. Some effects of certain communication patterns on group performance. *Journal of Abnormal and Social Psychology,* 1951, **46,** 38–50.

Miller, G. R., and Bacon, P. Open- and closed-mindedness and recognition of visual humor. Unpublished paper, Michigan State University, 1967.

Miller, G. R., and Hewgill, M. The effect of variations in nonfluency on audience ratings of source credibility. *Quarterly Journal of Speech,* 1964, **50,** 36–44.

Miller, G. R., and Lobe, J. Opinionated language, open- and closed-mindedness, and response to persuasive communications. *Journal of Communication,* 1967, **17,** 333–341.

Norton, D. Problems in experimental design. *American Journal of Mental Deficiency,* 1959, **64,** 370–383.

Orne, M. The nature of hypnosis: Artifact and essence. *Journal of Abnormal and Social Psychology,* 1959, **58,** 277–299.

Orne, M. On the social psychology of the psychological experiment: With particular reference to demand characteristics and their implications. *The American Psychologist,* 1962, **17,** 776–783.

Pierce, A. The subconscious again. *Journal of Philosophy, Psychology, and Scientific Method,* 1908, **5,** 264–271.

Ring, K. Experimental social psychology: Some sober questions about some frivolous values. *Journal of Experimental Social Psychology,* 1967, **3,** 113–123.

Rokeach, M. *The open and closed mind.* New York: Basic Books, 1960.

Rosenthal, R. *Experimental effects in behavioral research.* New York: Appleton-Century-Crofts, 1966.

Scriven, M. Views of human nature. In T. Wann (Ed.), *Behaviorism and phenomenology: Contrasting bases for modern psychology.* Chicago: University of Chicago Press, 1964. Pp. 163–183.

Shaw, M. Some effects of unequal distribution of information upon group performance in various communication nets. *Journal of Abnormal and Social Psychology,* 1954, **49,** 547–553.

Shaw, M. A comparison of two types of leadership in various communication nets. *Journal of Abnormal and Social Psychology,* 1955, **50,** 127–134.

Spence, K. The nature of theory construction in contemporary psychology. *Psychological Review,* 1944, **51,** 47–68.

Troldahl, V., and Powell, F. A short-form dogmatism scale for use in field studies. *Social Forces,* 1965, **44,** 211–215.

Walster, E., Berscheid, E., Abrahams, D., and Aronson, V. Effectiveness of debriefing following deception experiments. *Journal of Personality and Social Psychology,* 1967, **6,** 371–380.

4

Research Setting: Field Studies[1]

W. Charles Redding

For many years methodologists have talked about the supposed contrasts between *laboratory* studies and *field* studies. Without denying the usefulness in such analysis, this chapter will argue that this dichotomy is not the best way of describing the most important dimensions of research.

Probably the least ambiguous, although not necessarily the most valuable, way of defining field research is in terms of *locale*. Pending a more detailed analysis later in the chapter (pp. 137–146), this type of definition will be adopted. Scott (1965), in his discussion of field methods applied to the study of organizations, starts with the terminology of Hughes (1960, p. v): "Field work . . . refers to observation of people *in situ* [pp. 261–

[1] For several reasons, especially lack of space, the author has omitted detailed suggestions concerning a potentially lengthy list of practical problems commonly encountered in field locales (*e.g.,* gaining entry into organizations, relationships with "sponsors," and maintaining objectivity and rapport with subjects). As long as the supply lasts, a mimeographed document dealing with these matters may be obtained from the author, Communication Research Center, Department of Communication, Purdue University, Lafayette, Indiana 47907.

262]." But Scott elaborates by pointing out that the term *observation* should be taken in the broadest sense, including

> ... all the kinds of techniques which have been employed to examine behavior in naturally occurring groups — human beings "on the hoof" — as opposed to studies of *ad hoc* groups conducted in the laboratory [p. 262].

Like Zelditch (1962), Scott makes the important point that field research need not refer to any single methodology or technique.

However, as field research was originally developed by anthropologists and sociologists during the last several decades, the term "field study" has frequently been used as roughly synonymous with certain methods (as well as locales); thus, many writers refer to such methods as nonquantitative participant observation or descriptive surveys when they speak of field studies. In this manner, the quite different concepts of *method* and *locale* have become confused in many treatments of field research. (This topic will be explored in more detail on pp. 137–146.)

For present purposes, then, the more parsimonious definition of field studies will be accepted, denoting investigations conducted "outside the library and laboratory and '[in] the field' [Carter, 1958, p. 78]." It is not surprising that until very recent times substantially all that has been known about the vast universe of phenomena called human communication behavior has been the fruit of observations made in the field (including those recorded in the documents and materials of history). Especially since the end of World War II, researchers affiliated with a variety of academic departments and disciplines have been applying the methods of laboratory experimentation to the study of communication. For a while there was a great clamor to be rigorously "scientific" in communication research; this frequently meant that the laboratory was substituted for the field.

However, in the last few years many voices, including those of laboratory experimentalists themselves, have been raised to question the universal validity and applicability of the laboratory approach, particularly in the study of the complex, dynamic, and multivariate phenomena of human communication (Katz, 1953; Brunswik, 1956; Hovland, 1959; Hughes, 1960; Homans, 1962; Orne, 1962; McGuigan, 1963; Rosenthal, 1963; R. Hyman, 1964; Clevenger, 1965; Klintz, Delprato, Mettee, Persons, and Schappe, 1965; Nebergall, 1965; Scott, 1965; Weick, 1965, 1967; Jaques, 1966; Redding, 1966; Bakan, 1967; Barnes, 1967; Burns, 1967; Roy Turner, 1967; S. L. Becker, 1968; Thayer, 1968; Tompkins, 1968; Haiman, 1969; Kibler and Barker, 1969; G. R. Miller, 1969; Thompson, 1969). A dominant theme expressed by a number of spokesmen emerged in two recent research conferences sponsored by the Speech Association of America (New Orleans, February 1968; Chicago, August 1968); this theme could be epitomized in such words as the following: "Laboratory experimentation is fine, but we must explore more thoroughly the possibilities of communication research carried out in 'real-life' field settings (Kibler and Barker, 1969; *Summary Report: Conference on Social Engagement, 1968*). We shall look at some of the reasons supporting this recommendation in later sections of this chapter.

The main concern here will be to propose a basic rationale for so-called field research, with special reference to the study of human communication behavior. Such topics will be considered as the bases of categorizing field studies, the problems associated with scientific validity, and alleged differences between laboratory and field settings. Criteria will be suggested for describing and analyzing field versus laboratory research; in fact, it will be argued that the conventional dichotomy should be replaced by other schemes. This chapter is not a "cookbook" of procedural prescriptions. In the first place, there already exists a substantial literature suggesting long lists of do's and don't's for the field researcher. Most of these recommendations consist of empirical generalizations based on the personal experience of numerous investigators; very few, if any, could be regarded as established scientific principles or even as rules of thumb applicable to all cases. Moreover, since a revisionist view of the laboratory-field dichotomy will be proposed on pp. 137–146, it will be urged that relatively few features of the field study as conventionally defined cannot be subsumed under the basic rubrics of scientific inquiry in general.

Even assuming that the topics were germane to the objectives of this chapter, space does not permit detailed discussion of many methodologies frequently identified with field research which in themselves are quasi disciplines, *e.g.,* sampling surveys or polls, interviewing techniques, participant observation, and historical-critical methods applied to public address situations. Those interested in detailed accounts of the more-or-less accepted formulations of field research applicable to the whole range of behavioral science are referred to such competent and comprehensive sources as the following (this list is arbitrarily restricted to bound volumes, omitting the vast number of titles to be found in journals and monographs): Lerner and Lasswell (1951); French (1953); Katz (1953); H. Hyman (1955); Carter (1958); Westley (1958); Selltiz, Jahoda, Deutsch, and Cook (1959); Adams and Preiss (1960); Junker (1960); R. Hyman (1964); Kerlinger (1964); Richardson, Dohrenwend, and Klein (1965); Scott (1965); Weick (1965, 1967); Barnes (1967); Burns (1967); McCall and Simmons (1969). Especially useful are the anthologies containing contributions from numerous authors: Lerner and Lasswell (1951); Festinger and Katz (1953); Nafziger and White (1958); Adams and Preiss (1960); March (1965); Vroom (1967); McCall and Simmons (1969).

The present chapter will take a broader methodological view of the term "field studies" than that of Kerlinger (1964, p. 387), for example, who restricts the concept to scientific inquiries exclusively of an ex post facto nature. Under this heading Kerlinger includes only those designs providing for the discovery of relationships among "variables . . . in life situations," and in which hypotheses are tested. In the present context, any research is arbitrarily classified under the label "field study" if it is conducted in a *locale perceived to be primarily real-life rather than laboratory,* and if it meets accepted criteria of "productive scholarship" and the spirit of "scientific inquiry," as these terms are explicated, for example, by Westley (1958, pp. 204–213). This means, therefore, that field studies may or may not be quantitative, may or may not be experimental, and may or may not test formally stated hypotheses.

COMMUNICATION STUDIES CONVENTIONALLY CLASSIFIABLE AS FIELD RESEARCH

It should be helpful at this point to proceed inductively and to note a random sample of communication studies which may be regarded as illustrations of field research. (No evaluative inferences should be drawn from the order in which examples are mentioned; furthermore, if disproportionate attention seems to be focused on studies with which the present writer has been associated, the reason is obviously that he has firsthand knowledge of them.)

Experimental and Quasi-Experimental Field Studies

We may begin by mentioning one of the earlier field investigations of communication; actually this was a field *experiment,* although the subjects were not aware that they were participating in an experiment. Verplanck (1955), concerned with investigating reinforcement theory, instructed. his experimental assistants (students) to conduct "natural" conversations in everyday social settings with the subjects (also college students). During the middle third of each conversation, the experimental assistant responded to the subject's opinion statements with positive reinforcement (*e.g.,* "You're right"), and during the last third with negative reinforcement or no reinforcement.[2]

STUDIES OF RUMOR

A number of field studies using varying designs and varying degrees of quantitative or experimental features have addressed themselves to serial transmission of messages, especially rumors. One of the earliest, for example, conducted by Festinger, Cartwright, Barber, Fleischl, Gottsdanker, Keysen, and Leavitt (1948), traced the spread of a rumor about alleged Communist influence in a wartime housing project. It is interesting to note that from this one study three principles of rumor behavior were generated: "external control," "cognitive unclarity," and "integrative explanation." Two other field studies of rumors (Caplow, 1947; Peterson

---

[2] Kerlinger (1964, pp. 377–378) and Jones and Gerard (1967, pp. 539–542) arrive at different interpretations of the Verplanck study.

and Gist, 1951) emerged with findings somewhat at variance with those of Festinger *et al.;* Caplow, for instance, found that in wartime military units the accuracy of rumors was quite high.[3]

Another famous rumor study is that of Davis (1953a, b), examining how "grapevine" messages were transmitted among the entire managerial-supervisory population of a small manufacturing plant. He collected data with ingeniously designed written forms reporting grapevine messages about real events in the company; hence, his design could be called a variant of a natural experiment. From this study emerged the well known "ECCO" ("episodic communication channels in organization") concept and the notion of a "cluster chain" to explain the grapevine network. More recently, Sutton and Porter (1968) attempted a partial replication of Davis' original study and came up with quite different findings. And Davis himself (1968) has extended his interests in the direction of "chain-of-command oral communication" in business organizations.

ORGANIZATIONAL STUDIES

It is not surprising, in fact, that many communication studies have been conducted in various kinds of formal organizations, such as industries, hospitals, and government agencies. Organizations already exist "out there" without having to be created ad hoc; most of the time they are typically undergoing various kinds of changes or innovations which can provide naturally occurring independent variables; and they present a rich — although bewildering — array of communication events. As Scott (1965) has observed: "Most of what we know today about organizations and the behavior of their members is known on the basis of field studies [p. 261]."

The Dahle (1954) study represents one of the earliest and at the same time most ambitious field researches in organizational communication. Because he actually exercised controls and manipulated independent variables, Dahle conducted what is properly called a field experiment. In fact, there were three separate experiments: one with college students, one with employees in a small industrial plant, and one with personnel of a large retail mail order company. Experimental treatments consisted of varying modes of transmitting real-life organizational information — such as "oral only," "written only," and "oral and written" combined.

Another attempt to perform a controlled experiment with design and measurement techniques roughly approximating those of laboratory conditions was the field research of Miraglia (1963). This study was concerned with "the effects, in actual on-the-job performance, of a training program in face-to-face oral communication . . . for supervisory nurses [p. iv]." Like Dahle, Miraglia introduced a replication feature by conducting supposedly equivalent experimental training courses in two separate hospitals.

---

[3] Caplow's study, incidentally, is entirely nonquantitative and descriptive (being based on notes he made while he was in wartime service).

The Miraglia study is noteworthy for its use of a variety of measuring instruments, including those related to criteria of job performance. In addition to several paper-and-pencil questionnaires and tests, Miraglia devised instruments intended to secure (a) perceptions by subordinates of supervisors' on-the-job communication behavior; (b) perceptions by subordinates of supervisors' supervisory effectiveness; and (c) perceptions by superiors of the supervisors' supervisory effectiveness. The Miraglia design used control groups with before measurements and two after measurements, one immediately and one four months later. As is frequently the case in field experiments, Miraglia was compelled to make a number of compromises with the ideals of experimental controls (see pp. 139–140 for more on this common problem).

NATURAL FIELD EXPERIMENTS

Although not focusing on communication behavior per se, Lawrence (1958) depended heavily on certain communication behaviors as criteria, or indicators, of major dependent variables. The basic design of this study was that of a natural field experiment, although sample sizes were very small and only very limited forms of experimental controls were used. The setting was a supermarket chain in which a decentralization of managerial structure had been initiated; this decentralization represented, in a global sense, the independent variable. Before-and-after assessments of managerial behavior were made by the researcher, with a time spread of as long as two years. Among Lawrence's most important means of describing interpersonal interaction between members of superior-subordinate pairs was observing and recording oral communication encounters. Adapting a category scheme from Bales's (1950) well known Interaction Process Analysis (see Chapter 13), he observed and categorized (using a stopwatch) such behaviors as total talking time, time spent in asking questions, time spent in giving information, and time spent in rendering opinions.

Nonexperimental Designs

For obvious reasons, nonexperimental designs have been much more common in organizational field studies than have designs which would satisfy rigorous experimental criteria. However, elaborate and precise quantification techniques combined with careful selection of samples have frequently characterized studies which stop short of laboratory conditions for testing causal hypotheses. Simons (1961), for example, compared the communication attributes of two criterion groups of supervisors in a large urban hotel — those rated highest and those rated lowest in terms of overall supervisory success. In order to do this, the researcher was compelled to create a variety of measuring devices and to persuade the hotel management to install a system of evaluating the job performance of supervisors.

In a companion study, Pace (1960) employed similar techniques to examine analogous relationships between oral communication attributes of sales representatives and their sales effectiveness. He devised an ingenious method for arriving at a reasonably precise numerical criterion measure of sales effectiveness based on dollar sales (taken from company records) in relation to hours spent on the job. Both Simons and Pace administered an extensive inventory of questionnaire items, including some quantitative tests, in face-to-face interviews; they also recorded in rating scale units their evaluations of the subjects' actual oral communication behavior as observed in the data gathering interviews.

Smith (1967) attempted to discover measurable communication correlates of interpersonal sensitivity (roughly equivalent to empathy) in a carefully selected sample of 60 industrial supervisors in a large automotive manufacturing plant. This study involved an unusually large number of quantitative instruments and devices, including attitude and self-description scales, a specially created empathy instrument, and an event recording machine (with which two observers categorized details of communication behavior, such as eye contact, during two-person interviews). The researcher also invented ingenious computer based data recording instruments, making it possible for the subjects to indicate responses directly on computer print-out sheets.

Kelly (1962) sought to determine whether a relationship exists between listening competence and supervisory effectiveness. In his central research project (excluding some peripheral studies), he worked with the entire supervisory population of a medium-sized plant manufacturing electrical products. In order to determine various kinds of validity of listening tests, he ran correlations among three different listening tests (one of which he himself devised), as well as between the listening tests and measures of personality and of general mental ability. He also collected data by directly observing the listening demeanor of the supervisory subjects, having employees rate their supervisors on this same attribute, having superiors rate supervisors, and interviewing the subjects themselves.

Studies Devising and Validating Measuring Instruments

An important type of investigation in behavioral science has for many years been the attempt to devise and validate one or more measuring instruments. For obvious reasons, such studies commonly make crucial use of data collected under field conditions. Pyron (1964) was attempting to construct a reliable and valid written instrument for assessing the communication attitudes of first-level industrial foremen. The type of instrument he proposed to develop was a forced choice scale (see Chapter 5, pp. 169–170). Freshley (1955) worked with a sampling of industrial managers and created a multiple choice test whose items were brief problem incidents incorporating communication principles extracted from the literature.

Descriptive Field Studies

A number of field studies have been designed basically to discover "what is going on" in organizations. Sometimes they are built on formally stated hypotheses, sometimes they attempt to supply answers to research *inquiries* couched in the form of direct, open-ended questions, and frequently they address themselves to both hypotheses and questions. For example, Richetto (1969) wanted to find out whether a theoretical statement of personal influence processes would accurately describe the real-life situation encountered in selected units of the George C. Marshall Space Flight Center (NASA), Huntsville, Alabama. The main thrust of his research was directed to testing five formal hypotheses, in turn based on a theory proposed to Richetto by Tompkins. Three of Richetto's hypotheses were:

1. There exists in the organization an informal network of local influentials . . . who influence other members of their sub-groups in the areas of: (1) *task* influence, (2) *political* influence, and (3) *social-emotional* influence.

2. These local influentials possess one or more of the following characteristics which constitute "credibility" in the Aristotelian, Hovland, and Bauer models of persuasion:
   (1) Expertise
   (2) Trustworthiness
   (3) Good Intent

   .   .   .   .   .

5. When credibility ratings are compared between a subject's selected informal influential and that subject's immediate supervisor, the former will receive a higher credibility rating.

He also posed six research inquiries which were not amenable to statistical testing. For example:

1. How does the formal organizational-communication structure differ from the informal structure?
2. What, if any, specific techniques in . . . persuasion do local influentials utilize . . . [pp. 20–21]?

It should be noted that research inquiry questions may take either of two general forms, depending in turn on which one of two theoretical frames of reference may be in the mind of the investigator. He may ask (a) *"What is out there?"* or (b) *"What, if any, relationships exist among specified phenomena* (whether they are cause to effect or of concomitant variation)?" For example, in his field study of communication attitudes and perceptions in the total supervisory-managerial populations of two divisions within the same manufacturing company, Minter (1969) proposed three broad questions. The first was of the "what is out there" type:

1. What are the attitudes and perceptions, relevant to selected communication factors, of several "vertical" levels of supervisors, managers, and executives within each of the two divisions of the company [p. 28]?

But his second and third questions were concerned with relationships, the second with the possible concomitant variations between communication phenomena and position on the hierarchical ladder within each division, and the third with variations between the same communication phenomena and the factor of technological climate, which was postulated as a basic difference between the two divisions.

The field studies of Nilsen (1953), Level (1959), Sanborn (1961), and Tompkins (1962) were attempts primarily to answer the first type of question, "What's out there?" However, all their inquiries were influenced by existing theory in that research was directed into specific channels in an effort to determine whether certain theoretical constructs or assertions could be verified in the real-life situation. Furthermore, all the studies were at least subordinately concerned with examining relationships among certain phenomena. Nilsen, in one of the earliest systematic investigations of communication in complex business or industrial enterprises, actually studied three different organizational settings. His data collecting methods were interviews, a written questionnaire, and direct on-the-job observation. His conclusions, couched as tentative generalizations extrapolated from findings in the three settings, ranged from the narrow and specific to the broad and abstract. For example, he concluded that group meetings should not be restricted solely to ad hoc crisis situations; he also suggested that a general need for ego-enhancement underlies the entire communication climate of an organization.

Level, working in a small midwestern bank with a total managerial and employee population of less than 60, focused particularly on the degree to which nine selected communication principles appeared to be valid descriptors of actual communication behavior in the bank. Sanborn, using similar design and constructs, gathered data from a large sample (over 400) of managers and employees in national, regional, and local units of a nationwide sales organization.

Tompkins was one of the very few investigators to attempt an academic, systematic study of communication within a labor union. He collected data (using interviews, an information test, direct observation, and a modified semantic differential) from three levels of personnel within the Brotherhood of Painters, Decorators and Paperhangers: international headquarters staff, business representatives in a district council, and a randomly chosen sample of rank-and-file members in the St. Louis area.

Although carefully phrased with appropriate reservations and qualifications, the conclusions in all four studies are examples of generalizations. Such generalizations are sometimes tentative confirmations of existing hypotheses; sometimes they cast doubt on such hypotheses; sometimes they propose new theoretical constructs (such as "communication satisfaction" by Level and "semantic/information distance" by Tompkins) or new hypotheses (such as the role of ego-enhancement needs by Nilsen). In addition to generalizations, such studies also typically report specific findings applied explicitly to the unique field setting in which the research is conducted. In all investigations, however, even the most descriptive or exploratory, the collection of data is purposeful and guided by preexisting formulations: concepts, constructs, pragmatic rules of thumb, or formally stated hypotheses.

CLASSIFYING AND EVALUATING FIELD STUDIES

Whether intentionally or not, when writers in the field of methodology propose classification schemes applicable to the great variety of field studies encountered in the behavioral sciences, they use labels connoting value judgments beyond objective description. For this reason, *classifying* and *evaluating* will be considered together. Such common terms as "experimental," "correlational," and "exploratory" typically describe a hierarchy of values — in descending order of scientific sophistication — as well as an axis for characterizing types or purposes of field research.

The Place of Field Research in Research Taxonomies

(1) In a book published more than fifteen years ago (and recently reissued), Festinger and Katz (1953) provided a basic taxonomy of research methodology which has pervasively influenced the thinking of all sorts of persons calling themselves behavioral scientists. This book presents an overall view of methodology and divides the subject into four general parts: research settings, sampling procedures, techniques of data collection, and procedures for analyzing. "Field studies" are classified in this scheme as one of four "research settings"; the other three are "sample surveys," "experiments in field settings," and "laboratory experiments." Citing Festinger and Katz, Kerlinger (1964), in his widely used textbook on behavioral research, lists the same four types — but he calls them "major categories" of scientific research, rather than "settings." Such a categorization, as he points out, "stems from two sources, the distinction between experimental and nonexperimental research and that between laboratory and 'field' research [p. 375]."

(2) R. Hyman (1964, pp. 43–53), in his brief but comprehensive introduction to psychological inquiry, identifies three basic categories, but he considers them as falling under the heading of "getting the facts." In his terminology, the categories are "naturalistic studies" (including, as a

variant, the "clinical method"), "differential methods" (including especially the "correlational method"), and "experimental methods." What Hyman calls "naturalistic studies" obviously would fall entirely into any category as broad as field research; similarly, the "correlational method," which he defines as investigating a "relationship between two or more variables as they exist in nature," includes work carried out in the field (for example, sample surveys).

(3) Another influential and generalized treatment of research methodology in the social sciences is that of Selltiz *et al.* (1959). These authors discuss their taxonomy in terms of research design, which in turn is divided into two large classes according to whether *causal* relations may be inferred at a high level of probability:

(I)   Exploratory and descriptive studies
(II) Studies testing causal hypotheses — primarily experiments, although several quasi-experimental designs are also considered useful in the attempt to discover causal relations

For most purposes, then, the classificatory scheme proposed by Selltiz *et al.* boils down to a tripartite set of categories:

(1) exploratory
(2) descriptive
(3) hypothesis testing (chiefly experimental)

In his definitive survey of field methods applicable to the study of organizations, Scott (1965, p. 267) accepts this schema as useful although imperfect, regarding it as based on research *purpose*.

COMPARISON

Naturally, these published classification systems often overlap. For example, Katz (1953, pp. 74–76) omits a separate category of descriptive studies, apparently including these under "exploratory"; first, he suggests that all field studies are "of two major types: exploratory and hypothesis-testing." But after characterizing exploratory studies as those which are designed "to see what is there rather than to predict relationships," he also concedes that from such studies "may come knowledge about important relationships between variables" (even though "more definite proof of these relationships comes from hypothesis-testing"). Then he explicitly proposes:

> There are at least two levels of exploratory studies. At the first level is the discovery of the significant variables in the situation; at the second, the discovery of relationships between variables [p. 75].

Some writers would restrict hypothesis testing to experiments or quasi experiments (*e.g.*, Selltiz *et al.*, 1959); others would declare that hypotheses can also be tested in field studies of a nonexperimental nature (Scott, 1965,

p. 268; Kerlinger, 1964, p. 387). However, it is important to observe that some writers have in mind hypotheses stating *causal* relations; others are referring to hypotheses stating *correlational* relations (this issue will be taken up shortly). The received conventional wisdom of methodologists is very clear: that only experimental designs (whether in the laboratory or in the field) yield findings of high reliability on cause-to-effect relationships.

The fact of the matter is that *no single classificatory scheme* of research methods in general and field methods in particular has been accepted. Not only do different writers use different terms for the same things and the same terms to refer to different things, but the bases of the category systems vary from one authority to another. Some of the commonest of these bases are:

— stage of the total inquiry (early or late)
— setting of the inquiry (contrived or real-life)
— exploration or hypothesis testing
— comparative or causal objectives
— degrees of control by the researcher
— degrees of quantification, precision, measurement

The conclusion seems inescapable: *since there are a number of different bases on which to erect classificatory schemes, no single scheme is adequate to describe all the varieties of behavioral research — especially field research.*

Value Judgments Commonly Applied to Field Research

When Kerlinger (1964, p. 360), for example, advances a basic dichotomy between experimental and ex post facto research, he is doing much more than merely categorizing; he also identifies at least three major weaknesses as *inherent* features of all ex post facto research, and his entire discussion leaves little doubt that any ex post facto study yields conclusions more equivocal and less reliable than those of properly executed laboratory experimental research. Kerlinger does concede that ex post facto studies are a necessary part of the total scientific endeavor. He defines them as dealing with a situation wherein "the independent variable or variables have already occurred"; thus, the researcher "starts with the observation of a dependent variable" and "studies the independent variables in retrospect." He then states his conclusion:

> This [*i.e.*, the acceptance of plausible but spurious findings] is a danger in experimental research, but it is *less* of a danger than it is in ex post facto research because an experimental situation is so much easier to control [p. 372].

> Where one must be careful with experimental results and interpretations, one must be doubly careful with ex post facto results and interpretations [p. 373].

Since by definition in Kerlinger's frame of reference all field studies of a nonexperimental design are ex post facto, it follows that they occupy a lower place in a theoretical hierarchy of scientific values than experimental studies. Kerlinger's views may be fairly described as typical of the ideology which has dominated behavioral science for a considerable period of time.

Indeed, any field study probably should be scrutinized for vulnerability with one or more of the following questions:

—To what degree has the researcher been able to exercise controls over the relevant variables?

— To what degree has the researcher been able to specify his concepts, constructs, and categories?

— To what degree has the researcher been able to achieve precision in measurement units and procedures?

— To what degree has the researcher any justification for generalizing beyond the particular case or cases he has studied?

— Whether he can generalize safely or not, to what degree does his design permit conclusions about *causal relations,* or must he be careful to restrict himself to inferences about *correlations?*

Obviously, such questions are fundamental, but other chapters of this book deal with them fully. Hence, only a brief review of selected methodological issues will be included here to provide a rationale for recommendations which will follow later in the chapter.

CAUSALITY AND THEORY

Many writers have maintained that the most important — or perhaps even the sole — ultimate goal of all science is *discovering* and *testing theories* which yield hypotheses subject to tests for predictability. Thus, in a basic text on the logic of science, Nidditch (1960) declares:

> One aims at discovering a law or group of laws governing the sets of facts. The scientific formulae . . . have to lead to correct predictions. . . . Unless there are empirically testable consequences, a formula about facts can rationally be neither supported nor subverted; if there can be no evidence for it or against it, it is useless . . . [p. 157].

Braithwaite (1955) has identified the function of science as establishing general laws enabling the researcher "to make reliable predictions of events . . . [p. 1]." Following this line of reasoning and citing Braithwaite's testimony for support, Kerlinger (1964) asserts flatly that "the basic aim of science is theory" and says that theories consist of "explanations [p. 10]."

Of course, even the most dedicated advocates of *causality* as the ultimate object of scientific search concede that in the kind of inductive procedures the investigator is compelled to use if he is concerned with empirical data (rather than with formal deductive systems in the abstract) there can never be absolute certitude about cause-to-effect relations. As Selltiz *et al.* (1959) put it:

> It must be stressed that such evidence [*i.e.*, evidence meeting appropriate criteria] merely provides a reasonable basis for inferring that X is or is not a cause of Y; it does not provide absolute certainty . . . we can never be certain that the relationship has been conclusively demonstrated [p. 88].

The logician Holmes (1939) states the point in vivid, down-to-earth terms:

> No one ever saw, smelt, tasted, heard or felt a cause. . . .
> It is demonstrable that wherever we "find" causal connections, the only elements which we actually experience are the *contiguity* of two events and the *priority* [in time] of one of them. . . .
> That events are connected in nature by a cause-and-effect series is another of our assumptions . . . we can never know whether or not it is true [p. 207].

However, fallible or not, the notion of causality — with its corollary of theory building — is closely linked to the oft-repeated principle that scientific endeavor deals with groups or sets and cannot work with unique, individual cases. Since a large body of field studies consists of in-depth accounts of single cases (individuals, communities, organizations, small groups, etc.), this principle is of pivotal importance to the field researcher. Nidditch's (1960) concise statement represents the great majority of views in the published literature on methodology:

> Science is concerned with generality, not with particularity. . . .
> The scientist deals with individual facts in order to discover the properties of the whole set of phenomena to which the individual facts belong; his interest is in sets of facts rather than in their members as such [pp. 156–157].

Throughout his text, Kerlinger (1964) emphasizes this point of view; for example: "Relations are the essence of science [p. 80]" and "Relations are always between classes or sets of objects [p. 81]." Because all scientific data must be objective and reproducible, argues R. Hyman (1964), it follows that

> If the event . . . is a unique historical incident that cannot be repeated for others to observe, then the event has no status as a scientific fact. The facts of science have nothing to do with particular and unique occurrences [p. 37].

Thus, it comes about that the hardnosed methodologists relegate many field studies, and most especially the so-called one-shot case study (the intensive description or analysis of a single phenomenon), to the lowest possible dungeon of prescientific or preexperimental designs. Campbell (1957) could find no sources of validity whatever in the one-shot study — since such a study lacks the absolute minimum characteristic of being able to make at least one comparison. And, following Campbell's rationale, Kerlinger (1964) says that single-case studies are "scientifically worthless" if not "badly misleading [p. 294]."

VALIDITY

If causality and theory are basic concepts in all scientific research, then it is easy to understand the familiar concern with *validity*. And it is easy to see that valid findings depend on such well known characteristics as *control* and *reliability*. In fact, the single attribute of control is frequently discussed as a sine qua non of all scientific investigation. "Psychological inquiry," declares R. Hyman (1964), "is *controlled* inquiry [p. 42]."

Since the concept of validity is discussed in other chapters of this book (see especially Chapter 1, pp. 41–43), no more need be done here than to recall the crucial distinction between *internal* and *external* validity. This issue has been expounded with great acuity in a highly influential article (and further elaborated in later publications) by Campbell (1957). Briefly stated, the concept of internal validity refers to the degree to which the experimental treatments actually produced any differences in behavior; internal validity is described as the *basic minimum* or the sine qua non of any experiment. External validity refers to *generalizability:* to what extent the findings may be generalized to other situations — including other populations, other settings, other variables, other measurement devices, etc.

Internal validity. The factor of control, obviously an important prerequisite for internal validity, is therefore understandably singled out by many writers as the most critical difference between experimental and non-experimental research, and also by other writers as the most intractable problem facing any kind of field research, whether experimental or not. Festinger (1953), for example, distinguishes between laboratory experiments and field experiments on the basis of two criteria: the degree to which the investigator is able to "create a specially suited situation, and the degree of precision in the control and manipulation of variables [p. 137]." Restricting himself to the narrower definition of "field study" adopted by Katz (1953), French (1953) differentiates "field study" and "field experiment" primarily in terms of *design:*

> The field experiment involves the actual manipulation of conditions by the experimenter in order to determine *causal* relations, whereas in the field study the researcher . . . [determines] *correlations* [p. 99; italics supplied].

The next link in the chain of reasoning in investigating causal relations is exercising controls — especially manipulating one or more experimental (independent) variables "in order to test some hypothesis [French, 1953, p. 101]." In a perceptive discussion of experimental and field research as applied to speech communication, Clevenger (1965) insists that manipulating an independent variable is an essential feature of any experiment, but goes ahead to argue that descriptive (or field) studies may also test hypotheses:

> In the instance of the hypothesis relating prior attitude to attitude change, it seems perfectly clear that the hypothesis can be tested by descriptive study as surely as by experiment; and, indeed, some propositions can be tested only by means of descriptive study. For instance, one might conjecture that in formal public speaking situations in the United States, speakers nowadays talk faster than speakers used to. This question can be resolved by descriptive study only ... [p. 10].[4]

External validity. But over and beyond the necessity of control in order to achieve internal validity, field studies face the problem of generalizability — or external validity. Many methodologists have addressed themselves to this troublesome question. The reader is familiar with the common charge that it is risky to generalize from the supposedly artificial and highly restrictive conditions of the laboratory experiment to the real world. As French (1953) observes:

> The laws which hold for such restricted situations may not apply without changes to the more complex settings of real life. Usually a field experiment is not subject to such artificiality and thus avoids this problem of generalizing to real-life situations [p. 100].

Clevenger (1969) proposes a plausible general rule of thumb particularly applicable to the obviously complex nature of most human communication events:

> ... the farther one moves away from basic physical and biological data toward personal-psychological and social data, the greater grows the number of factors that may perturb a given effect; hence, the greater the difficulty of generalizing from an experiment to similar effects in a naturalistic setting. ... the pathway from experiments in persuasion to the engineering of political consent has yet to be found [p. 158].

---

[4] The example used by Clevenger to support the claim that descriptive research may be used to test hypotheses may perhaps more accurately be described as a natural or naturalistic experiment, in which the researcher capitalizes on an event that occurs without reference to any intervention on his part. Such events may be either acts of nature, such as floods, or acts of man, such as corporate mergers or political speeches. In the article cited here, Clevenger suggests that a hypothesis about the effect of initial audience attitude on amount of attitude change following a persuasive speech could be tested by means of studying audience responses before and after one of the Nixon-Kennedy encounters in 1960.

It would hardly be an exaggeration to assert that the chief motivation for conducting field research, especially field experimentation, has been to validate hypotheses and variables in the so-called real world. Addressing his remarks primarily to those interested in laboratory and field studies of attitude change, Nebergall (1968) puts the issue in sharp focus when he asks:

> . . . are we in the laboratory because of a confidence that the experiments we conduct there will tell us things we want to know about the world outside the laboratory or are we there because that's the place we can most conveniently work? Stated more formally, this is the problem of ecological validity (Orne, 1962). An experiment is ecologically valid if it permits appropriate generalization from the laboratory to the non-experimental situation. . . . ecological validity needs to be established and not presumed [p. 53].[5]

As French (1953) has made clear, a field experiment may reduce the problem of generalization in either of two ways; first, it may avoid the risks of applying conclusions based on studies of college sophomores to such populations as scientists or bank clerks; second, it can test out "hypotheses proved in laboratory experiments but not yet sufficiently studied in field settings [pp. 103–104]." For example, lively discussion has ensued for years among behavioral scientists regarding the well known and numerous inconsistencies in findings between laboratory (especially paper-and-pencil) indicators of attitude change and other more real-life behaviors (such as contributing money to a campaign). This is not the place to review the arguments that have filled many journal pages on this issue; Cronkhite (1969) has already done this, with both wit and perspicuity. But one obvious conclusion can be drawn from the whole dialogue, especially for those communication researchers investigating persuasion or attitude change: it is indeed hazardous to generalize from the constraints of the laboratory to the dynamics of the real world (Hovland, 1959; Festinger, 1964; Nebergall, 1965, 1968; Rokeach, 1966; G. R. Miller, 1967; S. L. Becker, 1968).

Finally, it must be noted that directly contradictory claims are frequently made about field studies: on the one hand, field research is held by some authorities to be the essential method of validating or at least correcting laboratory findings; on the other hand, field research is held by others to be inherently so deficient in controls that it falls short of internal validity, while at the same time it is based on unrepresentative sampling so that it fails to satisfy the criteria of external validity. Of course, many experts view internal and external validity as inversely correlated, in a sense; thus, there is serious doubt that any single study can meet fully and

---

[5] Kerlinger (1964, p. 302) identifies three aspects of external validity, of which *ecological* (generalizability to other social settings) is only one. The others are *sample* and *variable* validities.

simultaneously the requirements of both kinds of validity (Campbell, 1957; Kerlinger, 1964, pp. 301–302). The safest assertion on this matter would seem to be that nothing *inherent* in field research (defining field research now primarily in terms of mere *locale*) renders it either "better" or "worse" than laboratory research.

Three Kinds of Inquiry: Descriptive, Correlational, Causal

Methodologists have long delighted in drawing basic distinctions among research endeavors, such as descriptive versus experimental, descriptive versus explanatory, experimental versus correlational, and correlational versus causal. For example, H. Hyman (1955) applies to the specific problems of conducting large scale sampling surveys basic logical concepts derived from general principles of scientific methodology. He divides surveys into two large classes, *descriptive* and *explanatory*. A descriptive survey, as the name implies, is concerned with "sheer description of some phenomenon [p. 66]"; or, more exactly, "precise measurement of one or more dependent variables [p. 68]." An explanatory survey attempts to uncover causal relationships between "one or more . . . dependent variables, and one or more causes or independent variables [p. 66]."

As has been indicated earlier, the conventional scientific wisdom has usually identified the investigation of cause-and-effect relationships with experiments designed to test hypotheses (ideally derived from broader statements called theories). H. Hyman (1955) has put this judgment into explicit and concise phraseology: "The scientific model for the study of cause-and-effect relationships is the *controlled experiment,* in which the responses of an experimental group . . . are compared with those of an equivalent control group [p. 243]." French (1953), whose distinction between *causal* and *correlational* designs was quoted on p. 119, declares that "the field experiment can distinguish between independent and dependent variables, whereas the field study can only establish correlations among variables [p. 107]."

Cronbach (1957) spoke of *experimental* and *correlational* as the two disciplines of psychology. Although he stressed the factors of control and manipulation of conditions in order to test hypotheses, he based his analysis on the source of variations rather than the presence or absence of causal relations per se, stipulating that in the experiment the investigator is dealing only with "variation he himself creates" while "the correlator finds his interest in the already existing variation between individuals, social groups, and species [p. 671]." Weick (1965), in commenting on Cronbach's position, very carefully makes the point that causal relations may be assumed or examined in either experimental or correlational designs:

> Correlational methods imply that past experience is the critical determinant of behavior, whereas experimental methods inflate the role of the present situation [p. 195].

Clevenger (1965) was quoted on p. 120 as supporting a similar view — that *descriptive* studies, in which the researcher exercises no control over independent variables, may test hypotheses; such hypotheses would commonly be concerned with cause-to-effect relationships:

> With the growing influence of anthropology upon the field of speech, we will witness in the next few years a great increase in the proportion of descriptive studies which test hypotheses, and many of these will be of a general theoretical nature [p. 10].

In the same article, Clevenger proposes that the only essential difference between experimental and descriptive (*i.e.,* correlational) studies lies in the *control* by the experimenter.

Similarly, Kaplan (1964) identifies instituting controls as the crucial feature of experimentation; but, unlike Clevenger, he argues that these controls need not always take the particular form of manipulation of the independent variable by the researcher:

> Experimentation, when it is conceived sufficiently broadly . . . consists in making observations in circumstances so arranged or interpreted that we have justification for analyzing out the factors relevant to our particular inquiry [p. 162].

Also unlike Clevenger (who apparently includes *natural* experiments under the heading of descriptive studies, as previously discussed), Kaplan (p. 164) points out that even in experimental situations where independent variables are manipulated, manipulation may or may not be the result of the scientist's intervention — it may be that the researcher capitalizes on changes in the environment introduced by public officials, organizations, etc.

CAUSAL RELATIONSHIPS

The whole rationale of hypothesis testing, then, may be viewed as one prominent feature of the conventional scientific wisdom. However, opinions differ on whether all hypotheses subject to testing need to deal with cause-to-effect relationships: it is possible to hypothesize that X and Y are correlated (they *co-vary*) in a specified manner, without suggesting anything about cause. Furthermore, it is even possible for so-called correlational designs at least to postulate certain kinds of causal relations; by dividing his subjects according to such factors as age, sex, race, or income, the researcher is probably in many instances assuming cause-effect relations, as Weick and Cronbach make clear. And, of course, field research may or may not incorporate experimental controls, may or may not be intended to investigate causal relations.

However, the *conventional* rationale of modern behavioral research, as much of the discussion in earlier sections of this chapter demonstrates, certainly regards testing hypotheses under conditions providing for experimental controls as primarily an undertaking addressed to discovering cause-and-effect. This rationale, as Kaplan shows, is derived from the dominant *reconstructed logic* of modern science, not to be confused with the actual logic in use which describes the way successful scientists proceed. The reconstructed logic is an idealized system, created after the fact, purporting to prescribe the reasoning patterns which scientists *ought* to employ in their research. When the reconstructed logic is "mathematically elegant, precise, and powerful . . . its attractions are nearly irresistible [p. 11]." Such an elegant logic is the "hypothetico-deductive method" (see Chapter 1, pp. 12–13) which has for a long time been the most widely accepted reconstruction in modern science:

> According to this reconstruction, the scientist, by a combination of careful observation, shrewd guesses, and scientific intuition, arrives at a set of postulates governing the phenomena in which he is interested; from these he deduces observable consequences; he then tests these consequences by experiment, and so confirms or disconfirms the postulates [pp. 9–10].

Kaplan not only doubts the relevance of this reconstructed logic to such fields as theoretical physics; he suspects it may not be a useful description of the most fruitful research rationales in the behavioral sciences.

In the study of communication behavior, then, the field researcher must on the one hand take confidence in the realization that he can perform scientifically respectable work without necessarily using all the controls of laboratory experimentation and without always seeking causal relationships; but on the other hand, he cannot escape the fact that field studies are an especially inviting refuge for the dilettante who boasts of the "richness" of his data and claims that subtle insights make unnecessary the application of such criteria as internal or external validity. Weick (1965) quotes with approval the jolting admonition of Zigler (1963) that "collections of concepts gained through naturalistic observations have a striking characteristic — they are quite refractory to disproof [p. 206]."

This very liability has stirred many critics of historical descriptions of public speaking events to pose the question: "Yes, very interesting, but what can we learn from it?" Like any other researcher, the field researcher must subject his design and his data gathering procedures to close scrutiny to ascertain the extent to which he is justified in answering any one or more of three basic questions:

(1) Does this study offer a reasonably accurate and unbiased description of significant phenomena as they exist in the real world?

(2) Does this study offer reasonably reliable and valid findings to support inferences that two or more sets of phenomena bear some sort of significant relationship to one another?

(3) Does this study offer findings to justify an inference which goes beyond correlation, to establish reasonable grounds for stating cause-to-effect relationships?

Simons (1961) is a convenient example of a researcher who delineated with great clarity two fundamental kinds of analysis applied to his data. He stated as his primary purpose the investigation of "relationships (if any) which may exist between selected dimensions of 'internal communication behavior' and supervisory 'success' [p. 3]" on the part of two specially selected samples of supervisory personnel in a large urban hotel. Since his design called for comparing "more successful" and "less successful" supervisors, obviously the primary analysis was comparative, *i.e.,* correlational. But, by combining data from both groups of subjects (the high and the low) into one large aggregate, he was also able to describe what he termed the "modal" communication attributes of the combined samples. However, these modal trends were not simply reported in the form of gross numerical quantities; hypotheses of a noncausal nature were drawn from a body of accepted practices or recommendations by recognized authorities in the field. The data were then analyzed statistically to determine to what extent the majority's responses were congruent with such hypotheses at a selected level of confidence that such findings were not due to chance. Simons explicitly stated early in the thesis that "this study could not attempt to isolate direct, linear, cause-and-effect relationships [p. 4]." In fact, since high and low groups were compared for *differences* in communication attributes, even a direct correlation was impossible to estimate; rather, a correlational logic furnished the rationale for applying statistical tests to differences between the two groups.

As Simons phrased his basic design: "The present study may be described, methodologically, as *both* a critical inquiry (determination of *relationships*) and a descriptive survey (determination of *prevalent behavior*), carried out as a 'field case study' in a single company [p. 5]." The way he formulated and applied some of his specific hypotheses is worth quoting:

> For the purpose of determining whether differences existed between criterion groups, the responses of the high-rated groups were separated from responses of the low-rated groups. Wherever possible, each question was treated as a sub-hypothesis of the general hypothesis that *good supervisors are good communicators; bad supervisors are the opposite.* [NOTE: Simons made no assumptions concerning any possible cause-to-effect relations in either direction in these hypotheses.] In these cases one-tailed tests were employed. Where, in the researcher's judgment, the literature . . . did not seem to indicate a "preferred" response, two-tailed tests were used. . . . The hypotheses underlying the use of the above tests of differences between groups will now be formally stated:
>
> 1. *Directional* (one-tailed test). The high-rated supervisory group in this study will yield responses indicating more "preferred" communication behavior than will the low-rated supervisory group.
>
> 2. *Non-Directional* (two-tailed test). Differences in responses to certain communication items between high- and low-rated groups will be greater than chance [pp. 89–90].

This example could be supported by many others, of course. For example, Williams and Sundene (1965), in a field investigation of certain effects of a public relations speech (involving both theoretical and pragmatic objectives), were careful to sort out causal from noncausal inferences based on their findings:

> Perhaps the most interesting theoretical implication was the finding of significant interrelationships between consummatory and instrumental responses to the speech. Unfortunately, however, from a methodological standpoint, these results are a product of the weakest portion of the study. First, it is important to realize that the present data support no interpretations of consummatory effects as *causing* instrumental effects — only that both responses, in some cases, tended to vary together as an *effect* of hearing the speech [p. 168; second italicized word supplied].

This example is especially interesting since the researchers designed the study so that *some* results could be attributed as cause-to-effect phenomena (the speech being the cause or independent variable; the audience responses, the effect or dependent variable), but others could only be interpreted as correlational.

When Brooks (1965, 1967) executed an ingeniously designed field study (actually a natural experiment) on the effects of campaign speeches by President Johnson and Senator Goldwater on real-life listeners, he posed five carefully worded hypotheses. The first four dealt with causal relations; the fifth — couched in terms of predicting differences — was concerned with a correlational relationship, actually based on a prediction that the two phenomena in question would *not* be causally connected.

The general implication from this entire discussion remains: the researcher (any researcher, but perhaps especially the field researcher, since he may be more likely to overlook basic logical criteria of design) should specify as precisely as possible those aspects of his procedures which permit description of the status quo, those which justify various kinds of correlational inferences, and those which justify cause-to-effect conclusions.

THE LABORATORY-FIELD DICHOTOMY

Unquestionably, many field studies have been defended on the grounds that various shortcomings are inherent in laboratory experimentation (of course, the reverse is also true). Chapters 1 and 2 take up basic issues of research design, and specific attributes of laboratory setting are discussed in Chapter 3, so only a representative sampling of arguments will be reviewed here.

Criticisms of Laboratory Experiments

It is common knowledge that in recent years a swarm of critics has descended upon the laboratory experimentalists in all the behavioral sciences and particularly in communication research. Obviously, a venerable and oft-repeated charge, couched in a variety of ways, is that the laboratory experiment is somehow *too artificial,* too far removed from real life to permit valid generalization from more or less trivial phenomena in the laboratory to the really important events of the world outside:

> ... no matter how precisely researchers are able to refine their instruments, no matter how precise their techniques of statistical manipulation become, no matter how carefully they are able to construct experiments which tap with greater and greater sensitivity more and more precise variables — unless researchers keep a constant and rigorous check on the way their propositions relate to the real world they will be in serious difficulty. A communication theory must relate to people. It must relate to the day-to-day behaviors which these people exhibit and to the kinds of communication responses they make in all kinds of situations every day of their lives. Those kinds of behaviors need to be measured where they are found. Unfortunately, they are often not found in the classroom or in the laboratory [Nebergall, 1965, p. 16].

Basing his recommendations on a Skinnerian skepticism concerning unobservable and "overly complicated constructs of intervening variables, such as attitude," S. L. Becker (1968) pleads for more detailed descriptions of real-life communication situations:

> One possible reason for our failure to consider various processes in our research or the interaction of a larger series of the variables which are probably relevant in any given communication situation, is that we have a paucity of useful descriptive data about such situations. We need a great deal of careful and complete observation and description of a varied sample of communication situations [p. 67].

Clevenger (1969), in contrast to Becker, insists that communication research should endeavor to be even *more* theory oriented than it has typically been in the past; but, although he starts from premises somewhat different from Becker's, Clevenger also makes a strong case for the value of field research. Like Nebergall, he is concerned that the researcher can only observe "the event in its natural setting" if he is to verify "that an effect which appears to take place in the laboratory retains its potency when transplanted into the sort of real-life situation to which it is hoped experimentally-derived principles will generalize [p. 157]." Therefore, he argues:

> ... if an effect is so slight or unstable that it cannot be observed in a natural setting, then it is perhaps not worth the investment of substantial time and resources in experimental research. . . .

.   .   .   .   .

> . . . researchers should devote more attention to field studies. *They impose the rigor of reality on theories, requiring a completeness of specification not usually demanded in the experimental setting. . . .* Because experiments so readily control these variables (which all too often are referred to as "extraneous"), attention tends to be diverted away from the effects of such variables. In the field study they cannot be ignored; thus, *such studies represent the ultimate test of scholars' understandings* [p. 157; italics supplied].

G. R. Miller (1969) adopts a more sweeping view, declaring that "like many other behavioral scientists, speech researchers are victims of an experimental 'hangup' [p. 60]." He argues that the listener brings a large body of significant variables, which he calls "Information 2," to a typical speech situation, representing the residuum of all that has happened to him before he listens to the speech. These relevant parameters are typically neglected, in Miller's opinion, by the laboratory experiment. Hence, he quotes the words of the psychologist Carl Rogers with approval: "We may have to go back and do much more naturalistic observation, make more of an attempt to understand people, behavior, and the dynamics of things [p. 59]." Commenting on Miller's paper, Haiman (1969) sees a number of deficiencies in experimental research, and he urges investigators to devote a "major share of their efforts" to field research, if they hope to make their work "more relevant to the real problems of contemporary society [p. 139]."

COUNTERARGUMENTS

It is only fair to note in passing that thoughtful commentators have proposed convincing counterarguments to these and similar charges against experimentalism. A review of such rebuttals would be outside the scope of the present chapter. However, the reader is referred, for example, to two papers by Weick (1965, 1967) which subject the attacks on experimental method to searching but fair-minded scrutiny. For example, Weick shows that "experiments are *both* artificial and realistic" and contends that therefore "there is little warrant to the assumption that the greater the similarity between the experimental and field situations, the greater the generality of the experimental outcomes. Realism," he continues, "is instrumental to various research goals" and "blanket indictment of experiments because of their artificiality is meaningless and distracting [1965, p. 207]." Again, he argues that using hypotheses in experimental work does not necessarily "induce myopia" or cause the researcher to miss important variables; on the contrary, he holds that hypotheses can "frequently direct attention to new areas rather than force a neglect of them [1967, p. 14]." But since the present chapter takes as its province a wide variety of field research formats — including field experiments — the arguments against many features of laboratory experiments would also apply, of course, to field experiments insofar as they were successful in meeting the narrow demands of the laboratory. The issues and the criteria applicable to laboratory settings discussed in Chapter 3 are therefore equally relevant to field experiments and need not be repeated here.

SPECIFIC CHARGES AGAINST LABORATORY EXPERIMENTS

It may be helpful to supply for the sake of perspective a cursory listing of some of the most common charges brought against laboratory experiments. These may be listed under a variety of headings, but three categories keep recurring in the literature:

— influence of the experimental environment, or setting
— influence of the experimenter (on the subjects)
— influence of the subjects (on the experimenter)

Under these three heads, Barnes (1967, pp. 80–89) organizes his discussion of "the problem of classical design and experimenter influence." They are about the same as the classification of experimental constraints given by R. Hyman (1964, p. 43): those in the observer, those in the environment, and those in the subject. Weick (1965), however, writes that "all experimental situations include at least three components: a setting, a task, and subjects [p. 197]." The factor of "task" can easily be included under influences of the experimenter.

Another way of organizing criticisms of the experimental method is provided by Weick (1967, pp. 36–48). In discussion which is both searching and definitive, he identifies four problems of internal validity and five problems of external validity. No prospective communication researcher should proceed with the design of either laboratory or field studies before studying the implications of these nine problems.

Barnes (1967) has conducted an excellent survey of the literature dealing primarily with field *experiments* (and with special reference to the study of changes in human organizations). So much of this survey, however, exposes issues relevant to any kind of experimental research and to any kind of field experiment in particular that there is no need to traverse the same ground in any detail here. The reader is urged to examine his paper for full documentation of the problems discussed.

Noting that such writers as French (1953) and Seashore (1964) stipulate that field experiments must adhere to the strict standards of experimenter control prescribed for the laboratory in order to achieve proper levels of validity, Barnes correctly points out that this position leaves the field experimenter faced with a real dilemma. He must somehow resolve the conflict between "research objectives and practical objectives [p. 79]." The result is that

> The field experimenter is thus left with an ideal (classical design), a prescribed role (manipulator and controller of variables), and little hope of achieving either in an organizational [or field] setting. . . .

> At this point, the would-be field experimenter must make a choice. He either must work toward an apparently hopeless ideal of classical design and experimenter influence, or else he must begin to revise his goals and procedures [pp. 79–80].

However, Barnes finds a way out of the dilemma. After exploring the state of affairs confronting those who are employing classically designed laboratory experiments, he concludes that "problems of field experimentation are not all in the field" and that a number of "serious issues plague laboratory experimenters as well [p. 80]." At this point Barnes surveys relevant literature demonstrating that laboratory experiments are commonly troubled by undesired (and usually unmeasured and unaccounted for) influences stemming from the experimental environment itself, the experimenter, and the subjects (interacting with the experimenter).

After citing the work of such researchers as Orne (1962), Milgram (1965), and Orne and Evans (1965), he concludes that "environmental influence may determine subject behavior more than the experimental treatment does and yet go disregarded as a major influence [p. 84]." He reviews the well known studies of McGuigan (1963) and Rosenthal and his associates (*e.g.,* Rosenthal, 1963) dealing with subtle and previously undetected ways in which the experimenter exercises a distorting influence on the behavior of his subjects (even of animals). The heart of the matter is that "different experimenters come up with different findings from the same experiment [p. 85]." Barnes agrees with the conclusion drawn by Klintz *et al.* (1965, p. 224):

> Wherever an experimenter-subject relationship exists, the possibility also exists for *E* [the experimenter] to complicate his data. . . . It appears that experimental psychology has too long neglected the experimenter as an independent variable [p. 86].

The very fact, Barnes argues, that the field experimenter is likely to be in a position from which he can exercise little if any control over his subjects (compared to the classical laboratory situation) can actually mean that the problem of extraneous experimenter influence is "probably less crucial in field experiments than in laboratory experiments [p. 88]."

However, the third type of problem — that in which the subjects exert unplanned influence on the researcher — is very probably more indigenous to the field than to the laboratory. Books and articles on field studies in such disciplines as sociology and anthropology are commonly preoccupied with discussions of relationships between the observer and his subjects, emphasizing the benefits and the hazards involved in permitting the subjects to establish friendship (or even power) relations with the observer. Subject influence on the researcher is especially likely to be a knotty problem in those field studies where the investigator chooses to depend on selected "informants" — specially chosen key individuals in an organization, for example, as contrasted with randomly chosen subjects — for most or even all of his data. Scott (1965, pp. 291–294) provides a perceptive analysis of informant roles and functions, identifying three common ways in which they serve researchers: as representative subjects (a risky procedure), as surrogate observers, and as experts. In any of these roles, informants present the field researcher with both dangers and opportunities.

Objections to the Basic Logic of Experimental Design

Some critics of recent years, whether explicitly advocating field research or not, have at least implicitly built a case for it by leveling sweeping charges against the entire rationale of experimentalism. Some of these attacks focus on one vital feature, others represent a scattered or general broadside.

PROBLEMS IN HANDLING VARIABLES

For example, Brunswik (1955, 1956) has chosen to single out what he regards as an almost fatal vulnerability lying at the very heart of classical experimental design. It is his opinion that experimental requirements too frequently force the researcher either to tie together or to separate multiple variables in a manner not true to their operation in the real world; such a fallacy, in his view, is encouraged by the prescription for independent and dependent variables. S. L. Becker (1968, pp. 71–72) feels strongly that even our most advanced multivariable experimental designs are inadequate for the study of the true *process* nature of communication phenomena.

INADEQUACY OF STATISTICAL METHODS

Sidman (1960) is representative of a group of critics who in recent years have been experiencing varying degrees of disenchantment with the adequacy of accepted statistical methods and the inferences associated with them "to further their research [R. Hyman, 1964, p. 75]." In his view, for example, too many inferences made from the sample concerning the form and parameters of the parent population are too rarely justified, "for there are an infinite number of distributions from which to choose [p. 44]." Since all conventional methods of hypothesis testing based on the brilliant advances in probability statistics by R. A. Fisher make pivotal use of theoretical distributions of statistical concepts, Sidman's critique penetrates to the core of typical experimental methodology:

> Particularly risky, because of its circularity, is the once general practice of deducing the properties of the parent distribution from the data one is testing. This practice is now [1960] declining in popularity. Even the so-called distribution-free statistics do not wholly escape from this dilemma, however, for some distribution is always required as a baseline with which to compare the empirical observations. . . . Science is presumably dedicated to stamping out ignorance, but statistical evaluation of data against a baseline whose characteristics are determined by unknown variables constitutes a passive acceptance of ignorance [pp. 44–45].

Pursuing this line of reasoning further, Sidman challenges the adequacy of all statistical inferences based on *group* rather than *individual* variations — although he is careful to point out that he by no means rejects the applicability of such statistics in every case. When he suggests that an "experimental manipulation produces an irreversible change in . . . an individual's behavior [p. 52]," Sidman could easily be referring to speech communication; although compensatory utterances and other behaviors may follow any act of human communication, words once spoken can never be un-spoken. Speech behavior, then, in at least many respects, may come under the category of "irreversibility" proposed by Sidman:

> If true irreversibility should be encountered, there is a straight-forward solution available: *to study such processes as they occur in nature.* . . . Group statistics is certainly not the answer. . . . a group function may have no counterpart in the behavior of the individual . . . [pp. 52–53; italics supplied].

INADEQUACY OF THEORETICAL CONSTRUCTS

Writing primarily from his work in operant conditioning, Sidman follows the well known strictures of Skinner against the use of theoretical constructs (see, for example, Skinner, 1950; Evans, 1968). Hence, he is no opponent of experimentation per se; in fact, he is an experimentalist. But his arguments and those of others who take analogous positions (R. Hyman, 1964, pp. 75–81) demonstrate certain limitations in the basic logic underlying conventional experimental designs; and they have been used to justify conducting many kinds of field studies in which highly elaborate and precise statistical manipulations (based on group averages and variances) are considered inappropriate, if not impossible.[6]

Although not explicitly advocating Sidman's conclusion that relatively nonstatistical field studies should be preferred over statistical-experimental research, Clevenger (1969) applies a similar line of argument to the problems of scientific investigation in speech communication:

> As a general rule, the less reliable the theory and the measurement techniques of a given discipline, the more powerful are the statistical techniques it employs. One does not need statistical procedures applied to photometer data to tell the difference between night and day. . . .
> Greater recognition of this principle would prove beneficial to speech-communication research. . . . Researchers ought to be looking for variables that make large and unmistakable differences rather than for more refined techniques for measuring very small or highly probabilistic differences between effects [pp. 161–162].

[6] Weick (1965, pp. 196–197), himself a strong defender of experimental methods in social science, recommends that careful attention be devoted to Sidman's criticism of the traditional approach to experimentation and statistical inference. See also R. Hyman (1964, pp. 72–101) for a comprehensive and balanced discussion of these topics.

INADEQUACY OF INFERENTIAL METHODS

It is perhaps ironical that currently approved methods of making inferences from experimental data, depending as they do on reasoning from samples to populations (in order to permit generalization), fail to guarantee external validity, *i.e.,* the ability to generalize. Kerlinger (1964), a powerful and convincing advocate of closely controlled experimentation combined with probability statistics ("the laboratory experiment," he says, "is one of man's greatest achievements"), speaks of "conceding the lack of representativeness (external validity) [p. 382]" of the laboratory experiment.

Admitting that debates are still going on among competent advocates supporting various plausible positions, the researcher may still be pardoned if he asks the question: "When field studies are attacked for 'looseness' and inability to justify generalization, and when many critics can demonstrate that generalization is also risky from laboratory experiments testing hypotheses with probability statistics, from what *is* it possible to generalize?" The rather obvious answer, at this point, would seem to be that *no single rubric of research methodology or of statistical inference can offer a watertight guarantee of generalizability* from one study — or even from a group of studies — to different subjects, different measurement techniques, different applications of the same variable, or different environments. In the view of the author, this proposition assumes added force when applied to conditions typical of human speech communication behavior: it is notoriously difficult to generalize from one set of speaker or message variables to another. One "fear appeal" is difficult to equate with another; one "informational message" may not be comparable with another; speaker "ethos" in one study turns out to be different from a superficially similar "ethos" in another study, etc. (Bellamy and Thompson, 1967; Bowers and Phillips, 1967; Tompkins, 1967). It is probably safe to assert that disappointments are the rule rather than the exception for those investigators who attempt to replicate the findings and conclusions from any prior communication study.[7]

Minter (1969) investigated a large number of construct variables among the total supervisory-managerial populations in two divisions of a large manufacturing company. In subjecting his data to an unusually large number of quantitative comparisons and analyses, he decided that with minor exceptions the rationale of sampling (probability) statistics was not applicable to his data.

In essence, Minter was probably applying — although without conscious intent — some of the principles recommended by Sidman and Clevenger. Working with a fairly small number of subjects (65 supervisors and man-

---

[7] After this chapter was written, Thompson (1969) published a perceptive critique of quantitative and experimental methodology in speech communication. He argues convincingly that, especially because of multidimensionality inherent in both independent and dependent variables, generalizability from experimentation in speech communication is especially hazardous. He suggests that there may be features of human communication behavior which make inapplicable "the assumptions basic to the model on which experimental research rests [p. 63]."

agers) comprising the entire relevant populations of supervisory-managerial personnel in the two divisions of the company, he collected huge quantities of in-depth information, rather than a few facts skimmed off the top of a large sample. Most of the interpretive analyses of these data had to be improvised ad hoc in terms of the shapes of the numerous frequency distributions. For example, in order to determine the extent to which subjects on different hierarchical levels revealed congruent perceptions and attitudes relevant to specified communication concepts, it became necessary to devise what was called "congruence analysis"; in this manner

> . . . it was possible to compare responses of two or three contiguous levels of supervisory or managerial personnel to the same items. "Two-level" congruence was recorded whenever similar responses were found from interviewees occupying two contiguous hierarchical levels in the same department (e.g., manager *vs.* foreman; foreman *vs.* supervisor). For example, "2-level" congruence occurred when a manager's response was considered the same as his foreman's. "Three-level" congruence occurred when, in addition, a majority of responses from that same foreman's subordinate supervisors were coded the same as those of both the foreman and the manager (i.e., manager *vs.* foreman *vs.* supervisors) [Vol. 1, pp. 78–79].

SCIENTISM

Even after ignoring the numerous humanistic writers and lecturers who for years have inveighed against "scientism," one can assemble a respectable band of stalwarts who themselves have been trained as behavioral scientists but express grave misgivings about experimental methods in the behavioral sciences. For example, such reputable names as Lewin and Homans are included in a list of several antagonists compiled by Weick in his discussion of the "folklore" about experiments:

> What can be observed reliably is socially meaningless and what is socially meaningful cannot be observed reliably [Lewin, 1951, p. 155; quoted by Weick, 1967, p. 7].

> Some social scientists will do any mad thing rather than study men at firsthand in their natural setting [Homans, 1962, p. 259; quoted by Weick, 1967, p. 7].

Skinner (Evans, 1968) charges that the accepted scheme of scientific experimental methodology fails to describe accurately what successful behavioral scientists actually do. Thayer (1968) joins Skinner in arguing that conventional methods are incapable of handling one important and pervasive feature of human behavior (especially of communication behavior), "serendipity." It is Thayer's view that communication outcomes can be described along a continuum from the inevitable at one end to the impossible at the opposite pole, with the possible and the serendipitous between. Following the reasoning of such writers as Kuhn, Toda, and Shuford, and others, Thayer declares that we must recognize

> ... that the notion of cause or causation is an irrelevant (or at least redundant) concept in science. Whenever the description of a phenomenon is adequate, the nature and direction of "cause" is implicit in that description ... [p. 4].

Like many others, Thayer speaks in terms of "misguided scientism [p. 1]," mistakenly supposed to be "appropriate to any and all questions [p. 6]," and attributable to an unseemly scramble on the part of behavioral scientists "to legitimate themselves by emulating the physical sciences [p. 2]":

> There's certainly nothing basically wrong with trying to emulate success! But the difficulty goes deep. To get right to the heart of that difficulty . . . the "closed" theories of statistical mechanics as well as the more "open" or probabilistic orientations of quantum theory in physics both presume a homogeneity of classes of objects, as well as an infinity of classes. And these are basic assumptions or presumptions which specifically do not hold for living things — especially not for the "human" aspects of human behavior [p. 2].

He deplores the "frantic striving for legitimation that attracts the softest of the soft sciences to the kind of scientism that the hardest of the hard sciences have long since matured out of [p. 2]."

A number of critics have been charging that behavioral scientists have jumped on the wrong bandwagon by imitating the rationale of the supposed methodology of the established sciences, especially physics. In the passage quoted by G. R. Miller (1969) on p. 128, Carl Rogers speaks of harboring a modest hope that a devotion to *naturalistic observation* may eventually give rise to "a real psychological science, not an imitation of physics, a human science that should have as its appropriate subject, man [pp. 59–60]." Tompkins (1968) adds his voice:

> Most academic fields have their god. Physics seems to be the god of Psychology; and Psychology seems increasingly to be the god of Speech. We then seem to be imitating an imitator — and those in a position to know tell me that the Physics emulated by Psychologists is an outdated, outmoded Physics. . . . let us take a look at the field we are imitating — Psychology.
>
> It is a field of positive results (i.e., progress is made by rejecting the null hypothesis). Psychological journals publish practically nothing but positive results. This means that fully five per cent of their pages represent Type One errors. Conceivably, this could be as high as 100%.

. . . . .

An applied mathematics professor told me last summer that he had observed an increasing number of social science students in his

classes. Wondering what they were up to, he began to read the research literature of the social sciences. He was appalled. He was
appalled by the misapplication of statistics, but even more he was
appalled by the air of preciseness and objectivity the researchers
assumed once they had numbers with which to play [p. 2].

Many of these sweeping attacks seem to focus especially on alleged
faults in the basic hypothetico-deductive logic of conventional experimentalism. Among communication researchers taking this position are
Thayer (1968) and G. R. Miller (1969, pp. 60–61), who quotes the
psychologist Bakan (1967) to the effect that behavioral experimentation
frequently fails to be "really empirical."

In any event, after considering the pronouncements of Bakan and Rogers,
Miller concludes that what is called for is "more naturalistic observation
(i.e., empirical research) and less experimentation," including specifically
more "intensive case studies of the information processing behaviors of
one or two persons [p. 61]." Such a conclusion is indeed one logical consequence of these kinds of arguments. However, insofar as such attacks are
directed against the basic logic of scientific research in behavioral science,
they can also be aimed at so-called scientific studies carried out in the field
as well as against laboratory experiments. Furthermore, we should consider thoughtfully the point made by Kaplan (1964) that when behavioral
science is accused of imitating physics, the attack may be missing the target:

> . . . the presumption is certainly in favor of those operations of the
> understanding which have already shown themselves to be so pre-
> eminently successful in the pursuit of truth. What *is* important . . .
> is that behavioral science should stop trying to imitate only what a
> *particular reconstruction claims* physics to be [p. 11; italics on final
> clause supplied].

Kaplan (1964) and Tompkins (1968) seem to be agreeing that the
logic of experimental physics, supposedly the object of unthinking imitation by the behavioral scientists, is not necessarily the logic actually being
employed by modern physicists. However, critics like Tompkins and
Thayer (1968) argue that even if the reconstructed logic of physics were
the real one, it fails to fit many of the phenomena characteristic of human
communication behavior.

G. R. Miller (1969), citing Rogers in his support, draws the conclusion
that naturalistic observations or intensive case studies carried out in the
field are now to be emphasized in communication research. Whether such
a conclusion is the ineluctable corollary of the premises (the charges
against the rationale of experimentalism) is probably a moot question because of the dubious validity of the conventional distinctions drawn between laboratory and field. If, for example, it turns out that there is no
inherent difference in kind — but only one of degree — between these two
settings, then the arguments both for and against the accepted logic of

scientific method will apply with equal force to both laboratory and field. We now turn to a consideration of this pivotal issue.

A Proposed Revision of the Laboratory-Field Dichotomy

In spite of a long tradition supporting the notion that laboratory and field represent two contrasting research entities, many writers have confessed difficulty in drawing a clear boundary between the two. For example, French (1953) defines a field *experiment* in terms of "some *real* existing social situation in which the phenomena to be studied are commonly found [p. 100; italics supplied]." Attention is called to the crucial word "real." As French himself goes on to add: "By implication, it is not an 'artificial' situation created in a research laboratory [p. 100]." In other words, the terms "laboratory" and "real" have typically been posed as opposite terminals on an axis, obviously leading inexorably to the inference that laboratory settings must be *un*real. But we should note how French continues his discussion:

> This distinction, however, is not nearly so clear-cut as it seems at first glance, for *it is not important whether the social phenomena occur in a building called a laboratory* rather than in a school or some other "real" social situation. . . . The distinctions between "artificial" laboratory experiments and "real" field experiments are, therefore, *matters of degree* . . . [pp. 100–101; italics supplied].

Festinger's (1953) position is a bit puzzling. On the one hand, he admits that the distinction between field experiments and laboratory experiments is in many cases "difficult to maintain" and he writes in terms of "*degree* of control [p. 137; italics supplied]" exercised by the researcher. But, on the other hand, he also declares:

> A laboratory experiment need not, and *should not,* be an attempt to duplicate a real-life situation. If one wanted to study something in a real-life situation, it would be rather foolish to go to the trouble of setting up a laboratory experiment duplicating the real-life condition. . . . The laboratory experiment should be an attempt to create a situation in which the operation of variables will be clearly seen under special . . . conditions. . . . In the laboratory . . . we can find out exactly how a certain variable affects behavior or attitudes under special, or "pure," conditions [p. 139; italics supplied].

Furthermore, his discussion seems to suggest that the laboratory is *inherently* artificial when he writes that "in the laboratory, by setting up an artificial situation, we should be able to verify, elaborate, and refine our knowledge . . . [p. 141]." However, Festinger comes to grips with what the present writer regards as the most crucial issue when he speaks of reality as a cognitive phenomenon; in other words, he is clearly implying that reality or artificiality is a function of *perception:*

> All . . . situations are, in a sense, "real" for the subject, and all of them, likewise, are experiments from the point of view of the investigator. . . . the situation in which one places the subject can be "real" for him in that it brings into play powerful forces, regardless of whether or not it is cognitively an experimental situation for him [p. 153].

Weick subjects the reality-artificiality issue to close analysis in two of his methodological papers. In the present author's opinion, he rightly regards "artificiality" as a "dangerous label . . . because it focuses attention on pseudo issues . . . [1967, p. 13]." If reality is assumed to ensure the ego-involvement of subjects in the experimental events, then, as Weick argues, it is obviously a fact of common observation that in many cases "laboratory experiences are *more* vivid, and feelings are expressed *more* openly, than in everyday life, because inhibitions are fewer [1965, p. 248]." The concepts of "novelty" and "artificiality" are frequently assumed to be the same thing (1967); hence, it is important to realize that although the experimental situation may confront the subject with unfamiliar events and surroundings, the laboratory setting itself "is still real" — it is not something out of *Alice in Wonderland.* However, an extremely important question is raised when Weick reminds us to be concerned with "the *goals* of people who participate in experiments [1967, pp. 10–11; italics supplied]":

> Subjects often are concerned with more than just the task assigned by the experimenter. It is this spread of concern to issues such as deciphering the purposes of the experiment and predicting what is a "healthy" or "safe" response, that many persons equate with artificiality [1967, p. 11].

Reality, then, is in the mind of the perceiver. In some cases, the experimenter may perceive that he has created a real-life facsimile, but the subjects may perceive it as an artificial creation of the experimenter. In other cases the situation may be exactly the reverse. But Kaplan (1964) has identified the nub of the issue when he reminds us that "the experimental situation is not to be contrasted with 'real life' but at most only with *everyday life* [p. 169; italics supplied]." And it is clear that he is referring here to the subject's *perception* of what is everyday as being familiar, not out of the ordinary.

Obviously, then, it is unjustified to speak of "laboratory" or "field" settings for research as though they were absolutes, existing out in space independent of a human perceiver. As Roy Turner (1967) has epitomized the matter:

> . . . the proposed dichotomy between experiments and what Festinger calls "real-life situations" is an untenable one; clearly, experiments . . . *are* social situations and possess the properties common to such scenes. Given that experimenters, in the course of their daily lives,

can induce subjects (in the course of *their* daily lives) to comply with the demands of the experiment, we can legitimately claim that *one social scientist's experiment is his colleague's "natural" scene* [p. 27; italics on final clause supplied].

Therefore, as Turner (p. 28) rightly argues, any investigator should treat as an integral part of his data the subjects' definition (*i.e.,* perception) of the research situation.

Researcher Control and Subject Perceptions

So we may deduce at least two reasons for the breakdown of the laboratory-field dichotomy as a description of what really goes on. First, as many writers have testified, the differences between so-called laboratory conditions and those of real (or everyday) life are matters of degree rather than kind. As Kaplan (1964) has observed, the real issue is "the extent to which the subject being experimented on is *responsive* to those features of the context that have been controlled [p. 165; italics supplied]."

The second reason for questioning the laboratory-field dichotomy is even more basic, for it suggests that realism is not the most important way of characterizing research settings — even if it be granted that degrees of realism permit no firm boundary lines. The position urged here is that analyzing research situations in terms of realism (or artificiality) diverts attention to an incidental, if not a false, issue. Instead of describing a research setting in terms of the degree to which it approximates real life, we should examine every scientific study with two fundamental questions in mind:

(1) *To what extent does the researcher exercise controls?*

(2) *How do the subjects actually perceive the relevant phenomena in the research situation?*

For convenience, these two factors may be labeled *researcher control* and *subject perceptions.*

If the logical implications of this position are followed, *no single continuum — such as the conventional laboratory-field — will yield the most useful analysis of research settings.* Rather, at least two would be required: one for degrees of researcher control and the other for degrees of subject perceptions. In fact, there are probably two different types of subject perceptions, for each of which a separate continuum could be constructed:

(a) the degree to which subjects perceive that conditions are significantly different from everyday life

(b) the degree to which subjects recognize the researcher as a researcher (assuming subjects perceive such differences at all)

Since the topic of control was considered in an earlier section, little need be added here. General agreement among methodologists supports researcher control as a sine qua non of experimental design (Kaplan, 1964, pp. 161–162; Clevenger, 1965, p. 10; Weick, 1965, p. 198). However, it should be remembered that controls are commonly exercised in nonexperimental as well as experimental studies (for example, in classifying subjects or gathering data). Furthermore, the term "control" must not be taken in a narrow sense. Especially in recent years, writers have spoken of two general kinds of control, manipulative and statistical (Weick, 1965, p. 198). Kaplan (1964), for example, warns that not all controls are "manipulative in character"; they may take the forms of establishing test and control groups, or of "processing the raw data, as in the application of techniques of multivariate analysis [p. 162]."

The position proposed here is that the subjects' *perceptions* of the situation constitute as important a feature of research as the controls imposed by the investigator. (Hence, issue is taken with the single-criterion approach enunciated in a statement of the Social Science Research Council in 1954, declaring that the distinction between laboratory experiment and field study is in the "degree of control exerted over the events being studied [Carter, 1958, p. 78].") The terms "laboratory" and "field," however defined by whatever researcher, are inadequate analytical concepts insofar as they confound the two factors of researcher control and subject perceptions. If these terms are used to denote degrees of realism, then we must declare that a given study is a laboratory study if the subjects perceive it as such, or a field study if the subjects so perceive it.

REVISED CLASSIFICATION OF LABORATORY AND FIELD STUDIES

Probably because the human mind must categorize in order to make sense of the world, typologies abound. But because the world defies any set of categories, all typologies are imperfect. The most ingenious taxonomic schemes, when exposed to the test, are found either to include or to exclude too much. The following set of categories is therefore proposed in the full knowledge that any given investigation may easily be subsumable under more than a single category.

CASE 1 SUBJECTS PERCEIVE DEVIATIONS AS RESEARCHER INDUCED

Case 1-a Controlled experiment

In this case, the subjects perceive (accurately) that something out of the ordinary is going on and that some kind of investigation is involved. Such deviations, in the properly executed controlled experiment, embrace two general kinds of researcher intervention: controls over primary events (manipulation of relevant variables; control of extraneous factors) and controls over data gathering procedures. In Case 1-a, the subjects perceive at least significant portions of *both* kinds of controls. A further subdivision would be possible, based on whether the subjects perceive the manipulation of relevant variables for what it really is, or whether (as is so often true) the researcher has been able to mislead them into believing that he is investigating something other than his real variables.

Case 1-b   *Controls related to data gathering only*

This case is intended to describe those situations in which (a) the researcher is making no attempt to manipulate or control variables as such; (b) he is intervening for the purpose of gathering data; (c) the subjects correctly perceive that information is being gathered for research purposes of some kind (although they need not, and usually do not, have insight into all the objectives or procedures). Under Case 1-b would obviously fall a great number of descriptive and analytical "field studies" in the conventional sense of the term, especially those in sociology and anthropology, as well as most sampling surveys. Again, a further subdivision might be useful if the researcher wished to focus attention on the degree to which the subjects are intended to perceive (or actually do perceive) the true purposes of the study.

CASE 2   SUBJECTS PERCEIVE DEVIATIONS, BUT AS UNRELATED TO RESEARCHER

In this case, the subjects perceive that something unusual is occurring, but they do not attribute it to a researcher. There are three identifiable conditions under this heading:

Case 2-a   *Controlled experiment*

In this case, events are being modified by the researcher in some sort of experimental design, but the subjects are unaware of the research related aspects of the situation.

Case 2-b   *Natural experiment*

Events are occurring because of factors (either human or physical) independent of researcher intervention; but the researcher is utilizing such events "opportunistically [French, 1953, p. 99]" as variables in an experimental design (*e.g.*, a tornado, an assassination of a public figure, a corporate merger). Subdivision would be possible if it were desired to specify whether such natural events were known or predicted in advance, or whether the investigator created his design post hoc without opportunity for planning or data gathering prior to the relevant occurrences.

Case 2-c   *Nonexperimental study*

This category differs from Case 2-b only in that the researcher chooses not to use (or cannot use) a truly experimental design.

It should be noted that from the standpoint of the subjects' perceptions Cases 2-a, 2-b, and 2-c are all the same; they differ in the perceptions and behaviors of the researcher. It should also be noted that two or more categories may be required to describe different phases of the same investigation. For example, it is quite common that subjects participate in either a controlled or a natural experiment without realizing that anything related to research is happening, but then at a later point in the course of events various data gathering instruments or procedures (*e.g.*, questionnaires, tests, interviews) are introduced. At this point the investigation which would have been classifiable under Case 2-a or 2-b would be Case 1-a or 1-b. The study as a whole would be described as, for example, Case 2-a + 1-a, since two significantly different types of subject perceptions would be involved.

CASE 3   SUBJECTS PERCEIVE NO DEVIATIONS FROM EVERYDAY ROUTINES

In this case, regardless of what the researcher may be doing, the subjects perceive no significant variations whatever from ordinary, everyday phenomena. As with Case 2, three identifiable subclasses may be listed:

Case 3-a   *Controlled experiment*

Case 3-b   *Natural experiment*

Case 3-c   *Nonexperimental study*

The point to stress here is that although *something* out of the ordinary is taking place, whether or not induced by the researcher, the subjects remain totally ignorant of it.

Since it is quite common for different kinds of subject perceptions to take place at different stages in the course of a single investigation, the researcher is advised to give careful thought to this matter as a part of his advance planning. For example, it might be feasible to represent predicted subject perceptions on a graphic time line:

Predicted Subject Perceptions during Study

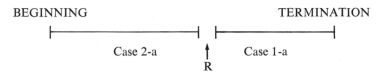

BEGINNING   TERMINATION

Case 2-a   R   Case 1-a

At point marked R, data gathering procedures such as interviews or questionnaires are introduced.

The hypothetical situation pictured above is illustrated by the Hughey (1966) experiment, conducted in a university environment. Using a sample of more than 1,700 college undergraduates, the investigator devised a simulated real-life situation in which the subjects were exposed to a persuasive speech — with varying accompanying messages attributed to real personages on the staff — purporting to be part of a campaign to establish a student operated bookstore at the university. For some time prior to the beginning of the experiment, a persistent and well publicized effort actually had existed to enlist student support for the establishment of such a bookstore. With the exception of only a few isolated individuals, none of the student subjects realized that any kind of research was taking place — until, of course, they received certain written instruments on which they were to record various kinds of responses (a subsample was also drawn, whose members were interviewed by the investigator). No pre-tests were administered, although certain essential information about the subjects had been collected by means of an instrument which had been presented in a totally different context as a routine feature of the course. In these and other ways, the researcher attempted, with a high degree of success, to create an experimental situation which would meet one of his basic criteria by "giving an air of plausibility and reality." In other words, so far as the subjects were concerned and in terms of their perceptions, this was not an experiment at all prior to the point at which data gathering instruments appeared.

Other criteria were congruent with this one:

1. The topic of the communication should offer the opportunity for a high degree of ego-involvement.

2. The communicator should be linked intimately and vividly with the message.

3. The communication should offer the opportunity for making a formal or informal commitment to the speaker's proposal [1968, p. 1].

The third criterion is worth special attention not only because it had to do with creating the illusion of reality, but because it also called for *behavioral* indicators of attitude over and above the typical paper-and-pencil scales. The experimenter introduced three measures of commitment. One was a Thurstone-type scale (validated by peers of the experimental subjects) corresponding to the conventional instrument generally used to measure effects of a stimulus speech on an audience. But the other two devices represent methods rarely used in this type of experiment: the "Will-Join scale" elicited from each subject an estimate of how far he was willing to go in lending the use of his name or in participating in an active campaign to support the speaker's objectives; the "Money index" gave each subject an opportunity to indicate how much (if any) actual cash he was willing to pledge in the campaign. (It is interesting to note that cumulative pledges of money came to a figure in the thousands of dollars.)

With all this realism and plausibility, the question may logically be raised: "What psychological impact did the experiment have on the subjects after they discovered that they had in a sense been duped?" In fact, this question is perhaps subsidiary to the larger issue of ethics (see Chapter 3, pp. 98–102), and the present writer is unable to offer a neatly packaged answer. The experimenter reported in personal conversations that a few subjects voiced resentment and many expressed disappointment (some going so far as to say that they were now sufficiently motivated to go out and actually campaign for a student operated bookstore). A conscientious effort was undertaken by the researcher to debrief all subjects in question-and-answer sessions and even in personal interviews when requested, with the purpose of explaining the theoretical significance of the study and the supposedly justified reasons for perpetrating the series of deceptions. The results of these post-experimental explanations were considered by the researcher to be on the whole quite satisfactory.

However, there was reason to wonder whether an entire generation of undergraduates in one university experienced a permanent loss of faith in the credibility of their instructors. Thus, even if the subjects agreed on the basis of ex post facto explanations that they had been deceived for a worthy cause, the fundamental ethical problem remains: people *were* deceived, and they were deceived about a real-life issue on which many of the subjects felt strong emotional commitments.

In the final analysis, each reader must decide for himself whether the ingenious stratagems so successfully employed by Hughey to manipulate subject perceptions were ethically justified in that particular situation. Even more important than resolving this question for the Hughey experiment is the necessity for any researcher to think through in the planning stages of a study the ethical — as well as the practical — implications of his proposed procedures. He must be especially vigilant when he expects to be dealing with Case 2 or Case 3 types of subject perceptions. For example, the ethical problems are compounded when the subjects do not even know that they have been studied and do not perceive the researcher as a researcher (if they perceive him at all), as in the dramatic field investigation undertaken by Festinger, Riecken, and Schachter (1956). To use R. Hyman's (1964) descriptive terminology, the researchers "infiltrated a group whose members believed that the world would come to an end on a specified day [p. 43]." Festinger *et al.* were therefore compelled to participate as bona fide believers; as a result, anything they did or anything they failed to do when action was expected by the group inevitably exercised an influence on the events being observed. An especially sticky problem arose when the scientists left the group and published their account, since the group members were now likely to discover that they had been duped. As Scott (1965) remarks, "Most groups take a dim view of people who tell lies to insiders and reveal secrets to outsiders [p. 274]."

The argument being pressed here is that investigators considering the relative merits of so-called laboratory and field research are likely to be diverted to peripheral matters if they think of the laboratory-field continuum merely in terms of the locale in which the study occurs. True, locale is obviously a factor to be taken into account. But, as French (1953) has rightly observed in words quoted earlier in this chapter, "It is not important whether the . . . phenomena occur in a building called a laboratory rather than in . . . some . . . 'real' social situation [p. 100]." Actually, locale is important only insofar as it significantly influences either or both of the two really basic factors: (a) the degree of control available to the researcher and (b) the ways in which the subjects perceive the relevant phenomena.

Subject perceptions, in turn, are likely to be the chief determinants of such important matters as:

— the extent to which subjects will respond to the relevant or to the irrelevant (unintended) stimuli in the research environment, especially when an effort is made to outguess the experimenter (Weick, 1967, p. 11)

— the extent to which subjects will be ego-involved in the topics or tasks with which they are dealing

In fact, it could be argued that ego-involvement is itself definable in terms of perceived importance. The ego-involvement issue is of particular concern to communication researchers whose studies focus on persuasion or attitude change, for they must face a dilemma recognized for many years as a methodological hazard: whether to use deeply involving real-life issues on which no measurable shift may occur or superficial issues producing shifts from which it is difficult to generalize.

The point is that *neither* field nor laboratory settings per se are guarantors of subject involvement. The researcher must decide whether the particular purposes and design of his proposed investigation call for high or low levels of involvement. Having made this decision, he should then consider ways and means of obtaining the kinds of subject perceptions most appropriate to his research objectives. Whether these perceptions are most easily produced in a so-called natural setting or in an experimenter contrived laboratory then becomes simply one more practical detail to be worked out. But the decision on locale should follow the decisions about researcher controls and subject perceptions.

In the Hughey study, the decision to create a classroom environment in which a persuasive message would be presented (even though the situation was recognized as an obvious deviation from ordinary routines) came quite late in a long series of other decisions prior in both time and logic on such matters as the theoretical derivations of hypotheses, the kinds of variables and criterion measures to be used, and the desired level of ego-involvement on the part of the subjects.[8] Why inquire, then, whether this was a laboratory or a field setting? The answer would depend not only on which criteria were being applied (*e.g.,* is the classroom environment real life?), but especially on how the subjects perceived it. The Hughey study exhibited the *controls* of a laboratory experiment but the *subject perceptions* (up to a certain point) of a naturalistic field study. Thus, it is argued that no single continuum is adequate to describe the settings of research, and, in particular, that the conventional laboratory-field dichotomy fails to provide a valid basis for analyzing such settings.

THE STEREOTYPE OF FIELD RESEARCH AS PRELIMINARY OR SECOND RATE

It has become traditional to view field studies as preliminary, prescientific labor, useful only to clear away the underbrush before undertaking the main task of erecting elegant theoretical structures. The notion is widespread that much, if not most, field research is preliminary to the truly scientific work of hypothesis testing (Kerlinger, 1964, p. 388); it is frequently identified solely with the early or "natural history" stage of inquiry, its chief value deriving from the questions it raises rather than from its actual findings (R. Hyman, 1964, p. 46). However, competent observers have also suggested that controlled laboratory experiments can be used for exploratory as well as hypothesis testing ends (Weick, 1967, pp. 9–10). Clevenger (1969) would also allow an important place for experimentation as a predecessor of field research, but for somewhat different reasons:

> . . . why bother with experiments? Because prior to the time when researchers are ready to test a complete theory in the field, they need to explore it systematically and to guarantee themselves from time to time that they are moving in the right directions. It is precisely because a field study demands such a complete grasp of details that it represents an inefficient way to launch a new area of research [p. 157].

[8] For discussions of the ubiquitous ego-involvement problem in research dealing especially with persuasion and attitude change, the reader is referred to such sources as Hovland (1959); Nebergall (1965, 1968); M. Sherif, C. Sherif, and Nebergall (1965); Clevenger (1969); Cronkhite (1969).

Priority of Field and Laboratory Research

The researcher, then, may select any of several points of view regarding the supposed priority (in time) of field studies vis-à-vis laboratory experimentation, and he can find authoritative opinion to support whatever position he adopts. He may decide that in opening up a new area of investigation he should begin with naturalistic observation and descriptive field studies. Or he may decide that he should begin with laboratory experimentation and then follow up with validating experimental or descriptive studies in the field. Or he may decide that regardless of which one comes first the only true road lies in alternating laboratory and field studies — a conclusion almost universally recommended (*e.g.,* Katz, 1953; Hovland, 1959; Nebergall, 1965, 1968).

The One-Shot Case Study

Moreover, even the much maligned one-shot descriptive case study can indeed yield valuable scientific conclusions if it is planned with reference to specified theoretical constructs. A single study — or better yet a series of studies — can at least provide sound evidence that a given theory does *not* apply to specified situations. As Kaplan (1964) has observed, "Important scientific propositions have the form of universals, and a universal can be falsified by a single counterinstance [p. 37]." Kerlinger and others have been cited earlier in this chapter (pp. 118–119) to the effect that the single case study has virtually no scientific value largely because it does not provide for the essential feature of comparison (Kerlinger, 1964, pp. 293–295; Campbell, 1957, p. 298). Such an evaluation would seem to be justified only for those one-shot studies — if any really exist — undertaken to describe phenomena in a total theoretical vacuum: to find out what is "out there" just for the sake of doing it, without comparing *observed* events and *expectations* of events. Such expectations may or may not, at a given stage of inquiry, take the form of hypothetico-deductive statements or fully developed theories. It must be remembered that the prerequisite of comparison can be satisfied in more than one way: Case A may be compared with Cases A_1, A_2, A_3 . . . A_n; specified factors (variables) within Case A may be compared with one another; or single Case X may be studied as a potential counterinstance to a stated hypothesis or theory.

DESCRIPTIVE STUDIES

A well known illustration of a single descriptive case study explicitly designed to determine the applicability of an established theory to a specified set of conditions is Cyert, Simon, and Trow (1956). This is a detailed, step-by-step account of a real-life decision in a company on the feasibility of using electronic data processing equipment. The investigators stated at the very outset of their report that "it is extremely doubtful whether the only considerable body of decision-making theory . . . available in the past

— that provided by economics" offers an adequate explanation of actual human decision making "in large organizations operating in a complex world [p. 237]." They then announced it as their aim to ascertain whether the traditional theory or a revised theory would better take account of the decision making processes in the specific case studied. As a result of their intensive observation (involving neither manipulation nor quantification), the authors offered the carefully qualified conclusion that the traditional theory was indeed inadequate; on the basis of this single study, they then generated a new theory, or at least hypothesis, founded on the construct of programmed versus nonprogrammed decisions. Thus we have a one-shot case study deliberately designed for two purposes: (1) to search for a counterinstance of an existing theory and (2) to provide a source for new hypotheses or constructs. The authors clearly pointed out that generalization was risky, but surely this study should not be dismissed as possessing no significant scientific value.

Even investigations going no further than thorough and intensive description of existing phenomena (related, of course, to some meaningful frame of reference or to a specified theory) have been praised by behavioral scientists as useful *scientific* endeavors. Although characterizing the anthropological type of intensive case study as representing "only the first step in science" because of weaknesses in quantification and controls, Katz (1953) declares that "this type of study provides a great deal of information about a community or a culture with a remarkable economy of effort"; and he warns that quantification, by concentrating on "easily measured variables, may focus on microscopic and trivial factors and miss the significant processes in group functioning [p. 64]." He speaks for a respectable body of commentators when he concludes that

> . . . the great strength of the field type of study is its inductive procedure, its potentiality for discovering significant variables and basic relations that would never be found if we were confined to research dictated by a hypothetical-deductive model. *Thus, the field study and the survey are the great protection in social science against the sterility and triviality of premature model building* [p. 75; italics supplied].

At various points in this chapter a number of behavioral scientists, especially those concerned with the study of human communication, have been cited for their recommendations urging greater allocation of research energies to "field" studies.[9] The word "field" is enclosed in quotation marks, since it is fairly clear that these writers are using the term in the restricted sense of real-life (versus artificial) settings, but without specifying the factor of subject perceptions.

[9] See, for example, S. L. Becker (1968), Clevenger (1969), Haiman (1969), and G. R. Miller (1969).

Scott (1965) is addressing his remarks explicitly to researchers investigating complex organizations, but it is interesting to communication students to observe that he goes so far as to suggest that researchers in the future should be expected to be "less and less inclined to think in terms of . . . hypotheses" and more concerned with "theoretical models which generate numerous implications, each of which becomes a proposition guiding field observations." As a consequence, he feels that "the most important contribution of field research in the future may be the collection of detailed descriptive information [p. 269]."

Conclusion

To summarize the argument offered in this chapter, we may conclude that both attacks on and defenses of field research are frequently misguided. Sometimes they center on the secondary issue of locale (*i.e.,* so-called real-life versus so-called artificial settings). At other times, they focus on the prime issue of researcher induced modifications, or experimental controls. But all too frequently, writers appear to assume that researcher controls automatically produce artificiality which in turn automatically destroys external validity. Both these assumptions have been shown to be unacceptable as universal principles insofar as they fail to take into account at least three facts: (1) that reality is better described as a continuum of infinite gradations rather than as a phenomenon existing as one pole of a dichotomous category; (2) that this continuum is primarily a function of subject perceptions; (3) that these perceptions vary more or less independently of the locale in which the research happens to be conducted.

Anyone declaring, therefore, that the nonexperimental field study is ipso facto a "scientific weak cousin of laboratory and field experiment [Kerlinger, 1964, p. 390]" must be understood as arbitrarily defining it as inherently deficient in researcher control. Although certainly defensible (given certain premises about the concept of control), this definition is just as certainly vulnerable. Likewise, he who advocates field research on the grounds that results of laboratory experimentation can be validated only in naturalistic environments (*e.g.,* Clevenger, 1969) must be understood as arbitrarily defining laboratory settings as unreal. Confronted with this assumption, one should inquire: "*Who* is perceiving either the laboratory or the field setting as natural?"

The position adopted in this chapter is that a real-life setting is not necessarily important or desirable (or undesirable) for its own sake; rather, what is important is that a given investigation be conducted in a locale — whether it be labeled "laboratory" or "field" — which offers the optimum combination of researcher controls and subject perceptions. A so-called natural setting is natural or artificial only as it is perceived by the relevant individuals, typically, the researcher(s) and the subject(s). Therefore, what one researcher may consider to be a laboratory locale may be perceived by another researcher or especially by his subjects as a naturalistic locale; and what one investigator regards as a real-life setting his subjects may perceive as a contrived experiment. This chapter agrees with those critics who have questioned the supposedly inherent reality of field studies and inherent artificiality of laboratory studies; it agrees with those critics who have pointed out that subjects (depending on their perceptions of the total situation) *may* be more ego involved in some laboratory settings than in some natural settings.

The study of human communication behavior should be appropriate to its basic subject matter, and this subject matter is frequently characterized by phenomenally high levels of fluidity, multidimensionality, subtlety, and nonrepetitiveness. Furthermore, since symbolic or communicative behaviors are obviously among the most uniquely human of all human behavior, the communication researcher is especially likely to find himself dealing with ego-involved responses; or, put another way, superficial responses are in many cases trivial communication events. The kinds of communication variables most urgently in need of study are probably the kinds most difficult to capture in any setting perceived by the subjects to be nonrealistic. However, it is also a fact of common observation that the most meaningful acts of human communication are imbedded in a complex maze of other interacting factors; in other words, the systems approach is highly recommended to communication researchers. Insofar as conventional laboratory experimentation fails to deal appropriately with all these attributes of human communication behavior, nonlaboratory approaches have been strongly urged by many recent researchers. Again, however, there is not necessarily any virtue in a precipitate rejection of laboratory studies in a mad rush to do research in the field (the allegedly real world). The laboratory is also *one* real world, as perceived by those involved in it. The same logic, of course, compels the researcher to rid himself of those stereotyped views of field studies as endeavors forever consigned to earlier and less sophisticated stages of inquiry.

A field study, then, is simply any kind of research carried out in a specified locale which is perceived by specified perceivers (particularly the subjects) as being free of significant researcher related deviations from everyday life. It may have any conceivable design, any conceivable controls, and any conceivable data gathering techniques available in the entire repertory of science. A field study per se is neither more nor less scientific than a so-called laboratory study.

Once field research has been defined in terms of who perceives it as "field," it may appropriately be used in any of the familiar rationales: exploratory, descriptive, correlational, and causal (hypothesis testing). Some competent authorities would recommend field studies especially for exploratory and descriptive research; other authorities, just as competent, feel that the supposedly more complex character of real-life settings argues for field research as the culminating, theory validating effort of scientific inquiry — especially in the study of human communication. This chapter holds that both sides in this friendly controversy are right and wrong. Once the investigator has carefully delineated his problem and thought through the optimum combination of researcher controls and subject perceptions it requires, then and only then need he address himself to the pragmatic, ad hoc decision regarding the locale in which the study will be conducted.

To assist the communication researcher in his decision making, as he considers the setting of his investigations, this chapter has proposed that he examine the extent to which identifiable parts of any study may usefully be categorized under one or more of three combinations of researcher controls and subject perceptions. For purposes of convenience, these three combinations were called Case 1, Case 2, and Case 3:

CASE 1   Subjects perceive deviations (from everyday routine) as researcher induced

CASE 2   Subjects perceive deviations, but as unrelated to researcher

CASE 3   Subjects perceive no deviations from everyday routines

It is suggested that this mode of analysis be substituted for the conventional laboratory-field dichotomy.

References and Selected Readings

Adams, R. N., and Preiss, J. J. (Eds.) *Human organization research: Field relations and techniques.* Homewood, Ill.: Dorsey, 1960.

Argyris, C. Creating effective relationships in organizations. *Human Organization,* 1958, **17,** 34–40.

Back, K. W. The well-informed informant. *Human Organization,* 1956, **14,** 30–33.

Bain, R. K. The researcher's role: A case study. In R. N. Adams and J. J. Preiss (Eds.), *Human organization research.* Homewood, Ill.: Dorsey, 1960. Pp. 140–152. (Modified from original article in *Human Organization,* 1950, **9,** 23–28.)

Bakan, D. *On method: Toward a reconstruction of psychological investigation.* San Francisco: Jossey-Bass, 1967.

Bales, R. *Interaction process analysis.* Cambridge, Mass.: Addison-Wesley, 1950.

Barnes, L. B. Organizational change and field experiment methods. In V. H. Vroom (Ed.), *Methods of organizational research.* Pittsburgh: University of Pittsburgh Press, 1967. Pp. 57–111.

Barnlund, D. C. *Interpersonal communication: Survey and studies.* Boston: Houghton Mifflin, 1968.

Bavelas, A., and Barrett, D. An experimental approach to organizational communication. *Personnel,* 1951, **27,** 366–371.

Becker, H. S. Problems of inference and proof in participant observation. *American Sociological Review,* 1958, **23,** 652–660.

Becker, H. S. Problems in the publication of field studies. In A. J. Vidich, J. Bensman, and M. R. Stein (Eds.), *Reflections on community studies.* New York: John Wiley, 1964. Pp. 267–284.

Becker, H. S., and Geer, B. Participant observation: The analysis of qualitative field data. In R. N. Adams and J. J. Preiss (Eds.), *Human organization research.* Homewood, Ill.: Dorsey, 1960. Pp. 267–289.

Becker, S. L. New approaches to audience analysis. In C. E. Larson and F. E. X. Dance (Eds.), *Perspectives on communication.* Milwaukee: Speech Communication Center, University of Wisconsin at Milwaukee, 1968. Pp. 61–77.

Bellamy, M., and Thompson, W. N. Stability of attitude as a predeterminer of experimental results. *Speech Monographs,* 1967, **34,** 180–184.

Berelson, B. *Content analysis in communication research.* Glencoe, Ill.: The Free Press of Glencoe, 1952.

Bowers, J. W., and Phillips, W. A. A note on the generality of source-credibility scales. *Speech Monographs,* 1967, **34,** 185–186.

Braithwaite, R. *Scientific explanation.* Cambridge, Eng.: Cambridge University Press, 1955.

Brooks, W. D. A study of the relationships of selected factors to changes in voting attitude of audiences listening to political speeches of President Johnson and Senator Goldwater. Unpublished doctoral dissertation, Ohio University, 1965.

Brooks, W. D. A field study of the Johnson and Goldwater campaign speeches in Pittsburgh. *Southern Speech Journal,* 1967, **32,** 273–281.

Brunswik, E. Representative design and probabilistic theory in functional psychology. *Psychological Review,* 1955, **62,** 193–217.

Brunswik, E. *Perception and the representative design of psychological experiments.* (2nd ed.) Berkeley: University of California Press, 1956.

Bruyn, S. T. *The human perspective in sociology: The methodology of participant observation.* Englewood Cliffs, N.J.: Prentice-Hall, 1966.

Burns, T. The comparative study of organizations. In V. H. Vroom (Ed.), *Methods of organizational research.* Pittsburgh: University of Pittsburgh Press, 1967. Pp. 113–170.

Campbell, D. T. Factors relevant to the validity of experiments in social settings. *Psychological Bulletin,* 1957, **54,** 297–312.

Campbell, D. T., and Stanley, J. C. *Experimental and quasi-experimental designs for research.* Chicago: Rand McNally, 1966.

Caplow, T. Rumors in war. *Social Forces,* 1947, **25,** 298–302.

Carter, R. E., Jr. Field methods in communication research. In R. O. Nafziger and D. M. White (Eds.), *Introduction to mass communications research.* Baton Rouge: Louisiana State University Press, 1958. Pp. 78–127.

Clevenger, T., Jr. The interaction of descriptive and experimental research in the development of rhetorical theory. *Central States Speech Journal,* 1965, **16,** 7–12.

Clevenger, T., Jr. Research methodologies in speech-communication. In R. J. Kibler and L. L. Barker (Eds.), *Conceptual frontiers in speech-communication.* New York: Speech Association of America, 1969. Pp. 144–165.

Cohen, A. R. Upward communication in experimentally created hierarchies. *Human Relations,* 1958, **11,** 41–53.

Cronbach, L. J. The two disciplines of psychology. *The American Psychologist,* 1957, **12,** 671–684.

Cronkhite, G. L., Jr. Out of the ivory palaces: A proposal for useful research in communication and decision. In R. J. Kibler and L. L. Barker (Eds.), *Conceptual frontiers in speech-communication.* New York: Speech Association of America, 1969. Pp. 113–135.

Cyert, R. M., Simon, H. A., and Trow, D. B. Observation of a business decision. *Journal of Business,* 1956, **29,** 237–248.

Dahle, T. L. An objective and comparative study of five methods of transmitting information to business and industrial employees. *Speech Monographs,* 1954, **21,** 21–28.

Davis, K. Management communication and the grapevine. *Harvard Business Review,* 1953 (January–February), **31,** 43–49. (a)

Davis, K. A method of studying communication patterns in organizations. *Personnel Psychology,* 1953, **6,** 301–312. (b)

Davis, K. *Human relations in business.* New York: McGraw-Hill, 1957.

Davis, K. Success of chain-of-command oral communication in a manufacturing management group. *Academy of Management Journal,* 1968, **11,** 379–386.

Dexter, L. A. Role relationships and conceptions of neutrality in interviewing. *American Journal of Sociology,* 1956, **62,** 153–157.

Evans, R. I. *B. F. Skinner: The man and his ideas.* New York: Dutton, 1968.

Festinger, L. Laboratory experiments. In L. Festinger and D. Katz (Eds.), *Research methods in the behavioral sciences.* New York: Holt, Rinehart & Winston, 1953. Pp. 136–172.

Festinger, L. Behavioral support for opinion change. *Public Opinion Quarterly,* 1964, **28,** 404–417.

Festinger, L., Cartwright, D., Barber, K., Fleischl, J., Gottsdanker, J., Keysen, A., and Leavitt, G. A study of a rumor: Its origin and spread. *Human Relations,* 1948, **1,** 464–486.

Festinger, L., and Katz, D. (Eds.) *Research methods in the behavioral sciences.* New York: Holt, Rinehart & Winston, 1953.

Festinger, L., Riecken, H. W., and Schachter, S. *When prophecy fails.* Minneapolis: University of Minnesota Press, 1956.

French, J. R. P., Jr. Experiments in field settings. In L. Festinger and D. Katz (Eds.), *Research methods in the behavioral sciences.* New York: Holt, Rinehart & Winston, 1953. Pp. 98–135.

Freshley, D. L. A study of the attitudes of industrial management personnel toward communication. Unpublished doctoral dissertation, Ohio State University, 1955.

Glaser, B. G. The constant comparative method of qualitative analysis. *Social Problems,* 1965, **12,** 436–445.

Gold, R. L. Roles in sociological field observations. *Social Forces,* 1958, **36,** 217–223.

Goode, W. J., and Hatt, P. K. *Methods in social research.* New York: McGraw-Hill, 1952.

Guest, R. H. Categories of events in field observations. In R. N. Adams and J. J. Preiss (Eds.), *Human organization research.* Homewood, Ill.: Dorsey, 1960. Pp. 225–239.

Guetzkow, H. Communications in organizations. In J. G. March (Ed.), *Handbook of organizations.* Chicago: Rand McNally, 1965. Pp. 534–573.

Gullahorn, J., and Strauss, G. The field worker in union research. In R. N. Adams and J. J. Preiss (Eds.), *Human organization research.* Homewood, Ill.: Dorsey, 1960. Pp. 153–165.

Haiman, F. S. A response to "Out of the ivory palaces." In R. J. Kibler and L. L. Barker (Eds.), *Conceptual frontiers in speech-communication.* New York: Speech Association of America, 1969. Pp. 136–139.

Holmes, R. W. *The rhyme of reason.* New York: D. Appleton-Century, 1939.

Homans, G. C. The strategy of industrial sociology. In G. C. Homans (Ed.), *Sentiments and activities.* New York: The Free Press of Glencoe, 1962. Pp. 257–268.

Hovland, C. I. Reconciling conflicting results derived from experimental and survey studies of attitude change. *The American Psychologist,* 1959, **14,** 8–17.

Hughes, E. C. Introduction: The place of field work in social science. In B. H. Junker, *Field work: An introduction to the social sciences.* Chicago: University of Chicago Press, 1960. Pp. v–xv.

Hughey, J. D. An investigation of two selected methods of modifying credibility on the immediate and delayed effectiveness of a speaker. Unpublished doctoral dissertation, Purdue University, 1966.

Hughey, J. D. Research Abstract No. 20. Lafayette, Ind.: Communication Research Center, Department of Speech, Purdue University, 1968.

Hyman, H. *Survey design and analysis: Principles, cases and procedures.* Glencoe, Ill.: The Free Press of Glencoe, 1955.

Hyman, R. *The nature of psychological inquiry.* Englewood Cliffs, N.J.: Prentice-Hall, 1964.

Jaques, E. The science of society. *Human Relations,* 1966, **19,** 125–137.

Jones, E. E., and Gerard, H. B. *Foundations of social psychology.* New York: John Wiley, 1967.

Junker, B. H. *Field work: An introduction to the social sciences.* Chicago: University of Chicago Press, 1960.

Kahn, R. L., and Mann, F. Developing research partnerships. *Journal of Social Issues,* 1952, **8,** 4–10.

Kaplan, A. *The conduct of inquiry.* San Francisco: Chandler, 1964.

Katz, D. Field studies. In L. Festinger and D. Katz (Eds.), *Research methods in the behavioral sciences.* New York: Holt, Rinehart & Winston, 1953. Pp. 56–97.

Kelly, C. M. "Actual listening behavior" of industrial supervisors, as related to "listening ability," general mental ability, selected personality factors and supervisory effectiveness. Unpublished doctoral dissertation, Purdue University, 1962.

Kennedy, J. L. A "transition-model" laboratory for research on cultural change. In R. N. Adams and J. J. Preiss (Eds.), *Human organization research.* Homewood, Ill.: Dorsey, 1960. Pp. 316–323.

Kerlinger, F. N. *Foundations of behavioral research.* New York: Holt, Rinehart & Winston, 1964.

Kibler, R. J., and Barker, L. L. (Eds.) *Conceptual frontiers in speech-communication.* Report of the New Orleans Conference on Research and Instructional Development, February 1968. New York: Speech Association of America, 1969.

Klintz, B. L., Delprato, D. J., Mettee, D. R., Persons, C. E., and Schappe, R. H. The experimenter effect. *Psychological Bulletin,* 1965, **63,** 223–232.

Larson, C. E., and Dance, F. E. X. (Eds.) *Perspectives on communication.* Milwaukee: Speech Communication Center, University of Wisconsin at Milwaukee, 1968.

Lawrence, P. R. *The changing of organizational behavior patterns: A case study of decentralization.* Boston: Graduate School of Business Administration, Harvard University, 1958.

Lazarsfeld, P. F. Evidence and inference in social research. In D. Lerner (Ed.), *Evidence and inference.* New York: The Free Press of Glencoe, 1959. Pp. 107–138.

Lerner, D., and Lasswell, H. D. (Eds.) *The policy sciences.* Stanford, Cal.: Stanford University Press, 1951.

Level, D. A., Jr. A case study of human communications in an urban bank. Unpublished doctoral dissertation, Purdue University, 1959.

Lewin, K. *Field theory in social science.* New York: Harper, 1951.

Mann, F., and Likert, R. The need for research on the communication of research results. *Human Organization,* 1952, **11,** 15–19.

March, J. G. (Ed.) *Handbook of organizations.* Chicago: Rand McNally, 1965.

McCall, G. J., and Simmons, J. L. *Issues in participant observation: A text and reader.* Reading, Mass.: Addison-Wesley, 1969.

McGuigan, F. J. The experimenter: A neglected stimulus object. *Psychological Bulletin,* 1963, **60,** 421–428.

Milgram, S. Some conditions of obedience and disobedience to authority. *Human Relations,* 1965, **18,** 57–76.

Miller, G. R. A crucial problem in attitude research. *Quarterly Journal of Speech,* 1967, **53,** 235–240.

Miller, G. R. Communication and persuasion research: Current problems and prospects. *Quarterly Journal of Speech,* 1968, **54,** 268–276.

Miller, G. R. Human information processing: Some research guidelines. In R. J. Kibler and L. L. Barker (Eds.), *Conceptual frontiers in speech-communication.* New York: Speech Association of America, 1969. Pp. 51–68.

Miller, S. M. The participant observer and over-rapport. *American Sociological Review,* 1952, **17,** 97–99.

Minter, R. L. A comparative analysis of managerial communication in two divisions of a large manufacturing company. Unpublished doctoral dissertation, Purdue University, 1969. 4 vols.

Miraglia, J. F. An experimental study of the effects of communication training upon perceived job performance of nursing supervisors in two urban hospitals. Unpublished doctoral dissertation, Purdue University, 1963.

Nafziger, R. O., and White, D. M. (Eds.) *Introduction to mass communications research.* Baton Rouge: Louisiana State University Press, 1958.

Nebergall, R. E. A critique of experimental design in communication research. *Central States Speech Journal,* 1965, **16,** 13–16.

Nebergall, R. E. Attitude change through persuasion: The laboratory and the field. In C. E. Larson and F. E. X. Dance (Eds.), *Perspectives on communication.* Milwaukee: Speech Communication Center, University of Wisconsin at Milwaukee, 1968. Pp. 52–59.

Nidditch, P. H. *Elementary logic of science and mathematics.* Glencoe, Ill.: The Free Press of Glencoe, 1960.

Nilsen, T. R. The communication survey: A study of communication problems in three office and factory units. Unpublished doctoral dissertation, Northwestern University, 1953.

Northrop, F. S. C. *The logic of the sciences and the humanities.* New York: Macmillan, 1947.

Oleson, V. L., and Whittaker, E. W. Role-making in participant observation: Processes in the researcher-actor relationship. *Human Organization,* 1967, **26,** 273–281.

Orlans, H. Ethical problems in the relations of research sponsors and investigators. In G. Sjoberg (Ed.), *Ethics, politics, and social research.* Cambridge, Mass.: Schenkman, 1967. Pp. 3–24.

Orne, M. T. On the social psychology of the psychological experiment. *The American Psychologist,* 1962, **19,** 776–783.

Orne, M. T., and Evans, F. J. Social control in the psychological experiment: Anti-social behavior and hypnosis. *Journal of Personality and Social Psychology,* 1965, **1,** 189–200.

Pace, R. W. An analysis of selected oral communication attributes of direct-selling representatives as related to their sales effectiveness. Unpublished doctoral dissertation, Purdue University, 1960.

Peterson, W., and Gist, N. Rumor and public opinion. *American Journal of Sociology,* 1951, **57,** 159–167.

Piersol, D. T. A case study of oral communication practices of foremen in a midwestern corporation. Unpublished doctoral dissertation, Purdue University, 1955.

Pyron, H. C. The construction and validation of a forced-choice scale for measuring oral communication attitudes of industrial foremen. Unpublished doctoral dissertation, Purdue University, 1964.

Read, W. H. Upward communication in industrial hierarchies. *Human Relations,* 1962, **15,** 2–15.

Redding, W. C. The empirical study of human communication in business and industry. In P. E. Ried (Ed.), *The frontiers in experimental speech-communication research.* Syracuse, N.Y.: Syracuse University Press, 1966. Pp. 47–81.

Richardson, S. A. A framework for reporting field-relations experiences. In R. N. Adams and J. J. Preiss (Eds.), *Human organization research.* Homewood, Ill.: Dorsey, 1960. Pp. 124–139. (Modified from earlier version in *Human Organization,* 1953, **12,** 31–37.)

Richardson, S. A., Dohrenwend, B. S., and Klein, D. *Interviewing: Its forms and functions.* New York: Basic Books, 1965.

Richetto, G. M. Source credibility and personal influence in three contexts: A study of dyadic communication in a complex aerospace organization. Unpublished doctoral dissertation, Purdue University, 1969.

Riecken, H. W. The unidentified interviewer. *American Journal of Sociology,* 1956, **62,** 210–212.

Ried, P. E. (Ed.) *The frontiers in experimental speech-communication research.* Syracuse, N.Y.: Syracuse University Press, 1966.

Robinson, W. S. The logical structure of analytic induction. *American Sociological Review,* 1951, **16,** 812–818.

Rokeach, M. Attitude change and behavioral change. *Public Opinion Quarterly,* 1966, **30,** 529–550.

Rosenthal, R. On the social psychology of the psychological experiment. *The American Scientist,* 1963, **51,** 268–283.

Rosenthal, R. The volunteer subject. *Human Relations,* 1965, **18,** 389–406.

Rubenstein, A. H., and Haberstroh, C. J. Field study techniques. In A. H. Rubenstein and C. J. Haberstroh (Eds.), *Some theories of organization.* (Rev. ed.) Homewood, Ill.: Irwin and Dorsey, 1966. Pp. 685–711.

Sanborn, G. A. An analytical study of oral communication practices in a nationwide sales organization. Unpublished doctoral dissertation, Purdue University, 1961.

Scott, W. R. Field methods in the study of organizations. In J. G. March (Ed.), *Handbook of organizations.* Chicago: Rand McNally, 1965. Pp. 261–304.

Seashore, S. E. Field experiments with formal organizations. *Human Organization,* 1964, **23,** 164–170.

Selltiz, C., Jahoda, M., Deutsch, M., and Cook, S. W. *Research methods in social relations.* (Rev. ed.) New York: Holt, 1959.

Sherif, C., Sherif, M., and Nebergall, R. E. *Attitude and attitude change: The social judgment-involvement approach.* Philadelphia: W. B. Saunders, 1965.

Sidman, M. *Tactics of scientific research.* New York: Basic Books, 1960.

Simons, H. W. A comparison of communication attributes and rated job performance of supervisors in a large commercial enterprise. Unpublished doctoral dissertation, Purdue University, 1961.

Sjoberg, G. (Ed.) *Ethics, politics, and social research.* Cambridge, Mass.: Schenkman, 1967.

Skinner, B. F. Are theories of learning necessary? *Psychological Review,* 1950, **57,** 193–216.

Smith, R. L. Communication correlates of interpersonal sensitivity among industrial supervisors. Unpublished doctoral dissertation, Purdue University, 1967.

Summary report: Conference on Social Engagement. Sponsored by the Speech Association of America, Chicago, August 1968. New York: Speech Association of America, 1968.

Sutton, H., and Porter, L. W. A study of the grapevine in a governmental organization. *Personnel Psychology,* 1968, **21,** 223–230.

Thayer, L. On theory-building in communication: IV. Some observations and speculations. Unpublished presidential address delivered at the annual convention of the National Society for the Study of Communication, New York, April 1968.

Thompson, W. N. An assessment of quantitative research in speech. *Quarterly Journal of Speech,* 1969, **60,** 61–68.

Tompkins, P. K. An analysis of communication between headquarters and selected units of a national labor union. Unpublished doctoral dissertation, Purdue University, 1962.

Tompkins, P. K. The McCroskey-Dunham and Holtzman reports on "Ethos: A confounding element in communication research." *Speech Monographs,* 1967, **34,** 176–178.

Tompkins, P. K. Future research strategies in communication. Paper presented at the annual convention of the Central States Speech Association, Chicago, April 1968.

Tooley, J., and Pratt, S. Who will watch the brain watchers? *Behavioral Science,* 1964, **9,** 3 (letter to the Editor).

Turner, Ralph H. The quest for universals in sociological research. *American Sociological Review,* 1953, **18,** 604–611.

Turner, Roy. The ethnography of experiment. *The American Behavioral Scientist,* 1967, **10,** 26–29.

Verplanck, W. The control of the content of conversation: Reinforcement of statements of opinion. *Journal of Abnormal and Social Psychology,* 1955, **51,** 668–676.

Vidich, A. Participant observation and the collection and interpretation of data. *American Journal of Sociology,* 1955, **60,** 354–360.

Vidich, A., and Bensman, J. The validity of field data. *Human Organization,* 1954, **13,** 20–27.

Vidich, A., and Shapiro, G. A comparison of participant observation and survey data. *American Sociological Review,* 1955, **20,** 28–33.

Vroom, V. H. (Ed.) *Methods of organizational research.* Pittsburgh: University of Pittsburgh Press, 1967.

Wax, R. H. Reciprocity in field work. In R. N. Adams and J. J. Preiss (Eds.), *Human organization research.* Homewood, Ill.: Dorsey, 1960. Pp. 90–98. (Modified from Reciprocity as a field technique, *Human Organization,* 1952, **11,** 34–41.)

Webb, E. J., Campbell, D. T., Schwartz, R. D., and Sechrest, L. *Unobtrusive measures: Nonreactive research in the social sciences.* Chicago: Rand McNally, 1966.

Weick, K. E. Laboratory experimentation with organizations. In J. G. March (Ed.), *Handbook of organizations.* Chicago: Rand McNally, 1965. Pp. 194–260.

Weick, K. E. Organizations in the laboratory. In V. H. Vroom (Ed.), *Methods of organizational research.* Pittsburgh: University of Pittsburgh Press, 1967. Pp. 1–56.

Westley, B. H. Scientific method and communication research. In R. O. Nafziger and D. M. White (Eds.), *Introduction to mass communications research.* Baton Rouge: Louisiana State University Press, 1958. Pp. 201–239.

Whyte, W. F. *Man and organization.* Homewood, Ill.: Irwin, 1959.

Whyte, W. F. Interviewing in field research. In R. N. Adams and J. J. Preiss (Eds.), *Human organization research.* Homewood, Ill.: Dorsey, 1960. Pp. 352–374.

Williams, F., and Sundene, B. A field study in effects of a public relations speech. *Journal of Communication,* 1965, **15,** 161–170.

Zajonc, R. B., and Wolfe, D. M. Cognitive consequences of a person's position in a formal organization. *Human Relations,* 1966, **19,** 139–150.

Zelditch, M., Jr. Some methodological problems of field studies. *American Journal of Sociology,* 1962, **67,** 566–576.

Zigler, E. Metatheoretical issues in developmental psychology. In M. Marx (Ed.), *Theories in contemporary psychology.* New York: Macmillan, 1963. Pp. 341–369.

Zima, J. P. The conseling-communication of supervisors in a large manufacturing company. Unpublished doctoral dissertation, Purdue University, 1968.

Part Two

RESEARCH METHODS AND INSTRUMENTS

Complementarity in Measurement

PHILIP EMMERT

The problem a quantitative researcher faces in the behavioral sciences bears a striking resemblance to the problem a doctor faces during the treatment of a patient. Both the doctor and the behavioral scientist must accurately describe the phenomenon under investigation, be it an illness or some facet of the communication process.

Consider the doctor faced with a patient who complains of a pain in his chest. He may do a number of things, depending on what he knows of the patient's medical history: (1) he may ask the patient to describe the pain verbally; (2) he may ask the patient to point to the location of the pain; (3) he may listen to the area in question with a stethoscope; (4) he may check the patient's blood pressure; (5) he may record the patient's height and weight; (6) he may x-ray the patient; (7) he may test a sample of the patient's blood; (8) he may take an electrocardiographic reading. The doctor then synthesizes these varied measures into a statement about the patient's condition, the cause of his pain, and the treatment required. But if he bases his diagnosis only on the electrocardiographic reading or only on the recorded height and weight, the patient will probably think the doctor has not obtained enough information for an accurate picture of his physical state.

Unfortunately, in communication science many generalizations have been made on the basis of just such severely limited information. Consider attitude change. Studies have been conducted in which the one measure of self-esteem is the extent to which a subject says he is like his ideal (Cohen, 1959); studies have determined attitude change by only one measuring instrument (Anderson, 1959). Because of pragmatic considerations or an awareness of the inadequacy of certain instruments, the experimenter chooses a single measure which he thinks will best describe the attitudes of subjects before, immediately after, and possibly several weeks after treatment. He analyzes his measurements and then diagnoses and prescribes. He assumes that he can describe attitudes with a single instrument accurately and completely enough to describe attitude change.

But a number of scholars working on attitude change have been quick to observe that a single instrument does not truly measure all the dimensions of an attitude. In developing new methods of measuring attitudes to improve or replace existing inadequate measurement techniques, they have discovered that though it is possible to make certain inferences about the state of a person's mind or about his behavior at any one time on the information derived from a single instrument, the single technique which will do the whole job has yet to be found; it is necessary to use a number of instruments for a complete picture of the phenomenon under observation. Just as a doctor describes a person's physical condition with more than one measurement, the behavioral scientist must describe a person's behavior with more than one instrument.

To see this problem in another light, let us consider the nature of some measuring techniques. If we were to conduct a study of racial attitudes, we could approach the problem of measurement with any of a number of instruments.

(1) We could construct some Likert scales (Chapter 7) and ask subjects to respond on these attitudes. Through this technique we could plot a point on an evaluative continuum which would represent an individual's attitude.

(2) We could ask our subjects to write essays about different races and then subject them to content analysis to determine the differences in affective words included in the essays for each race (Chapter 10).

(3) We could ask each subject to respond to bipolar adjectives describing each race under study, using the technique of semantic differentiation (Chapter 6).

(4) We could ask our subjects to arrange evaluative statements about race in piles representing how much or little the subject thinks each statement applies to the race. This would be *Q*-sort technique (Chapter 5).

(5) We could measure palmar perspiration, heartbeat, or respiration rate as we expose subjects to pictures of people of different races, expecting some correspondence between these physical phenomena and the affective state of the subject (Chapter 14).

The point is that each of these approaches could be used to measure racial attitudes. Not only would each of them produce a measure that could be interpreted as a measure of attitude, each would also measure *something different*. Any one of these methods provides the experimenter not only with a magnifying glass to examine attitudes, but also with blinders to exclude information. Thus, a subject will be perfectly aware that he is telling us his attitude when he marks a Likert scale; however, he may not be aware of what he is telling us when he writes an essay that is later subjected to content analysis. The subject tells us different things under each condition by including and excluding different information. Thus, I can measure my daughter's height with a yardstick; but if I choose to use only her height to describe her size, I exclude information about her weight. The problem of measurement, then, is not just selecting *an* instrument to measure a phenomenon, but rather selecting instruments that can measure different aspects of the phenomenon.

This multimethod approach is similar to the concept of complementarity developed by the physicist David Bohm (1957). Observing the atom presented no small problem to physicists because the very acts of measurement, observation, etc., changed it. Bohm suggested the desirability of the partial description of the atom by scientists in various fields, a combined effort to achieve a more complete picture. He called this process of combining diverse descriptions of a phenomenon "complementarity."

Cornwell (1967), applying this concept to the study of the speech process, suggested that a phenomenon as complex as speech could not be understood by any one conceptual tool or discipline; that, indeed, the complexity itself required the combined approaches of such areas as history, sociology, political science, psychology, rhetoric, etc. This combination of approaches, he felt, would produce a more comprehensive view of what occurs when man speaks to man.

Without combining approaches, the experimenter who studies attitudes using *Q*-sort technique may well have an understanding of the subjects' attitudes, but his understanding will come to him through *Q*-colored glasses. The problem likewise affects the researcher who uses the semantic differential, Likert-type scales, or any other single method of measurement. In all cases the experimenters are able to see only that part of the phenomenon under investigation which their chosen measurement instruments will permit them to see. Furthermore, what they see is necessarily refracted according to the characteristics of the measurement method, just as light is refracted by the lenses in a pair of glasses. So, just as it has been possible to show the existence of an "experimenter effect" (Rosenthal, 1966; Friedman, 1967), it is also possible to talk of a "methodology effect" or an "instrument effect" — that bias or distortion of observations in an experiment resulting from the kind of measurement methods or instruments used.

Because of the difficulties which can result from the "methodology effect," complementarity in measurement is a desirable goal for behavioral scientists. Since each measurement method has its own bias and distortions, a variety of instruments may mean a more complete picture of the object of investigation. In the hypothetical example of the study of racial attitudes, for example, the problem is not choosing *an* instrument to measure attitudes, but rather being informed enough to know what instruments in *combination* will produce the best description of attitudes.

It is hoped that this book will help to free communication researchers from depending on one or two measuring instruments and/or experimental designs. If this happens, we should be closer to the goal of complementarity in experimental research.

References and Selected Readings

Anderson, N. H. Test of a model for opinion change. *Journal of Abnormal and Social Psychology*, 1959, **59**, 371–381.

Bohm, D. *Causality and chance in modern physics*. London: Routledge & Kegan Paul, 1957.

Cohen, A. R. Some implications of self-esteem for social influence. In C. Hovland (Ed.), *Personality and persuasibility*. New Haven: Yale University Press, 1959. Pp. 102–120.

Cornwell, C. Complementarity in rhetorical studies. Paper presented at the meeting of the Central States Speech Association, Indianapolis, 1967.

Friedman, N. *The social nature of psychological research: The psychological experiment as a social interaction.* New York: Basic Books, 1967.

Rosenthal, R. *Experimenter effects in behavioral research.* New York: Appleton-Century-Crofts, 1966.

5

Q-Sort Technique

William D. Brooks

Q-sort technique was developed independently by William Stephenson (1935) and Sir G. H. Thomson (1935). However, the first comprehensive analysis of the methodology was not published until 1953 by Stephenson, and the majority of Q-sort studies have been conducted since that time. Q methodology as initially advocated by Stephenson stemmed from a form of factor analysis (R technique) on test responses of a large random sample of subjects in order to discover groups of tests which correlated highly and thus seemed to be measuring the same factor. However, Stephenson (1953) suggested that instead of correlating test responses, an investigator could correlate persons, *i.e.,* he could correlate the test results of two or more selected subjects. The method traditionally used to gather the data for correlating persons is called "Q-sort technique." The prefixing letter Q has no particular significance; it simply came to be used to identify these procedures by historical accident (Block, 1961, p. 11).

The two terms "Q-sort technique" and "Q methodology" are sometimes confused. Although they are related and are often used in concert, they are not identical. They will be carefully differentiated in this chapter in the same way Stephenson (1965, p. 134) distinguishes them. The term *Q methodology* has been used to refer to Q correlation, responses by card sorting, a specialized use of questionnaire items, forced responses so that data falls into a preestablished distribution, and factor analysis of Q correlations. *Q-sort technique* has consistently referred to a specific method of eliciting responses, namely card sorting. It is a sophisticated form of ordering statements, adjectives, or objects by rank. This chapter, of course, is primarily concerned with Q-sort technique.

The Q-sort procedure involves the selection of a set of objects — verbal statements, single words, phrases, pictures — related to the concept to be studied. When the objects are statements, phrases, or adjectives, they are placed on cards (one to a card), the cards are shuffled, and the subject is instructed to sort the cards into a set of piles (usually from seven to eleven) according to the extent of his agreement with the statements. The purpose of the sorting is to get a conceptual representation of the sorter's attitude toward the subject being considered — "what is in his head." By varying the instructions, Q-sort technique can be used in a number of ways. The experimenter can instruct the subject to describe himself as he was, as he is, as he would like to be, as perceived by his family, friends, superiors, subordinates; he may ask the sorter to apply the statements to another person — a political candidate, for example; finally, the statements may be sorted by judges, therapists, teachers, or experimenters to describe the attitudes, personality, or behavior of patients, contestants, students, or other classes of subjects.

Although the Q sort as envisioned by Stephenson was intended to serve as a tool within the broader framework of his Q methodology, it has proved compatible with numerous research problems in the behavioral sciences. What makes the Q sort most advantageous in behavioral description is that the individual provides his own frame of reference. The Q sort is an objective, organized method for studying many aspects of man's internal and external behavior. Examples of studies which have used Q-sort technique are Block (1952, 1954, 1955, 1956); Rogers and Dymond (1954); Hilden (1958); Goldberg (1962); Cassel (1965).

Rogers and Dymond wanted to discover the relationship between an individual's image of himself as he is and his ideal image, between his real image and his image of the ordinary person, and between his ideal image and his other person image. In addition, they wanted to know how these relationships changed as the result of psychotherapy. Each subject in the study was given a set of 100 cards, each printed with a personal characteristic statement such as:

> I am a hard worker.
> I really am disturbed.
> I am likable.
> I am a submissive person.
> I am easily angered.
> I tend to hurt people's feelings.

I like to work with others.
I am physically attractive.

Each subject was instructed to sort the cards to describe *himself as he was,* placing the statements least descriptive of himself at one extreme and those most descriptive of himself at the other extreme. The subjects were required to put the cards into nine piles with a specified number of cards in each pile. Then each subject was told to sort the cards a second time to describe his *ideal self* and a third time to describe the *ordinary person.* The subjects then entered psychotherapy and after a period of treatment again carried out the three sorts. Rogers and Dymond investigated the correspondence between self-image and ideal image, self-image and ordinary person image, and ideal image and ordinary person image before and after therapy. They tested the differences between the means of the correlations and also summarized the data into a single score for each subject which they called an "adjustment" score.

Although the Rogers and Dymond study is typical of many using *Q*-sort technique in that it is concerned with self-image and other person images, the technique is easily adaptable to communication research, including attitude studies. Subjects might be asked to sort sets of statements about foreign policy, labor-management relations, or presidential candidates according to the extent of their agreement or disagreement with each statement.

SPECIAL PROBLEMS IN USING Q-SORT TECHNIQUE

Any experimenter using *Q*-sort technique has to resolve at least three special problems: item selection, forced or unforced choice in sorting, and analysis of the data.

Item Selection

The first step in preparing a *Q* sort is to collect a set of statements dealing with the topic to be studied. No stipulated number of statements must be selected for the *Q* set, but for statistical stability and reliability, the number should probably be neither less than 50 nor more than 100. The items or statements may be obtained in various ways, depending on the topic: they may be developed so as to conform to a particular theory of behavior, personality, leadership, persuasibility, and the like: or they may be selected at random from a carefully defined population of items. Such a population of items might be all statements used in written, open-ended self-descriptions; words used in personality inventories; statements occurring in conversations; statements occurring in speeches given by beginning speech students; statements in newspapers, plays, books, or interviews with the subjects.

Types of Q Sets

UNSTRUCTURED Q SET

When a population of statements has been carefully defined and the statements comprising it gathered, the experimenter can draw random statements from it to make up the Q set. Such a set of items is called an *unstructured Q* set because the items have been selected without regard to the factors involved in the theory. The only criterion for selecting the items is that they apply to one broad variable. Most Q studies have used unstructured Q sets (Wittenborn, 1961).

Rogers and Dymond (1954) developed their Q set from reading therapy protocols and from a list of statements clients made about themselves. Block (1961, pp. 52–57), in constructing his California Q set for the assessment of personality, selected 90 personality variables viewed by his contemporary clinicians as representing a comprehensive coverage of the personality domain, and then wrote a theoretically based statement for each. He then spent some 60 hours discussing with experts the clarity, importance, and relevancy of each item; finally, he deleted, revised, or added items as the consensus of the experts dictated. Knapp (1963, pp. 43 and 44), in a study of adult education students' attitudes, selected statements for the Q sort he devised from the findings of previous studies, personal experience reports of experts, and from hypotheses formed from a knowledge of the subject to be studied.

STRUCTURED Q SET

When items are created to correspond to a particular theory or set of hypotheses, they are collectively known as a *structured Q* set. This method of building Q sets is especially advantageous to the testing of theory. Since the instrument is constructed to embody the theory, the sorting of the items by known types of individuals can *test the hypotheses* generated by the theory. The use of Q sorting to build and test theory is an important suggestion of Stephenson (1953, pp. 65–85) that probably should not be ignored. By deriving Q-sort statements from some theoretical framework, one can build theory into the research tool and better test theory in operational terms. This task can be accomplished by selecting the theoretical variables to be included and developing a certain number of Q-sort statements for each variable (Stephenson, 1953, 1967). Olson and Gravatt (1968, p. 15) wrote three positive and three negative items for each category or cell. This particular approach for building a structured Q set has been used by Kerlinger (1956), Rawn (1958), Hess and Hink (1959), and Olson (1967). Olson and Gravatt (1968, pp. 14–15) have argued that the structured Q set is superior to the unstructured Q set because the statements used in unstructured Q sets are generally selected without much concern for how they represent the population being studied or how relevant they are theoretically; research studies using unstructured Q sets are of less value because they have no theoretical base, and theories continue to remain untested.

When creating or selecting Q-sort statements, it is important to keep in mind that the statements must really represent the concept for which they are written. If one is testing a particular theory, the statements should be selected with that theory clearly in mind. Goldberg (1962, p. 255) has suggested that if the concept one is studying has three or four identifiable subareas, then there should be an equal number of statements for each area; if a single category concept is being studied, then there should be an equal number of positive and negative statements related to the concept. Sherif and Hovland (1953, p. 135) have suggested that statements of three kinds should be used in Q sets: very pro statements, very con statements, and ambiguous or neutral statements. Cronbach (1953) advises:

> So far as present research indicates, almost any set of statements can be the basis for investigation of correlations between persons. . . . Until we penetrate the problem more deeply, I can suggest these criteria. First, statements, while logically bearing on the same domain, should represent a large number of continua. . . . Second, statements being compared should have about the same average degree of desirability over the entire population. . . . Third, each statement should have substantial variance, in that different persons put it in different places [p. 380].

Although items may be carefully formulated, some usually seem irrelevant to some sorters. In his review of Cassel's *Leadership Q-Sort Test,* Stephenson (1965) says: "It is always the case, in a well constructed Q-sample, that the individual will find that most of the statements don't matter to him [p. 135]." The characteristic of the sorter selecting items that are relevant for him and ignoring items that are irrelevant for him is a strength of the Q-sort technique because the subject is permitted to respond with "his" items and categories rather than the experimenter's.

After the statements for the Q set have been selected and printed on cards, and each card has been numbered for ease of recording the data, the experimenter asks the next question: should he use a forced or unforced sort?

Types of Sorts

FORCED SORT

A forced sort procedure requires the subject to place a predetermined number of cards in each pile; the experimenter thus specifies the shape and scatter of the distribution curve.

Here is a forced *Q*-sort distribution of 90 items:

Most like me								Least like me		
3	4	7	10	13	16	13	10	7	4	3

This is a rank order continuum from "Most like me" to "Least like me" with varying degrees between the extremes. The center pile with 16 cards is neutral. The statements in this pile may be ambiguous to the sorter or may be left over after he made other choices. The three statements or items in the pile at the extreme left are the statements the sorter believes to be most like himself, while the three statements or items in the pile at the extreme right are the statements the sorter believes to be least like himself. Some sample distributions that have been used in forced sorts are 5-8-12-16-18-16-12-8-5 for a nine-category, 100-item sort (Block, 1961); 2-5-7-10-12-12-10-7-5-2 for a ten-category, 72-item sort (Knapp, 1963); and a 2-4-11-21-26-21-11-4-2 for a nine-category, 102-item sort (Goldberg, 1962). The following *Q*-sort distributions are recommended because they conform to the suggested platykurtic (less concentrated around the mean than normal) distribution and have enough categories to be reasonably sensitive to subtle differences among subjects.

$n = 60$

	2	3	6	11	16	11	6	3	2	
2	3	4	7	9	10	9	7	4	3	2

$n = 70$

2	3	5	8	11	12	11	8	5	3	2
	4	6	9	10	12	10	9	6	4	

$n = 80$

2	4	6	9	12	14	12	9	6	4	2
	4	6	10	12	16	12	10	6	4	

$n = 90$

3	5	8	10	12	14	12	10	8	5	3
	4	8	10	16	18	16	10	8	4	

The number of cards in each pile is not important as long as there are more cards in the center piles than in the end piles so that the distribution approaches a normal curve.

UNFORCED SORT

The unforced sort method allows the subject to place each item in the pile in which he judges it to belong regardless of the number of items already in that pile. The number of piles is specified as in the forced choice, but since the sorter is free to make a spontaneous arrangement of items, the final distribution may have any shape and scatter.

Some arguments for and against both points of view are given as follows.[1] If a free choice is allowed, one subject may evaluate more items as extremely characteristic or extremely uncharacteristic than a second subject. This means that the researcher cannot control the shape or scatter of the distributions, *i.e.*, one distribution may be a normal curve, one may be positively skewed, or one may be negatively skewed. Some experimenters view this lack of control over the shape and scatter of the distribution as a serious problem. Block (1961, p. 72) has pointed out that some persons may simply be less assertive about their perceptions and thus place fewer items in the extreme positions, while others may place more items in the extreme positions and thus tend to dominate the consensus (average) judgment through the disproportionate weighting caused by the larger variance of their responses. On the other hand, Cronbach (1953, p. 378) believes that the scatter and distribution of items are sources of important information and that this information may be lost by using a forced sort procedure. Sherif and Hovland (1953) explained what kind of information is revealed by the shape and scatter of the distribution when they stated:

> The placement of items is affected by the attitudes of the judges. Using the typical Thurstone-type of attitude scaling (method of equal-appearing intervals), in which a specified number of categories is fixed by the experimenters and the scale values are determined by the frequencies with which the items are placed in each category, characteristic displacements of judgments, depending on the pro and con attitudes of the judges, were found. Neutral items particularly were displaced toward the extremes of the scale, the result being that items were piled up in certain of the prescribed categories to the detriment of others, with characteristic gaps in between. Various experimental checks indicated that this concentration of items by specified subjects was *not* due to carelessness, but to the *S*'s *personal involvement* in the issue [p. 135].

Cronbach and Gleser (1954) strongly emphasized the same point when they stated:

> This forcing is of dubious value. It does insure variance in the responses and eliminates response sets. However, it discards possibly important information about differences in scatter, and gives data to which analysis of variance cannot properly be applied [p. 328].

---

[1] Among those who have written in favor of the forced choice method are Stephenson (1953), Livson and Nichols (1956), Hilden (1958), and Block (1961). Among those opposing the forced choice sort are Mowrer (1953), Sherif and Hovland (1953), and Cronbach and G. C. Gleser (1954).

Block (1961) devised a study to test whether or not important information was lost through the forced sort procedure. He required judges to sort freely a set of items and then asked them to use a forced sort on the same items. He found that the information revealed by the shape of the distribution in the free choice sort was also available in the forced choice sort. When the subjects' unforced sorts were correlated with their forced sorts, the mean for the 55 correlations was found to be .94 and only two correlation coefficients were below .90. Block further stated:

> The instance described above is not an isolated finding. In almost all *Q*-sort circumstances the psychological meaning or reliable distribution differences — both subject-based and judge-based — is also available or could be made available from examination of *Q*-item content [p. 77].

Hess and Hink (1959) concluded that free and forced sorts do not give strikingly different results.

Some researchers have criticized the forced sort on statistical grounds: the forced sort violates the assumption of independence. The opportunity for a card to be placed in any pile is reduced each time another card is assigned to a pile, *i.e.,* the response to one item is affected by responses to other items. At least four rebuttals can be made to this criticism: (1) all forced choice procedures violate the assumption of independence, thus making *Q* sorting no different from other commonly used instruments in the behavioral sciences; (2) when a *Q* sort is properly administered, subjects understand that they are free to take any item from the pile into which it has been sorted and place it in any other pile; (3) the violation is so minute that "it is doubtful that too much is risked in *Q*-statistical situations, if there is a fairly large number of items [Kerlinger, 1966, p. 594]"; (4) the requirement for statistical significance in *Q* sorts may be raised from the .05 level to the .01 level.

Another criticism of the forced sort procedure is that it constrains the subjects and they do not like to do the sorting. However, it has been the experience of the author that most individuals enjoy the *Q*-sorting procedure. Kerlinger (1966, p. 595) has observed the same response and also has related an incident showing that even for the few who feel constrained and question the procedure, test-retest sorts correlate highly: one of Kerlinger's colleagues questioned the procedure and indicated that if he had to do it over again the results would be different. Eleven months later he did the sort again and the coefficient of correlation between the two sorts was .81. A similar experience occurred in another study (Brooks and Platz, 1968); four speech professors were sure they would not sort the items in the same way a second time, but when they sorted the items a second time, the test-retest correlation coefficients ranged from .77 to .84.

Among those who have raised arguments against the free choice sorting procedure is Block (1961). He summarized his reasons for opposing the free choice method as follows:

(1) The unforced *Q*-sorting procedure obscures recognition of the correspondences existing among evaluations of personality where the forced *Q*-sorting procedure permits a clear assessment of degree of equivalence. . . .

(2) The unforced *Q*-sorting procedure tends to provide fewer discriminations than the forced *Q*-sorting procedure and consequently, is more susceptible to the Barnum effect, the tendency to say very generally true things about an individual. . . .

(3) The unforced *Q*-sorting procedure is not more reliable than is the forced *Q*-sorting procedure. . . .

(4) The unforced *Q*-sorting procedure does not appear to provide information not also, and more easily, assessible through the forced *Q*-sorting procedure.

(5) The unforced *Q*-sorting procedure provides data which is unwieldy and at times impossible to work with where the forced *Q*-sorting procedure provides data in a convenient and readily processed form [p. 78].

Similarly, Livson and Nichols (1956) made a strong plea for the forced choice sort: "Recent evidence is cited supporting the conclusion that, in most *Q*-sort applications, a prescribed forced distribution should be used [p. 165]."

A majority of the studies using *Q*-sort technique have used the forced sort procedure. However, the individual experimenter must decide for himself which procedure he can best justify for his particular study.

Analyzing Q-Sort Data

A third major question to be considered by an experimenter using *Q*-sort technique concerns the type of analysis he should perform on the data. The various possibilities fall into two general classifications, analysis of item-by-item comparisons and analysis of the similarity between or among entire *Q* sorts.

COMPARING ENTIRE Q SORTS

Q sorts have generally been analyzed in terms of their correlations or similarities. One way to do this is to test the correspondence of *Q* sorts with a criterion *Q* sort (conceptual sort or defining sort). Brooks and Platz (1968), in studying concept of self as a communicator, used a criterion sort acquired by having several expert communicators sort the *Q* items. Cassel (1965) used a similar procedure to develop a criterion sort for his Leadership *Q*-Sort Test. For certain research questions, an experimenter may want to discover whether subjects in one group correlate more highly with a criterion sort than subjects in a second group. Thus, the experimenter may not necessarily be interested in a comparison of item-by-item placement, but in an overall comparison of Q sorts. The majority of Q studies of this nature have used product-moment correlations. For determining the relationship between the two Q sorts, the following formula may be used:

$$r = 1 - \frac{d^2ip}{2N\sigma_{D^2}}$$

where (d^2ip) is the squared difference between the Q values (the values assigned to the piles) of corresponding statements, (N) is the number of statements, and (σ_{D^2}) is the standard deviation of the Q set (Block, 1961, p. 101).

Cronbach and Gleser (1953) have criticized the use of r as a test for correlation and have proposed an alternative, the D test, for use on Q-sort data:

$$D = \sqrt{\Sigma_j d^2}$$

in which (j) is any of the variates (items) — a, b, c, and so on — and (d) is the difference between scores on a given statement or item. However, Block (1961, p. 101) has shown that when the data result from a forced choice sort, r may be properly used. It is when an unforced choice sort is used that the D test may be necessary.

If one wishes to know whether two rs are significantly different, one must convert the rs into standard scores and determine the significance of the difference by a t test. It should be stressed that it is important to treat the rs as scores rather than as correlation coefficients when using a t test to determine the significance of the difference between the rs.

A second approach to analyzing Q sorts in a global way is factor analysis.[2] It is often to the experimenter's advantage, especially in exploratory studies, to group subjects on the basis of their Q sorts and then to analyze the independent sources of information in order to determine the correlations of group membership. Factor analysis enables one to reduce the number of variables to those few which appear to be most responsible or most active in the process he is studying. Once the factors are discovered through factor analysis, the difference between factor based groups may be evaluated parametrically, when the assumptions are met, by the t test or the F test. If the distributions of the Q values of the two groups being compared are reasonably symmetrical and have variances that are not too divergent, then the t test may be used to test the significance of the difference between means of two groups or the F test for three or more groups. Non-

---

[2] Examples of studies using this approach include Block (1952), Beck (1954), Monro (1955), Guertin and Jenkins (1956), and Apfelbaum (1958).

parametric methods are necessary when the assumption of normality cannot be made, *i.e.,* when the scores the statistics are based on do not appear to be normally distributed, and when the two sets of scores have grossly unequal variances. In such situations, the Mann and Whitney (1952) test may be used when comparing two groups, and the Kruskal and Wallis (1952) test may be used for three or more group comparisons.[3] If one is concerned with the relative frequency of factor based groups, the Chi-square test may be used.

ITEM ANALYSIS

The second general type of analysis that may be used with *Q*-sort data is item-by-item placement comparisons. One may make such comparisons in at least two ways. Item placements in one *Q* sort may be compared with item placements in a second *Q* sort, or item placements for one group can be compared with item placements for a second group.

The first type of analysis might be performed on two judges' *Q* sorts of the same speaker, or two experts' *Q* sorts of the theoretical ideal speaker. In the first example, ratings could be compared and more uniform evaluation standards might emerge. In the second example, areas of agreement and disagreement could be discovered so that more accurate theoretical concepts could be formulated.

Block (1961, pp. 91–93) has suggested that an informal method of determining whether the difference between the placements of an item in two sorts is significant is to note the items in the two sorts differing by three or more intervals. One may also determine statistically whether or not an item placement difference is significant.

The second type of item placement analysis is comparing the item placements of one group of individuals with the item placements of a second group of individuals. One could, for example, compare the item placements of a *Q* set for a group of debaters with the item placements of the same *Q* set for a group of nondebaters, or of speech majors with nonspeech majors.

The procedure for analyzing the item placement would be to select the item, sum the scale values of the item for all the individuals in one group, and determine its mean value. The same thing would be done on that item for the second group and the difference between the means would be tested for significance by parametric or nonparametric tests as required by the nature of the data. For example, one could select Item 7 in a 100-item sort and find which of the nine piles it had been placed in by Sorter 1. If Item 7 was placed in the pile having a value of 3 (values having been assigned from 0 to 8 for the nine piles or categories), the 3 value is recorded. The placement of Item 7 by Subject 2 is discovered and that value recorded. This continues for each subject in Group A until all the

---

[3] These tests may also be found in Walker and Lev (1953).

values for Item 7 are recorded. These values are then summed and the mean value for Item 7 for Group A is determined. The same procedure is performed for Group B and the mean value for Item 7 for Group B is determined. The difference between the two means for the item can then be tested for the degree of significance.

Q-SORT RELIABILITY AND VALIDITY

Reliability is traditionally demonstrated by a high correlation between results obtained on two or more performances with an instrument. However, the very nature of Q sorts makes difficult the determination of reliability through such usual approaches as split halves, alternate forms, or matched items. In a self-sort (statements are arranged according to how they describe the sorter) or an ideal sort (statements are arranged according to how they describe what the sorter would like to be) the researcher has no prior knowledge of the sorter's conception of himself or of his ideal and so items cannot be matched or groups of statements split into halves of equal significance. However, other methods of determining the reliability of Q sets have been used.

Hilden (1958) approached the problem of determining the reliability of his Q set from sampling theory. He suggested that a universe of statements could be established in some systematic way and then sets of statements (several Q sets) could be randomly drawn from the universe of statements. Random sampling theory suggests that these sets should be alike, and thus one could compare two of these equal sets, when sorted as two sorts by the same individual, in order to test for reliability. Hilden's study revealed a high reliability for his Q sets ($r = .94$).

Block (1956) has approached the problem of determining the reliability of Q sets in a different way. He has suggested the technique of gathering multiple but independent observer evaluations and correlating the consensus score of one set of observers with the consensus score of an equivalent second set of observers.

Frank (1956) used the test-retest method and found the reliability of the Q sorts to be quite high, with correlation coefficients ranging from .93 to .97. Hess and Hink (1959), using the test-retest method, have reported reliabilities as high as .95 and .99. Olson and Gravatt (1968) tested the reliability of their forced choice Q set by having 44 college students complete the same Q sort twice with approximately two weeks intervening between the two administrations. Test-retest reliabilities ranged from .59 to .93 with an average correlation of .80.

Although the validity of Q sorts has not been extensively and systematically investigated, several researchers have defended it.[4] Block (1961) has argued that the Q sort he devised has an "intrinsic" or "face validity

---

[4] See Mowrer (1953, p. 354), Sherif and Hovland (1953, p. 141), and Block (1961, p. 29).

[p. 29]": the empirical relationships that emerged were coherent with the theoretical framework that prompted the search. His *Q* set had a kind of reciprocal validation. From the outset, the validity of a *Q* set rests on a "reasonable" relevance of the operations to the construct under investigation.

Summary

Q-sort technique is a method of eliciting responses by having the subject sort a series of items that relate to a given concept into a prescribed number of piles along a descriptive continuum. The method has received support from several research areas because of its alleged objective measurement of internal behavior. Its use in research conducted in the areas of personality, psychiatry, and education, as well as its increasing use in other areas of study, suggests its applicability to communication research.

References and Selected Readings

Apfelbaum, B. *Dimensions of transference in psychotherapy.* Berkeley: University of California Press, 1958.

Beck, S. J. The six schizophrenias. *Research Monographs of the American Orthopsychiatric Association,* 1954, No. 6.

Block, J. A. The assessment of communication: II. Role variations as a function of interactional context. *Journal of Personality,* 1952, **21,** 272–286.

Block, J. A. A differential approach to the officer selection problem. *IPAR Research Report,* 1954.

Block, J. A. The difference between *Q* and *R. Psychological Review,* 1955, **62,** 356–358.

Block, J. A. Comparison of the forced and unforced *Q*-sorting procedures. *Educational and Psychological Measurement,* 1956, **16,** 481–493.

Block, J. A. *The Q-sort method in personality assessment and psychiatric research.* Springfield, Ill.: Charles C Thomas, 1961.

Block, J. A., and Bailey, D. E. *Q*-sort item analyses of a number of MMPI measures of personality, interest, and intellect. *IPAR Research Report,* 1954.

Block, J. A., and Gough, H. G. An application of the *Q*-sort technique to the California Psychological Inventory. *Technical Memorandum,* No. OERL TM-55-8. Maxwell Air Force Base, Ala.: Officer Educational Research Laboratory, May 1955.

Brooks, W. D., and Platz, S. M. The effects of speech training upon self-concept as a communicator. *The Speech Teacher,* 1968, **17,** 44–49.

Buros, O. K. (Ed.) *The sixth mental measurements yearbook.* Highland Park, N.J.: Gryphon Press, 1965.

Burt, C. Correlations between persons. *British Journal of Psychology,* 1937, **28,** 59–96.

Burt, C. *The factors of the mind.* London: London University Press, 1946.

Burt, C., and Stephenson, W. Alternative views on correlation between persons. *Psychometrika,* 1939, **4,** 269–281.

Cassel, R. N. Leadership *Q*-sort test. In O. K. Buros (Ed.), *The sixth mental measurements yearbook.* Highland Park, N.J.: Gryphon Press, 1965. Pp. 280–284.

Cattell, R. B. On the disuse and misuse of *P, Q,* and *O* techniques in clinical psychology. *Journal of Clinical Psychology,* 1951, **7,** 203–214.

Cohen, J. An aid in the computation of correlations based on *Q*-sorts. *Psychological Bulletin,* 1957, **54,** 138–139.

Cronbach, L. J. Correlations between persons as a research tool. In O. H. Mowrer (Ed.), *Psychotherapy theory and research.* New York: Ronald Press, 1953. Pp. 376–388.

Cronbach, L. J., and Gleser, G. C. Assessing similarity between profiles. *Psychological Bulletin,* 1953, **50,** 456–473.

Cronbach, L. J., and Gleser, G. C. Review of W. Stephenson, *The study of behavior. Psychometrika,* 1954, **19,** 327–331.

Dunnette, M. D., and Hoggatt, A. C. Deriving a composite score from several measures of the same attribute. *Educational and Psychological Measurement,* 1957, **17,** 423–434.

Frank, G. H. Note on the reliability of *Q*-sort data. *Psychological Reporter,* 1956, **2,** 182.

Gaito, J. Forced vs. free *Q*-sorts. *Psychological Reporter,* 1962, **10,** 251–254.

Gleser, J. An aid in calculating *Q*-sort factor arrays. *Journal of Clinical Psychology,* 1955, **11,** 195–196.

Goldberg, A. The *Q* sort in speech and hearing research. *Asha,* 1962, **4,** 255–257.

Goodling, R. A., and Guthrie, G. M. Some practical considerations in *Q*-sort item selection. *Journal of Consulting Psychology,* 1956, **3,** 70–72.

Guertin, W. H., and Jenkins, R. L. A transposed factor analysis of a group of schizophrenic patients. *Journal of Clinical Psychology,* 1956, **12,** 64–68.

Hess, R. D., and Hink, D. L. A comparison of forced vs. free *Q*-sort procedure. *Journal of Educational Research,* 1959, **53,** 83–90.

Hilden, A. H. *Q*-sort correlation: Stability and random choice of statements. *Journal of Consulting Psychology,* 1958, **22,** 45–50.

Jones, A. Distribution of traits in current *Q*-sort methodology. *Journal of Abnormal and Social Psychology,* 1956, **53,** 90–95.

Kerlinger, F. N. The attitude structure of the individual: A *Q* study of the educational attitudes of professors and laymen. *Genetic Psychology Monographs,* 1956, **53,** 283–329.

Kerlinger, F. N. *Foundations of behavioral research.* New York: Holt, Rinehart & Winston, 1966.

Knapp, M. An analysis of motivational factors of adults in university and college adult speech education courses in the greater Kansas City area, 1963. Unpublished Master's thesis, University of Kansas, 1963.

Kruskal, W. H., and Wallis, W. A. Use of ranks in one-criterion variance analysis. *Journal of the American Statistical Association,* 1952, **47,** 583–621.

Livson, N. H., and Nichols, T. F. Discrimination and reliability in *Q*-sort personality descriptions. *Journal of Abnormal and Social Psychology,* 1956, **52,** 159–165.

Mann, H. B., and Whitney, D. R. On a test of whether one of two random variables is stochastically larger than the other. *Annals of Mathematical Statistics,* 1952, **47,** 50–60.

Meehl, P. E. Wanted — A good cookbook. *The American Psychologist,* 1956, **11,** 263–272.

Monro, A. B. Psychiatric types: A *Q*-technique study of 200 patients. *Journal of Mental Science,* 1955, **101,** 330–343.

Morsh, J. E. The *Q*-sort technique as a group measure. *Educational and Psychological Measurement,* 1955, **15,** 390–395.

Mowrer, O. H. *Q* technique: Description, history, and critique. In O. H. Mowrer (Ed.), *Psychotherapy theory and research.* New York: Ronald Press, 1953. Pp. 316–375.

Nunnally, J. C., Jr. An investigation of some propositions of self-conception: The case of Miss Sun. *Journal of Abnormal and Social Psychology,* 1955, **50,** 87–92.

Olson, H. D. Student attitudes toward marriage. *College Student Survey,* 1967, **1,** 71–78.

Olson, H. D., and Gravatt, A. G. The *Q* sort as an attitudinal measure. *College Student Survey,* 1968, **2,** 13–22.

Rawn, M. L. An experimental study of transference and resistance phenomena in psychoanalytically oriented psychotherapy. *Journal of Clinical Psychology,* 1958, **14,** 418–425.

Rogers, C. R., and Dymond, R. F. (Eds.) *Psychotherapy and personality change.* Chicago: University of Chicago Press, 1954.

Ruesch, J., Block, J., and Bennett, L. The assessment of communication: I. A method for the analysis of social interaction. *Journal of Psychology,* 1953, **35,** 59–80.

Schill, W. J. Unforced and group response to a *Q* sort. *Journal of Experimental Education,* 1966, **34,** 19–20.

Schill, W. J. The use of the *Q* technique in determining curriculum content. *California Journal of Educational Research,* 1961, **12,** 174–184.

Sheldon, S. M., and Sorenson, G. A. On the use of *Q* technique in educational evaluation and research. *Journal of Experimental Education,* 1960, **29,** 143–152.

Sherif, M., and Hovland, C. I. Judgmental phenomena and scales of attitude measurement: Placement of items with individual choice of numbers and categories. *Journal of Abnormal and Social Psychology,* 1953, **48,** 135–141.

Stephenson, W. Correlating persons instead of tests. *Character and Personality,* 1935, **4,** 17–24.

Stephenson, W. Some observations on *Q* technique. *Psychological Bulletin,* 1952, **49,** 483–498.

Stephenson, W. *The study of behavior.* Chicago: University of Chicago Press, 1953.

Stephenson, W. Review of Cassel's leadership Q-sort test. In O. K. Buros (Ed.), *The sixth mental measurements yearbook.* Highland Park, N.J.: Gryphon Press, 1965. Pp. 133–135.

Stephenson, W. *The play theory of mass communication.* Chicago: University of Chicago Press, 1967.

Sundland, D. The construction of Q sorts: A criticism. *Psychological Review,* 1962, **69,** 62–64.

Thomson, Sir G. H. On complete families of correlation coefficients and their tendency to zero tetrad differences. *British Journal of Psychology,* 1935, **26,** 63–92.

Walker, H. M., and Lev, J. *Statistical inference.* New York: Henry Holt, 1953.

Wittenborn, J. R. Contributions and current status of Q methodology. *Psychological Bulletin,* 1961, **58,** 132–134.

6

Semantic Differentiation

DONALD K. DARNELL

The semantic differential is a technique of measuring meaning or attitudes dating from at least two articles in Volume 49 of the *Psychological Bulletin* (Osgood, 1952; Osgood and Suci, 1952). The first five years of the history of the SD is summarized in *The Measurement of Meaning* by C. E. Osgood, G. J. Suci, and P. H. Tannenbaum (1957). Hundreds of studies have used it for a variety of purposes ranging from predicting a political election to identifying changes in personality structure. The limits of its application seem to be determined only by the imagination of experimenters.

To speak of *the* semantic differential is misleading, for it is not an instrument like the *F* scale or MMPI. Semantic differentiation is a *procedure* that involves rather standard scaling practices and a variety of analytical methods. The critical attributes of *a* semantic differential seem to be bipolar adjectives on seven-interval scales like the following:

good ＿＿ : ＿＿ : ＿＿ : ＿＿ : ＿＿ : ＿＿ : ＿＿ bad

clean ＿＿ : ＿＿ : ＿＿ : ＿＿ : ＿＿ : ＿＿ : ＿＿ dirty

safe ＿＿ : ＿＿ : ＿＿ : ＿＿ : ＿＿ : ＿＿ : ＿＿ dangerous

tender ＿＿ : ＿＿ : ＿＿ : ＿＿ : ＿＿ : ＿＿ : ＿＿ tough

Subjects (*S*s) respond to concepts like ME, BOULDER, WAR, THE DEMOCRATIC PARTY, or EDUCATION by checking the scales to describe each concept. The concepts are selected, of course, according to the experimenter's interest. The scales may be specially constructed for a particular task or selected from existing sets by any of several criteria. Most commonly (and unfortunately), scales are selected to represent the major factors from previous general factor analyses. The appropriate method of analyzing SD data depends on the question the experimenter wants to answer or the hypothesis he desires to test.

Differences in the patterns of check marks on the scales are assumed to represent differences in meanings of the concepts judged and/or differences in groups of subjects judging the same concepts. Since the results of an SD study differentiate a set of concepts on the semantic dimensions represented by the scales used, the name "semantic differential" is appropriately descriptive.

THE BIRTH OF A TRADITION

The originators of the SD started out to find the dimensions of meaning. They presumed a *semantic space* in which concepts could be located and a finite number of independent dimensions serving to differentiate the positions of concepts within that space. With this orientation, Osgood *et al.* (1957) selected a set of 20 concepts (nouns) that were "as diversified in meaning as possible . . . and . . . familiar to the subjects . . . [p. 34]." They then constructed 50 scales from the adjectives used most frequently by *S*s in a word association test. The responses of 100 *S*s on the 50 scales to the 20 concepts were then submitted to factor analysis to determine the number of orthogonal (independent) dimensions represented by the set of scales.[1] The data from all concepts were pooled so that the responses of one *S* to 20 concepts were treated as equivalent to the responses of 20 *S*s to a single concept. Three factors which accounted for nearly half the total variance in scale markings[2] were identified: evaluation, potency, and activity.

---

[1] "Dimensions" here means "clusters" or "bundles" of scales that are related to each other but unrelated to other bundles. Factor analysis starts by computing the correlation between each scale and every other scale. From these correlations one determines by visual inspection or computation which scales form bundles and which bundles measure essentially different things. In judging a variety of solid objects, one might find, for example, that some scales measure height, some measure width, and some measure depth, but there is no relation among these dimensions across the set of objects.

[2] Ideally, if all the scales were perfectly reliable, all the variations in the judgments obtained would reflect real differences in the objects judged. A complete factor analysis of such data would then account for all the variance in the data. Actually, such perfect scales do not exist; if a scale is repeated in a measuring instrument, it will not correlate perfectly with itself. Some of the variance in judgments is simply error. Factor analyses are therefore terminated when the addition of a new factor will make a statistically insignificant reduction in the residual (error) variance. As in skimming cream from a pan of milk, one stops when he cannot see the difference between what he is taking off and what he is leaving behind.

Other similar analyses have tended to confirm these factors, and although other factors have been identified, they do not appear to be as powerful as these first three. Consequently, a tradition has developed that an SD should contain at least some scales from each of these three factors, although potency and activity scales are sometimes used merely to mask the evaluative intent of the questionnaire (Kerrick and McMillan, 1961).

Another study (Osgood *et al.*, 1957, p. 47) of historical importance obtained scales a different way: an extensive list of 289 pairs of adjectives was drawn from Roget's *Thesaurus* and then reduced to 76 pairs (the capacity of the available computer) by eliminating all but one of any set consistently judged by *S*s to mean the same. One hundred *S*s again judged 20 concepts (again selected to be different in meaning) on these 76 scales. This time an eight-factor solution was obtained, but the three strongest factors were similar to those obtained in the previous study, and the last five factors accounted for less of the total variance than the first factor alone. Many studies since these two have simply selected scales to represent the three factors, occasionally experimenting with a few additions (Semans, 1957; Nebergall, 1958; Rabin, 1959; Rosen, 1959; Springbett, 1960; Triandis, 1960a).

Darnell (1964) used the same 20 concepts as the first analysis, the 50 scales from the first analysis, and 25 additional scales from the thesaurus study. A principal axis factor analysis with varimax rotation was performed on these data. For the 50 scales taken from Osgood's first study, a four-factor solution was obtained. The evaluation and potency factors were nearly identical to the earlier ones, but the activity factor was less clear. An eight-factor solution was obtained for the total set of 75 scales, and the results were comparable to those obtained in the thesaurus study. Numerous other studies have shown similar results even when the *S*s were from different cultural backgrounds and the instrument was strained by the process of translation (Osgood *et al.*, 1957; Osgood, 1967). This kind of evidence clearly supports the comparability of factor structures across subjects and explains why so many studies use scales representative of these three factors. But powerful as it is, there are exceptions which will be discussed later.

The factor analytic procedure is not, however, a necessary part of the SD, so the general evidence for the reliability and validity of the scaling procedure must be considered in detail.

Reliability

There is evidence that *S*s can respond to scale-concept items reliably (Osgood *et al.*, 1957, Ch. 4; Norman, 1959). Norman tested reliability of the instrument for individuals and reported a median test-retest (four weeks intervening) reliability coefficient of .66. Osgood *et al.* reported an overall test-retest (immediate) reliability coefficient of .85. Further, Osgood *et al.* indicate that approximately 64 per cent of scale items will be marked identically when repeated with the same Ss and that the average distance between test and retest marks is almost always less than one scale unit. Less than 5 per cent of the time will an individual's marks differ by as much as two scale units. Osgood *et al.* also indicate that the reproducability of scale markings is somewhat higher on evaluative scales than on potency and activity scales.

Mitsos (1961, pp. 433–434) found that scales selected by Ss as "relevant to the class of concepts being judged" yielded higher factor scores than "any scales" or "infrequently chosen scales." This is probably indicative of higher reliability. Common sense suggests that scales Ss can agree are relevant or literally applicable to the concept being judged should be more reliable (*i.e.,* used more consistently) than scales that are related metaphorically or by some momentary association. Ambiguity of concepts should also affect the reliability of measurement.

Generally speaking, the reliability of the SD is not as high as it should be, but given the availability of alternatives and some evidence of predictive validity, the SD is reliable enough to warrant use. A kind of negative evidence of reliability is provided by Osgood's (Osgood *et al.,* 1957, p. 34) comment that Ss sometimes agree so well on the rating of a particular concept on a particular scale that correlations are spuriously low or indeterminate due to the lack of variance in the SD scores. This is given, in fact, as a justification for summing across concepts in the factor analyses reported above.

Validity

The question of validity of the SD is complex. One must first decide what he wants to measure before he can reasonably ask if a particular instrument measures it. As the SD is extremely flexible, it is probably not equally valid for all possible applications. Second, in matters of validity, it is practically impossible to separate the measuring instrument from the procedure of analysis. Third, validity of the SD is probably affected by the relevance of the scales to the concepts judged, so both scales and concepts must be considered in estimating validity. Finally, validity may be viewed as a property of the inferences drawn from data and is, therefore, involved with the interpretation of the data as well as the data themselves.

In arranging concepts in semantic space, the SD has high *face validity* in that "most people would have clustered these concepts in much the same way without using the differential (Osgood *et al.,* 1957, p. 141)." However, with specific scales this is not always the case. Smith (1961) found, for example, that in his particular application the *hot-cold* scale seemed to be the best available measure of the strongest factor, although Ss could neither apply nor interpret it in that context. On another occasion Smith's (1959) subjects seemed to treat *worthless* and *meaningless* as positive values, which hardly makes common sense. An isolated case of multiple personality was analyzed from SD data with results that compared well with conclusions of clinicians in contact with the subject over a period of time (Osgood and Luria, 1954).

Most of the evidence on SD validity relates exclusively to the evaluative dimension. It is possible, for example, to differentiate Democrats and Republicans by their SD responses to a set of political concepts (Osgood *et al.*, 1957, p. 142). Correlation of five evaluative scales with Thurstone attitude tests on THE CHURCH, CAPITAL PUNISHMENT, and THE NEGRO produced coefficients of .74, .81, and .82 respectively. These correlations are all significant at the .01 level and are not significantly lower than those obtained by correlating each of the instruments with itself by test-retest. This and other evidence argues that evaluative scales may be used as reasonably valid and extremely efficient measures of attitude toward a broad range of objects.

As a measure of meaning, the value of the SD is highly questionable. J. B. Carroll (1959), in his review of *The Measurement of Meaning,* says, "If this is a factor analysis of 'meaning' in any degree whatsoever, it is a factor analysis of the three dimensions underlying a series of adjectival scales and not necessarily the dimensions inherent in the stimuli involved [pp. 67–68]." He goes on to argue that in selecting scales or concepts one could establish dimensions almost at will. Roger Brown (1958) says, "The differential solves none of the problems of meaning posed by philosophers and does not even observe the distinctions of which they feel the most confident [p. 114]."

Osgood *et al.* (1957) note in their summary chapter, after discussing some of the evidence of concept-scale interaction, "It now seems less likely that we will be able to discover a single set of scales which represent an adequate set of factors and which are stable across whatever concepts may be judged [p. 326]."[3] Smith (1959, 1961, 1962) noted that each new set of concepts he used produced a different factor structure, even though he started with scales selected from Osgood *et al.*'s three major factors. Osgood, Ware, and Morris (1961) discovered that when a homogeneous set of concepts was used, the classic three factors collapsed into a single evaluative factor and some new factors appeared.

There are numerous other instances of concept-scale interaction reported in the SD research literature, and each one challenges the validity of the method of analysis and the most popular interpretation of the SD. On the other hand, this seems to be the best possible evidence for the validity of the scaling procedure. It indicates in an unmistakable (and unintentional) fashion that *S*s do respond differentially to concepts on the bipolar adjectival scales.

It has been indicated that although it is extremely difficult to separate

---

[3] The quotation cited here constitutes an admission that context affects meaning. The surprising thing is that it had to be made at all.

the scaling procedure from the method of analysis and interpretative assumptions, it seems necessary to do so in order to make a reasonable statement about the validity of the SD. The scaling procedure itself seems to be a reasonably valid index of selected internal states of people; at least for those scales which S sees as relevant to the concepts judged, the scaling seems consistent with common sense and with S's other behavior. Concept-scale interaction, although attesting to the validity of the controlled association procedure, raises a seemingly insurmountable obstacle to the interpretation of a general factor analysis of a limited number of scales and a heterogeneous set of concepts.

Smith (1961) argues, "This [concept-scale interaction] necessitates, for any special area of investigation in which the semantic differential is to be used, a specific factor analysis to determine the important factors and the scales which measure them [p. 8]." There is a simpler solution for those who are not equipped to do factor analyses or are interested primarily in the evaluative (attitudinal) dimension of the SD. But before going on to describe it, let us consider some of the "causes" of concept-scale interaction.

CONCEPT-SCALE INTERACTION

The evidence that concept-scale interaction does occur is overwhelming. If its causes can be explained, however, perhaps it can be viewed as a merit rather than a demerit of the SD. One important reason for concept-scale interaction is easy to identify: the dimensions on which classes of events differ must be different from the dimensions on which members of a class differ. That is, the differences between a public speech and a dramatic production are not the same as the differences between two speeches or two dramatic productions.

In a typical SD factor analysis, data from a set of concepts are pooled. Osgood *et al.* (1957) comment that in early studies concepts were selected to be "as diversified in meaning as possible so as to augment the total variability in judgments . . . [p. 34]." This augmenting the variability to make the correlation analysis feasible has confounded the issue. Osgood *et al.* (1961) demonstrated that the within-concept variance has a relatively small effect on the factor structure, so the factor structures actually depend on the differences among concept classes, which will necessarily change as the set of concepts changes. Consequently, the factor structure which has been replicated so many times does not describe any single concept in the experiment or any other set of concepts.

Other reasons for concept-scale interaction are the assumptions necessary for correlation analysis that the relation between scales is linear and that the polarity of each scale is constant. Both of these assumptions are demonstrably false in specific situations. If it is meaningful to say that good PICKLES are sour but not too sour, then in a certain range of pickles the relation between *sweet-sour* and *good-bad* should be curvilinear, undetectable by linear analysis. Odds are that *good-bad* and *fast-slow* have a curvilinear relation when applied to the concept CLOCK. Darnell (1966) found that 37 of the 75 scales in his study changed polarity at least once across the 20 concepts. With the scale *hard-soft,* for instance, *hardness* seems to be good with regard to AMERICA, PATRIOT, COP, STATUE, SWORD, and BOULDER. But softness is better for the concepts LADY, SYMPHONY, MOTHER, LAKE, BABY, and FEATHER. The popular appeal of *hot* PIZZA and *cold* BEER gives further demonstration of polarity change.

The point of all this is that there are some potential values of the SD that have been too long ignored. The validity of the SD in speech communication is admittedly questionable if one adopts the whole procedure or accepts blindly the results of earlier studies. On the other hand, if one makes appropriate adaptations in the method of analysis, it may be uniquely suited to discovering loaded language for a particular persuasion topic, to exploring the relative effectiveness of persuasive appeals, for measuring the reactions to particular kinds of speech disorders, or structuring measurable responses to theatrical performances.

It seems advisable at this time to discard the idea of "semantic space" since this construct has served its purpose. It has held together a theoretical structure which has stimulated and facilitated research. It now appears that neither the construct nor the theoretical structure has any relevance to problems of communication. What difference does it make if a person's SELF-concept is located near his concept of SODA POP? Do the descriptive terms *sweet, bubbly, stimulating,* and *refreshing* mean the same when applied to SPIRIT and SPRITE? What difference does it make that a particular FISHING LURE is seen as extremely *strong* and quite *active,* if these attributes are indeed independent of the choice behavior of fish and fishermen? What difference does it make that a particular POLITICIAN is seen as *dynamic,* if that does not effect the votes he can win? What value has the information that an individual prefers *active* to *passive* CARROTS, if the individual is rational in most other respects? Or, for that matter, what can one do with the information that he prefers *good* CARROTS to *bad* ones?

The point is that most of us are *not* interested in what the SD has produced so far. Nor are we likely to become interested in anything produced under the assumptions in the SD tradition. The SD's value lies in predicting and explaining choice behavior. Some use of the evaluative dimension of the SD has been made in this context, and (as mentioned earlier) it provides most of the evidence for the validity of the SD (Osgood *et al.,* 1957, pp. 141–142). But nothing is gained from the tautological explanation that S chose X over Y because he prefers X, and there's nothing really new in predicting an election by taking a straw vote from a sample of voters, even if a different form of balloting is used.

If these primarily evaluative scales are used without attention to concept-scale interaction, they are simply complex preference ballots which may be less valid than other balloting procedures because of their complexity. The evaluative scales most frequently used do not even have the advantage of subtlety. Kerrick and McMillan (1961) have demonstrated that Ss can identify these scales and respond differently to them when threatened, even when evaluative scales are imbedded in a set of nonevaluative scales.

OTHER OBJECTIONS

There are other reasons for objecting to the traditional method of analysis which have not been taken into account even by those who have proposed separate factor analyses for each new concept or set of concepts (Triandis, 1960b; Smith, 1961). Gulliksen (1958) points out that because of these objections methods other than correlation analysis should be considered. The first of these objections has to do with the question of equal intervals in the SD data. In order to interpret correlation analysis, one must assume that the data intervals are equal. Osgood *et al.* (1957, pp. 146–152) report evidence that the intervals of the nine most frequently used scales are equal enough to produce no significant distortion. This evidence is hardly surprising since these scales have been selected because they behave most predictably in the analysis which assumes equal intervals. It says nothing, however, about scales that have behaved less predictably. The fact that an extremely *soft* BRICK can do serious damage to an extremely *hard* HEAD seems sufficient reason for skepticism about the equality of scale intervals, at least across concepts. Of course, this example also contains shifting anchor points on scales, changes in meaning, and contextual contamination, but these are all related to the assumption of equal intervals.

A second, and connected, objection to the traditional analysis has to do with the nature of "oppositeness." Carroll (1959) points out that not all adjective pairs are opposite in the same way, and that no particular justification is given for selecting opposite meaning adjectives. Osgood's (1957) general approach seems to imply that the adjective pairs should be logical contradictories (a *bad* APPLE is *not good* and vice versa) or at least contraries, but he allows a neutral position meaning "neither," which suggests the weaker contrary interpretation of "opposite." He even allows that a neutral mark may indicate an equal association with the two ends of the continuum, which implies the still weaker subcontrary relation. Some scales used (*e.g., sweet-sour, red-green, rational-intuitive*) are bounded by logically independent terms, not "opposite" in any accepted sense. Some terms are relative (*e.g., commonplace, alive*), and some are absolute (*e.g., unique, dead*), but all are treated the same way in the traditional analysis.

Considering all these objections, it is not clear what, why, or how the SD differentiates. It seems advisable, as we have indicated, to discard the concept of semantic space and the assumptions that go with it. Having no better alternative, one may still choose to use the scaling procedure, but he should be prepared to defend the specific instrument in the specific application.

AN ALTERNATIVE

Another rationale for using adjectival scales to obtain judgments of concepts suggests alternative methods for selecting scales and for analysis that should be applicable to a wide range of problems in speech communication. A primary assumption of this approach is that our major interest in the instrument is in the evaluative dimension and in predicting choices. This assumption is reasonable because evaluative scales provide most of the evidence for validity of the SD, because the evaluative dimension is the most stable of all dimensions, and because the evaluative dimension accounts for more than half the variance that can be accounted for in semantic judgments.

Outside the semantic space framework there is no justification for any dimension of judgment independent of evaluative judgments. Further, it seems clear that nonevaluative judgments are artifacts of concept-scale interaction and the factor analytic procedure. That is, probably all judgments or discriminations have either direct or indirect evaluative significance. One can reason, then, that any judgments or discriminations people make consistently enough to represent them in their vocabulary by adjective pairs very probably have evaluative significance (relate to choice behavior) to some class or classes of events.[4] The problem, then, is to discover what dimensions of variation people recognize in a particular class of events and how these dimensions relate to their choices or preferences within that class.

Another plausible supposition is that every reliable preference must relate to at least one *observable* variable in the class of events from which the choice is made. This is not to say that the person choosing is consciously aware of the observable variable or of its relation to his choice behavior, although preferences consciously related to observables are probably more reliable. If we are genuinely interested in predicting evaluative preferences, we must assume law-like relations between evaluations and observables, attempt to formulate those relations, and attempt to discover the related observable variables in each class of events pertinent to our interest. Following is a proposed adaptation of the SD that provides a means of discovering the significant dimensions of judgment in any class of events and a start on the formulation of the relational laws.

Suppose you are interested in predicting a choice that some person is going to make. You might ask him what he thinks he will choose. Assuming that he has an opinion and that he will receive no new relevant information before choosing, his answer should enable you to predict with better than chance success. To understand a choice after the fact, you could ask why the choice was made and cull a plausible answer from the variety of

---

[4] "Class of events" means a set of related things. The name of the set or class corresponds to "concept" in the earlier discussion. The change in terminology is an attempt to shift the emphasis from the name to the things named. It may be helpful to think about "differences among politicians," for example, rather than "variance within the concept POLITICIAN."

answers. But what you will get, after all, is an ex post facto explanation or rationalization that is inevitably contaminated by the decision maker's reaction to post-decision dissonance.

On the other hand, you can ask (before or after) in what ways the things in the relevant class differ and which of these differences are meaningful to the choice. With SD type scales, you can ask both of these questions at the same time, ask them in a subtle way that is less likely to make the respondent defensive, and obtain data that can be integrated objectively to formulate a prediction or explanation of the choice.

Method

The procedure for this alternative method is straightforward. One starts with the name of the class from which the choice is to be made (HOUSES, JOBS, AUTOMOBILES, PRESIDENTIAL CANDIDATES) and as large a set of SD-type scales as the situation and imagination will allow. Ss are instructed to respond to the "best imaginable example" and the "worst imaginable example" of the class on each scale with discriminable marks ("B" and "W" for "best" and "worse," for example). An S might then indicate by marking

PRESIDENTIAL CANDIDATES

rational __B__ : ____ : ____ : ____ : ____ : __W__ : ____ irrational

that he prefers his presidential candidates to be extremely rational and that he can't imagine an extremely irrational candidate. But in response to the class name AUTOMOBILE, where he probably would not see *rationality* as a dimension of variability, he might very well put both marks in the middle of the scale.

If a group of Ss respond in this fashion to a concept on a set of scales, one can determine whether they agree significantly on the polarity of a given scale. (The method for doing this will be described in some detail on pp. 192–193.) If Ss agree on the evaluative significance of a particular dimension for a specific class of events, one may infer that that dimension is one component of the decision that they may make to select one member of that class rather than other members of the class. If a group were to respond as in the example above, one would expect them, other things being equal, to vote for the more rational of two presidential candidates. But other things are seldom equal, so one would want to include a number of other scales such as *large-small, active-passive, young-old, strong-weak, safe-dangerous,* and *experienced-inexperienced* to improve the predictive accuracy of the instrument. (Note that the scales suggested here have, for the most part, been found to be independent of evaluation across concepts, but they are quite plausibly related to evaluation within this particular class of events.)

There are three primary advantages to this procedure over the usual factor analysis: (1) It allows one to find those dimensions of judgment that are used consistently by a group of people as evaluative dimensions for a specific concept without making the untenable mathematical assumptions required by the factor analysis.[5] (2) By finding those dimensions that are evaluative for a specific concept but which are not generally evaluative, one is more likely to obtain honest (nondefensive) answers about attitudes. Kerrick and McMillan (1961) found that a group that knew their attitudes were being measured showed much less tendency than a naïve group to change their attitudes as measured by evaluative scales, and some tendency to change in the "wrong" direction. Nonevaluative changes, however, were no different for informed and naïve groups. (3) To the extent that dimensions identified as evaluative for a specific concept class have objective content, and to the extent that the set of events from which a choice is to be made has observable differences, this procedure allows making predictions of choice without actually polling the voters.

Since the criteria for making a particular kind of decision must be more stable than the judgments themselves (the variations in judgments of a particular kind must contain the variations in the criteria and the variations in the events judged), it makes sense to try to discover these criteria. With knowledge of these general criteria and knowledge of the differences in a particular class of events from which a selection is to be made, one can predict the choice without asking anyone for his preferences in that particular set. For example, in our culture, a man in his lifetime makes many AUTOMOBILE choices. There are good economic reasons for wanting to predict those choices.

We can take three different approaches to predicting the car a given individual will buy next year. (1) We can ask him what one he will probably buy, but his answer can be no better than the stability of his criteria and his prediction of the alternatives he will be offered. (2) We can compare the choices he has made in the past and try to discover inductively the criteria that he used, reasoning that he will probably use these criteria again. However, we must wait until his choice is actually made to test the accuracy of our inductive process. (3) We can ask him for his criteria, deduce the choices he should have made in the past, test our deductions against his previous choices, and (assuming our deductions are supported) predict the kind of automobile he will choose. Our general prediction becomes specific as soon as *we* see the new models, and we even have, from the previous tests, an estimate of the kinds of errors likely to be associated with such a prediction. The third alternative is obviously the most desirable.

It seems to follow, then, that it is better to use subject time and research resources to discover the criteria that influence people in making choices

---

[5] The untenable assumptions referred to concern equality of intervals, linearity, constancy of polarity, and anchor point (see pp. 185–186).

rather than to take straw votes, whether the choices are automobiles, Presidential candidates, persuasive speeches, or some other class of interest.

Not all of this argument has been substantiated by experimental results. It has been shown, however, that the "best-worst" procedure outlined above can plausibly differentiate evaluative dimensions (criteria) for each concept class, and that the results are quite distinct from the factor analytic results (Darnell, 1966). In the research leading to these conclusions 75 scales were used, including the 50 from the first analysis by Osgood *et al.* (1957, p. 37) and an additional 25 selected from their thesaurus study (pp. 53–61). The extra 25 scales were selected for their nonevaluative factor loadings to compensate for the predominately evaluative first set. The concepts (set names) used were the same 20 used by Osgood *et al.* (p. 34) and were chosen so the results of the new study would be directly comparable to the earlier work.

Groups of 28 to 39 college students were instructed to respond to "best" and "worst" examples of each of five concepts on all 75 scales. For example, given a scale such as *large-small* and the concept TORNADO, *S* was instructed to mark a "B" in the appropriate slot on the scale for the best tornado he could imagine and a "W" on the same scale describing the worst tornado he could imagine. The instructions specifically allowed *S* to place both marks in the same scale interval.

It was assumed that if an *S* did not discriminate evaluatively among members of a concept set, or if his discriminations were not related to the particular scale dimension, he would place both marks in the same interval. On the other hand, it was assumed that if he did separate the two marks, he was preferring one end of the scale for the concept judged. To eliminate random indications of polarity, however, a particular scale was said to have an evaluative discrimination capacity for a particular concept if, and only if, a significant proportion of the *S*s agreed on the polarity of the scale.

The sign test was used to determine significant agreement. Following the procedure described by Siegel (1956), an *S* who placed both marks in the same scale interval was scored a tie and dropped from the sample. Left preferences were scored plus (+) and right preferences scored minus (−). Then the number of pluses or minuses (whichever was smaller) was referred to a table of critical values for the sign test to determine whether the agreement among *S*s differed from a chance distribution of responses. Two-tailed tests were made at the 5 per cent level of significance. Since 20 independent tests were performed on each scale, it was necessary to allow for the chance occurrence of significant values. It was determined, however, that four significant values on a given scale would permit the inference (at the 95 per cent level of confidence) that the scale discriminates for at least one of the 20 concepts.

The results were as follows: 72 of the 75 scales were evaluative for one or more of the concepts. *Strong-weak* and *active-passive,* which have been identifying scales in factors orthogonal to evaluation in numerous factor analyses, ranked 14.5 and 23, respectively, in number of concepts for which they discriminate. *Light-heavy, large-small, hard-soft, calm-excitable,* and *hot-cold,* all of which had been key scales in nonevaluative factors, showed an evaluative capacity for at least one of the 20 concepts.

Hard-soft, large-small, wide-narrow, and *near-far* had a noticable "flip-flop" tendency. That is, they reversed polarity from concept to concept, which would account for their low correlations with *good-bad* across concepts.

The facts that one scale (*kind-cruel*) discriminated evaluatively for 18 of the 20 concepts and another (*pungent-bland*) for none, and that one concept (LADY) was differentiated by 59 scales and another (RUSSIAN) by only 6 scales point up the need for some such analysis on each concept class in which one is interested.

The *good-bad* scale, incidently, ranked ninth in discriminative power, failing to differentiate 5 of the 20 concepts (SIN, TORNADO, FIRE, FRAUD, and RUSSIAN).

A standard form of the SD was administered to essentially the same subjects one week after the first test. Factor analyses of these data compared well with earlier studies, effectively blocking the alternative explanation that the results of the "best-worst" test (Darnell, 1964) were produced by an unusual sample of people.

This study shows, at least, that Ss can rationalize their preferences within a framework of bipolar adjectival scales, and that in doing so they use scales that have been considered independent of evaluation. Further research is needed to establish the predictive validity of criteria selected in this manner, but the method does provide a simple and objective way of selecting scales that reasonably ought to be related to preferential decisions.

The simplicity of this technique makes it feasible for a researcher to extend his imagination in constructing scales and to allow Ss, working independently, to reduce the set to a workable number of predictive variables. Scales which are not psychologically bipolar, which have unstable meanings even in the context of a specific concept, or which have different *values* in the population and hence low predictive value are precisely the ones most likely to be eliminated by the procedure suggested here.

Given a set of scales selected by the "best-worst" procedure, one could proceed to a prediction by either of two routes. Taking the evaluative dimensions identified by a group of Ss, one could turn to the set of events from which a choice is to be made (*e.g.,* PRESIDENTIAL CANDIDATES) and score the choices against the criteria. As suggested earlier, to the extent that the selected criteria (scales) refer to observable characteristics of the events (taller, louder, faster, etc.), one should be able to score the alternatives and make a reasoned prediction. Of course, if only subjective criteria are obtained (better, kinder, fairer, etc.), little has been gained.

Alternately, under certain circumstances one could take the scales selected by the "best-worst" method (Phase I) back to the Ss (or to a second independent sample from the same population) and administer them (Phase II) as a single response SD instrument and obtain judgments of the *N* individual choices. Having established the relevance and polarity of the scales in the first phase, it should be relatively easy to determine from the second set of data which of the alternatives is preferred by the sample of respondents and some insight into the reasons why.

One might view this whole procedure as the development of a diagnostic rating scale (Phase I) and its application by a panel of experts (Phase II). Of course, the final result depends not only on care and good judgment but on the representativeness of the sample or samples employed.

Summary

This chapter has attempted to give a brief overview of a research methodology called the semantic differential.[6] This survey has led to the conclusion that a number of untenable assumptions are made in the traditional type of SD analysis. An alternative has been suggested which may circumvent most of those assumptions. However, the alternative also makes assumptions, and pending further research the reader must decide which set of assumptions is the more plausible or useful.

The alternative to the factor analytic approach involves a two-step procedure. The first phase is aimed at selecting SD scales which have a reliable capacity to discriminate evaluatively within a specific class of events. The second phase involves using the selected scales for obtaining relative evaluations of a set of alternatives in order to predict choices. The instrument one obtains by following this suggested procedure is specific to a particular class of events, but for that very reason is presumed to be more sensitive than the general instruments obtained from factor analyses of responses to a variety of different classes of events. The evidence of concept-scale interaction in SD research is believed to warrant this presumption.

It seems clear that one can put together instruments using seven-interval scales bounded by bipolar adjectives, and that one can obtain useful information from such an instrument if it is carefully constructed and validated for the specific application. It is even clearer that wide popularity is no reason for using a semantic differential or, for that matter, any other measuring instrument or research methodology.

References and Selected Readings

Brown, R. Review of C. E. Osgood, G. J. Suci, and P. H. Tannenbaum, *The measurement of meaning. Contemporary Psychology*, 1958, **3**, 113–115.

[6] Readers who wish to extend their knowledge of semantic differential technique will find Snider and Osgood (1969) particularly helpful.

Carroll, J. B. Review of C. E. Osgood, G. J. Suci, and P. H. Tannenbaum, *The measurement of meaning. Language,* 1959, **35,** 58–77.

Darnell, D. K. A technique for determining the evaluative discrimination capacity and polarity of semantic differential scales for specific concepts. Unpublished doctoral disseration, Michigan State University, 1964.

Darnell, D. K. Concept scale interaction in the semantic differential. *Journal of Communication,* 1966, **16,** 104–115.

Gulliksen, H. Review of C. E. Osgood, G. J. Suci, and P. H. Tannenbaum, *The measurement of meaning. Contemporary Psychology,* 1958, **3,** 115–119.

Kerrick, J. S., and McMillan, D. A., III. The effects of instructional set on the measurement of attitude change through communication. *Journal of Social Psychology,* 1961, **53,** 113–120.

Mitsos, S. B. Personal constructs and the semantic differential. *Journal of Abnormal and Social Psychology*, 1961, **62,** 433–434.

Nebergall, R. E. An experimental investigation of rhetorical clarity. *Speech Monographs,* 1958, **25,** 243–254.

Norman, W. T. Stability characteristics of the semantic differential. *American Journal of Psychology,* 1959, **72,** 581–584.

Osgood, C. E. The nature and measurement of meaning. *Psychological Bulletin,* 1952, **49,** 197–237.

Osgood, C. E. Semantic differential techniques in the comparative study of cultures. In L. A. Jakobovits and M. S. Miron (Eds.), *Readings in the psychology of language.* Englewood Cliffs, N.J.: Prentice-Hall, 1967. Pp. 371–397.

Osgood, C. E., and Luria, Z. A blind analysis of a case of multiple personality using the semantic differential. *Journal of Abnormal and Social Psychology,* 1954, **49,** 579–591.

Osgood, C. E., and Suci, G. J. A measure of relation determined by both mean difference and profile information. *Psychological Bulletin,* 1952, **49,** 251–262.

Osgood, C. E., Suci, G. J., and Tannenbaum, P. H. *The measurement of meaning.* Urbana: University of Illinois Press, 1957.

Osgood, C. E., Ware, E. E., and Morris, C. Analysis of the connotative meanings of a variety of human values as expressed by American college students. *Journal of Abnormal and Social Psychology*, 1961, **62,** 62–73.

Rabin, A. I. A contribution to the "meaning" of Rorschach's inkblots via the semantic differential. *Journal of Consulting Psychology,* 1959, **23,** 368–372.

Rosen, E. A cross-cultural study of semantic profiles and attitude differences: (*Italy*). *Journal of Social Psychology*, 1959, **49,** 137–144.

Semans, C. B. Use of the semantic differential with lobotomized psychotics. *Journal of Consulting Psychology*, 1957, **21,** 264.

Siegel, S. *Nonparametric statistics.* New York: McGraw-Hill, 1956. Pp. 68–75.

Smith, R. G. Development of a semantic differential for use with speech related concepts. *Speech Monographs,* 1959, **26,** 263–272.

Smith, R. G. A semantic differential for theatre concepts. *Speech Monographs,* 1961, **28,** 1–8.

Smith, R. G. A semantic differential for speech correction concepts. *Speech Monographs,* 1962, **29,** 32–37.

Snider, J. G., and Osgood, C. E. (Eds.) *Semantic differential technique: A sourcebook.* Chicago: Aldine, 1969.

Springbett, B. M. The semantic differential and meaning in non-objective arts. *Perceptual and Motor Skills,* 1960, **10,** 231–240.

Triandis, H. C. Some determinants of interpersonal communication. *Human Relations,* 1960, **13,** 279–287. (a)

Triandis, H. C. A comparative factoral analysis of job semantic structures of managers and workers. *Journal of Applied Psychology,* 1960, **44,** 297–302. (b)

Attitude Scales

PHILIP EMMERT

The study of attitudes, not surprisingly, has been profoundly influenced by attitude measurement. However, the literature dealing with attitude measurement often does not consider the nature of attitudes. Many discussions of measurement have compared attitude scales to scales of physical phenomena (Thurstone, 1931) and the measurement of attitudes to the measurement of length, weight, speed, and so on. These comparisons and analogies imply that such a thing as *an* attitude exists which can be located as a point on a continuum just as the physical phenomena can be located on an abstract linear continuum.

The validity of this assumption is open to question. Though it has been demonstrated repeatedly that subjects *can* state their attitudes as points on a continuum, it has never been shown that a single point on a continuum is a valid representation of a subject's feeling about an attitude object. A major question to be examined in this chapter is whether an individual holds a *single* attitude about an attitude object which can be represented validly by a *single* point on a continuum.

Of the many methods of attitude measurement extant, the following three have received the most attention and use: the method of equal appearing intervals (Thurstone and Chave, 1929), the method of summated ratings (Likert, 1932), and the semantic differential technique (Osgood, Suci, and Tannenbaum, 1957). The first two of these approaches will be covered in this chapter (see Chapter 6 for the semantic differential technique). This chapter will also discuss a way of measuring attitudes of acceptance, rejection, and noncommitment, and ego-involvement (C. Sherif, M. Sherif, and Nebergall, 1965). Though still in the early stages of development, this approach seems to promise a more direct relationship with human behavior than the other methods.

EQUAL APPEARING INTERVALS[1]

A major step in attitude research was the development of the method of equal appearing intervals for the measurement of attitudes by Thurstone and Chave (1929). Not only has this approach been widely used, it has had an undeniable effect on the development of other scaling methods. At the very least, it has been the criterion measure with which other newer scales have been compared and validated.

Procedure

(1) The experimenter gathers statements concerning the psychological object of interest in a number of ways, from taking statements from newspapers to simply creating statements "from scratch." He needs a large and fair sampling of all possible statements that could be made about the psychological object. Obviously, the selection will include statements at the extremes of the continuum favorable and unfavorable to the object and statements at all other points. About 100 to 130 of these statements should be printed separately on cards for sorting purposes.

(2) Eleven cards labeled A through K are placed in front of each subject, with the two end cards (A and K) identified as favorable and unfavorable and the middle card (F) identified as neutral. Subjects are then asked to sort the statement cards into the 11 piles according to the degree of favorableness or unfavorableness the statement on each card expresses toward the psychological object under investigation.

It should be noted that only the two end positions (A and K) and the middle position (F) are identified; the other intervals are left undefined. Thus, the letters on the cards appear to represent equal intervals. It is possible that if the experimenter attempted to label each interval, he might use terms that did not appear to the subjects to be equally apart. This method of attitude measurement assumes that the subjects do indeed perceive the intervals as equal, and the assumption enables the experimenter to assign values from 1 to 11 to the piles for computational purposes.

Statements do not have to be on cards to obtain the initial judgments. Studies have been done using 11-point graphic rating scales beside each

[1] The author acknowledges the influence of Edwards (1957) on his thinking in the sections on equal appearing intervals and the method of summated ratings.

statement, 11 one-inch lines beside each statement, and IBM answer sheets as methods for obtaining subject judgments. All these approaches have apparently worked equally well.

In this step of the procedure, it should be mentioned that studies have been done using anywhere from 300 subjects (Thurstone and Chave, 1929) to 50 subjects (Uhrbrock, 1934) in the initial judging of the statements. The correlations between scale values obtained from these two groups was .99. This is obviously quite satisfactory, as have been similar correlations between other studies using groups of varying sizes.

(3) Once the statements are assigned on the 11-point continuum, the value for each statement can be determined. This value can be either the mean or median of each statement distribution. Thurstone and Chave relied on the median value of each statement as the most typical value for that statement.

(4) Obviously, it is possible for more than one of the statements to have the same or nearly the same median value. Therefore it is necessary to have an additional standard for evaluating the statements. Thurstone and Chave chose the interquartile range, or Q, as an indicator of the variation of judgments of statements. In this method, the experimenter seeks a group of 20 to 22 statements with scale values approximately equally spaced on the 11-point continuum and with small Q values. When several statements have similar scale values (that is, they fall at nearly the same point on the continuum) the experimenter should select those with the smallest interquartile ranges (Q values).[2] The statements selected are then arranged in random order for presentation to subjects.

(5) The subjects are instructed to select those statements with which they agree and those with which they disagree. By considering those statements the subjects agree on, an attitude score can be obtained. This score can be either the mean or median of the scale values of the statements selected by the subjects.

Reliability and Validity

The reliability and validity of a scale should be considered before using any method. In general, the method of equal appearing intervals has been satisfactorily reliable. According to Edwards (1957, p. 94), a common practice for determining reliability has been to construct two comparable forms of the attitude scale. This is easily accomplished by selecting a second set of statements having small Q values which are relatively equally spaced along the continuum. Both forms of the scale can then be administered to the same subjects and the results correlated. The correlation is considered as a measure of the reliability of the scales. Typically, reliability coefficients above .85 have been reported using this procedure.

[2] See Edwards (1957, pp. 86–92) for formulas for computing the median and Q values.

Questions concerning the validity of this method are not as easily answered as questions of reliability; however, this is not a shortcoming peculiar to this method. According to Shaw and Wright (1967, pp. 15–32) valid scales can be constructed using this method, but the validity greatly depends on the attitude being measured and the skill of the experimenter developing the scale. Questions have been raised about Thurstone and Chave's procedures and their effect on the validity of the scales. One questionable practice is the selection of statements in the initial judging procedure: Thurstone and Chave rejected judgments from any subject who placed 30 or more statements in any one of the 11 intervals. They assumed that any subject who did this was either careless in making his judgments or did not understand the instructions and was not diffentiating among the statements. However, it is possible that these subjects were not careless but held extreme opinions concerning the phenomena being scaled which caused them to distribute their judgments differently from subjects with moderate views. This was the major thrust of a study by Hovland and M. Sherif (1952), an attempt to replicate an earlier study by Hinckley (1932).

Hovland and Sherif predicted that eliminating the responses of those subjects who put more than 30 cards in one classification would systematically eliminate the responses of subjects with extreme opinions. Working with black and white judges of pro- and anti-black attitudes, Hovland and Sherif supported their prediction. Using Thurstone and Chave's practice of eliminating responses of subjects who placed 30 or more statements in one category, they discovered that over 75 per cent of the black judges and 66 per cent of the white judges with pro-black attitudes were eliminated. Both these groups showed a tendency to place statements considered neutral or moderately favorable toward black people in categories at the unfavorable end of the continuum. A similar though not as pronounced effect was noted in the opposite direction for the anti-black white subjects.

Hovland and Sherif suggest that these results could have been caused by a lack of ability on the part of subjects with extreme views to discriminate between adjacent statements at the end of the continuum opposite their own position, or that the results might have indicated differences in the individual judge's perception of the category intervals. Hovland and Sherif lean toward the latter explanation since the rank ordering of the statements is very similar for all groups. At any rate, their study does call into question eliminating judgments of subjects who place more than 30 statements in one interval. At the very least, their study refutes the notion that these subjects are careless or undiscriminating. Rather, it suggests that prior attitudes cause subjects to skew their sorting.

Evidence contrary to that of the Hovland and Sherif study had been supplied by earlier studies (Hinckley, 1932; Pintner and Forlano, 1937). It is interesting to note Hinckley's discussion on the displacement of statements:

One tendency which revealed itself in the sortings of some subjects was the bunching of statements in one or more piles to the apparent detriment of the other piles. This phenomena of bunching at the extremes was noticed in the case of certain of the white subjects, but was especially noticeable in the Negro subjects. Since the 114 statements are distributed with fair uniformity over the entire scale, marked bunching is a sign of careless sorting. If more than a fourth of the statements are assigned to any one pile, it will leave less than three-fourths to distribute over the remaining ten piles. Furthermore, the individual who sorts the statements in this fashion often ignores some of the piles completely. On the assumption that this bunching was due to poor discrimination and carelessness, every case having 30 or more statements in any one pile was automatically eliminated from consideration, and the results were not recorded [p. 288].

It should be pointed out that not only were the scale values for statements in both the Hinckley study and the Hovland and Sherif study almost the same, but both studies reported this "bunching" effect by similar subjects. The difference between the two studies is that Hinckley assumed that this was the result of carelessness and discarded the judgments of those subjects, whereas Hovland and Sherif analyzed the nature of subjects who bunched their statements. In light of the Hovland and Sherif analysis, the Hinckley assumption does not appear justified. This suggests that *the nature of the population that does the initial judging is an important consideration in the construction of an attitude scale using the method of equal appearing intervals.* A criterion for selecting subjects to do the initial sorting may well be that they should be as much as possible like the subjects who will ultimately fill out the scale. Another may be that the method of equal appearing intervals is best suited to attitude objects which are less involving than the topic of race was to the Negro and Caucasian subjects. In any case, these studies do show that caution must be exercised when constructing a scale using this method.

SUMMATED RATINGS

Although the method of equal appearing intervals preceded the method of summated ratings, the later approach to attitude measurement has enjoyed great popularity. Since its development by Likert (1932) it may have been used to a greater extent than the Thurstone scales. The reasons for its popularity, though not quite as valid today as they were 25 years ago, are enumerated by Edwards and Kenney (1946) who suggest that Likert scales appear to take less time to construct than Thurstone scales, that Likert scales are at least as reliable as Thurstone scales, if not more so, and that scales constructed by the Likert method yield results comparable to Thurstone results. Because of the reliability of Likert scales and because of the possibility that this method may be less time consuming, Likert scales have been widely used in attitude studies.

The amount of time it takes to construct the scales is no longer as important as it was then, since, as was pointed out earlier in this chapter, the number of subjects required for the initial judgments of statements need not be as high as Thurstone first believed; and also, since the development of computer science, it is possible to perform the computation necessary to construct a Thurstone scale with far greater ease than when the method was first developed.

Procedure

(1) The first step in constructing a summated rating scale is to select a large number of statements about the attitude object which meet Likert's (1932) criteria for items: (1) The statement should be an expression not of fact but of desired behavior or of value. (2) Conciseness, clarity, and straightforwardness should always be goals in formulating the items. (3) The statements should be worded so that reactions to them will be toward both ends of the continuum, with some in the middle — that is, they should be distributed all along the continuum. Likert does not require statements to which the responses are at the extreme ends of the continuum. (4) The statements should be so worded that about half the items corresponds to half the continuum, while the other half of the items corresponds to the other half of the continuum. These two kinds of statements should be distributed on a random basis throughout the test.

(2) Each of these statements is assigned to a graphic scale of either five or seven intervals on a continuum ranging from "agree" to "disagree." These continua can be arranged so that they run horizontally or vertically beneath the statements.

(3) Subjects are instructed to indicate the extent to which they agree or disagree with each statement by placing a mark in the interval on the continuum which shows how close to either the "agree" or "disagree" end of the continuum they feel they belong. Edwards (1957, pp. 156–157) suggests that scores derived with the method of summated ratings should not be interpreted independently of the distribution of scores of a defined group. Thus, *when constructing the scale one should always use subjects as similar as possible to those who will ultimately respond to the finished scale.* In fact, Nunnally (1967, pp. 514–588) suggests that all circumstances surrounding the initial preparation of the Likert scale should be as similar as possible to those in which the completed scale will be used. He even suggests that if the responses in the final situation will be anonymous, the responses of the judges in the initial step should also be anonymous.

(4) In the case of a seven-interval scale, the end of the continuum that is "unfavorable" is scored as 0, while the "favorable" end is scored as 6.

Thus, if a subject chooses the "very strongly agree" interval on a scale which has been paired with a statement worded favorably toward socialized medicine, and if we are measuring his attitude toward socialized medicine, then this response would be scored as 6.

(5) The individual item responses are summed to produce a total score for each subject. Each score is then divided by the number of statements on the test to produce a mean score for each subject, which actually is a placement of all the subject's responses — *i.e.,* his attitude — on the seven-point continuum.

(6) In order to determine which statements to keep for the final test, the experimenter performs an item analysis by dividing the subjects into the top and bottom quartiles in terms of their total scores. He then compares the mean scores for the high and low group on each of the statements. If the mean response for a statement was significantly higher for those in the high group than for those in the low group, the experimenter keeps that statement. Another common approach is to calculate the correlation coefficient for the responses on each statement for all subjects with the total score for all subjects. From those statements that correlate positively with the total score, the statements with the highest correlation coefficients are retained. Statements correlating negatively but strongly with the total score should have the values reversed on the continua. Statements with low correlations should not be used on the final attitude test. Both procedures assume that some common factor — the attitude under investigation — causes statements to discriminate between the high and low groups as in the first procedure or to correlate highly with the total score for all subjects as in the second procedure. For the construction of the final test approximately 20 to 25 items should be chosen. These should be the items that correlated most highly with the total score and/or the items whose t and r values were highest.

(7) Edwards (1957, p. 155) suggests that in the actual construction of the scale approximately half the statements should be worded so that they are favorable to the attitude object, with the "very strongly agree" response having a value of 6, while the other half of the statements should be worded unfavorably toward the attitude object, with the "very strongly agree" response having a weight of 0. This minimizes the possibility that a subject responding to the scale might acquire a response set as a result of all the statements being worded either favorably or unfavorably.

Reliability and Validity

Questions of reliability and validity of the scales constructed by the method of summated ratings are somewhat different from those of the method of equal appearing intervals, though they are just as problematic. The reliability of Likert scales has been a source of some controversy, largely because of some early studies comparing the Thurstone and Likert methods. Likert (1932) himself began the controversy. His study seemed to indicate that a scale could be constructed using Thurstone's approach, and then most of the selected items could be used according to the Likert approach, with resulting reliability coefficients as high or higher than they were with the original Thurstone scale.

Others later attempted to examine the same question with diverse results (*e.g.*, Ferguson, 1939; Edwards and Kenney, 1946). Only Edwards and Kenney actually used the two separate methods to construct attitude scales "from scratch;" the other studies all used one basic method and then attempted to adapt statements chosen with the first method for use with the second method. When reporting their results, Edwards and Kenney concluded that "the coefficient of .92 between the Likert and one of the Thurstone scales is surely sufficiently high to establish the fact that it is possible to construct scales by the two methods which will yield comparable scores [p. 82]." Edwards (1957), after reviewing the work in this area, went a little further when he concluded that "there is no reason to doubt that scales constructed by the method of summated-ratings will yield reliability coefficients as high as or higher than those obtained with scales constructed by the method of equal-appearing intervals [p. 162]." It would be safe to say that, even with Likert scales of less than 20 statements, reliability is not a problem.

The questions concerning the validity of the scales constructed by the method of summated ratings are both similar to and different from those regarding scales constructed by the method of equal appearing intervals. A problem of primary concern is again equality of units. The comments made by Hovland and M. Sherif (1952) on the possibility that the distortions and displacements observed in their research might have been caused by the individual judge's perception of the size of the category intervals in Thurstone scales might be equally applicable to Likert scales. Subjects who hold extreme views on a topic or whose egos are involved with it may perceive the equality of units in a Likert scale on the topic as unequal. In fact this is one of the reasons Shaw and Wright (1967) have suggested that Likert scales "probably should be treated as ordinal scales [p. 24]." Even though we cannot yet answer this question definitely, it does give cause for exercising caution when interpreting results from Likert scales that deal with highly involving topics and topics on which people are likely to have extreme views.

A second problem might come from assuming that the middle interval of the scale represents an undecided opinion. A subject could possibly mark the interval that has a value of 6 on half the items and the interval with a value of 0 on the other half, thus producing a total attitude score of 3. An experimenter might conclude that the subject had no opinion on this particular topic, when, in fact, the subject had very definite attitudes that counterbalanced each other. However, this probably could not happen often enough to be a matter of major concern if the Likert procedures are carefully followed. Certainly, the process of item analysis should eliminate all but the remotest possibility of this occurring.

SOCIAL JUDGMENT-INVOLVEMENT APPROACH

The objective of both methods of attitude measurement discussed thus far has been to locate a point on a continuum which represents an attitude. This is not true of techniques derived from the social judgment-involvement approach. Rather, the theoretical basis for the procedures developed by M. Sherif and C. Sherif (1967) and others assumes that a person's attitude involves not only the point on a continuum which the person would consider most acceptable, but also all other points on that continuum which he can also accept, plus that point on the continuum he considers most objectionable. In addition, the Sherifs also suggest that those points on the continuum which are neither acceptable nor objectionable are important to any person's attitude. Without knowledge of these different aspects of a person's attitude, the Sherifs would say that we simply do not have enough information to predict or theorize about attitudes.

Before discussing the procedures involved in this approach to attitude measurement, we should note that the approach is relatively new and thus is not buttressed by the years of testing by both critics and supporters that have gone into the methods already discussed. We are fortunate to have the results of the extensive work of the Sherifs and their associates; we are less fortunate in not having at our disposal the work of such qualified critics of this approach as M. Sherif himself was of Thurstone's approach.

An understanding of the Sherifs' measurement techniques requires some familiarity with their theoretical approach to attitudes. We will consider briefly some of the primary concepts in this approach, although more complete explanations are available elsewhere (Hovland and M. Sherif, 1961; C. Sherif *et al.*, 1965; M. Sherif and C. Sherif, 1967). The principal concepts of the social judgment-involvement approach to attitudes include:

(a) *Latitude of acceptance:* that position on an attitude continuum which is most acceptable to an individual, plus all other positions that are acceptable.

(b) *Latitude of rejection:* that position on an attitude continuum which is most unacceptable to an individual, plus all other positions which are unacceptable.

(c) *Latitude of noncommitment:* all positions on an attitude continuum which are not included in either the individual's latitude of acceptance or his latitude of rejection.

(d) *Assimilation and contrast effects.* When an object of judgment differs only slightly from an anchor, displacement toward the anchor, or assimilation, occurs. When an object of judgment is increasingly discrepant from the anchor, the difference is exaggerated, and contrast effects occur.

(e) *Ego-involvement.* The social judgment-involvement approach predicts that the number of categories used in making judgments about attitude objects is inversely related to the degree to which the individual's ego is involved in the attitude. Typically, as an individual is more ego-involved in an attitude, his latitude of acceptance tends to narrow and his latitude of rejection tends to widen.

The relationships between latitudes of acceptance, rejection, and non-commitment and the methods of measurement associated with this approach should become clear during the presentation of these concepts. The relationship between assimilation and contrast effects and measurement may not be quite so obvious. If we assume that an individual's attitude (as represented by the single most acceptable point on the continuum) is the anchor with which all other points on a continuum are compared, and if this anchor is extreme, the individual would perceive the points on the continuum to be farther from his anchor than they actually are; clearly a contrast effect is likely to occur because of the discrepancy between this anchor point and all other points on the continuum. Likewise, an assimilation effect results in the individual perceiving those points on the continuum near the anchor point as being more similar to the anchor than they actually are.

The implications of contrast and assimilation effects are of great importance to attitude measurement. If these effects interact with other variables, then observing them would be most helpful to any study concerned with attitudes. For example, salience of attitude has been found to interact with perception of statements on an attitude continuum using the methods about to be presented (Hovland and M. Sherif, 1961). Thus, the value of these methods is that they measure far more than just one part of an attitude (the single point on the continuum); with them we can measure a number of points and their relationship to each other, giving us a much more complete picture of the attitude we are measuring.

Two procedures have been developed by the Sherifs in their studies — the method of ordered alternatives and the own-categories procedure — to assess the latitudes of acceptance, rejection, and noncommitment. However, the own-categories procedure supplies more information on assimilation and contrast effects by allowing the subjects to bunch their judgments (see pp. 207–208) and using this bunching as one basis for analysis. These methods are still in the early stages of development, even after years of work. M. Sherif and C. Sherif (1967) comment, "In these early stages of development, the pretension is to demonstrate the kind of measurement techniques required by an adequate theory. Many technical improvements and elaborations are feasible . . . [p. 108]." It is the hope of the author of this chapter that presentation of these embryonic methods of measurement may stimulate the refinement of these methods for improved attitude research in the future.

Method of Ordered Alternatives Procedure

(1) A large number of statements about the attitude object are gathered, much as in the method of equal appearing intervals, representing the range of possible positions which can be taken by an individual regarding the attitude object. In one reported study (C. Sherif *et al.*, 1965, pp. 27–47), these statements were drawn from interviews and discussions with active proponents of the two major political parties in an election rather than from subject judgments. It has been suggested that the statements on the ends of the continuum should in no way be moderate. The researchers comment, "The extreme statements were deliberately designed to prevent a ceiling effect, that is, a restriction of the range of positions caused by too moderate items at the extremes [pp. 27–28]."

(2) These statements are sorted from most to least favorable. Judges or the experimenters may do the sorting, but judges are probably preferable to avoid distortions of individual set. No assumptions about the size of the intervals are made and no scale values are assigned to the statements.

(3) On the basis of the sorting, nine statements are retained that represent clearly differentiated positions, ranking from one end of the continuum to the other.

(4) The set of nine statements is duplicated on four sheets of paper, which are given to the subjects. The subjects are then instructed to indicate (a) on the first sheet, the most acceptable statement in the set; (b) on the second sheet, other acceptable statements in the set; (c) on the third sheet, the most objectionable statement in the set; (d) on the fourth sheet, other objectionable statements in the set.

(5) The combined statements from the first two sheets give each subject's latitude of acceptance. By combining the chosen statements from the third and fourth sheets we have each subject's latitude of rejection. The statements omitted from all four sheets show each subject's latitude of noncommitment. These latitudes are quantified in terms of the number or mean number of statements to be found in each latitude.

Own-Categories Procedure

(1) As in the method of ordered alternatives, a large number of statements (100 or more) regarding the attitude object are gathered, representing all possible positions that could be taken on the issue under study. Each statement is placed on a card.

(2) The cards are given to subjects, who are instructed to sort the statements into *any number* of piles (each pile represents a category, or judgment interval) so that all the statements in each pile seem to "go together." The experimenter defines only one category — "extremely favorable." For example, the experimenter would tell subjects asked to sort statements about black people only that one pile must be completely

favorable to black people. The subject would then decide for himself how many intervals he would use in sorting the cards in a continuum of favorableness.

(3) After the cards have been sorted, each subject is asked to number the piles consecutively from one end of the continuum to the other, beginning with the number 1.

(4) The piles are then secured tightly so that the subjects can no longer shift cards from one pile to another.

(5) Finally, the subjects are asked to label one pile "most acceptable" and one pile "most objectionable." They are then asked to label all other piles containing acceptable statements as "acceptable," and all other piles containing objectionable statements as "objectionable." By combining the piles labeled "most acceptable" and "acceptable," and the piles labeled "most objectionable" and "objectionable," we have a measure of the individual's latitudes of acceptance and rejection. We also have a measure of attitude, because the number of categories used by subjects is an indication of ego-involvement. The greater the ego-involvement, the fewer categories used by the subjects, and vice versa.

Reliability and Validity

Questions of reliability and validity concerning the social judgment-involvement approach to attitude measurement are considerably different from those associated with the methods of equal appearing intervals and summated ratings. Reports of reliability coefficients are not in the literature, but the reliability of the instrument has been indicated by different means.

C. Sherif *et al.* (1965) reported that in a study of the 1960 Presidential campaign they repeated measurements of the same subjects with the following results: "The similarity of the patterns of response just before the election and a week or so earlier is striking. With only slight variation, the patterns are similar [p. 41]." Even though this indicates that consistency of results is possible with this approach to attitude measurement, the evidence concerning the reliability of these measurement techniques is incomplete and inconclusive.

The validity of the social judgment-involvement approach is more easily demonstrated. C. Sherif *et al.* approached the question of construct validity by comparing the measurements obtained from five different criterion groups: (1) mature black students admitted to a newly integrated state university; (2) younger black students attending an all black university in an all black community; (3) pro-black white students who were members of an equal rights organization; (4) "average" white students at a state university; and (5) a few students who indicated anti-black attitudes on a paper-and-pencil test. Using the own-categories procedure, the researchers discovered that these groups did order statements and sort numbers of categories in keeping with predictions made by the social judgment-involvement approach to attitudes. "That is, more frequently than others, they [Group I] did use fewer categories and put a disproportionate number of items in the extremely unfavorable category. Conversely, the few anti-Negro whites available, on the average, placed fewer items in the extremely unfavorable category than any other criterion group [p. 112]." The authors concluded that the results showed an order of scores "as would be predicted if the number of categories and the tendency to pile up items in the extremely unfavorable category were a function of relative ego involvement in a *favorable* stand on the issue [p. 113]." These results tend to meet the criteria for construct validity discussed by Nunnally (1967): "(1) specifying the domain of observables, (2) determining to what extent all, or some, of those observables correlate with each other or are affected alike by experimental treatments, and (3) determining whether or not one, some, or all measures of such variables *act* as though they measure the construct [p. 87]." Although C. Sherif *et al.* did not manipulate treatments, the five groupings of students served a similar, though less controlled, purpose. The same researchers (pp. 27–41) reported similar results indicating the construct validity of the method of ordered alternatives in their study of the 1960 Presidential campaign.

Summary

The first two methods of attitude measurement discussed in this chapter have dominated attitude research since the late 1920s. The assumptions underlying these techniques have been responsible for a theoretical conception of attitudes which treated an attitude as a point on a continuum. The validity of this assumption went untested for many years until the Sherifs began research which resulted in the social judgment-involvement approach to attitudes, and with it, the method of ordered alternatives and the own-categories procedure as new techniques of attitude measurement.

The author feels that the assumptions of equal intervals, attitude as a point on a continuum, and the independence of judges' ratings from judges' attitudes are no longer tenable in light of the evidence presented by the Sherifs and their associates. Therefore, it seems invalid to continue using the method of equal appearing intervals and the method of summated ratings by themselves as indicators of attitudes in scholarly studies. A more justified approach to the measurement of attitudes appears to be a combination of the methods discussed in this chapter, for example, the method of ordered alternatives, the own-categories procedure, and the method of summated ratings. Nunnally (1967) has suggested a similar approach to measurement: "Because constructs concern domains of observables, logically a better measure of any construct would be obtained by combining the results from a number of measures of such observables than by taking any one of them individually [p. 86]."

In addition, the use of all three techniques would provide information about attitudes which may be more theoretically defensible by the social judgment-involvement approach, while providing information by the method of summated ratings which might be more easily handled statistically since the scores are not in frequency form. Possibly, comparing results using each method may also provide new information about attitudes and the ways people verbalize their attitudes that might not be available in any other way. In conclusion, the author of this chapter feels that though there are shortcomings in all the approaches discussed, the information which could be provided by a combined approach would be valid enough both theoretically and statistically for meaningful studies of attitudes.

References and Selected Readings

Blalock, H. M., Jr., and Blalock, A. B. *Methodology in social research.* New York: McGraw-Hill, 1968. Pp. 60–111.

Edwards, A. L. *Techniques of attitude scale construction.* New York: Appleton-Century-Crofts, 1957.

Edwards, A. L., and Kenney, K. C. A comparison of the Thurstone and Likert techniques of attitude scale construction. *Journal of Applied Psychology,* 1946, **30,** 72–83.

Ferguson, L. W. The requirements of an adequate attitude scale. *Psychological Bulletin,* 1939, **36,** 665–673.

Ferguson, L. W. A study of the Likert technique of attitude scale construction. *Journal of Social Psychology,* 1941, **13,** 51–57.

Fishbein, M. *Attitude theory and measurement.* New York: John Wiley, 1967.

Francis, R. G. Scaling techniques. In J. T. Doby (Ed.), *An introduction to social research.* New York: Appleton-Century-Crofts, 1967. Pp. 187–212.

Green, B. F., Jr. Attitude measurement. In G. Lindzey (Ed.), *Handbook of social psychology.* Vol. 1. Cambridge, Mass.: Addison-Wesley, 1954. Pp. 335–369.

Hinckley, E. D. The influence of individual opinion on construction of an attitude scale. *Journal of Social Psychology,* 1932, **3,** 283–296.

Hovland, C. I., and Sherif, M. Judgmental phenomena and scales of attitude measurement: Item displacement in Thurstone scales. *Journal of Abnormal and Social Psychology,* 1952, **47,** 822–832.

Hovland, C. I., and Sherif, M. *Social judgment.* New Haven, Conn.: Yale University Press, 1961.

Kerlinger, F.N. *Foundations of behavioral research.* New York: Holt, Rinehart & Winston, 1965. Pp. 483–488.

Likert, R. A technique for the measurement of attitudes. *Archives of Psychology,* 1932, **140,** 1–55.

Manis, M. Comment on Upshaw's "Own attitude as an anchor in equal-appearing intervals." *Journal of Abnormal and Social Psychology,* 1964, **68,** 689–691.

Manis, M. Rejoinder to Upshaw's reply. *Journal of Abnormal and Social Psychology,* 1964, **68,** 693.

Nunnally, J. C., Jr. *Psychometric theory.* New York: McGraw-Hill, 1967.

Osgood, C. E., Suci, G. J., and Tannenbaum, P. H. *The measurement of meaning.* Urbana: University of Illinois Press, 1957.

Pintner, R., and Folano, G. The influence of attitude upon scaling of attitude items. *Journal of Social Psychology,* 1937, **8,** 39–45.

Prothro, E. T. The effect of strong negative attitudes on the placement of items in a Thurstone scale. *Journal of Social Psychology,* 1955, **41,** 11–17.

Shaw, M. E., and Wright, J. M. *Scales for the measurement of attitudes.* New York: McGraw-Hill, 1967.

Sherif, C., and Sherif, M. (Eds.) *Attitude, ego-involvement and change.* New York: John Wiley, 1967.

Sherif, C., Sherif, M., and Nebergall, R. *Attitude and attitude change.* Philadelphia: W. B. Saunders, 1965.

Sherif, M., and Sherif, C. Attitude as the individual's own categories: The social judgment-involvement approach to attitude change. In C. Sherif and M. Sherif (Eds.), *Attitude, ego-involvement and change.* New York: John Wiley, 1967. Pp. 105–139.

Thurstone, L. L. The measurement of social attitudes. *Journal of Abnormal and Social Psychology,* 1931, **26,** 249–269.

Thurstone, L. L., and Chave, E. J. *The measurement of attitude.* Chicago: University of Chicago Press, 1929.

Uhrbrock, R. S. Attitudes of 4430 employees. *Journal of Social Psychology,* 1934, **5,** 365–377.

Upshaw, H. S. Own attitude as an anchor in equal-appearing intervals. *Journal of Abnormal and Social Psychology,* 1962, **64,** 85–96.

Upshaw, H. S. A linear alternative to assimilation-contrast: A reply to Manis. *Journal of Abnormal and Social Psychology,* 1964, **68,** 691–693.

There is not properly an Art of Observing. There may be rules for observing. But these, like rules for inventing, are properly instructions for the preparations of one's own mind; for putting it into the state in which it will be most fitted to observe, or most likely to invent. They are, therefore, essentially rules of self-education, which is a different thing from logic. They do not teach how to do the thing, but how to make ourselves capable of doing it. They are an art of strengthening the limbs, not an art of using them.

[Mill, 1852, p. 217]

Rating Scales

Samuel L. Becker

Rating communicative behaviors (such as discussion) or the artifacts of those behaviors (such as essays) is generally thought to be useful only for pedagogical purposes. This is unfortunate because, properly used, rating can be an important tool for communication research. Rating simply means describing an individual, group of individuals, behaviors, or artifacts of behaviors in terms of one or more numerical scales. Thus, for example, one might rate a particular discussion group on a seven-point scale according to the degree of cooperation displayed. Rating is a means of obtaining quantified descriptions when it is inappropriate simply to count or measure in other ways. Thus, through rating, one can measure such varied concepts as leadership, voice quality, degree to which the style of a message is adapted to the interests or needs of its intended audience, speech fright, cooperation within a group, or balance or attractiveness of a visual message.

Descriptions of human beings, their behaviors, or the products of their behaviors fall into one of two general types, either self-description by the individuals being studied or observation and description of those individuals by others. Rating applies to the latter category, along with content analysis and measures of physiological states. Attitude tests, personality tests, and other indicators of self-perception fall into the former category. Which category of measure is more valid for any given study depends to a large extent on the purpose of the study and the phenomenon being studied.

Ratings are often especially useful where the subject of study is inadequate as a direct source of information or where some other measurement technique would disrupt the process being studied. Properly designed, rating procedures need not disrupt most communication transactions. In contemporary terms, they tend to be less obtrusive or reactive than most measurement procedures.

This is not to say that the measurement obtained is not affected by the rating procedure. A rating is not purely a description of the individual or object being rated; it is rather a description of the individual or object *and* the individual(s) doing the rating. Thus, it is like any other form of measurement. Measurement, by definition, yields a description of the relationship between the measuring instrument and the object measured; it does not yield some property intrinsic to the object alone. This does not mean that a rating or any other measurement is useless for helping us to understand an object. It does mean that, as with any form of measurement, controls, reliability, and evidence of validity are critical. The bulk of this chapter will be concerned with suggestions for maximizing control, reliability, and validity in rating. It also means that describing the raters and their preparation for a task is as important in reporting one's study as describing the objects or behaviors rated and the scales on which the rating is done. In discussing rating, Kerlinger (1966) has said that

> . . . the observer is both a crucial strength and a crucial weakness. . . . The strength and weakness of the procedure is the observer's power of inference. If it were not for inference, a machine observer would be better than a man observer. . . . The strength is that the observer can relate the observed behavior to the constructs or variables of the study: he brings behavior and construct together. One of the recurring difficulties of measurement is to bridge the gap between behavior and construct. Competent observers and well-made observations help bridge this gap [p. 505].

In considering the use of ratings in a study, it is essential to realize that rating procedures involve almost all the problems of any form of measurement, especially any form of psychological measurement. Green (1954) has described measurement as

> . . . *the assignment of numerals to objects, events, or persons, according to rules.* . . . The result of a measurement is a *scale.* A scale comprises the set of numerals given to the objects by using a certain rule of assignment [p. 337].

METHODS OF RATING

There are four basic methods of rating: rank order, paired comparison, comparison with a set of examples which exemplify a range of the attribute being considered, and numerical rating on some standard scale. Some scholars substitute letters or descriptive terms for numbers on this last type of scale, but the results are essentially the same.

Rank Order

The rank order method of rating is probably best exemplified by how a judge votes in a speech or beauty contest: he gives one contestant first, one second, and so forth. He does not need to be concerned with how *much* better or prettier one contestant is than another, but simply who is best, who is next best, who is next, and so on, until he runs out of contestants. If he has difficulty distinguishing between the speaking quality or beauty of some of the contestants, he may sometimes declare a tie between two or more of them, *i.e.*, he may use tied ranks.

Whether the objects are girls being ranked on the quality of their physical beauty or abstract visual stimuli being ranked on degree of visual complexity, the judgment task is essentially the same. The experimenter must only decide beforehand and inform those doing the ranking whether tied ranks are permissible. This decision should be based on the way the rankings are to be used in the research. For certain purposes it may be desirable to force a respondent to avoid tied ranks.

In general, ranking provides the least information because one can get identical sets of rankings for objects which are quite similar and objects which are extremely different. In addition, the difficulty of the ranking task increases tremendously as the number of objects to be ranked increases. The number that can be reliably ranked will vary with the type of object, the dimension on which they are ranked, and the relative homogeneity of the group. In general, ranking must probably be restricted to six to ten objects in a group.

Paired Comparison

For many types of objects, paired comparison is the most reliable method of rating. In this procedure, each object is compared with every other object. For example, if one is rating pictorial balance, each visual stimulus will be judged against each of the other stimuli in turn. This is an excellent procedure when one is judging a small number of objects and each object is the kind that can be examined again and again, juxtaposed with each of the others. This would be the case in comparing certain visual stimuli, brief sounds, or short pieces of prose. Rating complete speeches is more difficult; it is impossible for all practical purposes if the speeches are live. In addition, if there are many objects in the set, the comparison task is extremely time consuming since the number of comparisons is equal to $\frac{N!}{2(N-2)!}$. Thus, with only 10 objects, there are 45 comparisons to be made.

Comparison with a Set of Examples Exemplifying a Range

This procedure probably has the least applicability to communication research problems. The rater is asked to judge which one of a set of standard objects is most similar on the relevant dimension to the object being judged. Thus, if raters are to judge voice quality, they might be reminded of five persons with whom they are familiar and told that a particular one is an example of "superior" voice quality, another represents "good," another "average," another "poor," and the fifth "very bad." The rater is then told simply to judge other voices he hears by these five. If the five criterion voices are not familiar to a rater, he can be exposed to recordings of them. He can even listen to them again, periodically, while in the midst of his rating task, to refresh his memory.

Though this basic procedure has limited usefulness in communication research, a variation of it could prove extremely useful: instead of the experimenter setting the range within which judgments are to be made and exemplifying the end points of that range, each subject must set the range and end points for himself. The procedure is probably best explained with an example from a study by Guilford and Holley (1949). These scholars were interested in studying the dimensions on which individuals make various sorts of aesthetic judgments of visual stimuli. Each judge was given 115 designs. He was to examine the entire set and place the one he thought was most attractive and the one he thought was least attractive on the ends of a row to serve as anchoring points for a seven-step equal appearing interval scale (see Chapter 7, pp. 198–201). Each of the remaining designs was to be placed on one of seven piles within this range, each pile to be thought of by the rater as representing one of those seven steps. (This procedure is similar, of course, to the sorting process of Q-sort methodology [see Chapter 5]. An experimenter could also use an adaptation of the own-categories procedure [see Chapter 7, pp. 207–208] described by Sherif, Sherif, and Nebergall [1965], in which a rater uses as many categories as he wishes in classifying objects.)

Standard Scale

This is the type of scale used for most rating tasks in communication research. In general, judges are told the dimension on which the objects are to be rated and are given labels for the end points of the scale (*e.g.,* "very well organized" — "very poorly organized"; "very complex" — "very simple"; "very interesting" — "not at all interesting"). Sometimes scales which go from a positive to a negative extreme label the zero or neutral point. Some researchers have even seen fit to label all points on a scale (*e.g.,* "excellent," "good," "fair," "poor"). Others have used numerical values to label the points on a scale. Little evidence indicates that these differences in labeling affect the substantive outcomes of one's research. Therefore, the procedure to use should depend on one's evaluation of which will be most meaningful to the particular judges for the particular judgments they are being asked to make.

Innumerable studies have compared the results obtained with the various types of rating scales, especially speech rating scales. Thompson (1943, 1944), for example, compared results from paired comparisons, rank ordering, linear scales, letter grade scales, and scales with descriptive terms. Brooks (1957a) compared a forced choice scale which he developed with a numerical scale. Morrison and Vernon (1941), working with written material, compared what they termed the "impressionistic" and the "analytic" methods of rating. Though some differences in reliability were obtained, the surprising finding is the similarity of results obtained from these varied procedures when the same concepts or dimensions were rated. This is not to say that there were *no* differences, however. If one is doing a study in which small differences are significant, these variations in type of rating scale may be extremely important.

As a matter of fact, even finer differences in scale format can be decisive. Madden and Bourdon (1964), for example, found significant differences among ratings done on standard scales with slightly different formats when men in the air force were rated on such qualities as knowledge, adaptability, and resourcefulness. Among the seven variations in format they compared were horizontal scales and vertical scales, scales with bars dividing the steps and scales without such bars, scales with the positive end at the top and scales with the positive end at the bottom, and scales in which the end points were labeled more and less extremely (*e.g.,* "above average" versus "very much more than average").

The point of all of this is that when one is looking only for very gross differences, or some rank ordering of stimuli which vary widely on the dimension being scaled, the rating procedure tends to make little difference. However, when one is seeking greater precision, searching for smaller differences, or discriminating among more homogeneous stimuli, greater attention must be given to the rating procedures used. Considering our present state of knowledge, for most such studies one should pre-test his rating procedures very carefully.

A hasty survey of the communication studies which have used rating data shows many variations of these rating methods. One in particular deserves mention here because of its possible applicability to a wide range of communication problems. Specifically, it is useful where one wants continuous ratings of a message as an individual is being exposed to it, so that comparisons can be made among the parts of the message as well as between one message and another. Each judge is given a switch, potentiometer, or some other device for rating each instant of a speech, film, radio program, drama, or whatever, as it is in progress. These ratings are recorded on moving tape or electronically, along with cues indicating to which part of the stimulus judges were being exposed at each point (Brockhaus and Irwin, 1958; Becker, 1960b, 1964). One variation is a paper-and-pencil procedure in which raters make discrete ratings at set time intervals rather than continuous ratings (Becker, 1960b, pp. 263–264). A number is flashed on the screen each time the judges are to make a rating. This technique has been used to get semicontinuous ratings of films and television programs on the "interesting-uninteresting" dimension. At least two scholars have used continuous ratings of these types to study the relationship between ratings of interest and retention of information associated with the various parts of messages (Twyford, 1951; Becker, 1964).

Whatever the object (or behavior) and dimension rated and the type of scale used, the basic problems of scale construction, reliability, and validity remain the same. Most of the remainder of this chapter will be devoted to these closely related concerns.

RATING SCALE CONSTRUCTION

Establishing the Purpose

One must begin with a clear idea of the *purpose* for which the rating is to be obtained. (This will be discussed in greater detail in the validity section, pp. 226–228.) If one were interested in the relationship between manifest cooperativeness in a discussion group and the degree to which the group can agree on a solution to a problem, he might develop a different procedure for rating cooperativeness than if he were interested in the relationship between manifest cooperativeness and the satisfaction participants derived from the discussion. The procedure should be determined, in part, by one's theoretical position or by the reasons one has for expecting to find such a relationship. One might expect cooperativeness to affect agreement because one conceives of cooperativeness as the effort to find common ground in a set of arguments. On the other hand, one might expect cooperativeness to affect participants' satisfaction because cooperativeness is conceived of as manifest efforts to help others develop and clarify their ideas. These two conceptions of cooperativeness are clearly not independent; however, they are independent enough so that one might need to develop different procedures for rating them. (As a matter of fact, the independence of these two sets of cooperativeness ratings and the relative power of each to predict satisfaction and agreement are themselves empirical questions that may be worth answering.)

Clarifying the Concept

Considering the purpose of one's study and the rationale for one's question or hypothesis, the next step is to develop as complete an image of the concept to be rated as possible. Here one might take a cue from those philosophers who have explicated the meanings of terms. William James (1890) for example, had a firm foundation for developing a set of rating scales when he completed his explication of the term "prudence."

> Suppose, for example, that we say a man is "prudent." Concretely, that means that he takes out insurance, hedges in betting, looks before he leaps. . . . As a constant habit in him, a permanent tone of character, it is convenient to call him prudent in abstraction from any one of his acts [p. 147].

Such an explication offers ideas for scales to use in rating a concept. For rating most concepts, having a number of scales instead of one is important for two reasons: it increases reliability (as will be demonstrated later) and, in many cases, each individual scale or indicator has only a probabilistic relationship to the underlying concept. For example, one may decide that the concept of quality in theme writing means, to most individuals, that the purpose of the theme is clear, the content contributes to the purpose, the language is adapted to the audience, sentences are well constructed, the best overall organization for the purpose is used, and a minimum number of faults show up in the mechanics of writing. However, the same individuals might possibly label a theme high in quality that was not perfect on one or more of these counts. In other words, no one indicator has a perfect relationship to the underlying concept. By using ratings of a number of these indicators and calculating some overall score that takes all the individual ratings into account, one increases the probability of having a fruitful rating of the concept.

It is possible, of course, to specify the indicators to too great an extent, so that one negates one of the major advantages of the rating method — to measure an aspect of objects or phenomena which is so complex that all of its relevant dimensions are impossible or impractical to specify. Thus, if one is devising a scale for rating hostility in a discussion group, one needs to give the observers some examples of behaviors which would indicate hostility. However, one must impress upon raters that the list of examples is not exhaustive and that there are no absolute weights for each indicator of hostility. An attempt to be exhaustive will probably increase reliability but may decrease validity because the definition of the construct becomes so restricted that it bears little resemblance to the idea one wanted to study initially. This is a type of minimax problem. What is the maximum amount of reliability one can obtain through specification, with the minimum degradation of validity? There is no absolute answer to this question. It will vary with the purposes and conditions of each study.

Analyzing Scales

Once a researcher has a set of indicators or scales for a concept to be rated, there is still a question of whether each scale is measuring a relatively independent aspect of the concept. When Becker (1962) factor analyzed the data from a set of 10 scales assumed to be indicators of 10 dimensions of speech quality, he found that the 10 scales were, in fact, measuring only three dimensions. The ratings on organization, material, analysis, and subject correlated so highly that the hypothesis was tenable that all were measures of precisely the same dimension. Likewise, the ratings of adjustment, fluency, body, voice, and articulation and pronunciation were found to vary dependently and so seemed to be measures of the same dimension. Only the language ratings seemed to be somewhat independent of the others. Thus, the 10 rating scales apparently represented only three dimensions of the concept "speech quality," not 10. In addition, and probably even more important, in studies using as a criterion the total score over all 10 rating scales (which was usually the case), the researcher was unknowingly probably giving more weight to delivery than to analysis-content and more to each of these than to language: there were, in effect, five ratings of delivery, four of analysis-content, and one of language. This is acceptable if it is consistent with the researcher's concept of speech quality. If it is not, he needs to add or delete scales accordingly. For example, if he decides that all three of these dimensions should have equal weight, he should have an equal number of scales for each. On the other hand, if he conceives of speech quality as being more the result of analysis-content than of delivery or language, he might want four rating scales loaded on the analysis-content dimension and two each on the delivery and language dimensions.

For even greater control of the relative weight given to each indicator or dimension of a concept being rated, one would want to consider the variance in the ratings on each scale. If the variances for all Becker's 10 scales are roughly equivalent, each scale contributes equally to the variance in the total score. On the other hand, when ratings on one scale are much more varied than ratings on another scale, the former scale has much more effect on the variance in total score. For example, if the ratings were done on seven-step scales and the ratings for analysis clustered around the 4 on the scale while the ratings for subject were spread evenly over the entire seven steps, the latter scale would be contributing more to the variance in the total score and, hence, would have more effect on any difference obtained between experimental groups. If it appears desirable to overcome this discrepancy, one can define analysis a bit more clearly to help judges make finer discriminations, or one can give judges additional training until they can make finer distinctions on this scale and begin using the total scale for ratings.

In the initial stages of some studies, one may be interested in a concept for which he does not have a very clear image and may devote a major part of the research to clarifying the concept. He would probably begin with a large number of scales and study the relationships among them and, perhaps, the relationship of each to some other variables. Carroll (1960), for example, was interested in an empirical clarification of the concept of prose style. He developed 29 rating scales which he believed tapped various dimensions of style. Among these were such scales as "subtle-obvious," "abstract-concrete," and "personal-impersonal." He also developed 39 objective measures, including number of syllables in a standard length passage, percentage of intransitive verbs, number of gerunds, etc. He then selected 150 English prose passages of roughly equal length from a variety of sources, including novels, newspaper stories and editorials, speeches, legal documents, and a collection of mediocre high school English compositions. He obtained a score for each passage on each of his 39 objective measures and then had eight judges rate each passage on each of the 29 rating scales. The total of the eight judges' ratings as the score on each scale gave 68 scores or measures for each passage which he correlated and factor analyzed. From these analyses, he found six meaningful dimensions of style that he could measure. One of these, which he labeled "characterization," could be measured reliably only with some of the objective measures. Three of them, "general stylistic evaluation," "abstractness," and "seriousness" could be measured reliably only by rating scales. And two of the dimensions, "personal affect" and "ornamentation," could be measured reliably either by rating scales or some of the objective methods. By studying both the rating scales and the objective measures which loaded heavily on each of the dimensions, Carroll was able to discover a good deal about prose style. In addition, he had some rating scales which could be used for obtaining reliable measures of what appeared to be most of the major dimensions of prose style. This assumes that his initial selection of rating scales was a representative sample of the population of rating scales that are relevant to prose style. Since he had studied style for many years, and since he apparently included every scale he could think of which appeared to be relevant, the assumption appears fairly sound.

Many other scholars did similar analyses of rating scales which appeared relevant to speech performances. Using 61 scales, Monroe (1937) found nine factors; using 35 scales, Price (1961) found six factors; using 50 scales, Bowers (1965) found nine factors. The factors found in these three studies were similar. Their differences, and the difference in number of factors found, appear to be at least partly due to the different sample of scales each started with and the somewhat different analytical procedures used in each study. Williams, Clark, and Wood (1966) did a similar analysis of debate ratings and found four factors. They labeled them "argument," "vocal correctness," "apparent character," and "overall delivery."

Because so many communication scholars are concerned with the concept of "source credibility" or, in rhetorical terms, "ethos," several developmental studies have been designed to produce a set of rating scales which can be used in studies of this concept. Exemplifying these is the study by McCroskey (1966). Rather than the usual sorts of rating scales, though, McCroskey used Likert-type scales. Each scale consists of a statement about an object and the rater is to indicate whether he strongly agrees, agrees, is undecided, disagrees, or strongly disagrees. Thus, the format of the instrument and the rater's task are like the instrument format and task in many types of attitude measurement. Clearly, rating procedures and attitude measurement procedures are not independent. The critical difference is in degree: whether one is using a procedure primarily to obtain a measure from which he can infer something about the object judged or a measure from which he can infer something about the individual doing the judging. This difference too often becomes blurred in practice. It is exceedingly important that one keep the distinction in mind as he develops his measurement procedures and, especially, as he tests the validity of his procedures.

Developing Scales for Communication Research

There are few helpful guidelines in developing indicators or rating scales for many of the concepts relevant to communication which one might want rated in a study. As a matter of fact, many communication concepts have been talked about in such vague and nonempirical language that it is difficult to develop a very clear image of what they mean. "Creativity" is an example of such a concept. Even a quick review of the literature on creativity shows that the term has been used to mean a great variety of quite different things. Yet for some communication research purposes the concept may be valid. In any case, we would assume at least initially that there are various kinds of creativity, and in developing rating scales for measuring them, we need to limit ourselves to a fairly homogeneous set of situations.

For example, let us say that we are interested in measuring the degree to which individuals are "creative" scholars. (The procedure is probably just as applicable for any other sort of creativity or almost any other sort of concept.) Some individuals insist that creativity cannot be measured. Yet these same individuals generally label some scholars creative and some noncreative. We must assume that this labeling is not a random process; consciously or not, they must have noticed something in the behavior or work of certain scholars which caused them to conclude that those scholars are creative. They must have noticed something else in the behavior or work of other scholars which caused them to conclude that those scholars are not creative. Or they may have remarked the presence of some things in one group and the absence of those things in the other group.

If some knowledgeable observers tried to make a list of the cues which help them discriminate between creative and uncreative scholars, we would have the beginnings of a set of rating scales. We could see which cues our observers agreed on and then we could test them to see whether they discriminated between two sets of scholars who we were certain represented two extremes in creativity. For this purpose, we should use a new set of observers or raters. On the basis of these results, we could refine our scales and test again, repeating the process until we had a set of scales trained observers could make reliable judgments with and which would result in ratings which discriminated among scholars who we were certain varied on this trait.

A similar procedure which can be used to develop rating scales for judging a concept is to have observers keep a record over some period of time of "critical incidents,"[1] behaviors which strike them as representative of one extreme or the other of the concept. Such a procedure might be used, for example, in developing a set of indicators of creativity in writing among fifth grade youngsters. With a group of teachers keeping diaries for this purpose, one would develop a meaningful set of rating scales in a relatively short period.

In developing or selecting rating scales for use in a study, one must meet two major criteria, reliability and validity.

RELIABILITY

Three major types of scale reliability must be considered when using rating in most communication studies: intrarater reliability, interrater reliability, and intraobject reliability. Intrarater reliability is the degree of agreement of a rater with himself when he judges the same object at different times. Interrater reliability is the degree of agreement among different raters judging the same object. Intraobject reliability is the degree to which an object is consistent when it is sampled in different ways or at different times. For example, we know that almost all persons vary from one day to another and from one topic to another in the quality of their speaking. The greater this variance, the lower the intraobject reliability when one is trying to infer the speaker's skill from a single speech.

Intrarater Reliability

Intrarater reliability has seldom been studied, though it is obviously important. Two researchers who did study it found that judges of speeches are not as consistent as one might believe. Drushal (1939), for example, found that when four trained teachers rated a group of recorded speeches on "general effect of delivery" three times at one-week intervals, the correlation between the ratings for the first and second hearings was .76, and .73 between the second and third hearings. The criterion measure was the sum of the four teachers' ratings of one speech at one time. Huckleberry (1950) had three trained judges rate each of a set of recorded speeches twice and found the rank difference correlation between the two sets of ratings to be .55. Higher intrarater reliability was found by Anderson and Traxler (1940) for theme rating. They found that the total of two judges' ratings of themes at two different points in time correlated at .89 in one study and .93 in another. However, the rating in this study was largely of mechanical aspects of the writing, rather than what one might call substantive aspects like ideas or analysis. Adding the latter types of scales would undoubtedly have lowered reliability.

[1] This procedure was developed by John Flanagan (1954).

From the various studies which have been done on rating reliability, four clear findings about intrarater reliability have emerged: (1) A judge's reliability will increase with training (Hurd, 1942). (2) His reliability will be higher if he is forced to distribute his ratings among six to seven steps on a scale, rather than rating on a two- to four-step scale or being allowed to bunch his ratings on two to four steps of a longer scale (Becker and Cronkhite, 1965). (3) His reliability will be higher if the concept to be rated is broken down into a series of indicators, each to be rated independently, and the total score used as the criterion, rather than rating the concept itself on a single scale (Bradshaw, 1930; Becker, 1960a). As a matter of fact, there is even some evidence that a judge's rating of a speech on the single scale of "general effectiveness" will be more reliable if the judge first rates the more microscopic qualities or attributes of a speech and then rates "general effectiveness" (Clevenger, 1964). Rating individual aspects of the object first apparently increases the probability that various raters will consider most of the same attributes in rating the overall or general quality of the object. (4) A judge's reliability will vary with the heterogeneity (on the dimension rated) of the objects rated. For example, in rating visual complexity, ratings will be more reliable when the stimuli are distributed in a wide range of complexity than when they cluster within a narrow range. Related to this, Knower's (1940) findings on speech ratings indicate that objects or individuals ranked at the ends of the distribution are rated with greater reliability than those in the middle. (For example, a judge is more consistent in his ratings of very good and very poor speakers, but he has difficulty with those who are just so-so.)

The first two points above are obviously closely related, though not synonymous. One of the goals of the sessions for training judges is to help them learn to make finer discriminations. The training will also make them more consistent in the discriminations they make. In addition, even trained judges tend to bunch ratings around the middle point on a scale. Therefore, directions to judges must stress the importance of avoiding this tendency.

Though training raters can increase reliability, it is important to note that it is not always appropriate. For example, in some studies, part of the purpose might be to discover something about the ways naïve audiences perceive some communication object or behavior. Rating scales could be used on which members of these audiences record their perceptions. Training these subjects would alter their responses and hence invalidate the ratings.

Interrater Reliability

Interrater reliability is affected by all the points noted for intrarater reliability plus some additional ones. The most important point is that interrater reliability increases with the number of judges whose ratings are added, though it does not increase in a linear fashion. The greatest increase in reliability will come as one goes from rating by a single judge to rating by a few judges. As the number of judges is increased still further, the gain in reliability becomes relatively smaller until the point is reached where additional judges add virtually nothing to the reliability coefficient. This point obviously is reached more rapidly with trained judges than untrained judges. Bryan and Wilke (1941) found that the interrater reliability coefficient for untrained judges was .66 when the sum of five raters was used, .83 when the sum of 10 raters was used, and .91 when the sum of 20 was used. Though the absolute value of obtained reliability has varied in studies using other types of raters and when other concepts or objects were rated, the general finding of the way reliability increases and diminishes with number of raters has been the same.

It was indicated earlier that intrarater reliability is higher for trained than untrained judges. In addition, trained judges will agree with each other more than untrained judges will; that is to say, interrater reliability is also higher for trained than untrained judges. However, some evidence shows that using the sum of a series of ratings of discrete aspects of an object rather than using a single overall rating will reduce the discrepancy between trained and untrained judges (Wiseman and Barker, 1965).

Where value judgments may be involved in ratings, one of the results in a study by Knower (1940) is important. He found that even trained judges agree more definitely on speaking characteristics of which they disapprove than on those of which they approve.

Researchers have studied the effect on reliability of many other rater variables, such as sex of rater (Bryan and Wilke, 1942; Haiman, 1949; Hildreth, 1954), age (Bryan and Wilke, 1942), and personality (Bostrom, 1964). One communication scholar (Clevenger, 1963) even examined, in effect, whether the libido of male judges affected their ratings of the excellence in speaking by females (he found that it did). The results from these studies probably have little generalizability beyond the very specific behaviors or concepts rated. On the other hand, the effect of a closely related variable — attitude — is relevant to a great many communication studies. A wide variety of studies gives evidence that the attitude of judges toward the content of a message can affect their ratings of other aspects of the message (Knower, 1935; Miller, 1964). One must carefully control for this factor, especially in any study involving the rating of persuasive messages or their sources.

Intraobject Reliability

Intraobject reliability has been the least studied type of reliability. This negligence is probably due in part to the fact that intraobject reliability is not a relevant problem for all types of communication studies using ratings. For example, it would not be a problem in rating visual complexity. The problem is extremely important, however, where one is rating performance as a measure of speaking or writing skill. Some obvious technical difficulties in assessing intraobject reliability independently of rater reliability have been overcome in at least two studies, one of reliability in theme writing and one of reliability in speech making. In the former, Traxler and Anderson (1935) concluded that the reliability of the ratings of trained judges was relatively high while the reliability of pupil performance in writing English compositions was low. Marine (1965), on the other hand, concluded that the consistency or reliability of student speaking performance was greater than the reliability of student raters. The differences between these studies must be viewed with caution since expert raters were used in one study and student raters in the other, and different types of rating were employed. Additional research on the problem should be done before one uses ratings of a single performance as an index of performance skill.

Maximum reliability is not necessarily the goal of every rating procedure: in general, it is not worth the cost. One's goal should rather be enough reliability to insure detecting the minimal differences or relationships one wants to detect. For example, if one were comparing two methods of teaching writing, one could probably detect the most minute difference between experimental groups by a lengthy and arduous training process, refinement of the rating instrument over a long series of pre-tests, and the use of 20 to 30 judges for each sample of written work with which subjects are tested. Thus, one can get statistically significant differences where the differences are so small they make no practical difference. In developing rating instruments and procedures, it is important to ask how large a difference must be to be meaningful and then plan accordingly.

The most generally applicable and probably the best method for estimating the reliability of a set of ratings is the intraclass correlation method developed by Robert Ebel (1951). The method is described in a number of statistics textbooks as well as in the original journal article.

VALIDITY

Validity is one of the most difficult problems encountered by a researcher. The problem is not lessened by such questions as, "But does that rating procedure measure his *real* writing skill (or speaking skill or whatever)?" These questions, as generally asked, are meaningless. They are related to what is unfortunately the usual definition of validity. This definition is some variation of "Validity is the capacity of an instrument to measure what you say it measures," in other words, a type of operational definition in reverse.

A better definition of validity is the *usefulness* of the measure for your particular purpose. It is not fruitful to speak of validity independently of purpose, as a measure may be valid for one purpose, but not another. A particular speech rating may be valid as a predictor of how credible a speaker will be perceived to be by a particular audience, but it may not be valid as a predictor of whether the speech will alter the attitudes of listeners toward its thesis.

Many developers of tests have "validated" an instrument by correlating scores obtained with it and scores obtained from the same subjects with another instrument which presumably measures the same concept. There are two fallacies in this procedure. The scores could correlate extremely well, yet neither set have much predictive power for the relevant criterion. On the other hand, the two sets of scores could correlate with each other poorly and yet each correlate equally well with the relevant criterion, *i.e.,* have equal predictive power.

There are no general ways to test validity. One must simply think through the purpose of his study, what he believes should be predictable from his ratings, and then develop rating scales and procedures consistent with that purpose and, if possible, pre-test to see whether they are in fact consistent.

Influences on Validity

A number of tendencies among raters may reduce validity for most purposes. Some, such as the influence of a female speaker's sex appeal on ratings of speaking performance, were mentioned above. In addition, what has been termed the "halo effect" can be seen, for example, if one takes an essay, presents it to one group of judges in neatly written form with no grammatical errors and to another group of judges in a messy form with a number of striking grammatical errors, and has each judge rate the "quality of the ideas" in the essay. The neatly and correctly written essay will almost certainly be rated higher in "quality of ideas" because the form in which it is presented acts as a "halo," affecting a reader's perceptions of the other qualities of the object.[2]

Similarly, the order in which objects are presented to judges can affect the ratings they receive, as both Knower (1940) and Becker (1953) have shown for speech ratings. Judges vary in the degree to which they tend to be severe or lenient in their ratings. To some extent this is probably a matter of different anchors or standards against which each is judging the objects; to some extent it is probably a difference in personality. In any case, like all the problems of raters which affect validity, this can be minimized with proper training sessions for the raters who are to be used in a study.

The sampling of the objects to be rated may also have an influence on validity as well as reliability. Again, the particular method of sampling should depend on the purpose of the study. If the purpose involves speaking or writing *skill* of subjects, one must decide how to sample the speaking or

---

[2] Some evidence for this generalization is presented in the studies mentioned on p. 225 which have found a great deal of common variance among the ratings of different aspects of objects. See also Ruechelle (1958).

writing to be rated. How long should each example be? How many and what kind of samples should be obtained for each subject? In what form should the messages be when judges are exposed to them? For some types of oral communication, one must decide whether judges are simply to hear the messages, both see and hear them, or perhaps just read transcripts of the speeches. Clearly, the decision depends in large part on the purpose of one's study. However, some research may be relevant to one's decision in certain cases. Gilkinson (1941) found that when judges were rating "general speech effectiveness," their reliability was higher when they only heard the speech rather than when they both saw and heard it or when they only read the manuscript. Reliabilities in the latter two cases were roughly equivalent. However, there was a high correlation between the ratings obtained from judges who both saw and heard the speeches and those who only heard them, but virtually no correlation between the ratings of those who saw and heard the speeches and those who only read the manuscripts. In other words, when judges rated the oral presentation and the oral and visual presentation, they seemed to be measuring the same or equivalent things. On the other hand, when they rated the manuscript (on the same speech rating scale), they seemed to be measuring quite different things.

Another study relevant to the decision of exposing judges to only the aural cues or to both the aural and visual cues is one by Gauron and Dickinson (1967). The study found that when psychiatrists were given a case history of a patient and then exposed to a motion picture of the patient being interviewed, they were significantly more "comfortable" about their diagnoses than when they had to make diagnoses on the basis of the case history alone. ("Comfortableness" was defined as the psychiatrist's emotional satisfaction or happiness.) On the other hand, the film had little effect on the diagnoses. Thus, the researchers confirmed their hypothesis that "psychiatrists prefer to see patients in order to *feel* better about their conclusions." These results are probably generalizable to the behaviors and attitudes of raters of some other forms of communication. Thus an experimenter must discriminate between the cues judges need for reliable and valid ratings and the cues judges may want for extraneous reasons.

On all questions of sampling, defining the objects to be rated, procedures for rating, etc., one should be able to make sound decisions if he considers the matters noted in the reliability and validity sections above, carefully pre-tests, and applies common sense.

STATISTICAL TREATMENT OF RATING DATA

Much of the literature disagrees about which statistics are most appropriate for describing and testing rating data. Some scholars contend that only nonparametric statistics may be used legitimately. Others contend that the use of parametric statistics is defensible except where there are gross departures from the assumptions of normal distributions of scores and homogeneity of variance. One of the most interesting arguments involves the question of whether the intervals on rating scales are "equal." At one time, many scholars spent a great deal of time developing scales in which the intervals were "psychologically equivalent." But this kind of developmental research has diminished probably because the concept of "psychologically equivalent steps on a rating scale" has little useful meaning and makes little practical difference to results. A safe rule of thumb is to use the statistical procedures that are most precise and that seem most appropriate to the particular problems, unless there is clear evidence that the data depart so far from one or more of the assumptions that misleading results are likely to be obtained from these procedures. In that case, it is probably wise to turn to statistical procedures which are not dependent on those assumptions, even though they are less ideal for the original purposes or, as is usually the case, provide a less precise test of the hypotheses.

Although these suggestions are imprecise, they imply that the researcher must have clearly defined purposes in his study, a high degree of familiarity with the phenomena being investigated, a "feel" for his data, and a great deal of common sense. Without these four attributes, the most precise instructions to a budding researcher are worthless.

USES OF RATING SCALES

Because of the variety of purposes for which rating methods have been and can be used in communication research, no single study can serve as an example of how to use them. In some studies ratings are used as the dependent variables, in others they are used to define the independent variables, and in still others they are used as control variables. For example, one can manipulate a message variable in order to test the effect on ratings of the message. Or one can select a group of messages which have been rated high on some quality and another group rated low and test for differences in the learning or attitude change they cause in an audience. Or one can manipulate one variable in messages, use ratings as a check to insure that the messages are equivalent on other dimensions, and test for still other effects the messages may have on an audience.

Whether as dependent, independent, or control variables, ratings have been used to describe a wide variety of phenomena. They have been used to describe almost every aspect of the behavior manifested by a speaker, writer, or actor, from the degree to which he displays "fear" in the communication situation or the "quality" of his voice or handwriting to the degree to which he is perceived as "generally effective" or "natural." Some researchers have had sources of various types rated on "credibility," "trustworthiness," and "competence." Visual stimuli, from motion pictures to random designs, have been rated on everything from "balance," "visual complexity," and "rhythm" to degree of "high or low key" lighting. Rating techniques have been used to describe such various aspects of discussion sessions as the "quality" of the overall discussion, the "opinionatedness" of individual statements within the discussion, the "quality" of the solution to a problem achieved by a group, the "attractiveness" of the group, and the "leadership" of individual members of the group. Ratings have been used to describe degrees of violence displayed by various incidents in television dramatizations and to determine whether a mother "structures" her child's activities during mother-child interactions.

There are innumerable experiments on pedagogical methods in speech and English which have used ratings as *dependent variables* or criterion measures. Typical of these is the study by Becker and Dallinger (1960) comparing three methods of teaching communication skills. Two of the eight criterion measures were ratings. One was the rating of expository themes which each student was given two hours to write. Each theme was rated by a judge on six seven-interval scales; purpose, content, organization, sentence structure, diction, and mechanics. On the post-test, each theme was rated by at least two experienced raters. The criterion measure was the mean of the ratings of both judges over all scales for each student. The second criterion measure was the rating of a four-minute argumentative speech which each student was given fifty minutes to prepare. Each speech was rated by three to five experienced judges on eleven scales: central idea, analysis, supporting material, organization, language, adjustment to speaking situation, bodily action, voice, articulation and pronunciation, fluency, and general effectiveness. The criterion was the average rating given on all scales by all judges for each subject.

Attneave (1957) and Gunkle (1963) used ratings as *independent variables* to categorize sets of stimuli so that measurements could be made of the objects in each category and tests run to determine which physical variables could account for the differences in rating. Gunkle studied the vocal variables associated with perceiving differences in spontaneity. He had naïve judges (sampled from the population to which he wished to generalize) rate the spontaneity in each of a large set of recordings. Each judge rated each utterance on a single seven-step scale which was labeled "nonspontaneous" on one end and "spontaneous" on the other. Some of the recordings were of actual conversation, some were of actors reading transcribed bits of conversation, and some were of actors performing from memory these same bits of conversation. Gunkle selected the utterances whose mean spontaneity ratings were in the top quartile and the utterances whose mean spontaneity ratings were in the bottom quartile. He tested the significance of the difference between these two sets of utterances in temporal patterns of phonation, phonation time ratio, mean rate, and changes in rate.

Attneave was interested in the physical attributes of two-dimensional shapes which cause them to be perceived as varying in complexity. His stimuli were 72 "random" shapes varying on such dimensions as curvedness, symmetry, number of turns, and angular variability. Judges were again untrained because he wanted to generalize about the variables in stimuli which affect their probability of being perceived as complex by *untrained* persons. Each judge rated each of the shapes on a labeled seven-step rating scale. Attneave's description of his procedure is a model for those who may be writing up studies in areas where slight differences in procedure can seriously affect results:

> Procedure — The shapes were displayed, in a white-on-black figure-ground relationship, by projecting them individually to the front wall of the room in which Ss were seated. Each S was provided with a seven-category rating form containing a line for each shape and columns headed 'Extremely Simple,' 'Very Simple,' 'Simple,' 'Medium,' 'Complex,' 'Very Complex,' and 'Extremely Complex.' The instructions given contained no definition, either explicit or implicit, of the terms 'Simple' and 'Complex.'
>
> Before actually making their ratings, the Ss were shown all 72 shapes in rapid succession (2-sec. exposure each) in order that they might, from the beginning, adapt their rating behavior to the range of stimuli with which they were to deal. In displaying the shapes for rating, each was exposed for 10 sec. with a negligible interval between stimuli.
>
> The Ss served in four approximately equal groups which differed only in the ordering or sequence of stimulus presentation. The first sequence was a random permutation of the 72 stimuli, the second was an 'inside-out' reordering of the first, and the third and fourth were reversals of the first two [p. 223].

Typical of the way in which ratings have been used as *control variables* is a study by Lana (1963) on the interaction of topic controversy and the order of presentation of persuasive messages. Lana used four messages, one for and one against Picasso and one for and one against the use of nuclear weapons. He attempted to make them comparable by giving them approximately the same length and basing each on five points within the general framework of the topic. In as many cases as possible, each favorable point on an issue was developed as a point against the issue for the opposing argument. Not satisfied that he had adequately controlled the equality of his messages, he selected ten subjects from the population to which he wished to generalize to rate the clarity of presentation, consistency of argument, excellence of style, and overall effectiveness in changing opinion of each message. The results showed that the pro and con messages were comparable on these dimensions. If they had not been, he undoubtedly would have rewritten and retested them, repeating the process until he was satisfied that he had adequately controlled for those variables.

Summary

This chapter has suggested some rules for observing — some procedures which can strengthen research. Rank order, paired comparison, comparison with examples, and numerical rating scales have been described, and procedures have been suggested for developing new sets of scales or indicators for a concept and means of increasing validity and intrarater, interrater, and intraobject reliability. Most important of all is the suggestion that, before one begins making decisions about methods of rating, one should clearly specify the purpose of his study and the purposes for which he is obtaining rating data. These are necessary bases for determining whether the kind of rating methods one selects and the way one uses them are the most fruitful for the study. Rating procedures can be useful tools for research if one follows the suggestions outlined here and emulates the careful and intelligent ways the authors of the last four studies used ratings.

References and Selected Readings

Anderson, H. A., and Traxler, A. E. The reliability of the reading of an English essay test — A second study. *School Review,* 1940, **48,** 521–530.

Attneave, F. Physical determinants of the judged complexity of shapes. *Journal of Experimental Psychology,* 1957, **53,** 221–233.

Becker, S. L. The ordinal position effect. *Quarterly Journal of Speech,* 1953, **39,** 217–219.

Becker, S. L. An analysis of speaking and writing ratings. Unpublished paper, University of Iowa, 1960. (a)

Becker, S. L. Reaction profiles: Studies of methodology. *Journal of Broadcasting,* 1960, **4,** 253–268. (b)

Becker, S. L. The rating of speeches: Scale independence. *Speech Monographs,* 1962, **29,** 38–44.

Becker, S. L. Interest, tension, and retention. *AV Communication Review,* 1964, **12,** 277–291.

Becker, S. L., and Cronkhite, G. L., Jr. Reliability as a function of utilized scale steps. *The Speech Teacher,* 1965, **14,** 291–293.

Becker, S. L., and Dallinger, C. A. The effect of instructional methods upon achievement and attitudes in communication skills. *Speech Monographs,* 1960, **27,** 70–76.

Belson, W. A. The effects of reversing presentation order of verbal rating scales. *Journal of Advertising Research,* 1966, **6,** 30–37.

Blumberg, H. H., DeSota, C. B., and Kuethe, J. L. Evaluation of scale formats. *Personnel Psychology,* 1966, **19,** 243–259.

Bostrom, R. N. Dogmatism, rigidity, and rating behavior. *The Speech Teacher,* 1964, **13,** 283–287.

Bowers, J. W. Report on the effectiveness of speech instruction in the rhetoric program. Unpublished paper, University of Iowa, 1965.

Bradshaw, F. F. The American Council on Education Educational Rating Scale: Its reliability, validity, and use. *Archives of Psychology,* 1930, **18** (119). (Entire issue.)

Brockhaus, H. H., and Irwin, J. V. The Wisconsin Sequential Audience Analyzer. *Speech Monographs,* 1958, **25,** 1–13.

Brooks, K. The construction and testing of a forced-choice scale for measuring speaking achievement. *Speech Monographs,* 1957, **24,** 65–73. (a)

Brooks, K. Some basic considerations in rating scale development: A descriptive bibliography. *Central States Speech Journal,* 1957, **9,** 27–31. (b)

Bryan, A. I., and Wilke, W. H. A technique for rating public speeches. *Journal of Consulting Psychology,* 1941, **5,** 80–90.

Bryan, A. I., and Wilke, W. H. Audience tendencies in rating public speakers. *Journal of Applied Psychology,* 1942, **26,** 371–381.

Carroll, J. B. Vectors of prose style. In T. A. Sebeok (Ed.), *Style in language.* Cambridge, Mass.: M.I.T. Press, and New York: John Wiley, 1960. Pp. 283–292.

Carter, L., Haythorn, W., Meirowitz, B., and Lanzetta, J. The relation of categorizations and ratings in the observation of group behavior. *Human Relations,* 1951, **4,** 239–254.

Clevenger, T., Jr. The influence of sex appeal upon ratings of speaking performance. *Worm Runner's Digest,* 1963, **5,** 35–39.

Clevenger, T., Jr. The influence of scale complexity on the reliability of ratings of general effectiveness in public speaking. *Speech Monographs,* 1964, **31,** 153–156.

Doll, R. E. Peer rating validity as a function of rater intelligence and rating score received. *USN School of Aviation Medical Research Report,* 1963, No. 24. Project No. MR005.13–5001, Subtask 12.

Drushal, J. G. An objective analysis of two techniques of teaching delivery in public speaking. *Quarterly Journal of Speech,* 1939, **25,** 561–569.

Ebel, R. L. Estimation of the reliability of ratings. *Psychometrika,* 1951, **16,** 407–424.

Edwards, A. L. *Applications of ranking in film research and the statistical analysis of ranks.* USN Special Devices Center project, No. SDC 269–7–59. Port Washington, N. Y., 1955.

Flanagan, J. The critical incident technique. *Psychological Bulletin,* 1954, **51,** 327–358.

Gauron, E. F., and Dickinson, J. K. The influence of contact with the patient on diagnostic decision making in psychiatry. Paper presented at the meeting of the American Psychiatric Association, Detroit, May 1967.

Gilkinson, H. Indexes of change in attitudes and behavior among students enrolled in general speech courses. *Speech Monographs,* 1941, **8,** 23–33.

Green, B. F. Attitude measurement. In G. Lindzey (Ed.), *Handbook of social psychology.* Vol. 1. Cambridge, Mass.: Addison-Wesley, 1954. Pp. 335–369.

Greenwood, J. M., and McNamara, W. J. Interrater reliability in situational tests. *Journal of Applied Psychology,* 1967, **51,** 101–106.

Guilford, J. P. *Psychometric methods.* New York: McGraw-Hill, 1954.

Guilford, J. P., Christensen, P. R., Taffe, G., and Wilson, R. C. Ratings should be scrutinized. *Educational and Psychological Measurement,* 1962, **22,** 439–447.

Guilford, J. P., and Holley, J. W. A factorial approach to the analysis of variance in esthetic judgments. *Journal of Experimental Psychology,* 1949, **39,** 208–218.

Gunkle, G. N. Vocal cues to the perception of spontaneity. Unpublished doctoral dissertation, University of Iowa, 1963.

Haiman, F. S. An experimental study of the effects of ethos in public speaking. *Speech Monographs*, 1949, **16**, 190–202.

Heynes, R. W., and Lippitt, R. Systematic observational techniques. In G. Lindzey (Ed.), *Handbook of social psychology*. Vol. 1. Cambridge, Mass.: Addison-Wesley, 1954. Pp. 370–404.

Hildreth, R. A. An experimental study of audiences' ability to distinguish between sincere and insincere speeches. Unpublished doctoral dissertation, University of Southern California, 1953. Abstract in *Speech Monographs*, 1954, **21**, 146–147.

Hoffman, L. R. A note on ratings versus choice as measures of group attraction. *Sociometry*, 1962, **25**, 313–320.

Huckleberry, A. W. The relationship between change in speech proficiency and change in student teaching proficiency. *Speech Monographs*, 1950, **17**, 378–389.

Hurd, M. A study of the relationships between voice and personality among students of speech. Unpublished doctoral dissertation, University of Minnesota, 1942.

James, W. *Principles of psychology*. New York: Henry Holt, 1890.

Kerlinger, F. N. *Foundations of behavioral research*. New York: Holt, Rinehart & Winston, 1966.

Knower, F. H. Experimental studies of changes in attitude: I. A study of the effect of oral argument on changes of attitude. *Journal of Social Psychology*, 1935, **6**, 315–345.

Knower, F. H. A study of rank-order methods of evaluating performances in speech contests. *Journal of Applied Psychology*, 1940, **24**, 633–644.

Lana, R. E. Controversy of the topic and the order of presentation in persuasive communications. *Psychological Reports*, 1963, **12**, 163–170.

Madden, J. M., and Bourdon, R. D. Effects of variations in rating scale format on judgment. *Journal of Applied Psychology*, 1964, **48**, 147–151.

Marine, D. An investigation of intra-speaker reliability. *The Speech Teacher*, 1965, **14**, 128–131.

McCroskey, J. C. Scales for the measurement of ethos. *Speech Monographs*, 1966, **33**, 65–72.

Mill, J. S. *A system of logic*. New York: Harpers, 1852.

Miller, G. R. Agreement and the grounds for it: Persistent problems in speech rating. *The Speech Teacher*, 1964, **13**, 257–261.

Monroe, A. H. The measurement and analysis of audience reaction to student speakers — Studies in attitude change. *Studies in Higher Education* (Bulletin of Purdue University), 1937, **38** (1). (Entire issue.)

Morrison, R. L., and Vernon, P. E. A new method of marking English composition. *British Journal of Educational Psychology*, 1941, **11**, 109–119.

Pence, O., and Richards, G. An empirically derived rating scale for inter-collegiate discussion sequences. *Journal of Communication*, 1956, **6**, 69–76.

Price, W. K. Derivation of a rating scale for public speaking. Unpublished paper, University of Wisconsin, 1961.

Ruechelle, R. C. An experimental study of audience recognition of emotional and intellectual appeals in persuasion. *Speech Monographs,* 1958, **25,** 49–58.

Sherif, C., Sherif, M., and Nebergall, R. E. *Attitude and attitude change.* Philadelphia: W. B. Saunders, 1965. Pp. 92–126.

Thompson, W. N. Is there a yardstick for measuring speaking skill? *Quarterly Journal of Speech,* 1943, **29,** 87–91.

Thompson, W. N. An experimental study of the accuracy of typical speech rating techniques. *Speech Monographs,* 1944, **11,** 65–79.

Thompson, W. N. *Quantitative research in public address and communication.* New York: Random House, 1967. Pp. 177–203.

Traxler, A. E., and Anderson, H. A. The reliability of an essay test in English. *School Review,* 1935, **43,** 534–539.

Twyford, L. C. A comparison of methods for measuring profiles of learning from instructional films. Unpublished doctoral dissertation, The Pennsylvania State University, 1951.

Williams, F., Clark, R. A., and Wood, B. S. Studies in the dimensionality of debate evaluation. *Journal of the American Forensic Association,* 1966, **3,** 95–103.

Wiseman, G., and Barker, L. L. A study of peer group evaluation. *Southern Speech Journal,* 1965, **31,** 132–138.

9

Analysis of
Verbal Behavior

Frederick Williams

A chapter title like this one is presumptuous indeed. The materials on verbal behavior or even the analysis of verbal behavior would make a modest size library. Prolificacy of research and theory is but one reason for this abundance; a more troublesome reason is that so many kinds and facets of behavior are loosely referred to as *verbal* behavior.

However, within the framework of this volume, we can see the necessity for sometimes assessing the linguistic details of verbal expression, particularly those details which may better enable us to understand the functional aspect of language — that is, *communication*. In other chapters, the analysis of language is used as a basis for making inferences about "content" in communication (Chapter 10), or for objectively characterizing qualities of "style" (Chapter 11). This chapter centers more on the details of language behavior per se — how these details can be characterized in the production behavior of encoders, how they enter into the analysis of language samples, how they may serve in the description of messages that decoders are responding to.

A Perspective on the Problem

Whenever a communication researcher refers to processes of *encoding* and *decoding,* he is making tacit assumptions about the nature of the language user, as well as the nature of the language code. The main premise of one cluster of these assumptions is that a group of human beings, by convention, may share a common system for verbal symbolization, that is, a common *language.* The linguist calls such a group a *speech community;* he abstracts from his observations of individuals in this community a description of their system for expression. This description, in both discovery procedure and report, is essentially qualitative; it characterizes the sounds, the minimal forms, and the constructional regularities of expression. The linguist is not particularly concerned with the individual user of a language; he is more concerned with the system for expression that unites a group of individuals.

Another cluster of assumptions focuses on the individual capabilities of the language user — his propensity for language, his functional knowledge of an expression system induced from his linguistic experiences. Descriptions of such capabilities fall within the realm of the psychology of language, or, more recently, in sharper focus within a field called *psycholinguistics.* These descriptions are qualitative in specifying the schema of expression, but they are essentially quantitative when referring to the dynamics of behavior. If we were to say that the linguist describes language, we could add that the psycholinguist describes how the user behaves with language.

Given the foregoing kinds of assumptions, the communication researcher's most direct interest in language is in exploring the functional aspects of expression in a communications situation. What aspects of language are exercised by an encoder? What variables influence these aspects? What aspects of language have predictable consequences on decoders? Although the communication researcher must draw from the descriptions provided by the linguist and psycholinguist in order to answer these questions, he must go one step further. If he is to study language, his goal is to describe how man exercises his linguistic capabilities in a functional sense, that is, how the characteristics of language enter into the larger framework of the characteristics of communication.

Plan of the Chapter

In broadest perspective, two initial linguistic tasks concern the communication researcher — specification and quantification. *Specification* is defining the characteristics of expression that are the focus for inquiry. Some of these, such as the sounds, the minimal forms, or the constructional patterns of expression can be based directly on definitions or descriptions provided by the linguist. In this chapter we refer to these characteristics as having *linguistic* bases for specification. There are other characteristics, however, which can be only partially based on linguistic criteria. These, including such concepts as the word, parts of speech, and utterance structures, we refer to as having *quasi-linguistic* bases for specification. Finally, there are characteristics whose bases for specification are more behavioral than linguistic per se. Articulatory operations, hesitation phenomena, and the like have been called *production* bases for specification.

Quantification, of course, plays a key role in communication research design. Since we are concerned with the characteristics and regularities of behavior, most of our descriptions and schemes for analysis are statistical in nature. We have grouped these under three headings — (1) *production characteristics;* (2) *frequencies, patterns, and measurements;* (3) *cloze procedure.* The first refers mainly to the various procedures for describing production rate. The second incorporates a variety of procedures where description consists of enumerating units and unit sequences. The third, a technique for assessing language predictability, has been given special prominence because it has been successfully and substantially applied in communication research.

Another section of the chapter outlines a sample study illustrating research into language variables. The study, which reports the results of a factor analysis of part-of-speech usage, should be of methodologic interest to researchers who are concerned with the types of inferences that can be drawn from the specification and enumeration of these grammatical units. The results of the study have not been published before.

The aim of this chapter might best have been summarized by the title *Ways to Analyze the Language Characteristics in the Messages that Encoders Transmit and that Decoders Respond to.* But such a title would violate what we communication researchers are always telling one another about our own use of language.

BASES FOR SPECIFICATION

Linguistic Bases

One of the problems in becoming acquainted with the contemporary literature in linguistics is the two current competing viewpoints which are both relevant to the needs of the communication researcher. One of these, generally within the realm of *descriptive linguistics,* concerns itself mainly with methods for linguistic investigation and description and stresses that linguistics is an empirical science. The other, typically called *generative* (or *transformational*) *grammar,* aims more for linguistic theory than description and does not take the position that linguistics is an empirically based science. Let us outline these two viewpoints in more detail, particularly as they pertain to the communication researcher.

DESCRIPTIVE LINGUISTICS

A relatively elementary text on descriptive linguistics (*e.g.,* Gleason, 1961) will explain that language involves both *expression* and *content*. The expression system is what we describe when we talk about the basic sound units (*phonemes*), the basic forms (*morphemes*), and the arrangements or constructions of forms (*syntax*) which make up a given language. A person (called an *informant*) is talking about content when he tells us, for example, that "bat" and "pat" mean something different to him, or that the "s" in such expressions as "dogs" and "books" means more than one, or that the difference between "John hit Mary" and "Mary hit John" is in who is doing the hitting. In simplified terms, the descriptive linguist's task is to discover, to classify, and to label distinctions in expression that are correlated with distinctions in content. His report describes mainly what he has discovered about the expression system of a language, namely its phonologic, morphologic, and syntactic characteristics. Presumably, his discoveries came after objective observation.

The reader who is venturing for the first time into the literature of descriptive linguistics very soon discovers a strong concern with scientific method and how it is applied to rigorous definition of linguistic phenomena. In the area of American linguistics, much of this scientific attitude dates back to Leonard Bloomfield and his landmark book *Language* (1933). Although some parts of *Language* are now obsolete, it is a good first book for any communication researcher seriously interested in descriptive linguistics.

GENERATIVE GRAMMAR

Much of what is written about generative grammar stems from Noam Chomsky's *Syntactic Structures* (1957), a brief monograph which sets forth the goals and an outline for a new linguistic theory. It emphasizes the need for a formalized general theory of linguistic structure, contrasted with what Chomsky calls "the desire to purify well-established methods of linguistic analysis [p. 5]." Chomsky attempts to reveal the shortcomings of traditional structural analysis and further illustrates how a mentalistic conception of a linguistic theory is preferable to an empirically based one. Within this mentalistic conception, linguistic description has the form of a body of generative rules. It does not empirically describe a sentence as one would observe it in speech or writing; it describes the rules which in a mentalistic sense underlie the generation (creation) of a sentence. These rules cannot be directly observed in speakers. On the contrary, the generative grammarian must intuit these underlying rules from the language and, to some extent, his observation of performance.

In Chomsky's terms, a grammar of a language would be all the rules of that language, rules which would underlie the creation and understanding of the sentences of that language. If this sounds like a radical departure from descriptive linguistics, it indeed is. In no mild terms, linguists disagree about the merits of generative grammar, and this provides a confusing picture for the communication researcher who anticipates only a brief excursion into the literature of linguistics in order to answer a question or two. The interested researcher should try *Syntactic Structures* (Chomsky, 1957), *Current Issues in Linguistic Theory* (Chomsky, 1966), then perhaps *Aspects of the Theory of Syntax* (Chomsky, 1965). Fodor and Katz (1964) have compiled a book of readings which treat various topics concerning this approach to language. Bach's *An Introduction to Transformational Grammars* (1964) is worthwhile reading as an example of a textbook on generative grammar. Finally, Miller (1962, 1965) describes the relevance of this type of grammar to the psychologist of language.

DESCRIPTION

Despite the contrast in the above viewpoints, it is possible to gain some introduction to the details of linguistic description by briefly considering the three main levels mentioned earlier — namely, *phonology, morphology,* and *syntax.* No matter what viewpoint one takes in linguistic description, it is important to understand that the structure of language is hierarchical, and that the various strategies for linguistic description all involve specifying this hierarchy in one way or another. Figure 1 illustrates simply the hierarchical levels of language.

Phonologic level. Beginning at the base of the hierarchy shown in Figure 1, we could specify the utterance as a discrete series of spoken events

FIGURE 1

A Sample Utterance

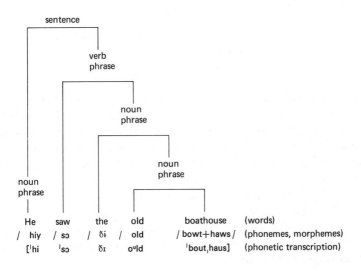

He	saw	the	old	boathouse	(words)
/ hiy	/ sɔ	/ ði	/ old	/ bowt+haws /	(phonemes, morphemes)
[ˈhi	ˈsɔ	ðɪ	oᵘld	ˈboutˌhaus]	(phonetic transcription)

by transcribing these events into symbols from the *phonetic* alphabet (and usually enclosed by brackets). Each symbol in this alphabet presumably has a one-to-one correspondence with a given speech sound. We can think of an inventory of such symbols as an inventory of the sounds susceptible to specification in any language, and the symbols themselves as written transcriptions of these sounds. If in a given study we wished to write a detailed description of the sounds of utterances, we would typically use phonetic transcription. Or we might use similar transcription when we wanted to indicate to an oral reader the precise pronunciation characteristics of an intended stimulus utterance. Source material on phonetic transcription may be found in such texts as Van Riper and Smith (1954) or Thomas (1958).

However, phonetic transcription itself says little about linguistic specification. As described above, it represents only the sounds of speech. Linguistic specification on the phonological level comes when we describe how the sounds of speech represent particular classes of sounds that are basic to a given language. Such classes can be thought of as the "sound building blocks" of a language; they are called *phonemes*. We call them classes or categories of sounds because each phoneme typically is susceptible to some variation in how it is articulated. Thus, even though phonemes have letters as symbols (usually enclosed between slashes), they do not have a one-to-one correspondence with the sounds used to express them. Consider, for example, the /r/ phoneme as it would vary in articulation in such words as "tree," "around," "groom," and "argosy." If you listen carefully to the pronunciation of these words, or feel the position of your own articulators during pronunciation, you will note subtle differences in expression of the /r/. Most schemes for phonemic transcription of the sound segments of English comprise around 33 to 40 different specifications. Gleason (1961) for example, lists 33:

> (consonants) /p b t d k g ě j f v θ ð s z š ž m n ŋ l r/
> (vowels) /i e æ ɨ ə a u o ɔ/
> (semivowels) /y w h/ [p. 50]

Thus far in our discussion of phonology, we have designated only sound segments in utterances. Accompanying these phonological segments are further phonological features of *intonation* and *stress,* often called *suprasegmentals*. Although the specifications of these phenomena vary among linguists, we can describe some of the following which are classed by Gleason (1961, p. 50) as phonemes in English.

Four *levels of stress* are designated as primary / ´ /, secondary / ^ /, tertiary / ` /, and weak / ˇ /.

The *open transition* /+/ may be expressed as a very brief pause, prolongation of a sound, a weakening of voicing, or a contrast in degree of aspiration (like an [h] sound).

Three types of *clause terminals* specify combined pitch, volume, and pausal characteristics of a clause ending; they include fading / ⤢ /, rising / ⤴ /, and sustained / → /.[1]

Four *levels of pitch* range from low /1/ through mid /2/ and high /3/ to extra high /4/.

Adding the above 12 suprasegmental phonemes to the previously listed 33 segmentals provides a basis for the phonemic specification of English utterances. Although any person who knew the symbol scheme could render orally an utterance transcribed phonemically, the symbols would not be an exact guide to pronunciation; they are not intended as such. Suggested readings on phonemics include Trager and Smith (1957), Hockett (1958), and Gleason (1961).

Morphologic level. The next level of specification in Figure 1 involves units which are either single phonemes in themselves or else combinations of phonemes. The simplest definition of units on the level, *morphemes*, is that they are minimal units of expression that have particular correlations with meaning. For example, as a unit of expression, the morpheme "boat" /bowt/ cannot be further divided so that all of what remains has a correlation with meaning in English. Compare this morpheme, however, with the expressions "boats" /bowts/, "boathouse" /bowthaws/, and "boathouses" /bowthawziz/. Each of these illustrates how combinations of morphemes enter into the construction of what we loosely call *words*. For example, in "boats" we find the morpheme "boat" combined with the phoneme /-s/, which in this case is a morpheme indicating plural in English for words like "boat," "dog," "book," and so on. In "boathouse" we have the combination of the morphemes "boat" and "house"; or in "boathouses," we have added the plural morpheme to this combination. Note in this latter example a variant in the expression of the plural morpheme, that is, /ziz/ as against /s/. Morphemes that can occur alone (like "boat" and "house") are called *free forms*; morphemes that can occur only in some attached position (like -s) are called *bound forms*.

Specifying the morphemes of a given language typically involves two main objectives. Given a sample of utterances for analysis, the first is the task of segmenting the utterances into minimal units of expression which have particular correlations with meaning — that is, identifying the morphemes in the sample. The second task is classifying morphemes according to their roles in the structure of a language. Classifications are loosely akin to what we call parts of speech, except that in linguistic research the lay parts of speech ("A noun is a person, place, or thing") are largely unworkable. Instead, linguistic classification depends on how given morphemes distribute in common structural contexts (for example, one class would distribute in

---

[1] In some schemes these are classified as the *double cross juncture* / # / (corresponding to / ⤢ /), the *double bar juncture* / ‖ / (/ ⤴ /) and the *single bar juncture* / | / (/ → /).

the context: "The _____ is/are good."), and how bound forms enter into combinations — *e.g., as affixes* — with classes of free forms.

From a practical standpoint, most of what we have briefly discussed about morphology reflects how a linguist deals with words in a language. Strictly speaking, he is not interested in words, except in describing the vocabulary, but in the units of expression that by virtue of the system of the language correlate with particular meanings. On one level of the language hierarchy, the linguist can describe morphemes as they are substructured by the phonemic system of a language. On a higher level of the hierarchy he can describe how morphemes themselves enter into structural sequences — that is, the syntactic regularities of a language. Within this hierarchy the word is not a useful structural unit, at least to the linguist. But if a communication researcher is at all concerned with specification of the properties of words in English, particularly with affixes, he should consult resource material in morphology, for instance Nida (1949), Elson and Pickett (1960), and Gleason (1961). We will have more to say about words in a subsequent section of this chapter (pp. 246–247).

Syntactic level. As shown in Figure 1, the syntactic level completes the specification of the utterance under analysis. Literature in descriptive linguistics does not always consistently define where the morphological level ends and the syntactic level begins, but when we consider the alternative patterns which link morphologic units in English, we are quite clearly making syntactic specifications. Most nonlinguists have some notion of this level of analysis as a carryover from their days of "diagramming" sentences as an exercise in school grammar. For example, we could specify the sample utterance as follows:

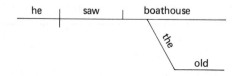

This diagram divides the subject and predicate parts of the sentence, then further divides the verb from the object, and also indicates which words modify these basic sentence parts. All such diagrams were attempts to specify the structural patterns in sentences, a goal not too far removed from the linguist's purpose in syntactic analysis.

By contrast, what we have shown in Figure 1 is one way a descriptive linguist would specify a syntactic hierarchy. This hierarchical outline, called a *tree diagram,* was formed by a procedure known as *immediate constituents* analysis, or *IC* analysis for short. In order to describe this procedure it is necessary to understand the distinction between a *construction* and a *constituent.* First, the minimal combination of two morphologic forms is called a construction. In turn, the two forms which enter into this construction are its immediate constituents. Thus, for example, "old" and "boathouse" are the immediate constituents of one of the constructions labeled "noun phrase" in Figure 1. Next, constructions themselves may become constituents of higher level constructions in the structural hierarchy. Again, for an example, we could say that the noun phrase we just considered ("old boathouse") and the morpheme which precedes it ("the") are the immediate constituents of the next higher level noun phrase shown in Figure 1. This layering of immediate constituents and constructions continues until we reach the maximal construction, usually the sentence. In most cases we view the sentence as the upper boundary of syntactic analysis since it does not enter as a constituent into any higher level construction. By the same token, we can view the morpheme as the lower boundary of syntactic analysis since it has no lower level syntactic constituents.

As illustrated in Figure 1, immediate constituents are usually two in number for each level of construction, although this is a point of some disagreement among linguists. Syntactic specification, then, can be based on the hierarchy of (usually) binary divisions or combinations made for a given utterance. This specification can be further augmented by labeling the constructions that are defined in the analysis, for example, "noun phrase," "predicate," and so on. The logic of *IC* analysis dates back to Bloomfield (1933) and has been given some degree of systemization by Wells (1947) and Nida (1949). The key problem in *IC* analysis comes in knowing and applying the criteria that govern the location of constituent divisions. Street (1967) provides a good review of such criteria. There are, of course, other schemes for specifying syntactic structure, ranging from simplified school grammars (*e.g.,* Roberts, 1956) to relatively detailed procedures for the formal analysis of English structure (*e.g.,* Fries, 1952).

This section has briefly outlined some of the bases for linguistic specification found in the literature of descriptive linguistics. If a communication research design necessarily incorporates phonologic, morphologic, or syntactic specification, the researcher is advised to consult the pertinent linguistics literature or else enlist the aid of a professional linguist.

A final note pertains to linguistic description which is founded in one way or another on a generative theory of grammar. As mentioned earlier, this viewpoint differs radically from what one encounters in descriptive linguistics: an utterance is described by defining the abstract rules which underlie it. In addition to the references previously cited, the reader may wish to consult Chomsky and Halle (1968) for a discussion of the phonological component of such a grammar, or Katz and Postal (1964) for a discussion that incorporates the syntactic and semantic components in an integrated description. McNeill's paper "Developmental psycholinguistics" (1966) attempts to define the syntactic rules underlying the word combinations observed in the utterances of young children.

Quasi-Linguistic Bases

As stated earlier, most communications studies involving the analysis of language concentrate on its functional aspects. That is, they are often less concerned with detailed and formal linguistic analysis than with specifying the units of language that seem to have some functional reality to the language user. Thus, while phonology, morphology, and syntactics best reveal to us the essence of the language code, such concepts as the word, the classification of words as parts of speech, and the gross aspects of utterance structures often become relevant when dealing with language in communications studies. This is not to say that the communication researcher can overlook the more formal concepts of linguistic analysis, but that he may often have to look beyond them to a level of specification which most directly relates to his concern with communication behavior.

THE WORD

Although the word is not a useful concept to the linguist, it seems to be an important concept to the psychologist or psycholinguist. As discussed earlier, the word is not a necessary unit in the formal analysis of language. When linguists discuss the definition of the word, it is usually to reemphasize the point that there is no rigorous guide to its specification, at least among the strategies of descriptive linguistics. If, then, the word is a concept to be studied, how can it be defined, or at least adequately specified for psychological investigation? For one thing, there seems little hazard in assuming that the word is a convention of language not too much unlike such concepts as the sentence or the paragraph. Although we typically discover such units by observing details in the written form of language, such as the spaces between words in spelling or the inventories of words in dictionaries, there are psychological grounds for their definitions. The psycholinguist Osgood (1963), for one, has argued in favor of the word (or "word-like" units) as being a key psychological unit in verbal behavior. Much of his evidence in support of this argument comes from observing how a person corrects himself while speaking (Maclay and Osgood, 1959). When only a part of a word is seemingly uttered in error by a speaker, he will typically correct himself with entire word units. Psychological theories of verbal behavior which revolve around learning theory constructs (*e.g.,* Skinner, 1957; Mowrer, 1960) tend to focus on the word as a minimum psychological unit of utterance.

Phonology holds little basis for the specification of words. In normally phrased continuous speech, open transitions $/+/$ will sometimes occur between what we usually consider as words, but this is not a consistently predictable phenomenon either within or among speakers, nor is the open transition found only between words. In short, no adequate articulatory or even acoustic basis exists for defining words in normal speech. However, if we ask a person to reduce his speech rate successively, he will typically increase the intonation-type junctures between words until most of the words of, say, a sentence will sound as if they were a series of unrelated units being read from a list. Decreasing a speaker's rate still more, however, will usually result in the appearance of these junctures between the major parts and eventually the syllables of words. (Such junctures can be considered in terms of the *phonetic syllable* and the *breath group,* concepts discussed in a subsequent section.)

If word specification is to be undertaken in a study and the research does not involve any more than the usual incidence of compound words which raise questions about hyphenization and the like (*e.g.,* is "overall" one word?), most native speakers of English can be depended on to give consistent identifications of word units when transcribing speech to writing. It is usually necessary to develop ad hoc criteria for specification involving numbers (is "five hundred and sixty-eight" five words?), contractions, abbreviations (is "UN" one word?), and proper names (is "John Paul Jones" three words?). Most problems involving hyphenated words and the like can be resolved by consulting a good dictionary. Of course, if messages in a study are already encoded in a written form, it is usually satisfactory to define words by the writer's divisions among the letter sequences.

As discussed earlier, morphology allows us to talk about the structural properties of words. Perhaps most useful is the notion of structural complexity. In terms of structure, a *simple* word is one comprised of a single minimal free form morpheme. A *complex* word contains a minimal free form morpheme and bound form; a *compound* word is a combination of free form morphemes. Further, if it is desired, these basic specifications may be elaborated on by counting the free and bound form morphemes found in words. Structural complexity, however, does not necessarily imply psychological complexity, although some schemes for assessing readability or comprehensibility take into account the number of syllables in words (Flesch, 1946). There also appear to be certain statistical relations between word lengths and their frequency of occurrence in usage. This topic as well as the use of word frequency lists will be discussed in the section on quantification.

PARTS OF SPEECH

Among the various schemes for classifying words, identifying words as different parts of speech has been used in a wide variety of communication-type studies. Essentially, an adequate linguistic classification of parts of speech groups together those words which function similarly in the grammatical patterns of sentences. Given such classification, description can run in two different directions of the language hierarchy. As mentioned earlier, the classification can be morphologic, that is, it can define the different structural features and roles assumed by morphemes. On the other hand, the occurrence and sequence of parts of speech can to some degree define the structural patterns of utterances. The best example of the latter approach is found in Fries's (1952) procedures for the structural analysis of English. He begins with part-of-speech identification according to criteria which he has devised, then, based on this identification, he specifies syntactic structures as various sequences of parts of speech, including immediate constituents analysis.

Most of the communication studies involving part-of-speech classification have focused on its syntactic implications, although no study to the author's knowledge has pursued the interpretation of parts of speech with the rigor of the aforementioned work by Fries (1952). Typically, the research has involved classifying and enumerating the parts of speech occurring in messages under study, and interpretations are based mainly on the frequencies different classes exhibit.

The lay conception of parts of speech usually reflects the eight or so categories defined in the various traditional or "school" grammars (see Gleason, 1965, pp. 114–137). The main objection to such grammars is that they offer an oversimplified and often nonrigorous set of word categories. In fact, it is a rare linguist who does not in many ways try to avoid the shortcomings in traditional classification schemes, even to the point of altogether avoiding the term "part of speech." Among the factors contributing to the lack of rigor in traditional schemes is their frequent stress on the meanings of words, as, for example, when they classify a noun as "the name of a person, place, or thing" or a verb as an "action word." Most of the more rigorous classification schemes avoid meaning and center instead on structural features of the words themselves, as well as on the syntactic environments in which the words are found. If a researcher is considering specifying parts of speech, he will be safest if he adopts a scheme grounded entirely in structural criteria. Gleason (1965) gives an excellent overview of the different part-of-speech classification schemes. For English, probably the most fully developed as well as most thoroughly explained scheme is found in Fries (1952), although he departs from such traditional labels as "noun" and "verb" and substitutes in their place a series of categories identified by numbers and letters. Perhaps the easiest scheme for the untrained person is described by Roberts (1956). However, Roberts describes his scheme in the context of a school text on grammar, and its examples serve more for pedagogical purposes than as a guide to the analysis of English.

Most persons who have experience in part-of-speech coding would probably agree that, given an adequate classification scheme, usually about 90 per cent of the words encountered can be easily and unambiguously coded. The problem lies in adequately classifying fragmentary constructions, nongrammatical constructions, single-word utterances, and the like. In the author's experience, some words (perhaps around 5 per cent) can never be confidently coded.

That most words can be easily classified on structural criteria is shown by the comparative success of computerized routines developed for classification. One, known as the *Wisconsin Syntactic Coder* or *WISSYN* (Stolz, Tannenbaum, and Carstensen, 1965), takes keypunched text as input and produces part-of-speech symbols as output. It is capable of classifying words in context with up to 93 per cent accuracy, as compared with expert hand coding assumed to be 100 per cent accurate, and at the rate of approximately 2000 words per minute. Lindsay (1960), Klein and Simmons (1963), and Kuno and Oettinger (1963) have reported other computerized routines.

SYNTACTIC UNITS

Identifying parts of speech leads to procedures for specifying the larger units of linguistic structure. Also, some syntactical bases for specifying structural units avoid altogether the consideration of parts of speech.

As mentioned in the preceding section (p. 248), Fries's (1952) study of English structure entailed procedures in which, given the identification of parts of speech, he could specify how combinations of parts of speech define the larger structural units of utterances. It is easiest to think of Fries's specifications as proceeding from parts of speech as the basic grammatical elements of utterances, then to see how these basic elements combine into constructions (*phrases*) of various types. The most basic combinations involve the modification patterns observed among words in English. For example, the phrase patterns involving a word like "cat" (designated a Class 1 word by Fries), can be specified by designating modifier words like "the" (A) and "red" (3):

A1: "the cat," "a house," "three men"
A31: "six big men," "the red house," "a bad boy"

Or basic sentence patterns can be specified (Fries designates a verb-type word as Class 2):

12: "Birds sing."
A123: "The cat is black."

By referring to Fries's grammar, one can determine a specification, or a "formula," as Fries calls it, for the majority of phrase structures found in English. Of particular interest to the communication researcher is that Fries was analyzing and describing spoken American English (telephone conversations); thus his examples are realistic and not confined to the neatly consistent and seldom heard sentences and phrases found in most school textbooks on grammar.

The problem with using parts of speech for defining structural units is that the same sequence of given parts of speech may underlie different higher level structures. For example, most schemes would classify as adverbs both the words "upstairs" and "quickly" in the sentences "The men upstairs hit me" and "The men quickly hit me." Even though these two sentences have the same part-of-speech sequence, in the first the adverb modifies the noun phrase "the men," but in the second the adverb modifies the verb. In other words, just knowing the parts of speech in the two sentences would not be enough to determine the layers of phrase structure.

Perhaps the best basis for specifying structural units in communication studies involving English is either the logic of immediate constituents analysis (described on pp. 244–245) or the simple definition of structural units. If the researcher takes the latter approach, he can begin by deciding what structural units are pertinent to his investigation; then he can consult an English grammar for their specification criteria. Suppose, for example, the researcher is interested in clauses (subject-verb constructions) and their different patterns. He will find the descriptions of ten basic patterns in Roberts (1962) and an even more detailed list in Gleason (1965). The researcher can then proceed to classify the clauses in his own messages by matching them with the descriptions from a reference grammar. He can apply a similar strategy to phrase structures within clauses, if he desires this level of specification. The main problem in specifying any level of structural units is that the categories for classification can often become so numerous that identification as well as subsequent statistical analyses become difficult. For example, in unpublished research conducted by a colleague of the author, the detailed specification of clause types entailed some 40 categories. Currently the best single source for specifying syntactic units in English is Gleason's *Linguistics and English Grammar* (1965).

A study by Williams and Naremore (in press) illustrates how criteria for linguistic and quantitative description can be combined to some advantage in describing the degree of syntactic structuring found in a language sample. In analyzing social class differences in a sample of some 25,000 words, the researchers proceeded briefly as follows: (1) Utterances were segmented according to clause terminals (#). (2) Sequences between terminals were further segmented into maximal syntactic units — that is, sequences of words related by some common syntactic structure. (3) A modified form of immediate constituents analysis was applied and divisions between parts of the structures were coded according to the "rank" of the cut and the phrase environment in which it occurred. The following sentence illustrates the coding:

$$1_s \quad 9 \quad 8_j \quad 2_j \quad 1_j$$
$$\text{\# The / boy / ate / the / green / candy \#}$$

The numerical scheme represents an ordinal scale of divisions, ranging from the highest level in this example (9, between subject and predicate) to the lowest (1, or divisions between words modifying one another). Alphabetical subscripts in this example include "s" for subject noun phrase and "j" for object phrase.

Obviously, the foregoing procedure involves more than can be shown in a simple example. In brief, the procedure incorporates three types of information: hierarchical "rank" of cuts, the environments of cuts, and sequential data. By various computerized routines, Williams and Naremore were able to develop such information into summary statistics pertaining to a given language sample and eventually to differences between samples.

Production Bases

In this section we turn to types of specification that involve phenomena circumstantial to the production of language rather than language characteristics themselves. Such phenomena include behavioral factors of language production, the acoustic characteristics of speech, and the pausal and hesitation characteristics of encoding behavior.

SPEECH PRODUCTION

It is possible to specify speech sounds as the operations of the oral articulators, a method of specification usually labeled *physiologic* or *articulatory* phonetics. The traditional literature of this area usually treats the articulatory specifications of vowel and consonant sounds separately. For vowel sounds specification entails describing the tongue position and height, and sometimes the shape of the lips as well. Tongue position refers to where on the tongue the sound is made, *front, center,* or *back;* height means where in the mouth the tongue is when the sound is made, *low, mid,* or *high;* lip shape usually refers to how much or little the lips are rounded during production. For example, the English vowel [i] (as in "b*i*t") is placed at the front of the tongue, and the tongue is high in the mouth. Compare it with [ɔ] (as in "l*a*w"), which is generally back and low.

Consonants are usually specified by three variables: *place,* or the combination of articulators involved; *manner,* the type of sound that is made; and *voicing* — whether the sound is voiced or voiceless. Thus, for example, the place of the [p] sound is *bilabial* (lip combination), the manner is classified as a *stop* (involves closure of the air passage), and the sound is *voiceless.* The [b] sound is also a bilabial stop, but it is *voiced.* Compare these with, say, the [f] sound, which is *labiodental* (lips and teeth), *fricative* (very narrow air passage), and *voiceless.* Guides to specifying speech sounds by the foregoing schemes can be found in such texts as Miller (1951) or Gleason (1961). It should be noted, however, that this type of specification is very crude. For a review of the problems involved in articulatory specification the reader should consult Peterson and Shoup (1966a).

For the communication researcher in particular larger units of production are worthy of mention. One of these is the *syllable,* or more precisely, the *phonetic syllable.* As speech production takes place, a pulsating effect occurs due to the unequal amounts of air required for vowel as against consonant production. About one-third of the syllable occurrences in English consists of a burst of speech comprising a vowel-type sound bordered by consonant-type sounds. Most of the remaining are either consonant-vowel or vowel-consonant combinations. These syllables are not always the same as the syllabic divisions in an English dictionary, although many overlap. As a production phenomenon, phonetic syllables can be viewed as the more or less minimal segments of serial production that are susceptible to specification in continuous speech. To illustrate, when a person speaks words as slowly as possible, his bursts of speech will typically be phonetic syllables and not usually any lesser unit. As will be subsequently discussed, the syllable is a desirable unit for use in specifying speech rate. Also, some contemporary psycholinguistics literature sees the syllable as a unit of psychological significance (Osgood, 1963).

A larger unit of speech production is the *breath group*. Specifying this unit reflects the operation of the respiratory cycle in speech production. Since phonation takes place only during the expiratory phase of respiration, the speaker must interrupt himself for periods of respiratory inspiration. The breath group is the speech segment which begins on an expiratory phase and terminates (with some predictable exceptions) as fundamental frequency and amplitude of phonation both drop, when a pause occurs. Such termination is the same phenomenon that often underlies the identification of what was described earlier as a fading clause terminal /$\searrow$/, a double cross juncture /#/, or what is sometimes also called a *terminal juncture*. However, these suprasegmentals may also occur within a breath group. Although the breath group is viewed primarily as a physiological phenomenon, some linguists also think it has psychological significance (Lieberman, 1967), since presumably a speaker must somehow plan or gauge his linguistic structures to be compatible with his respiratory cycle. A study by Loban (1963) illustrates how terminal junctures can be used to segment samples of verbal behavior. Loban's purpose was to compare the language of children of various ages. In analyzing sequences of their speech, Loban chose as a basic level of segmentation bursts of speech that fell between terminal junctures; he called these *phonological* units.

It might be noted in passing that defining terminal junctures, phonological units, and the like is not as easy a basis for specification as it might seem at first. Where a terminal juncture might occur, other phenomena often intrude, such as hesitation devices or even other intonational signals (*e.g.,* a question intonation). In short, a variety of supplementary criteria must augment specification based on terminal junctures in order to avoid confounding by other phenomena which either replace terminal junctures or disguise them.

SPEECH ACOUSTICS

With the advent of modern electronic instrumentation, the acoustic analysis of speech has burgeoned. Much of it has involved use of the *sound spectro-*

graph, a device which visually displays the basic acoustic parameters of frequency, amplitude, and complexity across a time continuum, making it possible to study the acoustic patterns of speech sounds. The research in this area usually comes under the label of *acoustic phonetics,* for example, the work described in Ladefoged's *Elements of Acoustic Phonetics* (1962). Peterson and Shoup (1966b) and Lehiste (1967) review the methodological and theoretical problems.

Development of a device known as the *pattern playback* has also given impetus to a substantial amount of research in acoustic phonetics and speech perception. This device functions just opposite to the sound spectrograph; it takes visual patterns as input and produces synthesized sound as output. Research has typically involved varying the graphic displays of input patterns and studying the consequences on perception of the synthesized output, a process generally known as "speech analysis by synthesis." Sections of Denes and Pinson's *The Speech Chain* (1963) present some basic orientation to this field and a collection of research papers edited by Wathen-Dunn (1967) contains some good reviews of perceptual research in this area.

PAUSAL PHENOMENA

Implicit in most lay conceptions of speech production is that articulation proceeds (or should proceed) in relatively coherent, uninterrupted grammatical sequences. The real picture of speech, particularly of spontaneous speech, is quite the contrary. Most articulation is marked by a variety of gaps in production, and it is sometimes the task of the researcher to specify which of these gaps are phenomena of linguistic significance, and if not, to determine what their significance might be, if any at all. Although the literature is not consistent on this point, the term *pause* sometimes implies a more or less "regular" feature of production, whereas *hesitation* implies an irregularity, an intrusion or disruption in production.

Most schemes for the phonological analysis of speech include within their classification of intonation features pausal phenomena which somehow serve as structural signals. In this sense, such phenomena have phonemic significance; they are a part of the language code. Pauses, or slight silent gaps in production, most often come within this category as the suprasegmentals discussed earlier — namely, the open transition $/+/$ and the three clause terminals $/\rightarrow \searrow \nearrow/$. Often accompanying these types of pausal phenomena are other pauses which appear to serve a *rhetorical* function. Often complemented by facial expression and gestural movements, they sometimes convey the impression that a speaker is carefully deliberating on what he is about to say; or, if they occur antecedent to a key word, they tend to place emphasis on that word in context. Literature on rhetorical pauses and similar devices is sketchy and diverse; some of it may be found in works on oral reading (*e.g.,* Aggertt and Bowen, 1956), and some in linguistics (see especially Bloomfield, 1933; Bloch, 1946).

HESITATION PHENOMENA

As mentioned above, hesitation implies that a speaker's production has been unavoidably disrupted. In some cases disruption may take the form of a silence intervening in the stream of speech, the type of silence that might appear superficially similar to a rhetorical pause. Maclay and Osgood (1959), among others, classify this type of silence as an *unfilled pause*, subjectively based on the specification that the silence seems of "unusual length" to a listener. This basis for specification, however, may result in biasing the identification and location of hesitation silences according to their grammatical context. In a study of the perception of silences in speech, Boomer and Dittmann (1962) found that the durational threshold for identifying silences was lower when they occurred within grammatical phrases as compared with silences occurring between such phrases. In short, we may be extra sensitive to pauses which occur within phrases and relatively less sensitive to pauses between phrases (where they typically occur).

Originally, Goldman-Eisler (1956) distinguished between silences which patterned with grammatical junctures and were often accompanied by respiratory activity and silences which were not at grammatical junctures and had minimal respiratory activity. In a series of studies, Goldman-Eisler (1958a, b; 1961a, b) and Goldman-Eisler, Skarbek, and Henderson (1965a, b) presented evidence to support the hypothesis that the latter type of silence was symptomatic of encoding decision activity on the part of the speaker. In other words, they advanced the conclusion that some hesitation silences are for purposes of verbal planning. In a number of the aforementioned studies all silences exceeding 250 milliseconds, independent of their grammatical location, were included in the analyses. The number of such silences and the total amount of time spent in these silences was usually combined in a ratio with the number of words in the spoken message (as in a "pause-length" ratio). The results of an experiment reported by Webb, Williams, and Minifie (1967) questioned whether respiratory activity is a distinction between pauses which do or do not involve decision activity; it appeared that decision behavior during pausing did not necessarily coincide with the lack of respiratory activity.

A number of studies have involved the attempt not only to specify different types of hesitation phenomena, but to relate their incidence to either decision activity as discussed above or to an alternative notion that hesitations are symptomatic of anxiety in the speaker's behavior. Mahl (1956, 1959a, b), for example, has reasoned that speech, as a finely coordinated skill sequence, is particularly susceptible to disruption due to anxiety. Originally, Mahl (1956) listed eight types of disruptions:

(1) *Ah:* filled pausing (excluding "er," "um," etc.).

(2) *Sentence correction:* correction in the form or content of the expression while the word-to-word progression occurs; this must be

sensed by the listener as an interruption in the word-to-word sequence.

(3) *Sentence incompletion:* an interruption; the sentence is clearly left incomplete, and the communication proceeds without correction.

(4) *Repetition:* the serial and superfluous repetition of one or more words, usually only one or two.

(5) *Stutter:* when only a part of a word is repeated.

(6) *Intruding incoherent sound:* when a sound is uninterpretable to the listener and intrudes without itself altering the form of the expression, and when the sound cannot be clearly identified as a stutter, omission, or a tongue slip.

(7) *Tongue slip:* neologisms, the transposition of words from their correct serial position, and the substitution of an unintended word for an intended word.

(8) *Omissions.*

By counting the occurrence of the foregoing items and the number of words in a patient's speech, Mahl (1956) proposed the following "Speech Disturbance Ratio":

$$\text{SDR} = \frac{N \text{ speech disturbances}}{N \text{ words spoken by patient}} \quad [\text{p. 2}]$$

In subsequent research (Kasl and Mahl, 1958, 1965), "ah" was omitted from the foregoing ratio because the researchers found it did not correlate with measures of manipulated anxiety in speakers. This modified ratio is known as the "non-ah ratio." Mahl (1956) has also studied silences, but mainly as an overall ratio ("silence quotient") of the number of seconds of silence to the number of seconds available for a patient to talk.

A study by Maclay and Osgood (1959) dealt mainly with a specification of the linguistic distribution of hesitation phenomena. They reduced Mahl's eight categories to the following four:

(1) *Repeats:* all repetitions of any length that are judged to be nonsignificant semantically.

(2) *False starts:* all incomplete or self-interrupted utterances.

(3) *Filled pauses:* all occurrences of vocalized hesitation devices.

(4) *Unfilled pause:* all hesitations not classifiable into the preceding three categories, mainly silences of unusual length and non-phonemic lengthening of phonemes.

The main thrust of Maclay and Osgood's findings was that the aforementioned types of hesitations were biased in occurrence toward particular types of linguistic contexts. This led them to believe that such phenomena were clearly related to the psychological processes involved in encoding behavior. Their interpretations related to both the decision activity and the emotional implications of hesitation phenomena. Blankenship and Kay (1964) reported a roughly similar distributional study which also reduced Mahl's original categories. Implications of this study referred mainly to the decision point interpretation.

Whether some hesitations are indicative of encoding choice points, encoder anxiety, or both is a topic undergoing current investigation by a number of researchers (see Levin and Silverman, 1965; Tannenbaum, Williams, and Hillier, 1965; Tannenbaum *et al.,* 1967). Suffice it to say that though the current evidence is potentially interesting to communication researchers, much research remains to be done.

QUANTIFICATION

As described at the outset of this chapter, when the communication researcher is studying verbal behavior, he is typically concerned with how language users are using or are reacting to certain specified aspects of language. His focus, since it centers on the dynamics of behavior, is essentially *quantitative* in orientation. Most of this section will discuss a variety of strategies for quantitative description. Most of these strategies involve the enumeration and statistical treatment of some specified unit of language or production behavior. Some involve using statistical regularities to describe *patterns* of language behavior. And in some, description is based on gauging behavior in a language prediction situation.

Production Measurements

SPEECH RATE

Speech rate is often expressed as words per minute (*wpm*), or as the amount of time taken to produce a message of a given length. Both of these measures leave something to be desired. The main problem with the former measure is that words, of course, vary substantially in length. If we want to compare the speech rates of different persons or rates involved in different types of utterances, we may be hard pressed to assume that word length differences will not confound our measurements. Because syllables, or more precisely *phonetic syllables,* are far more consistent in length than are words, they are a more desirable unit of rate measure. Moreover, the syllable, by its definition, is a closer reflection of a production phenomenon than is the word. Obviously, there may be conditions under which even differences in syllable length might confound measures of rate differences, but differences in syllable length are far less likely than differences in word length. One might consider using phonemes to measure speech rate, except that phonemic specification entails far more work than syllabic specification, and one encounters the further question of whether the phoneme is realistically a production unit in either physiological or psychological terms.

It is also useful to understand the distinction between *articulation rate* and speech rate. As its name implies, articulation rate refers to the speed at which sound units are produced, but it omits from consideration the time devoted to silences occurring in the stream of speech. As Goldman-Eisler (1956), among others, has pointed out, differences in speech rate are due primarily to differences in pause time rather than differences in articulation rate itself. In other words, the changes in a person's speech rate are due primarily to the incidence and durations of silences in the stream of production rather than changes in speed of the movements of the articulators. Articulation rate itself is relatively invariant both within and among speakers (Goldman-Eisler, 1956), although some evidence (Minifie, 1963) shows that it may vary as a consequence of a speaker's loudness efforts.

The main problem in reporting rate as the time taken for a standard segment of output (*e.g.,* "minutes per 500 words"), as Carroll (1966) has pointed out, is that the harmonic mean rather than the arithmetic mean should be used when averaging such times. Moreover, rate gauged in terms of the number of units per unit of time (as in "syllables per minute") is usually normally distributed over different persons or over different conditions, whereas measures of rate in terms of the number of units of time per unit of utterance are usually skewed positively.

In short, the most convenient and adequate measure of speech rate is in terms of syllables per unit of time, and it should be remembered that variations in rate are primarily a function of pause time rather than speed of individual articulations. Other selected papers on speech rate include Darley (1940), Gibbons, Winchester, and Krebs (1958), Hutton (1954), Schwartz (1961), Shearn, Sprague, and Rosenzweig (1961). An unpublished paper by Carroll (1966) presents a good general review of the topic.

Unit Frequencies, Patterns, and Measurements

A number of investigations have tried to establish frequency norms for the various types of linguistic units. Phoneme frequencies in English are reported in studies by Dewey (1923) and Voelker (1935), and Zipf (1935) has studied their frequencies in 12 different languages. Counts of English syllable patterns are reported in such studies as Dewey (1923) and French, Carter, and Koenig (1930). And, as discussed in two subsequent sections, other researchers have subjected words and parts of speech to a variety of frequency studies. For the communication researcher, the norms illustrated in these studies are useful for quantified descriptions of usage or perhaps even stylistic characteristics. It is possible, for example, to examine the "fit" between unit frequencies observed in the language of a specified encoder population and the frequencies reported in the so-called normative studies. One can use unit frequencies to compare encoder populations or the consequences that different encoding conditions or modalities have on these populations. Numerous studies have described speech development in children by comparing unit frequencies observed for different age groups (*e.g.,* McCarthy, 1930; Templin, 1957). Similar frequency norms have been used in studying the stylistic characteristics of authors (*e.g.,* Yule, 1944; see readings in Leed, 1966) or speakers (Paisley, 1967).

WORD FREQUENCIES

Among other things, Zipf's (1935) early study of word frequencies in various languages revealed two reliable statistical characteristics of words. One of these, called the *law of abbreviation,* indicates that the more frequently used words of a language tend to be its shorter ones (by syllabic or spelled length). Another regularity associated with word frequency is that a language tends to have fewer *different* high frequency words as against a far greater variety of low frequency words. Put another way, we tend to use a few words again and again and many words rarely. This regularity is sometimes called the *rank frequency* law. Both of the above laws are statistical in nature; they give us a general picture of regularities, but they are not useful in characterizing or explaining individual word usages. We can easily think of individual exceptions to both laws.

It is possible to conceive of using the above laws in communication-type studies. For one thing, they paint a statistical picture of certain parameters of word usage which can help in interpreting statistics found in our own samples. If we have relatively large samples of words from speakers or writers who have encoded under different conditions, we can find out whether the law of abbreviation or the law of rank frequency obtains within our samples, as well as whether the samples differ among themselves. We might expect, for example, departures from the law of abbreviation in scientific writing (longer words will have greater than normal frequencies), or in comic books (shorter words will have greater than usual frequency). Undertaking these types of analysis, however, implies some major problems. Large samples, say 50,000 to 100,000 words, are necessary; further, the best equations for expressing the laws are questionable. Zipf's (1935) book is good introductory reading on this topic. Later papers by Carroll (1938, 1966) and Yule (1944) illustrate some of the problems and applications of frequency analyses.

WORD LISTS

Another way in which researchers have used word frequencies is in *word* or *frequency lists.* Such lists are useful when a researcher wishes to prepare messages containing "common" words, "rare" words, or the like. They can also be used for reference if a researcher undertakes to gauge the normative frequency characteristics of words found in messages encoded by populations under study, or in messages obtained under various experimental conditions. The most well known of these lists is *The Teacher's Word Book of 30,000 Words* (Thorndike and Lorge, 1944). The two main shortcomings of this list are that it is based on printed materials, thus raising questions about its applicability to spoken language, and, of course, that there have been changes in English usage since 1944. One well known compilation of spoken words is the list prepared by French, Carter, and Koenig (1930), which is not only out of date but may have incorporated sampling problems. The lists were compiled from telephone conversations and involved only sampling certain part-of-speech classes during different monitoring periods. More recently a frequency list of some 250,000 spoken words was published in the *Journal of Verbal Learning and Verbal Behavior* (Howes, 1966).

WORD VARIETY

One way to describe verbal diversity is by plotting the regression line generated by the rank frequency relation mentioned earlier. As word variety increases in a sample, the slope of this line becomes less steep. However, there are a number of easier ways to describe variety in word usage. Perhaps the most straightforward is counting the number of *different* words (called *types*) in a sample. Obviously, a main shortcoming of this approach is that if samples are to be compared with one another, they must be of equal length. But a more subtle problem is also involved: as samples get successively smaller, the smaller is the probability that the "rare" words (and hence, diversity) will be indicated. Unless sample sizes are equalized and unless they are relatively large (see Carroll, 1938), counts of different words are apt to be a misleading index of verbal diversity, particularly if we are trying to characterize a person's lexical repertoire. However, if we are assessing the diversity of words that encoders use in a relatively structured situation — that is, if we are describing the person in a given encoding task — the objections to counting the number of different words used are somewhat lessened.

One way of avoiding the sampling problem, as suggested by Carroll (1938), is to count the average number of words intervening between the occurrences of the most frequently used word in a message. Presumably, in the message of a person using a greater variety of words more words intervene, on the average, between occurrences of the most frequent word. One distinct advantage of this procedure is that it does not entail laboriously listing every different word in a message.

Probably the most typical index of word variety is a ratio between the number of different words found in a sample (*types*) and the total number of words (*tokens*). This is known as the *type-token ratio*, usually abbreviated *TTR*. The more types that occur relative to tokens, and thus the larger the magnitude of the ratio, the greater is the diversity of vocabulary. But like counts of different words, this ratio, too, raises a sampling problem. The smaller the size of the sample, the smaller is the probability for different words to appear; hence the bias is to reduce the magnitude of the *TTR*. Again, therefore, both size and equality of sample sizes are a problem. One way of equalizing sample sizes is to calculate what is called the *mean segmental TTR*. In this procedure, the researcher samples messages by extracting from them segments of equal length, say, 100 or so words. *TTR*s are calculated for each segment, then averaged for the message. Several papers have been published on the topic of *TTR*s, including variations on the basic ratio and ways of interpreting and applying it (Carroll, 1938; Chotlos, 1944; Johnson, 1946). Without going into detail on the point, it should be obvious that the logic of *TTR* can be applied to other than word units.

Carroll (1964) suggested one further procedure for avoiding the sample size problem in indices of diversity. This entails dividing the type count by the square root of double the token count.

WORD SEQUENCE LENGTH

Another commonly used measure involving word frequencies is counting the number of words relative to some larger unit of discourse. Among these, *sentence length* has probably received the widest application. As subsequently discussed, it enters into readability formulas (Flesch, 1946), has been used to study stylistic characteristics of authors (Yule, 1944), and has had numerous applications in the study of language development in children (McCarthy, 1930; Templin, 1957).

Basically, there are no outright objections to measuring sentence length, so long as a researcher can specify what he means by a *sentence,* a definition subject to some dispute among linguists (Gleason, 1965, pp. 330–331). As anyone who has tried to define sentences in oral materials will probably already know, many utterances in speech are less than sentences in construction, and when sentence-like sequences are segmented, problems arise in determining their independence as grammatical units. For example, consider defining the "sentences" in this transcribed utterance of a ten-year-old boy:

> Well and then the the king told a uh soldier to go and turn out the electricity so when he um turned off the electricity all the generators stopped and so all the electricity that was going through the generators stopped and so all the electricity that was going through the door stopped Flash Gordon. . . .

Unless a researcher carefully describes his criteria for sentence specification (as well as for word specification), statistics of words per sentence are likely to be meaningless.

Usually, however, the most major problem with sentence length measures is that researchers often mistakenly use them to index sentence or structural complexity. Consider, for example, the following five-word sentences:

    (i) "Because Jane came, Bill left."
   (ii) "Jane came and Bill left."
  (iii) "The big boy hit him."

The first two sentences share the same two clauses, but because (i) involves a subordinate relation and (ii) only a coordinate relation, we would usually consider the clauses in (i) as more structurally integrated than in (ii). The number of words in these sentences does not enable us to reveal the grammatical distinction made when we call (i) a "complex" sentence and (ii) a "compound" sentence, or, even more unfortunately, when we compare these with (iii) which we often call a "simple" sentence.

The problem looms even larger when we carefully consider what we mean by "complexity." Is it intended to reflect strictly grammatical criteria, such as the relative complexity of tree diagrams (discussed on pp. 244–245), or the numbers and kinds of generative rules that might underlie a given pattern? Do we mean complexity in a psychological sense — that the creation or comprehension of a given structure requires more "effort," "planning," or "grammatical decisions" than an alternative one? Or do we mean both — grammatical as well as psychological complexity? Needless to say, the notion of complexity is elusive. But it seems clear that measures of words per sentence often do no more than confound the matter.

READABILITY FORMULAS

A variety of procedures incorporate frequency statistics in formulas for estimating the "readability" of prose materials. Perhaps the best known of these is the *Flesch index* (Flesch, 1946) which incorporates counts of syllables per 100 words (W) and average sentence length (S) in the following formula:

$$\text{Reading ease} = 206.84 - 0.85W - 1.02S$$

The index, or reading ease score, varies between 0 (unreadable) and 100 (easily readable). Though the potential utility and the widespread application of this formula may seem impressive, the original research on which it was based is not (Flesch, 1944). Many materials violate the bases of the index. Flesch's index may be a handy rule-of-thumb gauge of readability or style, but it has little justification as a description of readability.

Flesch (1946) has also provided a formula for measuring the so-called *human interest* quality of prose. It incorporates a count of "personal words" (w: nouns of sexed gender, personal pronouns, and the like) per 100 words and of "personal sentences" (s: direct quotations, questions, requests, and the like) per 100 words in the following formula:

$$\text{Human interest} = 3.64w + 0.31s$$

This formula, probably even more than reading ease, is no more than a rule-of-thumb index of more popular than scientific interest.

A number of alternative techniques have been proposed as readability measures; some have been popularized as have Flesch's indices, others have been developed and tested under more exacting research conditions. The best sources for reviews of such techniques are a monograph by Chall (1958) and a book by Klare (1963).

SYNTACTIC INDICES

As mentioned in the discussion of word sequence lengths, measures of syntactic structure (or syntactic complexity) are sometimes desired in a research design. This is a most challenging problem, for in most conceptions of syntax, we are jointly concerned with the hierarchical as well as the sequential patterns of structure, and it is difficult to reflect both in a single measure. Sequential segments (words, phrases) can, of course, be counted, but there is the question of what structural "layer" to include. We can think of word sequence lengths as enumerating the "surface" features of sentence structure, at the expense of describing the "deeper" features (in the sense of the different layers and their interrelations in a tree diagram). As subsequently discussed, we can also consider the statistical patterns of part-of-speech sequences,[2] but again, this may overlook the deeper features of syntactic structure.

On the other hand, we can try to measure directly the hierarchical features of structure and, in a sense, try to gauge the structural "depth" of sentences. Goldman-Eisler *et al.* (1965a) have described one procedure of this type, called the *subordination index* (*SI*) as "the proportion of subordinate propositions in the total number of propositions (proposition being a group of words in grammatical sequence, dependent upon a verb, and making complete sense) [p. 86]." For example, the sentence

"When I saw the box which was on the table, I immediately liked it."

would have a subordination index of .67; two of the three propositions are subordinate. Or in the sentence examples given earlier (i–iii, p. 260), only the first (i) incorporates subordination ($SI = .50$); the others have none ($SI = 0$). By examining English constructions that approximate what Goldman-Eisler *et al.* call "propositions," we can see that this measure is sensitive to the incidence of such hierarchically integrated units as subordinate clauses ("When I saw the box") and relative clauses ("which was on the table"). It is not clear in the description of this procedure (or else it is the arbitrary decision of the researcher) whether such clausal constructions as the following should be counted as subordinate propositions:

> It snowed <u>and so I stayed in.</u>
> <u>Wanting to be rich</u> is a good idea.
> The best suggestion was <u>that we leave.</u>

---

[2] This problem is the topic of the Stolz (1964, 1965) studies described in a subsequent section of this chapter (see pp. 265–266).

However, given the necessary decision criteria for determining subordinate propositions, the subordination index has proved useful in some recent studies (Goldman-Eisler *et al.,* 1965a; Tannenbaum *et al.,* 1967, 1968).

Another procedure for gauging hierarchical structure originated with Yngve's (1960, 1961) conception of "syntactic depth." Stated in brief, Yngve theorizes that an encoder creates a sentence by following a processing pattern that approximates a hierarchical outline of that sentence's structure (similar to the tree diagram in Figure 1, p. 241). The sequence of processing is from top to bottom (in the sense of moving down the branches of a tree diagram), yet, because production is from left to right, this sequence must proceed first to the leftmost word (moving down the leftmost branch of the diagram), then back to the hierarchical level which leads to the second word, and so on. One way of quantifying the structural characteristics of a sentence, but primarily in terms of their "processing" implications, is to count the number of "steps" that would be required for production of the entire sentence. Each step is roughly akin to the differentiation of a constructional unit (*e.g.,* "the man") into its immediate constituents: ("the" and "man"). Yngve's theory also has an additional measurement feature. Since the processing sequence must accommodate the leftmost elements first, it is often necessary to store temporarily (in a memory system) the as yet undifferentiated elements. In Yngve's reasoning, sentence processing is most efficient when there are minimal numbers of elements that must be temporarily postponed or stored during the processing sequence. It is this concept — the number of necessary postponements — that underlies his concept of the structural *depth* of sentences. Thus, in this case, a particular type of hierarchical pattern, one which contributes to depth, can be gauged with precision.

Certainly concepts such as Yngve's depth hypothesis refer more to the psychological implications of syntactic complexity than they do to the structural descriptions of sentences themselves. But this is a topic of substantial interest to psycholinguists (see Miller, 1962, 1965), and no doubt it is relevant to some problems in communication research.

Williams and Naremore (in press) suggest a final type of syntactic index. This scheme undertakes a series of immediate constituent divisions for English sentences and then ranks these divisions in an order ranging from the most major division (between two independent clauses) to the most minor division (a two-word modification pattern in a phrase). One of the reasons for assigning numbers to the different divisions is to define an *ordinal scale* of the different levels on which constituents are divided in English sentences. With some exceptions,[3] ordinality is achieved in this scheme; thus

---

[3] One major problem is the treatment of embedded clausal constructions. Dependent clauses are initially segmented (placed in parentheses), then successively segmented (placed in double parentheses, triple parentheses, etc.) until some arbitrarily imposed limit has been reached. Relative clauses are arbitrarily segmented to Level "5."

the numbers themselves can serve in certain measures of syntactic hierarchy.

ORDER APPROXIMATIONS

There are also statistical methods for describing language patterns. If a person were to select randomly letters of the English alphabet, we would have a string of letters that would seem to bear no relation to the patterns of letters that we often see in English spelling. Based on an example given by Shannon (1949, p. 13), the randomly selected string might look like this (adding a selected "space"):

XFOML RXKHRJFFJUJ

The above string is known as a *zero-order approximation;* the incidence of letters is unrelated to the frequencies and patterns of usage. The same type of approximation can be illustrated in terms of such other units as phonemes, words, or parts of speech, for example, words (Miller, 1951):

COMBAT CALLOUS IRRITABILITY
MIGRATES DEPRAVED TEMPORAL [p. 84]

Units involved in randomly selected zero-order approximations have an equal probability of occurrence, which, of course, units of natural language do not have.

Suppose, by contrast, we were to select individual units by their frequencies in a language; this gives a *first-order* approximation. If we were selecting English letters, units such as "e" or "o" would have a far greater probability of occurrence than, say, "q" and "x." Some examples of first-order approximations in English are (Shannon, 1949):

Letters: OCRO HLI RGWR NMIELWIS [pp. 13–14]

Words: REPRESENTING AND SPEEDILY [p. 14]
IS AN GOOD APT OR COME CAN [p. 14]

First-order approximation still does not reflect the statistical regularity of patterns, only the relative occurrence of individual units. However, suppose we were to determine selections by the frequency of joint occurrence; this is known as a *second-order* approximation. Beginning with the letter "q," for example, we could confidently expect that the next letter in English spelling would be "u." In a second-order approximation, the third letter would be biased by the prior occurrence of the "u" (excluding the "q"). The fourth letter would be biased by the occurrence of the third letter, and so on. An example of second-order letter approximation in English is (Shannon, 1949):

ON IE ANTSOUTINYS ARE T INCTORE ST [p. 13]

Similarly, in a *third-order* approximation, each unit is biased in occurrence by the two preceding units; the occurrence of a unit in a *fourth-order* approximation is biased by the three preceding units. Such approximations can be extended to a *fifth-order,* a *twentieth-order,* or even an *infinite-order* approximation. An example of a *seventh-order* English word approximation is (Miller and Selfridge, 1953):

RECOGNIZE HER ABILITIES IN MUSIC
AFTER HE SCOLDED HIM BEFORE [p. 185]

As can readily be seen in the above examples, second-order and above approximations begin to characterize pattern regularities of a language; in a haphazard way, some even make "sense" to a reader (or even more to a would-be poet). However, it should be remembered that such frequency based patterns reflect mixtures of the grammatical and pragmatic factors which influence the patterns in language. They are only a crude statistical map of linguistic regularities. They have been used most in psychological studies of verbal perception, where, for example, it has been found that the higher the order approximation of a contrived verbal pattern is to a person's language, the greater is the probability that it will be perceived or recalled accurately (see Miller and Selfridge, 1953). Nevertheless, order approximations are still another crude way to describe or manipulate language characteristics. A major methodological problem in using order approximations is obtaining the frequency data on which they are based. When considering the statistical patterns of even short sequences of words, for example, the variety of sequences reaches fantastic proportions.

There are, however, some easier ways to obtain patterns something like order approximations, including a method (discussed next) that focuses on part-of-speech frequencies and a variety of procedures for having persons try to predict language units or sequences (discussed subsequently).

PART-OF-SPEECH SEQUENCES

Stolz (1964, 1965) has described a procedure in which the conditional probabilities among parts of speech can serve as a crude index of grammatical structure. Imagine, for example, that we have a relatively large sample (Stolz used 68,000 words) of messages, and that we have assigned the words their part-of-speech classifications. With computerized procedures it is not difficult to obtain frequency counts of sequences of limited length (say, up to five members). This is far more feasible with parts of speech than with words because we are dealing only with a limited number of different individual units as against a very large number of different units if words were counted.

Given the sequential statistics of parts of speech, it is then possible to calculate probabilities of individual unit occurrences. For example, for a first-order approximation, we can determine the probability of individual part-of-speech units by their individual frequencies of occurrence in the text. Or for second-order approximations, we can construct sequences based on the probabilities of two-unit occurrences, and so on for three-unit, four-unit, and five-unit sequences. However, as Stolz has done, we can describe these sequences in terms of *conditional probabilities* among their individual units rather than the probabilities of entire sequences per se. Thus, for example, given that, say, a noun has occurred, we can describe the probabilities of the various parts of speech that could serve as the next unit in sequence. Such probabilities are *conditional* in that they are relative to what has occurred in the preceding context. Stolz's procedures have made it possible to calculate conditional probabilities relative to the occurrence of up to five units of either antecedent or subsequent context, or up to a four-unit bilateral context. In short, these conditional probabilities allow us to characterize the statistical regularities within part-of-speech sequences, a description somewhat akin to what is reflected in the order approximations discussed earlier.

The two Stolz studies illustrate ways to use conditional probabilities of parts of speech as a research tool. In the first (1964), conditional probabilities were incorporated in a *constraint* index of part-of-speech sequencing. This index allowed for describing language that was characterized by a greater variety in usage of the different parts of speech and different sequence patterns, as against language characterized by a lesser variety. This index was applied in the comparative study of spoken and written messages from the same encoders. In the second study (1965), conditional probabilities were used to calculate a statistic which described the relative structural *bond* at junctures between part-of-speech sequences in English sentences. For example, two sequences which had a high probability of cooccurrence would have a high bond value in the juncture between them. Stolz used his bond statistic to see whether conditional probability data from part-of-speech frequencies could predict the kinds of structural divisions described in syntactic tree diagrams.

PREDICTABILITY SCHEMES

Another way of describing the statistical regularities of language sequences involves presenting persons with part of a language sequence (or some other relevant stimulus), then having them "guess" what follows. Miller and Selfridge (1953), for example, developed order approximations among English words not by counting words in a message sample, but by recording what words Ss provided when they were given one or so words and told to complete a sentence. Second-order approximations were gained by providing a S with one word, having him supply a second word, then presenting a different S with this second word, and having him supply a third, and so on. Thus, second-order approximations are based on eliciting or "tapping" verbal habits in a prediction situation rather than the frequency of two-word occurrences.

There are numerous variations in predictability schemes. Goldman-Eisler (1958a), for example, tried to define points of linguistic "uncertainty" in previously recorded utterances by having persons guess or reconstruct them in a word-by-word sequence. She gauged uncertainty by the number of guesses it took to reproduce each original word. However, among predictability schemes, one called *cloze procedure* has received the most attention in communications studies.

Cloze Procedure

The term "cloze" was coined from the Gestalt psychology concept of closure, for example, that a person witnessing an almost completed figure — say, a circle — would tend to complete the figure by mentally closing the gap. Taylor's (1953) original application of this concept to "language closure" involved systematically deleting words in prose manuscripts (usually every fifth word), then requesting *S*s to close the gaps by filling in the missing words. To the extent that a person could supply the deleted (original) words, the message was judged more or less readable to him as a decoder. A *cloze score* is the number of correctly replaced words. Although cloze procedure was introduced as a readability gauge, it has had many diverse applications. We will review some of these.

READABILITY, COMPREHENSION, AND LISTENABILITY MEASURES

In two early studies, Taylor (1953, 1957) compared readability measures involving cloze procedure with measures derived by the Flesch (1946) and Dale and Chall (1948) procedures. He found significant positive correlations among the three measures, and these seemed unaffected by variations in the every-fifth-word mutilation pattern, by variations in the order of administering the passages for word prediction, or by scoring only exact word replacements as against also counting synonyms in the prediction score.

Taylor (1957) also reported a study where armed forces personnel were administered a cloze test both prior to and after studying subject matter related to messages sampled from an Air Force manual. Selected results included: (1) post-study cloze scores were higher than pre-study scores; (2) there were high positive correlations between cloze scores and a recall-type comprehension test; (3) there were significant positive correlations between cloze tests and scores on the *Armed Forces Qualification Test*; (4) these results generally prevailed across three different cloze deletion schemes — viz., a comparison among schemes involving every *n*th word, only "hard" words, or only "easy" words. Taylor interpreted these results as evidence that cloze scores measure comprehension, aptitude (in the sense of "ability to understand"), and can, to some degree, withstand variations in word deletion schemes. In view of the latter interpretation, Taylor noted that the every *n*th-word deletion scheme seemed to provide more "stable, reliable, and discriminating [p. 26]" scores than the other two versions. Other relatively early reports of cloze procedure describe its use in measuring the readability of newscopy (Hvistendahl, 1958), measuring the readability of Korean prose materials, comparing written and spoken communication, and gauging foreign language acquisition (Taylor, 1956).

A quite natural extension of cloze procedure is to apply it to spoken materials in a manner paralleling, if possible, applying it to written messages. Although Taylor (1956) briefly mentioned its application to spoken materials, more detailed accounts were subsequently provided by Williams (1962), Weaver and Kingston (1963), and Dickens and Williams (1964). Williams' (1962) procedure involved marking a sound tape at every fifth-second interval, then replacing the word spoken at that point (or the word nearest that point) with an equal length of tape on which white noise had been recorded. Immediately following each spoken sentence, a five-second length of unrecorded tape was inserted for each deletion incorporated in the preceding sentence. As *S*s heard the tape, they were instructed to try to write down during the response periods between sentences the words that had been deleted from the preceding sentence.

No doubt readability, comprehension, or even listenability can to some useful degree be measured by cloze procedure. One point to bear in mind is that cloze measures of readability or listenability must be taken from *some* decoder population, even though the purpose may be gauging the materials rather than the reader or listener per se. Or on the other side of the coin, if cloze procedure is to measure the decoder's capabilities in comprehension, there is the necessary specification: comprehension of what? Thus, whether the measure is intended to describe messages or people, two populations contribute to measurement variance — the "population" of message materials on the one hand, and the population of decoders on the other. As will be subsequently discussed, other important sources of variation may contribute to cloze scores, perhaps even so much so under certain conditions that neither readability nor comprehension is what is directly being measured.

Another point concerns the type of deletion scheme in cloze procedure. As Taylor (1954) mentions, an every-fifth-word pattern seems to suffice for studies of readability or comprehensibility. Usually this involves random selections of a starting point in a message, then replacing every fifth word with some type of deletion indicator, usually 10 spaces of typed underscoring. Although Taylor presents evidence that different starting points in a message will generally result in the same range of cloze scores, the generality of this evidence and its implications may be severely limited. In a series of unpublished pilot studies involving language samples from *Reader's Digest*, Tannenbaum and Williams found that different fifth-word deletion schemes sometimes led to significantly different cloze scores for a given message. Different every-fifth-word patterns tended to incorporate different numbers of *lexical* (nouns, verbs, adjectives, adverbs) as against *function* words in the deletion sample. As subsequently discussed in this section, function words — the structural markers of a sentence — typically have high cloze scores, often with twice the percentage of replacement as lexical words, which more or less convey the content of a message. In the *Reader's Digest* samples, some fifth-word patterns seemed almost to synchronize with the structural patterns of phrases, leading to a relatively greater inclusion of function words than other deletion patterns. When this was the case, cloze scores were substantially higher than in the alternative deletion patterns. In subsequent research, the problem was combatted with two strategies. First, rather than deleting every fifth word, 20 per cent of the words in a message were deleted in a pattern based on random numbers, usually allowing at least one word and not more than seven words to intervene between two deletions. Second, cloze scores were separately calculated for lexical and function word types. Following this procedure, responses tended to vary more on lexical replacement scores than on function word scores, which raises the question whether the two scores should ever be combined. They may indeed be two quite distinct "grammatical populations," and their combination may confound any useful interpretations of results. Also, this distinction carries serious consequences for the statistical analyses of cloze scores, including whether variances found for replacement of the two types can be combined as a legitimate estimate of measurement error. Or, when variance is strongly influenced by function word replacement, the resulting estimate of measurement error may be so small that it makes psychologically trivial differences in mean cloze scores statistically significant.

A final point to think about concerns the interpretation of cloze scores, qua measurement scale, as an index of readability, listenability, or comprehension. In Taylor's (1953) reasoning, the more words a person can replace, the more readable or comprehensible is the material to him. One's initial reaction is to consider cloze scores as reflecting a continuous measure of readability or comprehension, ranging, say, in percentage scores from 0 to 100. But this is misleading, particularly when considering relatively high percentages of word replacement. Suppose, for example, that a person were able to correctly replace all deleted words in a message. With only slight exception, we could no doubt agree that the message was "readable" or "comprehensible" to him; but a high cloze score also indicates that a message was *redundant* to the respondent. That is, it gave him a minimal degree of "new information." Obviously, then, messages which yield relatively high cloze scores are not desirable messages from a communication standpoint; they communicate nothing new to the receiver. Unfortunately, nobody has systematically investigated this problem, although Taylor (1954) mentions an *optimal* readability score, which would be something less than 100 per cent closure. Needless to say, this point, too, raises serious questions regarding the noncritical use of cloze procedure to measure readability or comprehension. But perhaps most of all it raises the key question: What is it that cloze scores truly measure?

THE NATURE OF CLOZE MEASUREMENTS

Two studies partially answer the above question, and they also suggest how to use cloze procedure as a research tool. Taylor's (1954) dissertation presented, among other things, a more detailed picture of word predictability measures than was previously available. Briefly, Taylor demonstrated how an array of response words for a given deletion or the individual response arrays for a series of deletions could be described in terms of three measurements expressed as percentage components: (1) *cloze percentage*, or the proportion of the response words comprising verbatim replacements; (2) *misdirection*, or response words which were agreed upon by Ss but which were not verbatim replacements, and (3) *actual remaining relative entropy*, or an index of the degree of unique, nonverbatim replacements. These three percentages are complementary: they sum to 100 per cent in every case. Though there is not enough space here to describe Taylor's procedures for calculating these components, we can discuss their practical interpretation.

A high cloze percentage resulting from a series of replacements indicates that the words were redundant to the decoder. Because of his knowledge of the message topic, knowledge gleaned from the message context, or other reasons, the respondent has been able to replicate the word selection of the original encoder. Rather than reflecting readability and the like, we might say that cloze percentages most directly reflect *redundancy* in the prediction situation. Or, as Taylor describes it, we could say that cloze percentage gauges the correspondence between the verbal habits of the encoder and decoder. Misdirection measures a type of *deviate constraint*, in contrast to the foregoing redundancy reflected in exact replacements. Here, knowledge leads to decoder agreement in replacements, but these replacements do not correspond with the units originally encoded in the message. In a sense, the decoders are "agreeing to disagree" with the original encoder. The greater the misdirection percentage, the more *stylistic* deviations between the habits of the encoder and decoders, at least in word choice. The final percentage component, actual remaining relative entropy, characterizes the opposite of redundancy or constraint; it is an index of *randomness* (or in information theory terms, *entropy*) in the prediction situation. In contrast to cloze and misdirection percentages, the uncertainty percentage reflects that neither have decoders been able to bring to bear the necessary knowledge for reproducing the original words, nor is there enough constraint to result even in any agreement among decoders.

Taylor's three percentage components thus characterize a total picture of the response components reflected in cloze procedure. Consider these components in reverse order. Some persons' lack of applicable knowledge or cues in the prediction situation results in randomness among their responses. Knowledge and cues constrain some persons' responses to be in consensus with one another, but different from the original encoder's choices. Finally, knowledge and cues may make a word entirely redundant.

Taylor mainly applied these measures in a word-by-word analysis of the text of brief sample messages. He obtained prediction data for every word in context by administering to five different samples of the same decoder population five different every-fifth-word deletion versions of the messages, the first version starting with deletion on the first word, the second version starting on the second word, and so on. These data allowed him to describe a word-by-word prediction "profile" for continuous text, thus indicating loci of redundancy, misdirection, and uncertainty. Needless to say, this type of all-word analysis seems to be an ingenious strategy for studying language contexts. But perhaps a major problem with it arises in comparing the predictability of adjacent words in context. Their differences in predictability are confounded by differences in the deletion patterns. A reader interested in this procedure or some variation of it should consult Taylor's report.

The second paper bearing on the nature of cloze measurements is by Weaver and Kingston (1963). These researchers conducted a factor analysis of score intercorrelations of commercially available reading, listening, and language ability sub-tests and eight cloze-type tests, including word replacement in both spoken and written messages. Among the three main factors Weaver and Kingston extracted, the one they labeled *redundancy utilization* seemed most to reflect cloze scores and similar prediction-type behavior on other tests. In comparing this factor with others labeled "verbal comprehension" and "rote memory, flexible retrieval," Weaver and Kingston saw cloze procedure as measuring some aspects of reading and listening behavior that are not measured by the more standard tests. But in the main, they concluded that cloze scores were a measure of redundancy utilization.

APPLICATIONS OF CLOZE PROCEDURE

Considering the foregoing discussion, one may measure readability, listenability, or even comprehensibility with cloze procedure only by making some major assumptions. What cloze procedure seems to index is redundancy in the prediction situation, or, more practically, the correspondence between the word choices of encoders and decoders (the persons who are replacing words). A few recent studies illustrate this type of application, gauging encoder-decoder agreement or correspondence in word selection. Fillenbaum and Jones (1962), for example, gauged the correspondence between the verbal habits of aphasic (verbal impairment related to brain damage) patients and nonaphasic, normal individuals by having the latter undertake word replacement in messages obtained from the former. Robinson (1965) used a similar approach in comparing social class differences in language. Clark, Williams, and Tannenbaum (1965) assessed the effects of shared referential experience on encoder-decoder "language agreement" by cloze procedure. More recently, Odom, Blanton, and Nunnally (1967) used cloze procedure in a study comparing the language capabilities of deaf and hearing Ss.

Some research similar to Taylor's (1954) earlier discussed investigation has centered on linguistic factors affecting word predictability: variations in the immediate contextual environment of deletions, including the amount of context (Oléron, 1960; MacGinitie, 1961; Fillenbaum, Jones, and Rapoport, 1963); the position of context (Aborn, Rubenstein, and Sterling, 1959; MacGinitie, 1961); whether the decoder knows the grammatical form class of the deleted item (Tannenbaum, Williams, and Clark, 1969). Some of these studies (*e.g.,* Aborn *et al.,* 1959) used a score based on grammatical replacement (called *FC*, or form class score). Thus, in addition to gauging verbatim replacement (*V* score), they assessed predictability as the degree to which respondents could replace a deletion with a word that was the same part of speech as the original item, apart from whether or not they correctly replaced the word itself. This has been taken as an index of *grammatical closure*, or *syntactic correspondence* between encoder and decoder. Further, Fillenbaum and Jones (1962) used a ratio defined as V/FC which indicates the degree of verbatim replacement as "adjusted" for differences in grammatical replacement. Tannenbaum *et al.* (1965) applied these measures when attempting to describe both lexical and grammatical uncertainty in the linguistic contexts of speech hesitations.

Darnell (1963) suggests a further and potentially useful application of cloze procedure. He assessed the consequences of varying a message's structure by obtaining word predictability data from successively disorganized revisions of the original message. As described in a study of Phillips (1965), it seems reasonable to assume that the differences in cloze scores between a version of a message with its sentence-by-sentence order as originally encoded and a version with randomized sentence order would be a psychological gauge of message organization. That is, the more the cloze score of the original version would exceed that of the randomized version, the more it would seem that the order of sentences, or message structure, would contribute to word replacement. Though Phillips' study did not bear directly on this issue, his results did indicate the potential utility of a cloze-based index of message structure. Certainly, however, there is need for further research into the use of cloze procedure as a structural index, including consideration of the structural segments to be manipulated and the type of words best scheduled for the deletion scheme.

SAMPLE STUDY[4]

The study reported here is intended to illustrate a communication research design which centers directly on the analysis of language behavior. It incorporates the tasks of specification and quantification discussed in the two previous main sections of this chapter. The report is also intended to be of methodological interest to communication researchers who for one reason or another may use part-of-speech frequencies to describe language behavior.

[4] This research was conducted jointly by the author and Mr. William Phillips as a project of the Speech Experimental Laboratory at the University of Wisconsin under support from the Wisconsin Alumni Foundation and the Institute for Research on Poverty. The results have not been published before.

Problem

Among the objective strategies which have been applied in studying language behavior, identifying and counting parts of speech have received no little attention. They have been applied in studies ranging from style in speech and writing to the assessment of linguistic deviations accompanying certain speech disorders, and even to the language associated with the cognitive or emotional states or sociological circumstances of encoders.[5] Despite this widespread application, such studies have not always clearly revealed the relation between individual part-of-speech frequencies and the syntactic component of language behavior.

In some cases, the individual frequencies have been interpreted as syntactic units themselves, without reference to the larger structures into which they enter. This obviously restricts description to only a characterization of the incidence of syntactic "elements" observed in behavior, rather than the patterns structured by these elements. Moreover, such a description is uneconomical; it must be based on a number of measures equal to the number of different parts of speech. In other cases, this problem has been only slightly alleviated by combining certain individual frequencies into ratios. Thus, for example, the ratio of adjectives to nouns is a crude index of noun modification — "crude" or "partial," since, of course, nouns are modified by other words in addition to adjectives, and verbs by words other than adverbs. We are not likely, either, to construct adequately more complex ratios, since our knowledge of English grammar indicates that many parts of speech can enter into more than one type of modification pattern, thus introducing ambiguity into the interpretation of such ratios.

The question leading to the sample study originated from the reasoning that part-of-speech frequencies could be susceptible to multivariate analysis. That is: Might an array of individual part-of-speech frequencies, taken as syntactic measures, be reduced through factor analysis to a set of fewer, more basic variables or "dimensions" of syntactic behavior?

Individual part-of-speech frequencies, after all, are not all independent of one another. Certain frequencies, or even clusters of frequencies, should vary together, reflecting how particular types of phrase structures require the use of particular parts of speech. Consider the incidence of noun phrases, for example. Unless a pronoun functions as a noun phrase, we would expect a noun to occur. And if a noun occurs, there is a high probability that a determiner will occur, and perhaps a lesser probability that an adjective will occur. We can base such expectations to some extent on a knowledge of the phrase and clause patterns of English grammar or the knowledge of the statistical patterns among parts of speech, such as Stolz (1964, 1965) described in the studies discussed on pp. 265–266. The present study anticipated that if the intercorrelations among part-of-speech

---

[5] See, for example, Carroll (1960); Osgood (1960); Bernstein (1962); Blankenship (1962); Jones, Goodman, and Wepman (1963); Knabe, Nelson and Williams (1966).

frequencies revealed a salient factor structure, the factors could be meaningfully interpreted as expectations based on a knowledge of English syntax. At best, such an analysis promised to reveal if relative usages of individual parts of speech might be reduced to a more integrated description of syntactic performance.

Generally, the research involved obtaining messages under conditions presumed to affect syntactic patterning differentially. Words in these messages were coded for part-of-speech identification, and the intercorrelations among the relative frequencies of the individual classes were subjected to a factor analysis. The goal in interpreting the rotated factor matrix and in selected subsequent analyses was describing syntactic performance which, although based on part-of-speech frequencies, would avoid some of the usual shortcomings.

Method

MESSAGES

The messages subjected to analysis were written responses by Ss (undergraduate college students) to a set of three captionless cartoons previously used in language behavior studies (Goldman-Eisler, 1961a). The choice of written rather than oral messages was relatively arbitrary except that written messages would bypass the necessity for making transcriptions of spoken messages and would possibly offer more in the way of syntactic complexity and variety for subsequent analyses. Additionally, the messages represented the manipulation of two variations in encoding conditions, each undertaken for purposes of inducing further syntactic variety in the messages, and for purposes of subsequent comparative analyses.

The main variation in message encoding conditions was that some Ss were required to present a verbal *description* of a cartoon, others to abstract its subtle meaning (labeled an *abstraction*). Prior research has indicated that this manipulation leads to anticipated differences in cognitive demands on encoding behavior (Goldman-Eisler, 1961a), as well as corollary manifestations in the syntactic structure of verbal responses (Goldman-Elsler et al., 1965a). Asking for a description is intended to induce a series of verbal representations of the items within the cartoon as they are serially experienced by the observer. The language is relatively concrete and is marked by specificity of description. By contrast, abstraction presumably requires synthesizing and interpreting the totality of items in the cartoon, thus prompting language marked by substantial clause integration and less marked by specificity of description.

A second variation in encoding conditions involved manipulating whom S was told to anticipate as an audience for his messages, a "college professor" or a person identified as a "fifth grader." Presumably, encoders will vary their overall syntactic patterns from the relatively complex (for the professor) to the relatively simple (for the fifth grader). For the sample

study, the assumption was that the results of this manipulation would interact with the syntactic contrasts anticipated between the description and
abstraction conditions. Specifically, differences between descriptions and
abstractions were expected to be greater in the professor audience condition
than in the alternative condition.

Altogether, 120 messages were included in the analysis, representing
the total responses of 40 Ss, each S responding to all three cartoons, and
four subgroups of 10 Ss being randomly assigned to each of the four basic
encoding conditions — *i.e.*, description-professor, description-fifth grader,
abstraction-professor, and abstraction-fifth grader.

GRAMMATICAL CODING

The procedure for part-of-speech classification was a 12-category scheme
which followed closely the criteria incorporated in the *WISSYN* computer
program (Stolz *et al.*, 1965) discussed on pp. 248–249. The researchers
chose this scheme mainly because they anticipated that should the investigation prove successful, the statistical description of syntactic performance
could be fully computerized by adding further processing routines to the
already available *WISSYN* program. However, to bypass the necessity for
keypunching the language sample and to omit classification categories not
deemed pertinent to the investigation, the coding was conducted by hand.
Table 1 (p. 276) outlines the reduced classification scheme.

Analyses and Results

The first three columns of figures in Table 2 present summary data for
the various parts of speech coded in the overall sample. Of passing interest
to us are the mean relative frequencies of the 12 parts of speech, indicating
how various proportions of the sample were subsumed within the different
grammatical classes. Each entry is the frequency of an individual part of
speech divided by the total number of words (17,064) in the sample.
Nouns and verbs together made up approximately 36 per cent of the words,
and such classes as modifying verbs, intensifiers, and subordinators together
accounted for slightly less than 5 per cent. Where these grammatical classifications were comparable with other studies (*e.g.*, Stolz, 1964), their relative frequencies correspond roughly to previous findings. For each part of
speech, Table 2 also presents the standard deviations (s) of its overall
distribution. These values indicate how much within the overall sample
each part of speech was susceptible to variation in relative frequency distribution — such variation reflecting a confounding of individual encoder
differences and differences due to the various encoding conditions. To
facilitate comparing variability across the different parts of speech, coefficients of variation ($100s$ divided by M) are also given in Table 2.
From a practical viewpoint, values of *c.v.* indicate the relative susceptibility
of each grammatical class to variation in relative occurrence. If the primary

TABLE 1

Parts of Speech

Name	Sample Frame
Noun	We saw the ______. (The) ______ is/are here.
Verb	He ______ it. Bob ______ rich. He ______.
Adjective	The ______ man left. It seemed ______. They are very ______.
Adverb	He walked ______. The barn ______ was old.
Pronoun	(*Word list*) ______ left the dog ______ John bought.
Determiner	(*Word list*) He shot ______ wolf. I saw ______ father.
Auxiliary	He ______ walking. He ______ go.
Intensifier	He was ______ unhappy.
Modifying verb	He ______ to go.
Preposition	(*Word list*) She walked ______ the house. He got there ______ walking.
Subordinator	(*Word list*) He ate ______ he was hungry. He knew more ______ I did.
Connector	(*Word list*) They arrived ______ we left. John ______ Mary arrived.

TABLE 2

Means, Standard Deviations, Coefficients of Variation and Rotated Factor Matrix of Part of Speech Frequencies Relative to Total Words in Messages

Part of speech	Mean	*s*	*c.v.* (%)	Factors I	II	III
Noun	.217	.048	22	−.09	−.89	−.05
Verb	.143	.030	21	−.85	−.21	−.29
Adjective	.079	.035	44	−.10	−.52	−.35
Adverb	.056	.029	52	−.05	.18	−.60
Pronoun	.088	.047	55	−.84	.02	−.14
Determiner	.170	.053	31	.07	−.84	−.03
Auxiliary	.057	.026	46	−.42	−.07	−.64
Mod. Verb	.016	.015	94	−.29	.13	−.86
Intensifier	.012	.010	83	−.03	−.15	.38
Preposition	.101	.034	34	.08	−.80	.08
Subordinator	.021	.018	86	−.55	−.07	−.37
Connector	.045	.022	51	−.75	−.25	.08

research interest is the differential usage of the various parts of speech as it may vary as a function of individual encoder differences or differences due to encoding conditions, those classes having relatively high *c.v.* values should be most susceptible to variation. Thus, for example, the relative frequencies of nouns and verbs (basic sentence constituents) should be less prone to differ in usage than, say, modifying verbs, intensifiers, or subordinators (relatively optional constituents).

DIMENSIONALITY OF USAGE

As previously discussed, the main question was whether the relative frequencies of grammatical classes, taken as variables symptomatic of syntactic performance, could be reduced through factor analysis to a set of fewer variables or dimensions. A factor analysis was performed, and the results are also presented in Table 2.[6]

Of the total variance (12.0) assumed in the analysis, a variance of 7.5 was accommodated by the three *factors* (I, II, III) shown in Table 2. This means that within the assumptions of the factor analysis, approximately 63 per cent of the total variance in terms of the intercorrelations among the 12 parts of speech was redefined in terms of the three factors, or dimensions. The question then was: Could these three dimensions be given meaningful interpretations in view of the goal at hand?

Factor I. Approximately 89 per cent of the variance of Factor I is attributable to four variables — viz., relative frequencies of verbs, pronouns, subordinators, and connectors. In other words, Factor I primarily reflects the concomitant variation of these four parts of speech. The fact that these particular parts of speech were involved and that they varied together suggested a dimension of *clausal incidence* for the following reasons. First, the occurrence of verbs in the present classification scheme is an indicator of the occurrence of basic predicate units (recall that verbs which modified other verbs were classified separately as modifying verbs). This reasoning alone, however, does not resolve whether such predicate units were simple sentence constructions in themselves or whether they were clausal constituents within complex sentences. The accompanying occurrence of the three other parts of speech sheds light on the interpretation. Pronouns in the present classification scheme are symptomatic of clausal units in at least two ways. Relative pronouns (*e.g.*, "He liked the car *that* I bought") introduce linked constructions. Other pronouns (*e.g.*, "Mary is my sister, I like *her*") are often used in clauses in order to avoid repeating a word from another clause in a sentence. Further, the occurrence of a subordinator ("*Because* he came, I left") always signals a modifying clause. Finally, one function of a connector ("John came *and* Mary left") is to relate two

---

[6] This was a principal components analysis (ones in the diagonals) coupled with varimax rotation using the University of Wisconsin Computer Center library's program IMAGE.

clauses. Although the data are not unequivocal on this point, the foregoing suggests the occurrence of clauses in complex sentence constructions.

In varying the encoding conditions under which the messages were obtained, the researchers anticipated that if interpretable factors were found in the analysis, it would then be possible to reinforce their interpretation by comparing results across message conditions. For this purpose, the relative frequencies of the four parts of speech (verb, pronoun, subordinator, connector) having the highest loading on Factor I were subsumed (arithmetic mean) as a *factor score* for each *S*. These scores were then subjected to a 2 x 2 analysis of variance having dimensions corresponding to the message and audience conditions (omitting the distinctions in cartoons). Table 3 summarizes the results of the analysis.[7] If we assume, as described earlier in this report, that the abstraction condition would lead to a greater degree of clause integration than the description condition, the results for Factor I scores appear to be in line with expectations. The mean score is significantly greater (under "Audience Combined" in Table 3) for abstractions than descriptions.

TABLE 3

Factor I Scores
(Verb, Pronoun, Subordinator, Connector)

Message	Audience		
	Prof.	*5th G.*	*Combined*
Description	.060	.065	.063*
Abstraction	.084	.088	.086
Both	.072	.077	

* Message main effect significant ($p < .05$); $F = 5.28$, $d.f. = 1/36$.

As discussed earlier, the manipulation of anticipated audience was expected to interact with the effects of the two message conditions. However, this was not realized in the factor analysis. There were no significant interactions between the message type and audience conditions, and an inspection of the cell means (under "Audience" in Table 3) indicates that for both professors and fifth graders as anticipated audiences, the Factor I score means for abstractions exceed those for descriptions. Evidently, the audience variable had little effect on this dimension of performance.

In sum, Factor I was identified as a dimension of *clausal incidence,* an interpretation based on the relatively high factor loadings of verbs, pro-

---

[7] To conserve space, only the *F* ratios for the hypothesis tests indicating statistical significance rather than the entire analysis of variance summary tables are reported for this and the subsequent analyses.

nouns, subordinators, and connectors, as well as differences among the message conditions.

Factor II. The main variables which accounted for approximately 93 per cent of the variance on Factor II (Table 2) were the relative frequencies of nouns, adjectives, determiners, and prepositions. As described as an example at the outset of this report, we would expect to find the relative frequencies of nouns, adjectives, and determiners varying together since they are constituents of noun phrases. Also, we can add that determiners and adjectives are the main constituents in elaborating the constructions of noun phrases. Prepositions, too, enter with prepositional phrases into the elaboration of noun phrases, but prepositional phrases can also modify verbs. They probably occur in this factor mainly because prepositions typically require an object nominal, which itself is often a noun and its modifiers (as in "by *the house*"). Assuming this explanation, Factor II was labeled as *nominal incidence elaboration*, owing to its reflection of noun phrase characteristics.

If, as was assumed at the outset, descriptions would incorporate detailed accounts of the referends in the cartoons, whereas abstractions would not concentrate on such detail, we should again expect differences due to the message conditions. This also assumes, of course, that the incidence and elaboration of noun phrases (or the relative incidence of the four parts of speech loading highly on Factor II) are symptomatic of increasing the descriptive details of expression. Again factor scores were calculated, this time for the mean of the relative frequencies of nouns, adjectives, determiners, and prepositions. Table 4 presents results of a similar 2 x 2 analysis of variance. Incorporating the foregoing assumptions, the results are again in line with expectations. The Factor II mean score for descriptions exceeds the mean for abstractions, thus indicating a greater degree of nominal incidence elaboration in the former condition than in the latter. Again, however, the anticipated interaction with the audience variable was not realized.

TABLE 4

Factor II Scores
(*Noun, Adjective, Determiner, Preposition*)

Message	Audience		
	Prof.	*5th G.*	*Combined*
Description	.161	.156	.159*
Abstraction	.133	.118	.126
Both	.147	.137	

* Message main effect significant ($p < .05$); $F = 7.43$, $d.f. = 1/36$.

In brief, Factor II was labeled as *nominal incidence elaboration,* and it reflected the relative occurrence of nouns, adjectives, determiners, and prepositions.

Factor III. The third factor (Table 2) reflects mainly the relative occurrence of adverbs, auxiliaries, and modifying verbs, together accounting for some 87 per cent of the variance on this factor. Clearly, the loading of auxiliaries and modifying verbs on Factor III points the elaboration of verb constructions. That adverbs also loaded relatively high on this factor suggests that their relative incidence, in these messages at least, was mainly in the role of verb modifiers rather than in their other possible modification roles. If we assume these interpretations, Factor III seems best labeled as *verbal modification.*

Unfortunately, the distinction between description and abstraction does not lend itself to clear expectations concerning a differential degree of verb modification. It could be argued that descriptions would incorporate a greater attention than abstractions to details of actions as well as to items within a cartoon. On the other hand, a reasonable counterargument is that an abstraction would require communicating subtle distinctions concerning actions portrayed in the cartoons. An analysis (Table 5) of scores calculated for Factor III provided no evidence of any distinctions between the message conditions. Of the factors heretofore examined, it was the only one that did not lead to a significant main effect due to the differences in message types. But as can be seen in Table 5, there is a significant main effect due to the audience variable, indicating a greater degree of verb modification when the encoder anticipated a professor as reader rather than a fifth grader. Apparently, if a difference due to audience sophistication was to be found, it was observed only in terms of this aspect of grammatical usage. However, at best, these results are only of heuristic value. Factor III, then, was taken as indicative of *verbal modification,* an interpretation based on the relative incidence of adverbs, auxiliaries, and modifying verbs, but without the additional support of distinctions among the message conditions.

TABLE 5

Factor III Scores
(Adverb, Auxiliary, Modifying Verb)

Message	Audience		
	Prof.	*5th G.*	*Combined*
Description	.052	.033	.043
Abstraction	.051	.035	.043
Both	.052*	.034	

* Audience main effect significant $(p < .05)$; $F = 4.21$, $d.f. = 1/36$.

Discussion

The key aim in the sample study was to examine whether the individual relative frequencies of parts of speech might be reduced through factor analysis to a set of fewer, more basic variables or dimensions of syntactic behavior. In the main, the results of this inquiry are largely affirmative. The initial analysis did reveal a salient factor structure, and the dimensions were interpretable when gauged against the patterns of English syntax. Further, at least two of these dimensions coincided with expectations based on the distinctions in message encoding conditions. Considering these results, there are some implications of both theoretical and practical consequence.

DIMENSIONALITY OF PERFORMANCE

For one thing, it seems evident that at least some of the larger constructional patterns of English can "survive," or be reflected, in the multivariate analysis of the frequencies of their elements. Or put into more elaborate terms: the results of the sample study indicate that the factor structure, which we might call a *grammar of performance,* does provide a crude approximation to at least some aspects of the structural hierarchy of English as defined by a formal grammar. But like most statistical descriptions, the picture is a gross and perhaps fragmentary one of language itself.

On the other hand, because it derives from how the user has employed language, the picture may be a kind of necessary chart for plotting the functional role of language in communication behavior. Here we are referring to the consequences that the distinctions in encoding conditions had on the factor scores. The variance defined in the factor structure reflects among other things variations in the individual relative frequencies due to the differences in encoding conditions. In other words, one of the reasons that the present three factors were revealed was presumably variation in the functional demands of the different encoding situations. For example, in view of the findings, we can assume that an *S* faced with the task of encoding an abstraction tended to use a greater relative number of verbs, pronouns, subordinators, and connectors than an *S* who was encoding a description. The very basis for this assumption — that the variance among *S*s within an encoding condition was substantially exceeded by the variance between conditions — is evidence of the functional reality of the obtained factor and, hence, its relevance to the demands of the encoding situation. In short, we can view the present factor structure as a rough map of the linguistic consequences of the functional demands on communication imposed by the manipulation of encoding conditions. This kind of "map" is what we were referring to when, in the beginning of this chapter, we said that the goal in this type of research is to describe how people exercise their linguistic capabilities in a functional sense, that is, how the characteristics of language enter into the larger framework of the characteristics of communication.

RESEARCH IMPLICATIONS

The present results are not much of a basis (nor could they be) for assuming that the three dimensions of *clausal incidence, nominal incidence elaboration,* and *verbal modification* provide an overall structure having generality across different types of encoders and encoding situations. For one thing, the encoders in this study were drawn from a population highly homeogeneous in their verbal habits and capabilities. Whether or not the same factor structure or even a meaningful structure would obtain for another population, and particularly for a heterogeneous population, is a question for further research. Bernstein (1962), for example, has described the distinction between the language of the working and middle classes in Great Britain in terms of syntactic contrasts. It seems reasonable that the dimensions of such contrast could be revealed by a factor analysis focusing on *S*s' differences as the main source of variation.

By the same token, we would expect the factor structure to vary with the demands of the encoding situation. In the design of the sample study, the assumptions concerning the abstraction-description distinction had the benefit of the prior research conducted by Goldman-Eisler and her colleagues (Goldman-Eisler, 1961a; Goldman-Eisler *et al.,* 1965a) and were reinforced by the new findings. What are some other situational distinctions that might be researched? Without going into detail, they could range from differences between types of messages (as in abstraction compared with description), topics of messages, and the modalities of the messages (speech as against writing), to the differences between the types of actual or anticipated audiences. As for the last distinction, audience differences, the contrast between professors and fifth graders, particularly when writing about cartoons, may have been too minimal or ambiguous to have had detectable consequences on the first two factors. Certainly, too, we could have more confidence in this type of manipulation if the encoder were given ample evidence of the characteristics and existence of the specified audience, and, further, if we had an independent measure of his recognition and acceptance of this specification. In sum, a viable focus for subsequent research is the relation between the different functional demands of encoding situations and the attendant consequences on the factor structure.

SOME PRACTICAL NOTES

The main utility of the techniques in the sample study is that they facilitate quantified description of syntactic aspects of response behavior, and the analyses — from part-of-speech classification to the factor analysis and even to comparison among samples — could be entirely accomplished by computer. But, as discussed on pp. 247–249, parts of speech as well as completely statistical descriptions are not the most adequate bases for characterizing the syntactic component of language. With this point in mind, we suggest that the procedures described in the sample study are probably best for exploratory purposes. That is, we can take advantage of their potential for computerization and economy of usage in order to perform initial studies of encoding situations. We can then use the gross pictures provided by these procedures for conducting more revealing and linguistically accurate descriptions of syntactic behavior.

RESEARCH PROSPECTIVES

In the major sections of this chapter we have discussed the analysis of verbal behavior chiefly as the specification and quantification of verbal or behavioral units of language. The result is, in most cases, a statistical description of some facet of language or language behavior. Perhaps we can best conclude this chapter by reviewing in a general way how these descriptions enter into the design of communications studies.

Language as an Independent Variable

As discussed in the chapter on stylistic analyses (Chapter 11), the problem in research designs describing the characteristics of messages as an independent variable concerns the consequences of these characteristics on the behavior of decoders. Some such designs are exploratory in strategy. They involve specifying and enumerating a variety of message characteristics, then, through the use of multiple regressional analyses, attempting to relate these characteristics to such facets of decoder behavior as comprehension, attitude, and the like. Although we criticized the use of the Flesch indices as research tools, their "formulas" illustrate what we are describing here — that is, the regression of psychological variables (such as *reading ease* or *human interest*) on variables reflecting message characteristics (word length, sentence length, personal words, etc.).

More in the way of hypothesis testing designs are involved when we actually manipulate language characteristics for the purpose of studying their consequences on decoder behavior. For example, given the definition of characteristics that appear related to the comprehensibility of message materials, the next step is to manipulate these characteristics as the independent variable in an experimental design. We might call investigations of the foregoing type, whether they explore or test a hypothesis, *decoding* studies.

Language as a Dependent Variable

Of course, the purpose of other research designs is studying language behavior in encoding. In such designs, which we might call *encoding* studies, language becomes the dependent variable. These designs, too, can be exploratory and descriptive, as when we assess the characteristics of some set of existing messages and attempt to attribute certain usage of these characteristics to specific authors, modalities, or situations of encoding. When language is the dependent variable in an experimental design, the actual circumstances of encoding are manipulated for purposes of studying the consequences on language behavior. The investigation of part-of-speech frequencies, reported earlier as the sample study, was a design of this type.

Summary

At the outset of this chapter we said that the linguistic concern of the communication researcher is mainly how the characteristics of language enter into the larger framework of the characteristics of communication. Or, put another way, it is the functional aspect of language that falls within the purview of the communication researcher. Throughout this chapter we have seen numerous schemes for specifying and quantifying verbal phenomena. If we were to review thoroughly the communication oriented studies using such procedures, we would encounter such substantive topics as effects of message structure on decoder behavior (*e.g.,* Beighley, 1954; Gulley and Berlo, 1956; Darnell, 1963), stylistic characteristics (Matthews, 1947; Bowers, 1963), and contrasts between speech and writing (Blankenship, 1962; DeVito, 1966; Gibson *et al.,* 1966; Gruner, Kibler, and Gibson, 1967), to name a few.

Despite the availability of the many procedures for analyzing the language component in communication, we still have little of theoretical consequence to show for it. Research has added many "bits and pieces" to our already fragmentary knowledge of the linguistic details of communication, but to date very little has been done to integrate them into meaningful theoretical constructs of the functional aspects of language. Specifically, we mean those constructs which would map the way from linguistic theory to communication theory. One need only read the sections devoted to language in such compilations of papers as Smith's *Communication and Culture* (1966) or Dance's *Human Communication Theory* (1967) to grasp this lack. Phrased in the bluntest of terms: the linguistic parameters of a communication theory remain essentially obscure. Communication researchers have the tools and the scientific attitude necessary to reveal the functional aspects of language. They should set about the task.

References and Selected Readings

Aborn, M., Rubenstein, H., and Sterling, T. D. Sources of contextual constraint upon words in sentences. *Journal of Experimental Psychology,* 1959, **57,** 171–180.

Aggertt, O. J., and Bowen, E. R. *Communicative reading.* New York: Macmillan, 1956.

Bach, E. *An introduction to transformational grammars.* New York: Holt, Rinehart & Winston, 1964.

Beighley, K. C. An experimental study of the effect of three speech variables on listener comprehension. *Speech Monographs,* 1954, **21,** 248–253.

Bernstein, B. Social class, linguistic codes and grammatical elements. *Language and Speech,* 1962, **5,** 221–240.

Blankenship, J. A linguistic analysis of oral and written style. *Quarterly Journal of Speech,* 1962, **48,** 419–422.

Blankenship, J., and Kay, C. Hesitation phenomena in English speech: A study in distribution. *Word,* 1964, **20,** 360–372.

Bloch, B. Studies in colloquial Japanese: II. Syntax. *Language,* 1946, **22,** 200–248.

Bloomfield, L. *Language.* New York: Henry Holt, 1933.

Boomer, D. S., and Dittmann, A. T. Hesitation pauses and juncture pauses in speech. *Language and Speech,* 1962, **5,** 215–220.

Bowers, J. W. Language intensity, social introversion, and attitude change. *Speech Monographs,* 1963, **30,** 345–352.

Carroll, J. B. Diversity of vocabulary and the harmonic series law of word-frequency distribution. *Psychological Record,* 1938, **2,** 379–386.

Carroll, J. B. Vectors of prose style. In T. A. Sebeok (Ed.), *Style in language.* Cambridge, Mass.: M.I.T. Press, and New York: John Wiley, 1960. Pp. 283–292.

Carroll, J. B. *Language and thought.* Englewood Cliffs, N.J.: Prentice-Hall, 1964.

Carroll, J. B. Problems of measuring speech rate. Paper presented at a conference on speech compression, University of Louisville, Louisville, Ky., 1966.

Chall, J. S. *Readability: An appraisal of research and application.* Columbus: Ohio State University Bureau of Educational Research, 1958.

Chomsky, N. *Syntactic structures.* The Hague: Mouton, 1957.

Chomsky, N. *Aspects of the theory of syntax.* Cambridge, Mass.: M.I.T. Press, 1965.

Chomsky, N. *Current issues in linguistic theory.* The Hague: Mouton, 1966.

Chomsky, N., and Halle, M. *The sound pattern of English.* New York: Harper & Row, 1968.

Chotlos, J. W. Studies in language behavior: IV. A statistical and comparative analysis of individual written language samples. *Psychological Monographs,* 1944, **56,** 75–111.

Clark, R. A., Williams, F., and Tannenbaum, P. H. Effects of shared referential experience upon encoder-decoder agreement. *Language and Speech,* 1965, **8,** 253–262.

Dale, E., and Chall, J. S. A formula for predicting readability [and] Instructions. *Educational Research Bulletin,* 1948, **27,** 11–20, 28, 37–54.

Dance, F. E. X. (Ed.) *Human communication theory: Original essays.* New York: Holt, Rinehart & Winston, 1967.

Darley, F. L. A normative study of oral reading rate. Unpublished Master's thesis, State University of Iowa, 1940.

Darnell, D. K. The relation between sentence order and comprehension. *Speech Monographs,* 1963, **30,** 97–100.

Denes, P. B., and Pinson, E. N. *The speech chain.* Baltimore: Williams and Wilkins, 1963.

DeVito, J. Psychogrammatical factors in oral and written discourse by skilled communicators. *Speech Monographs,* 1966, **33,** 73–76.

Dewey, G. *Relative frequency of English speech sounds.* Cambridge, Mass.: Harvard University Press, 1923.

Dickens, M., and Williams, F. An experimental application of cloze procedure and attitude measures to listening comprehension. *Speech Monographs,* 1964, **31,** 103–108.

Elson, B., and Pickett, V. B. *Beginning morphology-syntax.* Santa Ana, Cal.: Summer Institute of Linguistics, 1960.

Fillenbaum, S., and Jones, L. V. An application of cloze technique to the study of aphasic speech. *Journal of Abnormal and Social Psychology,* 1962, **65,** 183–189.

Fillenbaum, S., Jones, L. V., and Rapoport, A. The predictability of words and their grammatical classes as a function of rate of deletion from a speech transcript. *Journal of Verbal Learning and Verbal Behavior,* 1963, **2,** 186–194.

Flesch, R. F. Marks of readable style: A study in adult education. Unpublished doctoral dissertation, Columbia University, 1944.

Flesch, R. F. *The art of plain talk.* New York: Harper, 1946.

Fodor, J. A., and Katz, J. J. (Eds.) *The structure of language.* Englewood Cliffs, N.J.: Prentice-Hall, 1964.

French, N. R., Carter, C. W., and Koenig, W. The words and sounds of telephone conversations. *Bell System Technical Journal,* 1930, **9,** 290–324.

Fries, C. C. *The structure of English.* New York: Harcourt, Brace, 1952.

Gibbons, E. W., Winchester, R. A., and Krebs, D. F. The variability of oral reading rate. *Journal of Speech and Hearing Disorders,* 1958, **23,** 591–593.

Gibson, J. W., Gruner, C. R., Kibler, R. J., and Kelly, F. J. A quantitative examination of differences and similarities in written and spoken messages. *Speech Monographs,* 1966, **33,** 444–451.

Gleason, H. A. *An introduction to descriptive linguistics.* New York: Holt, Rinehart & Winston, 1961.

Gleason, H. A. *Linguistics and English grammar.* New York: Holt, Rinehart & Winston, 1965.

Goldman-Eisler, F. The determinants of the rate of speech output and their mutual relations. *Journal of Psychosomatic Research,* 1956, **1,** 137–143.

Goldman-Eisler, F. Speech production and the predictability of words in context. *Quarterly Journal of Experimental Psychology,* 1958, **10,** 96–106. (a)

Goldman-Eisler, F. The predictability of words in context and the length of pauses in speech. *Language and Speech,* 1958, **1,** 226–231. (b)

Goldman-Eisler, F. Hesitation and information in speech. In C. Cherry (Ed.), *Information theory — Fourth London symposium.* Washington: Butterworths, 1961. Pp. 162–174. (a)

Goldman-Eisler, F. The significance of changes in the rate of articulation. *Language and Speech,* 1961, **4,** 171–174. (b)

Goldman-Eisler, F., Skarbek, A., and Henderson, A. Cognitive and neurochemical determination of sentence structure. *Language and Speech,* 1965, **8,** 86–94. (a)

Goldman-Eisler, F., Skarbek, A., and Henderson, A. The effect of chlorpromazine on speech behavior. *Psychopharmacologia,* 1965, **7,** 220–228. (b)

Gruner, C. R., Kibler, R. J., and Gibson, J. W. A quantitative analysis of selected characteristics of oral and written vocabularies. *Journal of Communication,* 1967, **17,** 152–158.

Gulley, H. E., and Berlo, D. K. Effect of intercellular and intracellular speech structure on attitude change and learning. *Speech Monographs,* 1956, **23,** 288–297.

Hockett, C. F. *A course in modern linguistics.* New York: Macmillan, 1958.

Howes, D. A word count of spoken English. *Journal of Verbal Learning and Verbal Behavior,* 1966, **5,** 572–604.

Hutton, C. L., Jr. A psychophysical study of speech rate. Unpublished doctoral dissertation, State University of Iowa, 1954.

Hvistendahl, J. K. Language ability as a factor in cloze scores. *Journalism Quarterly,* 1958, **35,** 353–354.

Johnson, W. *People in quandaries.* New York: Harper, 1946.

Jones, L. V., Goodman, M. F., and Wepman, J. M. The classification of parts of speech for the characterization of aphasia. *Language and Speech,* 1963, **6,** 94–107.

Kasl, S. V., and Mahl, G. F. Experimentally induced anxiety and speech disturbances. *The American Psychologist,* 1958, **13,** 349.

Kasl, S. V., and Mahl, G. F. The relationship of disturbances of hesitations in spontaneous speech and anxiety. *Journal of Personality and Social Psychology,* 1965, **1,** 425–433.

Katz, J. J., and Postal, P. M. *An integrated theory of linguistic descriptions.* Cambridge, Mass.: M.I.T. Press, 1964.

Klare, G. R. *The measurement of readability.* Ames: Iowa State University Press, 1963.

Klein, S., and Simmons, R. F. A computational approach to grammatical coding of English words. *Communications of the A.C.M.,* 1963, **10,** 334–347.

Knabe, J. M., Nelson, L. A., and Williams, F. Some general characteristics of linguistic output: Stutterers versus nonstutterers. *Journal of Speech and Hearing Disorders,* 1966, **31,** 178–182.

Kuno, S., and Oettinger, A. G. Syntactic structure and ambiguity in English. In *Proceedings of the 1963 Joint Computer Conference.* Baltimore: Spartan Books, 1963. Pp. 397–418.

Ladefoged, P. *Elements of acoustic phonetics.* Chicago: University of Chicago Press, 1962.

Leed, J. (Ed.) *The computer and literary style.* Kent, Ohio: Kent State University Press, 1966.

Lehiste, I. *Readings in acoustic phonetics.* Cambridge, Mass.: M.I.T. Press, 1967.

Levin, H., and Silverman, I. Hesitation phenomena in children's speech. *Language and Speech,* 1965, **8,** 67–85.

Lieberman, P. *Intonation, perception, and language.* Cambridge, Mass.: M.I.T. Press, 1967.

Lindsay, R. K. The reading machine problem. Unpublished doctoral dissertation, Carnegie Institute of Technology, 1960.

Loban, W. D. *The language of elementary school children.* Champaign, Ill.: National Council of Teachers of English, 1963.

MacGinitie, W. H. Contextual constraint in English prose paragraphs. *Journal of Psychology,* 1961, **51,** 121–130.

Maclay, H., and Osgood, C. E. Hesitation phenomena in spontaneous English speech. *Word,* 1959, **15,** 19–44.

Mahl, G. F. Disturbances and silences in the patient's speech in psychotherapy. *Journal of Abnormal and Social Psychology,* 1956, **53,** 1–15.

Mahl, G. F. Exploring emotional states by content analysis. In I. De S. Pool (Ed.), *Trends in content analysis.* Urbana: University of Illinois Press, 1959. Pp. 89–130. (a)

Mahl, G. F. Measuring the patient's anxiety during interviews from "expressive" aspects of his speech. *Transactions of the New York Academy of Sciences,* 1959, **21,** 249–257. (b)

Matthews, J. The effect of loaded language on audience comprehension of speeches. *Speech Monographs,* 1947, **14,** 176–186.

McCarthy, Dorothea. The language development of the preschool child. *The Institute of Child Welfare Monograph Series,* 1930, No. 4.

McNeill, D. Developmental psycholinguistics. In F. Smith and G. A. Miller (Eds.), *The genesis of language.* Cambridge, Mass.: M.I.T. Press, 1966.

Miller, G. A. *Language and communication.* New York: McGraw-Hill, 1951.

Miller, G. A. Some psychological studies of grammar. *The American Psychologist,* 1962, **17,** 748–762.

Miller, G. A. Some preliminaries to psycholinguistics. *The American Psychologist,* 1965, **30,** 15–20.

Miller, G. A., and Selfridge, J. A. Verbal context and the recall of meaningful material. *American Journal of Psychology,* 1953, **63,** 176–185.

Minifie, F. D. An analysis of the durational aspects of connected speech samples by means of an electronic speech duration analyzer. Unpublished doctoral dissertation, State University of Iowa, 1963.

Mowrer, O. H. *Learning theory and the symbolic processes.* New York: John Wiley, 1960.

Nida, E. A. *Morphology: The descriptive analysis of words.* (2nd ed.) Ann Arbor: University of Michigan Press, 1949.

Odom, P., Blanton, R. L., and Nunnally, J. C., Jr. Some "cloze" technique studies of language capability in the deaf. *Journal of Speech and Hearing Research,* 1967, **10,** 816–827.

Oléron, P. Reconstitution de textes français ayant subi divers taux de mutilation. *Psychologie Française,* 1960, **5,** 161–171.

Osgood, C. E. Some effects of motivation on style of encoding. In T. A. Sebeok (Ed.), *Style in language.* Cambridge, Mass.: M.I.T. Press, and New York: John Wiley, 1960. Pp. 293–306.

Osgood, C. E. On understanding and creating sentences. *The American Psychologist,* 1963, **18,** 735–751.

Paisley, W. J. Minor encoding habits: II. Extemporaneous speech in the Kennedy-Nixon debates. Unpublished report, Institute for Communication Research, Stanford University, 1967.

Peterson, G. E., and Shoup, J. E. A physiological theory of phonetics. *Journal of Speech and Hearing Research,* 1966, **9,** 6–57. (a)

Peterson, G. E., and Shoup, J. E. The elements of an acoustic phonetic theory. *Journal of Speech and Hearing Research,* 1966, **9,** 68–99. (b)

Phillips, W. A. Inter-sentence constraint in orally encoded messages. Unpublished Master's thesis, University of Wisconsin, 1965.

Roberts, P. *Patterns of English.* New York: Harcourt, Brace, 1956.

Roberts, P. *English sentences.* New York: Harcourt, Brace & World, 1962.

Robinson, W. P. Cloze procedure as a technique for the investigation of social class differences in language usage. *Language and Speech,* 1965, **8,** 42–55.

Schwartz, M. F. Differential effect of instructions upon the rate of oral reading. *Journal of the Acoustical Society of America,* 1961, **33,** 1801–1802.

Shannon, C. E. The mathematical theory of communication. In C. E. Shannon and W. Weaver, *The mathematical theory of communication.* Urbana: University of Illinois Press, 1949. Pp. 3–91.

Shearn, D., Sprague, R., and Rosenzweig, S. A method for the analysis and control of speech rate. *Journal of the Experimental Analysis of Behavior,* 1961, **4,** 197–201.

Skinner, B. F. *Verbal behavior.* New York: Appleton-Century-Crofts, 1957.

Smith, A. G. (Ed.) *Communication and culture.* New York: Holt, Rinehart & Winston, 1966.

Stolz, W. S. Syntactic constraint in spoken and written English. Unpublished doctoral dissertation, University of Wisconsin, 1964.

Stolz, W. S. A probabilistic procedure for grouping words in phrases. *Language and Speech,* 1965, **8,** 219–235.

Stolz, W. S., Tannenbaum, P. H., and Carstensen, F. V. A stochastic approach to the grammatical coding of English. *Communications of the A.C.M.,* 1965, **8,** 399–405.

Street, J. C. Methodology in immediate constituent analysis. In I. Rauch and C. T. Scott (Eds.), *Approaches in linguistic methodology.* Madison: University of Wisconsin Press, 1967. Pp. 89–114.

Tannenbaum, P. H., Williams, F., and Clark, R. A. Effects of grammatical information upon word predictability. *Journal of Communication,* 1969, **19,** 41–48.

Tannenbaum, P. H., Williams, F., and Hillier, C. S. Word predictability in the environments of hesitations. *Journal of Verbal Learning and Verbal Behavior,* 1965, **4,** 134–140.

Tannenbaum, P. H., Williams, F., and Wood, B. S. Hesitation phenomena and related encoding characteristics in speech and typewriting. *Language and Speech,* 1967, **10,** 203–216.

Tannenbaum, P. H., Wood, B. S., and Williams, F. Effects of feedback availability upon generation of left- and right-branching sentence structures. *Language and Speech,* 1968, **11,** 12–19.

Taylor, W. L. "Cloze procedure": A new tool for measuring readability. *Journalism Quarterly,* 1953, **30,** 415–433.

Taylor, W. L. Application of "cloze" and entropy measures to the study of contextual constraint in samples of continuous prose. Unpublished doctoral dissertation, University of Illinois, 1954.

Taylor, W. L. Recent developments in the use of "cloze" procedure. *Journalism Quarterly,* 1956, **33,** 42–48, 99.

Taylor, W. L. "Cloze" readability scores as indices of individual differences in comprehension and aptitude. *Journal of Applied Psychology,* 1957, **41,** 19–26.

Templin, M. Certain language skills in children: Their development and interrelationships. *The Institute of Child Welfare Monograph Series,* 1957, No. 26.

Thomas, C. K. *An introduction to phonetics of American English.* New York: Ronald Press, 1958.

Thorndike, E. L., and Lorge, I. *The teacher's word book of 30,000 words.* New York: Teachers College, Columbia University, 1944.

Trager, G. L., and Smith, H. L. *An outline of English structure.* Washington: American Council of Learned Societies, 1957.

Van Riper, C. G., and Smith, D. E. *An introduction to general American phonetics.* New York: Harper & Row, 1954.

Voelker, C. H. Technique for a phonetic frequency distribution count in formal American speech. *Archives néerlandaises de phonétique expérimentale,* 1935, **11,** 69–72.

Wathen-Dunn, E. (Ed.) *Models for the perception of speech and visual form.* Cambridge, Mass.: M.I.T. Press, 1967.

Weaver, W. W., and Kingston, A. J. A factor analysis of the "cloze" procedure and other measures of reading and language ability. *Journal of Communication,* 1963, **13,** 252–261.

Webb, R., Jr., Williams, F., and Minifie, F. D. Effects of verbal decision behavior upon respiration during speech production. *Journal of Speech and Hearing Research,* 1967, **10,** 49–56.

Wells, R. S. Immediate constituents. *Language,* 1947, **23,** 81–117.

Williams, F. An experimental application of the semantic differential and "cloze" procedure as measurement techniques in listening comprehension. Unpublished doctoral dissertation, University of Southern California, 1962.

Williams, F., and Naremore, R. Social class differences in children's syntactic performance: A quantitative analysis of field study data. *Journal of Speech and Hearing Research,* in press.

Yngve, V. A model and an hypothesis for language structure. *Proceedings of the American Philosophical Society,* 1960, **104,** 444–466.

Yngve, V. The depth hypothesis. *Proceedings of Symposium in Applied Mathematics,* 1961, **12,** 130–138.

Yule, G. U. *The statistical study of literary vocabulary.* London: Cambridge University Press, 1944.

Zipf, G. K. *The psycho-biology of language: An introduction to dynamic philosophy.* Boston: Houghton Mifflin, 1935.

10

Content Analysis

John Waite Bowers

Berelson (1952) has defined content analysis as "a research technique for the objective, systematic and quantitative description of the manifest content of communication [p. 18]." This definition excludes the inferential leaps analysts make from their descriptions of messages to the antecedents and consequences of those messages. Although this exclusion is desirable in an abstract definition of content analysis, adhering to it in an explication of the method would result in a sterile treatment. Descriptions of messages are useful to students of communication only insofar as they lead to helpful inferences about the process of communication, and the process goes beyond the messages. Thus, Berelson qualifies his definition with the assumption "that inferences about the relationship between intent and content or between content and effect can validly be made, or the actual relationships established [p. 18]." To deny this assumption, of course, would be to deny the lawfulness of communicative behavior. Nevertheless, to generalize that inferences *can* validly be made and to assert for a particular study that inferences *are* validly made are two different claims. Probably the most common objection to content analyses is that inferences derived from them are based on an oversimplified conception of the lawful relationships in communication processes. In content analysis, safety is in thought, not in numbers; like any method, it can be abused.

Some communication scholars distinguish between content analysis and stylistic analysis (see Chapter 11). That distinction will not be preserved in this chapter, since an analyst searching for relationships among messages, their antecedents, and their consequences typically uses any clues available to him. Some may be "what" clues, while others may be "how" clues. Although he may distinguish between these two kinds of clues to tidy up his conceptual schemes, he does not need to distinguish between them methodologically. Thus, some of the illustrations in this chapter concentrate on semantic features of messages, others on syntactic features.

The peculiar virtue of content analysis as a method in psycholinguistic, rhetorical, and literary research is that it guards against distortion by selective perception. Once the analyst has established his sample and procedures, he must include as data all relevant material. He exercises selectivity only in choosing his sample and establishing his category system. The traditional critic, on the other hand, is free to emphasize or omit material as best suits his prejudices or momentary assumptions. A traditional critic, for example, might read this chapter and conclude in a review: "Bowers depends heavily on Berelson's (1952) *Content Analysis in Communication Research.*" He might support this statement by writing: "In the very first paragraph, Bowers mentions Berelson's name twice, quotes him directly twice, and accepts his definition of content analysis." Someone who had not read the chapter might find this plausible evidence for the original generalization.

The analyst, however, would require frequency counts of all statements attributable to published sources before making a judgment about Bowers' dependence on or independence of Berelson. He might say: "Of the X number of statements attributable to published sources, Y, or less than a fifth, can be traced to Berelson. However, the analytical method used here gave extra weights of .5 to attributable statements appearing in the first paragraph and extra weights of .5 to those statements identified as 'definitional.' These extra weights increase Berelson's proportion of total attributable influence to nearly a fourth. Berelson's work exerted more influence on Bowers than any other single source, but considerably less than all other sources combined."

The analyst is obviously more informative than the traditional critic, as he avoids distortion and ambiguity. The critic implies that the first paragraph is typical of the whole; the analyst shows that it is not. The critic's phrase "depends heavily upon Berelson" is ambiguous; the analyst shows exactly how heavily. The critic vaguely implies that extra weight should be given to early statements and definitional statements; the analyst makes explicit and quantifies those assumptions. The critic's summary suggests that potential readers should avoid Bowers if they have read Berelson. The analyst implies that something different, if not new, may be found in Bowers.

THE METHOD

In general, content analysis consists of the following steps: (1) formulating general hypotheses; (2) selecting the sample of messages to be analyzed; (3) selecting categories and units; (4) if necessary, formulating judgmental procedures; (5) if necessary, selecting a control or normative sample of messages to analyzed; (6) reformulating general hypotheses in terms of categories and units; (7) selecting the criterion for accepting or rejecting hypotheses; (8) tabulating; (9) applying the criterion. These steps do not necessarily occur in this order.

Formulating General Hypotheses

The origin of hypotheses is the same for content analysis as for any other technique of the social sciences. Hypotheses may come from hunches or common sense (spoken messages differ syntactically from otherwise equivalent written messages [DeVito, 1967]). Or they may be attempted extensions of elaborate theories of human behavior (high anxiety interferes with the performance of complex tasks and therefore produces stereotyped verbal behavior [Osgood, 1960]). Or, most often, they may be derived from some previous research and are attempted extensions of low order laws (positive reinforcement increases the incidence of statements of opinion in spontaneous conversation [Krasner, 1958]). Hypotheses may be almost purely descriptive (the intensity of evaluative assertions can be reliably measured [Osgood, Saporta, and Nunnally, 1956]) or almost purely predictive (hesitations in spontaneous speech will occur almost always before content rather than function words [Blankenship and Kay, 1964]).

Regardless of the sources and functions of the general hypotheses, they should bear some relationship to a relevant research problem. Otherwise, the analyst is likely to row about aimlessly on what Alexander George (1959) calls a "fishing expedition [p. 15]." His generalizations will be post hoc interpretations of his data. An undirected search in verbal materials is open to the same objections as impressionistic criticism. A student of communication who says, "I'm going to do a content analysis of John L. Lewis' speeches" is justifiably suspect. Instead, he should be saying, "I'm going to find out _____ by doing a content analysis of John L. Lewis' speeches." Counting for the sake of counting is not really useful after kindergarten.

Selecting the Sample

In many studies the analyst is confronted with far too much matter for practical treatment. In general, he must be guided by sampling theory in deciding what to analyze and what to omit. However, content analysis presents some special sampling problems.

An analyst might set out to define elements of a topic from the entire range of communication. However, any sampling procedure using random choices is likely to eliminate from the study both extremes. For this analyst, *any* sampling is unwise. He will do better to narrow the topic of his research and analyze all materials relevant to that topic. By sampling, he will probably eliminate the very materials that are most interesting to him: the extremes that set the outer limits on the range. In his study of communications about General Gordon, for example, Willy (1962) analyzed by sanctions *all* available material relevant to Gordon. To make the study practical, he limited his consideration to material published during a rather short period of time. Studies concerned with ranges of communication behavior should treat whole populations, not samples, of messages.

A cluster of problems for the analyst results from thinking about samples in terms of people. As people have relatively constant traits, he may expect the messages they produce to have relatively constant traits too. If the analyst thinks that way, he is likely to say to himself, "It doesn't really make much difference what messages or what parts of messages I select. After all, I'm trying to find out about John L. Lewis' development as a speaker. So I'll just use the first thousand words of eight speeches from his early period and the first thousand words of eight speeches from his late period." This is probably oversimplified, because messages have characteristics of their own. The analyst can identify those characteristics conceptually, independent of the people producing the messages. For example, Lewis' early speeches may differ from his late speeches, but the early parts of a single speech are also likely to differ from the later parts. If they do, then the analyst will be justified only in drawing conclusions about changes in the introductions (first thousand words) of Lewis' speeches from his early to his late period. He could avoid this by sampling randomly from among the statements or paragraphs of entire speeches in the early and late periods. He could be even more exact by stratifying his sample so that he could analyze separately changes in introductions, bodies, and conclusions of speeches from Lewis' early period to his late period.

Similar problems confront almost any analyst who must sample. Early parts of spontaneous conversations, psychotherapeutic interviews, group discussions, or works of fiction are likely to be systematically different from later parts. In his sampling, therefore, the analyst must confront the problem of selection within messages as well as among messages. "The first thousand words" is seldom a reasonable solution.

Some ingenious and lucky analysts, especially those concerned with problems in or about the mass media, occasionally find that their sampling has already been done for them. Davis (1965), for example, was interested in popular arguments surrounding the introduction of three new mass media: motion pictures, radio, and television. Discussing his sample, he cogently argues:

Since this study treats popular persuasion over a sixty-five-year period, certain limitations were necessary in the interests of practicality and manageability. The first such limitation related to the primary source material. Ideally, a study of this kind would gather its data from as wide a variety of sources as possible: speeches, pamphlets, newspapers, sermons, books, and magazines. Such a wide range is hardly practical, however, if the study is to cover in depth argument over a number of years. Therefore, the decision was made to focus the investigation on the main stream of discourse as represented in the national periodical press. From Theodore Peterson's *Magazines in the Twentieth Century* I established a comprehensive list of periodicals ranging from the mass-circulation, general-interest magazines to special-interest, limited-circulation journals. Since nearly all of the magazines on this list were indexed in the *Readers' Guide to Periodical Literature,* I used the *Readers' Guide* to find the individual articles from the periodicals on the Peterson list [pp. 4–5].

Reference sections of libraries are useful spots, even for content analysts.

Selecting Categories and Units

Two terms standard in the literature of content analysis are *category* and *unit.* Illustrations from analyses of nonverbal data are useful in explicating these terms.

ILLUSTRATIONS

Suppose we are interested in testing various hypotheses about money and human behavior. We are a low budget operation with no federal or foundation support, so we must proceed with only a little expense to ourselves.

The communication department that employs us has a staff lounge equipped with a large coffee urn. Next to the urn are a cardboard box with a slot in the top and a sign reading "Coffee 10¢." The box can be opened so that a coffee drinker can drop in money of larger denomination than a dime and make his own change. The departmental secretary empties the coin box at 5:00 P.M. daily.

Down the hall from our departmental offices is the social psychology department, with a similar coffee setup. We determine that the two urns dispense the same amount of coffee daily. We decide that our cardboard box and the coin box in the social psychology department will be the arenas for testing whatever hypotheses we can devise.

Our first hypothesis is that the members of the social psychology department are more affluent and free-spending than the members of our department. We predict that this difference will influence coffee buying behavior. Our reasoning goes this way: Suppose that, on a given morning, a member of the communication staff and a member of the social psychology staff approach their respective coffee machines simultaneously. Each reaches into his pocket and discovers that the only change he has is a quarter. Each opens the coin box next to the machine only to find it empty. We predict that from this point on their behavior will differ. The affluent social psychologist will drop in his quarter, telling himself that he will get his change later or that he will drink two and a half cups of coffee before he pays again. The communication scholar, on the other hand, will do one of three things. (1) He may walk down the hall to find out whether anybody else in the department has change for a quarter. (2) He may forego his cup of coffee. (3) He may take his cup of coffee without paying, telling himself that he will drink now and pay later. As often as not, however, he forgets to pay later. If the members of the two departments behave in the way we predict, then after the respective urns have been in operation a half-hour every morning the social psychology coin box should contain more money of a denomination higher than a dime than the communication coin box.

We can test our hypotheses in a way analagous to a content analysis. After getting permission from the two departments to open and inspect the coin boxes at 9:30 every morning, we begin to collect our data. To get as much information as possible, we decide to sort the money into every denomination rather than only a dime or less and a quarter or more. Over a two-week period, we simply count the number of pennies (Category I), the number of nickels (Category II), the number of quarters (Category III), the number of half-dollars (Category IV), the number of dollars (Category V), and so on. For this study, then, the various denominations of money are our *categories.* Our *units,* the things we count, are the coins and bills themselves.

An economist from the building next door hears of our study, admires our ingenuity, and decides to test a hypothesis of his own. He suspects that coin collectors in the social research departments of the university are having a significant effect on the local distribution of coins. Since our coffee urns are patronized exclusively by social scientists, he sees the coin boxes as a good place to test his hypothesis. Since old coins are generally more valuable to collectors than new coins, he reasons that our coin boxes should contain, at the time of collection, a smaller proportion of old coins than is normally available in the United States. He is already armed with normative data — the distribution of coins by date as they are circulated through a metropolitan bank.

If the members of the two departments behave in the way the economist predicts, they should (1) be reluctant to part with old coins and (2) select old coins from the box in making their own change. Possibly (3) an especially ardent collector in each of the departments inspects his department's coin box at 4:30 P.M. daily, extracts the old coins, and replaces them with new. Given any of these conditions, the proportion of old coins in the boxes should be smaller than in the normal United States run of coins.

The economist also tests his hypothesis in a way analogous to a content analysis. He inspects the two coin boxes at 5:00 P.M. daily and sorts the coins by date instead of denomination. His categories are 1889 (Category I), 1890 (Category II), 1891 (Category III), 1892 (Category IV), and so on. For his study, the *categories* are dates of origin. His *units,* the things he places into categories, are the coins themselves.

Frequently, a content analyst wants to test hypotheses requiring more complex category systems than dates and denominations. He sometimes is interested in the contingent patterns his units follow in relation to more than one variable. Our coffee urns and coin boxes can illustrate this kind of analysis, too.

Still interested in the relative affluence and spending behavior of scholars in social psychology and communication, we devise a more elaborate test of our hypothesis. We reason that payday should be a more relevant variable for people in communication than for people in social psychology. Since our university pays us on the first of every month, we decide that the denomination difference we looked for earlier should increase as distance from the last payday increases. More communication scholars should be getting their coffee on the cuff the day before payday than the day after. This relationship should not hold as strongly for social psychologists.

To test our hypothesis, we select a six-month period that does not include February. To make the data for the various months comparable, we decide to skip one day (probably the sixteenth one) in months that have 31 days. Each day at 5:00 P.M. we sort the money in each of the two coin boxes. This time, however, we use a category system that has two dimensions, (1) denomination and (2) days elapsed since last payday. If our hypothesis holds, we should be able to perceive a contingency between the two variables for the communication department but not for the social psychology department. Our *categories* in this study are pennies/first day since payday (Category I), nickels/first day since payday (Category II), and so on; pennies/second day since payday, nickels/second day since payday, and so on. Our *units,* again, are the coins themselves.

ESTABLISHING CATEGORY SYSTEMS

Much of the recent research in content analysis has been essentially methodological (establishing category systems for general use in various disciplines) rather than experimental (testing specific hypotheses). This research is based on the assumption that category systems can provide realistic tests of behavioral hypotheses. Many of these efforts have designed category systems explicitly for content analysis by computer.

The most ambitious project of this type is the set of procedures described by Stone, Dunphy, Smith, Ogilvie, and associates, in their book, *The General Inquirer* (1966). It is having a strong influence both on content analysis as a method and on the generalizations possible in various disciplines. Anyone planning a serious analytic study should read it.

In it, Stone characterizes the method this way:

> It is useful to liken the Inquirer to an energetic, compulsive, but stupid clerk who has been trained in content analysis mechanics. This clerk has no ideas of his own but waits for the specification of categories and scoring procedures supplied by the investigator. Once these instructions are received and not found to be self-contradictory, the clerk is able to apply them systematically to endless amounts of data [p. 68].

In short, the Inquirer, as a set of computer systems, saves work but not thought. In fact, instructing the computer requires more rigorous thought than most scoring procedures employing human coders, for the human coders can be assumed to have some judgmental facilities. This assumption does not hold for the computer.

The Inquirer uses a set of categories (tags, in Inquirer jargon) and a dictionary, both supplied by the investigator. Given a body of text punched on computer cards, it counts the occurrence of words in its dictionary subsumed under each of the tags. Some Inquirer systems include two sets of tags, first-order, to which all words in the dictionary belong, and second-order, to which some words might also be referred. In one system, for example, Dunphy (p. 183) notes that the word "sword" belongs to TOOL as its first-order tag, and to DANGER-THEME, MALE-THEME, SIGN-STRONG, and MILITARY as second-order tags.

The General Inquirer (pp. 169–170) discusses a number of dictionaries which had been devised for various disciplines. Among them were the Harvard III Psychosociological Dictionary, the Stanford Political Dictionary, Namenwirth and Brewer's adaptation of the Harvard III Dictionary for the analysis of editorial comment on international affairs, the McPherson Domestic Political Dictionary (used by Smith, Stone, and Glenn together with the Harvard III Dictionary for analyzing presidential acceptance speeches), the Colby Anthropological Dictionary, the Alcohol Dictionary used by Kalin, Davis, and McClelland, a Product Image Dictionary described by Stone, Dunphy, and Bernstein, and the Need-Achievement Dictionary.

Since *The General Inquirer*'s illustration of the Need-Achievement Dictionary's use includes contingency categories, it deserves further discussion here. The Need-Achievement Dictionary is comparatively small. It classifies about 855 words in 14 categories. Using the Inquirer system, it enables the computer to duplicate human judgments in locating evidence of the need for achievement in Thematic Apperception Test (TAT) responses. As Ogilvie and Woodhead note in Stone *et al.*, "It is only concerned with detecting the existence of an expressed need for achievement, and all words irrelevant to such a need are discarded [p. 191]." Hence, some of its tags are COMPETE, SUCCESS, FAILURE, AFFECT-POSITIVE, and AFFECT-NEGATIVE.

Clearly, one statement in a TAT response might be a more significant sign of the need for achievement than another, even when the two statements contain words belonging to the same tags. The Inquirer users therefore devised rules for the computer that would score certain words in a category only if they were preceded (or, sometimes, followed) by certain words in another category. For example, one rule instructs the computer to score occurrences of words belonging to the NEED tag if they are followed in the same sentence by words belonging to the COMPETE tag. Thus, the machine scores as need-achievement statements like "He is *determined* [NEED] to *win* [COMPETE]," and "He *wants* [NEED] to *excel* [COMPETE]." Another rule carries the contingency across sentence boundaries. A series of statements indicates need-achievement if a word belonging to the SUCCESS tag is followed in the same or the succeeding sentence by a word belonging to the AFFECT-POSITIVE tag. This rule would score as need-achievement a series of statements such as: "He received lots of *recognition* [SUCCESS] for his efforts. This *pleased* [AFFECT-POSITIVE] him very much [pp. 200–201]."

Ogilvie and Woodhead find that TAT responses scored by the Inquirer method agree from 82 to 86 per cent with judgments by trained scorers. This should be evidence that in many analyses the use of contingency rather than simple classificatory categories increases interpretive rigor.

Some recent work in syntactic category systems has aimed at increasing their meaningfulness as bases for inferences in various disciplines. Williams[1] for example, used content analysis together with factor analysis in an attempt to discover whether part-of-speech frequencies might be converted into more general categories.

Williams analyzed responses of subjects to a set of three captionless cartoons. Forty subjects had been divided into four groups, each receiving a different set of instructions: (1) Describe the cartoons. Anticipate that the audience for your description will be a college professor. (2) Abstract the subtle meaning of the cartoons. Anticipate that the audience for your abstraction will be a college professor. (3) Describe the cartoons. Anticipate that the audience for your description will be a fifth grader. (4) Abstract the subtle meaning of the cartoons. Anticipate that the audience for your abstraction will be a fifth grader. Williams expected his part-of-speech analyses to show systematic differences among the four groups. He also expected factor analysis of his data to show that parts of speech could be efficiently combined in fewer categories without significant loss of information.

Using a part-of-speech classification derived from Roberts' (1956) *Patterns of English,* Williams assigned each word in his sample to one of 12 categories. These categories depended on structural features and syntactic environment rather than extralinguistic reference. A noun, for example, was defined as any word that would fit into the frames: "We saw the _____. (The) _____ is/are here." This is a syntactic en-

[1] For a more complete account of the previously unpublished results of this research, see Chapter 9, pp. 272–283.

vironment criterion. A determiner was defined as any word that matched a word on a list (structural features) and would fit into the environmental frames: "He shot _____ wolf. I saw _____ father."

After categorizing each word for each subject, Williams correlated the frequencies with which the 12 parts of speech occurred across the messages. He then factor analyzed the correlations to discover whether the parts of speech could be grouped for "more parsimonious and meaningful descriptions of syntactic performance."

Williams found that his analyses grouped the 12 parts of speech into three factors, or dimensions: (1) *clausal incidence,* a measure of sentence complexity, including relative frequencies of verbs, pronouns, subordinators, and connectors; (2) *descriptive specificity,* relative frequencies of nouns, adjectives, determiners, and prepositions; and (3) *verb modification,* relative frequencies of adverbs, auxiliaries, and modifying verbs. (One part of speech, "intensifiers," did not fit clearly into any of the dimensions, but its heaviest loading was on verb modification.)

The real test of the new category system came when Williams attempted to interpret the data he had gathered in the four message-type/anticipated-audience conditions in the light of the three dimensions. He used analysis of variance to arrive at the following results: (1) The clausal incidence dimension is stronger in abstraction messages than in description messages (Williams had predicted this result). (2) The descriptive specificity dimension is stronger in description messages than in abstraction messages (Williams had predicted this result). (3) The verb modification dimension is stronger in messages directed at a college professor than in messages directed at a fifth grader (although Williams had not predicted this result, it certainly appeals to common sense).

Williams concludes from his research that "perhaps more than the usual can be said when part-of-speech techniques are applied to study, for example, style in language, the characteristics of different language encoders, and the consequences that different encoding conditions impose upon language performance." Essentially the same values are found in any study that succeeds in relating and refining categories for content analysis.

Another ingenious attempt to establish a category system useful for certain kinds of research is Paisley's (1967a) work in "minor encoding habits." His definition of a minor encoding habit includes the following criteria:

(1) It should not be prominent; otherwise it may be imitated, consciously or unconsciously, by others.

(2) It should be executed mechanically, with little feedback for self-criticism; otherwise the communicator may vary it for effect. Another way of saying this: it should exhibit low variance within a communicator's works.

(3) Its use should not be dictated wholly by convention (*e.g.,* the halo in Renaissance paintings). Another way of saying this:

It should exhibit high variance between the works of communicators being compared.

(4) It should not be so rare that examples cannot be found in each work. Frequency of occurrence should be high relative to the sampling error.

(5) Its frequency of occurrence should remain nearly constant whatever the topic or mood of the work, *if* comparisons are being made across topics or moods [pp. 2–3].[2]

Paisley's work was prompted by the work of Giovanni Morelli and Bernard Berenson in art criticism. Paisley notes that Morelli "exposed scores of mislabeled Renaissance works in Italian and German galleries by comparing the execution of fingernails, earlobes, and other small details [p. 2]." In music, Paisley (1964) himself "showed that simple pitch transitions were reliable indicators of the styles of Bach, Handel, Haydn, Mozart, Beethoven, Mendelssohn, and Brahms. Even the difficult discrimination between Haydn and Mozart was strongly established [Paisley, 1967a, p. 2]."

In verbal communication, Paisley (1967a) counts as minor encoding habits mainly function words, "words that are more important syntactically than semantically — conjunctions, prepositions, articles, and so on [p. 1]." He cites the work of Mosteller and Wallace (1964), who, in trying to decide whether Madison or Hamilton had been the author of 12 disputed *Federalist* papers, used as discriminators words like *to, there, on, of, by, an, also,* and *upon.* Such discriminators established with a probability of three million to one that Madison, not Hamilton, wrote the papers.

Paisley's (1967a) own recent work has been an exploration of the minor encoding habits of John F. Kennedy and Richard Nixon in their extemporaneous speech during the "great debates" of 1960. As shown by his description of his procedures, Paisley was careful in selecting his sample:

> The task of creating high-quality transcripts of the debates had already been completed by Clevenger, Parson, and Polisky (1962). From these transcripts, the first 2500 words uttered extemporaneously by each man in each debate were keypunched for computer processing. The sample of 2500 extemporaneous words per man per debate is only a few words below the total available in the shortest debate. . . .
>
> The problem of what constitutes an extemporaneous utterance was treated ingenuously: opening and closing statements were omitted, but all answers to newsmen's questions were considered to be extemporaneous. Undoubtedly both candidates anticipated certain questions and discussed answers with their advisers, but it is unlikely that an agreed-upon answer could be reproduced verbatim at the lectern. And, of all the words in an answer prepared hours or days beforehand, it is unlikely that those involving minor encoding habits would be well remembered [p. 4].[2]

[2] Reprinted by permission of the author.

Paisley began by searching for minor encoding words to use as discriminators between the extemporaneous speaking of the two men. He instructed the computer to compile a list of all words occurring an average of at least once every hundred words in either man's speech. This produced a list of fifteen words: *a, and, for, have, he, I, in, is, it, of, that, the, this, to,* and *we*. However, Paisley notes that not all of these words can be considered minor encoding habits. For example, since the frequencies for "I" and "we" are negatively correlated across the debates, Paisley infers that they were competing for insertion in the same contexts. If so, the two men were exercising choice, and the words are major, not minor, encoding habits. From this analysis, Paisley also found that Kennedy and Nixon did not overlap in the four debates in the incidence of *have, of, that,* and *this*.

A second analysis compiled the 132 most common, reasonably context-free words in the debates, from which Paisley selected 10 words for each man as the basis for a test in which their performance in the first three debates would be used to predict their performance in the fourth debate. The words he used to mark Kennedy were *of, two, if, which, second, the, than, so, and,* and *a*. Nixon's markers were *the, they, only, course, have, as, this, is, one,* and *he*. Using these words, Paisley found that each man's fourth speech matched his minor encoding style as inferred from the first three speeches.

Paisley also analyzed the debates to find differences between Kennedy and Nixon at the phrase level, a level including minor encoding habits in the selection of word combinations. He found, for example, that Nixon used a construction in which *also* linked a subject and a predicate ("let me also point out") 25 times, while Kennedy used such a construction only twice. Kennedy, on the other hand, used "*I* (do not) *believe*" 45 times to Nixon's nine.

Although to date category systems involving minor encoding habits have been used only in establishing authorship, they do hold promise for other kinds of research. As Paisley (1967a, pp. 13–15) notes, the system seems to have especially strong potential for attempts to establish patterns of stability in verbal behavior, verbal norms for reference and membership groups, and communicator preoccupations and personal values.

Formulating Judgmental Procedures

Obviously, most content analyses ideally establish categories and units that make disagreement among coders impossible. But since many interesting variables are not at present amenable to such precise description, the analyst must often depend on human judgments. This presents the problem of intercoder reliability. Judges must agree among themselves in assigning units to categories to produce worthwhile results. This section will suggest procedures for reducing intercoder disagreement. It will not describe statistical tests of reliability, since many are available in standard sources.

In general, an analyst requiring judgments from his coders should attempt to increase reliability by the following steps: (1) He should define his categories with words whose common meanings denote the variables he is interested in. (2) He should define his units carefully, so that his coders will know, for example, whether they are to make judgments on words or sentences. (3) He should survey material similar to that which he intends to analyze to discover the relative difficulty of the judgments to be made. (4) He should prepare a list of instructions as explicit as possible for his coders to use in assigning units to categories. This list of instructions should include illustrative material and possibly a dictionary specifying certain units for certain categories analogous to the General Inquirer systems described earlier. (5) He should test these instructions by having coders attempt to use them on material similar to that which will be coded in the main analysis. (6) He should then check the coders' reliability. (7) If necessary, he should revise his instructions and test again.

Depending on what variables interest the analyst, these procedures may be long and painstaking or short and simple. Osgood *et al.* (1956) require a 55-page article to describe the scoring procedure they call "Evaluative Assertion Analysis." This is a system for scoring communications that measures a communicator's attitudes toward terms eliciting wide evaluative disagreement. Since many analysts use attitudinal data, a brief description of the system is in order. Osgood *et al.* provide two definitions:

> (1) Attitude objects . . . are signs whose evaluative meanings vary extremely with the person producing or receiving them. [Most proper nouns are attitude objects.] (2) Common-meanings are signs whose evaluative meanings vary minimally with the person producing or receiving them, . . . signs upon whose evaluative meanings users of a common language have to agree in order to communicate. [Words like *good, bad, traitor, masochist* are common-meanings.] [P. 49.]

The method has four definable stages which Osgood *et al.* describe in detail:

> *Stage I* involves the identification and isolation of attitudinal objects within the messages being analyzed; arbitrary "nonsense" symbols are then substituted for the attitudinal objects and the material transcribed. *Stage II* involves the translation of this transcribed message material into an exhaustive set of evaluative assertions relating to attitudinal objects. In *Stage III* the assertions and common meaning evaluations are assigned directions and weights [on a scale from extremely favorable to extremely unfavorable]. Finally, in *Stage IV*, the assertions relating to each attitudinal object are collected and averaged in terms of common meaning evaluation; this operation allocates each attitudinal object to an evaluative scale [p. 48].

Using this procedure, they find that trained judges almost always correlate with each other in the 80 and 90 percentiles.

Gouran (1968) was able to use a much simpler system in his attempts to establish relationships among contributions in problem solving group discussions. His units were contributions, which he defined as "the continuous flow of language by one individual to the point at which another individual initiates a continuous flow of language, and the first individual discontinues his flow of language." He found these units easy to isolate.

Gouran's judges were untrained freshman students at the University of Iowa. He used a different set of judges for each of his 15 categories. Each set of judges rated each contribution in a pilot study sample on a seven-point scale. For example, the four judges in the "amount of information" category received the following instructions:

> On the following pages are 50 contributions of individuals who participated in five different discussions. I would like for you to read each item carefully and then assign it a number between 1 and 7 depending on the amount of information you think it contains. A statement is said to be informative if it contains facts, statistics, and opinions of qualified sources which bear directly on some aspect of the question being discussed. If you think the statement is *extremely informative,* assign it a rating of 7. If you think that it is *extremely uninformative,* assign it a rating of 1. If you think that the statement falls midway between these extremes, assign it a rating of 4. Use the values 2, 3, 5, and 6 to indicate degrees of informativeness other than those specified above. Consider the following examples:
>
> (1) "According to the Secretary of Defense in the last issue of *U. S. News,* we spent $20 billion to finance the war in Viet Nam last year."
>
> (2) "According to some authorities, domestic spending has to be cut if we are to finance the war in Viet Nam adequately."
>
> (3) "Well, myself, I think we ought to pull out of Viet Nam."
>
> The first statement seems to be very informative. You would probably assign it a rating of 6 or 7. The second statement is somewhat informative, but the information which it contains is not as specific as that contained in the first. You would probably assign it a rating of 3 or 4. The final statement is not very informative at all. You would probably assign it a rating of 1.

Using Ebel's (1951) method of estimating reliability of judges, Gouran found that with these instructions, untrained judges produced a reliability index of .862 in the "amount of information" category for a group of four.

Gouran wrote similar detailed instructions for rating contributions in the other 14 categories. Some of the categories were:

> *Clarity of expression.* A statement is said to be clear when an individual hearing or reading it feels confident that he understands what its maker means.

Opinionatedness. A statement is said to be opinionated when it expresses a feeling, belief, or judgment, the factual basis for which is not apparent in the statement itself.

Controversy. A statement is said to be controversial if it is possible to disagree with it.

Provocativeness. A statement is said to be provocative if it reflects a desire or willingness on the part of its maker to have another person make an overt response to it; that is, it seems to invite or welcome responses.

Other categories were friendliness, cooperativeness, emotionality, relevance, competence, redundancy, interest, objectivity, agreement, and orientation. Using the definitions he had devised in a pilot study, Gouran found reliability indices high enough to permit similar analyses in the body of material of primary interest to him.

In addition to the steps leading to intercoder reliability, the Gouran study also illustrates two levels for conceptualizing categories. Gouran's categories were the 15 variables. For a given judge concerned with a single variable, the categories were the possible ratings he could assign to a contribution: 1, 2, 3, 4, 5, 6, or 7.

Selecting the Control or Normative Sample

Many content analyses are experimental. That is, they aim to establish rigorous relationships between antecedent variables and consequent content variables by controlling and manipulating the situations in which content is elicited. These studies require comparison rather than simple description, and like all experimental work they must have both an experimental and a control sample.

Frequently the analyst can produce his own control sample. Gouran, for example, was interested in the characteristics of contributions and their relationships in problem solving discussions that reach consensus. His control sample was contributions from discussions conducted under identical circumstances that did not reach consensus. Ogilvie, Stone, and Shneidman (Stone *et al.,* 1966, pp. 527–535) wanted to establish the characteristics of suicide notes. They used in their sample genuine notes written by suicides who were male, Caucasian, Protestant, native born, and between the ages of 25 and 59.

> For comparative purposes, simulated suicide notes were obtained from nonsuicidal individuals who were also male, Caucasian, Protestant, and native born, and who were matched with genuine note writers with respect to age and occupational level [pp. 527–528].

Sometimes the analyst finds it impossible to replicate conditions in order to produce his own control sample. He then must search for normative data in other sources (*e.g.,* lists of most frequently used words).

Whatever his method, the analyst must determine the conditions that produced his control sample so that his experimental sample can be realistically compared with it. Paisley (1967b) has described eight types of norms that can be expected to affect any message:

(a) The *"all-language"* norm. For English or any other symbol system there is an hypothetical grand norm that might be estimated by comprehensive sampling of variations. . . . A good example is the norms for present-day American English created by Francis from an eclectic random sample of one million words.

(b) The *channel* norm. By channel I mean to encompass both sense modality and medium. English, for instance, is both heard and seen. Within each of these modalities, there are several media. Written English in a note to oneself, in a personal letter, in the newspaper, and in a scientific article will exhibit differences specific to these channels. All four may be more similar, however, than any one is to *spoken* English.

(c) The *structural* norm. Within the set of encoding acts directed toward any channel, there will be differences specific to the implicit structure of each act. Does the writer believe he is producing prose or verse? . . . Does the speaker believe he is presenting a speech or making an offhand comment? . . .

(d) The *topic* norm. Of greatest significance when words are the chosen content elements, the topic norm simply reminds us of the necessity of using different symbols, and common symbols in different proportions, when treating different topics. . . .

(e) The *situational* norm. Whatever the channel, whatever the structure or package, whatever the topic, the encoder finds himself in one of many unique situations. Does he face a friendly or hostile audience? . . . Is the situation relaxed or stressful? . . . These components of the situation could be separated into norms pertaining to the audience, the encoding environment, the encoder's emotional state, and so on. . . .

(f) The *regional* norm. . . . It is the local realization of the all-language norm. It is primarily the norm of the community in which the encoder learned to make himself understood.

(g) The *familial* norm. At least in the case of language, intensive shaping of encoding behavior occurs in the family. Beyond regional norms, or even in opposition to them, the encoder's childhood family is a second source of norms that he will bring to the situation with him.

(h) The *individual* norm. Partly derived from regional and familial norms, partly a result of his schooling and unique experiences, the individual's own norm is a strong theme on which channel, structure, topic, and situation will play variations [pp. 18–21].[3]

[3] Reprinted by permission of the author.

The analyst must attempt to control or manipulate all these sources of variation if his comparisons are to be rigorous. In Paisley's analysis of the Kennedy-Nixon debates, summarized on pp. 301–302, all norms except regional, familial, and individual were constant. Since regional norms probably make little difference to the encoding characteristics with which he was concerned, he could attribute the differences he found to familial and individual norms.

Reformulating General Hypotheses

Once the analyst has established his category system and, if necessary, devised reliable judgmental procedures, he is in a position to reformulate his general hypotheses. He can specify in terms of his study how he expects the incidence of units in one category to differ from the incidence in another. He can predict the existence of contingencies among simple categories, and, if he has the nerve, he can predict the strength of those contingencies.

A good way to make this reformulation clear and simple is to construct mock tables before actually tabulating, showing the relationships the analyst expects to find among his categories. They need to be neither elaborate nor more specific than the analyst cares to make them.

Suppose, for example, that an analyst, after hearing and reading the speeches of politician X, decides that the man has paranoid tendencies. This politician seems to think that he and the members of his party are the victims of a clandestine conspiracy. The analyst searches the psychological literature to find symptoms of paranoia and translates them into content categories that can be reliably counted and/or judged. Then, employing Paisley's normative system, he finds another politician who speaks on the same topics as the first, who belongs to the same party as the first, who has a position comparable to the first's, and whose family and regional background is similar to the first's.

One symptom of paranoia might be references to an unspecified other person or persons who pose a threat. Another might be the absence of information (*e.g.,* names of persons) necessary for an observer to establish or refute the actuality of the threat. Reformulating the term "paranoid" in terms of his categories, the analyst might construct the following mock table to show his hypothesis:

Type of Statement	Paranoid Politician	Control Politician
Unspecified other plus threat	+ +	
Presence of names plus places plus times		+ +

If he has been careful to construct categories relevant to his aims, the analyst can construct similar mock tables for all the categories and contingencies in his design. If his study is very strongly grounded in previous research, he might even be able to replace the plus signs with numbers.

Selecting the Criterion

Like all behavioral scientists, the content analyst has a responsibility to report his findings so that chance differences are accounted for. If sampling is involved in his study, he must establish statistically that the differences he reports are real rather than random. Because the analyst often is concerned with differences and contingencies among frequencies, the Chi-square statistic is especially useful to him. When rating procedures make it possible for him to apply scores to his units, however, he can use parametric statistics such as analysis of variance.

Regardless of what statistical procedure they use, social scientists generally agree that differences which would occur less than one time in 20 by chance (the .05 level of significance) can be considered real. If the analyst suspects very strong differences, he can set his criterion at the .01 level, or even the .001 level. But he should remember that the criterion, once set, is not alterable. He is no longer free to report as "significant" any differences that do not meet it.

Tabulating

Although this chapter is not the place for an extended treatment of methods for tabulating data, the analyst should keep in mind certain general precautions. He should tabulate his data so that he does not lose easily available information that might be useful to him later. For example, if he were analyzing several speeches by a single speaker, he would be foolish not to keep the data from each speech separate even though he does not intend to treat them separately. Second, he should establish a tabulating system that follows the text as closely as possible so that his coders do not have to search back and forth among the columns. Third, he should try to organize his tabulation system so that the categories to be compared occur close together on the tabulation pad. Finally, the analyst will usually be wise to enter his tabulations on pads amenable to computer keypunching. Even if he does not intend to use a computer in his analysis, he may later wish to duplicate his data by computer print-outs.

Applying the Criterion

At last all the preliminary steps are completed. The analyst has arranged his data to show the relationships among his critical variables. He has executed the appropriate statistical tests and decided which results reach the criterion of significance he has established earlier. All that remains is to write the report.

SAMPLE STUDY

Houck and Bowers (in press) conducted a study to test the proposition that the effects of regional dialects as cues to regionally bound norms differ in persuasive speeches when the main propositions of those speeches are relevant to the norms and when they are irrelevant. Specifically, the hypotheses were: (1) For audiences of northern college students, northern dialects in persuasive speeches will produce more favorable judgments of the speeches than southern dialects. (2) This effect will be enhanced when the propositions of the speeches are relevant to regional norms.

Two speeches, one relevant to regional norms (opposing integration of southern colleges) and one irrelevant to region (opposing government aid to needy college students) were recorded twice, once in a northern and once in a southern dialect, by each of two speakers, both of whom could produce at will either their native southern or their acquired northern dialect. The speeches were played in various combinations to randomly selected classes in the freshman speech and composition course at the University of Iowa. Each group of subjects heard two speeches, one in a northern and one in a southern dialect, one on one topic and one on the other topic, one by one speaker and the other by the other speaker.

The study incorporated two measures of judgment. The principal one was a six-scale semantic differential test of the competence and trustworthiness of the two speakers on their topics. Statistical analysis for this measure revealed that, as anticipated, the northern dialect in the speech irrelevant to region was significantly more effective on the trustworthiness dimension and much more effective on the competence dimension than its southern counterpart. For the topic relevant to regional norms, however, the anticipated effect was partially reversed. On the competence dimension, the southern dialect was slightly, but significantly, more effective than the northern. On the trustworthiness dimension, the difference between the two dialects for the integration speech was not significant. The semantic differential measure, then, showed the expected dialect effect for the irrelevant topic. For the relevant topic, the anticipated enhancement of this effect did not occur and, in fact, was reversed on the competence dimension.

The other measure of judgment was an attempt to use content analysis on the subjects' responses to two open-ended questions: (1) In a sentence or two, give your reaction to the first speech. (2) In a sentence or two, give your reaction to the second speech. An impressionistic reading of the responses led to the tentative conclusion that, although the speeches differed from each other *only* in dialect, subjects tended to rationalize their judgments with other criteria.

General Hypotheses

The first general hypothesis, derived from a cursory inspection of the data, predicted that dialect would not figure prominently in subjects' open-ended responses to the speeches. The second general hypothesis predicted that patterns in the open-ended responses would reinforce the patterns found with the semantic differential measure. That is, responses would be much more favorable to the northern dialect in the speech against government aid to needy students than to its southern counterpart and slightly more favorable to the southern dialect in the speech against integration of southern colleges than to its northern counterpart.

Sample of Messages

The entire range of open-ended responses (256 in all) was analyzed. This was assumed to be a sample from the population of potential northern audiences.

Categories and Units

The normal criteria for judging a speech fall into three categories: content, language, and delivery. Houck and Bowers further subdivided them to form six categories and added a "general" category. In order to retain any explicit comparisons subjects made between the two speeches, a "comparison" section was added for each of the seven categories.

To make categorizing easier, Houck and Bowers compiled a simple dictionary placing key words into the categories. Each response was judged in each of the categories listed below in capital letters. The comparison categories were used only when the subject explicitly expressed relative judgments of the two speeches he heard. Listed below each category are key words from the dictionary, which, of course, do not cover all cases.

LOGIC
  argument
  bias
  convincing*
  fallacy
  generalization
  idea
  point (noun)
  prove
  reasoning

EMOTION†
  bigot
  prejudice

SUPPORT
  convincing*
  evidence

  example
  figures
  instance
  specific

STYLE
  conciseness
  organization

DELIVERY

DIALECT

GENERAL
  interesting

ALL ABOVE CATEGORIES
  (comparison)

---

* All judgments based on "convincing" without qualification were categorized both in LOGIC and in SUPPORT.
† All judgments of EMOTION were also entered in LOGIC.

Judgmental Procedures

Each response was entered in each category according to the following coding system: 0 = unfavorable comment; 1 = favorable comment; 2 = no comment; 3 = ambivalent comment. In the comparison categories, of course, the system had to be different, and the following code was used: N # S = speech subject heard in northern dialect was compared favorably to speech subject heard in southern dialect; S # N = speech subject heard in southern dialect was compared favorably to speech subject heard in northern dialect; N = S = subject explicitly compared the two speeches but favored neither over the other; 2 = no comment.

This system was found to be reliable. An independent coder corresponded 93 per cent of the time with the original coder[4] on the 216 judgments involved in the responses of 10 randomly selected subjects. The errors that did occur were minor. Once, for example, the independent coder entered an unfavorable judgment in the SUPPORT category when the original coder had used the LOGIC category. Once, the independent coder entered a GENERAL judgment as unfavorable when the original coder had rated it ambivalent.

Control Sample

Since Houck and Bowers were interested only in comparing available responses to northern and southern dialects on the two topics, they had no need for further control or normative samples.

Reformulating Hypotheses

(1) Responses in the data explicitly mentioning dialect should be relatively rare. (2) The favorableness of the responses should follow the pattern of the semantic differential results:

Dialect	Integration	Government Aid
Southern	+	
Northern		+ + +

Selecting the Criterion

Inspecting the tabulated data revealed that statistical tests would be unrealistic for EMOTION, STYLE, DELIVERY, DIALECT, and all the comparison categories because only a few subjects had mentioned them. This inspection confirmed the first hypothesis, that explicit mentions of dialect would be rare. In fact, only 21 of the 256 reactions contained any mention of dialect.

[4] Mrs. Eleanor Gilroy.

Houck and Bowers decided to execute Chi-square contingency tests (significance level .05) on the remaining categories of LOGIC, SUPPORT, and GENERAL to determine the extent of the relationship between dialect variations and favorableness or unfavorableness of response on both topics (Tate, 1955).

Applying the Criterion

The table below shows the distribution of frequencies of favorable and unfavorable responses to LOGIC, SUPPORT, and GENERAL in the four conditions. It indicates that, as anticipated, the open-ended responses reinforced the semantic differential results. Only slight differences existed in the responses to the two dialects on the integration topic. In the government aid topic, the northern dialect elicited more favorable and fewer unfavorable responses than the southern dialect. The semantic differential measure also had shown these relationships.

For a contingency test of this kind, a Chi square of 3.84 is necessary for significance at the .05 level. None of the six tests executed reached this criterion. The tests for contingency between dialect and favorable judgments of SUPPORT and GENERAL on the government aid topic approached it (Chi square equaled 3.45 for both).

The obvious conclusion is that content analysis as used in this study is a less discriminating dependent variable than the six semantic differential scales. However, content analysis did make possible the interesting discovery that subjects rarely cite dialect as a basis for judgment of competence and trustworthiness even though it operates as one.

Type of Response	Southern Integration	Northern Integration	Southern Govt. Aid	Northern Govt. Aid
LOGIC				
Favorable	14	12	20	27
Unfavorable	30	31	23	17
SUPPORT				
Favorable	7	7	11	19
Unfavorable	15	16	16	10
GENERAL				
Favorable	17	16	25	34
Unfavorable	35	33	29	19

Summary

Content analysis is a means to an end, the end being determined by the analyst's scholarly interests. Typically, an analytic study requires nine

stages: (1) formulating general hypotheses; (2) selecting a sample of messages to be analyzed; (3) selecting categories and units; (4) formulating
judgmental procedures; (5) selecting control or normative data; (6) reformulating general hypotheses in terms of categories and units; (7) selecting the criterion for accepting or rejecting hypotheses; (8) tabulating; (9)
applying the criterion.

References and Selected Readings

Berelson, B. *Content analysis in communication research.* Glencoe, Ill.: The
Free Press of Glencoe, 1952.

Blankenship, J., and Kay, C. Hesitation phenomena in English speech: A study
in distribution. *Word,* 1964, **20,** 360–372.

Budd, R. W., Thorp, R. K., and Donohew, L. *Content analysis of communications.* New York: Macmillan, 1967.

Clevenger, T., Parson, D. W., and Polisky, J. B. The problem of textual accuracy: Texts of the debates. In S. Kraus (Ed.), *The great debates: Background, perspective, effects.* Bloomington: Indiana University Press, 1962.
Pp. 341–430.

Davis, R. E. Response to innovation: A study of popular argument about new
mass media. Unpublished doctoral dissertation, University of Iowa, 1965.

DeVito, J. A linguistic analysis of spoken and written language. *Central States
Speech Journal,* 1967, **28,** 81–85.

Ebel, R. L. Estimation of the reliability of ratings. *Psychometrika,* 1951, **16,**
407–424.

Garvin, P. L. (Ed.) *Natural language and the computer.* New York: McGraw-
Hill, 1963.

George, A. Quantitative and qualitative approaches to content analysis. In I.
de S. Pool (Ed.), *Trends in content analysis.* Urbana: University of Illinois
Press, 1959. Pp. 7–32.

Gerbner, G., Holsti, O. R., Krippendorff, K., Paisley, W. J., and Stone, P. J.
(Eds.) *The analysis of communication content.* New York: John Wiley,
1969.

Gouran, D. An investigation of variables related to consensus in group discussions of questions of policy. Unpublished doctoral dissertation, University
of Iowa, 1968.

Houck, C., and Bowers, J. W. Dialect and identification in persuasive messages.
Language and Speech, in press.

Krasner, L. Studies of the conditioning of verbal behavior. *Psychological
Bulletin,* 1958, **55,** 148–170.

Mosteller, F., and Wallace, D. W. *Inference and disputed authorship: "The
Federalist."* Reading, Mass.: Addison-Wesley, 1964.

Osgood, C. E. Some effects of motivation on style of encoding. In T. A. Sebeok
(Ed.), *Style in language.* Cambridge, Mass.: M. I. T. Press, and New York:
John Wiley, 1960. Pp. 293–306.

Osgood, C. E., Saporta, S., and Nunnally, J. C., Jr. Evaluative assertion analysis. *Litera,* 1956, **3,** 47–102.

Paisley, W. J. Identifying the unknown communicator in painting, literature, and music: The significance of minor encoding habits. *Journal of Communication,* 1964, **14,** 219–237.

Paisley, W. J. Minor encoding habits. II: Extemporaneous speech in the Kennedy-Nixon debates. *Odd Papers in Communication Research,* 1967, No. 1. (a)

Paisley, W. J. Studying the expression of style as encoding behavior. *Odd Papers in Communication Research,* 1967, No. 2. (b)

Pool, I. de S. (Ed.) *Trends in content analysis.* Urbana: University of Illinois Press, 1959.

Roberts, P. *Patterns of English.* New York: Harcourt, Brace & World, 1956.

Sebeok, T. A. (Ed.) *Style in language.* Cambridge, Mass.: M. I. T. Press, 1960.

Stone, P. J., Dunphy, D. C., Smith, M. S., Ogilivie, D. M., and associates. *The General Inquirer: A computer approach to content analysis.* Cambridge, Mass.: M. I. T. Press, 1966.

Tate, M. W. *Statistics in education.* New York: Macmillan, 1955. Pp. 479–482.

Willy, T. G. The agitation in Parliament and England over Charles George "Chinese" Gordon and his mission to the Soudan; January, 1884, to February, 1885. Unpublished doctoral dissertation, University of Iowa, 1962.

11

Stylistic Analysis

MERVIN D. LYNCH

Writers generally define communication as a process in which meaning is shared between a communicator and his audience (Ogden and Richards, 1923; Morris, 1946; Osgood, Suci, and Tannenbaum, 1957). Research studies have focused on three main elements of the process: the communicator, the message, and the audience. The message consists of the signs which convey the meanings, connotative and denotative, shared in the communication process. In communication research the message provides both the dependent variable data for measuring such phenomena as propaganda intent and communicator performance, and the independent stimuli for inducing persuasive and informational effects.

Distinct methodologies have been developed for research at each level of the communication process. Two in particular, content analysis and stylistic analysis, are currently used in message research. Content analysis measures the semantic aspect or the "what" of a message (see Chapter 10). After selecting more or less mutually exclusive categories and units, the content analyst counts the number of units within each category found in some sample of messages. Inferences are made from these counts about such factors as communicator intent and persuasive efficacy of the communication.

Stylistic analysis measures the syntactic aspect or "how" of a communication message. For some message sampling, the stylistic analyst counts such features of the message as parts of speech, punctuation units, words, and characters, and computes ratios on some of these counts. Using these ratios, he compares individual styles of writing and/or predicts judgmental responses to the message.

Of the two methods, content analysis has received the more systematic and thorough consideration in the literature (Berelson, 1952; Pool, 1959; P. J. Stone, Dunphy, Smith, Ogilvie, and associates, 1966), but stylistic analysis has an earlier historical basis — Lorge (1939, 1944) reports that the Talmudists used frequency counts on messages in 900 A. D. to distinguish usual from unusual meanings, and Gray and Leary (1935) report that stylistic considerations were involved in vocabulary treatments in McGuffey Readers as early as 1840. However, precedence does not indicate thoroughness. Although there are isolated instances of the application and use of stylistic indices and somewhat extensive research on one index (readability), the methodologies involved in stylistic analysis have not to date been fully elaborated elsewhere.

The major purpose of this chapter is to present one such methodological explanation. The procedures involved in the development of stylistic indices and their application in measuring one stylistic variable are presented and evaluated in terms of their validity and reliability.

Logic of Stylistic Analysis

Early approaches to the study of message style were primarily descriptive in that stylistic measures were used to differentiate patterns of literary usage. Berelson (1952) reports that Yule (1944) excluded the possibility that Gerson wrote "De Imitatione Christi," Chambers (1930) established the dates of works of Shakespeare, and Oliphant (1927) determined dates for works by Beaumont and Fletcher. Similarly, by applying rather crude stylistic measures to literary works, Miles (1946) characterized types of poetry, and L. A. Sherman (1893) demonstrated a historical trend toward stylistic simplicity in poetry and prose. Useful as descriptive stylistic measurement may be, these indices provide little more than grounds for subjective speculation about communication variables.

Stylistic analysis has subsequently proceeded more along analytic than descriptive lines. Judgmental measurements are taken on some communication variable for a sampling of messages. These scores are then predicted from frequency counts or ratios of such counts made on the stylistic stimulus attributes in each message.

The steps involved in analytic stylistic analysis are few and straightforward.

(1) The first step is *selecting and/or developing a working judgmental measure* for particular communication variables. For instance, in the work

on readability, available standardized measures of comprehension were selected and used to develop the various readability measures. However, there are few working judgmental measures available for other communication performance variables, and most stylistic analyses to date have required the development of a judgmental measure.

(2) The next step is *selecting stylistic attributes* which correlate with and hence may be used as predictors of the variable being studied. Though communication variables are primarily judgmental phenomena, various nonjudgmental correlates may be used for indirect assessment of particular communication variables. This assessment involves counts on attributes such as words, syllables, adjectives, verbs, and other features of the message where variations in frequency may accompany but not necessarily be causally associated with variations on the judgmental measure.

These attributes can be either drawn from findings of prior factor analyses (see p. 319) on similar message variables or selected by intuition and/or subjective inspection. Techniques of correlation and factor analysis are applied to the data to see which attributes do correlate with the communication variable and which are independent.

(3) After a sampling of messages has been selected, *counts are made* on each chosen attribute and ratios are computed among some of these counts. In most stylistic analysis to date, the samplings of messages studied have been diverse but by no means random. Many samplings have been taken from standardized comprehension tests so that it was possible to control for differential readability while studying other possibly related variables. Other messages have been selected from sources such as the Bible, Ferlinghetti, newspaper articles, and so on. In order to control for differential passage length, attribute counts are made for each passage and ratios formed among them.

(4) *Judgments are obtained* from subjects on each of the messages (they were predicted from the ratios and/or counts on the various stimulus attributes). Statistical techniques of correlation and factor analysis are used to determine the best set of message attribute predictors.

(5) *Multiple regression analysis is applied* to determine the adequacy of the prediction and to generate a regression equation which may be employed as an indirect measure of the judgmental variable (see Chapter 2).

SOME CONCEPTS OF STYLISTIC ANALYSIS

Judgmental communication variables reside primarily in the mind of the recipient of the communication. However, this approach to stylistic analysis assumes that the communication may contain various syntactic correlates or counterparts which act as stimuli to evoke or elicit judgmental responses.

Possibly such correlates may be used in regression analysis to generate correlate indices for indirect measurements on the judgmental variable.

Measuring perceptual response phenomena in terms of the physical characteristics of the stimulus has been a long-standing research aim of some psychologists. For example, Attneave (1957) found that in scaled judgments of stimulus complexity an appreciable proportion of variance was explained by various physical characteristics; similarly, Arnoult (1960) showed that a substantial proportion of the variance of judgments of size, familiarity, and meaningfulness was explained by various stimuli; and Tannenbaum and Elliott (1961) have had some success in estimating semantic judgments of colors, random two-dimensional shapes, and abstract sculpture from stimulus attributes.

Various writers have suggested the possibility of such objective correlates of syntactic counterparts in communication messages. Eliot (1955) proposed that "various feelings, inhering for the writer in particular words or phrases or images" will be expressed in his writing which in turn will "evoke the same feeling in the reader." Carroll (1960, 1964) called language symbols "verbal mediating processes" which provide some of the internal stimuli and stimulus producing responses which "initiate the process of overt responses." According to Sanford (1942), language is a vehicle of personality as well as thought, and when a person speaks, he tells us not only about the world but also "through both form and content about himself." In a sense, the search for such correlates has been a major aim of studies on readability by Flesch (1946, 1948, 1949, 1950, 1951, 1960) and others, by Carroll (1960, 1964) on attributes of prose, and by Husek and Suci (1961) on style attributes in mental health communications.

METHODS USED IN STYLISTIC ANALYSIS

A major problem encountered by the developers of stylistic measures was that there existed few, if any, acceptable measures of the relevant judgmental response variable. One concern of stylistic analysis has been developing valid measures of the judgmental response variable and applying these measures to selected samplings of messages to provide a criterion for deriving an indirect measure. Stylistic counts are made on various message attributes, ratios are formed from these counts, and factor analysis is applied to select the most sensitive set of correlates. Multiple regression analysis is then applied to generate regression equations which may be used as indirect measures of the judgmental variable.

The statistical procedures of correlation, factor analysis, and multiple regression analysis are often used at various stages in developing stylistic measures. *Correlation* is a procedure for estimating the degree of association between measurements on pairs of variables. When measurements are available on numerous variables, it is possible to compute estimates or correlations for all pairs of variables; this is called a correlation matrix.

Factor Analysis

Some highly correlated variables may not be independent, *i.e.,* they may be separate measures for the same phenomenon. Factor analysis can determine the independent relationships among such variables. The term *factor loading* describes the estimate of the correlation of each variable to some hypothetical construct which is called a factor or dimension. Each factor is labeled in terms of the cluster of variables which have high loadings or correlations on the construct.

Factor loadings are computed from the correlation matrix — those variables having the highest intercorrelations and low correlations with other variables generally have the highest factor loadings, and hence are the most designative of a factor. In stylistic analysis, factor analysis is used in three ways: (1) to define empirically the judgmental concept, *i.e.,* to determine the dimension of judgment; (2) to select the variables most designative of each factor, as they are the variables which may be used in measuring judgments; (3) to select the best set of correlates and hence the most parsimonious set of predictors for use in measurement.

Multiple Regression Analysis

One step in a stylistic analysis is predicting scores for each judgmental variable from the message correlates. Multiple regression analysis makes it possible to determine the extent of the relationship between two or more independent variables and a dependent variable. The estimate of the size of this relationship is called a multiple correlation. The square of the multiple correlation is the percentage of variance explained in the dependent variable by the independent variables; for instance, in stylistic analysis it is the percentage of variance explained in judgmental scores by the message correlates. Multiple regression is also used to generate an equation for predicting scores on the judgmental measure. Multiple regression gives coefficients which will provide an indirect measure of a concept when multiplied by counts on the message correlates of that concept.

Judgmental Measures

Since judgmental concepts may differ in various ways, methodological approaches to measurement will differ according to the response variable being measured. Measures of recall, the semantic differential, and Q methodology have all been used for indexing responses to concepts such as COMPREHENSION, SENSATIONALISM, HUMAN INTEREST, and CREATIVENESS. There are undoubtedly many other such variables to which judgmental measures may be applied.

RECALL

COMPREHENSION has generally been treated as a phenomenon of learning and is defined as the potential ease of understanding in a communication message. Various recall tests have been constructed for measuring it. Some of this work has been directed simply toward measuring reading ability. Other studies have used recall tests as the main criterion in studying the possible effects of intentional manipulation on such variables as amplification, compression, choice of typeface, and use of clauses of varied lengths (Patterson and Tinker, 1932; McCluskey, 1940; Wilson, 1944; Coleman, 1964).

In comprehension tests, an individual is usually asked to read a passage and then take a test rating his recall of the material in the passage. There are various forms of recall tests; one used rather commonly is the multiple-choice test where an individual is given several possible answers for each question and asked to indicate his choice.

Often recall tests have been constructed and applied which have not been adequately assessed for reliability or validity. Results of these tests may be attributed to the unreliability of the measures as readily as to the particular stimulus being studied. To solve this problem, standardized measures of recall have been constructed for indexing comprehension ability. Notable among these are tests described in studies conducted by Thorndike (1915; 1916a, b; 1921), Haggerty (1917), Monroe (1918), C. R. Stone (1922), McCall (1922), McCall and Crabbs (1926), and Courtis (1925). One in particular, the McCall-Crabbs Standard Test Lessons in Reading (McCall, 1922; McCall and Crabbs, 1926) has found widespread acceptance and use. In the McCall-Crabbs test subjects are required to read a short paragraph and answer multiple-choice questions. For instance:

> The wind wanted a man to take off his coat. The wind blew and blew, but the man held his coat closer and closer about him. The sun wanted the man to take off his coat. The sun smiled and smiled, and the man gladly took off his coat.
>
> 1. The wind a) hid; b) was wise; c) smiled; d) blew
> 2. What smiled? a) man; b) sun; c) wind; d coat
> 3. This story is about the a) sun and man; b) sun and wind; c) sun, wind, and man; d) wind and man

Other such tests have been developed. Some are considerably more sophisticated; some represent expansions on the McCall-Crabbs procedures, including outstanding efforts by the Educational Testing Service. The major aim of all standardized measures is to index what Gray and Monroe (1929) and Gray and Leary (1935) have called the individual's ability to grasp the essential meaning of a passage.

These standardized recall measures have also provided a general index of a message's ease of understanding or its clarity. In this application, recall measurements are used to locate the average level of COMPREHENSION for specially selected passages. In various studies, counts have been made on numerous stylistic indices in these passages and comprehension scores predicted for them through multiple regression techniques. Using such analytic procedures, researchers like Gray and Leary (1935), Flesch (1946, 1948, 1949, 1950, 1951, 1960), Farr, Jenkins, and Patterson (1951), and Gunning (1952) have developed readability formulas for measuring level of COMPREHENSION in communication messages.

SEMANTIC DIFFERENTIAL

The semantic differential (see Chapter 6) is a measure of individual connotations comprising a series of continua between polar adjective opposites on which individuals rate their reactions to some general concept. It is a technique, not a general methodology of measurement. It provides data useful in isolating and identifying dimensions of meaning on a concept such as SENSATIONALISM, but it does not provide a ready-made index for measuring the degree of sensationalism in a passage. To apply the semantic differential to the measurement of sensationalism, it is necessary to (1) permit each individual to use his own standard of judgment, (2) combine multidimensional ratings into one index, and (3) measure degree of sensationalism along an ordered continuum.

SENSATIONALISM is a concept which resides primarily in the mind of the beholder, and the standard of judgment on this concept may vary from one individual to another. To index sensationalism on passages with the semantic differential, ratings are obtained on the same set of scales on the standard SENSATIONAL NEWS and on each passage. For instance, individuals might rate the concept SENSATIONAL NEWS on semantic differential scales as follows:

SENSATIONAL NEWS

good ____ : ____ : ____ : ____ : ____ : ____ : ____ bad

fast ____ : ____ : ____ : ____ : ____ : ____ : ____ slow

weak ____ : ____ : ____ : ____ : ____ : ____ : ____ strong

A subject may rate SENSATIONAL NEWS as extremely good or extremely bad, quite good or quite bad, slightly good or slightly bad, or neutral. He also rates SENSATIONAL NEWS in terms of its fastness or slowness, weakness or strongness. Ratings on two or more passages are then compared to determine their relative similarity in meaning to the standard.

Tannenbaum and Lynch (1960, 1962), for example, obtained ratings on a variety of scales on the concept SENSATIONAL NEWS. First, they selected scales from various sources that seemed to describe attributes of the concept SENSATIONALISM. Several such studies were conducted as the scale selection was successively refined, until finally 10 scales were isolated which seemed to represent best the dimensions of judging SENSATIONALISM. To index SENSATIONALISM in a passage, individuals were asked to rate both the standard concept SENSATIONAL NEWS and the concept in each message on the 10 scales.

In their haste to analyze semantic differential data, researchers more often than not have ignored the multidimensional nature of their measurement technique. They have obtained ratings on semantic differential scales representing various dimensions of meaning and have compared ratings on two or more concepts on individual scale or dimensional scores, but not on a single index of meaning. Three main avenues have been used with semantic differential data to determine the similarity in meaning between profile ratings on pairs of concepts which could be applied to the measurement of sensationalism.

One procedure extensively used in semantic differential data analysis has been computing mean scores on each adjective pair scale for both the standard SENSATIONAL NEWS and the ratings for a passage and comparing these means scale by scale. A passage adjudged more active, more excitable and less mature than the standard on scales *active-passive, excitable-calm,* and *mature-immature* could be labeled as sensational. Where these scales have been derived by factor analysis, they should not be taken as meaningful features on the concept at issue but as representors of each dimension of meaning judgment. Each scale rating represents a fragmented aspect of meaning, and the inferred whole (SENSATIONALISM) may not be equalled by the sum of the independent parts. Further, a scale-by-scale measure does not provide an index of the degree to which the sensationalism of two or more passages may be compared, but only a statement that a passage is or is not sensational as inferred from the individual scale ratings.

A second procedure used with semantic differential data has been computing mean scores for each dimension of meaning on a concept; the standard scores on each dimension of meaning relevant to sensationalism judgment are indexed by this procedure — an advantage over the scalewise method of analysis — and a judgment about sensationalism inferred from the mean rating for the three dimensions of *excitement, activity,* and *evaluation.* Were ratings on a passage adjudged more exciting, more violent, and less favorable in evaluation than the standard of SENSATIONAL NEWS, a passage could be taken to be sensational. The dimensional constructs in and of themselves have little theoretical utility. The main reason for using the semantic differential is measuring meaning, and meaning is an especially useful variable in measurement operations. The dimensions represent individual aspects of meaning, and taken separately they do not serve the same function as the more general concept; as with the scalewise analysis, sensationalism would have to be inferred from the sum of these three parts.

A preferable approach to measuring concepts like SENSATIONALISM with the semantic differential is to use a multidimensional index which combines the ratings across scales and dimensions of the semantic differential, with degrees along a continuum of sensationalism judgment. The D-square procedure (generalized distance function), for example — used in the Tannenbaum and Lynch (1960, 1962) studies on SENSATIONALISM — provides an index of the similarity between two profiles of judgment (such as ratings on a passage and ratings on a standard) according to the following formula:

$$D = \sum_{i=1}^{n} (X_{ij} - X_{ik})^2$$

where i is a scale, j is a concept, k is a concept, and n is the number of scales.

This index has been applied in a variety of useful ways to provide a measure of some theoretically useful constructs. For example, it has been applied as a measure of identification where the D value is computed between semantic differential ratings on the concept MYSELF and the concept of another individual such as Wyatt Earp. The smaller the D value, the greater the degree of identification between an individual and, in this instance, Wyatt Earp. It has also been applied to index the degree of idealization of political candidates in research on the 1960 and 1964 elections. In these studies, semantic differential ratings were obtained on the same set of scales on each candidate and on the ideal candidate for a political office. The D value was computed between ratings for the idealized and actual candidate, and this D value provided the index of degree of idealization of each candidate; the smaller the D value, the more idealized a candidate was judged. The D-square procedure has also found use as a sociometric index where the D values on semantic differential ratings of concepts are computed between persons rather than concepts. Groups of persons are compared in terms of the homogeneity of their concept ratings. The smaller the D values, the greater the homogeneity in meaning.

In the Tannenbaum and Lynch (1960, 1962) studies of sensationalism, the D value was computed between the ratings on the selected semantic differential scales on the concept SENSATIONAL NEWS and on each passage, and the D values for two or more passages were compared. The larger the D value, the less sensational a passage was judged; the smaller the D value, the more sensational a passage was judged. Since the D was computed between the ratings on each passage and the standard for each individual, for measurement purposes each individual served as his own control — a major advantage from a methodological viewpoint. The D-square procedure's application for purposes of measuring sensationalism may be visualized in Figure 1. If there are ratings of two messages (A and B) and the concept SENSATIONALISM (S), they may be allocated as separate points in a multidimensional space. (They are presented in two dimensions in Figure 1, p. 324).

In using the D value in dependent variable analyses, several questions have arisen. For example, in computing the D value, equal weight is assigned to ratings at equal intervals on either side of the standard, and this

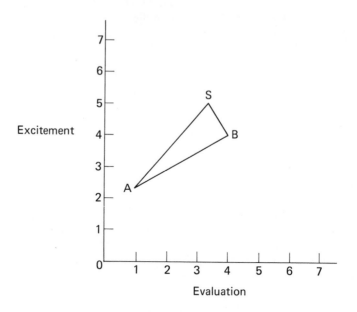

FIGURE 1

Sendex scale ratings on two dimensions of sensationalism judgment (excitement and evaluation) for two messages (A and B) and for the concept SENSATIONAL NEWS (S). The multidimensional measure (D) is applied to index the sensationalism judgments for A and B respectively as the geometric distance from A to S and B to S.

has led to some question about directionality. In using the D value with semantic differential data, the major question is the degree of similarity to the standard, not the particular position of ratings on individual scales. For instance, the more similar in meaning a rating is to the standard of SENSATIONAL NEWS, the more sensational is a passage judged. Direction is interpreted as a more or less sensational judgment, and, hence, a larger or smaller D value.

Researchers to date have assumed that the D value is normally distributed, and this has justified the use of parametric statistics in D-value analysis. The accuracy of this assumption is open to question, but determining the distribution for each set of D-value data would be time consuming and probably unproductive, since parametric statistics (such as the analysis of variance) are powerful enough to accommodate considerable departure from normality. At this point in methodological sophistication, it is perhaps better to assume the data are normally distributed and get on with the research work than to be mired by the slight possibility of data so skewed that they may not be analyzed by parametric procedures.

Q METHODOLOGY

Some concepts involve self-referent more than general connotations. CREATIVENESS, for example, can be defined by individuals with high creative aptitudes. *Q* methodology (see Chapter 5), a means of measuring such self-referent concepts, is the appropriate measure for indexing judgments of CREATIVENESS.

Lynch and Collier (1966) and Lynch and Bowman (1967) have used *Q* methodology to study CREATIVENESS. Individuals of varying creative aptitudes — as judged by some measure such as the Remote Associates Test (S. A. Mednick, 1962; M. T. Mednick, S. A. Mednick, and Jung, 1964; M. T. Mednick, S. A. Mednick, and E. V. Mednick, 1964; K. F. Reigel, E. M. Riegel, and Levine, 1966) — read and sorted each of the selected message stimuli along a forced normal continuum from most to least creative. These sorts were scored and the scores were subjected to correlation and factor analysis to determine the dimensionality of CREATIVENESS judgments. The factor accounting for the largest proportion of the common factor variance (creativeness) was designated by individuals with high creative aptitudes. This factor was also the major dimension of judgment of CREATIVENESS in writing. Factor composites in standard normal form were obtained by applying Spearman's (1927) weightings, computed from loadings on the factor, to weight the observation data for each message. These factor composites generally ranged from +2 to −2 and provided an index of CREATIVENESS for each message with scores on a continuum from most to least creative.

Selecting Correlates

The primary aim in stylistic analysis is to identify clusters of message attributes which may relate to and be predictive of the judgmental variables, and which may be used to derive a regression equation for indirect measurement. Possible message attributes are almost infinite in number; counts and comparisons have been made on such indices as sentences, words, and part-of-speech frequencies. In other studies, ratios such as adjectives to verbs, words per sentence, and syllables per 100 words have been computed and used for analysis.

To count all such attributes and form all possible ratios would be an unwieldy task. However, some research has attempted to reduce the dimensions of message style (Gray and Leary, 1935; Carrol, 1960; Husek and Suci, 1961; Lynch and Bowman, 1967; Lynch, Nettleship, and Carlson, 1968). This research, typical of stylistic analysis, involved counting message attributes, computing ratios, and performing correlation and factor analysis. Some general dimensions of writing style have emerged from these analyses.

Gray and Leary (1935) were perhaps the first to attempt to designate general stylistic constructs. From an inspection of the intercorrelations among 44 stylistic variables measured on 48 passages, they selected 24 which correlated substantially with measurement on comprehension. These were called elements of reading difficulty. They did not perform a factor analysis on their data, but Lynch and Bowman (1967) did and found six dimensions of style in the Gray and Leary data: *complexity, sentence length, redundancy, lexical diversity, phrase emphasis,* and *syllable range.* Husek and Suci (1961) expanded the Gray and Leary list to include some judgmental measures and applied them to 70 rather disparate passages. Using factor analysis, 10 factors were isolated; four of these were identified as *word difficulty, sentence difficulty, negative versus passive content tone,* and *readership appeal.*

Working along similar lines, Carroll (1960) obtained measurements on 29 semantic differential scales and 39 stylistic attributes on 150 written samples of 300 words each. From a factor analysis of this data, he isolated six general factors of prose style: *general stylistic evaluation, personal affect, ornamentation, abstractness, seriousness,* and *characterization.* These factors were strongly oriented toward factors of connotation rather than style. Lynch performed a factor analysis on stylistic measures made on messages, as part of the sensationalism research discussed on pp. 321–324, including 37 stylistic and four judgmental measures on each of the 24 messages. He found five general factors which seemed to be more stylistically oriented than Carroll's: *complexity, emotiveness, readability, pausality,* and *indirectness.* Lynch *et al.* (1968) carried out a factor analysis on 26 stylistic measures and one judgmental measure made on 36 written messages. The smaller number of stylistic measures reflects choices based on findings of prior research. From this analysis seven factors emerged and were labeled *emotiveness, readability, consistency, syntactic dispersion, productivity, complexity,* and *personalism.*

Although the findings of these factor analytic studies are by no means conclusive, they do provide a relatively good "feel" for the types of stylistic dimensions prevalent in communication messages. Some factors have emerged in several studies and/or seem especially sensitive to measurement on various judgmental concepts. These factors and their respective measures are as follows:

(1) Some index of *productivity* with measures on frequency of words or sentences. Johnson (1939) suggested that word frequency can be "a gross but in some respects very useful, measurement." He reported that Davis (1939) and M. Smith (1939) employed this measure and found "wide individual differences in spoken and written verbal output," and "marked variability in the output for any given individual." Lynch and Kays (1967) and Lynch and Swink (1967) found these measures sensitive discriminators between the performances of high and low creative persons in writing.

(2) An index of *sentence length* with measures on ratios of words to sentences and characters to sentences. Johnson (1939) reported that some researchers have found a positive relationship between sentence length usage and mental age, and D. H. Sherman (1939) found a negative relationship between sentence length and descriptive adequacy. In this connection, Johnson (1939) proposed that abstraction should vary directly and comprehensibility indirectly with measures on sentence length. Zipf (1935) in his studies of language usage found a stable positive relationship between magnitude and length of sentences. In his studies of reading comprehension, Flesch (1946, 1948, 1949, 1950, 1951, 1960) found that sentence length was a major correlate of comprehension and incorporated this measure into his readability formula.

(3) Some index of *consistency* with measures on such variables as characters per sentence, syllables per sentence, function words per sentence, and characters per word. These measures indicate both the frequency of occurrence and the dispersion of each attribute. Some of these measures were found to be sensitive discriminators between performances of high and low creative persons in writing activities (Lynch and Kays, 1967; Lynch and Swink, 1967).

(4) Some index of *lexical diversity* with measurement on the type-token ratio (*TTR*), formed by dividing the total number of words into the total number of different words (see Chapter 9, pp. 259–260). This index was originated independently by Zipf (1935) and by Johnson and Tuthill (1938). It has been employed in studies of language by Hockett (1938), Jersild and Ritzman (1938), and Carroll (1960). Johnson (1939) proposed that the *TTR* was a sensitive measure of vocabulary, degree of frustration, degree of disorientation, and the stimulation value of a situation. Osgood and Walker (1959) found it a sensitive discriminator between suicide and pseudocide notes, and Lynch *et al.* (1965) found it a major correlate of human interest in writing.

(5) An index of *syntactic dispersion* with measures of variance in strings of three, four, and five parts of speech. This measure, developed by Lynch and Quinn (1967), seems to be a sensitive discriminator between communication performances of high and low creative persons and a major correlate of creativeness in writing (Lynch and Collier, 1966; Lynch and Bowman, 1967; Lynch and Kays, 1967; Lynch and Swink, 1967).

(6) Some index of *abstraction* with measures on the ratio of abstract to total nouns and finite to total verbs. Various indicators of abstraction have been proposed by Sanford (1942) and Carroll (1960); Flesch (1950) and Gillie (1957) have presented specific measures. Lynch and Bowman (1967) found the ratio of abstract to total nouns to be a significant correlate of creativeness, and DeVito (1965, 1967) found the number of

abstract nouns and finite verbs to be sensitive discriminators between oral and written communication.

(7) An index of *complexity* with measures on the ratio of syllables to hundred words and characters to words. Zipf (1935), using measures of word length, found an inverse relationship between word length and frequency. Johnson (1939) and Skalbeck (1939) show that word length as indexed by syllables, phonemes, or letters is an "extraordinarily reliable measure." Measures formed from syllable counts are frequently used in the various readability formulas, especially those of Flesch (1946, 1948, 1949, 1950, 1951, 1960) and Gunning (1952). Lynch and Bowman (1967) found that the index of complexity was a major correlate of creativeness. Rickert (1927), in trying to explain why Perley (1927) found that syllable usage distinguished between works of Shakespeare and Marlow, proposed that monosyllables indicate "force and curtness" and polysyllables indicate complexity. Findings from studies by Bear (1930) and McCluskey (1935) reported by Gray and Leary (1935) show that syllables differentiate between easy and difficult passages.

(8) An index of *redundancy* with a measure on the ratio of function words per sentence. Function words include the articles, prepositions, and conjunctions — the metalinguistic connectives. Using function words as discriminants, Mosteller and Wallace (1964) provided conclusive evidence that Madison, not Hamilton, wrote 12 disputed *Federalist* papers. L. A. Sherman (1893) proposed that the use of function words as conjunctions is reduced when style matures in much the same way a child reduces his use of primer sentences as he grows older. In contrast, Rickert (1927) argued that increased use of such connectives will yield a "developed" style while reduced use will produce a "suggestive" style. Perhaps they can be reconciled by the theory that adults are able to understand a suggestive style of communication and therefore tend to eliminate redundancy in writing. Lynch (1962) found such a reduction in a study of editing practices and procedures.

(9) An index of *pausality* with a measure on the ratio of internal punctuation to sentences. This measure, used in analyzing written messages, appears to be a counterpart to measures of pause duration in speech communication. Tannenbaum and Lynch (1962) found this to be a correlate of sensationalism, and Lynch and Bowman (1967) found it to be a correlate of creativeness.

(10) An index of *personalism* with measures on the ratios of personal to total words, personal to total sentences, and the Flesch human interest score. Flesch (1948, 1960) believed measures of personal words and sentences could designate human interest, and he derived a human interest formula based on these ratios. In studies by Lynch *et al.* (1968), the

Flesch human interest score was found to be one, but not the only, correlate of human interest.

(11) Some index of *emotiveness* with measures on the modification ratio, variance in modification, degree of sensationalism, and degree of human interest. The modification ratio — the ratio of adjectives plus adverbs to nouns plus verbs — is closely related to adjective-verb ratios developed and applied by Busemann (1925), Rickert (1927), and Boder (1940). It was shown to be a sensitive indicator of psychological stress (Osgood and Walker, 1959) and a correlate of sensationalism (Tannenbaum and Lynch, 1960, 1962) and human interest — both of which are themselves indices of emotiveness.

(12) Some index of *readability* with measures such as those of Gray and Leary (1935), Flesch (1946, 1948, 1949, 1951, 1960), Dale and Chall (1948), and Gunning (1952). The studies of comprehension discussed in this chapter (Lynch and Bowman, 1967; Lynch and Kays, 1967; Lynch and Swink, 1967; Lynch, Kent, and Carlson, 1967; Lynch *et al.,* 1968; Lynch, 1969) have used revised forms of the various regression formulas computed by Powers, Sumner, and Kearl (1958) using more up-to-date and adult level measures of comprehension. Readability formulas like Flesch's (1946, 1948, 1951, 1960) are generally believed to index the speed and ease of reading a particular passage.

Sample Study

The procedures involved in stylistic analysis and some of the methods presented previously may be clarified by examining a sample study. Some recently completed work on the development of a measure of human interest seems especially well suited for this purpose. Lynch *et al.* (1967, 1968) identified dimensions of human interest, and from this research developed and applied an instrument to measure human interest called the Human Quotient Index (HQdex). The work reported in these two papers illustrates the various steps of stylistic analysis as well as some methodological problems unique to the measurement of human interest.

The research summarized in the two reports involved defining the problem, developing an index to measure it, and testing the validity of the index. Scales and concepts were selected in both definition and measurement; once a judgmental measure was developed, an objective correlate index of human interest was derived. This derivation involved choosing message and style attributes and generating a multiple regression equation which could be applied as an indirect or objective correlate measure of human interest.

Defining the Problem

The steps in defining the problem (reported in the 1967 paper) were similar to those in other research endeavors, including (1) selecting the problem, (2) surveying the literature, (3) defining the judgmental variable, (4) selecting concepts and scales, and (5) applying factor analysis and multiple regression analysis.

(1) *Selecting the problem.* Human interest has been a central concept in communication, and Hughes (1940) has called it "the universal element in the news." It seemed to be an intriguing dependent variable which should be indexed if one is to assess communication performance — a major goal in stylistic analysis.

(2) *Surveying the literature.* The researchers reviewed the extant literature and definitional materials on human interest and found that most definitional work had been classificatory: definers had used intuitive, presumedly expert judgment to categorize message content as thematic (Hughes, 1940), straight news (Hohenberg, 1960), and "test tube" (Corbin, 1928). The only relevant research work had been done by Flesch (1948, 1960), who developed his own index of human interest. He used a measure of comprehension as a judgmental criterion and ratios of personal to total words and personal to total sentences as message correlates. But the resulting index accounted for less than 20 per cent of the variance in comprehension. In instances where it was applied, it failed to discriminate appropriately between messages judged high and low in human interest (Klare, Mabry, and Gustafson, 1955); hence, there was reason to doubt its validity and develop a new measure.

(3) *Defining the judgmental variable.* The first step toward measuring human interest was to define the concept of human interest so that it would be amenable to measurement. Stylistic analysis assumes that such communication concepts are part of the total judgmental meaning elicited by a message. But what aspect of meaning is involved in human interest? The choice is between connotation — the affective or feeling aspect of meaning — and denotation — the factual aspect of meaning.

In the sample study, human interest was considered a connotative phenomenon — one residing primarily in the mind of the recipient of the message. The semantic differential was chosen for this study in preference to Q methodology because it measures individual general connotations rather than self-referent concepts.

(4) *Selecting concepts and scales.* Flesch (1948, 1960), among others, in discussing human interest, has called it the "human element," the "human feature," and the "human quality in writing." The sample study was focusing on news writing, and the concept selected was HUMAN QUALITY IN A NEWS STORY because individuals could rate it on scales as active-passive, weak-strong, and good-bad.

The semantic differential is simply a technique of measurement. It does not provide a set of standardized scales for all concepts, and some scale selection and subsequent refinement is usually necessary. For this study,

140 scales were chosen which seemingly ascribed or attributed human qualities in writing. Some of these scales were selected from *Roget's Thesaurus,* some from prior research by Carroll (1960), and some from various studies with the semantic differential (Osgood *et al.,* 1957; Tannenbaum and Lynch, 1960). An analysis including all 140 scales would have been more desirable, but the available factor analysis procedure would accommodate only 41 scales. Twenty judges, graduate students in journalism, circled the adjective in each of the 140 pairs which best signified the concept HUMAN QUALITY IN A NEWS STORY. From these ratings 41 pairs were chosen on which judges either generally agreed or generally disagreed. (This method should produce scales representing the various dimensions of human interest judgment, but one can never be certain.)

(5) *Factor analysis.* To determine the dimensionalities of judging human interest, factor analysis was applied to ratings made on these selected semantic differential scales. Three such factor analyses were carried out to arrive at a stable set of dimensions and a refined selection of scales. Lynch *et al.* (1967) applied factor analysis to data obtained on these scales from 54 adult subjects and isolated six factors: *evaluation, sensitivity, personalism, appearance, substance,* and *complexity.* The sample was subsequently enlarged to 221 by an area sampling of adults and these data were subjected to factor analysis. From this analysis five factors emerged, labeled *evaluation, personalism, complexity, substance,* and *constraint.*

Lynch *et al.* (1968) obtained ratings on 17 of these scales against the concept HUMAN QUALITY IN A NEWS STORY from 114 college students, using the scales which were most designative on each of the factors isolated in prior studies, *i.e.,* those with the highest factor loadings. Four identifiable factors — *personalism, evaluation, complexity,* and *constraint* — seemed to account for more than 60 per cent of the common factor variance. These four factors appeared to be rather stable dimensions of human interest judgment, inasmuch as they emerged with similar salience and scale selections on all three factor analyses. However, a method of indexing human interest on all four dimensions still had to be developed.

Developing the Judgmental Measure

As in the definitional research, the semantic differential was chosen as the appropriate procedure for obtaining measures of human interest judgment. In all, 13 semantic differential scales — those most salient on each of the four dimensions — were selected for measurement purposes. (The percentage of variance provides an index of salience.) This selection seemed especially appropriate because these scales represented the criteria that a diversity of individuals in previous studies used in making judgments of human interest.

Although the semantic differential is a technique for measuring human interest judgment, it does not provide a direct index of the degree of human interest in a communication message. Individuals may differ in their standards for judging human interest: some may rely on personalism, some on evaluation, others on constraint; some may use all these dimensions but differ in their degree of response on each dimension. Thus, a rating which represents high human interest for one person may indicate moderate or low human interest for another. Because of this problem, the sample study used a measurement procedure which permitted each individual to be his own control.

The generalized distance measure D — a multidimensional measure of meaning when applied with the semantic differential — was used to index human interest. In this procedure semantic differential ratings were obtained from individuals on various communication messages and on the standard concept HUMAN QUALITY IN A NEWS STORY. The D statistic was applied to index the similarity or difference in meaning between the profiles for the standard concept and each message; hence, each individual became his own control. The smaller the D value between semantic differential profiles of a given message and that of HUMAN QUALITY IN A NEWS STORY, the more similar in meaning they were, and the greater the degree of human interest in that message. Conversely, the larger the D value between the scale profiles for a message and the standard concept, the less similar in meaning they were, and the smaller the degree of human interest in that message.

VALIDITY TEST

The validity of this type of measure must ultimately rest on the logic of the operational definition. However, it is possible to provide some evidence by showing that this measure will differentiate between messages categorized on some other basis as high and low in human interest. Such a finding may be taken as evidence for *face validity* of the measure.

The aims of the 1968 study were to see if the judgmental measure of human interest it developed (HQdex) differentiated between messages categorized by another procedure (in this case the Q sort) as high and low in human interest, if they did so for various content typologies (categories determined individually by Q sort), and if they would apply generally. The 1967 study provided evidence on the applicability and validity of the HQdex. HQdex ratings were obtained on 45 messages from 45 adults who then Q-sorted the same 45 messages along a continuum from most to least human in quality. This method provided an independent categorizing of stories as high and low in human interest, and a means to determine typologies of human interest content prevalent in the 45 messages.

A factor analysis on the Q-sort data identified seven typologies of human interest content. They were labeled as *novelty, leisure, complexity, personalism, adversity, achievement,* and *orderliness.* Factor composites were formed by applying Spearman's (1927) weightings computed from factor loadings on each of the seven factors to weight the observation data. These composites, in standard normal form, were used to classify stories as high and low in human interest within each typology. The ten stories having the highest and lowest factor composite scores within each of the seven content typologies were then compared to the HQdex scores for the same stories. Analysis of variance was applied to make these comparisons. Findings showed that HQdex scores were significantly smaller ($p < .001$) for stories categorized high in human interest. There were neither differences among typologies nor a category by typology interaction; rather, the HQdex differentiated between categories similarly for all seven content typologies. Thus, these findings support the validity and applicability of the HQdex as a measure of human interest.

Developing the Correlate Measure

The availability of a judgmental measure like the HQdex does not preclude the possibility that there may be features in the message which correlate with and may be used as an indirect index of the judgmental variable. The major aim of the sample study was to develop one such measure. This involved isolating correlates of the judgmental variable and using these correlates to derive an indirect measure of the HQdex scores.

SELECTING ATTRIBUTES

A total of 26 stylistic measures was selected. These included attributes of each of the 12 general dimensions of style (see pp. 326–329).

SELECTING MESSAGES

Lynch *et al.* (1968) selected from among the 45 written messages the 36 which were found to be designative as the most and least human in quality on each of the seven content typologies emerging from the *Q*-sort analysis. This provided a balance both in terms of content diversity and levels of human interest judgment.

SELECTING CORRELATES

Lynch *et al.* (1968) obtained ratings on each of these messages and on the HUMAN QUALITY IN A NEWS STORY on the scales of the HQdex from 114 college student subjects. The computed HQdex scores provided the dependent variable measurements for correlational analysis. Counts were subsequently performed on the various stylistic variables and the 26 measures were formed from these counts. These measures and the HQdex scores were subjected to correlation and factor analysis to select the most parsimonious set of predictors for generating a multiple regression equation.

Four clusters of style attributes were isolated which loaded on factors with the HQdex and had more or less low intercorrelations with each other. These were the main correlates of human interest and provided the most parsimonious predictors. They were as follows:

(1) An index of passage *complexity* with the ratio of syllables per 100 words being the best single correlate. All else being equal, the fewer the syllables per hundred words, the greater the degree of human interest in a ·nessage.

(2) Some index of *emotiveness,* with the variance in modification per sentence being the best single index. All else being equal, the less the variance in modification, the greater the degree of human interest in a message.

(3) An index of *lexical diversity,* with the type-token ratio (*TTR*) being the best single correlate. All else being equal, the smaller the *TTR,* the greater the degree of human interest in a message.

(4) Some index of *personalism* with the Flesch human interest score being the best single index. All else being equal, the higher the Flesch score, the greater the degree of human interest in a message.

MULTIPLE REGRESSION ANALYSIS

These four attributes were used as covariates in a multiple correlation and regression analysis. The HQdex was the main variate. A multiple correlation $(R = .73)$ — a value accounting for more than 53 per cent of the residual variance in the HQdex — was obtained. The computation of the multiple correlations made it possible to generate and apply a multiple regression equation as an indirect measure of human interest in communication messages. One equation was computed:

$$HQ' = 3.027 + .026X_1 + .602X_2 + .113X_3 - .006X_4$$

where HQ' = predicted HQdex scores
X_1 = syllables per 100 words
X_2 = (10) x (variance in modification per sentence)
X_3 = (10) x (type-token ratio)
X_4 = Flesch human interest score

and where the numerical values represent the constant α (alpha) and the respective β (beta) in the conventional regression equation. Once this equation was developed, it could be used to research various problems. Studies are currently being conducted employing the measure to study possible effects of human interest writing on candidate images in election reporting and to determine what effect, if any, human interest writing will have on newspaper readership.

EVALUATING STYLISTIC MEASURES

Developing measures in stylistic analysis is not enough; they must be tested for validity and reliability. Validity and reliability are evaluational tests, aids in the assessment of the efficacy of the measures; they are not substitutes for a logical analysis of the operations measures are based on. This may seem obvious, but it has been ignored by some who would substitute rigor for logic.

Validity

If an index measures what it is said to measure, it is said to have validity. Downie (1958) has proposed bases for evaluating a measure: (1) content validity, where a measure is shown by logical analysis to meet its specifications or objectives; (2) predictive validity, where ratings are taken on a criterion and correlated with ratings taken on a second measure at some later date, yielding a correlation or validity coefficient; (3) concurrent validity, where ratings on a criterion and on a second measure taken at the same time yield a correlation or validity coefficient; and (4) construct validity, where some test of hypothesis or logical analysis determines that the index is measuring the psychological construct it is said to measure.

Some researchers will defend the validity of an index on the soundness of the operational definition; others will carry out an empirical test and use the results as evidence for validity. However, the case for validity in stylistic measures, as with any other measurement procedure, must ultimately rest on the logical soundness of the premises linking the measurement procedure with the theoretical construct.

Some researchers prefer a more empirically based determination of validity. Typically, a hypothesis is formed from a theoretical construct and an index produced to measure that construct. The index may then be used to provide a test of the hypothesis: evidence is provided supporting *face validity*. Such evidence is not conclusive since in the hypothesis test a concomitant may have been measured instead of the stimulus; hence, the validity is only apparent and not demonstrated.

Evidence of face validity has been gathered for measures of sensationalism. News stories on three topics were intentionally encoded with high, moderate, and low sensationalism (Tannenbaum and Lynch, 1960), and measurements were taken on each story on the Sendex measure. The Sendex scores differentiated between conditions as hypothsized — *i.e.,* stories written most sensationally were rated most sensational, and those written least sensationally were rated least sensational. Similarly, a criterion measure (*Q* sort) was taken to classify messages as high and low in human interest, and measurements were obtained on these stories on the HQdex (Lynch *et al.,* 1968). The HQdex was shown to discriminate between high and low levels of human interest as hypothesized. Thus findings of these two studies support the face validity for the HQdex as a measure of human interest, and Sendex as a measure of sensationalism.

The correlate measures of communication concepts, such as comprehension, sensationalism, human interest, and creativeness, have been formed by multiple regression procedures. Where the judgmental measures have been shown to have face validity, the correlate measures will have predictive validity. The multiple correlation among correlate predictors and the judgmental criterion may be taken as a validity coefficient — in all these instances as large or larger than the usual .60 or under (Cronbach, 1960).

Reliability

Questions of reliability generally involve some aspect of *determinacy* or *uniformity*: how well does the index measure? Conditions of determinacy are satisfied when similar ratings are obtained each time a particular measure is applied to responses from the same individuals; conditions of uniformity are satisfied when similar ratings are obtained each time the measure is applied to different individual samplings.

Questions of reliability are appropriate at several stages in stylistic analysis. Computation of counts on some indices involves parsing messages, and coders may differ in classifying parts of speech. In studies of style, skilled grammatical coders have generally done the parsing and usually agree on about 90 per cent of it. Some computer procedures are used now and others are being developed (Lynch and Stolz, 1962; Stolz, Tannenbaum, and Carstensen, 1965; Clarke and Wall, 1965; Baxendale and Clarke, 1966) which will carry out parsing in a reasonably efficient and accurate manner. The use of the computer will satisfy the condition of reliability in coding since all computers using the same program are run on the same messages.

But correlate measures will not explain all the variance in the judgmental variable they index, raising a second question of reliability. The percentage of variance explained by each measure may be taken as an indicator of reliability. In stylistic measurement of variables like human interest, sensationalism, readability, and creativeness, correlate measures have accounted for more than half the variance in the judgmental criterion with less than four message correlates. Though this is an appreciable proportion of the residual variance, half remains unexplained; research is being done to isolate other stylistic correlates or more content oriented indices which will improve the reliability of these measures.

Summary

From the foregoing, it should be more or less apparent that the steps in stylistic analysis will generally proceed as follows (not precluding, of course, the possibility of steps unique to a particular measurement problem): (1) developing a working judgmental measure; (2) selecting relevant message attributes; (3) performing counts on each of these attributes and obtaining judgmental ratings on the same selection of communication messages; (4) predicting the judgmental responses from counts or ratios computed from the message attributes; (5) generating a regression equation which may be used as an indirect measure of the communication variable.

These steps are directed toward developing badly needed working stylistic measures. Various readability formulas are currently in use, and no doubt the measures being developed for such variables as human interest, sensationalism, and creativeness will be successfully applied.

Stylistic measures may be applied in various useful ways, for example, directly to the analysis of written messages without first obtaining criterion judgments of the messages, a time-consuming and relatively expensive procedure. They may be applied to evaluate statements about such factors as the relative degree of human interest, the relative degree of creativeness, or the extent of sensationalism in various written or spoken materials. Further, they may be applied as stimulus measures to determine the consequences in communication of factors like human interest and creativeness.

These stylistic measures seem especially well suited for analyzing historical materials (judgmental measures are not especially applicable to human judgments changing over time). Presuming that stylistic usage changes concurrently with individual judgments, it should be possible to measure values indirectly at any date in history with the appropriate stylistic measure. A constant relationship between style usage and values, of course, remains to be shown, though some analyses of style change over time suggest that it exists (Zipf, 1949).

One other application of stylistic analysis represents a departure from present procedures but nevertheless is intriguing. It involves estimating communicator intent from measures on message style, a problem involving propaganda analysis. It should be possible to obtain judgmental measures of a communicator's intent, and to estimate them from stylistic measures on written or spoken output. By regression analysis of stylistic measures on the judgmental index of intent, regression equations may be generated for propaganda analysis. A message style measure should provide better data than propaganda analysis techniques where inferences are made from intuition and subjective insight about communicator intent.

The research on stylistic analysis assumes that the objective correlate accompanies but is not causally connected to the dependent variable. The relationship indexed by an objective correlate measure is unidirectional, not biconditional, a consideration often forgotten in current applications of various readability formulas. When a writer or speaker wishes to communicate a given emotion, he presumably will encode certain signs into the message to convey his feeling. His choice of signs does not uniquely determine that his feeling will be communicated; hence, changing the signs which comprise a written or spoken message to conform to a correlate relationship (for instance editing a message to make it approximate more readable or sensational writing) may not yield a passage which will be judged more readable or sensational.

The difference between stylistic and content analysis is that one measures form and the other content. Both are quantitative approaches: when one counts attributes and computes ratios, one is quantifying. There are no qualitative tests for analyzing message content or style.

Although the two methods should be considered as distinct analysis procedures, they are by no means mutually exclusive. Content analysis measures some aspect of syntax; stylistic analysis indexes some aspect of content. However, the predominant factor indexed in either case will involve the syntactic feature in stylistic analysis and the semantic feature in content analysis. Thus, stylistic as well as content analysis should provide useful information about communication messages and their potential effects.

References and Selected Readings

Arnoult, M. D. Prediction of perceptual responses from structural characteristics of the stimulus. *Perceptual and Motor Skills,* 1960, **11,** 261–268.

Attneave, F. Physical determinants of the judged complexity of shapes. *Journal of Experimental Psychology,* 1957, **53,** 221–227.

Baxendale, P., and Clarke, D. Documentation for an economical program for the limited parsing of English: Lexicon, grammar, and flow-charts. *IBM Research,* 1966, No. RJ386.

Bear, M. V., reported in G. R. Johnson, An objective method of determining reading difficulty. *Journal of Educational Research,* 1930, **21,** 284.

Berelson, B. *Content analysis in communication research.* Glencoe, Ill.: The Free Press of Glencoe, 1952.

Boder, D. P. The adjective-verb quotient: A contribution to the psychology of language. *Psychological Record,* 1940, **3,** 309–342.

Busemann, A. *Die Sprache der Jugend als Ausdruck der Entwicklungsrhythmik.* Jena: Fischer, 1925.

Carroll, J. B. Vectors of prose style. In T. A. Sebeok (Ed.), *Style in language.* Cambridge, Mass.: M. I. T. Press, and New York: John Wiley, 1960.

Carroll, J. B. *Language and thought.* Englewood Cliffs, N. J.: Prentice-Hall, 1964.

Chambers, E. K. *William Shakespeare: A study of facts and problems.* New York: Oxford University Press, 1930.

Clarke, D., and Wall, R. An economical program for the limited parsing of English. *AFIPS Conference Proceedings, Fall Joint Computer Conference,* 1965, 307–319.

Coleman, E. B. The comprehensibility of several grammatical transformations. *Journal of Applied Psychology,* 1964, **48,** 186–190.

Corbin, C. *Why is news news?* New York: Ronald Press, 1928.

Courtis, S. A. *Why children succeed.* Detroit: Courtis Standard Tests, 1925.

Cronbach, L. J. *Essentials of psychological testing.* New York: Harper & Row, 1960.

Dale, E. A comparison of two word-lists. *Educational Research Bulletin,* 1931, **10,** 484–489.

Dale, E., and Chall, J. S. A formula for predicting readability. *Educational Research Bulletin,* 1948, **27,** 11–20, 37–54.

Dale, E., and Tyler, R. A study of the factors influencing the difficulty of reading materials for adults of limited reading ability. *Library Quarterly,* 1934, **4,** 384–412.

Davis, D. A study of repetitions in the speech of young children in relation to certain measures of language maturity and situational factors. *University of Iowa Studies in Child Welfare,* 1939.

DeVito, J. A. Levels of abstraction and listenability. *Today's Speech,* 1965, **13,** 12–14.

DeVito, J. A. Levels of abstraction in spoken and written practices. *Journal of Communication,* 1967, **4,** 354–361.

Downie, N. M. *Fundamentals of measurement: Techniques and practices.* New York: Oxford University Press, 1958.

Eliot, T. S., in Vivas, E. (Ed.), *Creation and discovery: Essays in criticism and aesthetics.* New York: Noonday Press, 1955.

Fairbanks, G., and Kodman, F., Jr. Word intelligibility as a function of time compression. *Journal of the Acoustical Society of America,* 1957, **29,** 636–641.

Farr, J. N., Jenkins, J. J., and Patterson, D. G. Simplification of the Flesch reading ease formula. *Journal of Applied Psychology,* 1951, **35,** 333–337.

Fisher, Sir R. A. *Statistical methods and scientific inference.* New York: Hafner, 1959.

Flesch, R. F. *The art of plain talk.* New York: Harper's, 1946.

Flesch, R. F. A new readability yardstick. *Journal of Applied Psychology,* 1948, **32,** 221–233.

Flesch, R. F. *The art of readable writing.* New York: Harper's, 1949.

Flesch, R. F. Measuring the level of abstraction. *Journal of Applied Psychology,* 1950, **34,** 384–390.

Flesch, R. F. *The art of clear thinking.* New York: Harper's, 1951.

Flesch, R. F. *How to write, speak and think more effectively.* New York: Harper's, 1960.

Gillie, P. J. A simplified formula for measuring abstraction in writing. *Journal of Applied Psychology,* 1957, **41,** 214–217.

Gray, W. S., and Leary, B. E. *What makes a book readable.* Chicago: University of Chicago Press, 1935.

Gray, W. S., and Monroe, R. *The reading interests and habits of adults.* New York: Macmillan, 1929.

Gunning, R. *The technique of clear writing.* New York: McGraw-Hill, 1952.

Haggerty, M. E. The ability to read: Its measurement and some facts concerning it. *Indiana University Studies,* 1917, **34,** 1–63.

Hockett, J. A. The vocabularies and contents of elementary school readers. *State of California Department of Education Bulletin,* 1938, No. 3.

Hohenberg, J. *The professional journalist.* New York: Henry Holt, 1960.

Hughes, H. M. *News and the human interest story.* Chicago: University of Chicago Press, 1940.

Husek, A., and Suci, G. J., in J. C. Nunnally, Jr., *Popular conceptions of mental health*. New York: Holt, Rinehart & Winston, 1961.

Jersild, A. T., and Ritzman, R. Aspects of language development: The growth of loquacity and vocabulary. *Child Development*, 1938, **9**, 243–259.

Johnson, W. Language and speech hygiene: An application of general semantics. *General Semantics Monographs*, 1939, **1**, 1–54.

Johnson, W., and Tuthill, C. Some semantic aspects of stuttering. *Proceedings of the American Speech Correction Association*, Cleveland, Ohio, 1938.

Klare, G. R., Mabry, J. E., and Gustafson, L. M. The relationship of human interest to immediate retention and to acceptability of technical material. *Journal of Applied Psychology*, 1955, **39**, 92–95.

Kuhlman, F. Mentality tests. *Journal of Educational Psychology*, 1916, **7**, 280–282.

Lorge, I. Predicting reading difficulty of selections for children. *Elementary English Review*, 1939, **16**, 229–233.

Lorge, I. Word lists as background for communication. *Teachers College Record*, 1944, **45**, 543–552.

Ludwig, M. C. Hard words and human interests. *Journalism Quarterly*, 1949, **26**, 167–171.

Lynch, M. D. A stylistic analysis on editing practices. Unpublished paper, The University of Wisconsin, 1962.

Lynch, M. D. Creativeness: Its meaning and measurement. Paper presented at the Convention of the International Reading Association, Kansas City, 1969.

Lynch, M. D., and Bowman, D. L. A correlate measure of creativeness. Unpublished paper, University of Missouri, 1967.

Lynch, M. D., and Collier, M. K. The meaning of creativeness. Unpublished paper, University of Missouri, 1966.

Lynch, M.D., and Kays, D. J. Some effects of distribution of writing tasks and creative aptitude on journalistic performance. *Journalism Quarterly*, 1967, **44**, 508–512.

Lynch, M. D., Kent, B. D., and Carlson, R. C. The meaning of human interest. *Journalism Quarterly*, 1967, **44**, 673–678.

Lynch, M. D., Nettleship, H. M., and Carlson, R. C. The measurement of human interest. *Journalism Quarterly*, 1968, **45**, 226–234.

Lynch, M. D., and Quinn, F. The development of the ISD. Unpublished paper, University of Missouri, 1967.

Lynch, M. D., and Stolz, W. S. Towards a computer analysis of syntactical structure of written English. Paper presented at the Convention of the American Association for Education in Journalism, Chapel Hill, N. C., 1962.

Lynch, M. D., and Swink, E. Some effects of priming, incubation, and creative aptitude on communication performance. *Journal of Communication*, 1967, **17**, 372–382.

McCall, W. A. *How to measure in education*. New York: Macmillan, 1922.

McCall, W. A., and Crabbs, L. M. *Standard test lessons in reading*. New York: Bureau of Publications, Teachers College, Columbia University, 1926.

McCluskey, H. Y. A quantitative analysis of the difficulty of reading materials. Reported in W. S. Gray and B. E. Leary, *What makes a book readable.* Chicago: University of Chicago Press, 1935. P. 103.

McCluskey, H. Y. An experimental comparison of reading the original and digest versions of an article. *Journal of Educational Psychology,* 1940, **31,** 603–615.

Mednick, M. T., Mednick, S. A., and Jung, C. C. Continual association as a function of level of creativity and type of verbal stimulus. *Journal of Abnormal and Social Psychology,* 1964, **69,** 511–515.

Mednick, M. T., Mednick, S. A., and Mednick, E. V. Incubation of creative performance and specific associative priming. *Journal of Abnormal and Social Psychology,* 1964, **69,** 84–88.

Mednick, S. A. The associative basis of the creative process. *Psychological Review,* 1962, **69,** 230–232.

Miles, J. *The vocabulary of poetry.* Los Angeles: University of California Press, 1946.

Monroe, W. S. Standardized silent reading tests. *Journal of Educational Psychology,* 1918, **9,** 303–312.

Morris, C. W. *Signs, language and behavior.* New York: Prentice-Hall, 1946.

Mosteller, F., and Wallace, D. *Inference and disputed authorship: "The Federalist."* Reading, Mass.: Addison-Wesley, 1964.

Ogden, C. K., and Richards, I. A. *The meaning of meaning.* New York: Harcourt, Brace, 1923.

Oliphant, E. H. C. *The plays of Beaumont and Fletcher.* New Haven, Conn.: Yale University Press, 1927.

Osgood, C. E., Suci, G. J., and Tannenbaum, P. H. *The measurement of meaning.* Urbana: University of Illinois Press, 1957.

Osgood, C. E., and Walker, E. Motivation and language behavior: A content analysis of suicide notes. *Journal of Abnormal and Social Psychology,* 1959, **59,** 58–67.

Patterson, D. G., and Tinker, M. A. Studies of typographical factors influencing speed of reading. *Journal of Applied Psychology,* 1932, **16,** 605–613.

Perley, I., cited in E. Rickert, *New methods for the study of literature.* Chicago: University of Chicago Press, 1927. Pp. 39, 142.

Pool, I. De S. *Trends in content analysis.* Urbana: University of Illinois Press, 1959.

Powers, R. D., Sumner, W. A., and Kearl, B. E. A recalculation of four adult readability formulas. *Journal of Educational Psychology,* 1958, **49,** 99–105.

Rickert, E. *New methods for the study of literature.* Chicago: University of Chicago Press, 1927.

Riegel, K. F., Riegel, R. M., and Levine, R. S. An analysis of associative behavior and creativity. *Journal of Personality and Social Psychology,* 1966, **4,** 50–56.

Sanford, F. H. Speech and personality. *Psychological Bulletin,* 1942, **39,** 811–845.

Sherman, D. H. An objective study of the ability of junior high school pupils to use descriptive language. Reported in W. Johnson, Language and speech hygiene: An application of general semantics. *General Semantics Monographs,* 1939, **1,** 9.

Sherman, L. A. *Analytics of literature.* Boston: Ginn, 1893.

Skalbeck, O. M. A statistical analysis of three measures of word length. Reported in W. Johnson, Language and speech hygiene: An application of general semantics. *General Semantics Monographs,* 1939, **1,** 10.

Smith, M. An investigation of the development of the sentence and the extent of vocabulary in young children. *University of Iowa Studies in Child Welfare,* 1939, **3** (5), 1–92.

Spearman, C. *The abilities of man.* New York: Macmillan, 1927.

Stephenson, W. *The study of behavior: Q technique and its methodology.* Chicago: University of Chicago Press, 1953.

Stolz, W. S., Tannenbaum, P. H., and Carstensen, F. V. A stochastic approach to the grammatical coding of English. *Communications of the A. C. M.,* 1965, **8,** 399–405.

Stone, C. R. Recent developments in silent reading tests. *Journal of Educational Research,* 1922, **6,** 102-115

Stone, P. J., Dunphy, D. C., Smith, M. S., Ogilvie, D. M., and associates. *The General Inquirer: A computer approach to content analysis.* Cambridge, Mass.: M. I. T. Press, 1966.

Tannenbaum, P. H., and Elliott, L. L. Factor structure of semantic differential responses to visual forms and prediction of factor scores from structural characteristics of the stimuli. *School of Aerospace Medicine Bulletin,* 1961, **62** (8), 1–8. Brooks Air Force Base, Texas: USAF Aerospace Medical Center (ATC), November 1961.

Tannenbaum, P. H., and Lynch, M. D. Sensationalism: The concept and its measurement. *Journalism Quarterly,* 1960, **37,** 381–392.

Tannenbaum, P. H., and Lynch, M. D. Sensationalism: Some objective message correlates. *Journalism Quarterly,* 1962, **39,** 317–323.

Thorndike, E. L. Measurement of ability in reading. *Teachers College Record,* 1915, **16,** 445–467, and 1916, **17,** 40-67. (a)

Thorndike, E. L. Measurement of achievement in reading: Word knowledge. *Teachers College Record,* 1916, **17,** 340–355. (b)

Thorndike, E. L. *The teacher's word book.* New York: Bureau of Publications, Teachers College, Columbia University, 1921.

Wilson, M. C. The effect of amplifying material upon comprehensions. *Journal of Experimental Education,* 1944, **13,** 5–8.

Yule, G. U. *The statistical study of literary vocabulary.* London: Cambridge University Press, 1944.

Zipf, G. K. *The psycho-biology of language: An introduction to dynamic philosophy.* Boston: Houghton Mifflin, 1935.

Zipf, G. K. *Human behavior and the principle of least effort.* Cambridge, Mass.: Addison-Wesley, 1949.

12

Nonverbal and Kinesic Research

LARRY L. BARKER AND NANCY B. COLLINS

Unlike most of the preceding chapters in this book, this chapter does not focus on a specific research tool or methodology, but rather on a frontier of communication research — nonverbal communication. Some of the parameters of nonverbal communication have been suggested by Ekman (1965):

> The interlacing of fingers, twist of a foot, slump of a shoulder, slant of a hip, curl of the lip, furrow of the brow, direction of gaze, and tilt of the head are instances of what we have called nonverbal behavior. All can occur simultaneously or separately, with or without speech, during an interaction or when an individual is alone, spontaneously or by contrivance.

> . . . . .

> Poets and politicians, psychotherapists and playwrights, dancers and anthropologists have all provided examples of and testimonials to the rich variety of information which can be carried by interactive nonverbal behavior. The claims vary from the modest hypothesis that nonverbal cues provide qualifications about how a verbal message should be interpreted, to notions that this mode of communication escapes conscious censoring and thus reveals the "true," primitive, or repressed side of personality [p. 390].

343

There has been a tendency to use the term *nonverbal communication* synonomously with the term *nonverbal behavior*. However, nonverbal communication is much broader than nonverbal behavior. A room devoid of behaving, living things communicates atmosphere and function. Static clothing communicates the personality of the wearer. So nonverbal behavior is actually a subclass of nonverbal communication and may be further subdivided into indicative and communicative behaviors: "A nonverbal act such as a foottap can be shown to be an indicator of an internal or external event or to be a communicator of a specific item or class of information; but these are two quite different questions which entail different methods of study [Ekman, 1965, p. 391]."

Nonverbal communication is defined in different ways, depending on the interests and perception of the definer. The broadest definition would suggest that nonverbal communication involves all communicative forms other than the spoken or written word. A more restricted definition of nonverbal communication is offered by Ruesch and Kees (1956). They perceive three distinct classes of nonverbal communication: sign language, object language, and action language. The "Current Developments in Communication Research"[1] section of the *Journal of Communication* has included at least 18 different classes of studies in its nonverbal category, encompassing several nonverbal communication forms in addition to those involved with nonverbal behavior: (1) animal and insect; (2) culture; (3) environmental surroundings; (4) gestural, facial expression, bodily movement, and kinesic; (5) human behavior; (6) interaction patterns; (7) learning; (8) machine; (9) media; (10) mental processes, perception, imagination, and creativity; (11) music; (12) paralinguistics; (13) personal grooming and apparel; (14) physiological; (15) pictures; (16) space; (17) tactile and cutaneous; (18) time.

Since the construct "nonverbal communication" encompasses such a variety of forms, communication scholars have developed a diversity of methodologies and criterion measures to assess the many different types and levels of nonverbal communication. Research in nonverbal communication has not only been descriptive and experimental but has also been concerned with developing strategies for coding and analyzing nonverbal events. Because of the breadth of nonverbal communication and the diversity of research tools and methodologies used to investigate it, a single chapter could not adequately treat all types of nonverbal communication research. Therefore, this chapter will attempt to survey briefly several types of nonverbal communication research and elaborate on two representative nonverbal communication methodologies — the kinesic notation system by Birdwhistell (1952) and the Visual Information Display and Retrieval System developed by Ekman, Friesen, and Taussig (1967). New directions and suggested modifications for nonverbal communication research will conclude the chapter.

[1] For an explanation of the classification system of the "Current Developments in Communication Research" section, see Borden (1965).

Taxonomic View of Nonverbal Research[2]

This section attempts to classify and define briefly several types of non-verbal communication research. Some forms of research included in the taxonomy are discussed in detail in other chapters in the text; the primary purpose of this section is to provide an overview of the types of research which have been identified as nonverbal, and to cite examples of studies for each type of research discussed.

(1) *Animal and insect.*[3] It is possible to build a case that some forms of animal and insect communication are actually verbal rather than non-verbal (*e.g.,* the sounds made by porpoises). However, most scholars regard animal communication as a set of nonverbal sounds which have meaning only in their presence or relative frequency. Much of the signifi-cant research in animal communication has been conducted by Sebeok (1965). Mammals like porpoises, dogs, cats, and monkeys have received primary attention thus far, but such insects as bees and ants have also been observed. Porpoises have received the most attention recently with ex-tremely promising results.

Most research with animals has involved coding and classifying sounds and attempting to relate the sounds to events or objects in the animal's immediate environment. Investigators are interested in both the transmis-sion and reception phases of animal communication. They seek to deter-mine which stimuli can be comprehended and acted on systematically by certain animals, what meaningful information animals can transmit to hu-man beings, as well as what symbols animals and insects use to communicate within their own species.

(2) *Culture.*[4] A group of social psychologists and social anthropolo-gists has recently become interested in a form of nonverbal communication research called "ethnomethodology,"[5] which investigates the impact of cul-tural and ethnic variables on the individual and society. Ethnomethodology involves several other forms of nonverbal communication, especially kinesics and paralinguistics.

Most of the cultural research to date has been descriptive and compara-tive. No independent variables are usually manipulated although cultural variables are "assigned" in the statistical analysis of cross-cultural and intracultural research. Dependent variables range along a wide continuum

---

[2] The use of the word *taxonomy* in this section does not include the concept of some hierarchical structure of categories. The categories are described in alphabetical order with no attempt at presenting them in any preconceived sequence. In addition, several classes are not mutually exclusive.

[3] Examples of animal communication studies are Sebeok (1965, 1967) and Lan-caster (1967).

[4] Examples of cultural nonverbal studies are Eisenstadt (1952), Boyenton (1965), and Willhelm (1967). See also Hall (1959).

[5] See Garfinkle (1967).

from gestural patterns to complex meaning systems based on elaborated nonverbal codes.

A major problem in cultural communication research has been the broad background required of the investigator. Ideally, a researcher interested in pursuing cultural communication research should have a substantial background in speech, linguistics, history, sociology, anthropology, and psychology, and a comprehensive understanding of the foreign languages involved. Team research would appear to be most profitable in cultural communication research.

(3) *Environmental surroundings.*[6] Although only limited research has dealt with the effects of environmental surroundings on receiving and transmitting communication, this area seems to have broad social implications. Architects, city planners, and educators, to name but a few, have been intuitively aware of the effect of surroundings on social attitudes and learning ability. To date the research in this area has concentrated on such topics as the effects of aesthetic surroundings on observers' perceptions of facial expressions on both short and long term bases. Independent variables have included the furnishings and decorations of different rooms. For example, in one study three rooms were decorated to represent beautiful, lovely, and average surroundings. Dependent variables have been primarily attitude and rating scales. Physiological measures would also appear to be fruitful as dependent measures in assessing the effects of environmental surroundings on communication behavior.

(4) *Gestural, facial expression, bodily movement, and kinesic.*[7] Since this area of nonverbal research is the primary emphasis in the last part of this chapter, it will not be discussed in depth at this point. The methodology of most nonverbal research involving human movement has been direct observation by trained recorders.

Observational schemes in movement research (*e.g.,* Birdwhistell, 1952) have been used primarily as dependent variables in communication research. However, researchers using other nonverbal methodologies such as stick figures or pictures have attempted to manipulate facial expressions and movement as independent variables. Recent investigations in kinesics and human movement have used mechanical and/or electrical recording devices and computers to assess this type of nonverbal communication.

(5) *Human behavior.*[8] The entire scope of human behavior may be viewed as an important form of nonverbal communication. Studies of be-

[6] Examples of environmental surroundings studies are Maslow and Mintz (1956); Mintz (1956); Wright and Barker (1957).

[7] Examples of such studies are Whiteside, Graybial, and Niven (1965); F. Williams and Tolch (1965); Hamalian (1965).

[8] Examples of behavioral nonverbal studies are Perkins (1965); Sattler (1965); Brehm and Behar (1966). Also see Berelson and Steiner (1964).

havior have ranged from sex drives to play and from games to voting and buying practices. Subjects have ranged from embryos to octogenarians. The complexity of human behavior has been reflected in the methodologies used in investigating it. Most methodologies have focused on observation schemes and coding human acts in a given context.

Independent variables have ranged from reward and punishment to exposure to different physical environments. Dependent variables have involved paper-and-pencil tests, observational schemes, and physiological measures.

Reliability and validity have been persistent problems in all forms of nonverbal research investigating human behavior. Problems of reliability are often present both in the samples of behavior observed and in the criterion measures designed to assess the behavior (see Chapter 1).

(6) *Interaction patterns.*[9] The research concerning human interaction has evolved primarily from social and educational psychologists. Bales (1950), developer of the Interaction Process Analysis (IPA) scheme, is considered a pioneer in the study of group interaction processes. Other investigators like Amidon and Hough (1967) have developed similar methodologies for observing interaction in the classroom. Most interaction analysis methodologies involve trained observers recording the events (both nonverbal and verbal) occurring in a group situation. Since the schemes are often rather complex and the coding of behavior involves intense listening and observing, one of the major inhibitors of interaction research to date has been the time required to train competent observers. (See Chapter 13.)

Independent variables in interaction research have included the following: size of group, role structure of group, leadership styles, task centered functions, group salience, and physical environment for interaction. However, the interaction analysis schemes have been primarily used as dependent variables in interaction research.

(7) *Learning.*[10] Not all forms of learning involve nonverbal communication processes because some learning is directly dependent on verbal symbols. However, several forms of presymbolic learning involve nonverbal communication. Most nonverbal learning research has focused on discrimination among complex visual stimuli and concept formation based on such discriminations. Learning theorists in psychology and education have provided a corpus of research in this form of nonverbal communication. Speech communication researchers have devoted limited attention to nonverbal communication studies involving a learning concept.

[9] Examples of interaction studies are Cogan (1956); Medley and Mitzel (1959); Felipe (1966).
[10] Examples of learning nonverbal studies are Findley and Brady (1965); Mabry (1965); Treisman (1965a).

Independent variables in learning nonverbal research include number of stimuli to be identified, color of stimuli, intensity of stimuli, time needed to discriminate among a number of stimuli, complexity of stimuli, and the conditions under which the stimuli are observed.

Examples of dependent variables in learning nonverbal research are frequency or correct responses in identifying or recalling information about the stimuli, and paper-and-pencil tests related to the stimuli presented.

(8) *Machine.*[11] In the twentieth century, machine communication is more than a research methodology in communication; it is a vital part of our everyday lives. Most machine communication involves the use of electronic or digital computers in which men transmit interrogative messages into the machine and the computer replies on the basis of stored information. The decision making potential of computer-type machines is unlimited when sufficient information has been stored in the machine.

Research in man-machine communication has focused primarily on technical concerns such as the most efficient ways to retrieve stored information. Other research has focused on machine systems for transmitting, receiving, and storing information in usable forms. A comprehensive discussion of the uses of computers in communication research is presented in Chapter 15.

Much developmental and trial-and-error research has dominated machine communication to date, for unlike much unexplored nonverbal research, immediate applications are apparent and almost no "basic research" is needed.

(9) *Media.*[12] Marshall McLuhan (1964) must be credited with stimulating much contemporary interest in the medium as a message form. However, media research precedes McLuhan's writings by several decades. Educators, advertisers, and politicians, in addition to communication researchers, have long been concerned with presentation modes of factual and persuasive messages.

Independent variables in media research are generally the media themselves. Television is contrasted with film, radio with television, books with lectures, and so forth. A large body of media research has concentrated on the relative effectiveness of television as an instructional medium. Most studies have compared information reception, interpretation, recall, and attitude change as a result of the media under which the message was transmitted. Dependent variables have been such measures as comprehension tests and attitude scales in educational research, voting behavior and attitude polls in political research, and product scales and attitude polls in advertising research.

---

[11] Examples of machine communication studies are Scheuch and Stone (1964); Starkweather and Decker (1964); Cooper (1966).
[12] Examples of media nonverbal studies are Amato (1964), Boyenton (1965), and Sissors (1965).

(10) *Mental processes, perception, imagination, and creativity.*[13] All the cognitive and affective processes in human intrapersonal communication may be classified as nonverbal or supraverbal. Research in these areas has been troubled by difficulties with the validity of investigating mental processes. However, several studies in perception and creativity have been conducted with conflicting and often unexpected results. Perception studies have focused on the conditions in which stimuli are perceived at the conscious and subconscious levels, and studies in creativity have attempted to define the construct and determine what mental processes contribute to creative acts. Some applied research has focused on the effect of teaching styles and strategies (*e.g.,* authoritarian versus democratic) on creativity in students.

Independent variables in perceptual research include intensity level of stimuli, duration of stimuli, and frequency of stimuli. Independent variables in creativity research have ranged from exposure to a series of creative exercises to electrical stimulation of the portions of the brain theorized to affect creativity. Dependent variables are often measures of sound or visual discrimination in perception research. In creativity research such dependent measures as creativity tests (usually paper and pencil), number of solutions to a problem, and actual creations (such as an essay, painting, or sculpture) are common.

(11) *Music.*[14] Music as a nonverbal communication form has been systematically studied by musicologists, psychiatrists, and physicists for several years. However, some of the most fruitful nonverbal research with music remains to be conducted. The therapeutic value of music, for example, although often hypothesized, has not been explored fully. Also, because music incorporates sound characteristics similar to human paralinguistic communication (*e.g.,* pitch, intensity, frequency, etc.), it should consequently be investigated as a message form as well as a medium of message transmission.

Independent variables in music research have included the variation of musical forms and patterns, intensity of music, harmonic changes, environmental differences, and noise effects. Dependent variables have included physiological measures of an individual's state of relaxation, attitude scales, and message comprehension (when delivered through or in conjunction with music).

(12) *Paralinguistic.*[15] Most paralinguistic research to date has investigated nonverbal communication variables such as voice quality, inflec-

[13] Examples of such studies are Evans (1965); Gersuni (1965); Latics, Weiss, Clark, and Reynolds (1965). A summary of research in creativity may be found in Parnes and Harding (1962).

[14] Examples of musical nonverbal studies are Rubin and Katz (1946); Mitchell and Zanker (1948); Hiller and Bean (1966).

[15] Examples of paralinguistic nonverbal studies are Black (1949), St. Onge (1956), and Markel (1965).

tion, intensity, and rate. In a sense these variables are not nonverbal and perhaps ought to be termed "extraverbal": they accompany and modify verbal messages rather than substitute for them. Research in paralinguistics has been conducted primarily by scholars in voice science, speech pathology, and audiology. The concept of "noise" has been introduced simultaneously with several paralinguistic variables in an attempt to provide more information about information transmission and reception. Paralinguistic methodologies have involved electronic or mechanical recording and modification of voice samples as well as the recording of speech samples for comparative purposes.

Considerable interest has recently been evinced in rate of speech and its effect on comprehension and persuasion. Research in compressed speech (speech that has been recorded and mechanically altered to increase rate without significantly changing the speaker's vocal quality or pitch) has primarily depended on machines such as the one developed by Fairbanks, Guttman, and Miron (1957) (see Chapter 14). Recently, however, computer technologists and communication scholars have developed computer programs which can compress speech without significant loss of quality. For a review of the literature on compressed speech methodologies see Lawton (1967).

(13) *Personal grooming and apparel.*[16] Behavioral scientists researching personal grooming and clothing attempt to test the hypothesis that one's appearance communicates something about one's personality. One of the earliest investigations in this area (Flugel, 1930) attempted to identify various types of clothes representing stereotyped personality traits. More recent personal appearance studies have been concerned not only with clothing but also with jewelry, makeup, hairstyles, and personal belongings.

Much of the research in this area of nonverbal communication has been descriptive, so no independent variables have been used. In research studying grooming and apparel, independent variables have included different types of clothing, jewelry, and other personal belongings, and degrees of makeup. Dependent variables in these experimental studies have been primarily in-depth standardized interviews, attitude scales, and rating scales attempting to explore perceptions of personality traits.

(14) *Physiological.*[17] Nonverbal research involving physiological variables has focused primarily on the body's reactions to visual and verbal stimuli. Such measures as respiration, galvanic skin response, heart rate, muscle tension, and palmar sweat have been used to establish relationships among bodily reactions and communication stimuli.

---

[16] Studies of communication through grooming and apparel include McKeachie (1952), Compton (1962), and Aiken (1963).

[17] Examples of physiological nonverbal studies are Treisman (1965a), White (1965), and Cronkhite (1966). For a comprehensive review of the literature see Mason (1961).

Most physiological research studies have incorporated some mechanical or electronic apparatus which is attached directly to subjects so that physiological responses may be recorded on paper graphs or magnetic tape for future analysis. This type of research has been criticized for the unrealistic environment in which the subjects must operate (*e.g.,* sitting in a chair with electrodes taped to six points of the body). The contention has been that such laboratory conditions do not exist in the "real world." In order to compensate for the artificiality of laboratory conditions, most researchers attempt to establish base line, or control, data for comparison with experimental data so that fear or general anxiety levels may be controlled statistically (*e.g.,* by using scores representing differences from the base line rather than the absolute magnitude of specific physiological reactions). In addition, new methodologies are being refined which do not involve direct contact with subjects. Theodore Clevenger and Ralph Behnke at The Florida State University are investigating using a telemetry system for recording heart rate similar to the system used with American astronauts. A small transmitter is attached to the subject which transmits heart rate data to a recording device without restricting movement with wiring. Several systems for measuring physiological reactions are presented in Chapter 14.

(15) *Pictures.*[18] Although pictorial nonverbal research has often been used as a methodology or independent variable in other forms of nonverbal research (*e.g.,* in facial expression and kinesic research), much has focused directly on the use of pictures and visual stimuli. The research questions asked in this form of nonverbal research have included: "What do people look at first when they see a picture?" (a critical question in newspaper and magazine advertising), "What colors appeal to people most?" and "What type of people do men and women like best to see in a picture?" Most of the interest in this form of research has stemmed from advertising, so much of the research has consequently been conducted outside the communication research laboratory.

Independent variables in pictorial nonverbal research, in addition to those suggested in the questions above, include relative size of objects in the picture, distance required to perceive the picture under varying light conditions, and size of photographs. Dependent variables are usually forms of recognition and recall of information in the picture, or, in the case of advertising research, the amount of sales resulting from the ad. Some dependent measures have involved pupillary dilation, pupillary constriction, and similar related physiological measures.

(16) *Space.*[19] Both physical and semantic space have been investigated as forms of nonverbal communication. Distance between message

---

[18] Examples of pictorial nonverbal studies are Clark (1965), Gollin (1965), and Bossart (1966).
[19] Examples of spatial nonverbal studies are Furbay (1965); Horowitz (1965); Watson and Graves (1966).

sender and receiver has been manipulated in investigations to determine if it affects attitude change and message acceptance. Some recent research has involved changing the seating arrangement of members in an audience to see if it makes them react differently to speakers and theatrical productions.

Studies in semantic distance have involved relative differences in meaning associated with verbal symbols transmitted by different communicators. The semantic differential has been widely used in the assessment of semantic space (see Chapter 6).

Spatial research has used such independent variables as actual distance between and among communicators, personality types of groups with differing semantic profiles, and the effects of physical space on speaker credibility and audience attitude toward a message. Dependent variables in spatial research have included the semantic differential, attitude scales, and comprehension tests.

(17) *Tactile and cutaneous.*[20] Communication through the skin (cutaneous) and sensory end organs (tactile) has received little systematic investigation by communication scholars. Research in the physiological and biological sciences as well as in the space program has contributed most to what is known about tactile communication. Geldard (1960) has conducted considerable research in this area and has suggested several methodological approaches to the study of cutaneous communication.

Among the independent variables in cutaneous communication investigations are strength of stimulus, mode of impulse transmission (primarily mechanical and electrical), and length of stimulus impulse. Such dependent measures have been used as comprehension tests, number of simultaneous messages received and decoded, and physiological responses such as muscle response, respiration, and heart rate.

A major problem in tactile communication research has been obtaining subjects. Much of the early research incorporated painful electrical impulses, and even the newer mechanical systems sometimes occasion mild discomfort to subjects which may bias research with tactile modes. Communication through the skin has limitless implications for communication systems in the space program; for example, astronauts can receive coded messages via mechanical sensory transmitters without diverting their attention from other tasks which may demand concentration. The primary advantage of cutaneous communication appears to be its capability for being transmitted and received simultaneously with other verbal and nonverbal messages.

(18) *Time.*[21] Time is frequently used as an independent variable in assessing the effects of other nonverbal communication forms and is itself

[20] Examples of tactile and cutaneous nonverbal studies are Geldard (1960), Julesz (1965), and T. Williams (1966).

[21] Examples of time nonverbal studies are Schwartz (1964), Kaswan and Young (1965), and Treisman (1965b).

a useful type of nonverbal communication. Silence — operationally defined as a measured period of time void of aural stimuli — is a widely recognized form of human communication, but little communication research thus far has incorporated silence and other forms of time. Only recently have experimenters begun to investigate this variable systematically and purposefully.

Independent variables in nonverbal time research include frequency of periods of silence or pauses, time lapse between message transmission and reception, and intervening amounts of time between reception of a message and response. Dependent measures in time research include tests of attitude or comprehension related to the manipulated time variable, behavioral changes recorded by observers, and physiological responses to silence during a segment of interpersonal communication.

MOVEMENT AND FACIAL EXPRESSION RESEARCH

Since gestural, facial expression, and other types of movement research are most closely related to speech communication, this section will focus in depth on these forms of nonverbal research. Human physical nonverbal behavior was first explored empirically in the 1920's. The range of disciplines in which such research has been conducted (*e.g.,* speech pathology and audiology, speech communication, clinical psychology, social psychology, cultural anthropology, sociology) is as extensive as the labels under which such research has been described (expressive behavior, person-perception emotion, and the communication dyad, to name but a few), and several writers have provided comprehensive reviews of the literature in physical nonverbal behavior (Brengelmann, 1961; Klein, 1963; Davitz, 1964; Barnlund, 1968 [Barnlund also includes in his review an extensive bibliography containing 133 references]).

Facial Expressions

Facial expressions have been the most widely studied of the various forms of movement. The commonest methodology in facial expression research has been presenting photographs of facial expressions to judges who then label the expressions or assign scale values to the photographs. One of the earliest investigators (Frois-Wittmann, 1930) took a series of 72 photographs of a male model's facial expressions of various emotions. The Frois-Wittmann series has been widely used in nonverbal research in recent years. In the original experiments, Frois-Wittmann (1) asked judges to name the emotion portrayed and (2) compared the answers with the emotion each pose was originally intended to portray.

In a series of later experiments, Schlosberg (1941) attempted to derive a set of scales for evaluating all the pictures in the series. Hulin and Katz (1935) used a technique similar to the Q sort (see Chapter 5): they had judges sort into stacks the pictures which meant the same thing to them. Koen (1966) used the Frois-Wittmann series as stimuli in an experiment to test the codability of facial expressions. The series was also used by Manis (1967) in an experiment to determine the ability of judges to match the facial expressions with written descriptions of these expressions. The Frois-Wittmann series has been used in many experiments trying to determine the kind and amount of information communicated by different facial expressions.

A second set of photographs also has been frequently used in nonverbal research. This set, posed by Marjorie Lightfoot and known as the Lightfoot series, presents a female model's facial expressions. Unlike the Frois-Wittman series, many of the Lightfoot pictures are not intended to portray any emotion. The experiments using the Lightfoot series (Engen, Levy, and Schlosberg, 1958, 1960; Abelson and Sermat, 1962) have studied the same aspects of communication as the previously discussed experiments.

Other investigators have developed their own set of pictures for facial expression research. For example, F. Williams and Tolch (1965) developed a set of pictures at The University of Wisconsin and incorporated them into a creative investigation of human facial expression.

Another methodology devised for facial expression study has been to ask subjects to attempt to communicate a range of emotions through facial expressions to a group of judges (Thompson and Meltzer, 1964; Osgood, 1966). The judges are separated from the subjects by a screen which permits them to see only the subjects' faces; subjects are rated on their ability to communicate the desired emotion to the judges.

With both photographs and live models the nonverbal messages were usually limited to facial expressions. Most of the experiments removed the facial expression from any context or from any relationship with an ongoing communication event. The experimenters have attempted to determine the meanings communicated by these facial expressions, as well as the best way to measure such meanings.

Posture and Body Position

Other experiments have concentrated on posture or body position as a means of communicating. Sarbin and Hardyck (1955) devised a series of stick figure drawings representing various postures. This Stick Figure Test was used experimentally to determine what each posture communicated to a group of judges. Rosenberg and Langer (1965) used the Stick Figure Test (Figure 1) and asked judges to rate each figure on six referent dimensions. This test, like the methodologies discussed above, eliminated context variables as well as all other aspects of the communication situation. The stick figures also replaced nonverbal communication with caricatures.

The difficulties to be overcome in movement research in nonverbal communication were summarized by Ekman (1964): "Research on body

FIGURE 1

Stick Figure Test

From B. G. Rosenberg and J. Langer, "A study of postural-gestural communication." *Journal of Personality and Social Psychology,* **2** (1965), 594. Copyright © 1965 by the American Psychological Association, and reproduced by permission.

movement and facial expression has had to deal with a phenomenon which is continuously occurring, has no readily apparent unit of measurement or method of evaluation, and is both difficult and expensive to record [p. 295]." The research methodologies discussed have attempted to deal with these problems. Rather than studying the phenomena as they occurred, the researchers isolated a series of single events. They used each experimental stimulus as the unit of measurement within the study and experimented with the method of evaluation. The stimuli in each experiment were relatively easy and inexpensive to record. The methodology of kinesics, an approach to the study of body movement as a means of communication, has provided different solutions to the complex problems involved in studying body movement and facial expressions.

KINESIC RESEARCH[22]

This section will focus on the kinesic analysis system proposed by Bird-whistell (1952) because it represents most of the observational systems for studying nonverbal human behavior, was one of the earliest systems developed, and has been the most widely cited in the literature. Examples of more recent methods of describing and recording nonverbal behavior may be found in articles by Sainesbury (1954); Jones and Nara (1955); Jones, O'Connell, and Hanson (1958); Jones and Hanson (1961); Dierssen, Lorenc, and Spitalerl (1961); Buehler and Richmond (1963).

The Birdwhistell observational system has stimulated communication researchers to approach nonverbal cues systematically in their investigations. Birdwhistell proposed that the initial focus of kinesics should be on deriving units of measurement which can be employed in the study of movement. According to Birdwhistell, the absence of units for measuring movement has hampered past research; without them, the study of body communication can never become a science: "Independent research may become communicable and testable by various scientists only when they are sure they are examining similar phenomena [p. 14]."

First, the kinesic approach considers movement as a basic and integral part of communication. Communication is seen as a multichannel system, with language representing only one channel. Second, until research indicates otherwise, all patterns of body movement are regarded as socially learned, rather than natural or inborn. Thus, all movement may be studied as part of communication.

Units and Methodology

The study of kinesics initially requires an understanding of the units of kinesics. Kinesic units are ranges of movement with the same meaning. In the experimental setting, subjects are asked if one movement or position means something different from another movement or position. If so, that movement or position is said to have *differential meaning*. No attempt is made to determine what is meant, but only whether or not one movement means something different from another movement. The movements which have the same differential meaning comprise a unit.

The basic kinesic unit is the *kine,* defined as the smallest particle of body movement with discriminational meaning. There are kines for all parts of the body capable of transmitting visible body motion. Some kines may have the same differential meaning. Those kines which can be freely substituted for each other without altering meaning are called *allokines.* In verbal language, for example, certain ranges of sounds are all accepted as meaning the same thing. That is, everyone's "p" sound is different, but in most

---

[22] A dictionary of kinesic terms appears on pp. 366–367 to aid the reader in understanding kinesic terminology.

cases we interpret all these different sounds as meaning "p." In the same way, different allokines are interchangeable. All the kines which are allo-kinic make up a *kineme*. The kineme, or group of allokines, is the smallest set of body movements with differential meaning. Birdwhistell hypothesized from his research that general American movement comprises approximately 50 to 60 kinemes.

Beyond deriving basic units, the kinesic methodology seeks to derive patterns of movement. No kine ever occurs alone; it always occurs within a pattern. For example, the wink never occurs in isolation, but always in conjunction with kines in other parts of the face and body. These patterns or complexes of body movement are termed *kinemorphs*. Gestures, for example, represent base kinemorphs, or kinemorphs which are explicitly defined by a particular culture. Even though many persons consider gestures the complete system of body movement communication, they actually are a very small and extremely formalized part of the patterned body movement with differential meaning.

In order to determine kinemorphs, researchers ask subjects to distinguish differential meanings in a lengthy series of kinesic patterns in which a single kine is varied each time. Such contrast series yield information on the significance of a particular kine in a particular kinemorph.

Several kinemorphs can be combined into a more complex pattern called a *kinemorphic construction*. Kinemorphic constructions are derived by the same process as for determining differential meaning.

The kinesic approach also includes a less difficult and less expensive means of recording movement, previously suggested by Ekman (1964). The system of kinesic recording is based on *kinegraphs,* pictorial symbols used to represent kines. Kinemorphs are represented by combinations of kinegraphs. For the purpose of recording, the body is divided into eight major areas, and each body area is transcribed in a different type of kine-graphic symbol (see Figure 2, pp. 358–359). Movement can be quickly and easily recorded by kinegraphic transcription without the use of mechanical equipment. In addition, because the observer's recording is standardized, the transcription can be analyzed and interpreted by someone else.

The derivation and recording of units are based solely on experimentation involving differential meaning. The research reveals only those units of movements which have differential meaning, not what the various movements mean. The meaning of movement patterns in communication is referred to as *social* or *contextual meaning.* Analyzing the social meaning of movement is similar to current theories about words; meanings of words are dependent on context and individual use, and so are the meanings of movements. Common meanings of words can be studied within a range of contexts, and individual differences can be compared to common usage patterns. In the same way, movements can be studied in context to determine their usual meanings.

FIGURE 2

Example of Kinesic Analysis

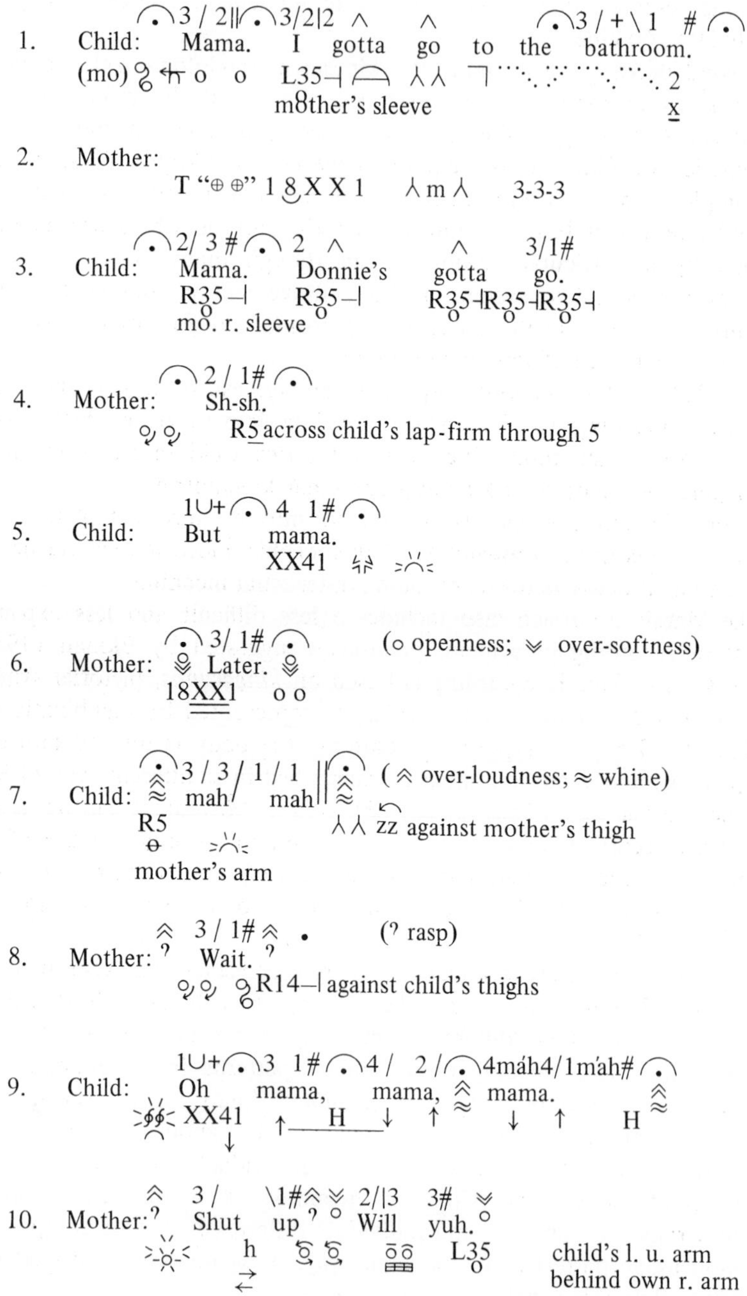

1. Child: Mama. I gotta go to the bathroom.
   (mo) mother's sleeve

2. Mother:
   T "⊕ ⊕" 1 8 X X 1   3-3-3

3. Child: Mama. Donnie's gotta go.
   R35 R35 R35 R35 R35
   mo. r. sleeve

4. Mother: Sh-sh.
   R5 across child's lap-firm through 5

5. Child: But mama.
   XX41

6. Mother: Later.   (○ openness; ⌄ over-softness)
   18XX1   o o

7. Child: mah/ mah   (⋏ over-loudness; ≈ whine)
   R5   zz against mother's thigh
   mother's arm

8. Mother: Wait.   (ˀ rasp)
   R14 against child's thighs

9. Child: Oh mama, mama, mama.
   XX41   H   H

10. Mother: Shut up Will yuh.
    L35   child's l. u. arm
    behind own r. arm

FIGURE 2 (*continued*)

*[Verbal account of the patterns of movement
represented by the kinesic symbols]*

Stress and intonation are indicated above the pertinent text, using symbols provided in Trager and Smith's *Outline of English Structure*; voice-qualifiers, *e.g.*, the drawl, are indicated by symbols developed by them. A phonemic transcription of the text is also provided. Kinesic symbols are given below the pertinent text, but merely illustrated, not translated. Those interested in a more detailed analysis are referred to the author's *Introduction to Kinesics*, University of Louisville Press.

1. This situation was observed on a bus. The little boy was seated next to the window. He seemed tired of looking out of the window and, after surveying all of the car ads and the passengers, he leaned toward his mother and pulled at her sleeve, pouted and vigorously kicked his legs.

2. His mother had been sitting erectly in her seat, her packages on her lap, and her hands lightly clasped around the packages. She was apparently "lost in thought."

3. When the boy's initial appeal failed to gain the mother's attention, he began to jerk at her sleeve again, each jerk apparently stressing his vocalization.

4. The mother turned and looked at him, shushed him, and placed her right hand firmly across his thighs.

5. The boy protested audibly, clenched both fists, pulled them with stress against his chest. At the same time he drew his legs up against the restraint of his mother's hand. His mouth was drawn down and his upper face was pulled into a tight frown.

6. The mother withdrew her hand from his lap and resettled in her former position with her hands clasped around the packages.

7. The boy grasped her upper arm tightly, continued to frown. When no immediate response was forthcoming, he turned and thrust both knees into the lateral aspect of her left thigh.

8. She looked at him, leaned toward him, and slapped him across the anterior portion of his upper legs.

9. He began to jerk his clenched fists up and down, vigorously nodding between each inferior-superior movement of his fists.

10. She turned, frowning, and with her mouth pursed, she spoke to him through her teeth. Suddenly she looked around, noted that the other passengers were watching, and forced a square smile. At the same time that she finished speaking, she reached her right hand in under her left arm and squeezed the boy's arm. He sat quietly.

[From R. L. Birdwhistell, "Background to Kinesics."] Reprinted by permission from *ETC: A Review of General Semantics,* Vol. XXV, No. 1; [pp. 14–15]; copyright 1955, by the International Society for General Semantics.

The basic method of this type of kinesic study is *context analysis*. Context analysis places given kinesic units in varying social contexts in order to derive meaning. Since meaning is not inherent in the movement itself, kinesics in no way attempts to construct a glossary of movements or gestures. Rather, as kinesics is based on undefined units, it allows for interpreting social meaning in context (see Figure 3).

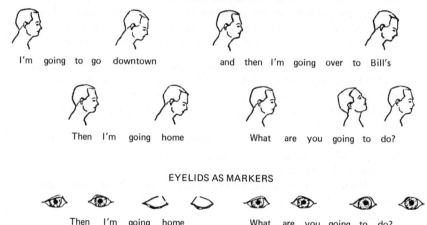

HEAD MOVEMENTS AS MARKERS

I'm going to go downtown   and then I'm going over to Bill's

Then I'm going home   What are you going to do?

EYELIDS AS MARKERS

Then I'm going home   What are you going to do?

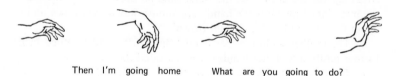

HAND MOVEMENTS AS MARKERS

Then I'm going home   What are you going to do?

FIGURE 3

Postural-Kinesic Markers of American Syntactic Sentences

From A. E. Scheflen, "The significance of posture in communication systems." *Psychiatry*, 1964, **27**, 321. Reprinted by permission of the author, the publisher, and the originator, Ray L. Birdwhistell.

The discovery of markers is a noteworthy example of the use of context analysis. Birdwhistell (1965) transcribed conversations and other communication events verbally and kinegraphically. In later analysis he eliminated all kinesic activity which did not accompany actual verbalization. In the remaining movements he discovered that certain movements always accompanied specific language behavior. For example, different movements characterized statements and questions. These movements were labeled *markers* for verbal behavior. Using context analysis on filmed psychiatric interviews, Scheflen (1964) discovered markers for larger units, such as a point made by one of the participants or a change of subject. Context analysis was used in these cases to determine the messages communicated by specific movements in a given context.

Although context analysis has been the primary method of establishing contextual meaning, kinesic data could be analyzed in other ways. The point is that the units and patterns of movement must be isolated first.

Appraisal of Kinesic Research

Kinesic observation systems like Birdwhistell's provide valuable contributions to the study of body movement in communication. Currently, however, they have several weaknesses. The experimentally derived basic kines and kinemorphs are abstracted units explained only by kinegraphs and abbreviated verbal descriptions. No pictures or examples are available to clarify precisely what the movement unit is.

A second major weakness is in the use of kinegraphs as a recording system. Although the system is rapid and relatively simple to use, the kinegraphs cannot be typed, nor are they adaptable for use with computers. As Birdwhistell (1965) suggests, this problem would be best solved by changing the recording symbols. A similar problem with such notational schemes is the tendency of the observer to simplify complex behavioral patterns and favor gross patterns of behavior rather than fine or latent bodily movements. This problem is a direct function of having both to observe and to make notations while attempting to record the event. Recent research has indicated that when such forced perceptual division occurs, comprehension is significantly reduced (Barker, Kibler, and Hunter, 1968).

A final weakness in the Birdwhistell system is that it does not provide for sampling nonverbal behavior but only for recording an entire event. This poses an unrealistic and uneconomical burden on a researcher who might profitably sample in his research.

Despite these weaknesses, the methodology of kinesics permits a rather sophisticated framework for research into body movement. The first and greatest advantage of the methodology is that it permits objectification in collecting and analyzing data on movement; it can supply objective units with differential meaning which are applicable to any communication situation. The observer's first task involves objective recording rather than making immediate subjective judgments concerning intended meaning. The ongoing event can thus be objectively recorded for later analysis. Prior methods of analyzing a nonverbal communication event were less objective because the researcher, being unable to record the entire range of action, was forced to choose those movements which he intuitively believed had meaning. Kinegraphic recording allows the collection of masses of data and eliminates the need for intuitive selection.

Objectifying data on movement also permits much more sophisticated experimental research. Movement, posture, and expression can be specified and manipulated by previously derived units. The nonverbal message need not be vague and poorly controlled, but can be subjected to experimental rigor. Any experiment where kinesic data are carefully specified can be replicated or its results can be safely compared to those in other similarly controlled experiments.

No single methodology is perfectly suited to all research in any field; many kinesic observation systems offer solutions to many methodological problems in movement research, providing units of measurement which permit rapid, inexpensive, and objective recording of these events. However, the following computerized system developed by Ekman *et al.* (1967) may prove even more valuable in future kinesic research.

A Computerized Approach to Kinesic Research

One of the mentioned weaknesses of the Birdwhistell notational scheme is the loss of specific detail caused by the divided perception of the observer-recorder. If the events to be analyzed were first recorded on motion picture film or video tape, this weakness could be significantly reduced by having the observer view the event a number of times and attend to different details of the event each time. Such a procedure would definitely increase the reliability and accuracy of the recorded observation, but the increased time and expense would make it unfeasible in most instances. In addition, the other weaknesses in the system would not be helped by this repeated viewing procedure.

Ekman and his associates (1967, pp. 3–4) have attempted to overcome some of the problems associated with notational schemes like Birdwhistell's by combining video tape recordings with a computerized storage and retrieval system for visual information. Their initial system, called VID-R (Visual Information Display and Retrieval), was in final stages of development at the time of this writing. The system was designed to satisfy five functional specifications which Ekman *et al.* deemed desirable for viewing and analyzing permanent visual records.

> (1) The operator should be able to view his record at various slowed and accelerated speeds.

> (2) Digital addresses for search and retrieval should ideally be stored for the smallest unit a recording unit can differentiate (24 separate addresses per second with sound motion picture film, 30 per second for video tape).

> (3) The operator should be able to find automatically any event within his record, retrieving this event by requesting an address or by using an index or measurement curve.

(4) Any series of events located in the record should be capable of being reorganized into a new record, in any predetermined sequence, for further viewing.

(5) The observer should have rapid access to a visual example which defines the meaning or the boundaries of any of the investigator's codes or measurement procedures.

By incorporating high speed video tape recording and viewing equipment with a computerized search system, the VID-R unit satisfies these desired functional characteristics.

COMPONENTS OF THE VID-R SYSTEM

The VID-R unit is designed to accept either 16mm film or video tape as the recording medium; however, all analyses are performed on video tape. One component of the system transforms motion picture films onto electronic video tape so that researchers can use existing film libraries and the flexibility of motion picture equipment in settings where video tape recording is not feasible or economical. In addition to the film-to-television chain, Ekman *et al.* list the following components of the VID-R system:

1. Two Sony PV 120U videotape recorders with complete remote control of the functions; playback, record, fast forward, rewind, variable slowed-motion, stop motion, variable high-speed playback, and stop.

2. One video-disc recorder capable of recording at least 20 seconds of video information and playback at high-resolution slowed and stop motion.

3. Three high resolution television monitors.

4. One Teletype ASR 33, keyboard-printer with papertape punch and reader. This is the means of operator-system communication.

5. One Digital Equipment Corporation PDP-8 programmed data processor. This low cost computer provides the logic for the operations to be described.

6. One video and audio interface to perform data transfers between the computer and recorders.

7. Three videotape recorder controllers capable of performing the instructions of the computer, to place the recorder into the proper motion to perform the task.

8. One or two high resolution Vidicon cameras for field recording [pp. 5–6].

OPERATING THE VID-R SYSTEM

If the original event is recorded on film, the first step in operating the VID-R system is to put the film onto video tape via the film-to-television chain. If the original event is recorded on video tape this transfer step is bypassed. When video tapes are used to record the event, each frame on the tape (162,000 in a 90-minute reel) is automatically numbered with a six-digit code, thus allowing eventual location of the unit of behavior recorded on the video frame. The code numbers are recorded directly on the tape in an area outside the viewing surface. The system is also designed to add the code numbers to the video tape when transferring from 16mm to the tape.

After the film-to-tape transfer has been completed and the frames have been coded, the operator is ready to view the video tape recording. He may view the recording at normal, slow, or high speeds and he may stop motion at any time. By using the high speed playback, a 90-minute reel of video tape may be viewed in approximately six minutes.

The next step in the operation begins the series of procedures which convert the videotaped events into data suitable for quantitative or categorical analysis. If the investigator desires to find all similar instances of an action or event, he finds the first frame where the desired action occurs on the tape and then instructs the computer to search for all similar events which follow and to record them in succession on a separate video tape. By repeating this procedure (for example with hand movements, facial expressions, leg movements, and so forth), the investigator can obtain an automatically edited tape containing only those specific actions or events with which he is concerned. He is thus completely freed from the time consuming task of viewing the tape over and over again to code or manually edit the tape in order to compare similar events or actions. The system also allows a sample action or event from a source outside the recording to trigger an automatic search for similar events or actions on the tape.

Instructions to and from the VID-R system are through the teletypewriter of the computer, thus providing a typed or a punched-tape record of codes, locations, and descriptions of all events on the video tape.

APPLICATIONS OF THE VID-R SYSTEM

The VID-R system has been developed primarily for use in analyzing nonverbal behavior occurring in psychiatric interviews, but the applications to other forms of nonverbal research are apparent. When the system is perfected and operationalized, it will be possible to develop a systematic dictionary of kinesic variables including specific models of each action or event. This will in turn provide a more theoretically sound basis for research in social kinesics and other forms of human nonverbal behavior. The system could also be applied to indexing film and taped libraries as well as programmed instruction involving visual concepts.

FUTURE DIRECTIONS FOR NONVERBAL AND KINESIC RESEARCH

Although countless studies have been tangentially related to the nonverbal communication process, few have been concentrated systematic attempts to investigate directly the nonverbal communication process. Future research needs to focus on the interrelationships between verbal and nonverbal communication as well as the relative effectiveness of nonverbal communication as an information imparting and persuasive communication form.

As was discussed earlier, the majority of experiments in movement have been limited to the study of facial expressions. Recognizing that a whole pattern of movement usually accompanies a facial expression would indicate a broader approach to the study of nonverbal communication of emotion. Although facial expression alone may still be studied, experimental research also could be conducted to determine the amount of information communicated by facial expression alone, as compared to the amount communicated by the same facial expression in concert with the entire bodily unit. Specifying units in facial and body stimuli is beginning to permit the manipulation of more complex variables in this area of nonverbal research.

Specifying kinesic units also will permit comparisons of results with other nonkinesic research methodologies. For example, the Frois-Wittmann and Lightfoot series could be analyzed separately in terms of kinesic units. The photographs could then be analyzed to determine the kinesic resemblances among them. Results obtained in these experiments could then be reanalyzed to determine whether or not those expressions which were labeled or scaled alike were kinesically similar. By compiling the results the researcher could find those kinemorphic ranges in the pictures which seemed to have similar meaning. From these results further experimentation could be conducted to determine whether similar kinesic patterns portrayed by other models communicated the same information to other judges. These changes would not alter the basic intent or results of the studies, but the revisions would provide additional data, make results comparable, and provide avenues for further research.

The kinesic methodology also will permit future analysis of complex communication events in context. Nearly all previous empirical research in body movement has removed the nonverbal event from its context. Facial expressions or postures out of context cannot be assumed to have the same meaning they would have in context. One obvious example is the psychiatric interview, which is far more than a series of postures and expressions. Using kinesic methodology and context analysis, Scheflen (1964) has begun to study the role of movement in this complex communication situation. He has analyzed films of such interviews to determine which kinesic variables always accompany or precede certain events and types of behavior. In this way he hopes to be able to identify common patterns and isolate deviations from the established patterns. Similar research could be conducted in other realms of nonverbal communication.

Some additional directions for future nonverbal research might include:

(1) Correlational studies between nonverbal acts and verbal messages

(2) Additional mapping of nonverbal patterns for use in later experimental studies

(3) Additional use of nonverbal cues as independent variables in communication research

(4) Research in the development and refinement of observational systems, observer training programs, and observation category validation procedures

(5) Computerized systems for mapping, coding, and analyzing nonverbal data (*e.g.,* VID-R)

The last direction appears to hold the greatest potential for nonverbal communication research in the not too distant future. Once the problem of directly coding nonverbal data is solved, the researcher can begin to study a broader range of relationships within the scope of nonverbal communication. Voice tracks and physiological measures (*e.g.,* heart rate, GSR, etc.) on the computer tape simultaneous with the visual images will make possible investigations of problems and relationships heretofore impossible to approach.

Dictionary of Kinesic Terminology

Act: a differential meaning pattern or kinemorph in any given area of the body which occurs in context

Action: a combination of two or more acts which occur simultaneously in context

Allokines: members of a class of movements, all of which have the same meaning or can be freely substituted for each other without changing the meaning

Context analysis: the method of determining social meaning by placing kinesic units and patterns in a given social context and determining meaning within that context

Contextual (*or* **Social) meaning:** the meaning a unit or pattern of movement communicates in a given situation

Differential meaning: variation in a unit or pattern of movement which makes it seem to mean something different from another unit or pattern

Kineme: one kine with all its allokines, forming the least class of body movements with differential meaning

Kine: smallest and simplest unit of movement which has discriminational meaning

Kinegraph: one of a set of transcription symbols for recording observed kinesic units

Kinemorph: a pattern of movement comprised of kines, including gestures

Kinemorphic construction: complex pattern of movement comprised of kines, including gestures

Kinemorphology: the systematic analysis of patterns of kines

Kinesics: a systematic, empirical study of body motion in order to determine the role of such movement in multichannel communication

Markers: particular movements which occur regularly in association with or in place of language arrangements and conversational stages in spoken English

Microkinesics: the part of kinesics which focuses on the derivation of units of movement

Prekinesics: the part of kinesics which deals with the physiological study of the limits of movement and the physiological determinants of movement

Social kinesics: the part of kinesics which deals with the study of units and patterns of movement in context in order to determine their function in communication

References and Selected Readings

Abelson, R. P., and Sermat, V. Multidimensional scaling of facial expressions. *Journal of Experimental Psychology,* 1962, **63**, 546–551.

Aiken, L. The relationships of dress to selected measures of personality in undergraduate women. *Journal of Social Psychology,* 1963, **59**, 119–128.

Amato, P. P. A comparative study of programmed instruction and video-taped lectures as part of a course in public speaking. *Speech Monographs,* 1964, **31**, 461–466.

Amidon, E. J., and Hough, J. B. (Eds.) *Interaction analysis: Theory, research and application.* Reading, Mass.: Addison-Wesley, 1967.

Bales, R. F. *Interaction process analysis.* Cambridge, Mass.: Addison-Wesley, 1950.

Barker, L. L., Kibler, R. J., and Hunter, E. C. An empirical study of overlap rating effects. *The Speech Teacher,* 1968, **17**, 160–166.

Barnlund, D. C. (Ed.) *Interpersonal communication: Survey and studies.* Boston: Houghton Mifflin, 1968.

Berelson, B., and Steiner, G. A. *Human behavior — An inventory of scientific findings.* New York: Harcourt, Brace & World, 1964.

Birdwhistell, R. L. *Introduction to kinesics.* Louisville: University of Louisville Press, 1952.

Birdwhistell, R. L. Background to kinesics. *ETC.,* 1955, **13**, 10–18.

Birdwhistell, R. L. Communication without words. In P. Alexandre (Ed.), *L'aventure humaine.* Paris: Société d'Etudes Litéraires et Artistiques, 1965. Pp. 36–43.

Black, J. W. Inflection of repeated messages. *Speech Monographs,* 1949, **16**, 217–220.

Borden, G. Current developments in communication research. *Journal of Communication,* 1965, **15**, 110–117.

Bossart, W. Form and meaning in the visual arts. *British Journal of Aesthetics,* 1966, **6,** 259–271.

Boyenton, W. The Negro turns to advertising. *Journalism Quarterly,* 1965, **42,** 227–235.

Brehm, J., and Behar, L. Sexual arousal, defensiveness and sex preference in affiliation. *Journal of Experimental Research in Personality,* 1966, **1,** 195–200.

Brengelmann, J. C. Expressive movements and abnormal behavior. In H. J. Eysenck (Ed.), *Handbook of abnormal psychology.* New York: Basic Books, 1961. Pp. 62–107.

Buehler, R. E., and Richmond, J. F. Interpersonal communication behavior analysis: A research method. *Journal of Communication,* 1963, **13,** 146–155.

Clark, H. Recognition memory for random shapes as a function of complexity, association value and delay. *Journal of Experimental Psychology,* 1965, **69,** 590–595.

Cogan, M. L. Theory and design of a study of teacher-pupil interaction. *Harvard Educational Review,* 1956, **26,** 315–342.

Compton, N. Personal attributes of color and design preferences in clothing fabrics. *Journal of Psychology,* 1962, **31,** 351–363.

Cooper, H. Put corporate information and data automation in perspective. *Systems and Procedures,* 1966, **17** (3), 10–14.

Cronkhite, G. Autonomic correlates of dissonance and attitude change. *Speech Monographs,* 1966, **33,** 392–399.

Davitz, J. R. (Ed.) *The communication of emotional meaning.* New York: McGraw-Hill, 1964.

Dierssen, G., Lorenc, M., and Spitalerl, R. M. A new method for graphic study of human movements. *Neurology,* 1961, **2,** 610–618.

Eisenstadt, S. N. Communication processes among immigrants in Israel. *Public Opinion,* 1952, **16,** 42–58.

Ekman, P. Body position, facial expression and verbal behavior during interviews. *Journal of Abnormal and Social Psychology,* 1964, **68,** 295–301.

Ekman, P. Communication through nonverbal behavior: A source of information about an interpersonal relationship. In S. S. Tomkins and C. E. Izard (Eds.), *Affect, cognition and personality.* New York: Springer, 1965. Pp. 390–442.

Ekman, P., Friesen, W. V., and Taussig, T. J. VID-R and SCAN: Tool and methods for the automated analysis of visual records. Paper presented at the National Conference on Content Analysis, The Annenberg School of Communications, University of Pennsylvania, Philadelphia, November 1967.

Engen, T., Levy, N., and Schlosberg, H. The dimensional analysis of a new series of facial expressions. *Journal of Experimental Psychology,* 1958, **55,** 454–458.

Engen, T., Levy, N., and Schlosberg, H. Woodworth scale values of the Lightfoot pictures of facial expressions. *Journal of Experimental Psychology,* 1960, **60,** 121–125.

Evans, C. R. Some studies of pattern perception using a stabilized retinal image. *British Journal of Psychology,* 1965, **1,** 121–133.

Fairbanks, G., Guttman, N., and Miron, M. Effects of time compression upon the comprehension of connected speech. *Journal of Speech and Hearing Disorders,* 1957, **22,** 10–19.

Felipe, N. Interpersonal distance and small group interaction. *Cornell Journal of Social Relations,* 1966, **1,** 59–64.

Findley, J. D., and Brady, J. Facilitation of large ration performance by use of conditioned reinforcement. *Journal of Experimental Analysis of Behavior,* 1965, **8,** 125–129.

Flugel, J. *The psychology of clothes.* London: Hogarth Press, 1930.

Frois-Wittmann, J. The judgment of facial expression. *Journal of Experimental Psychology,* 1930, **13,** 113–151.

Furbay, A. L. The influence of scattered versus compact seating on audience response. *Speech Monographs,* 1965, **32,** 144–148.

Garfinkle, H. *Studies in ethnomethodology.* Englewood Cliffs, N. J.: Prentice-Hall, 1967.

Geldard, F. A. Some neglected possibilities of communication. *Science,* 1960, **131,** 1581–1587.

Gersuni, G. V. Organization of afferent flow and the process of external signal discrimination. *Neuropsychologia,* 1965, **3,** 95–109.

Gollin, E. Perceptual learning of incomplete pictures. *Perceptual and Motor Skills,* 1965, **21,** 439–445.

Hall, E. T. *The silent language.* New York: Doubleday, 1959.

Hamalian, L. Communication by gesture in the Middle East. *ETC.,* 1965, **22,** 43–49.

Harrison, R. Nonverbal communication: Explorations into time, space, action, and object. In J. J. Campbell and H. W. Hepler (Eds.), *Dimensions of communication.* Belmont, Cal.: Wadsworth, 1965. Pp. 158–174.

Hiller, L., and Bean, C. Information theory analyses of four sonata expositions. *Journal of Music Theory,* 1966, **10,** 96–137.

Horowitz, M. Human spatial behavior. *American Journal of Psychotherapy,* 1965, **19,** 20–28.

Hulin, W. S., and Katz, D. The Frois-Wittman pictures of facial expression. *Journal of Experimental Psychology,* 1935, **18,** 482–498.

Jones, F. P., and Hanson, J. A. Time-space pattern in a gross body movement. *Perceptual and Motor Skills,* 1961, **12,** 35–41.

Jones, F. P., and Nara, M. Interrupted light photography to record the effect of changes in the poise of the head upon patterns of movement and posture in man. *Journal of Psychology,* 1955, **40,** 125–131.

Jones, F. P., O'Connell, D. N., and Hanson, J. A. Color-coded multiple image photography for studying related rates of movement. *Journal of Psychology,* 1958, **45,** 247–251.

Julesz, B. Texture and visual perception. *Scientific American,* 1965, **212** (2), 38–48.

Kaswan, J., and Young, S. Effect of stimulus variables on choice reaction times and thresholds. *Journal of Experimental Psychology,* 1965, **69,** 511–514.

Klein, Z. E. The nonverbal communication of feelings: A review of literature. Unpublished manuscript, 1963.

Koen, F. Codability of complex stimuli: Three modes of representation. *Journal of Personality and Social Psychology,* 1966, **3,** 435–441.

Lancaster, J. B. Communication systems of old world monkeys and apes in linguistics in communication. *International Social Science Journal,* 1967, **19,** 28–35. (Special Issue.)

Latics, V. G., Weiss, B., Clark, R., and Reynolds, M. Overt "mediating" behavior during temporally spaced responding. *Journal of Experimental Analysis of Behavior,* 1965, **8,** 107–116.

Lawton, R. E. Listening to rate controlled speech: A technique for improving education and communication in the Air Force and in industry. Unpublished Master's thesis, George Washington University, 1967.

Mabry, J. H. Discrimination functions based on a delay in the reinforcement relations. *Journal of Experimental Analysis of Behavior,* 1965, **8,** 97–103.

Manis, M. Context effects in communication. *Journal of Personality and Social Psychology,* 1967, **5,** 326–334.

Markel, N. N. The reliability of coding paralanguage: Pitch, loudness, and tempo. *Journal of Verbal Learning and Verbal Behavior,* 1965, **4,** 306–308.

Maslow, A. H., and Mintz, N. L. Effects of esthetic surroundings: I. Initial effects of three esthetic conditions upon perceiving "energy" and "well-being" in faces. *Journal of Psychology,* 1956, **41,** 247–254.

Mason, R. E. *Internal perception and bodily functioning.* New York: International Universities Press, 1961.

McKeachie, W. Lipstick as a determiner of first impressions of personality: An experiment for the general psychology course. *Journal of Social Psychology,* 1952, **36,** 241–244.

McLuhan, M. *Understanding media: The extensions of man.* New York: McGraw-Hill, 1964.

Medley, D. M., and Mitzel, H. E. Some behavioral correlates of teacher effectiveness. *Journal of Educational Psychology,* 1959, **50,** 239–246.

Mintz, L. Effects of esthetic surroundings: II. Prolonged and repeated experience in a "beautiful" and an "ugly" room. *Journal of Psychology,* 1956, **41,** 459–466.

Mitchell, S. D., and Zanker, A. The use of music in group therapy. *Journal of Mental Science,* 1948, **94,** 737–738.

Osgood, C. E. Dimensionality of semantic space for communication via facial expression. *Scandinavian Journal of Psychology,* 1966, **7,** 1–30.

Parnes, S. J., and Harding, H. F. *A source book for creative thinking.* New York: Charles Scribner's Sons, 1962.

Perkins, H. V. Classroom behavior and underachievement. *American Educational Research Journal,* 1965, **2,** 1–12.

Rosenberg, B. G., and Langer, J. A study of postural-gestural communication. *Journal of Personality and Social Psychology,* 1965, **2,** 593–597.

Rubin, H. E., and Katz, E. Aurotone films for the treatment of psychotic depressions in an Army general hospital. *Journal of Clinical Psychology,* 1946, **2,** 333–340.

Ruesch, J., and Kees, W. *Nonverbal communication.* Los Angeles: University of California Press, 1956.

Sainesbury, P. A method of recording spontaneous movements by time-sampling motion pictures. *Journal of Mental Science,* 1954, **100,** 742–748.

Sarbin, T. R., and Hardych, C. D. Conformance in role perception as a personality variable. *Journal of Consulting Psychology,* 1955, **19,** 109-111.

Sattler, J. A theoretical, developmental, and clinical investigation of embarrassment. *Genetic Psychology Monographs,* 1965, **71,** 19–60.

Scheflen, A. E. The significance of posture in communication systems. *Psychiatry,* 1964, **27,** 316–331.

Scheuch, E. K., and Stone, P. J. The General Inquirer approach to an international retrieval system for survey archives. *The American Behavioral Scientist,* 1964, **7,** (10), 23–28.

Schlosberg, H. A scale for the judgment of facial expressions. *Journal of Experimental Psychology,* 1941, **27,** 316–331.

Schwartz, M. F. The lengths of silence in initial *S*-plosive blends. *Speech Monographs,* 1964, **31,** 184–185.

Sebeok, T. A. Animal communication. *Science,* 1965, **147,** 1006–1014.

Sebeok, T. A. Animal communication in linguistics in communication. *International Social Science Journal,* 1967, **19** (1), 88–95. (Special Issue.)

Sissors, J. Some new concepts of newspaper design. *Journalism Quarterly,* 1965, **42,** 236–242.

Starkweather, J. A., and Decker, B. J. Computer analysis of interview content. *Psychological Reports,* 1964, **15,** 875–882.

St. Onge, K. R. A quantitative phonetico-syllabic method of duration analysis of the stream of speech. *Speech Monographs,* 1956, **23,** 247–254.

Tagiuri, R. Person perception. In G. Lindzey (Ed.), *Handbook of social psychology.* (2nd ed.) Vol. I. Reading, Mass.: Addison-Wesley, 1968. Pp. 395–449.

Thompson, D. F., and Meltzer, L. Communication of emotional intent by facial expression. *Journal of Abnormal and Social Psychology,* 1964, **68,** 129–135.

Treisman, M. Signal detection theory and Crozier's law: Derivation of a new sensory scaling procedure. *Journal of Mathematical Psychology,* 1965, **2,** 205–218. (a)

Treisman, M. The psychology of time. *Discovery,* 1965, **26** (10), 40–45. (b)

Watson, M. O., and Graves, T. Quantitative research in proxemic behavior. *The American Anthropologist,* 1966, **68,** 971–985.

White, E. H. Autonomic responsivity as a function of level of subject involvement. *Behavioral Science,* 1965, **10,** 39–50.

Whiteside, T. C. D., Graybial, A., and Niven, J. I. Visual illusions of movement. *Brain,* 1965, **88,** 193–211.

Willhelm, S. A reformulation of social action theory. *American Journal of Economics and Sociology,* 1967, **26,** 23–32.

Williams, F., and Tolch, J. Communication by facial expression. *Journal of Communication,* 1965, **15,** 17–27.

Williams, T. Cultural structuring of tactile experience in a Borneo society. *The American Anthropologist,* 1966, **68,** 27–39.

Wright, H., and Barker, R. *Midwest and its children.* Lawrence: University of Kansas Press, 1957.

13

Interaction Analysis

EDMUND J. AMIDON

Bales (1950) has defined interaction as the behavior of one person influencing the behavior of another in a face-to-face situation. Interaction analysis in its broadest sense is a method of describing and interpreting human interaction as it occurs in a specific group setting. The term was perhaps first used by Bales, and since the method has been applied mainly to studying interaction in the classroom, this chapter will discuss it in that context. Although much research in classroom behavior has been based on the rating scale (see Chapter 8), most recent research uses one of the various methods of interaction analysis.

The first section of this chapter will discuss the background and theory behind interaction analysis as a concept and the different systems that have been evolved for practicing it. The three dimensions on which classroom interaction is observed for analysis are briefly discussed, as well as the various methods of data collection and sampling units used by the different systems. Additional ramifications inherent or implied in certain systems will also be touched on.

The second section — and the bulk of the chapter — details the methodology of the 10-category Interaction Analysis system (Flanders, 1960b): how the classroom observer collects his data, how he uses it to describe classroom interaction, what interpretations and conclusions he can draw from it. A discussion of the limitations and validity of the system concludes the section.

The third section describes studies that have used Interaction Analysis for three different purposes: describing classroom interaction, using it experimentally, and applying it to teacher training.

BACKGROUND AND THEORY

The users of interaction analysis techniques have broadly identified three basic *dimensions* that the systems focus on: the affective, cognitive, and multidimensional. The affective systems generally examine such teacher behaviors as positive/negative reaction to students, praise, criticism, encouragement, acceptance, and support. The cognitive systems focus on the level of abstraction of a statement, logical processes, and the type of logical or linguistic function a particular behavior seems to serve in the classroom. Multidimensional systems attempt to identify factors from both dimensions, affective and cognitive. Some systems focus on verbal interaction, some on nonverbal, some on both. Some take as their subjects both the teacher and the students, some concentrate solely on the teacher or the students.

Data collection is usually handled in one of three ways: (1) The observer records the information directly into a category of behavior or codes the information using a category number or symbol. (2) He collects data with some sort of instrument, either a tape or video recorder, and from a typed script of the recording, he classifies the behavior into categories. (3) The observer takes handwritten notes of all behavior occurring in the classroom, the notes are typed, and then finally classified according to the various categories. The third method is not used very often.

The use of various coding or *sampling units* differs widely depending on the particular category system. A coding unit may represent simply a unit of time, a thought or verbal unit, a content area, or a sequence of two or more behaviors. At present, the more popular types of sampling include thought units and time units. Some of the more specific, sophisticated systems use combinations of time sampling and some type of sequential analysis.

Figure 1 diagrams the interplay of the three dimensions, the data collection methods, and the sampling units.

Dimensions of Interaction Analysis

AFFECTIVE SYSTEMS

The first and probably the most widely used types of interaction analysis systems are those generally classified as *affective*. Perhaps the earliest systematic approach to analyzing the social-emotional or the affective dimension was developed by H. H. Anderson and H. Brewer (1945). They used a continuum from integrative to dominative to analyze or classify the behavior of both teachers and pupils.

Using this general framework, the Withall (1949) Climate Index was developed and has since been used in various research studies. Withall's

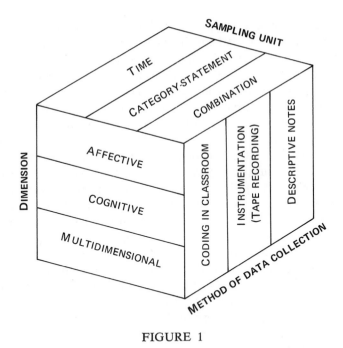

FIGURE 1

Framework for Classroom Observational Category System

system classifies teacher verbal behavior into seven categories: (1) supportive statements intended to reassure and commend the pupil; (2) accepting and clarifying statements intended to convey to the pupil the feeling that he was understood and to help him elucidate his ideas and feelings; (3) problem structuring statements or questions objectively proffering information or raising questions about the problem in an attempt to help the learner solve his problems; (4) neutral statements — polite formalities, administrative comments, verbatim repetition of something that has already been said — with no inferable intent; (5) directive or authoritative statements intended to make a pupil follow a recommended course of action; (6) reproving or deprecative remarks intended to deter the pupil from continued indulgence in present unacceptable behavior; and (7) self-supporting remarks intended to sustain or justify the teacher's position or course of action. Withall validated his system by comparing recorded pupil's comments and feelings of the climate in the classroom and ratings of a typescript of classroom interaction with data collected with the climate index and concluded that his method was useful in describing the general nature of classroom climate.

From 1950 until 1957 Flanders worked to refine the instrument of interaction analysis and also to replicate the results of Withall's study. Building on Withall's earlier work, Flanders (1960b) originated the system now known as Interaction Analysis (see pp. 378–401 for a detailed description of its latest updating). This is perhaps the most widely used category system in classroom research and identifies behaviors along a continuum from direct teacher influence to indirect teacher influence. The early work of Withall and Flanders indicated that a sample of teachers' verbal statements provides a general index for describing classroom climate.

A number of later category systems were made for the purposes of research and the training of teachers, modifying the approach of Flanders' Interaction Analysis system but retaining some of the basic categories or concepts. Such modified category systems include the Verbal Interaction Category system developed by E. J. Amidon and Hunter (1966a). Although this system was developed primarily to train teachers, its categories also have a potential use in the area of research. This system shifts the focus from indirect/direct teaching by defining teacher behavior as either statements of initiation or response. This same initiation/response division applies to statements by the children. Other modifications of the Flanders system are the Expanded Interaction Analysis system (E. J. Amidon, P. Amidon, and Rosenshine, 1968), the Multidimensional Analysis of Classroom Interaction system (Honigman, 1967a), a system for the analysis of instruction (Hough, 1967b), and a system for use in a foreign language (Moskowitz, 1966b).

Two other affective systems have been used in both research and teacher training. These include the system built by Joyce and Harootunian (1967) and a system developed by Spaulding (1962). Neither of these systems can be considered modifications of the Flanders Interaction Analysis system although they are similar. Another well known system used to study the affective dimensions in the classroom is the Marie Hughes (1962) category system, which focuses on the functions of teacher behavior in the classroom. The Hughes system originally used stenographic notes of all relevant classroom behavior, but more recently the system has used typescripts of tape recordings.

COGNITIVE SYSTEMS

B. O. Smith (1962) pioneered in the area of *cognitive* dimension with his attempts to develop a method for the logical analysis of the strategies teachers use in the classroom. Another of the early methods used to analyze teaching behavior was developed by Gallagher and Aschner (1963) using Guilford's (1956) framework for looking at the human intellect. This system uses four basic cognitive categories — cognitive memory, convergent thinking, divergent thinking, and evaluation — to analyze both the types of questions the teacher asks and the kinds of responses children make to these questions. In addition, a fifth category, routine remarks, includes prior statements that do not fall into one of the four categories mentioned above. Examples might include statements classified as affective behaviors in other systems or statements of classroom management.

As with many of the cognitive systems, the complexity of the Gallagher-Aschner system appears to make its application difficult in the field of teacher training. However, the four basic categories are a useful research tool for analyzing teacher-pupil interaction as well as for developing questioning skills in teacher training courses. The system appears to have its primary use in the analysis of thought processes in teacher-pupil verbal interaction. The relationship between the types of teacher questions and the types of pupil responses becomes a legitimate research question. Similarly, the relationship between types of task learning and the cognitive level of teacher statements provokes further questions for research. And, although this system has seldom been used as a feedback device, it offers promise for helping teachers analyze the types of questions they ask.

Perhaps the most recent cognitive system designed to analyze teacher behavior was developed by Bellack, Kliebard, and Hyman (1967). They have recently completed an analysis of what they term the teaching moves in the classroom as well as the teaching cycles which occur as various moves follow one another in sequence.

MULTIDIMENSIONAL SYSTEMS

Several category systems attempt to identify specific dimensions simultaneously, including the OSCAR system developed by Medley (1963) and the modified category system developed by E. J. Amidon (1966a). One of the more complex systems for analyzing classroom interaction is Multidimensional Analysis of Classroom Interaction (Honigman, 1967a). This system utilizes twenty categories including five student behavior categories and two miscellaneous categories. Although many are similar or identical to the Flanders Interaction Analysis categories, the Honigman system also includes a number of cognitive categories as well as modifications of the Flanders categories which indicate cognitive level in an otherwise undesignated teacher-student expression. Additional categories resulting from such modifications include emotional focus, modified pairs of categories, textual irrelevance, and empathic performance. Some data indicate that the Honigman approach covers a greater range of classroom behavior than the Flanders approach.

Methods of Data Collection

Interestingly enough, all the systems classifying interaction on the affective dimension, with the exception of Withall's, were designed to be used by a classroom observer who would classify directly into a category as he observed in the classroom. All the cognitive systems, on the other hand, were designed to classify from a typed script of a tape recording of classroom interaction. The multidimensional systems mentioned, in two cases modifications of the original interaction analysis system, are usable in direct observation; that is, the observer may classify the classroom interaction directly into categories.

Sampling Units

With the exception of Withall's system and Joyce and Harootunian's system, all the affective systems use *time* as a basic sampling unit (Joyce and Harootunian use a shift in content and Withall uses either words or phrases as the basic unit). In addition to the time sampling unit, the Flanders Interaction Analysis and related systems use *shifts* from one category to another as sampling units. This means that in addition to classifying every three or four seconds or whatever the stipulated time unit is, the observer must also classify shifts in categories even if they occur before time intervals elapse.

The basic sampling unit in the cognitive systems is always a *content* or cognitive unit. In the system of Bellack *et al.,* for example, the number of written lines in a one-category sequence is the unit. In the Gallagher-Aschner system as well, the category change indicates the length of the unit. In itself, then, unit length is the length of time that teacher or student behavior can be classified into a single category without the intervention of a second category. Smith uses a content change to indicate the length of the basic unit. The multidimensional systems of Honigman and Amidon both reflect the same sampling procedure used in the Flanders Interaction Analysis system, while the OSCAR uses a title change as the basic unit.

METHODOLOGY

Systematic observation has become increasingly popular as a method for studying the classroom. Techniques are available for studying one or a variety of aspects of classroom interaction. A recent survey (Simon, Boyer, and Moskowitz, 1967) identifies 26 separate category systems that are in use or have been in use in the last five years, seven of which are modifications of the original Flanders Interaction Analysis (1960b) system. The system selected for detailed description here is the 10-category Interaction Analysis system (E. J. Amidon and Flanders, 1967), a direct outgrowth and refinement of Flanders' original system.

General Observation Procedures

When recording, the classroom observer seats himself in a good position to see and hear the teacher and the children. He watches and listens for several minutes before attempting to code the verbal interaction. During this period the observer may detect nonverbal cues that will help him make accurate decisions in coding the verbal interaction, or he may identify certain behaviors as unintentional verbal ties. The observer may also watch for student reactions to various types of teacher influence. This preliminary period allows the observer to understand the classroom climate before actually coding the verbal interaction.

The observer then begins to tally, noting carefully the time he begins. He generally records for approximately 20 minutes. Sometimes periods up to 40 minutes must be coded, but experience has indicated that an observer may become fatigued after coding for longer than 20 minutes, making his tallying unreliable.

Figure 2 (p. 380) shows a sample tally sheet on which the classroom observer enters the appropriate category numbers. Note that this sheet is specifically designed for a five-minute observation at the rate of one tally every three seconds. Four of these sheets would be required for a 20-minute observation. Categories were originally specified to sample time; the observer noted the type of interaction occurring in the classroom at regular time intervals by writing down the number assigned to the appropriate category it fell into, or by marking a tally sheet in the column under the appropriate category heading. Now another sampling unit, category shifts, has been added to the recording procedure: an observer not only records one category every three seconds, he also notes changes in category occurring between the three-second intervals. When events of particular interest occur, the observer may wish to describe them briefly in a marginal note beside the appropriate tally.

OBSERVER TRAINING

Observer training requires learning the categories at several levels. First, the observer must memorize exactly what kind of behavior belongs to each category, and the category numbers, so that he never has to refer to the list of categories and their definitions while observing. Second, he must learn to identify specific categories during classroom interaction, usually accomplished in the beginning stages with audio tapes of actual teacher-pupil interaction.

Third, he learns to pace the timing of his coding. The best way to accomplish this appears to be constant feedback from the trainer during the early stages of tape listening and coding: after coding a minute-long segment of an audio tape of classroom interaction, the observer trainees should be told how many tallies they should have recorded. At first the observer trainees are invariably a little too slow. In their efforts to increase their rate of coding, they may find that they speed up during the relatively easy segments of classroom interaction (that is, when the same category is repeated for an extended period of time) and slow down when the shifts between categories are rapid. With constant feedback over six or eight hours of training, most observer trainees stabilize their coding to the appropriate pace of classification. The fourth step is classifying a real class.

It is important during the early stages of training that the observers be given the opportunity to listen to audio tapes from a variety of types of classroom situations. Feedback on the "correctness" of their coding during these audio tape sessions is of utmost importance. Therefore, a variety of

FIGURE 2

Tally Sheet

1._____	26._____	51._____	76._____
2._____	27._____	52._____	77._____
3._____	28._____	53._____	78._____
4._____	29._____	54._____	79._____
5._____	30._____	55._____	80._____
6._____	31._____	56._____	81._____
7._____	32._____	57._____	82._____
8._____	33._____	58._____	83._____
9._____	34._____	59._____	84._____
10._____	35._____	60._____	85._____
11._____	36._____	61._____	86._____
12._____	37._____	62._____	87._____
13._____	38._____	63._____	88._____
14._____	39._____	64._____	89._____
15._____	40._____	65._____	90._____
16._____	41._____	66._____	91._____
17._____	42._____	67._____	92._____
18._____	43._____	68._____	93._____
19._____	44._____	69._____	94._____
20._____	45._____	70._____	95._____
21._____	46._____	71._____	96._____
22._____	47._____	72._____	97._____
23._____	48._____	73._____	98._____
24._____	49._____	74._____	99._____
25._____	50._____	75._____	100._____

taped segments of classroom interaction accompanied by an expert's complete codings have been developed specifically for training Interaction Analysis observers (E. J. Amidon and P. Amidon, 1967a).

In order to develop maximum reliability, observers should be very familiar with not only the categories but certain ground rules (pp. 384, 386) as well. Trainees' reliability increases with time, with observing the nonverbal cues in a live classroom situation which accompany the verbal behavior of pupils and teachers, and with hearing and understanding the content of the class. In the early stages of observer training, trainees usually have difficulty listening to the content of a lesson. As they become trained in the use of the categories, they find that they are able not only to discern the specific categories but also to listen to and understand the content of the lesson being discussed.

Although these general procedures of observation and training apply to any interaction analysis system, they have been specifically adapted to the 10 categories and their modifications in what is now known as Interaction Analysis; conversely, these categories are particularly adapted to the method of observation sampling just described. People who have worked with classroom observation over the past several years have found that the observer coding in the classroom has great difficulty with more complex systems of classification.

Basic Interaction Analysis Categories

Before examining the 10 categories of Interaction Analysis, the reader should be aware of two guidelines for setting up categories used by the observer recording classroom interaction. First, enough categories should be available to the observer so that he can describe any occurrence at any time. Second, the categories should be mutually exclusive so that the observer cannot describe an occurrence with more than one category at any single recording time.

All classroom verbal behavior is classified into one of three basic divisions: teacher talk; student talk; and silence, confusion, or miscellaneous occurrences. Teacher talk has been further classified as indirect and direct.

TEACHER TALK: INDIRECT INFLUENCE

Category 1: Accepts feeling. This category is used when the teacher communicates acceptance of feelings expressed by the children. He does this in a number of ways. First, and probably most basic, the teacher simply uses a word or phrase which identifies the feeling of a child without criticizing the child for having the feeling. Or he relates the child's feeling to other people's feelings. Perhaps he tries to relate the feeling to the supposed cause of the feeling: "I guess we're feeling kind of blue today; I've often felt that way myself when I was disappointed"; "The class seems very excited about our trip to the dairy farm."

One kind of behavior which is often misclassified into this category is reassurance. Actually, a reassuring statement is rejection of feeling. When the teacher says, "Don't be upset about your test, it's not all that hard and I know you're very bright," he is, in fact, rejecting or ignoring the child's anxiety and concern about the test.

Category 2: Praises or encourages. Praise includes statements which evaluate a student's idea as right, good, or appropriate, for instance, "You are right, that answer is a good answer," or "I like that answer." *Encouragement* in Interaction Analysis means only statements that actually function to encourage the child to continue talking. The teacher's "Uh huh," "Okay," "Yes," "Um hmm," "Right," and "All right" during a child's hesitations are classified in Category 2 only if they do not inhibit pupil talk. Also included in Category 2 are statements which cause laughter, that is, *jokes* not said at the expense of a student.

In general, then, Category 2 includes direct, positive behavior communicating to the listener or the student "I like what you're doing," "What you're doing is good," "You're right," "Your answer is right," "That's good thinking," "That's a good idea."

Category 3: Accepts ideas. This category includes statements repeating, rephrasing, summarizing, or restating a student's idea. They communicate simply that the teacher has heard the child's statement; they do not communicate that the idea is right or wrong.

Category 4: Asks questions. This category includes questions about procedure or about content designed to elicit an answer from a student. Only questions which are legitimately designed to gain information, knowledge, or opinion from students are classified in this category; they may be broad in scope or very narrow. This category does not include rhetorical questions and questions which communicate sarcasm or criticism.

TEACHER TALK: DIRECT INFLUENCE

Category 5: Gives lecture. "Lecture" is a broad term, as used here, signifying facts, information, opinions, ideas, and orientation presented to introduce material to the class, review material, or focus the attention of the class on an important topic. Usually, information in lecture form is given in extended time periods. It may be given in response to a student question, or it may be presented to clarify a question the teacher has previously asked or is about to ask. Rhetorical questions are also included in this category. Category 5 is the most frequently used category in classroom Interaction Analysis.

Category 6: Gives directions. This category is used when the observer can predict an observable behavior on the part of a child or the class as a result of the teacher's instruction. "Observable behavior" is usually some physical action on the part of the child or children or a specific response which the teacher has demanded.

Category 7: Gives criticism. Criticism, as defined in the Interaction Analysis category system, is a statement designed to change a student's behavior from unacceptable to acceptable. In effect, the teacher is saying, "I don't like what you are doing, do something else." This category also includes statements in self-defense or justification of the teacher's behavior or authority, often difficult to detect when the teacher appears to be explaining the reasons for a lesson. Loosely, when the teacher is explaining the reasons why he should be telling the children what to do, why he is the one who makes the decisions, or why he is the one who should be listened to, he is justifying his authority. These statements also include statements of extreme self-reference in which the teacher asks a child or the class to do something as a favor to him.

Whenever the teacher is talking, Categories 1–7 and only 1–7 are used. Every three seconds, the observer must put down one of these seven categories as long as the teacher is talking. If the teacher is not talking, one of the following categories is used.

STUDENT TALK

Category 8: Student talk — response. Category 8 is used when the teacher directly initiates the contact or solicits the student's statement, and the response by the child is a predictable response, that is, statements of fact asked for in a question, or limited choice responses which give the student's feeling or opinion. An example is the answer "Columbus, in 1492" to the question "Who discovered America and when?" Another is the response to the teacher's question "Do you think we are doing the right thing in Vietnam?" The answer "Yes" would be classified "8". However, if the teacher asked Johnny the question and Alice answered it spontaneously, her answer would be classified "9".

Category 9: Student talk — initiation. In general, if the student raises his hand, is acknowledged, and makes a statement or asks a question, he has not been prompted by the teacher to talk. The appropriate category is "9". Also, when the child responds at some length to a very broad question asking for opinion or divergent thinking, the category is "9".

Distinguishing between the two categories of student talk is often very difficult. The criterion seems to be whether or not the observer can predict the general kind of answer that a student will give in response to a question. If the answer is not predictable, then the statement would be classified as a "9". If it is predictable, then the statement would be classified as an "8". In general, the kind of question asked gives a clue as to whether the student statement will be classified as an "8" or a "9". A broad question will give a clue that a "9" is likely to follow; a narrow question will give a clue that the student response is likely to be an "8".

MISCELLANEOUS

Category 10: Silence or confusion. This category includes everything not included in the other categories: periods of confusion in communication when it is difficult to determine who is talking, periods when a number of people in the class are talking at once, periods when there is no talking at all, and miscellaneous occurrences such as laughter, music, bells ringing.

A summary of these categories for Interaction Analysis is given on the following page.

Ground Rules[1]

Because of the complexities of problems involved in classification, several ground rules for use with Interaction Analysis were established (E. J. Amidon and P. Amidon, 1967a) which have been found to aid in developing consistency and reliability in categorizing teacher behavior. The rules have been useful in research and in teacher training at all grade levels and in several subject matter areas. There are 15 in all, and five follow as examples.

RULE 1

When not certain in which of two or more categories a statement belongs, choose the category that is numerically farthest from Category 5, except when one of the two categories in doubt is Category 10. Category 10 is never chosen if there is an alternate category under consideration; if there is any specific verbal behavior going on, it cannot be silence or confusion! Because those categories farthest from the center (5) of the continuum occur less frequently, the observer maximizes information by choosing the less frequently occurring category (except 10) when there is a choice. For example, if the observer is not sure whether it is a 2 or a 3, he chooses the 2; if in doubt between a 5 and a 7, he chooses a 7.

RULE 2

If the primary tone of the teacher's behavior has been consistently direct or consistently indirect, do not shift into the opposite classification unless a clear indication of shift is given by the teacher. The trained observer is in the best position to judge whether or not the teacher is restricting or expanding pupils' freedom of action. If the observer feels that the teacher's general

---

[1] Adapted from E. J. Amidon and P. Amidon, *Interaction analysis training kit: Level I.* Minneapolis: Association for Productive Teaching, 1967. By permission of the authors and the publisher.

Categories for Interaction Analysis

Minnesota, 1959

TEACHER TALK	**INDIRECT INFLUENCE**	1.* ACCEPTS FEELING: accepts and clarifies the feeling tone of the students in a non-threatening manner. Feelings may be positive or negative. Predicting or recalling feelings is included.
		2.* PRAISES OR ENCOURAGES: praises or encourages student action or behavior. Jokes that release tension, not at the expense of another individual, nodding head, or saying "um hm?" or "go on" are included.
		3.* ACCEPTS OR USES IDEAS OF STUDENT: clarifies, builds, or develops ideas suggested by a student. As teacher brings more of his own ideas into play, shift to Category 5.
		4.* ASKS QUESTIONS: asks a question about content or procedure with the intent that a student answer.
	DIRECT INFLUENCE	5.* LECTURING: giving facts or opinions about content or procedure; expressing his own ideas, asking rhetorical questions.
		6.* GIVING DIRECTIONS: giving directions, commands, or orders to which a student is expected to comply.
		7.* CRITICIZING OR JUSTIFYING AUTHORITY: making statements intended to change student behavior from non-acceptable to acceptable pattern; bawling someone out; stating why the teacher is doing what he is doing; extreme self-reference.
STUDENT TALK		8.* STUDENT TALK — RESPONSE: talk by students in response to teacher. Teacher initiates the contact or solicits student statement.
		9.* STUDENT TALK — INITIATION: talk by students which they initiate. If "calling on" student is only to indicate who may talk next, observer must decide whether student wanted to talk. If he did, use this category.
		10.* SILENCE OR CONFUSION: pauses, short periods of silence, and periods of confusion in which communication cannot be understood by the observer.

* *No* scale is implied by these numbers. Each number is purely classificatory; it designates a particular kind of communication event. To write these numbers down during observation is to enumerate, not to judge a position on a scale.

From E. J. Amidon and N. A. Flanders, *The role of the teacher in the classroom.* (Rev. ed.) Minneapolis: Association for Productive Teaching, 1967. Reprinted by permission of the authors and the publisher.

pattern of behavior expands the freedom of students to act, a slightly more direct statement in a very indirect pattern may tend to look, in contrast, like a more direct statement than it actually is. On the other hand, he must remain alert to momentary shifts to one of the more direct categories. Conversely, if the observer feels that the teacher has been consistently restrictive in his behavior, he is particularly careful in his use of the indirect categories.

RULE 3

The observer must not be overly concerned with his own biases or with the teacher's intent. Rather, he must ask himself the question, "How does this behavior affect the pupils' freedom?" If pupils see the teacher's "clever" statements as criticism, the observer uses Category 7 rather than Category 2. If the teacher says sarcastically how good the children are, again Category 7 is used. If a statement intended as a question restricts students' freedom, it must be classified as a direction. The effect of a statement on the pupils, then, and not the teacher's intent, is the crucial criterion for categorizing a statement.

RULE 4

If more than one category occurs during the three-second interval, then all categories used in that interval are recorded; therefore, record each change in category. If no change occurs within three seconds, repeat that category number. Generally an observer writes down a category number every three seconds, and the pace of recording is maintained at a constant level so that only one category number is written during this period. However, if there is a change in categories during this interval, the observer records the change. Within the three-second interval, for example, the teacher may ask a question, the child may answer, and the teacher may praise the child. The observer attempts to record all three categories.

RULE 5

Directions are statements that result (or are expected to result) in observable behavior on the part of the pupils. Examples of directions are: "Go to the board," "Read question 3," "Go to your seat." Some teacher statements sound like directions but cannot be followed by observed student compliance. Therefore they may not be classified "6". These statements often precede the actual direction; for example, "Let's get ready now to go to recess" is a statement of orientation (Category 5). But "Everyone in Row 5 is to get his coat" is a direction (Category 6).

Using and Interpreting Interaction Analysis

The preceding section explained a method of recording that preserves the chronological sequence of the types of teacher or student statements. The sequence of events in a classroom must be preserved for analysis. It is not enough to say that a teacher lectures 50 per cent of the time or that he criticizes 5 per cent of the time; we need to know when he lectures or criticizes, and what kinds of statements precede or follow lecturing or criticizing.

The following step-by-step example shows how an observer records his classroom data and sets it up for examination and interpretation. Say a fifth-grade teacher is beginning a social studies lesson. The observer has been sitting in the classroom for several minutes and has begun to get an idea of the general climate before he begins to record. The teacher says to the class, "Boys and girls, please open your social studies books to page 5." The observer classifies this as a 6 and follows it with a 10 because of the period of silence and confusion as the children try to find the page.

The teacher says, "Jimmy, we are all waiting for you. Will you please turn in your book to page 5?" (Observer records a 7 and a 6.) "I know now," continues the teacher, "that some of us had a little difficulty with, and were a little disturbed by, the study of this chapter yesterday; I think today we are going to find it more exciting and interesting." (Observer records two 1's for "reacting to feeling.") "Now, has anyone had a chance to think about what we discussed yesterday?" (Observer records a 4 for a question.) A student answers, "I thought about it, and it seems to me that the reason we are in so much trouble in Southeast Asia is that we haven't really had a chance to learn to understand the ways of the people who live there." (Observer records three 9's.)

The teacher responds by saying, "Good, I am glad you suggested that, John. Now let me see if I understand your idea completely. You have suggested that if we had known the people better in Southeast Asia, we might not be in the trouble we are in today." (This is classified as a 2, followed by two 3's.)

RECORDING DATA IN A MATRIX

The observer now has the following list of numbers:

$$
\begin{array}{ll}
& \left.\begin{array}{l} 10 \\ 6 \end{array}\right) \quad \text{1st pair} \\
\text{2nd pair} \quad \left(\begin{array}{l} 10 \\ 7 \end{array}\right) \quad \text{3rd pair} \\
\text{4th pair} \quad \left(\begin{array}{l} 6 \\ 1 \\ 1 \\ 4 \\ 9 \\ 9 \\ 9 \\ 2 \\ 3 \\ 3 \\ 10 \end{array}\right.
\end{array}
$$

(The 10s at the beginning and end of the sequence are explained in the discussion that follows.)

Notice in the listing above that the numbers have been marked off in pairs. The first pair is 10–6; the second pair is 6–10, etc. The observer now makes tabulations in a 10-row by 10-column *matrix* to represent pairs of numbers (see Table 1). The particular cell in which tabulation of the pair of numbers is made is determined by using the first number in the pair to indicate the row and the second number in the pair for the column. Thus, 10–6 would be shown by a tally in the cell formed by Row 10 and Column 6. The second pair, 6–10, would be shown in the cell formed by Row 6 and Column 10. The third pair, 10–7, is entered into the cell of Row 10 and Column 7, and so on. Notice that each pair of numbers overlaps with the previous pair, so that each number, except the first and the last, is used twice. It is for this reason that 10's are entered as the first and last numbers in the record; it is convenient to assume that each record began and ended with silence. This procedure also permits the total of each column to equal the total of the corresponding row. There should be one less tally in the matrix than there were numbers entered in the original observation record. In this case we started with 15 numbers and the total number of tallies in

TABLE 1

Sample Interaction Matrix

		Second 1	2	3	4	5	6	7	8	9	10		
	1	1			1								
	2			1									
	3			1					1				
	4							1					
	5												
First	6	1							1				
	7						1						
	8		1						11				
	9												
	10						1	1					
	Total	2	1	2	1	0	2	1	3	0	2	14	Matrix Total
	%												

Tables 1–9 from E. J. Amidon and P. Amidon, *Interaction analysis training kit: Level I.* Minneapolis: Association for Productive Teaching, 1967. Reprinted by permission.

the matrix is 14. This tabulation is shown in Table 1 in the extra cell labeled "Matrix Total."

Ordinarily, a separate matrix is made for each lesson or major activity. If the observer is categorizing 40 minutes of arithmetic and 20 minutes of social studies, he makes one matrix for the arithmetic and another for the social studies lesson. If a secondary teacher has a 30-minute discussion period followed by a 20-minute period of more structured lecture in another area, then the observer usually makes two separate matrices. Matrices are less confusing and more meaningful when they represent a single type of activity or work.

USING THE MATRIX TO DETERMINE GENERAL ASPECTS
OF CLASSROOM INTERACTION

The purpose of setting up observational data in a matrix is to make it examinable and interpretable as a description of the classroom interaction. The observer may describe the interaction in several ways, but he usually begins by determining the percentages of the different kinds of statements. The first step is computing the proportion of each category to the total observed classroom interaction. This is done by dividing each of the column totals by the total number of tallies in the matrix. Determining the percentage of total teacher talk in each of Categories 1 through 7 is done by dividing the total of each category by the sum of these seven categories. For example, Table 2 (p. 390) has 105 tallies in Columns 1–7. If 10 of these tallies are in Column 3, the 10 is divided by 105 and we find that the amount of teacher talk that falls into Category 3 is approximately 9.5 per cent of the total amount of teacher talk. The pattern of interaction that the teacher has used with the class will be evident when the percentages of all seven categories have been computed.

The total percentage of teacher talk, of prime importance in interpreting the matrix, is found by dividing the total number of tallies in Columns 1 through 7 by the total number of tallies in the matrix. There are 150 tallies in the matrix, 105 of which are in Columns 1–7. This teacher talked 70 per cent of the total time of the observation. To find the percentage of student talk, the total number of tallies in Columns 8 and 9 (42) is divided by the total number of tallies in the matrix — the students talked 28 per cent of the time. A total of three tallies in Column 10 divided by 150 shows that 2 per cent of the time was spent in silence or confusion.

Next the observer focuses on the relative number of indirect and direct teacher statements. The total number of tallies in Columns 1, 2, 3, and 4 is divided by the total number of tallies in Columns 5, 6, and 7 to find the ratio of indirect to direct teacher statements (I/D ratio). An I/D ratio of 1.00 means that for every indirect statement there was one direct statement; an I/D ratio of 2.00 means that for every two indirect statements there was only one direct statement, etc.

TABLE 2

A Typical Illustration

		1	2	3	4	5	6	7	8	9	10	
						Second						
	1	1				1			1			
	2		4	1					2			
	3		1	6	1				2			
	4			1	14				5			
First	5	1				48			6			
	6						1		4			
	7							4		1		
	8		2	2	5	6	4		11			
	9	1						1		9	1	
	10									1	2	
	Total	3	7	10	20	55	5	5	30	12	3	150 Matrix Total
	%	2	4½	6½	13½	36½	3½	3½	20	8	2	

A revised i/d ratio shows the kind of emphasis given to motivation and control in a particular classroom: the number of tallies in Columns 1, 2, and 3 is divided by the number of tallies in Columns 6 and 7. Categories 1, 2, 3, 6, and 7 are more concerned with motivation and control in the classroom and less concerned with the actual presentation of subject matter than Categories 4 and 5.

USING THE MATRIX TO DETERMINE SPECIFIC AREAS
OF CLASSROOM INTERACTION

The matrix provides the observer with a convenient device for analyzing the summarized teacher-pupil interaction data. It shows at a glance the categories that have heavy buildups of tallies, as well as the categories in which there are no tallies.

Tables 3 through 9 show how certain areas of the matrix describe the interaction more specifically. Table 3 indicates the area called the "content cross." Tallies in this area represent teacher statements consisting primarily of lecture; statements of opinion, ideas, and information; and questions about information and content that he has presented. A heavy concentration of tallies in this area indicates an emphasis on content.

TABLE 3

The "Content Cross"

Second

		1	2	3	4	5	6	7	8	9	10	
First	1											
	2											
	3											
	4											
	5											
	6											
	7											
	8											
	9											
	10											
	Total											Matrix Total
	%											

Table 4 represents the emphasis the teacher gives to using student ideas, extending and amplifying student statements, and accepting and enlarging on student feelings. It also includes stages of transition from one of these areas to the other. High frequency in these cells indicates the use of extended indirect influence by the teacher.

Table 5 indicates the cells representing the teacher's emphasis on criticism, giving lengthy direction, or moving from one of these types of influence to the other. In general, tabulations in this area suggest extended direct teacher influence and use of authority.

An important aspect of classroom interaction is the way the teacher responds to student comment. Table 6, Area A, represents direct response to student comment. Comparing the relative number of tallies in these two areas indicates the pattern of behavior used by the teacher in response to students at the moment a student stops talking.

Table 7 shows student talk. The tabulations that fall into Area A can indicate the kinds of teacher statements that tend to stimulate student talk. They help to answer the question "How do students in this classroom become involved in classroom interaction?" Area B represents student talk of two types: prolonged talk by one student and sustained talk by several students, not interrupted by teacher talk.

TABLE 4

Extended Indirect Influence

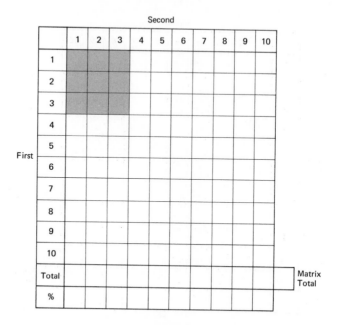

TABLE 5

Extended Direct Influence

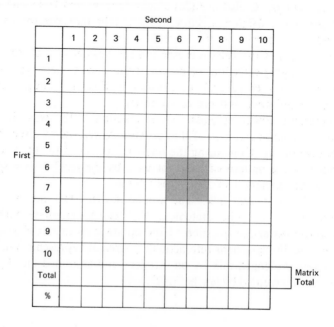

TABLE 6

Teacher Response to Student Comments

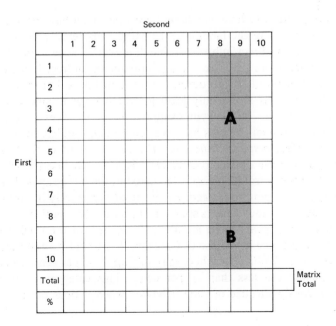

TABLE 7

Student Talk Following Teacher Talk

Table 8, Column 10 shows the kind of teacher or student talk that is followed by silence or confusion.

Table 9 shows the "steady-state" cells lying along the diagonal of the matrix. Only when the behavior remains in a single category for longer than three seconds will there be tallies in these cells. If, for example, there is a tally in the 1–1 cell, it means that the teacher was accepting or clarifying student emotion during a period of more than three seconds. Note particularly that these cells along the diagonal are the only cells in the entire matrix that identify continuous talk in a single category; all other cells are transitional cells representing movement from one category to another. A buildup in any one of these cells, except 10–10, indicates that that kind of communication is being extended. Either the teacher or a student is taking time to expand on the ideas being presented. Heavy loading in diagonal Categories 1–7 indicates that the teacher is being deliberate in communication, taking time to extend his ideas or those of the students. Above average or heavy loading in the 8 and 9 diagonal cells indicates that individual students are being permitted to expand their own ideas.

INTERPRETING MATRIX DATA

In developing an intensive description of a particular matrix, it is well to remember that only the individual teacher whose class the matrix reflects can make the final decisions about what behavior is "good" or "bad," "undesirable" or "desirable." Some predictions, however, can be made about the effects of certain combinations of behavior in the classroom. In this section the matrix will be systematically expanded in order to discuss consequences that can be expected for particular kinds of cell totals and cell buildups.

Teachers referred to here as "direct" are those who have been identified in the research and in the laboratory as using considerably more than the average amount of direct influence. The "indirect" teachers are those who have used much more than the average amount of indirect influence. The average percentages given are derived from matrices of junior high school teachers because this is the only level at which large numbers of classes have been observed. Subsequent examination of matrices of elementary teachers or high school teachers has revealed no major differences. *Average percentages reflect actual practice, not the best or most desired practices.* For example, a naturally indirect teacher is likely to become even more indirect after special training than is indicated in the paragraphs that follow.

Statements belonging to *Category 1* are used very rarely in any teaching style. The average time teachers spend in clarifying the emotions of students in the classroom appears to be less than .5 per cent of the total classroom time. Little difference in the use of Category 1 is found between direct and indirect teachers. Indirect teachers may use up to .5 per cent, while direct teachers usually use less than .1 per cent. This category is maintained because of the significance of such behavior when it does occur.

TABLE 8

Silence or Confusion

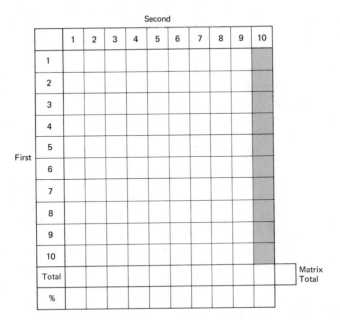

TABLE 9

Steady-State Cells

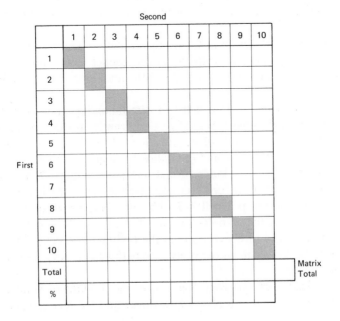

Direct and indirect teachers seem to use practically the same number of *Category 2* statements. The average amount of praise used is about 2 per cent of the total time of the classroom interaction. Many teachers are surprised to learn that the direct teacher uses as much praise as the indirect teacher. However, the 2–2 cell, which shows extended praise, is particularly significant. Almost twice as many tallies show up in it on the matrix of the indirect teacher.

The greatest difference between direct and indirect teachers is in acceptance or clarification of ideas (*Category 3*). Only about 2 per cent of the tallies of direct teachers fall into Category 3, but about 9 per cent of indirect teacher statements fall into it. Although some differences can be accounted for by subject matter area, fewer differences seem to be due to subject matter areas than to type of teacher. The tallies in Category 3, particularly in the 3–3 cell (further extension of student ideas), often distinguish between two types of teachers — the one who is alert to and using the relationship between a student's idea (whether right or wrong) and classroom content and the teacher who is apparently unaware of or does not care to use this relationship.

Category 4 and Category 5, although one indicates indirect and the other direct influence, will be discussed together since they seem to be closely related. The percentage of teacher talk that is questioning (*Category 4*) usually varies from 8 to 15 per cent. *Category 5* statements, or lecture, constitute 25 to 50 per cent of the total verbal behavior of teachers. There seems to be very little difference between the amounts of questions and lecture direct and indirect teachers use. Questions appear to constitute about 8 per cent of the verbal behavior of direct teachers and 11 per cent of the pattern of indirect teachers. No consistent differences appear to exist between the direct and indirect teachers in the amount of lecture used in the classroom.

In their use of *Category 6* behavior, direct and indirect teachers are often found to differ significantly, with the direct teacher using about 8 per cent and the indirect teacher only 4 per cent of the total interaction time in giving directions.

A look at *Category 7*, too, helps in discriminating between direct and indirect teachers: the two types differ significantly in the amount of time they spend in criticism and self-justification. The direct teacher criticizes about 5 per cent of the time and the indirect teacher less than 1 per cent of the time. Nor do the two kinds of teachers use Category 7 statements in the same way. Most of the criticism used by the direct teacher is extended criticism, which shows up in cell 7–7. The direct teacher also uses criticism after lecture (5–7), direction (6–7), and student talk (8–7 and 9–7). The indirect teacher, who rarely registers in the 6–7 and 7–6 cells, tends to distribute his use of criticism more evenly among the other categories than does the direct teacher.

The significance of *Category 8* is not in the amount of student talk it represents but rather that it shows how direct and indirect teachers induce pupil participation. In the matrix of the direct teacher, about 50 per cent of Category 8 tallies occur in the 4–8 cell, which represents answers to teacher questions. In the matrix of the indirect teacher the total in the 4–8 cell is closer to 30 per cent. A larger percentage of student talk in the 8–8 cell occurs in the matrix of the indirect teacher than in that of the direct teacher.

The differences are also significant in *Category 9*. Although there is very little difference in total percentages of Category 9 statements appearing in matrices of direct and indirect teachers, sustained student talk, shown in the 9–9 cell, occurs frequently in the matrix of the indirect teacher and infrequently in the matrix of the direct teacher. Students in the classroom of the indirect teacher, according to this information, express themselves more freely.

Category 10, which shows the total amount of silence or confusion in the classroom, is more heavily loaded in the matrix of the direct than the indirect teacher.

Limitations and Cautions

Some of the limitations in the use of Interaction Analysis are immediately evident. First, the system is designed for use only when the student and the teacher are engaged in verbal interaction; no record of nonverbal inter-action is made (although the system could be adapted to other forms of human interaction, both verbal and nonverbal). In certain teaching situa-tions, nonverbal communication may be important enough to warrant atten-tion, for instance when a class is broken up into small groups in which the teacher himself is not interacting with the children. (When the teacher is interacting with one of the small groups, however, this group can be observed in much the same manner as the total class.) Another limitation is that the system cannot be used when the teacher is using audio-visual aids or other tools which preclude talk.

One particular limitation inherent in the system warrants special atten-tion. Category 4 contains all types of teacher questions requiring pupil response. No allowance is made for different types of questions, *e.g.*, broad and narrow. Length of student response, indicated by several consecutive 8's, may reflect something about the kind of question, but specific informa-tion is still lacking in the matrix. Likewise, there is no indication whether student response is correct or incorrect; the cell indicating the ensuing re-sponse by the teacher (8–3) may or may not suggest the correctness of the student's reply.

Categories in this system, although fairly inclusive concerning teacher talk, are more limited in the area of student participation; for example, one student questioning another student is not reflected in the matrix, although many consecutive 9's indicating prolonged student conversation might lead an interpreter to guess that some student-to-student questioning indeed had occurred. Anger on the part of the student may also not be revealed on the matrix except perhaps by a 7 (a teacher reprimand) or a 1 (the teacher accepting feelings). In other words, no exact interpretations of student verbal behavior are provided in Interaction Analysis.

Recent work with Interaction Analysis has indicated that categories may be added to the existing system. As an example, the Expanded Interaction Analysis system developed by E. J. Amidon *et al.* (1968) follows.

The Expanded Interaction Analysis System[2]

1. Accepts Feeling:
   - 1a   Acknowledges Student Feeling
   - 1c   Clarifies Student Feelings
   - 1r   Refers to Student Feelings

2. Praises or Encourages:
   - 2P   Public Criteria
   - 2p   Private Criteria
   - 2w   Without Criteria

3. Accepts or Uses Ideas of Student:
   - 3a   Acknowledges Student Ideas
   - 3c   Clarifies Student Ideas
   - 3s   Summarizes Student Ideas

4. Asks Questions:
   - 4f   Asks Factual Questions
   - 4c   Asks Convergent Questions
   - 4d   Asks Divergent Questions
   - 4e   Asks Evaluative Questions

5. Lecturing:
   - 5f   Factual Lecturing
   - 5M   Motivational Lecturing
   - 5O   Orientational Lecturing
   - 5P   Personal Lecturing

6. Giving Directions:
   - 6c   Cognitive Directions
   - 6M   Managerial Directions

7. Criticizing or Justifying Authority:
   - 7P   Public Criteria
   - 7p   Private Criteria
   - 7w   Without Criteria

8. Student Talk — Predictable:
   - 8f   Factual Response
   - 8c   Convergent Response

[2] From E. J. Amidon, P. Amidon, and B. Rosenshine, *Skill development in teaching manuals.* Minneapolis: Association for Productive Teaching, 1968. Reprinted by permission of the authors and the publisher.

9. Student Talk — Unpredictable:

   9d   Divergent Response
   9e   Evaluative Response
   9i   Initiated Comment

10. Silence or Confusion:

   10s   Silence
   10c   Confusion

These additional categories show how the original ten categories may be expanded, making it possible for the observer to tailor his observational technique to the particular dimension of human interaction about which he is concerned.

Problems of Validity and Reliability

VALIDITY

The development of most psychological instruments is characterized by a number of studies which tend to validate the instrument and determine its reliability. Interaction Analysis is no exception, although the construct validity of the instrument is based on a conception of group climate or classroom social-emotional climate. This construct, developed at length in Chapter 1 of E. J. Amidon and Hough (1967), seems to be characterized by the feelings and attitudes that the members of the classroom group have toward one another, the subject they are studying, their teacher, and the work conducted in the classroom. Methods used to identify outside criteria for measuring the classroom climate have included supervisory ratings, behavior and reactions of the children, and in some cases objective observer ratings of classroom climate. The early studies of Withall and Flanders indicate that, in general, where children have more positive attitudes toward classes, teachers tend to be more indirect than teachers of classes in which children have more negative attitudes. These results were replicated in a foreign culture (Flanders, 1965b).

A more direct question of validity concerns the focus of the instrument itself. Interaction Analysis puts the classroom observer psychologically into the classroom group. The observer attempts to judge a teacher statement not on the basis of how he feels but rather on the effect the statement has on the group or a particular child in the group. If the instrument is valid, when the observer sees the teacher as accepting student ideas, the children should also be seeing their teacher as accepting their ideas and should be reacting by saying so. Conversely, when the observer notes that the teacher is criticizing the children, the children should also see the teacher as criticizing their ideas. Studies have attempted to compare observers' perceptions of teacher influence directly with the students' perceptions by asking the children questions based on the Interaction Analysis categories themselves: "Does your teacher accept your ideas?" "Does the teacher criticize you?" "Does the teacher praise your ideas?" "How much does the teacher talk?" In most studies (see E. J. Amidon [1959], J. P. Anderson [1960], and Kirk [1963] for three different types) the relationships between students' perceptions of teacher influence and Interaction Analysis data were congruent. That is, where the observer reported a particular type of influence, the children in the classes tended to perceive a similar type of influence.

More recent notions of the validity of Interaction Analysis have had to do with the relationship between teacher influence patterns and achievement of children in the classroom. If Interaction Analysis shows that certain teacher behavior patterns do or do not encourage achievement, then it can be used to predict achievement in the classroom. Interaction Analysis' validity as a prediction tool is much more significant than its validity as a tool simply to describe classroom climate, pupil attitudes toward the class, or pupil perceptions of the teacher.

The results of teacher education research using Interaction Analysis have added a further dimension to the question of validity as we think about what the category system is measuring and what it can do. Results of a number of studies (Kirk, 1963; Hough and E. J. Amidon, 1964a; Furst, 1965; Romoser, 1965; Zahn, 1965; E. J. Amidon, 1966b, 1967; Moskowitz, 1966a) clearly indicate that teachers who learn Interaction Analysis are more likely to be accepting, supportive, and less critical than teachers who are not taught Interaction Analysis. The results of these studies make it clear that Interaction Analysis is a tool that can be used to identify teaching patterns of teachers and to discriminate between groups of teachers who have received different kinds of training. It might seem logical since, in many cases, the training itself was Interaction Analysis training. However, Sorber's (1964) research compared two groups of teachers, both unaware of the Interaction Analysis categories. They, too, differed significantly in their use of certain Interaction Analysis behaviors.

RELIABILITY

The problem of reliability has received a great deal of attention in the research. Traditionally, reliability in Interaction Analysis has been thought of primarily as interobserver agreement for the same classroom observation, or consistency within the same observer across two observations. The problem with the second index of reliability is that it is difficult to assume that a teacher who is observed by the same observer over periods of time will produce the same behavior. In other words, a teacher might behave differently in six different classes or in the same class at six different times, so the data collected by the observer across the six observations could theoretically be different.

For the purpose of research, most interaction analysis projects have measured reliability with interobserver agreement. Determining observer agreement has depended on the specific category system used. In research studies using the interaction analysis system described here, observer agreement might be determined in a classroom situation by comparing the classifications of two trained observers and possibly one criterion expert or expert observer. Another method would be to have observers of different classes categorize a tape recording of a class which none of them had ever observed. A third method would be to check an observer against himself on a tape recording of a teacher he had already categorized after enough time has elapsed so that the observer does not remember the specific classifications he made before.

Agreement between two coders using typed scripts can be determined by having them code together the same typescript of a class. The same procedure could be used with tape recordings. With this method of determining reliability, observers are asked to resolve disagreement about particular classifications, thus modifying the whole notion of reliability. The problem of reliability here — agreement among the observers — is crucial when the observers are coding verbal classroom statements with no instrumentation available for checking out their classifications. Obviously, if their data are used for research purposes, the observers must be highly reliable.

An analysis of a number of tape recordings indicates that the major source of unreliability — lack of agreement between observers — is not in categorizing statements but in timing. When a lecture statement lasts for 10 seconds, two observers generally both classify it Category 5. But observers who are relatively fast may record four 5's in a period of 10 or 11 seconds, whereas an observer who is relatively slow may record three 5's in this same period. Although these differences are slight when considering a sequence of three or four 5's, they might become important when considering 20 to 40 minutes' worth of coding. These types of errors constitute the major source of observer unreliability; not hearing the teacher's statement or dropping a pencil are relatively unimportant.

INTERACTION ANALYSIS IN RESEARCH

Interaction analysis was developed originally as a research tool. Both Withall and Flanders used interaction analysis to identify and characterize classroom climates on the basis of the teachers' verbal statements. The bibliography gives some indication of the extent to which the instrument of interaction analysis is being used in a variety of research endeavors.

Interaction analysis has been used in three different basic types of research. The first is *descriptive*: characterizing the classrooms in terms of their interaction patterns. Descriptive research has been done in both elementary (Nelson, 1966; Soar, 1966a; Weber, 1967; Powell, 1968) and secondary (LeShier, 1965; Furst, 1967) schools, but not in colleges and graduate schools.

The second type of research is *experimental*: controlling teacher influence patterns as independent variables in order to determine relationships between patterns of teacher influence and certain other variables, for example, student achievement.

In *applied* research, teachers are trained to use interaction analysis as a research tool in observing themselves and their own classes. Then inter-action analysis is used to determine whether the training in the use of the instrument affects the teacher's interaction patterns in the classroom.

The following section discusses and describes examples of each of these three types of research and goes into one study of each type in detail.

Descriptive Research

Several studies have been largely descriptions of interaction in the class-room. Furst and Amidon (1962) observed 25 elementary school teachers in three subjects — reading, arithmetic, and social studies. Giammatteo (1963) analyzed interaction patterns of 130 elementary school teachers in language arts lessons. The results tended to support those of Furst and Amidon. Another study (Amidon and Giammatteo, 1965) compared teachers who were judged as superior by their supervisors with a randomly selected group of teachers. This study showed that superior teachers talked a smaller percentage of total class time, accepted and encouraged student ideas more, and made a greater effort to build on student ideas than did the randomly selected group of teachers.

As one of the earliest and most typical studies, the Furst and Amidon (1962) report will be described in detail. It attempted to determine if there were any differences in interaction patterns among six elementary grade levels and also among the subject areas of reading, social studies, and arithmetic.

PROCEDURE

Three socio-economic areas were identified: (1) intercity schools in Philadelphia, (2) a middle socio-economic area in Philadelphia, and (3) a high socio-economic suburban area. Approximately one-third of the observations were made in the intercity area, one-third in the middle socio-economic area, and one-third in the suburban schools. One hundred and sixty separate classroom observations were made between January and May of 1962. Twenty-five classrooms were observed at each grade level with a minimum of five classroom observations in each subject area for each grade level.

RESULTS

Results were reported as grade level comparisons and subject matter comparisons using a number of the statistics yielded by the Interaction Analysis system.

Relationship of indirect to direct teacher influence. The I/D ratio (overall index of indirectness or directness of a teacher) for Grades 1 and

2 in all subject areas was between 1 and 1.4, indicating that the teachers used more indirect influence than direct influence. The I/D ratio for arithmetic and reading in the third and fourth grades varied between .6 and .9, indicating more direct influence than indirect. In social studies, the I/D ratios for third and fourth grades were 1.2 and 1.32 respectively, or slightly more indirect. In fifth and sixth grades, I/D ratios were lower, .6 and 1.0 respectively. The revised or small i/d ratio (representing only Categories 1, 2, 3, 6, and 7, concerned with motivation control) in the first four grades was lower than the I/D ratios. In fifth and sixth grades, the revised i/d ratios were higher than the I/D ratios.

Teacher talk. Of the total interaction for first grade, teacher talk comprised 50 per cent. Some decrease was evident in second grade where only 45 per cent of the total talk was the teacher's. A slight increase of 47 per cent occurred in third grade, with a continued rise to 52 per cent in fourth grade. In fifth and sixth grades, teacher talk comprised 49 per cent of the total verbal behavior.

Student talk. Student talk made up 34 to 39 per cent of the total interaction in first and second grades, was down to between 33 and 36 per cent in third and fourth grades, and was down further to between 27 and 30 per cent in fifth and sixth grades.

Silence. Silence in first and second grades represented 15 per cent of the total lesson; in third grade it increased to 17 per cent; in fourth grade it was again down to 15 per cent. A definite rise was noted in fifth and sixth grades where silence was up to 20 per cent and then to 25 per cent.

Specific category totals. Praise (Category 2) represented 5 to 6 per cent of the total interaction in first and second grades, decreased to 3 per cent and 4 per cent in third and fourth grades, and was up in fifth and sixth grades to 4 per cent and 5 per cent respectively. Acceptance of student ideas (Category 1) represented 4 per cent in first grade, was down to slightly more than 2 per cent in second grade, and was slightly less than 2 per cent in third grade. It was up to 3.5 per cent in fourth, fifth, and sixth grades. Teacher questions (Category 4) represented 18 per cent of the total time in first, 16 per cent in second, and 15.5 per cent in third grade. In fourth grade, it was up to 17 per cent, was down again to 13 per cent in fifth grade, and was slightly less than 13 per cent in sixth grade. Lecture (Category 5) represented 9 per cent of total lesson time in first grade and increased with each grade level: 10 per cent in second grade, 14 per cent in third and fourth grades, and 21 per cent in fifth and sixth grades.

Direction giving (Category 6) decreased fairly consistently from first to sixth grade with some notable exceptions. The first-grade teachers used the most time for direction giving, although the third-grade teachers used more than the second-grade and nearly as much as the first-grade teachers. In two subject areas, reading and arithmetic, the third-grade teachers used as much or more direction giving than the first-grade teachers. The only consistent difference in the relative amount of directions given in different subject areas was in third and fifth grades, where teachers gave fewer directions in social studies than in other areas. The amount of direction giving decreased from third grade until sixth grade, and in the sixth grade directions were a very small percentage of the total classroom interaction.

Compared to other categories, there was very little time spent in criticism (Category 7) in any of the grades. There was an apparent decrease from first to sixth grade, with the first-grade teacher using the most criticism (3 per cent) and the sixth-grade teacher using the least (2 per cent).

Special cells in the matrix. One way to understand the relative emphasis of a particular teaching style from one grade level to another or one subject area to another is to identify the cells in the Interaction Analysis matrix that have the highest loading of tallies. In first grade, the cell indicating questions followed by student response (4–8) had the largest number of tallies. The second largest cell was the 8–8 or continued student response cell. These cells were large in all three subject matter areas. In second grade, the 8–8 was the largest cell in all subject areas, with the 4–8 and the 10–10 (continuous silence or confusion) cells next. The cells with the two heaviest frequencies in third grade for all subject areas were the 8–8 and the 10–10. However, in social studies, the 9–9 cell, indicating prolonged student initiated response, was the heaviest. In fourth grade, the cells containing the most tallies were the 4–8 and the 8–8, although in reading and arithmetic, teacher lecture followed by teacher lecture (5–5) was nearly as large as the other two cells. Arithmetic and reading in fifth grade had most tallies in the 10–10 cell with the 5–5 cell second. In social studies, the 5–5 cell was largest and the 10–10 and 8–8 were next. In sixth grade the 5–5 cell was the largest in reading and social studies and the 10–10 cell in arithmetic.

TRENDS AND CONCLUSIONS

Certain trends were clear as grade levels were compared with one another and subject matter areas were compared. In general, teachers appeared to be more indirect in the early grades and more direct in fifth and sixth grades. However, in the revised i/d ratio, fifth-grade teachers appeared to be more indirect and lower grade teachers more direct. Similarly, a direction in trends was indicated in the amount of teacher talk and student talk. Teacher talk, high in first grade, decreased in second grade. Although it increased in third and fourth grades, it was slightly less again in fifth and sixth grades. Student talk was highest in first and second grades. Teacher and student talk were both high in first grade because of the low occurrence of silence and confusion in the classroom. In first and second grades silence was lowest. It increased in third and fourth grades and became highest in sixth grade where 25 per cent of the observation was recorded in Category 10.

The specific categories of teacher talk indicated some trends that appeared worth noting. The almost total lack of tallies in Category 1 was a striking example. In no grade or subject area did the number of tallies in this category reach 1 per cent of the total. In only three classes observed, a second-grade social studies, a third-grade social studies, and a sixth-grade reading lesson, did the total in this category reach even half of 1 per cent. These three cases involved teachers who admitted to a philosophy of the teaching-learning process stressing acceptance of feelings. A somewhat surprising trend was observable in the amount of praise used at various grade levels. Praise was most used in first and second grades. It decreased to its lowest point in third grade and rose again in fifth and sixth grades. Comparing subject matter areas revealed that the greatest amount of praise used was in social studies and the least amount was in reading and arithmetic. In Grades 1, 2, and 3, however, teachers used the least amount of praise in reading, whereas in fourth, fifth, and sixth grades they used the least amount of praise in arithmetic. The patterns apparent in acceptance of student ideas were similar to those found in the use of praise. Accepting student ideas was highest in first grade, decreased in second grade, reached its lowest point in third, and then increased in fourth, fifth, and sixth grades. There was a clear trend in both question asking and lecture. Lecture was used least in first grade, then became higher with each succeeding grade level. The use of questions indicated a reverse trend. The first-grade teachers asked more questions than any of the others and the teachers of succeeding grades progressively fewer.

Experimental Research

From 1957 to 1959, Flanders investigated hypotheses on the effects of direct and indirect teacher influence and various conditions of goal perception on student achievement. In the first year of the study, the concept of teacher influence and goal perception was used with eighth-grade students in two areas — geometry and social studies — with a total of 560 geometry and 480 social studies students participating. Results of the experimental study in geometry are partially reported by Amidon and Flanders (1961, 1967) and Flanders (1965b). The results indicated that indirect teaching produced higher achievement among dependence-prone geometry pupils (pupils exhibiting low initiative and high reliance on the teacher) in the experimental group. Results for the first-year study were not clear in the social studies experiment.

The second year of the research project involved a field study that tested the same relationships as those tested the first year in the laboratory. Nine hundred students participated. Half of them were seventh-grade social studies students and half were seventh-grade geometry students. The 32 teachers, 16 in each area, were the regular classroom teachers. In the second-year study, predictions were made that students of indirect teachers would achieve more in both geometry and social studies than students of direct teachers. In both areas, although the mathematics teachers apparently used time differently from the teachers of social studies, the prediction was supported.

The section of the first-year laboratory study reported by Amidon and Flanders (1961), concerned with the relationship between teacher influence and the achievement of dependence-prone children in an eighth-grade geometry class, will be treated in detail.

PROCEDURE

The study employed a laboratory design in order to exercise experimental control of spontaneous behavior. First, the behavior of the teacher was controlled by training a single teacher to play the roles of both direct and indirect teacher. His statements in both roles were classified by an observer to make sure that the desired differences were great enough for students to notice. Second, of the total of 560 students participating, 140 who scored in the upper 25 per cent on a dependence-prone test developed by Flanders, Anderson, and Amidon (1961) were selected for the experimental population. Third, learning was controlled by using pre-tests and post-tests of geometry achievement. And fourth, for half the experimental groups the basic content material, presented in a tape recording, was organized so that the immediate learning goals were unclear; for the other half the immediate learning goals were made clear. The four treatments involved were:

> *Treatment* 1. Direct teacher influence, clear goals: 35 dependence-prone students
>
> *Treatment* 2. Direct teacher influence, unclear goals: 35 dependence-prone students
>
> *Treatment* 3. Indirect teacher influence, clear goals: 35 dependence-prone students
>
> *Treatment* 4. Indirect teacher influence, unclear goals: 35 dependence-prone students

Twenty students per session went to a spare room in a public school. First, a pre-test of geometry achievement and a test of dependence-proneness were administered. Second, a tape recording was played introducing the basic concepts of $C = D$ and Distance = Speed $\times$ Time, and geometric concepts and formulae concerning inscribed angles. For half the groups the recording explained clearly how this information could be used to solve problems; the other students were warned that they could not be sure how this information could be used. Third, in the direct treatments a teacher gave a 15-minute lecture, with a few questions, explaining the material and illustrating problems that could be solved. The content coverage was the same in the contrasting treatments. Fourth, the students spent about 15 minutes at their seats working practice problems. And fifth, the post-test of achievement was administered. The entire sequence lasted two hours. Later, the validity and reliability of the observers' judgments were verified by the tape recording that was made of every experimental session.

RESULTS

Control of teacher influence and goal perception. The manipulation of direct and indirect teacher influence occurred right after the tape recording when the teacher first came into contact with the students. The same role player acted as teacher in all treatments to eliminate the variables of personality and appearance. Table 10 classifies teacher statements according to interaction categories. The figures show the essential differences between the direct and indirect treatments: the teacher lectured and gave more directions in the direct treatments; he asked more questions and encouraged more student participation in the indirect treatments; he praised, encouraged, and clarified student ideas more frequently in the indirect treatments; and he criticized students more frequently in the direct treatments.

After the lectures and discussions and before the period devoted to practice problems, the students responded to a number of opinion items combined into a scale which measured their perceptions of the teacher's be-

TABLE 10

Percentage of Tallies in Interaction Categories

Category Definition	Treatment			
	1	2	3	4
Teacher talk:				
Praise and encouragement	1.35	1.61	17.04	14.90
Clarification and development of ideas suggested by students	2.48	0.92	15.78	16.10
Asks questions	2.58	1.73	28.07	30.04
Gives own opinions and facts (lectures)	63.10	61.40	13.52	15.97
Gives directions	8.67	10.36	0.28	0.27
Criticizes students	13.03	15.54	1.27	0.94
Student talk	5.07	5.29	16.47	17.17
No one talking	3.49	3.45	7.75	4.69
Total tallies on which the percentage figures are based	889	869	711	746

havior. An analysis of variance was made of these scale scores which indicated that the *F* ratio between the groups subjected to the direct and indirect influence treatments was 78.4 (*df* = 1/136). This was significant at the .01 level of probability. The mean scores indicated that students in the direct treatments more often saw the teacher as "telling us what to do," "firm and businesslike," "making plans for us," "critical of our ideas," "talking more than the students," and "not using student ideas or suggestions." In the indirect treatments, students often said the teacher was "finding out what we know," "relaxed and cheerful," "letting us make our own plans," "letting students talk," "using our ideas," and similar characteristics opposite to the direct pattern. The means and *F* ratio are presented in Table 11.

TABLE 11

Student Perception of Teacher Influence

Group	Mean	*F* between Direct and Indirect Groups
Direct influence	11.74	78.40
Indirect influence	18.84	

As expected, an analysis of observation data and of student perceptions of the teacher comparing the clear and unclear goal treatments showed no significant (*p* < .05) difference in teacher behavior. Also, no significant (*p* < .05) interaction effects were found in the analysis of variance. The interaction analysis data and measures of the students' perceptions showed that the differences between the direct and indirect approach did exist as required by the experimental design, were clearly seen by a trained observer, and were noticed by the students.

Paper-and-pencil measures of the clarity of goals (students were asked to solve geometry problems by applying the concepts the teacher had taught them) were made after the playback of the tape recording introducing the basic geometric concepts. An analysis of variance of these scale scores yielded an *F* ratio of 16.98 (*df* = 1/136, *p* < .01). An inspection of the means indicated that the results were consistent with the intended goal manipulation. The results showed that the immediate responses of students to the clear and unclear tape recordings were significantly different. The means and *F* ratio are found in Table 12.

Geometry achievement. Since achievement in geometry was the fundamental outcome variable analyzed in this study, the post-test was subjected to several analyses. The first analysis was comparing the post-test scores of the indirect and direct teacher influence groups. The *F* ratio found in this

TABLE 12

Student Perception of the Goal

Group	Mean	F between Clear and Unclear Groups
Clear goals	21.40	16.98
Unclear goals	26.13	

analysis was 7.67, which was significant at the .01 level. The means of the indirect teacher influence groups were significantly higher than the means of the direct teacher influence groups on the post-test measure. In order to reduce unaccounted-for error in the analysis of post-tests, two analyses of covariance controlling pre-test scores and intelligence scores were run. The F ratio between direct and indirect teacher influence groups was 10.03 when intelligence was controlled and 9.62 when pre-test scores were controlled. Again, those F ratios were significant at the .01 level, indicating the superiority of the indirect teacher influence group. For each of the analyses of covariance $df = 1/137$.

The analysis of variance and covariance just discussed yielded insignificant ($p > .05$) results when the clear and ambiguous goal perception groups were compared statistically. The interaction of goal perception and teacher influence also did not yield significant ($p > .05$) results. The F ratios found in these analyses are presented in Table 13.

TABLE 13

Analysis of Differences in the Means of Post-Test Scores with Various Factors Controlled Statistically

Source of Variation	df	F	Null Hypothesis
With no measure controlled:			
Interaction	1	—	Not rejected
Teacher influence	1	7.67	Rejected
Goal perception	1	—	Not rejected
Pre-achievement controlled:			
Interaction	1	2.71	Not rejected
Teacher influence	1	10.03	Rejected
Goal perception	1	—	Not rejected
Intelligence controlled:			
Interaction	1	1.08	Not rejected
Teacher influence	1	9.62	Rejected
Goal perception	1	1.13	Not rejected

The means of the indirect group were significantly higher than the means of the direct group. This was true both when intelligence and pre-test achievement scores were controlled and when they were not controlled. The means of the direct and indirect teacher influence groups are presented in Table 14.

TABLE 14

*Means of Direct and Indirect Groups
for Post-Achievement Measure*

Mean	Not Adjusted	Adjusted by Pre-Test Scores	Adjusted by Intelligence
Direct group	9.24	9.31	9.30
Indirect group	10.82	10.76	10.69

DISCUSSION

The measures of geometry achievement indicate that the dependence-prone students learned more in the classroom in which the teacher gave fewer directions, less criticism, less lecturing, more praise, and asked more questions which increased their verbal participation. This finding takes on added significance when compared with Flanders' (1965b) findings that the total group of 560 students failed to show the same significant differences under the same conditions. Moreover, when the independence-prone students (those in the twenty-fifth percentile on the dependency scale) were compared separately, no differences were found. Compared with students in general, dependence-prone students are apparently more sensitive to the influence pattern of a geometry teacher.

One implication of this study is that closer supervision through the use of direct influence, an all too common antidote to lower achievement, may be more harmful than helpful for dependence-prone students.

Applied Research

Flanders (1962) first attempted to use Interaction Analysis as a method for training teachers. The idea was that instead of training an observer to collect data about teachers in a large research project, the teacher himself should be trained to observe and analyze his own teaching, with an eye to developing and improving his teaching techniques. Hough and E. J. Amidon (1964a, b) applied this idea to the in-service training of teachers. Since they initiated their first project at Temple University, numbers of studies have been conducted on the effects of training in Interaction Analysis on student teachers' classroom behavior. These studies include Kirk (1963), Hough and E. J. Amidon (1964a, b; 1965), E. J. Amidon and Powell

(1965), Romoser (1965), Zahn (1965), E. J. Amidon (1966b, 1967), Hough and Ober (1966), Moskowitz (1966a), Simon (1966), Lohman (1967), and Gillman (1968). In some of these studies, the groups of teachers who were not taught Interaction Analysis underwent other specific kinds of experimental training. However, most of these groups received what we might call "traditional" training, although the specific type often differed from one study to another. In all events, the results of the studies appear to be conclusive. Student teachers taught Interaction Analysis differed significantly from groups of student teachers who were not taught Interaction Analysis. They were found to (1) take more time to accept new student ideas, (2) encourage a greater amount of pupil-initiated talk, (3) use less criticism, (4) use less direction, (5) be more accepting and encouraging in response to student ideas, and (6) have a more generally indirect teaching style.

Amidon and Powell's (1965, 1966) two-and-a-half-year study was designed to test the relationships between the training of cooperating teachers, certain course content, and the behavior of student teachers. The following hypotheses were tested:

(1) Student teachers taught Interaction Analysis are more indirect at the end of their student teaching experience than student teachers not taught Interaction Analysis.

(2) Student teachers supervised by those cooperating teachers who have been trained in Interaction Analysis are more indirect at the end of student teaching than student teachers working with cooperating teachers not trained in Interaction Analysis.

PROCEDURE

This study employed a two-by-two design in order to test the influence of two variables (student teacher training and cooperating teacher training) on certain measures of student teacher behavior and attitudes. These training variables are often considered to be the most important elements in the teacher education program. The experiment was carried out during three successive semesters in order to provide for replication under nearly ideal conditions.

Student teachers in Group I (see Figure 3) were taught Interaction Analysis in weekly two-hour lectures and weekly two-hour laboratories. In addition, they discussed problems they were having with their teaching in weekly two-hour seminars with a college faculty member. The cooperating teacher, using Interaction Analysis, observed the student teacher formally once every week for 30 to 40 minutes, and he spent one hour a week discussing the observation with the student teacher.

Student teachers in Group II were trained in the same way, except that the cooperating teacher, trained in learning theory, observed the student teacher formally without using Interaction Analysis.

FIGURE 3

The Four Experimental Groups

Course Content	Supervisory Cooperating Teacher Trained in	
	Interaction Analysis	Learning Theory
Interaction analysis and seminar	Group I	Group II
Learning theory and seminar	Group III	Group IV

Student teachers in Group III were taught learning theory in weekly two-hour lectures and weekly two-hour laboratories. In addition, they discussed problems they were having with their teaching in weekly two-hour seminars with a college staff member. They were also observed formally once a week for between 30 and 40 minutes by their cooperating teacher, who spent one hour a week discussing the observation with them. Although the cooperating teacher was trained in Interaction Analysis and may have used it in his observation, he was instructed not to discuss this tool or any of its terminology with the student teacher under any circumstances.

Student teachers in Group IV were trained in the same way as Group III, except that the cooperating teacher was trained in learning theory and not Interaction Analysis.

Obviously, two different types of training were used with both student teachers and their cooperating teachers. The courses in Interaction Analysis or learning theory given to the student teachers were identical to those given to the cooperating teachers except that the courses given to the student teachers were approximately 60 hours, while the courses for the cooperating teachers were 45 hours.

RESULTS

The first analyses compared directness and indirectness. The revised i/d ratios of the student teachers in the first two semesters showed no differences among the groups. In the third semester, however, the student teachers trained in Interaction Analysis had significantly higher revised i/d ratios than the student teachers trained in learning theory.

The I/D ratios (the second variable used as a test of the two hypotheses) were mixed for the first two semesters. The comparison of data in the third semester, however, produced a difference that was significant at the .05 level and approached the .01 level, supporting the first hypothesis.

The next measure of indirect-direct teaching was the revised i/d ratio for

Column 8. Hypothesis 2 was supported in the third semester ($p > .05$). The difference indicated that the Interaction Analysis group was significantly more indirect. In the first semester the differences were in the predicted direction, but significant only at the .10 level.

The next variable was the I/D ratio for Column 8. Again, as in the previous tests, the only .05 level difference was for the third semester and between types of student teacher training. However, the first-semester difference was in the predicted direction.

The revised i/d ratio for Column 9 showed significant differences in both the first and third semesters between the student teachers who learned Interaction Analysis and those who were exposed to learning theory. Again this supports the first hypothesis.

The I/D ratio for Column 9 included one large difference for the third semester which supported Hypothesis 1. There was also a trend in the predicted direction in the first-semester I/D ratio.

An analysis of the revised i/d ratio for Columns 8 and 9 produced one .05 difference in the first semester, a trend for the second semester, and a .10 level difference in the third semester. These three differences support the first hypothesis.

The I/D ratio for Columns 8 and 9 yielded similar results to the i/d ratio for Rows 8 and 9. That is, in the first semester the results tended to support Hypothesis 1 (.10 level), and in the third semester they also supported Hypothesis 1 (.01).

Analysis of the next variable, extended indirect influence, supported Hypothesis 2 in all three semesters. In the first and second semesters the differences were significant at the .05 level, and in the third semester the difference was significant at the .01 level.

Analysis of the extended direct influence variable produced no differences that were significant, although the slight differences were in the right direction in the first and third semesters.

The extended i/d ratio was significant in the first semester at the .01 level and in the third semester at the .05 level. The second semester was again not different, and therefore, as with previous variables, the second hypothesis was supported in the first and third semesters but not in the second.

The I/D ratio for Column 9 divided by the revised i/d ratio for Column 8 further analyzed a variable highly related to pupil achievement. Although the result in the third semester was significant (.05), all three semesters yielded data in the direction predicted in Hypothesis 1.

The revised i/d ratio for Column 9 divided by the revised i/d ratio for Column 8 produced large differences in any of the analyses, the proper direction to support Hypothesis 1.

Analysis of the three indirect categories (Categories 1–3) offered support for Hypothesis 1, but for Category 1 the differences for the three semesters never reached the .10 level. Category 2 was in the predicted direction in all three semesters, in the first semester at the .10 level, and in the third semester at the .05 level. Analysis of Category 3 yielded significant F ratios in the first (.10), second (.10), and third (.05) semesters. The analysis of these categories produces conflicting results for the second hypothesis.

The last index of indirectness used was analysis of the 3–3 cell. It offered support for the second hypothesis in the first ($F = 3.91$, $p > .10$) and second ($F = 5.36$, $p > .05$) semesters, but in the third semester, though the difference was in the right direction, the F ratio was below 1.

Table 15 presents a summary of the appropriate results for Hypothesis 2.

Of the 20 separate variables analyzed in each of the three semesters (60 separate tests), eight showed no difference or a trend in the direction not predicted in Hypothesis 1. Not one of these eight produced an F ratio of 1.0 or more. On the other hand, of the 52 tests resulting in the predicted

TABLE 15

Summary of Analysis Relevant to Testing of Hypothesis 2†

Variable		Student Teacher Training Semester			Cooperating Teacher Training Semester		
		1	2	3	1	2	3
104	(i/d)	1.37	+	3.39	−	+	+
105	(I/D)	+	−	6.50*	4.00	−	−
106	(i/d-8)	3.25	1.33	5.00*	−	+	+
107	(I/D-8)	1.09	−	5.50*	−	+	−
108	(i/d-9)	5.80*	+	5.50*	−	−	+
109	(I/D-9)	3.50	+	16.60**	1.25	−	−
110	(i/d-8+9)	5.33*	+	3.00	−	+	−4.00
111	(I/D-8+9)	3.67	−	21.00**	−	+	3.00
112	(Ex. ind.)	4.96*	4.62*	8.47*	−	−	−
113	(Ex. dir.)	+	−	+	−	1.28	1.50
114	(Ex. ind./ ex. dir.)	8.00**	−	6.71*	−	+	+
122	(i/d-9/ i/d-8)	1.80	+	+	−	+	+
123	(I/D-9/ i/d-8)	+	1.28	4.27*	−	+	−
129	(Col. 1)	1.20	2.65	1.79	1.47	−3.75	−
130	(Col. 2)	3.67	+	5.58*	2.46	+	−
131	(Col. 3)	3.80	4.19*	3.22	−2.38	+	−2.33
134	(Col. 6)	+	−	5.36*	+	+	2.01
135	(Col. 7)	4.75*	+	−	+	1.23	+
137	(Col. 9)	+	−	8.35**	+	−	−7.91**
139	(3-3 Cell)	3.91	5.36*	+	−	+	+

† A plus sign (+) indicates "in the predicted direction." A minus sign (−) indicates "not in the predicted direction." All F ratios without minus signs were in the predicted direction.
  * .05 level of probability
** .01 level of probability

direction, nine were significant at the .01 level. On the basis of these results, Hypothesis 1, that student teachers taught Interaction Analysis are more indirect at the end of their student teaching experience than student teachers not so taught, was supported.

The data did not give as clear a picture for Hypothesis 2. Of the 60 analyses, 30 were not in the predicted direction. Several of the differences in the wrong direction also produced F ratios above 1.0, and one was significant at the .01 level.

The results of the tests of Hypothesis 1, the single hypothesis that was accepted, do appear to have a potential impact on the field of teacher education. Apparently the immediate effect of teaching student teachers Interaction Analysis is that they become more indirect in working with pupils. Some evidence also indicates that the children perceive this effect, but it is inconclusive.

Specific Uses

The three studies just described indicate the primary uses of Interaction Analysis in research, but other research studies have used the tool in a number of different ways. The following list includes some of these more specific uses in educational research.

(1) Interaction Analysis has been used to describe interaction patterns existing in a particular school, a randomly selected group of teachers of specific grade levels, and/or specific subject matter areas (E. J. Amidon and Flanders, 1961; Nelson, 1964; LeShier, 1965; Moskowitz, 1966b; Pankratz, 1967).

(2) Interaction Analysis has been used to describe interaction patterns of teachers and then relate these patterns to other outside criteria by which these teachers have previously been identified (Davies, 1961; Spaulding, 1962; Amidon and Giammatteo, 1965).

(3) The instrument has been used to describe the development of teachers' interaction patterns over extended time. Only a few of these studies have been attempted; they usually span an academic year (Flanders, 1963a; Farrow, 1965; Gillman, 1968).

(4) Interaction Analysis has been used for controlling teaching styles in experimental studies on the effects of teacher behavior on student achievement in certain subjects (Lambert, 1961–1969; J. P. Anderson, 1963; Flanders, 1964, 1965b; Bidwell, 1967).

(5) The instrument has been used to measure teaching behavior at the beginning and at the end of an experiment in which some type of training of the teachers took place (Kirk, 1963; Hough and Amidon, 1964a; Furst, 1965; Hough, 1965b; Hough and Ober, 1966; Moskowitz, 1966a).

(6) It has also been used in contexts other than the classroom in which a leader is working with a group in somewhat the same way a teacher works with a group of students, for example, with counselling groups to analyze

the behavior of the counselor-counselee interaction, and in faculty meetings to analyze the behavior of the administrator (Amidon, 1965a).

(7) In recent years, it has been used most extensively to gather data about a leader's or teacher's behavior which can then be used as a basis for feedback in a training program. Though this kind of program is part of a research design, the instrument is often used simply as a feedback device in in-service and pre-service teacher education. In these contexts, it is often used in conjunction with video and audio tape recording (Flanders, 1962, 1963a, b; Amidon and Powell, 1965, 1966; Hill, 1966; Amidon, 1967; Amidon, Furst, and Mickelson, 1967; D. L. Wright, 1967).

Interaction Analysis has rapidly assumed national importance in education. Though it was at first used only as a research tool, its most recent application appears to be as a research tool and teacher training technique. It has become clear to most psychologists and educational psychologists using this approach that the instrument has useful applications not only in educational research and teacher education, but also in social work, counseling, and other areas of supervision and administration where people interact with one another in a face-to-face situation.

References and Selected Readings

Amidon, E. J. Dependent-prone students in experimental learning situations. Unpublished doctoral dissertation, University of Minnesota, 1959.

Amidon, E. J. The observational technique of interaction analysis applied to the classroom: Procedures and limitations. Paper presented at the annual meeting of the American Educational Research Association, Chicago, February 1963.

Amidon, E. J. A technique for analyzing counselor-counselee interaction. In J. Adams (Ed.), *Counseling and guidance: A summary view*. New York: Macmillan, 1965. Pp. 50–56. (a)

Amidon, E. J. Interaction analysis and its application to student teaching. *Association for Student Teaching yearbook*. Dubuque, Iowa: William C. Brown, 1965. Pp. 71–92. (b)

Amidon, E. J. Interaction analysis: Recent developments. Paper presented at the annual meeting of the American Educational Research Association, Chicago, February 1966. (a)

Amidon, E. J. Using interaction analysis at Temple University. Paper presented at the Conference on the Implications of Recent Research on Teaching for Teacher Education, sponsored by the National Association for Student Teaching and the University of Rochester, Rochester, January 1966. (b)

Amidon, E. J. *Project on student teaching: The effects of teaching interaction analysis to student teachers*. United States Department of Health, Education and Welfare, Office of Education, Cooperative Research Project No. 2873. Philadelphia: Temple University, 1967.

Amidon, E. J., and Amidon, P. *Interaction analysis training kit: Level I.* Minneapolis: Association for Productive Teaching, 1967. (a)

Amidon, E. J., and Amidon, P. *Interaction analysis training kit: Level II.* Minneapolis: Association for Productive Teaching, 1967. (b)

Amidon, E. J., and Amidon, P. *Teaching pattern analysis.* Minneapolis: Association for Productive Teaching, 1967. (c)

Amidon, E. J., Amidon, P., and Rosenshine, B. *Skill development in teaching manuals.* Minneapolis: Association for Productive Teaching, 1968.

Amidon, E. J., and Flanders, N. A. The effects of direct and indirect teacher influence on dependent-prone students learning geometry. *Journal of Educational Psychology,* 1961, **52,** 286–291.

Amidon, E. J., and Flanders, N. A. *The role of the teacher in the classroom.* (Rev. ed.) Minneapolis: Association for Productive Teaching, 1967.

Amidon, E. J., Furst, N., and Mickelson, J. The effects of teaching interaction analysis to student teachers. Paper presented at the annual meeting of the American Educational Research Association, New York, February 1967.

Amidon, E. J., Furst, N., Moskowitz, G., and Simon, A. An experimental course in pre-service education. *Classroom Interaction Newsletter,* 1966, **1** (2), 6–9.

Amidon, E. J., and Giammatteo, M. The verbal behavior of superior teachers. *Elementary School Journal,* 1965, **65,** 283–285.

Amidon, E. J., and Hough, J. B. *Interaction Analysis: Research, theory and application.* Reading, Mass.: Addison-Wesley, 1967.

Amidon, E. J., and Hunter, E. *Improving teaching: Analyzing verbal interaction in the classroom.* New York: Holt, Rinehart, & Winston, 1966. (a)

Amidon, E. J., and Hunter, E. Verbal interaction in the classroom. *Professional Reprints in Education,* No. 8605. Columbus, Ohio: Charles E. Merrill, 1966. (b)

Amidon, E. J., Kies, K., and Palisi, A. A fresh look at supervision. *The National Elementary Principal,* 1966, **45** (5), 54–59.

Amidon, E. J., and Powell, E. R. Interaction analysis as a feedback system in teacher preparation. Paper presented at the Association for Supervision and Curriculum Development meeting, Curriculum Research Institute, Washington, November 1965.

Amidon, E. J., and Powell, E. R. Interaction analysis as a feedback system in teacher preparation. In *The supervisor: Agent for change in teaching.* Washington: Association for Supervision and Curriculum Development, 1966. Pp. 31–46.

Amidon, E. J., and Simon, A. Implications for teacher education of interaction analysis research in student teaching. Paper presented as part of a symposium on interaction analysis and its application to student teaching, annual meeting of the American Educational Research Association, Chicago, February 1965. (a)

Amidon, E. J., and Simon, A. Teacher-pupil interaction. *Review of Educational Research,* 1965, **35,** 130–139. (b)

Amidon, P. *Skill development in teaching workbook.* Minneapolis: Association for Productive Teaching, 1968.

Anderson, H. H. The measurement of domination and socially integrative behavior in teachers' contacts with children. *Child Development,* 1939, **10,** 73–89.

Anderson, H. H., and Brewer, H. Studies of teachers' classroom personalities: I. Dominative and socially integrative behavior of kindergarten teachers. *Psychological Monographs,* 1945, No. 6.

Anderson, H. H., and Brewer, J. E. Studies of teachers' classroom personalities: II. Effects of teachers' dominative and integrative contacts on children's classroom behavior. *Psychological Monographs,* 1946, No. 8.

Anderson, H. H., Brewer, J. E., and Reed, M. F. Studies of teachers' classroom personalities: III. Follow-up studies of the effects of dominative and integrative contacts on children's behavior. *Psychological Monographs,* 1946, No. 11.

Anderson, J. P. Student perception of teacher influence. Unpublished doctoral dissertation, University of Minnesota, 1960.

Anderson, J. P. Conclusions concerning teaching influence, pupil attitudes and achievement. Paper presented at the annual meeting of the American Educational Research Association, Chicago, February 1963.

Aschner, M. J. The analysis of verbal interaction in the classroom. In A. A. Bellack (Ed.), *Theory and research in teaching.* New York: Bureau of Publications, Teachers College, Columbia University, 1961. Pp. 53–78. (a)

Aschner, M. J. The productive thinking of the gifted children in the classroom. Paper presented at the annual meeting of the American Educational Research Association, Chicago, February 1961. (b)

Aschner, M. J. A theoretical model for research in education. Paper presented at the annual meeting of the American Educational Research Association, New York, February 1967.

Aschner, M. J., Gallagher, J. J., Perry, J. M., Jenne, W., Afsar, S. S., and Farr, H. *A system for classifying thought processes in the context of classroom verbal interaction.* Urbana: Institute for Research on Exceptional Children, University of Illinois, 1965.

Bales, R. *Interaction process analysis.* Cambridge, Mass.: Addison-Wesley, 1950.

Bellack, A. A. (Ed.) *Theory and research in teaching.* New York: Bureau of Publications, Teachers College, Columbia University, 1963.

Bellack, A. A., Kliebard, H. M., and Hyman, R. T. *The language of the classroom.* U. S. Department of Health, Education and Welfare, Office of Education, Cooperative Research Project. New York: Bureau of Publications, Teachers College, Columbia University, 1967.

Biddle, B. J., and Ellena, W. J. (Eds.) *Contemporary research on teacher effectiveness.* New York: Holt, Rinehart, & Winston, 1964.

Bidwell, C. G. Student achievement in learning percent as affected by teaching method and teaching patterns. Unpublished doctoral dissertation, Temple University, 1967.

Davies, L. S. Some relationships between attitudes, personality characteristics, and verbal behavior of selected teachers. Unpublished doctoral dissertation, University of Minnesota, 1961.

Dawson, R. W. *Observer reliability and the classification of classroom communication.* Minneapolis: University of Minnesota, 1962.

Farrow, R. Changes in student teachers' verbal behavior. *Dissertation Abstracts,* 1965, **25,** 3991–3992.

Filson, T. M. Factors influencing the level of dependence in the classroom. Unpublished doctoral dissertation, University of Minnesota, 1957.

Flanders, N. A. Teacher-pupil contacts and mental hygiene. *Journal of Social Issues,* 1959, **15,** 30–39.

Flanders, N. A. Diagnosing and utilizing social structures in classroom learning. In N. B. Henry (Ed.), *The dynamics of instructional groups.* 59th yearbook of the National Society for the Study of Education. Chicago: University of Chicago Press, 1960. Pp. 187–217. (a)

Flanders, N. A. *Interaction analysis in the classroom: A manual for observers.* Minneapolis: University of Minnesota, 1960. (b)

Flanders, N. A. Interaction analysis: A technique for quantifying teacher influence. Paper presented at the annual meeting of the American Educational Research Association, Chicago, February 1961.

Flanders, N. A. Using interaction analysis in the in-service training of teachers. *Journal of Experimental Education,* 1962, **30,** 341–349.

Flanders, N. A. *Helping teachers change their behavior.* United States Department of Health, Education and Welfare, Office of Education, Project Nos. 1721012 and 7-32-0560-171.0. Ann Arbor: University of Michigan, 1963. (a)

Flanders, N. A. Intent, action and feedback: A preparation for teaching. *Journal of Teacher Education,* 1963, **14,** 251–260. (b)

Flanders, N. A. Teacher influence in the classroom. In A. A. Bellack (Ed.), *Theory and research in teaching.* New York: Bureau of Publications, Teachers College, Columbia University, 1963. Pp. 37–52. (c)

Flanders, N. A. Some relationships between teacher influence, pupil attitudes and achievement. In B. J. Biddle and W. J. Ellena (Eds.), *Contemporary research on teacher effectiveness.* New York: Holt, Rinehart & Winston, 1964. Pp. 196–231.

Flanders, N. A. Integrating theory and practice in teacher education. In *Theoretical bases for professional laboratory experiences in teacher education.* 44th yearbook of the Association for Student Teaching. Dubuque, Iowa: Association for Student Teaching, 1965. Pp. 59–68. (a)

Flanders, N. A. *Teacher influence, pupil attitudes, and achievement.* United States Department of Health, Education and Welfare, Office of Education, Cooperative Research Monograph No. 12. Washington: Government Printing Office, 1965. (b)

Flanders, N. A., and Amidon, E. J. Two approaches to the teaching process. *NEA Journal,* 1962, **51** (5), 43–45.

Flanders, N. A., Anderson, J. P., and Amidon, E. J. Measuring dependence-proneness in the classroom. *Educational and Psychological Measurement,* 1961, **21,** 575–587.

Flanders, N. A., and Havumaki, S. Group compliance to dominative teacher influence. *Human Relations,* 1960, **13,** 67–82.

Flanders, N. A., and Simon, A. Teacher effectiveness. In R. L. Ebel (Ed.), *Encyclopedia of Educational Research* (4th ed.), in press.

Fowler, B. D. Relation of teacher personality characteristics and attitudes to teacher-pupil rapport and emotional climate in the elementary classroom. Unpublished doctoral dissertation, University of South Carolina, 1961.

Furst, N. The effects of training in interaction analysis on the behavior of student teachers in secondary schools. Paper presented at the annual meeting of the American Educational Research Association, Chicago, February 1965.

Furst, N. The multiple languages of the classroom: A further analysis and a synthesis of meanings communicated in high school teaching. Unpublished doctoral dissertation, Temple University, 1967.

Furst, N., and Amidon, E. J. Teacher-pupil interaction patterns in the elementary school. Paper presented at Schoolmen's Week, University of Pennsylvania, Philadelphia, October 1962.

Gage, N. L. (Ed.) *Handbook of research on teaching.* Chicago: Rand McNally, 1963.

Gallagher, J. J. Expressive thought by gifted children in the classroom. *Elementary English,* 1965, **42,** 559–568.

Gallagher, J. J. A topic classification system in analysis of BSCS concept presentation. *Classroom Interaction Newsletter,* 1967, **2** (2), 20–22.

Gallagher, J. J., and Aschner, M. J. A preliminary report on analysis of classroom interaction. Merrill-Palmer Quarterly, 1963, **9,** 183–195.

Galloway, C. An exploratory study of observational procedures for determining teacher nonverbal communication. Unpublished doctoral dissertation, University of Florida, 1962.

Giammatteo, M. C. Interaction patterns of elementary teachers using the Minnesota categories for interaction analysis. Unpublished doctoral dissertation, University of Pittsburgh, 1963.

Gillman, R. A follow-up study on the effects of training in interaction analysis on the behavior of teachers. Unpublished doctoral dissertation, Temple University, 1968.

Guilford, J. P. The structure of intellect. *Psychological Bulletin,* 1956, **53,** 267–293.

Hayes, R. B., Keim, F. N., and Neiman, A. M. *The effects of student reactions to teaching methods.* Bureau of Research Administration and Coordination, Department of Public Instruction, Harrisburg, Pa. Cooperative Research Project No. 6-2056. September 1967.

Hill, W. M. The effects on verbal teaching behavior of learning interaction as an in-service education activity. Unpublished doctoral dissertation, Ohio State University, 1966.

Honigman, F. K. Testing a three-dimensional system for analyzing teacher influence. Unpublished doctoral dissertation, Temple University, 1966.

Honigman, F. K. *Multidimensional analysis of classroom interaction (MACI).* Villanova, Pa.: Villanova University Press, 1967. (a)

Honigman, F. K. *MACI abstract*. Philadelphia: Department of Curriculum and Instruction, School District of Philadelphia, 1967. (b)

Hough, J. B. The dogmatism factor in the human relations training of pre-service teachers. Paper presented at the annual meeting of the American Educational Research Association, Chicago, February 1965. (a)

Hough, J. B. A study of the effect of five experimental treatments on the development of human relations skills and verbal teaching behaviors of pre-service teachers. Unpublished paper, Ohio State University, 1965. (b)

Hough, J. B. Interaction analysis in a general methods course. *Classroom Interaction Newsletter,* 1966, **1** (2), 11–14.

Hough, J. B. Classroom interaction and the facilitation of learning: The source of an instructional theory. In E. J. Amidon and J. B. Hough (Eds.), *Interaction analysis: Theory, research and application*. Reading, Mass.: Addison-Wesley, 1967. Pp. 375–387. (a)

Hough, J. B. An observational system for the analysis of classroom instruction. In E. J. Amidon and J. B. Hough (Eds.), *Interaction analysis: Theory, research and application*. Reading, Mass.: Addison-Wesley, 1967. Pp. 150–157. (b)

Hough, J. B. Training in the control of verbal teacher behavior — Theory and implications. Paper presented at the annual meeting of the American Educational Research Association, New York, February 1967. (c)

Hough, J. B., and Amidon, E. J. *Behavioral change in pre-service teacher preparation: An experimental study*. Philadelphia: College of Education, Temple University, 1964. (a)

Hough, J. B., and Amidon, E. J. An experiment in pre-service teacher education. Paper presented at the annual meeting of the American Educational Research Association, Chicago, February 1964. (b)

Hough, J. B., and Amidon, E. J. The relationship of personality structure and training in interaction analysis to attitude change during student teaching. Paper presented at the annual meeting of the American Educational Research Association, Chicago, February 1965.

Hough, J. B., and Ober, R. L. The effects of training in interaction analysis on the verbal behavior of pre-service teachers. Paper presented at the annual meeting of the American Educational Research Association, Chicago, February 1966.

Hughes, M. *Development of the means for the assessment of the quality of teaching in elementary schools*. U. S. Department of Health, Education and Welfare, Office of Education, Cooperative Research Project No. 353, University of Utah, 1959.

Hughes, M. What is teaching? One viewpoint. *Educational Leadership,* 1962, **19,** 251–259.

Joyce, B. R., and Harootunian, B. *The structure of teaching*. Chicago: Science Research Associates, 1967.

Joyce, B. R., and Hodges, R. E. Instructional flexibility training. *Journal of Teacher Education,* 1966, **17,** 409–415.

Kirk, J. Effects of teaching the Minnesota system of interaction analysis to intermediate grade student teachers. Unpublished doctoral dissertation, Temple University, 1963.

LaGrone, H. F. *A proposal for the revision of the pre-service professional component of a program of teacher education.* U. S. Department of Health, Education and Welfare, Office of Education, Educational Media Branch, Contract No. OE3-16-006. Washington: American Association of Colleges for Teacher Education, 1964.

Lambert, P. *Classroom interaction, pupil achievement, and adjustment in team teaching as compared with the self-contained classroom.* U. S. Department of Health, Education and Welfare, Office of Education, Cooperative Research Project No. 1391, 1961–1969.

LeShier, W. S., Jr. An analysis of certain aspects of the verbal behavior of student teachers of eighth grade students participating in a BSCS laboratory block. Unpublished doctoral dissertation, University of Texas, 1965.

LeShier, W. S., Jr. The use of interaction analysis in BSCS laboratory block classrooms. Paper presented at the National Science Teachers Association Meetings, New York, April 1966.

Lohman, E. E. Differential effects of training on the verbal behavior of student teachers — Theory and implications. Paper presented at the annual meeting of the American Educational Research Association, New York, February 1967.

Lohman, E. E., Ober, R. L., and Hough, J. B. A study of the effects of pre-service training in interaction analysis on the verbal behavior of student teachers. In E. J. Amidon and J. B. Hough (Eds.), *Interaction analysis: Research, theory and application.* Reading, Mass.: Addison-Wesley, 1967. Pp. 346–359.

Medley, D. *Studies of teachers' behavior: Refinement of two techniques for assessing teachers' classroom behavior.* New York: Office of Research and Evaluation, Division of Teacher Education of the City University of New York, 1955.

Medley, D. Technique for measuring classroom behavior. *Journal of Educational Psychology,* 1958, **49,** 86–92.

Medley, D. Experiences with the OSCAR technique. *Journal of Teacher Education,* 1963, **14,** 267–273.

Mitzel, H. E. Teacher effectiveness. In C. W. Harris (Ed.), *Encyclopedia of educational research.* (3rd ed.) New York: Macmillan, 1960. Pp. 1481–1486.

Moskowitz, G. The effects of training in interaction analysis on the attitudes and teaching patterns of cooperating teachers and their student teachers. Unpublished doctoral dissertation, Temple University, 1966. (a)

Moskowitz, G. The Flint system: An observational tool for the foreign language class (Foreign language interaction system). Unpublished paper, Temple University, 1966. (b)

Nelson, L. N. The effect of classroom interaction on pupil linguistic performance. *Dissertation Abstracts,* 1964, **25,** 1789.

Nelson, L. N. Teacher leadership: An empirical approach to analyzing teacher behavior in the classroom. *Classroom Interaction Newsletter,* 1966, **2** (1), 18–21.

Ober, R. L. Predicting student teacher verbal behavior. Unpublished doctoral dissertation, Ohio State University, 1966.

Ober, R. L. Predicting the verbal behavior of student teachers. Paper presented at the annual meeting of the American Educational Research Association, New York, February 1967.

Oliver, D. W., and Shaver, J. P. The development of a multi-dimensional observation system for the analysis of pupil-teacher interaction. Paper presented at the annual meeting of the American Educational Research Association, Chicago, February 1963.

Pankratz, R. Verbal interaction patterns in the classrooms of selected physics teachers. In E. J. Amidon and J. B. Hough (Eds.), *Interaction analysis: Theory, research and application.* Reading, Mass.: Addison-Wesley, 1967. Pp. 189–210.

Perkins, H. Climate influences group learning. *Journal of Educational Research,* 1951, **45,** 115–119.

Powell, E. R. Some relationships between classroom process and pupil achievement in the elementary school. Unpublished doctoral dissertation, Temple University, 1968.

Proctor, V. A further refinement of the Wright observational schedule. Unpublished Master's thesis, Washington University, 1960.

Provo City Schools. *Patterns of effective teaching.* Second Progress Report of the Merit Study of the Provo Schools. Provo, Utah: Provo City Schools, 1961.

Romoser, R. C. Change in attitude and perception in teacher education students associated with instruction in interaction analysis. *Dissertation Abstracts,* 1965, **25,** 5770.

Schantz, B. M. B. An experimental study comparing the effects of verbal recall by children in direct and indirect teaching methods as a tool of measurement. Unpublished doctoral dissertation, The Pennsylvania State University, 1963.

Simon, A. The effects of training in interaction analysis on the teaching patterns of student teachers in favored and non-favored classes. Unpublished doctoral dissertation, Temple University, 1966.

Simon, A., Boyer, E. G., and Moskowitz, G. Programming pupil-teacher interaction. Paper presented at the annual meeting of the American Educational Research Association, Chicago, February 1966.

Simon, A., Boyer, E. G., and Moskowitz, G. *Mirrors for behavior: An anthology of classroom observation instruments.* Vol. 1–6. Philadelphia: Research for Better Schools, Inc., and The Center for the Study of Teaching, Temple University, 1967.

Smith, B. O. Conceptual frameworks for analysis of classroom social interaction. *Journal of Experimental Education,* 1962, **30,** 325–326.

Smith, B. O., Aschner, M. J., and Meux, M. *A study of the logic of teaching.* Urbana: University of Illinois, 1962.

Smith, B. O., and Ennis, R. H. *Language and concepts in education.* Chicago: Rand McNally, 1961.

Soar, R. S. Pupil needs and teacher-pupil relationships. Paper presented at the International Reading Association meeting, May 1965.

Soar, R. S. *An integrative approach to classroom learning.* U. S. Department of Health, Education and Welfare, Public Health Service, Final Report No. 7-R11MH02045. Philadelphia: Temple University, 1966. (a)

Soar, R. S. Teacher-pupil interaction and pupil growth. Paper presented at the annual meeting of the American Educational Research Association, Chicago, February 1966. (b)

Soar, R. S. Pupil growth over two years in relation to differences in classroom process. Paper presented at the annual meeting of the American Educational Research Association, New York, February 1967. (a)

Soar, R. S. Whiter research on teacher behavior. *Classroom Interaction Newsletter,* 1967, **3** (1), 1–3. (b)

Sorber, E. Classroom interaction patterns and personality needs of traditionally prepared first year elementary teachers and graduate teaching interns with degrees from colleges of liberal arts. Unpublished doctoral dissertation, University of Pittsburgh, 1964.

Spaulding, R. L. Some correlates of classroom teacher behavior in elementary schools. Paper presented at the annual meeting of the American Educational Research Association, Atlantic City, February 1962.

Storlie, T. R. Selected characteristics of teachers whose verbal behavior is influenced by in-service course in interaction analysis. Unpublished doctoral dissertation, University of Minnesota, 1961.

Suchman, J. R. *The elementary school training program in scientific inquiry.* Urbana: University of Illinois Press, 1963.

Taba, H. Patterns and levels of thinking in elementary class discussion sequences. Paper read at the meeting of the American Psychological Association, Philadelphia, August 1963.

Urbach, F. D. A study of recurring patterns of teaching. Unpublished doctoral dissertation, University of Nebraska, 1966.

Weber, W. A. Teacher and pupil creativity. Unpublished doctoral dissertation, Temple University, 1967.

Wilk, R. E. *A study of the relationship between observed classroom behaviors of elementary student teachers, predictors of those behaviors, and ratings by supervisors.* U. S. Department of Health, Education and Welfare, Office of Education, Cooperative Research Project No. 473. Minneapolis: College of Education, University of Minnesota, 1962.

Wilk, R. E., and Edson, W. H. Predictions and performance: An experimental study of student teachers. *Journal of Teacher Education,* 1963, **14,** 308–317.

Withall, J. The development of a technique for the measurement of social-emotional climate in classrooms. *Journal of Experimental Education,* 1949, **17,** 347–361.

Withall, J. The development of a climate index. *Journal of Educational Research,* 1951, **45,** 93–99.

Withall, J. Assessment of social-emotional climates experienced by a group of seventh graders as they moved from class to class. *Educational and Psychological Measurement,* 1952, **12,** 440–445.

Withall, J. Research tools: Observing and recording behavior. *Review of Educational Research,* 1960, **30,** 496–512.

Withall, J. *Impact on learners of climate created by the teacher.* Madison: Bureau of Audio-Visual Instruction, University of Wisconsin, 1963. (Film.)

Wright, D. L. A study of various types of training and feedback on the verbal behavior and attitudes of teachers. Unpublished doctoral dissertation, Temple University, 1967.

Wright, E. M. J. Development of an instrument for studying verbal behaviors in a secondary school mathematics classroom. *Journal of Experimental Education,* 1959, **28,** 103–121. (a)

Wright, E. M. J. A rationale for direct observation of behaviors in the mathematics class. In R. L. Feierabend and P. H. DuBois (Eds.), *Psychological problems and research methods in mathematics training.* St. Louis: Washington University, 1959. (b)

Wright, E. M. J. *A rationale for direct observation of verbal education.* U. S. Department of Health, Education and Welfare, Office of Education, Cooperative Research Monograph No. 3. Washington: Government Printing Office, 1960.

Wright, E. M. J. Interaction analysis in the Minnesota National Laboratory mathematics field study. Paper presented at the annual meeting of the American Educational Research Association, New York, February 1967. (a)

Wright, E. M. J. Teacher-pupil interaction in the mathematics classroom. *Observer's Manual,* Appendix No. 1, Technical Report No. 67-5, Minnesota National Laboratory, Minnesota State Department of Education, May 1967. (b)

Wright, E. M. J., and Proctor, V. *Systematic observation of interaction as a method of comparing mathematics lessons.* U. S. Department of Health, Education and Welfare, Office of Education, Cooperative Research Project No. 816, 1961.

Wright, E. M. J., and Proctor, V. Patterns and variability of verbal behaviors during problem solving in the typical subgroups of a high school geometry class. Paper presented at the annual meeting of the American Educational Research Association, Atlantic City, February 1962.

Zahn, R. D. The effect of cooperating teacher attitudes on the attitudes of student teachers. Unpublished doctoral dissertation, Temple University, 1964.

Zahn, R. D. The use of interaction analysis in supervising student teachers. Unpublished doctoral dissertation, Temple University, 1965.

Zahn, R. D. Helping the beginning teacher. *Classroom Interaction Newsletter,* 1966, **2** (1), 14–17. (a)

Zahn, R. D. Project Cope Camden opportunity for professional experience. *Classroom Interaction Newsletter,* 1966, **1** (2), 9–11. (b)

Zahorik, J. A. The nature and value of teacher verbal feedback. Paper presented at the annual meeting of the American Educational Research Association, New York, February 1967.

Part Three

RESEARCH TECHNOLOGIES

Technological Perspectives

William D. Brooks and Philip Emmert

Part Three of this book focuses on new technologies that appear to be especially promising for communication research specifically, as well as for research generally. It has often been true that the most revolutionary changes in scientific study have occurred through methodological and technological innovations rather than through grand theories. For example, the development and use of the microscope, the telescope, and the electron tube resulted in the emergence of new theories. Frequently, new devices and technologies allow new methods to be used to approach old problems or study new kinds of problems.

Chapter 14 describes many of the psychophysiological techniques and instruments now available to communication researchers. Mechanical-electrical-chemical devices, for example, are playing increasingly important roles in behavioral research and are destined to become basic and necessary to future research. Some devices are new and some are not, but their application to the study of communication is original. The establishment and development of communication research centers and laboratories equipped with such devices represent a great potential for change in communication research. Sometimes the potentials for research and the relationship between research and available technologies are subtle and may go unnoticed. The common concern of the contributors to this volume is that communication researchers and students use with greater sophistication the methods, instruments, and technologies already available.

For example, the development of computers (Chapter 15) has made it possible for communication scientists to raise new questions for study and to test old explanations more thoroughly and precisely. The vast potentialities created by faster data processing are of great significance in communication research, and perfected automatic scanners will multiply the possibilities even more.

The final chapter of this book is concerned with information retrieval technologies. Of course, information retrieval (Chapter 16), like the other technologies discussed in Part Three, is finding its way into many areas other than research, such as instructional management systems. However, information retrieval is of direct and paramount interest to the communicologist. Traditionally, communication scientists have been forced to deal with relatively small amounts of material and data in order to keep their research manageable. But information retrieval technologies now available permit more rapid retrieval and greater quantities of data.

The technologies discussed in Part Three of this book appear to be of special importance to future communication research. Disciplines concerned with communication-related problems are indebted to those who have pioneered in the development and application of sophisticated technologies. Many of these technologies and/or devices have been adapted from a number of different areas in the social-behavioral sciences, and one can only guess at the new directions communication research will take as a result of their widespread use.

We can be assured that the development and application of these devices in communication research will result not only in new answers to old questions about communication and human behavior, but will very likely result in the asking of new questions — questions we have been unable even to conceive of because of the limitations inherent in past methods. For the communication scientist, learning to use these new "scientific methods" is like acquiring a new language. With our increasingly technical "language" we shall be able to think new thoughts, whether it be thoughts about the design of an experiment or the development of a new theory. It is now up to behavioral scientists to apply these technologies productively to the study of human communication.

14

Psychophysiological Technologies

RALPH R. BEHNKE

INTRODUCTION

Students and scholars with a wide variety of training and interests have been attracted to the scientific study of human communication. The variety and complexity of reactions to a communication event probably account for some of that attraction. These reactions range from *overt* responses (such as voting, striking, or marching in protest) to *covert* responses (such as changes in heart rate, skin resistance, or the electrical activity of the brain). Psychophysiological measuring techniques deal with detecting, analyzing, quantifying, and interpreting these "hidden" responses of the body to the mind.

This chapter will introduce (1) some of the basic concepts in psychology, physiology, and research design which underlie psychophysiological measurement, (2) a description of the instrumentation typically used in this line of research, and (3) a review of selected psychophysiological experiments related to communication.

429

Rationale

Science, according to Goldstein (1964), may be defined as "the systematic accumulation of knowledge which imparts predictability to observation and so leads to an understanding and control of nature [p. 1]." In applying this definition of science to the study of communication, one might begin by constructing a framework in which a comprehensive analysis of a communication system can be carried out. This organizing framework, or model, seeks to optimize the process of inquiry. Initially, models are constructed from the observations (data) available at the time, but they must continually be modified to account for new data. The model and the data may be said to coevolve, since the model generates the hypotheses under which the data are collected and these data, in turn, tend to "update" the model.

Perhaps a model of human communication based on communication research will best represent "reality" when the data collecting processes are diverse. If so, experimental data on a wide variety of human responses should be collected; paper-and-pencil tests, interviews, and somatic responses would all tend to illuminate the model. In some instances, data collected under several different techniques appear to conflict with the model, but this is no reason for disowning these data nor the procedures and techniques for gathering them. On the contrary, it would be rather surprising if, in these early stages, very high correlations were consistently found between physiological and psychological responses.

Methods of data collection must be precise as well as diverse. Each of the various instruments and measuring techniques appears to have its peculiar problems, and physiological measurement is no exception. However, a good deal of research has been conducted which has greatly improved the sensitivity and fidelity of physiological instrumentation. In addition, basic research has focused on the problems in quantifying and interpreting physiological responses.

Therefore, under the criteria of diversity of approach and precision of measurement, physiological response measurement techniques may justifiably be included in the armamentarium of communication research.

The Concept of Activation

Activation theory serves as an integrating concept for much of the research on physiological response measurement. Since many covert responses to stimuli are accompanied by measurable releases of energy, the energy may be viewed as an index of level of "activation" or state of arousal of the individual (Duffy, 1962). The physiological changes and energy releases which result from some stimulus or activity amenable to measurement constitute a major concern of this chapter. Researchers frequently take measurements from several interactive subsystems of the body. In such studies, the definition of the term "activation" takes on increased complexity. Although many studies infer the activation level of subjects from a single physiological response index, a simultaneous observation of several responses is preferable.

Research studies related to communication have measured the activation level of a wide variety of responses including the activities of the heart, brain, skin, and muscles. Respiration depth, frequency and ratio of inhalation to exhalation, pulse pressure and frequency, and pupillary dilation have also served as dependent variables in studies examining some aspect of the process of communication. The goal of this line of research has frequently been to correlate physiological activation level with various types of behavioral measures. In instances where high correlations were found, the measures tended to validate each other. When low correlations were noted, theoretical explanations were submitted. In some instances where the verbal reports of subjects did not correspond with physiological data, it has been suggested that the physiological report may have been superior to the verbal report if subjects hesitated to admit having had a response (Syz, 1926). In instances where a process is presumed to be going on, and where directing a subject's attention to it is likely to contaminate the data, the responses over which the subject has little or no control may provide valuable information.

INSTRUMENTATION

The following general discussion of research instrumentation is succeeded by a detailed examination of the nature of several selected physiological parameters and a somewhat more specific description of some of the types of measuring instruments which have been used in this line of research.

Although interest in research instrumentation is not new to the twentieth century, many recent advances have stimulated the development of specialized instrumentation for research into the physiological processes in the complex behavior of man. A significant portion of the research literature relating to physiological responses and to the instrumentation employed in this kind of investigation may justifiably be labeled "communication research."

The recent upsurge in interest in physiological response measurement is probably associated with the increased commercial production of biomedical instruments. Although these instruments are directly related to those used by Galvani and Helmholtz, electronic technology and medical research have both contributed to the modern versions of these instruments.

The Measurement System

One of the characteristics of this modern hybrid instrumentation is its increased flexibility, usually indicated by the term *system*. In physiological measurement, a system is a basic group of physical, electrical, and electronic components which, in conjunction with a wide variety of accessories, provides for monitoring and recording a complex variety of physiological phenomena. A system usually provides for multichannel monitoring and recording of these phenomena. Frequently, the entire system is housed in a mobile cabinet (Figure 1).

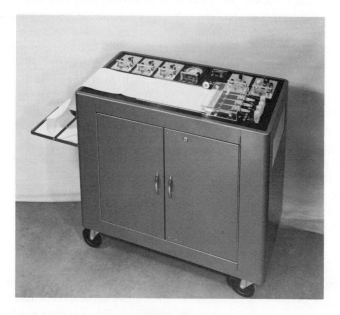

FIGURE 1

A Physiological Measuring System
Installed in a Mobile Cabinet

Courtesy E & M Instrument Co., Inc., Houston, Texas.

A typical measurement channel consists of three basic components: (1) the signal sensor or transducer; (2) the signal processor or amplifier; (3) the output indicator or recorder as shown in Figure 2. A measurement system is frequently made up of several channels (Figure 3).

If the parameter under measurement is not already electrical in nature, the transducer converts the primary signal from the subject into an electrical signal which varies in direct proportion to the magnitude of the primary signal. Since the output signal of the transducer is generally not strong enough to drive an indicator or recorder, it is electronically amplified in the processor. The output of the processor is most frequently fed to a read-out device such as a meter, a cathode ray oscilloscope, or a direct writing recorder using an ink pen, a heated stylus, or a beam of light. Or the output may be recorded on magnetic tape or transferred to punched cards for later analysis by a computer.

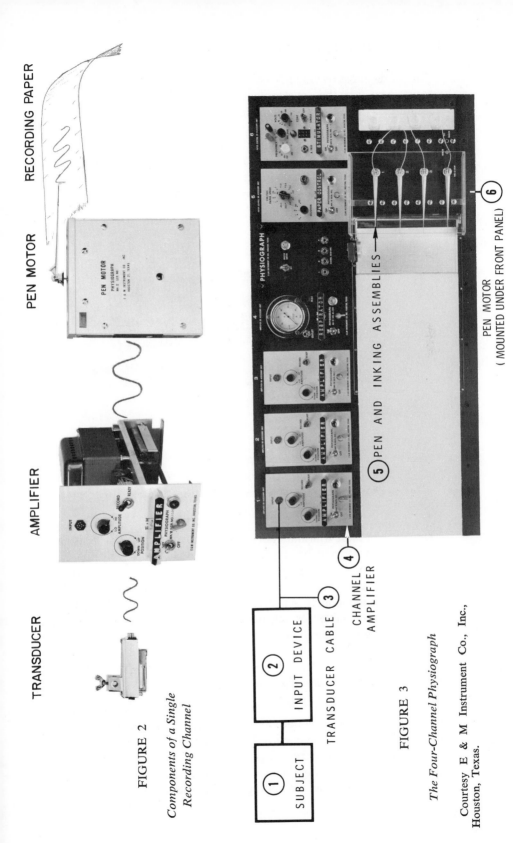

TRANSDUCER   AMPLIFIER   PEN MOTOR   RECORDING PAPER

FIGURE 2

*Components of a Single
Recording Channel*

⑤ PEN AND INKING ASSEMBLIES

① SUBJECT   ② INPUT DEVICE   ③ TRANSDUCER CABLE   ④ CHANNEL AMPLIFIER

⑥ PEN MOTOR
(MOUNTED UNDER FRONT PANEL)

FIGURE 3

The Four-Channel Physiograph

Courtesy E & M Instrument Co., Inc.,
Houston, Texas.

One of the most recent and significant advances in physiological response measurement was the development in electronics of miniature telemetric transmitters. These transmitters, containing transistorized circuitry and powered by mercury cells, permit the remote monitoring and recording of physiological data. The transmitters frequently weigh under 20 grams and exhibit a surface area not much larger than two standard postage stamps (Figure 4). They are worn under the clothing of the subjects, allowing them to move about unrestrained by wires and not distracted by laboratory measuring instruments.

FIGURE 4

*Miniature Transmitter
for Telemetering Physiological Data*
Courtesy E & M Instrument Co., Inc., Houston, Texas.

The range of these transmitters (which operate in the 88 to 108 megacycle FM band) is restricted by the legal power input allowed by the Federal Communications Commission. Although the effective range varies with environmental conditions, a usable range of 100 to 200 feet may be expected with a moderately sensitive receiver. At present, transmitters are commercially available for telemetering a variety of physiological phenomena including respiration, heart activity, skin responses, brain waves, and voice signals.

Commercial, Modular, and Homemade Equipment

Since instrumentation systems for physiological measurement may be more or less elaborate, the question of commercial equipment versus homemade equipment must frequently be considered. Commercial equipment is usually more attractive, reliable, compact, and expensive than is a homemade instrument. Totally homemade equipment is recommended only when (1) the builder has the appropriate knowledge and skill, (2) a commercially manufactured instrument for a particular application does not exist, or (3) funds to purchase a commercially built instrument are not available.

Modular instrumentation provides a possible alternative; a system carefully selected and assembled from manufactured components will usually exhibit the required accuracy at a significant reduction in expense. Wiring the component units together requires only a minimal knowledge of electronics and greatly reduces the probability of producing an inaccurate, unreliable, or even dangerous instrument. Several excellent source books describe in much greater detail the nature of each functional component subsystem in a total physiological measurement system (Goldstein, 1964).

Even an incidental inspection of the professional research journals in psychology, physiology, and medicine would indicate a significant increase of interest in developing and implementing new instruments and procedures for measuring human physiological responses. The following discussion will consider some of these responses, how they are measured, and their relationship to the process of communication.

SELECTED MEASURES

A review of the research literature demonstrates that assessing the general activation level may mean assessing a wide variety of physiological responses, and that these responses may be employed both singly and in combinations. Although each response has its own measurement and interpretation problems, some offer considerably more difficulty than others. For example, the continuous monitoring of blood pressure and studies of muscular tension often require the use of needle electrodes. Skin resistance, heart rate, volume change, muscular tension, and the electrical activity of the brain have been selected for further discussion because they are reasonably accessible for measurement. However, they do not necessarily exhibit fewer problems of quantification and interpretation. This section will include (1) a general description of each physiological response, (2) how each response is measured, (3) a waveform of each response, and (4) a report of research studies which have attempted to correlate physiological activity with other types of behavior.

Skin Resistance

Probably the most widely used single index of activation level is electrical skin resistance. When the gradual changing resistance of the skin to the passage of an electric current is observed over long periods of time, the phenomenon is labeled *basal resistance change;* a relatively large change observed over a short period of time is known as *galvanic skin response* (GSR). The GSR, according to McCleary (1950), appears to be the result of some presecretory change in the sweat glands. The *exosomatic* technique requires an electric current to pass through the skin and measures the apparent resistance of the skin. An alternate procedure, called the *endosomatic* method, measures the difference in electrical skin potential between two electrodes (GSP). Some investigators prefer the endosomatic technique since the passage of current through cells for any length of time will in itself produce changes in them (Wang, 1957).

Instrumentation for the measurement of skin resistance is relatively un-complicated. Two electrodes are placed on the subject's fingers, palms, or soles of the feet, making the subject part of a balanced electrical circuit. Changes in the skin resistance of the subject proportionally unbalance the circuit and a calibrated meter (or other read-out device) indicates the amount of resistance change. When the read-out device is a pen writing on moving paper, a graph results which plots resistance against time (Figure 5). Conductance, which is simply the mathematical reciprocal of resistance, is frequently used in displaying the data.

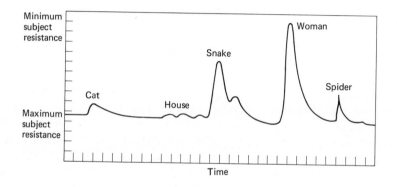

FIGURE 5

A Record of the Galvanic Skin Responses
of a Male University Student
While Listening to Stimulus Words

Since the construction and operation of the instrument is neither difficult nor particularly expensive, observation of the GSR is a good starting place for the researcher who wishes to try his hand at physiological response measurement. For a very simple, highly sensitive circuit which may be constructed for GSR measurement, see Zolik and Reinhard (1958) or Nichols and Daronge (1946).

The popularity of the GSR is probably related to its sensitivity and the speed with which it follows a stimulus. In a variety of studies, skin resistance has served as an index of attention, alertness, efficiency, difficulty, interest, and "emotion." Johnson (1959), in a series of skin resistance studies conducted for the United States Air Force, was concerned with the alertness of electronic equipment operators. He found that basal skin conductance measurements of these operators while performing their routine tasks correlated with independent measures of their alertness. In addition, he was able to determine whether they were awake or asleep.

In a more recent study, Behnke (1966) found moderate correlations between increased skin conductivity (GSR) and the ability of subjects to recall information which had been presented to them orally. In this procedure, the skin responses of subjects were recorded as they listened to short information loaded sentences presented by tape recorded speech. Generally, when a sentence elicited a large GSR, the subject was able to recall the information correctly on the post-test. All items on the post-test were classified according to item difficulty, and the highest correlations between galvanic skin response and information gain were noted for items of middle difficulty.

Leiderman and Shapiro (1963) compared skin response readings with the type of activity in which subjects were engaged during a 40-minute group discussion. The number of initiations made by each subject in the group was recorded and galvanic skin potential (GSP) was sampled at one-minute intervals. In this study, some major response differences were noted between men and women during the period the experimenters labeled as "learning to initiate decisions." Men showed an increase in mean basal GSP and a decrease in variability of the GSP; women showed a decrease in mean basal GSP and an increase in GSP variability.

Burstein, Fenz, Bergeron, and Epstein (1965) examined both GSR and GSP data while presenting differing degrees of psychologically disturbing verbal stimuli. Both GSR and GSP effectively measured the emotional impact of the stimuli. Although the researchers used a wide variety of quantification techniques in the study, they reported that they noted the most significant differences between GSR and GSP when the simple sum of all vertical deflections from the base line was used to quantify the responses. This experiment is of interest since it specifies the conditions under which the skin potential method is preferable to the skin resistance method.

The studies of skin response reported here reflect an interest in a diversity of subjects related to communication. Alertness, information gain, group interaction, and the measurement of the emotional impact of words are only a few of the specific areas in which psychophysiological experiments have been conducted.

Electrical Activity of the Brain

In a general sense an electroencephalographic recording (EEG) is a record of the electrical activity of the brain. Certain patterns of these electrical changes are associated with a variety of states of the individual including sleep, fatigue, alertness, and various "emotional" states such as fear and embarrassment. These rhythmic signals indicate varying electrical potentials in the nerve cells and reflect their sensitivity to stimulation. Early EEG studies showed that rhythmic oscillations of the greatest magnitude were observed when subjects were resting and not exposed to external stimulation. Under stimulation, these signals either decreased in amplitude or appeared to lose their rhythmic quality. It seemed as though the activity of the brain and the evoked electrical potentials were inversely related. The current interpretation of this paradox is that only comparatively large electrical potentials can be recorded by using surface electrodes on the scalp, and that potentials which are large enough to be recorded by this technique result from the summation of the discharges of many neurons. According to Duffy (1962),

> . . . sensory stimulation, as well as other types of stimulation, presumably has a desynchronizing effect on groups of cells that beat in unison. Hence, under these conditions the large rhythmic waves disappear and are replaced by faster waves of smaller magnitude or by the loss of rhythm in the EEG [p. 66].

Frequently EEG waveforms have been classified into types of waves, *alpha* (the large rhythmic waves) and *beta* (the smaller, high frequency oscillations) (Figure 6). Although this gross classification scheme has persisted for some time, it now appears to be falling into disfavor. The trend of classifying EEG signals according to more specific criteria such as (1) mean frequency, (2) mean amplitude, and (3) number of consecutive waves of the same amplitude may well dominate.

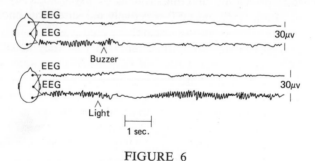

FIGURE 6

The effect of visual and auditory stimuli on the electro-encephalogram (EEG). Both stimuli blocked the alpha rhythm after a latency of about 0.4 seconds.

New techniques for analyzing and quantifying complex EEG waveforms continue to be developed. Darrow, Wilcott, Siegal, Stroup, and Aarons (1956) developed an electronic phase comparator which indicated and scored timing relationships of EEG signals from several pairs of electrodes attached to areas of the head corresponding to various regions of the brain.

Later experimenters (Darrow and Hicks, 1965) suspected that the phase or timing of these signals would show differences when evoked by different types of stimuli: (1) simple sensory, (2) "indifferent ideational," and (3) "disturbing ideational." The responses to these stimuli were recorded and analyzed according to patterns of phase relationships between EEGs of different areas of the brain. Although the differences in the EEG response patterns are too involved to discuss here, the major findings of the study were the significant differences in the timing relationships of the waveforms for the three stimulus classifications.

Cohen and Walter (1966) also analyzed variations in the EEG waveform for "meaningful" stimuli. In this study, symbolic and meaningful stimuli were presented to subjects tachistoscopically and the evoked EEG responses to the visual stimuli were averaged electronically. The complexity of the evoked waves was found to be related to the complexity of the stimuli. Subjects were presented with a "conditional" stimulus signalling the impending onset of the "imperative" stimulus which required a recognition or interpretation response. It was found that during the interval between the presentation of the conditional and the imperative stimuli, the waveform, which represented the averaged evoked EEG responses, exhibited a slow negative variation labeled the "expectancy wave." After the termination and recognition of the meaningful visual stimulus, a slow positive return was noted. Cohen and Walter found that responses to meaningful symbolic visual stimuli were more elaborate than responses to clicks and flashes of light.

The relation of complex features of the EEG wave to meaningful stimuli appears to warrant further research. Mean frequency, mean amplitude, number of consecutive waves of the same amplitude, phase relationship, and average of evoked responses are a few of the techniques that have been employed to quantify EEG responses in communication studies. The development of additional quantification techniques and electrode placements in future research may greatly increase the ability of the waveforms to describe the complex nature of a thoughtful human response.

Heart Rate

Records of the activity of the human circulatory system may also be used as indices of activation level. Popular measures of heart activity include the *arterial pulse,* the *electrical activity,* and *rate.*

The arterial pulse is measured by an instrument known as a *sphygmograph* which records the mechanical effect of the contraction (systole) phase of the heart action. The *electrocardiogram* (EKG) is a record of the electrical activity of the heart muscle. Heart rate is measured by attaching a sensitive microphone taped near the subject's heart to an electronic amplifier and counter. In cases where EKG instrumentation is available, the EKG waveform is fed directly to a *cardiotachometer* which senses and

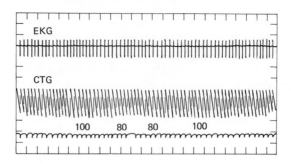

FIGURE 7

Sample waveforms of the electrocardiogram (EKG) and the cardiotachogram (CTG). An inverse relationship exists between heart rate and the amplitude of the CTG wave. The numbers 80 and 100 represent the number of beats per minute at those points in time.

counts the individual cycles of heart action (Figure 7). The latter technique is to be preferred since it uses simple electrodes instead of a microphone, thereby avoiding several sources of noise.

In a recent communication study which measured heart rate as an index of activation, Behnke and Carlile (1967) observed the heart rate patterns of speakers before, during, and after a five-minute extemporaneous speech. Situational artificiality was reduced in this study by using transistorized telemetric transmitters attached under the clothing and over the heart of the speaker (see p. 434). Members of the speaker's audience were not aware that an experiment was being conducted. Heart rate information was telemetered from the speech classroom to the laboratory, and a continuous chart recording was made of each speaker (Figure 8).

Moderate correlations were found between certain heart rate patterns and scores on paper-and-pencil tests which have been related to stage fright (such as Gilkinson's *Personal Report of Confidence as a Speaker* and Taylor's *Personality Scale of Manifest Anxiety*). In general, subjects whose patterns showed low levels of physiological adaptation throughout the speech reported lower levels of confidence and greater anxiety than did subjects whose patterns more nearly approximated their own patterns while at rest. Although procedures for the continuous monitoring of activation level during public performance are far from being well developed, they provide the stage fright researcher with physiological indices of a speaker's confidence or anxiety.

It is important to remember that the utility of particular physiological response measurements, like heart rate, as indices of anxiety or arousal may depend on many factors, for example, the nature of the experimental task

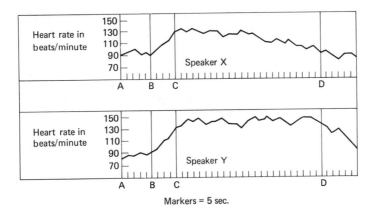

Markers = 5 sec.

FIGURE 8

Mean heart rate patterns of two public speakers. Speaker
Y, whose waveform shows less adaptation, reported less
"confidence" and more "anxiety" than Speaker X.
(A: subject is seated in the audience waiting to speak.
B: subject is called upon to speak. C: subject begins
speaking. D: subject returns to his seat.)

and the complexity of the environmental setting. Haywood (1963) investigated the anxiety induced by delayed auditory feedback (DAF).
Heart rate, pulse pressure, and palmar sweat measurements were taken
from subjects before and after reading a selection under DAF. Heart rate
was not significantly related to anxiety and showed no effects other than
adaptation. However, in this study anxiety was not clearly defined; it was
apparently inferred from what the experimenter believed to be an anxiety
producing task.

Concurrent recordings of heart rate and respiration are frequently taken
since respiration speed and depth affect heart rate. Huttenlocker and Westcott (1957) found that large and consistent heart rate changes were
associated with shallow, medium, and deep respiration patterns. Very slow
and deep breathing produced heart rate changes on the order of 25 beats
per minute during each breathing cycle. This experiment indicates the desirability of recording respiration patterns in studies which measure heart rate
in order to correct for major variations in breathing. The heart rate measure
appears to exhibit considerable promise in psychophysiological research
when proper control of interactive measures is exercised.

Changes in Volume

In addition to heart rate, changes in volume of various parts of the body
might serve as another index of the circulatory system's level of activation.

The volume of fingers, for instance, increases and decreases with vasodilation and vasoconstriction respectively. These changes are under the control of the autonomic nervous system, and they are measured with an instrument known as a *plethysmograph* (from the Greek root "plethysmos," an enlargement). Brown, Giddon, and Dean (1965) present an excellent detailed description of four plethysmographic measuring techniques: (1) *rheoplethysmography,* which serves as an index of blood flow, is limited to the fingertip, and senses changes in finger volume; (2) *electrical impedance plethysmography,* which measures the impedance (opposition to an alternating current) presented by intervening tissues and volume of blood which separate the two sensing electrodes; (3) *girth plethysmography,* in which an elastic tube encircles the part of the body under measurement and serves as a transducer which converts volume changes into an electrical waveform; (4) *photoplethysmography,* which detects variations in optical opacity of tissue (Figure 9). The transducer for a photoplethysmograph consists of a relatively high intensity light source mounted in close proximity to a photosensitive cell. Volumetric changes in the finger or other parts of the body, caused by pulsatile changes in blood volume, vary the amount of light permitted to reach the photocell (Figure 10). The consequent variations in the electrical output of the photocell comprise the waveform of the response.

In his descriptive research on the sleeping and waking states of subjects, Kleitman (1939) found that hand volume increased during sleep and relaxation and decreased during the process of awakening or during arousal by a variety of external stimuli. Davis, Buchwald, and Frankmann (1955) found that finger volume was significantly reduced by an auditory stimulus and that a high intensity tone produced significantly greater vasoconstriction than sounds of lesser intensity.

Berry (1957) recorded the continuous finger volume pulses of 16 male subjects during a rote learning task. He found that the mean volume pulse

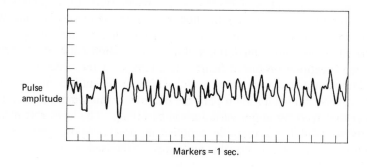

Pulse amplitude

Markers = 1 sec.

FIGURE 9

A Photoplethysmographic Representation
of the Pulsatile Changes in Finger Volume
of a Subject While Listening to a Television Newscast

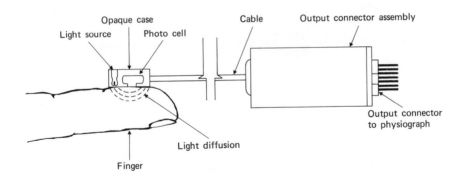

Opaque case

Light source   Photo cell   Cable   Output connector assembly

Output connector
to physiograph

Light diffusion

Finger

FIGURE 10

Pictorial Diagram of a Photoplethysmographic Transducer

Courtesy E & M Instrument Co., Inc., Houston, Texas.

correlated significantly with trials to criterion. From these records he was able to identify the rapid learners. Continuing his research, Berry (1960) measured finger volume decreases during mental problem solving. He found a significant correlation between number of decreases in finger volume and number of correct answers on the test. He suggested that the degree of vasoconstriction in the finger is an index of "quality of performance" in a simple verbal task.

As with most other physiological measures mentioned in this chapter, plethysmographic findings have been used as indices of the emotional state of the individual. Bigelow, Bryan, Cameron, Ferreri, Koroljow, and Manus (1955) found that the plethysmographic record revealed the presence of tension and concealed emotional reactivity of subjects.

Muscle Tension

The contraction of a muscle produces electrical signals which may be viewed as still another index of the level of activation. The record of this electrical activity is known as the *electromyogram* (EMG). Although physical measurements of muscular tension may be taken, the use of electrical and electronic instruments to measure and record muscle activity is becoming increasingly popular. Norris (1963) describes the essential components of a bioelectric instrument. Each circuit consists of two metal electrodes separated by body tissue and an electronic amplifier and recorder. Either surface electrodes or intramuscular (needle) electrodes may be used depending on the nature of the required data. Surface electrodes frequently summate the electrical signals generated by several muscles and are considerably less sensitive to weak signals. In communication research designs that do not need to pinpoint specific electrical potentials, surface electrodes

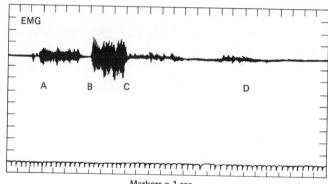

Markers = 1 sec.

FIGURE 11

An electromyogram of a subject listening to a humorous speech. Surface electrodes were attached to the right cheek. (A–B: chuckle. B–C: hearty laugh. C–D: smile.)

From D. B. Lindsley, "Emotions and the electroencephalogram." In M. L. Reymert (Ed.), *Feelings and emotions. The Mooseheart symposium.* (New York: McGraw-Hill, 1950), p. 241. Reprinted by permission of the author.

may be preferred to intramuscular electrodes for the sake of convenience. The waveform of a muscular response is represented in Figure 11.

Research on muscle tension reports that this index has been associated with "motivation," "attention," "imagination," and "thinking." Landis and Hunt (1939) demonstrate that levels of muscle tension comprise a continuum which describes the level of activation extending from deep sleep, on the one hand, to the startle response on the other. Duffy (1962) concludes:

> There appears to be much evidence to support the conclusion, that when other factors are constant, the degree of muscle tension varies directly with the significance and demands of the situation as interpreted by the individual, and that with this variation in tension, is associated a corresponding variation in the degree of alertness or effort [p. 57].

Research studies related to communication have been conducted in an interview setting (Sainsbury, 1955). High amplitude muscle potentials were recorded on an electromyograph while a simultaneous audio tape recording was made of the conversations. The experimenter identified stressful periods of the conversation when the subjects discussed certain topics which they had historically viewed as most disturbing. Periods of the EMG record were classified according to signal amplitude. The higher signal amplitudes were significantly related to the stressful periods of the interview. In situations which the individual interprets as demanding an increase of energy, the related increase in muscular tension appears to be a useful measure of arousal or activation.

Measurement Problems

Reliability

Several sources of variability in research studies employing physiological measuring instruments and techniques warrant discussion. One is in the measuring instruments themselves. Assuming that the design of the instrument is basically sound, that it has been initially calibrated and has demonstrated its reliability, the instrument user is still faced with the problem of maintaining a high level of calibration accuracy, since variations in signal processing contributed by the instrument itself are likely to invalidate the data. In spite of calibration procedures, periodic maintenance, and careful handling of the equipment, occasional failures must be anticipated. Such failures, especially when they occur while an experiment is in process, are very likely to impose major reductions in the efficiency with which an experiment may be conducted. The best defense against unexpected equipment failure is a backup system which includes duplicate components as well as standby personnel. Although such procedures increase the initial cost of a measurement system, they pay significant dividends in the long run.

Noise

Although the term *noise* may be expanded to include all signals which interfere with the desired signal or signals, we shall limit this discussion to some of the major types of instrument related noise. Specification sheets describing the essential characteristics of a research instrument generally describe its immunity to noise in terms of its *signal-to-noise ratio*. An acceptable signal-to-noise ratio would depend, of course, on the type of instrument, the nature of the signals it will measure, and the demands of the experimental design. Since the quality of the measurement is in the balance, the instrumentalist should be encouraged to learn as much as possible about the nature of noise and its elimination.

Experiments which require that electrodes be attached to the skin of the subject must deal with the problem of *contact* noise. Small currents generated by random electron movement develop small voltages at the point of contact. These currents comprise the noise signal in cases where the amplitude is large enough to fall within the spectral and sensitivity ranges of the measuring instrument. The problem of contact noise is accentuated when large, instable electrodes are used or when the electrodes are made of dissimilar metals.

In addition to the electrodes, all the electronic components in an instrument are possible sources of noise. Complete failure of the components and changes in their values due to overheating or mistreatment are typical instances of malfunction. The importance of very high quality components in research instruments is obvious. The fact that an instrument is commercially manufactured is in and of itself no guarantee that it meets high standards of quality.

Electrostatic and electromagnetic signals generated by other instruments and equipment moderately near the laboratory may be serious noise problems. The reduction of this type of noise is usually accomplished by a procedure called shielding, which consists of surrounding the more susceptible components with a wire mesh or metal shield attached to an earth ground. The shield intercepts the undesirable signals before they reach the sensitive components and shunts them to the ground. Depending on the severity of the problem, one or more components may require shielding. In addition to component shielding, a grounded metal screen frequently surrounds the entire experimental area. Quite often the subject himself is grounded.

It should be emphasized that the ground in physiological measurement must be a *good* earth ground; radiators, water pipes, and the metal conduit which encloses electrical wiring are not usually suitable. A copper grounding rod driven into moist earth and attached to the instrument by a copper braid is satisfactory. When several instruments are used simultaneously, their individual chassis should be connected together with copper braid and grounded. This point warrants considerable emphasis, since a multitude of problems and headaches may result from improper grounding and shielding. Even very limited experience with sensitive electronic instruments will demonstrate the importance of careful grounding.

Overgeneralization

We noted earlier that a wide variety of physiological responses have been inferred to indicate the physiological activation level of human subjects. In studies using a single index of activation, this inference may become exaggerated; according to Lacey and Lacey (1962), no single measure should be allowed to serve as an index of the total state of activation or arousal of an individual. In increasing numbers, authoritative sources in this line of research are indicating their preference for polygraphic or multi-response studies.

Individual Differences

Sources of variation probably more difficult to control and to understand than those in the measuring instruments are found in the subjects themselves. Alexander, Roessler, and Greenfield (1963) demonstrated the existence of certain biological rhythms which are not necessarily related to the experimental stimulus and which tend to complicate the interpretation of physiological response data. Their findings indicate that an individual's response to a stimulus may partially depend on that portion of the period in which the stimulus is presented. These biological rhythms vary among individuals and tend to increase the difficulty of (1) making comparisons between subjects and (2) replicating previous experiments.

Another possible source of confusion in interpreting physiological responses stems from the relationship of a subject's initial behavior with the behavior he exhibits when the stimulus is presented. As a general rule, the higher the basal or initial level of physiological activity, the smaller will be the response elicited by the stimulus (Wilder, 1957). So, unless basal or initial levels of each subject are taken into account, a major source of data contamination may be introduced into the research design.

Spontaneous Activity

Physiological "responses" not directly attributable to the controlled stimuli of the experiment (sometimes labeled spontaneous fluctuations) are another source of variability. When care is taken to estimate the amount of spontaneous response activity each subject produces, these fluctuations themselves may be viewed as an experimental variable. In general, high spontaneous activity has been related to higher levels of manifest anxiety. The importance of classifying the stability of subjects by their level of spontaneous response activity has been well documented (Stern, 1965).

The preceding discussion has touched on a few of the major sources of variability which concern scientists who wish to describe and interpret the covert response behavior of man. The problems and difficulties associated with this line of research are indeed thorny, but they are being combatted. Let us proceed to examine some of the apparent trends in psychophysiological research and speculate about the challenges of the future.

TRENDS AND CHALLENGES OF THE FUTURE

The future role of physiological measuring systems in communication research appears to depend in large measure on the growth and development of both communication theory and medical electronics. A good deal of basic research has already been done in the areas of instrument development, response quantification techniques, specific response patterns to classified stimuli, and the interaction of the various physiological processes. These will probably continue to prompt research, but no doubt more measures will be added to the traditional array. Perhaps many of the complex measuring techniques in this type of research, which at present require some sophistication in more than one field, will in the future be automated so that interested researchers with limited technological knowledge and experience can use them. For the present time and for the immediate future, however, psychophysiological research in communication seems to generate an excellent framework for interdisciplinary research. Even a cursory examination of the vast research literature dealing with physiological measurement would suggest not only an interest in basic research problems of methodology and measurement, but also serious attempts to apply these procedures to the solution of practical problems.

No doubt each point mentioned above merits considerably more attention and development; however, two particular major trends and challenges of psychophysiological research are at present generating considerable enthusiasm and will augment considerably the kinds of experiments that can be conducted.

Toward Decreased Artificiality of the Measurement System

The results of psychophysiological experiments conducted in a laboratory setting are frequently questioned. The atmosphere of the laboratory, the presence of the experimenter, and the movement restrictions imposed on the subject by the "wiring harnesses" attaching him to the measuring instruments can hardly fail to remind the subject that he is participating in an experiment. Any subsequent responses from the subject may be at least in part a consequence of this awareness. The development of lightweight transistorized telemetric transmitters (see p. 434) probably provides the most significant reduction of artificiality in an experiment; rapid advances in electronic microcircuitry will no doubt further decrease their size and weight. Subjects will then be able to wear telemetry equipment for such long periods of time and with such comfort that they will probably forget they have it on.

Telemetry not only allows the experimenter to reduce subject distraction, it also permits communication responses to be observed and recorded in a natural setting (one in which the behavior under observation would normally take place). The unnatural setting of the laboratory may now be replaced by the school auditorium, the coffee shop, the faculty lounge, or the interviewing office of a large corporation. In this way, normal communication behavior is less likely to be modified by a foreign experimental environment.

A side effect of this kind of experimental design is that it is less difficult to withhold certain types of information about the experiment from the subjects. For example, if the responses of the speaker are under observation, it may be possible to withhold all information about the experiment, including the fact that it is an experiment, from the audience since none of the equipment need be exposed to view. This makes it possible for the speaker to address a "natural" audience unaffected by awareness of the requirements of the experiment.

Possibly the next logical step in reducing the artificiality of the experimental setting caused by apparatus obviously attached to the subject is measurement by induction. Inductive measuring devices would sense and transmit physiological responses of subjects to the laboratory without direct connection to the subject. These instruments should significantly reduce the criticism leveled at the artificiality of many experiments using complex instruments in laboratory settings.

In addition to reduced artificiality of the experimental setting, the psychophysiological researcher may look forward to increased efficiency in data collecting and data processing procedures. The following discussion will consider some of the equipment and procedures which will make this possible.

Toward Increased Efficiency of the Measurement System

The impact of electrically and electronically aided instrumentation on the observation of psychophysiological phenomena related to communication has to date been modest. However, as improved methods of quantifying data develop, we may expect that interest in these technologies will become more widespread. The dynamic interest in improving instrumentation in both medicine and electronics lends an increased measure of predictable success to this line of research. With the development and refinement of these instrumentation and research techniques, research potentialities will develop which will far exceed the capacity of our present data collecting and processing procedures.

In recent years, electronic methods for presenting communication stimuli and for measuring and analyzing covert responses to communication events have become increasingly powerful tools for investigating psychophysiological correlates of human behavior. Future improvements for studies of this kind will include (1) increased variety of physiological responses which may be sensed and recorded, (2) increased flexibility in the variety and complexity of visual and auditory stimuli which may be systematically presented, and (3) minimized distraction value of extraneous stimuli not related to the questions under investigation.

The data collected in the kinds of experiments discussed earlier in this chapter usually consist of (1) subject responses recorded in one or more channels of analogue information and (2) time markers indicating that point on the record at which particular events or responses have occurred. Quite frequently such studies are conducted over relatively long periods of time and a great deal of information is collected. Manual processing techniques for these data are relatively crude and time consuming; they frequently influence decisions about how information may be extracted from the data, thereby reducing the overall efficiency of the experiment.

Speed, capacity, and logical ability make the general-purpose digital computer an obvious choice to assist in psychophysiological research. The large capacity of a single reel of magnetic tape greatly facilitates recording several channels of physiological data. The computer may then be programmed to recognize, extract, and quantify certain types or patterns of data on a single channel or to attempt to discover correlations between sets of data on several channels. In addition to these intraexperimental correlations, comparisons may be made between sets of data collected in several different experiments since both the data and the programs may be retained.

The flexibility of a computerized data recording and processing system must be compared with its expense. A system would become more efficient if the data conversion (which involves playing back prerecorded analogue magnetic tapes and converting these signals into digital form) could be accomplished by a central data conversion and processing system which would be available to a large number of researchers. This time sharing system tends to insure that the most expensive equipment in the total system operates at least under a normal work load.

The speed and accuracy of the computer provide several other advantages. Since large amounts of data may be recorded and processed very rapidly, the computer will assist in establishing narrow range response classifications for highly specified groups. The efficiency of the computer facilitates establishing norms for groups of a specific age, sex, weight, I.Q., or other criteria which appear likely to increase the meaningfulness of subject responses. The rapidity with which it may survey vast amounts of response data frees research personnel, who previously dedicated significant portions of their time to routine chores of data classification and analysis, to spend more time designing and conducting additional experiments. Finally, a widely generalized use of the computer in physiological measurement systems increases the probability of standardizing measurement techniques, which would facilitate replication of experiments and portions of experiments from which principles of wider applicability could be drawn.

Summary

The purpose of this chapter has been to introduce the reader to some of the basic concepts necessary to understanding and appreciating the role of psychophysiological technologies in communication research. It has examined (1) a research rationale, (2) the concept of activation, (3) selected physiological responses, (4) related electronic measuring devices, (5) some of the major measurement problems in this line of research, and (6) the implications for psychophysiological research of some recent developments in electronics and computer technology.

References and Selected Readings

Alexander, A., Roessler, R., and Greenfield, N. S. Periodic nature of spontaneous peripheral nervous system activity. *Nature,* 1963, **197,** 1169–1170.

Behnke, R. R. An exploratory study of relationship between galvanic skin response and information-gain. Unpublished doctoral dissertation, University of Kansas, 1966.

Behnke, R. R., and Carlile, L. W. Heart rate pattern as an index of anxiety in public speaking. Unpublished paper, Center for Communication Research, University of Texas, 1967.

Berry, R. N. The relationship of the magnitude of volume pulse to speed of rote learning. *The American Psychologist,* 1957, **12,** 414.

Berry, R. N. Changes in finger volume during a simple addition task. *Psychological Reports,* 1960, **7,** 446.

Bigelow, N., Bryan, L., Cameron, G., Ferreri, V., Koroljow, S., and Manus, G. A preliminary report on a study of correlation between emotional reactions and peripheral blood circulation using a strain gauge plethysmograph. *Psychiatric Quarterly,* 1955, **19,** 193–201.

Brown, C. C., Giddon, D., and Dean, E. Techniques of plethysmography. *Psychophysiology,* 1965, **1,** 253–265.

Burstein, K. R., Fenz, W., Bergeron, J., and Epstein, S. A comparison of skin potential and skin resistance response as measures of emotional responsivity. *Psychophysiology,* 1965, **2,** 14–24.

Cohen, J., and Walter, W. G. The interaction of responses in the brain to semantic stimuli. *Psychophysiology,* 1966, **2,** 187–197.

Darrow, C. W., and Hicks, R. G. Interarea electroencephalographic phase relationships following sensory and ideational stimuli. *Psychophysiology,* 1965, **1,** 337–346.

Darrow, C. W., Wilcott, R. C., Siegal, A., Stroup, M., and Aarons, L. Instrumental evaluation of EEG phase relationships. *Clinical Neurophysiology,* 1956, **8,** 333–336.

Davis, R. C., Buchwald, A., and Frankmann, R. Autonomic and muscular responses and their relation to simple stimuli. *Psychological Monographs,* 1955, **59,** 1–71.

Duffy, E. *Activation and behavior.* New York: John Wiley, 1962.

Goldstein, N. N. *Instrumentation methods for physiological studies.* Berkeley, Cal.: Operations Services Department, University of California Extension, 1964.

Haywood, H. C. Differential effects of delayed auditory feedback on palmar sweating, heart rate, pulse pressure. *Journal of Speech and Hearing Research,* 1963, **6,** 181–185.

Huttenlocker, J., and Westcott, M. R. Some empirical relationships between respiratory activity and heart rate. *The American Psychologist,* 1957, **7,** 414.

Johnson, G. E. Application of skin resistance in psychophysical studies. *USAF WADC Technical Report,* 1959. Pp. 59–688.

Kleitman, N. *Sleep and wakefulness.* Chicago: University of Chicago Press, 1939.

Lacey, J. I., and Lacey, B. C. The law of initial value in the longitudinal study of autonomic constitution: Reproductibility of autonomic responses and response patterns over a four-year interval. *Annals of the New York Academy of Sciences,* 1962, **98,** 1257–1326.

Landis, C., and Hunt, W. A. The startle pattern. New York: Farrar and Rinehart, 1939.

Leiderman, P. H., and Shapiro, D. A physiological and behavioral approach to the study of group interaction. *Psychosomatic Medicine,* 1963, **25,** 146–157.

Leiderman, P. H., and Shapiro, D. *Psychobiological approaches to social behavior.* Stanford, Cal.: Stanford University Press, 1964.

Lindsley, D. B. Emotions and the electroencephalogram. In M. L. Reymert (Ed.), *Feelings and emotions: The Mooseheart symposium.* New York: McGraw-Hill, 1950. Pp. 238–246.

Malmstadt, H. V., and Enke, C. G. *Electronics for scientists.* New York: W. A. Benjamin, 1963.

McCleary, R. A. The nature of the galvanic skin response. *Psychological Bulletin,* 1950, **47,** 97–117.

Nichols, R. C., and Daronge, T. An electronic circuit for the measurement of the galvanic skin response. *Journal of Experimental Psychology,* 1946, **59,** 149–151.

Norris, F. H. *The EMG: A guide and atlas for practical electromyography.* New York: Grune and Stratton, 1963.

Rosenblith, W. A. *Sensory communication.* Cambridge, Mass.: M.I.T. Press, 1961.

Sainsbury, P. Gestural movement during psychiatric interview. *Psychosomatic Medicine,* 1955, **17,** 458–469.

Stacy, R. W. *Essentials of biological and medical electronics.* New York: McGraw-Hill, 1960.

Stern, J. A. Stability-lability of physiological response systems. *Annals of the New York Academy of Sciences,* 1965, **134,** 1018–1027.

Syz, H. C. Observations of the unreliability of subjective reports of emotional reactions. *British Journal of Psychology,* 1926, **17,** 119–126.

Wang, G. H. The galvanic skin reflex: A review of old and recent works from a physiologic point of view. *American Journal of Physical Medicine,* 1957, **36,** 295–321.

Whitfield, I. C. *An introduction to electronics for physiological workers.* New York: Macmillan, 1959.

Wilder, J. The law of initial value in neurology and psychiatry: Facts and problems. *Journal of Nervous and Mental Disorders,* 1957, **125,** 73–86.

Woodworth, R. S., and Schlosberg, H. *Experimental psychology.* (Rev. ed.) New York: Holt, Rinehart & Winston, 1954. Pp. 107–185.

Yanof, H. M. *Biomedical electronics.* Philadelphia: F. A. Davis, 1965.

Zolik, E., and Reinhard, C. A transistorized psychogalvanometer. *Journal of General Psychology,* 1958, **59,** 299–300.

15

Computers and Communication Research

THEODORE CLEVENGER, JR.

Computers were developed as aids to rapid calculation in scientific fields using elaborate statistical and mathematical formulae; but once their full potential was realized they spread rapidly to business, adminstrative, and military applications as well as scholarly research in the arts, humanities, and social sciences. Nowadays it is virtually impossible to find any field of systematic inquiry to which computers have not made some significant contribution, and even in such disciplines as literary history and criticism the informed scholar needs to know something about their use.

Advanced research in communication has made increasing use of computers in recent years, and as knowledge and experience of electronic data processing methods and capabilities become more widespread among communication researchers, the field will depend still more on computers. The purpose of this chapter is to introduce the prospective researcher to the modern computer and to describe some of its present and possible applications in communication research.

WHAT IS A COMPUTER?

In the most fundamental sense, a computer is any device that will take a controlled information input, perform some predetermined operation on it, and return an information output showing the result of that operation. Though used today on an unprecedented scale, computers are hardly new. The Romans used arrangements of small pebbles ("calculi") to perform simple arithmetic, and the Chinese invented the abacus more than two thousand years before Columbus discovered America. Probably the first computer in the Western world was built around the mysterious prehistoric temple known as Stonehenge (Hawkins, 1965). Thirty-five hundred years ago, the preliterate inhabitants of England used it to predict startling astronomical events. By annually moving small stone markers around a circle of 56 holes surrounding the great trilithon arches (now known to have comprised an incredibly precise solar-lunar observatory), ancient priests were able to warn their people of impending eclipses and arrange suitable ceremonies to propitiate the gods.

Mechanical aids to calculation have received attention from many of the world's best minds. In the 1600's, William Oughtred made the first slide rule. In the same century both Pascal and Leibniz invented mechanical calculators. A model of Leibniz' machine is still in existence today (Kreiling, 1968). To multiply with it, the operator positions a set of knobs, one for each digit of the multiplicand. Then he turns a hand crank a number of times corresponding to the value of the multiplier. Each turn of the crank adds the multiplicand one more time. The crank is geared to a set of stepped cylinders which are in turn geared to numbered dials on the face of the machine, where the product may be read. The information input is controlled by the knob settings and by turning the crank; the operation of multiplication is performed by the gears and cylinders; and the information output is the display on the product dials.

In contrast to these crude calculating aids, the modern computer is fantastically complex. A machine in the IBM 7090 class has 50,000 transistors, 125,000 resistors, and 500,000 connectors, joined by roughly 20 miles of wire. It can do a quarter of a million additions or subtractions per second. It reads punched cards fast enough to consume the complete works of Shakespeare in less than an hour and routinely disgorges information at the rate of 600 printed lines per minute. Using magnetic tape input and output, it can work even faster. For example, it could read from tape everything written in the journals of the Speech Association of America and its regional affiliates up to 1965 in a little less than seven minutes. Moreover, it can perform all these operations — reading, calculating, and writing — at the same time.

Impressive as these facts may be, the really significant difference between the modern electronic computer and earlier calculating machines lies neither in complexity of construction nor in speed of operation, but in the capacity for internal storage of both data and computational instructions. Taken together, these allow a flexibility of operation that is approached by no other machine of man's invention, and they lay the foundation for uses of the computer in other than arithmetical computations. So extensive are these nonarithmetic applications, in fact, that the term "computer" has become something of a misnomer. To encompass the full range of applications, modern computers of the type that we shall be discussing in this chapter are better described as electronic data processing systems. Using computers and their peripheral systems is often called "electronic data processing," or EDP.

A typical computer designed for general research work will consist of at least five and perhaps as many as two dozen specialized components. For purposes of this discussion, however, it is profitable to think of such machines as containing four vital subsystems: (1) input-output ("I/O"), (2) storage, (3) arithmetic, and (4) control. Before proceeding to applications of the computer in communication research, we shall describe briefly the essential aspects of each of these subsystems.

Input-Output

The computer must have some way to take in information and put out results. Different computers solve this problem in various ways. Most general purpose computers have for the major input channel a card reader that converts holes punched through Hollerith or "IBM" cards into electrical signals, and for the major output channel a high speed printer. Let us consider these separately, taking up first the *card reader*.

In the usual application, each of the 80 columns of the standard IBM card can carry one unit of information, such as a single digit, letter, punctuation mark, or other symbol. There are 12 places in each column where a punch can be made. Starting at the bottom of the card and moving upward to the top, they are conventionally called the 9, 8, 7, 6, 5, 4, 3, 2, 1, 0, −, and + punches respectively. Letters and other symbols are designated by combinations of two punches in the same column. For example, "A" is represented by punching + and 1 in the same column; "8" is + and 2. Unless specially programmed, computers do not distinguish between capital and lower case letters; where letters appear they are all capitals. The 12 possible punches, taken in pairs, allow 60 different combinations per column. Thus, in addition to the letters and customary punctuation marks, it is possible to add special symbols (such as Greek letters or mathematical signs) that use combinations of punches not taken up by the ordinary ones. Such special symbols are used rarely, however, due to the cost of adding the equipment for punching the special symbols into cards and printing them out. It is partly for the same reason that, except when operating in the "binary mode" — a case we shall not consider here — computer inputs do not allow for more than two punches in each column of the card, even though more would provide for a much greater variety of input symbols.

The commonest output channel for general purpose research computers is a *high speed printer* that types a whole line of output information at a single stroke. Most printers can handle up to 120 columns of data on a line, including numbers, letters, symbols, and blanks. How much of this capacity is actually used depends on a program of instructions controlling the output and may be varied to suit the convenience of the user; but most programs use far less than the printer's 120-column capacity. No matter how many columns are used, the machine stamps roughly 10 lines of output per second onto fan-folded "tab" paper that feeds continuously into the printer.

Although the card reader is the commonest form of computer input and the high speed printer the commonest form of output, most computers are equipped to "read" and "write" on *magnetic tape*. Tape input is precisely analogous to card input, except that in place of holes punched in the card, the half-inch-wide tape carries tiny magnetic patches arranged in rows across its width. These magnetic spots are sensed by a reading head similar to that of a sound tape recorder as the tape moves over it at high speed on a cushion of compressed air. Like an ordinary tape recorder, the computer tape deck is also equipped to record, so the same unit can be used for both input and output.

At one time *punched paper tape* was commonly used for computer I/O, with one unit for reading prepunched tapes as input and another for punching tapes as output. Many older and slower machines still use paper tape, but punching errors are more awkward to correct on tape than on cards, and the paper tape must move rather slowly to avoid breakage. Consequently, widespread use of paper tape I/O has declined in recent years.

Three other special forms of I/O need to be considered before we move on to other subsystems of the computer. In addition to reading from punched cards, most computers are also equipped to *punch cards as output*. This procedure is commonly used when the output of one computer operation is to be stored externally for later use as input to a subsequent operation or analysis. Output cards are also punched when the user anticipates a need for more than one complete copy of his results. Instead of (or in addition to) getting a printed output, he will call for punched cards, which later can be fed through a printer-tabulator as many times as he desires copies of the output. The output cards may even be stored and used to produce additional copies years later.

Let us now consider two additional forms of input. Computer scientists have invested thousands of hours of research and development in *pattern recognition programs* that will enable computers to "read" directly from a printed (eventually even a handwritten) page. A photosensitive beam scans the page and records the dark and light areas as electronic signals. A special program inside the computer itself analyzes the pattern and "recognizes" the symbols which are then handled exactly as if they had been read in from a card reader or tape deck. At the time of this writing, the principal technical problems seem to have been solved, but the existing systems are relatively slow. Since they use the whole computer just for input (so that it cannot be used simultaneously for calculations or other processing), visual pattern recognition input systems are fairly expensive. Auditory pattern recognition programs that will allow the programmer to talk directly to the computer must wait for the perfection of automatic speech recognition programs. The technical problems in analyzing the acoustic speech wave are analogous to those encountered in visual pattern recognition but much more complex. When we know enough about our language to write the necessary programs, computers will be able to receive spoken instructions and data as easily as they can be read off the printed page.

One final form of input is used only in connection with remote time sharing systems in which several individuals use the same computer simultaneously from control consoles situated in remote locations. Some corporations make use of *telephone lines* to connect offices across the country to a single EDP system. Through special compilers and central control programs, each user actually occupies only a fraction of the computer's total capacity, yet gets output back almost as rapidly as if he had the entire machine to himself. Usually these remote consoles are like teletypewriters. The operator types his input on an ordinary-looking keyboard and signals the end of his problem. After a brief wait (sometimes less than a second) the typewriter begins typing out his results. At the time of this writing many universities and research facilities have access to time shared computers, and some look forward to the day when every campus department or research facility using computer time will have its own remote console.

We have spent considerable time discussing I/O systems because they represent the main point of contact between man and machine. We shall dispose more quickly of the remaining three subsystems: storage, arithmetic, and control.

Storage

The capacity for storing instructions and data makes the modern computer man's most versatile and sophisticated tool. In present-day machines all storage is based on tiny electrical components that behave like flip-flop switches: at a given moment, any individual component is either positive or negative, either on or off.

For example, a magnetic core memory consists of many thousands of tiny doughnuts made of a special iron alloy, each measuring one-fiftieth of an inch in diameter. The polarity or direction of magnetization in each of these ferrite cores can be switched 180 degrees by passing a current along wires running through the hole of the doughnut. By arbitrarily designating one of the directions as "0" and the other as "1," it is possible to store one binary digit ("bit") of information in each core. A second set of wires allows this stored information to be sensed, or "read out," on demand. A variety of electronic devices has been developed to perform the storage function, but they all operate in a similar way (Evans, 1966). If two of these binary storage units are combined so that they are "written" and "read" together, they can jointly represent four different symbols: 00, 01, 10, and 11. Five such units would allow 32 different combinations (00000, 00001, 00011, etc.). If we assigned a different symbol to each combination, this would provide enough storage to allow for all the letters of the alphabet plus most of the conventional punctuation marks. Thus, if we had 5,000 magnetic memory cores available for storage, we might group them into 1,000 sets of five cores each, and store in this memory bank up to 1,000 alphabetical characters and punctuation symbols, or perhaps 150 words of written material. A core memory with a storage capacity of 30,000 bits — not uncommon in a large computer — might then hold as much as 4,500 words of text.[1]

In general, there are three classes of storage in electronic data processing. The easiest to work with is *rapid access storage,* contained within the main computer itself. Information can be stored in and retrieved from this location almost instantaneously, but by its very nature the amount of rapid access storage is strictly limited. For most computers it is a few thousand bits. To augment this internal storage, large computers have *auxiliary storage* to the extent of several tens of thousands of bits. The difficulty is that storing and retrieving information take longer with auxiliary storage than with rapid access storage. And technology seems able to do little to improve the situation, since operating speed is limited by the rate at which an electric signal will travel along a wire (something approaching the 180,000 miles per second speed of light). Thus a coaxial cable connecting a core storage to its central computer interposes a considerable bottleneck in the operations, even though it is only 20 feet long. When both internal and auxiliary storage are inadequate to hold the data for a given problem, *tape storage* units are used. The same tape decks used for input and output can be used for slow access storage. Information is written onto the tapes with identifying magnetic labels attached. It is then read back into the computer on demand. The extreme slowness of the tape transport (compared to the speed of purely electronic storage media), plus the chance that a given piece of information may be several hundred feet downtape from the reading head at the moment it is needed, make tape storage and retrieval operations awkward. Except for the most routine operations, programming for optimum use of tape storage is difficult.

[1] As a matter of fact, one would ordinarily wish to use more than 32 different symbols in storing English language texts, so the basic storage unit would have to be larger than five bits. Moreover, a very high level of programming skill is required to use storage capacity as efficiently as this example would indicate. Consequently, a 30K core memory would, in any real application, be able to handle considerably less than 4,500 English words. The example was deliberately simplified in order to convey a basic understanding of the general way information is stored in computers.

Arithmetic

All of the actual computation done by a computer occurs in its arithmetic unit. As one might guess from the foregoing discussion of storage, the arithmetic of the computer is binary: it adds, subtracts, multiplies, and divides by manipulating chains of 1's and 0's. This is not nearly so easy to accomplish electronically as might at first appear, and we shall forego here any discussion of the actual construction of the arithmetic unit. We might note, however, that it can perform only one operation at a time. For instance, if the computer is instructed to add a long string of numbers it will perform somewhat like a human being; it will set a counter to 0, add the first number, then add the second to the first, then add the third to the total of the second and first, and so on, one number at a time. Of course, it does so very rapidly. If all of the data are in rapid access storage, some computers can add about a million numbers in four or five seconds, and they can process seven-digit numbers as fast as single digits.

The arithmetic unit of a general purpose computer can perform many operations that are not apparently numerical in character. For instance, many information retrieval, counting, and data sorting routines require that two symbols be compared to determine whether they are the same or different. The arithmetic unit can perform this operation by the simple expedient of subtracting the binary representation of one of the symbols from the binary representation for the other. If the remainder is 0, the two symbols are the same; if it is anything other than 0, they are different.

Control

A computer will perform only those operations that it has been instructed to perform, and the controlling instructions must be presented in painstaking detail. A list of instructions for performing some complete operation is called a *program*, a list of instructions for performing some integral part of a larger operation is called a *subroutine*. As in all such classifications, the distinction between programs and subroutines is entirely arbitrary. Some subroutines are more complex, require more detailed instructions, and take longer to execute than some programs. If the set of instructions is designed to be used alone, it is called a program; if it is designed to be used primarily as part of a longer control sequence, it is called a subroutine.

If you wrote out in elaborate detail the procedures you go through when adding a column of figures on a desk calculator, your description could be called a program. When you execute that program, unless you are a very practiced operator, you spend much more time remembering what to do next, looking up the next number, punching it into the keyboard, and pushing the "Add" button than the calculator spends grinding out the answer. If you use an electronic calculator, the discrepancy is truly enormous: from a percentage point of view, practically all the time required to add the figures is the time you spend remembering, looking, and punching.

Now suppose you had some way of setting up your program so that each step in getting ready to add the next number used up no more time than the electronic calculator took to perform the addition itself, and each new step was initiated the very instant the preceding step was complete. Your program would now run off automatically, and at very high speed, the only serious limitation being the rate at which new numbers could be brought into the calculator. This illustrates one great advantage conferred on a computer by internal storage of the control program. The instructions are represented by electronic signals located in a special section of the storage. As each step in the sequence is completed, the program goes on to the next without delay.

PROGRAMMING

Setting up the sequence of instructions that will be read into a computer to control its operations is called programming. It is useful to distinguish three different levels of programming, which vary in the amount of programming skill and awareness of the computer's hardware and circuitry required, and in the amount of detail required in the program sequence.

The most basic level of programming is done in the *language of the particular computer itself*. Its instructions are extremely detailed and require a close acquaintance with the computer's inner workings. Few "production" programs — programs written to obtain answers to particular questions, solve equations, compute correlations, calculate probabilities, etc. — are written in basic machine language. Most basic programming of this type is done to construct subroutines and compilers.

For example, FORTRAN is the *lingua franca* of scientific computer work, yet no computer is designed to accept directly programs written in FORTRAN. A *compiler* must first be written that translates the widely known FORTRAN instructions into the specific patterns of electrical impulses to which that computer is able to respond. Of course, it would be possible to require everyone intending to use a particular computer to learn its machine language, but this would be restrictive in two ways. First, it would work undue hardship on research workers using more than one computer or sending programs from one research center to another. Second, it would require much more time to write production programs, since a single FORTRAN instruction usually represents a long string of more detailed instructions in machine language. For instance, one of the commonly used FORTRAN subroutines is called:

$$Y = SQRTF \ (X)$$

The FORTRAN compiler converts this command into a sequence of several dozen detailed machine instructions for obtaining the square root of whatever appears in place of X within the parentheses, and storing the result in some location arbitrarily labelled Y. Without a compiler, the programmer would have to write out the entire sequence of instructions every time he wanted to extract a square root, a tedious chore. Very early computermen learned that it was easier to write compilers and store them in the machine where they could be called into play instantly to simplify programming operations and render the computer accessible to a wider family of users.

The second level of programming uses the *language of one of these compilers* to solve a problem. As you might suppose, many compilers — or languages — have been written to simplify the programming of different sorts of problems. FORTRAN is especially useful in scientific work, particularly where the data to be processed are entirely in numerical form. FORTRAN can deal with alphabetical and other symbolic data, but it does so awkwardly. LISP and PENELOPE are two of many languages available for processing textual materials in English. The IPL-V compiler was devised to facilitate list processing operations, especially where they are used in computer simulations of human thought processes (Newell, 1964). COBOL is the computer language of the international business community. It handles both numbers and words with relative ease and is the language of choice for most accounting and management problems.

Most production computer programs are written in the language of some compiler. To get some idea of what is involved at this level of control, examine the following FORTRAN program for obtaining the mean of a string of numbers:

```
        SUMX = 0
        NUM = 0.0

        READ (5,10) K
     10 FORMAT (F3.0)

    100 READ (5,11) INC
     11 FORMAT (F2.0)

        SUMX = SUMX + INC

        NUM = NUM + 1.0
        IF (NUM.GE.K) GO TO 200
        GO TO 100

    200 XMEAN = SUMX/NUM

        WRITE (6,12) XMEAN
     12 FORMAT (5X,F5.2)
        STOP
```

The first two instructions, "SUMX = 0" and "NUM = 0.0", create names for two storage cells that the machine will set up according to detailed instructions in the FORTRAN compiler, and "clear" both cells — set their value to 0. SUMX will be used to store the running total and NUM will be used to count how many numbers have been added to the total, but so far the computer does not "know" this.

The next two instructions tell the computer to read a card, give a name to the number it will find there, and where on the card to look for the number. "READ (5,10) K" in effect says, "Read the number that we shall call 'K' from input unit 5 (the card reader) and look for K in the location specified by the format statement numbered 10." "10 FORMAT (F3.0)" may be translated: "This is the instruction numbered 10. The card to which I refer contains a single number. You will find it in the first three columns of the card, and no significant digits follow the decimal point (*i.e.,* it is a whole number)." This set of instructions reads in a control card governing how many numbers (K) the machine will read before it calculates a mean. Every time he calculates a mean, the user will have to count his data cards and specify that number on this control card, which will be read in ahead of his data.

The next two statements tell the computer to read another card — in this case, a data card. "100 READ (5,11) INC" says: "This is the instruction numbered 100. (Remember my number, because you will need it later on.) From the card reader, read a number named 'INC' according to format 11." The only difference between format statements 10 and 11 is that format 11 specifies a two-digit number. This means that this program is limited to calculating the means of two-digit numbers. If a larger number is punched on the card, the machine will ignore everything but the first two digits, which it will treat as if they comprised a two-digit number. To expand the capacity of the program one would simply change the "2.0" to a larger number.

The next instructions tell the computer to add the value of INC, which it has just read, to whatever number is already stored in SUMX. For the first data card, this will of course be 0.

"NUM = NUM + 1.0" simply adds 1 to whatever value is stored in NUM. This instruction records the fact that a number has been added to SUMX.

Now we come to the first really remarkable instruction. The computer is told to make a decision about what to do next on the basis of a specified criterion. This instruction says: "If the value of NUM is now greater than or equal to the value of K, go to statement number 200 for your next instructions. Otherwise, simply go on to the next instruction below this." On the first card, of course, NUM equals 1, and presumably K is a much larger number, so the control unit goes to the next statement for instructions.

The next statement simply tells the machine to go back to instruction number 100, which starts again the sequence of reading a data card, adding its value to SUMX and tallying 1 in NUM.

Of course, sooner or later (when the last data card is read, summed, and tallied) NUM will equal K. At this point the computer goes to statement 200 for directions.

Statement 200 says: "Create a new number named 'XMEAN', and set it equal to the value that you get when you divide SUMX by NUM."

The next-to-last two statements print out the result of the calculation. The first of these translates: "Write with output unit 6 (the printer) the value of XMEAN, according to format 12." Statement 12 tells the printer to skip the first five columns on the left, and to print XMEAN in the next five columns, allowing two significant digits to the right of the decimal place.

The final statement is self-explanatory.

Programs may be written in the language of any compiler so that they are able to solve one problem only — the one the programmer has at hand when the program is written — or so that they are capable of solving not only that specific problem but a whole family of similar ones. To write a program that is general enough to solve a significant number of related problems is a challenge to the programmer's ingenuity, but such programs are extremely useful. The third and last level of computer programming is using such a *generalized program* to solve a particular computational problem.

The Biomedical Division of the UCLA Medical School, for example, developed an extensive library of general statistical programs that are currently in use at a very large number of computer centers. The entire library of programs has been stored in the computer, where any one may be called up by a single instruction. There are programs for simple statistics, such as the mean and standard deviation, correlation coefficient and Chi square, and there are more elaborate programs for factor analysis, complex analysis of variance, and multilinear procedures (Dixon, 1964). To use one of these programs, the programmer needs to write only a few instructions specifying just how he wants to use the program and the overall dimensions of his problem and data.

Note that as we have moved through these three levels of programming, we have required progressively less computer know-how on the part of the programmer. To write in machine language, the programmer must know a good deal about his particular computer and must write his program in very great detail. To write in a compiler language, such as FORTRAN, he needs to know very little about the computer and writes a much less detailed program, leaving it to the compiler to translate his rather global instructions into signals that the computer can use. To use a library program, such as the BMD series, he needs to know next to nothing about the computer and nothing at all about the compiler language in which the program was written. His instructions are extremely broad, and he relies on the program to generate the appropriate sequence of operations.

As the number of library programs available at a given computation center increases, the amount of technical sophistication required of the user drops off sharply. Before deciding that he is not sufficiently "computer-wise" to use EDP procedures in solving his research problems, the researcher is well advised to check the library programs available.

Applications in Communication Research

Having reviewed what a computer is and how it works, let us now consider how it can be used in communication research. We will find that the range of application is surprisingly broad, and because at the time of this writing the range has not yet been fully exploited, we sometimes will discuss possibilities in place of actualities. Moreover, because the research applications in communication bear close resemblance to applications in other fields, some of our concrete examples will be drawn from research in related areas.

It will be useful to discuss these applications under five broad headings: (1) numerical calculations, (2) computational linguistics, (3) information storage and retrieval, (4) analog-to-digital applications, and (5) simulation of complex processes.

Numerical Calculations

One thinks of the computer first in connection with high-speed *arithmetic,* for it is as very rapid calculators that computers have been used most. Computers do arithmetic at almost inconceivable speed. For instance, the program described above for calculating the mean will compute the average for almost 1,000 two-digit numbers in approximately 15 seconds, only a second or two being used in the actual calculations, with most of the time spent in "peripheral processing" — getting numbers in and results out. By altering the program slightly, it would be possible to obtain the mean of over a million numbers in less than half a minute of continuous operating time, an operation that would require days of human labor if done by hand. Moreover — and this is an important point — the computer result would be error-free; to be sure that the results obtained by hand were correct, it would be necessary to perform the whole operation a second time as a "check." If there were a discrepancy between the two results (and with a million numbers, there surely would be), the whole thing would have to be done a third time, perhaps a fourth, maybe even a fifth, until we were reasonably sure of having the right answer. Human beings make errors without realizing it; when the computer fails, it stops running the program and signals its error. When a computer program runs through to completion we know that its results are "correct" — that is, that the machine did correctly what the program told it to do.[2]

The foregoing example is somewhat artificial because a program that simple would seldom be used. Unless one did have to obtain the mean of several thousand numbers (a problem that seldom arises), he would probably do such brief and uncomplicated calculations on a desk calculator.

---

[2] Of course, if the program of instructions is faulty, the results will contain whatever errors were dictated by the program. Computers can detect purely mechanical programming errors, but if, for example, the programmer uses the wrong formula for calculating a certain value, the machine will faithfully execute the erroneous instructions.

Computers are particularly valuable for complex statistical computations such as analysis of variance, multiple correlations, and factor analyses.

In particular, *factor analysis* has come into its own only since the advent of the electronic computer. Factor analysis is an extremely complicated procedure for determining, among a fairly large set of variables, which ones tend to cluster together as factors. As applied to the construction of semantic differentials, for example, factor analysis helps to determine which scales are measuring the same basic dimensions of a semantic space. With this information a researcher not only can improve his semantic differential instrument by eliminating redundant or irrelevant scales, he can also know more accurately just what aspects of meaning his instrument as a whole is measuring.

Semantic differentials were unknown before the advent of EDP, partially because the work involved in calculating by hand the factor analysis for a differential of any significant size is almost inconceivable. The job begins with calculating the correlation between every scale and every other scale; for a semantic differential with 20 scales, this comes to 180 correlations. With 100 subjects involved in the experiment, each of these correlations might take an hour to do and check on a desk calculator; but once they are in hand the really complicated part of the analysis begins. All told, it might take an experienced and diligent worker a month to do the factor analysis of a 20-scale semantic differential, provided he didn't mind working overtime. If we now note that preliminary semantic differential scales often incorporate 50 to 100 scales, and if we remember that the number of correlations among these scales increases exponentially with the number of scales, it is not hard to understand why factor analysis was virtually unknown before the advent of the computer.

But computers make quick work of factor analysis. Recently, for example, a class analyzed a 24-scale semantic differential in one minute and 36 seconds of machine time, using a CDC 6400 computer. At the time of this writing, new equipment is coming onto the market that will reduce this time requirement by a factor of 10.

The foregoing examples should make clear that the computer has done something more than just speed up calculation in communication research; it has made a whole range of new mathematical techniques accessible for the first time. Because of the drudgery involved in complex mathematical and statistical calculations, problems in the past have been restricted to those which could be solved by relatively simple formulae. Electronic data processing at rates approaching the speed of light has effectively removed the old restrictions. There is now no practical limit to the size or complexity of the problems one can analyze; one is limited now only by the stretch of his imagination and the scope of his analytic skills. We can now tackle problems that we could only dream of 10 years ago. Thus, by quantitatively speeding up the rate of calculation, the computer has produced qualitative changes in communication research.

Computational Linguistics

When texts in some natural language such as Greek or English are prepared in machine-readable form, suitable analytic programs can be written to study the style of speeches, poems, novels, essays, plays, and other linguistic artifacts, as well as to study significant features of the language itself. Without concrete examples, the scope of computational linguistics and its applications in speech research can scarcely be realized; therefore in this section we will examine several communication related studies that suggest the range of computational linguistics as applied to communication research.

In 1859, mathematics Professor Augustus de Morgan of London's University College suggested that average word length might be characteristic of an author; but apparently he never followed up the suggestion with research. Around 1900, T. C. Mendenhall studied texts and found that word length alone tends to vary so much with subject matter as to be an unreliable indicator of authorship. However, in 1945, W. C. Wake found that different authors of works in the same literary form could easily be identified by the length of their sentences.

Even such simple stylistic statistics as *sentence and word length* are extremely tedious to gather by hand and are notoriously liable to error. Use of the computer to count, sort, and summarize removes all the tedium and most of the error and speeds up the process tremendously. Morton and Levison have pioneered the use of computers in literary detective work. Some of their earliest research (1966) dealt with the works of the Greek orators, which they found to be highly identifiable on the basis of very simple language statistics. More than 60 works attributed to Demosthenes, and more than 20 each attributed to Lysias and Isocrates were punched onto paper tape and fed through a computer that analyzed only sentence length distributions and the occurrence of two short, common words (roughly translated, "and" and "but"). The mean, median, and quartile range of the sentence distribution distinguished the genuine from the spurious works in all but a few cases, and these were resolved by reference to the relative frequencies of the two common words. Departures from this very regular pattern arose in only two cases: in one speech by Demosthenes where he quoted extensively from his opponent, and in one of the works of Isocrates where (as he reported elsewhere) he departed consciously from his usual style of composition. Morton and Levison must have been working with a relatively slow computer; they report that the complete analysis of each sample (averaging about 150 sentences) required two passes through the machine and about two minutes to complete. An efficient program on one of today's faster computers could complete the job in less than a minute.

A similar approach can be made to *variations in the style* of a given author. While evidence indicates that the distributions of sentence length and of certain very common words do not change for a given author (due either to subject matter shifts or to the passage of time), certain other features of his style may be highly variable, and this variability may be correlated with different "periods" in his career, with the audience he addresses, with changes of topic, or with many other variables. Computers can help to uncover these correlations.

For example, certain critics had observed intuitively that the poetic style of Dylan Thomas seemed to change significantly shortly after he began reading his verse over the BBC radio network in 1938. J. R. Ayer (1968) used a specially programmed IBM 1620 to study the objective bases of these observations. Using a greatly simplified concordance program (similar to those discussed in greater detail below), Ayer first made an alphabetical list of 5,000 different words used by Thomas in a representative selection of poems before and after 1938; then he counted the relative frequency of each word before 1938 and compared that figure with the relative frequency after 1938. The results showed unequivocally that lexical items indicative of high stylistic "density" — such as hyphenated compound words — abound in Thomas' poetry before 1938, but virtually disappear soon after that. On the basis of this and other evidence gathered with the computer, Ayer concludes that Dylan Thomas strove for greater clarity of expression when he sensed a living, listening audience beyond the microphone, and that this drive for clarity continued for the remainder of his career.

In both the preceding studies, the computer was used essentially as a high speed counter, but computational linguistics includes other approaches as well. One of these is exemplified by the research of Hultzen, Allen, and Miron (1964) into the *transitional frequencies of English phonemes*. Using a corpus of several thousand words (over 20,000 phonemes) carefully sampled from several types of prose, they tabulated the relative frequencies of second-, third-, and fourth-order strings of phonemes. One should note that simply generating the list of fourth-order strings is a job for a computer, since it involves working out every permutation of four different phonemes in the list of 44 English speech sounds. This results in a total of more than 7,500 speech sound patterns. The computer not only generated this list, it also counted the relative frequency of each string in the corpus of 20,000 phonemes, an undertaking that would be unthinkable without the aid of electronic data processing. The resulting tables are useful to information theorists, linguists, and anthropologists. Motley (1967) proposed the potential use of computers to compare transitional probabilities between standard English and the glossolalia produced by native English speakers.

Although we may be dazzled by the speed and accuracy with which computers perform such painstaking and time consuming tasks, we are perhaps too ready to believe that certain operations are beyond a computer's capacity. We regard the computer as suitable only for such clerkish jobs as counting, sorting, calculating, and performing other repetitive tasks. As the final example in computational linguistics, we shall consider one task that, until recently, would have been judged to lie beyond the capacity of any machine: *writing a brief abstract* of an article or story. While there are several "autoabstracting" programs that might be considered, we have chosen one that has particular significance for the theory of organization, a topic that has concerned teachers of speech since the earliest times.

The most natural way to obtain an abstract of an article or speech is to ask someone capable of understanding the subject matter to read it and either to select from the text or to compose a set of sentences that would allow a reader to decide whether he should read the original. The goal of autoabstracting is to make it unnecessary to use a person who understands the text, or, for that matter, any person at all.

The late S. N. Jacobson's (1966) autoabstracting program is built around a "dictionary of clues." This dictionary is based on a list of possible relations between sentences. The clues tell where to look for related sentences, how to detect a related sentence when it is encountered, and when to give up looking for a related sentence. When one of these "clues" occurs in the text, a prediction is set up which puts in motion a search for a connected sentence. When the connected sentence is found, it is indexed and its relation (subordinate, coordinate, or superordinate) to the original sentence is established. When the whole text has been treated in this way, a network of relations is established among the sentences that could be interpreted as a rearrangement of the entire text in sentence outline form. The abstract consists of reading out the string of sentences with the lowest order of subordination. For instance, a short abstract of a well composed three-point speech would consist of the subject sentence, then the three main points. A longer abstract would contain the primary subpoints, and so on.

Obviously, the program is only as good as its list of clues and their accompanying search criteria; but equally obviously, this list is subject to continual improvement. Not only can the program be improved through research, but the search for improved clues and criteria can enhance our understanding of how speakers organize their utterances and how listeners comprehend them. In this sense, the autoabstracting program qualifies as a simulation of two important communication processes, a topic that we shall consider in greater detail below.

Information Storage and Retrieval

As the literature in all academic fields proliferates, the task of locating previous research related to a current problem becomes increasingly more difficult. At the same time, the drudgery of working with card catalogs, indexes, tables of contents, and special abstract journals grows ever more tiresome and time consuming. The effort one must invest in literature searching goes up, along with the chance that a significant piece of information will be missed. Communication comes to this problem rather later than such fields as chemistry and psychology, where the literature has already grown to vast proportions. They have begun to use computers to solve their information storage and retrieval problems, and some areas of communication research will soon find it necessary to follow suit.

Computers may aid in the storage and retrieval of information in four significant ways: autoabstracting, high speed literature searching, generating special indices, and building concordances. The first of these procedures, *autoabstracting,* has been discussed on p. 468 and need not be dealt with here. We will simply note that if one had a long list of potentially valuable references, abstracts would reduce the work of scanning the documents. The abstracts could help one decide which titles needed to be examined in detail and which could be ignored. Since in many instances this could reduce the effort of the detailed search by half or more, it is clear that autoabstracting can be a material aid to information retrieval from a large file of documents.

For the most part, when one thinks of electronic information storage and retrieval, one thinks first of the *automatic literature search.* This may be accomplished in a variety of ways depending on the size of the file, the amount of effort that can be invested in preparing the file for storage, and the amount of detail required in the output. The simplest procedure from the computational point of view is to store indexed titles. Each document in the file is read by an indexer who labels it according to a set of prearranged categories. These category labels are stored along with the document title in computer memory or on magnetic tape. When conducting a literature search, the user employs these category labels exactly as he would a cross-reference index. He may retrieve all titles carrying any label, or any combination of labels, by entering the appropriate labels with a search command. The computer prints out the relevant titles, labeled by category.

The difficulty with *index storage* lies primarily in the fact that the categories relevant to research in a given field change, sometimes from year to year. Categories that were meaningful ten years ago may not be relevant today; meanwhile, new categories have arisen, and the documents filed at that time are not indexed for the new categories. If, for example, we had started an indexed retrieval system in 1950, such categories as "compressed speech," "semantic differential," "information theory," and "physiological response to communication" would not have been meaningful. Moreover, considerable literature would have accumulated in each of these areas before the indexers realized that a new category would be required for each. Meanwhile, many studies involving these concepts would have been indexed incorrectly.

The indexing problem has been solved in a variety of ways. One of these is to store the title of the article, or the title with an abstract, without index terms. Then at the time of search, the user specifies what words or combinations of words in the title or abstract indicate articles or books that may interest him. The computer simply reads through the titles and/or abstracts, looking for words that match the user's input; when a match is found, the title is printed out. Of course, if titles alone are used, the computer will overlook any article with an imaginative, nondescriptive title. In searching for articles about the enthymeme, for example, it would retrieve "Neo-classical Conceptions of the Enthymeme," but it would miss "Modern Variations on an Ancient Theme." By including a descriptive abstract, however, we avoid most of these potential oversights. (Remember that abstracts can be generated by computers.)

Using the methods described above, one can be reasonably sure of getting references to any documents mainly on the topic of his literature search, but none of these methods will locate references to documents in which the topic is mentioned in passing, as it were. The only way to obtain flexible retrieval of this kind of information is to store and scan the entire text. For example, in the key-word-in-context approach (KWIC), the computer reads systematically through each document, and whenever it encounters a match to the key word input, it prints out that word along with several words of context on either side of it. By reading the key word in context, the user is able to determine whether he needs to go to the original document for more detailed reading. If one selects the right combination of key words (an art in its own right), he can be sure of obtaining through this approach every direct reference to his topic contained in a very large file of documents. The time required for a KWIC search will vary somewhat with the number of relevant references located; for instance, in a file consisting of all of the publications of the Speech Association of America, it would take longer to conduct a KWIC search on the term "rhetoric" than on the term "dissonance," and the cost of the former print-out would be proportionally larger. However, it has been estimated that all the periodical publications of the Speech Association of America could be recorded on less than one reel of computer tape and electronically scanned in less than five minutes.

Once the KWIC approach has been implemented, it is available for other applications beyond producing references for individual users, for example, to create an index to a document or a file of documents. By reading in a list of key words to be indexed, one obtains a list of every occurrence of the word; moreover, each occurrence is embedded in enough context to tell the user how the word was used, and hence whether the passage the word occurs in is important to him. In 1964, the *American Political Science Review* published an index to its Volumes 1–57, obtained in this manner (Janda, 1964). The printed index is a photo-offset reproduction of the computer print-out of a KWIC program similar to those described here.

In addition to indexes, computers can produce other information retrieval aids to scholarship. The last example we shall mention here is *building concordances* with the computer. Concordances vary all the way from the *index verborum,* which is simply a list of all of the words that occur in a text, along with their locations, to the more voluminous concordance, which not only lists each location of the word (or concept), but prints out the sentence in which the word occurs. A program developed for Markman's (1964) concordance of Middle English poetry, and later applied to the Kennedy-Nixon debates, is of the former variety. A program that generates a more extensive (and expensive) output of the latter variety was developed by Smith (1964) of the IBM Corporation.

Concordance making is fraught with all the difficulties inherent in indexing any work, but with a due regard for the problems one can locate or devise a concordance program to satisfy a wide range of scholarly needs. Rhetorical scholars could probably benefit greatly from concordances of the important rhetorics, orations, and collections of critical works. Such aids to scholarship would not only ease the research burdens of theorist and critic alike, they would probably provide a stimulus to both analytic and comparative studies.

Information retrieval applications — autoabstracting, automatic literature search systems, index construction, and concordance building — are particularly relevant to humanistic research in communication. We turn now to an area of applications that is significant largely for the more scientific aspects of communication research.

Analog-to-Digital Applications

A digitizer, or analog-to-digital converter, takes some continuously varying input, such as a voltage, and converts it to discrete, stepwise units. Such a device is an important adjunct to a digital computer, since the digital machine has no circuitry for handling a continuous signal. Although presently rather expensive, analog-to-digital converters hold great promise for speech research, for they remove a great deal of the drudgery from research projects that rely on such mechanical measuring devices as sound level meters, frequency analyzers, and physiological measuring instruments.

Consider, for example, a study of the relation between muscle tension in the diaphragmatic region and the loudness of vocal tone. Muscle tension can be measured myographically and loudness by a sound level meter. Each of these measuring devices puts out a continuously varying voltage, which is usually displayed either on a meter or as a line on a moving graph paper in a strip chart recorder. If both lines were traced side by side on a two-channel recorder, it would be possible to compare the changes in muscle tension with changes in loudness, and to draw some conclusion about the relation between the two. However, to make a quantitative assessment of the relation, it would be necessary to convert the lines to a succession of numbers and to compare the numbers analytically, perhaps by means of a correlation formula.

It is at the point of converting the lines to sets of numbers that an enormous amount of effort is involved in both acoustic and physiological measurement. Conventionally, one would apply a calibration chart to successive points along the line (every tenth of a second, every second, or every five seconds, etc., as directed by the nature of the measure and the purposes of the research), convert the measurements to numbers, record the numbers in a table, and later punch the table onto IBM cards for detailed analysis. Obviously, this procedure represents a major bottleneck in any research project, a serious barrier to any but the most important, promising, and well financed studies.

The digitizer eliminates the bottleneck and expands the scope of feasible studies. Many digitizers can themselves be programmed like computers, so as to convert the analog signal in a variety of different ways — for example, by summing up or averaging over different time intervals. The input is taken in many instances directly from the acoustic or physiological measuring instrument and converted into whatever type of digital information the programmer desires. This digital information is written onto magnetic tape, which can then be fed as input to the main computer.

Clearly, this way of processing the data eliminates most of the effort of getting the information into the computer, thus saving a great deal of time. What is even more important, however, is that it allows the researcher to experiment with different ways of handling his data. If, for example, heart rate data are obtained by hand measurement techniques in five-second intervals, the experimenter has such a large investment in the data that he is not likely to perform a second analysis to determine whether three-second or seven-second intervals might produce more meaningful results. With the digitizer, the signal could be processed in a variety of different ways at very little additional cost, thus providing the researcher with greater flexibility in dealing with his basic heart rate data. In this instance we see again the same phenomenon that we have noted in other applications of computers to communication research: by quantitatively speeding up the analytic process, the computer makes available to us qualitative changes in the conduct of research.

Simulation

We come now to the last application to be discussed in this chapter: computer simulations of communication processes. What a simulation is and how it works can perhaps best be illustrated by an example from the specialized field of artificial intelligence.

Computers can be programmed to play certain games with surprising skill. In simple games, such as checkers, the computer operates in a fashion distinctly unlike a human being: it tries all the possibilities at every move, forecasts the results of each possibility several moves ahead, and selects the optimal move. Such games are "algorithmic," in that the possibilities are few and well defined enough to make feasible a neat "formula" for a winning strategy. A well programmed computer can always play such a game as well as any human, though its *modus operandi* is entirely different. But in more complex games, such as chess, the possibilities at each move are so vast and the ramifications of each choice so complex that not even the biggest computer can deal with them algorithmically. In such cases, the machine must be programmed to operate somewhat like a human. If the programmer bases his strategy for a chess program on what he observes good chess players to do, then his program is a simulation: it simulates the behavior of the human chess player.

In order to simulate an intelligent process, the programmer must of course understand the process as it operates in the natural setting. Consider, for example, the program reported by Evans (1966) at M. I. T. He describes a program written to recognize analogies between geometric figures. Given two figures bearing a certain relation to each other, the program was designed to find a similar relation between a third figure and one of five choices offered: "A is to B as C is to (D_1, D_2, D_3, D_4, D_5)". As presented in general intelligence tests, such questions have no uniquely correct answer; performance is graded on the basis of selections made by expert judges. Thus, no simple formula exists for their solution. Evans began by proposing a theory of four steps or processes the human brain might use in dealing with such relational problems: (1) One tries several descriptions of A and B in order to find how a description of A can be translated into a description of B. (2) One looks for aspects or parts of A that correspond to aspects or parts of C. (3) In each of the five possible "answer" figures (the D's), one looks for items that relate it to C as B is related to A. In a "hard" question, the relation will not be perfect for any of the choices, and its specifications must be loosened or weakened to some degree to permit the analogy. (4) By assessing the amount of weakening required for each of the five possible relations, one can select as the best answer the one whose relation to C requires the least modification to achieve a match of that relation to the relation between A and B.

This theory then became the basis for the simulation program. Writing in the programming language LISP, Evans translated the theory into a detailed and specific program for the computer. When tried on college entrance examination-type questions, Evans' program performs at about the tenth-grade level. To improve the program's performance, one would have to understand more fully just how better or more mature minds deal with the analogy problem. This would require not better programming, but a better theory of intelligent behavior; and herein lies perhaps the greatest potential of computer simulation — it provides us with an objective check on the validity of a theory that would otherwise prove too complex to test in a definitive way. If the simulation works, then the theory on which it is based is at least a *possible* description of the process for which the theory is supposed to account. To the extent that the simulation fails to produce valid results, its underlying theory cannot possibly be a valid description of the process and thus must be revised (Minsky, 1966).

Once we have in hand a trustworthy simulation program, we can use it to predict or estimate the consequences of certain trends or proposed courses of action. For instance, a politician seeking national office might want to predict the consequences of taking certain stands on particular issues during the campaign. Even though he were not crass enough to base all his decisions on such information, he might find it useful to know how many votes it would cost him in what states to come out strongly for or against this or that proposal. To get this information, he might use a simulation program.

In *The 480,* Burdick (1964) describes such a program supposedly developed by the Simulmatics Corporation for use in the 1960 Presidential election campaign. The program divides the national electorate into 480 voter categories on the basis of racial, religious, political, economic, geographic, and other considerations. To each category of voters is attached a set of attitudes and predispositions toward the major issues of the campaign, plus other information governing their voting behavior. Input to the program consists primarily of defined "stands" on particular issues. The program supposedly simulates the most general features of voter response, and the output specifies the effect on various groups of voters, which can then be translated into electoral votes gained or lost.

A different kind of program was developed by Abelson and Bernstein (1963) to simulate community referendum elections. A large number of actual people (ideally, a cross-section of the voting population) are represented anonymously and symbolically in the computer. For each person the representation contains demographic characteristics, attitudes toward the campaign arguments, frequency of exposure to news channels, attitudes toward key persons who might prove pivotal in the campaign, knowledge of the issues, frequency of informal conversation about the referendum, interest in the issue, initial position on the issue, and local voting history. The model specifies how each individual may change during the campaign, either through exposure to the media or through conversations with individuals. The standard local communication channels are represented in the computer, and for any cycle of the program they can be loaded with appropriate assertions from sources. The program computes the probable change in each individual as a result of the media coverage, then allows symbolic "conversations" between individuals which produce further changes. The simulation cycle is now complete, and results can be read out at this point, or a new cycle initiated by introducing new media coverage.

One of the objections often raised to social science theorizing is that it is too simplistic. For the most part, research consists of testing one proposition at a time, meanwhile trying to hold all other variables constant (a situation that never occurs in the natural social setting), and ignoring the dynamic nature of human affairs, in which changes on one variable produce chain reactions on others. Social scientists as well as humanistic theorists have recognized the validity of this argument for some time, but until the advent of computer simulation it seemed possible to do little about it. Now, however, it is possible to represent a theory of any imaginable complexity as a network of interconnected symbolic processes and to do preliminary "experiments" on the theory without using human subjects. At some point in the development of the simulation, the researcher will check its results against those obtained with actual human subjects. If the simulation and the live experiment produce similar results, then the theory underlying the simulation is a possible explanation-description of the human behavior; if not, the theory calls for revision. Once a workable simulation has been programmed, it can be used to predict the consequences of alternate courses of action.

Although simulations of related processes have been programmed in fields peripheral to communication, at the time of this writing the author is unaware of any that have been completed by programmers who specifically identify themselves with this field. Nevertheless, it can be predicted that simulation will play a key role in the development of theory and research in communication. Simulation is particularly appropriate where theory is complex and where direct experimentation on some of the variables is difficult or impossible because of the dynamic nature of the process. Since it is widely recognized that any adequate analysis of communication will prove both complex and dynamic, it seems likely that simulation holds the key to future theoretical development in the field and thus will play a significant role in the development of communication research.

References and Selected Readings

Abelson, R. P., and Bernstein, A. A computer simulation model of community referendum controversies. *Public Opinion Quarterly*, 1963, **27**, 93–122.

Ayer, J. R. Dylan Thomas in aural dimension. *Computer Studies in the Humanities and Verbal Behavior*, 1968 **1**, 6–9.

Borden, G. A. Computers and the field of speech. *Today's Speech*, 1966, **14** (2), 2–3 *et seq.*

Burdick, E. *The 480*. New York: McGraw-Hill, 1964.

Dixon, W. J. (Ed.) *Biomedical computer programs*. Los Angeles: Health Sciences Computing Facility, School of Medicine, University of California, 1964.

Evans, D. C. Computer logic and memory. *Scientific American*, 1966, **215** (3), 74–85.

Hawkins, G. S. *Stonehenge decoded*. New York: Dell, 1965.

Hultzen, L. S., Allen, H. D., Jr., and Miron, M. S. *Tables of transitional frequencies of English phonemes*. Urbana: University of Illinois Press, 1964.

Information networks. *Educom*, 1966, **1** (7).

Jacobsen, S. N. A modifiable routine for connecting related sentences of English text. In P. L. Garvin (Ed.), *Computation in linguistics: A casebook*. Bloomington: Indiana University Press, 1966.

Janda, K. (Ed.) *Cumulative index to the "American Political Science Review," Volumes 1–57: 1906–1963.* Evanston, Ill.: Northwestern University Press, 1964.

Kreiling, F. C. Leibniz. *Scientific American,* 1968, **218** (5), 94–101.

Marder, L. The computer and Shakespearean scholarship. *Shakespeare Newsletter,* 1964, **14** (6), 1.

Markman, A. Litterae ex machina. In J. B. Bessinger *et al.* (Eds.), *Literary Data Processing Conference proceedings.* New York: Modern Language Association, 1964.

McCameron, F. A. *FORTRAN logic and programming.* Homewood, Ill.: Irwin, 1968.

Minsky, M. L. Artificial intelligence. *Scientific American,* 1966, **215** (3), 246–264.

Morton, A. Q., and Levison, M. Some indications of authorship in Greek prose. In J. Leed (Ed.), *The computer and literary style.* Kent, Ohio: Kent State University Press, 1966. Pp. 141–179.

Motley, M. T. Glossolalia: Analyses of selected aspects of phonology and morphology. Unpublished Master's thesis, University of Texas, 1967.

RAND Corporation. *Information processing language — V manual.* (2nd ed.) A. Newell *et al.* (Eds.) Englewood Cliffs, N.J.: Prentice-Hall, 1964.

Smith, P. H. A computer program to generate a text concordance. In J. B. Bessinger *et al.* (Eds.), *Literary Data Processing Conference proceedings.* New York: Modern Language Association, 1964.

16

Information Storage
and Retrieval

Larry L. Barker

As the preceding chapter indicated, electronic computers have in recent years given new meaning to the phrase "information storage and retrieval." However, information storage and retrieval systems were in operation before the development of the present computerized systems. Book indexes and library card files, for example, were common several decades before the invention of electronic computers. The purpose of this chapter is to describe and illustrate contemporary information storage and retrieval processes in the light of the needs and interests of the communication researcher. A sample study is provided as a postscript to the chapter, illustrating how an actual information storage and retrieval system was developed and implemented.

"Information retrieval" will be used throughout this chapter as a short form of "information storage and retrieval." (It is understood that information must be stored before it can be retrieved.) The word "storage" needs no special definition in the framework of information retrieval, but "information retrieval" should be clarified. "Information retrieval" defined operationally is *bringing into availability and usefulness knowledge which has been stored.* The word "system" often is linked with the term "information retrieval." An "information retrieval system" is *a set of coordinated steps integrated into a computerized, mechanical, or manual system, allowing a user to store and retrieve information.*

Information retrieval is an integral part of the documentation process, the link between an author (or researcher) and the reader of the literature. It involves such steps as classifying, indexing, and retrieving the document. A brief overview of the documentation process should be useful in placing information retrieval in an operational framework.

The documentation process begins with the recording and storing of information. Recording usually takes the form of writing and publishing; storing involves placing the document (*e.g.,* book, journal, computer tape, or cards) in some storage facility (*e.g.,* memory bank of a computer, shelves in a library). Next, collections of documents are summarized and classified. Related documents are placed in the same "class" in order to make them more easily retrievable. Indexes are usually prepared at this point so that specific documents will be available with minimal "search" time (time to hunt through the documents to find the ones you want). Even so, the information is still of little value. It must be made available to the potential user before the documentation process is complete. This recalling of documents is information retrieval — the final step in the documentation process.

Types of Retrieval Systems

The term "information retrieval" is very general and perhaps misleading. Through common usage "information retrieval" has become synonymous with "reference retrieval," "document retrieval," or "fact retrieval." In reality, there are slight distinctions among these terms which should be noted, distinctions which can be made clearer by discussing the terms in the context of systems with which they are associated.

A *reference retrieval* system stores the titles of specific references. The user requests references concerning a particular topic, and the titles of all references in storage related to that topic are supplied. For example, an index published by the Speech Association of America (prepared by Franklin Knower) stores titles of articles and key terms describing articles published in *Speech Monographs, The Speech Teacher,* and *Quarterly Journal of Speech.* The user manually looks up in it key terms related to the concept or construct he is investigating (*e.g.,* "stage fright," "debate," "theatre-in-the-round," or "aphasia") and titles of related articles are provided. *Reader's Guide to Periodical Literature, Social Sciences and Humanities Index* (formerly *International Index*), and *Education Index* are additional examples of manual reference retrieval systems.

A *document retrieval* system produces complete copies of entire documents on request. The card catalogue of the library is such a system. The communication scholar searches the catalogue for all available books on a particular topic. The cards contain numbers which direct him to the books or documents he is looking for. Assuming that the books are on the shelves in the proper order, the document retrieval system operates smoothly. Document retrieval systems are being computerized because storing complete documents on computer tape or cards requires much less space than storing them on library shelves.

The *fact retrieval* system is the kind used by political parties to classify voters. When information about each voter has been stored in a computer, a politician can request the names of all voters who are Catholic, live in towns of over 100,000, voted Democratic in the past election, work in department stores, own two-story homes, or have three children. The computer can even print out multiple copies of mailing labels for the names supplied as a result of the request. Such a monumental task was almost impossible before electronic computers were available.

An actual *information retrieval* system goes one step beyond any of these, however. It not only can produce titles, documents, and facts; it can synthesize stored data and produce "new" information based on instructions given via a computer program. Since these systems must deal with specific concepts in addition to facts and references, they are extremely difficult to design and operate. In fact, only a handful of effective information retrieval systems has been developed to date (see Green *et. al.,* 1961). One of the most sophisticated is used by astronautical engineers to make decisions concerning spacecraft in flight. Data are transmitted to the computer from the spacecraft and many additional sources, and all information is stored in the "memory" of the computer. Through a series of complex computer programs the data are analyzed and the results of the analysis are stored along with the "raw data." The astronautical engineer can then ask the computer an actual question, such as "At what degree should the spacecraft reenter the earth's atmosphere in order to reduce its surface temperature?" and the computer can provide the answer (*i.e.,* "information") in a matter of seconds.

As this example illustrates, a true *information* retrieval system is extremely complex and thus quite expensive to set in operation. The three preceding types of retrieval systems are also rather complex, but they are considerably easier and less expensive to implement.

As the reader may have noticed, most of the casual references to "information retrieval systems" imply "reference, document, or fact retrieval systems." In most cases the umbrella term "information" is used to refer to one of the three specific *types* of information discussed above. In this chapter "information retrieval" will be used in the general sense, but the reader should keep in mind that the object of retrieval may be references, documents, facts, or other types of "information."

Using the example of the information retrieval system in the space program makes it necessary to distinguish data processing from data storage and retrieval. In the example given, both processing and retrieval systems were used. Data processing involves manipulating, replacing, changing, or adding to various bits of information or documents already in storage. (This was the phase of the example involving synthesizing the raw data and computing the optimal angle for reentry.) Data storage involves the reception and internalization of bits of information and/or documents by a computer, mechanical device, or manually prepared storage facility. (This was the reception and internalization of the raw data transmitted from the spacecraft and other sources in the "memory" of the computer.) Data retrieval involves bringing back into usefulness data which have been stored previously or, in the case of the space example, data which have been processed and stored.

MANUAL, MECHANICAL, AND COMPUTERIZED RETRIEVAL SYSTEMS

Information may be retrieved through manual, mechanical, or computerized systems. Before the refinement of electronic computers, most retrieval was by hand. Many scholars spent entire lifetimes developing indexes and concordances of the works of a single author. The *Bible* has been indexed and concorded by scholars throughout the ages, and thousands of lives have been spent preparing retrieval systems for this volume alone, not to mention the works of Shakespeare and Dante.

Manual systems are designed and executed by people, not machines. Routine tasks such as storing information and searching for information are performed without the aid of mechanical or electronic devices. Card files, indexes, directories, dictionaries, and bibliographies are familiar examples of manual information retrieval systems. The writing of letters requesting information might even be classified as a type of manual information retrieval system. Because of tradition and the complexity and expense of changing over to computers, many libraries still operate with manual information retrieval systems.

Some retrieval operations are cumbersome to perform by manual systems and yet not extensive enough to justify using electronic computers (*e.g.,* keeping a cross-indexed file of all articles related to a specific research topic so that searches may be made for a variety of articles depending on specific needs). For these "intermediate" retrieval problems there are *mechanical systems,* simpler and less expensive than a computer, which may be used. One of these is the edge-punched card system. Clevenger and Bowman (1964) explain the design of the cards:

> Edge-punched cards are similar to common unlined file cards with
> rows of one-eighth-inch-wide holes spaced around the edges of the

card, either four or five holes to the inch. . . . The central part of the card, front and back, may be used for written or reproduced information or may hold inserts or attachments, such as microfilm transparencies or microficards [p. 191].

Cards with material on a given subject are notched with a hand punch; for cross-referencing, as many notches may be made in a card as there are subjects to which the material on that card pertains. When the user wishes to retrieve information on a given topic from his deck of cards, he inserts a wire tumbler or needle into the deck at the hole signifying the topic; since the cards pertaining to that topic are notched at that hole, they fall away from the deck when the deck is suspended.[1]

Similar to the edge-punched card systems are the interior-punched card systems. As might be expected, the punches are made in the center of the cards rather than around the perimeters.[2]

The data stored in edge-punched and interior-punched card mechanical systems are usually titles of articles, key words pertaining to content of an article, authors' names, and other data useful in identifying the content of a particular reference. But occasionally it is desirable to have the entire document available for retrieval. Several systems may be coupled with mechanical systems like those described above which allow the user to retrieve entire documents. Examples are microfilm, microfiche, and aperture card systems.

Microfilming systems are growing in use and acceptance. Several new mechanical and computerized devices have been developed to record, duplicate, read, and perform searching operations on microfilmed material. The conventional microfilm reels are gradually being replaced by transparent film cards, called *microfiches*. A microfiche card contains several rows of images (approximately 75 documents per cubic inch), and it may be easily stored and handled.

One other storage system which has mechanical (and computerized) searching capabilities is the *aperture card*. Aperture cards are keypunched and contain one or more microfilm frames. The advantage of these cards is the combination of index and document in the same system. Aperture cards have been used extensively in engineering fields and in the United States missile and space projects to store vast amounts of data in a relatively compact space for immediate retrieval.

[1] Some commercial brands are E-Z Sort, Keysort, Zatocard, Unisort, Flexisort, Needlesort, Practa Data-Card, and Electrofile. The names and addresses of distributors of these systems may be found in Bourne (1963). Full instructions are included with each set. Edge-punched cards are usually 3¼" x 7½" or 5" x 8". A thousand 5" x 8" cards may be purchased for less than $4.50.

[2] Some commercial brands are Termatres, Trio, Omnidex, Findex, Brisch-Visten Feature Card, Keydex, and Find-It. The names and addresses of distributors of these systems may be found in Bourne (1963).

Computers will undoubtedly operate most retrieval systems in the near future. The Library of Congress estimates that about 30,000 scientific and technical journals are published in over 60 languages throughout the world. This means that approximately one to two million articles are published each year (Bourne, 1963). With such a mass of information being produced daily in addition to that already recorded, manual retrieval devices are becoming outmoded. Even by using the most modern computer systems it is impossible to locate much of the needed information. Sharp (1961) reported that a vice-president of a large corporation stated: "If a research job costs less than $100,000 it is cheaper to do the research than to find out if it has been done before [p. 34]." This is only a slight exaggeration; in several instances different companies have duplicated the same piece of research because the retrieval process was not developed well enough to make a search of the existing literature economically feasible.

The basic operations of any computerized retrieval system are input and output. Input (storage) functions include analyzing, encoding, and storing the information. Output (retrieval) functions include searching, identifying, and responding. An intermediary or auxiliary conjunction (Kent, 1962) is performed by the operator of the machine. His job is to maintain consistency between the input and output functions by translating the specified problem into the code of the stored information. Auxiliary conjunction between input and output is also maintained through devices in the computer program, such as subject authority lists, cross-references, or duplicate entries (Kent, 1962).

Though computers can scan documents at high speed, it does not necessarily follow that a computerized search will be faster or more desirable than mechanical or manual searching in a given setting. It could take several minutes to locate an item on a magnetic computer tape because the machine would have to scan all items on the tape before reaching the one requested in the search. The item might, on the other hand, be found in a matter of seconds in a card file or book index because of immediate access to these manual retrieval systems.

The use of computerized information retrieval systems has been limited by the expense and time involved in transferring manuscripts to cards or computer tape. Several researchers have been experimenting with visual pattern-recognition programs which permit the computer to decode accurately the words from the printed page and encode them in a machine language. Most of the visual pattern-recognition programs developed thus far have been relatively slow and expensive, but there are indications that such programs, when perfected, will make retrieval operations more efficient and less expensive (see Chapter 15, pp. 456–457).

As was suggested at the beginning of this chapter, the term "information retrieval" has come to be identified primarily with mechanical and computerized retrieval operations. It is in this context that the term will be used throughout the remainder of the chapter. The retrieval problems associated with mechanical and computer systems are similar, but distinctions will be made between them when necessary to help the reader perceive subtle differences.

USES OF INFORMATION RETRIEVAL IN COMMUNICATION RESEARCH

Although information retrieval as a research methodology is relatively new to the humanities and behavioral sciences, there are indications that its use is becoming widespread. Of the 120 research projects listed under "literature" in a recent issue of *Computers and the Humanities,* over half used computerized information retrieval systems in developing concordances and indexes of literature and speech manuscripts. An additional fourth of the studies in progress cited information retrieval computer programs as a research tool in investigations involving linguistics and content analysis. At some time or other most communication scholars will be involved in developing topical concordances, indexes, abstracts, and/or some form of content analysis (computerized content analysis is discussed in greater detail in Chapters 10 and 15). Lamb (1965) discussed these and several additional areas in which information retrieval techniques have been used successfully. A brief description of each use follows.

(1) *Content analysis.* Since two chapters in this book are devoted to content analysis, it will not be discussed at length here. Most of the content techniques discussed in Chapters 10 and 11 may be performed in conjunction with or by a mechanical or computerized information retrieval system. In general, the more complex and lengthy the project the more appropriate will be computerized information retrieval methods. When a small sample of data is used, some content analysis techniques can be performed more efficiently by hand or by a mechanical system like edge-punched cards. In content analyses using word counting, type-token ratios, and readability formulas, computerized retrieval systems are not only helpful but more accurate and efficient (Danielson and Bryan, 1953a, b, c).

Many kinds of content analysis are based on putting certain types of statements and words in a message sample into classes and determining the relative proportion of entries in each classification. As has been emphasized previously, though machines cannot make decisions concerning the emotional or logical nature of a word, they can count how many times the word appears in a given segment of the text. Classifying operations are easily programmed and are also components of larger information retrieval computer programs.

Standard categories of computer operations related to content analysis include indexing, classifying, abstracting, and processing full texts (Kent, 1962). Some of these operations, most of which relate in some way to content analysis, will be discussed further below.

(2) *Concording.* A concordance is an alphabetized list of entries with one entry for each word. It is an indexing procedure frequently used in organizing communication and other types of research literature. Each entry in the concordance has a list of references, with one reference for every occurrence of the word, syllable, or morpheme in the text. Each reference usually includes the word in the context in which it occurs, often with a coded reference number, such as the page and line where the word appears in the original text.

Though several types of concordance are useful in communication research, the two main types are selective and restricted concordances. The *selective* concordance is constructed when the user of a retrieval system is interested only in retrieving information about specific entries in the text. The user consequently supplies the operator (computer programmer or data processer) with a list of terms he is interested in, and the retrieval operation is confined to those items.

The restricted concordance is constructed when the user wants to retrieve information about all entries in a text except a few selected terms. The user gives the operator a list of words (such as "and," "or," "but," "that," etc.) he is not interested in, and the product of the search is a print-out of all entries in the text except those on the list.

Clevenger used retrieval techniques to develop a restricted concordance of the four 1960 Nixon-Kennedy debates. He related the following operations of his program:

> . . . the text of the debates was prepared on IBM cards with 70 or fewer characters to the line. Each document (in this case, each speech) was assigned a consecutive number and each line (that is, each card) was assigned a consecutive number. The first stage of the program simply transferred the cards to tape. The second stage of the program prepared a second tape which identified each word by associating with it a memory cell containing the line number and the document number in which the word appeared. In the third stage of the program the alphabetical list of words was printed out along with the location tags of each occurrence of each word. The sole exception to this general rule was a set of words which appeared on a common word list. These words were simply counted for frequency and their locations in the text were not printed in the final output.
>
> In order to perform these operations in this order we found it necessary to use three magnetic tapes. One of them contained the original language samples and this tape was preserved throughout the entire run against the possibility that something might go wrong in a later stage of the program. The other two tapes were used as scratch and record tapes.[3]

---

[3] Letter from T. Clevenger, Jr., October 9, 1965. Clevenger indicated that placing his list of "common words" in the proper phase of the program resulted in their not being included in the print-out. Consequently, the end product was "cleaner" and easier to analyze.

Concording information is usually the initial function of a literature-searching computer program. Consequently, a commercially available retrieval program for literature searching may be adapted to develop a concordance (p. 490). By stopping the operation of a program designed for literature searching after the concording sequence has ended, the user will receive a complete alphabetized concordance of his document or speech.

Though electronic computers are best suited to the development of concordances of lengthy documents and speeches, mechanical systems may be used for less enterprising projects. Kent (1962) reports the following steps in developing a concordance through the use of a punched-card retrieval system:

(1) A scholar marks the text (or speech) to indicate how it should be recorded on punched cards, noting the beginnings and endings of paragraphs and sentences, etc.

(2) Each line of text is keypunched into cards, with identifying reference to its place in the text. Words are not split between cards; rather, a word is started on a new card if it will not fit on the preceding one.

(3) The keypunching is verified and errors are corrected.

(4) The running text is divided into single-word cards by using a Cardatype machine which prints the context of a total card on the reverse of each card for a single word. (The Cardatype or card-operated typewriter reads cards and causes a typewriter to transcribe the punching onto some record).

(5) The single-word cards are sorted into alphabetical order, providing a concordance-index ready for use by a scholar [p. 86].

Concordances are quite useful in communication research. For example, a researcher could store in a computerized information retrieval system all speeches delivered by a political candidate. A concordance of the speeches could then be made, allowing the researcher to analyze recurring words, phrases, and "issues." In addition, by examining which speeches contained different types of issues, the investigator could study audience adaptation.

(3) *Word indexing.* The concordance mentioned above provides a complete index of all words in a given manuscript. Information retrieval systems can also be designed to provide other types of word indexes. By specifying a set of ground rules for selecting key terms for indexes, a computerized information retrieval system can provide a set of descriptor terms (terms which identify content in a given article, research report, or book) for literature stored in the system. Word indexing is useful in locating specific articles in a mass of unorganized literature. It is primarily a time-saving device for the researcher. Key-word-in-context (KWIC), uniterm indexing, and controlled indexing may be developed through computerized information retrieval systems. Researchers desiring specific information on any of these specific types of indexes should consult Kent (1962).

(4) *Determining authorship* (*or ghostwriting*). Computer programs have been developed which can help determine authorship of a particular message. The computer programs use several content analysis formulas and techniques which compare word usage and writing "style" in two or more messages. When a speaker or writer's verbal characteristics are known, they are put into the program as a "model." A message is then tested against the model to determine how its characteristics compare with the known characteristics of the author. Ghostwriting also may be detected through this technique.

(5) *Stylistic analysis.* Again, content analysis techniques may be coupled with information retrieval programs to investigate characteristics of literary and rhetorical style. By coding the message in advance, such elements as tropes and figures may be isolated, counted, and compared.

(6) *Deciphering undeciphered languages.* Through computerized information retrieval systems languages may be translated and deciphered. The technique involves developing a concordance of all words, noting the context and frequency of each. By carefully applying linguistic principles, the structure and meaning of the language may be inferred. It is important to note that information retrieval plays only a small part in this type of problem — but a very important one.

(7) *Making abstracts.* Computer programs have been developed to write abstracts of articles, research papers, and books. Abstracts are useful to the communication researcher when he must search a large body of literature on a given topic and then assimilate the information (Luhn, 1958; see also Chapter 15, pp. 467–468). The most common method of developing computerized abstracts is to reproduce the first and last paragraphs of articles or chapters of a book. This type of abstract usually provides enough information about the book or article to tell the user whether it justifies further investigation.

(8) *Text processing.* Communication scholars often forget that computers can process full texts. Libraries have used this technique to store entire documents on tape or film and then retrieve the sections requested by the user. Several similar text processing systems could be developed which would help communication researchers. For example, if a battery of tests related to communication skill were stored in a computer memory bank, the user could call for those items on each test which relate to communicator credibility, and the machine would print out a "new" test containing only credibility related items.

This list suggests but a few ways information retrieval has been used to date. As technology advances and computers (and computer programs) become more readily accessible, there should be vast potential for communication research incorporating retrieval methodologies.

Having viewed some of the basic uses of information retrieval in research related to communication, let us now look at the steps involved in putting an information storage and retrieval system into operation.

Storing and Classifying Information for Retrieval

The reader will remember that "information retrieval" is a short form of "information storage and retrieval." The *storage* of data for future retrieval is the subject of this section, and the emphasis will be on storing data for computerized information retrieval systems.

The "raw data" for storage may be in the form of articles, books, research papers, or manuscripts of speeches. The data usually will be printed and will need to be put into a form suitable for storing in a computer — on computer cards or magnetic tape.

Storing data for information retrieval is difficult to discuss in general terms because the data must be adapted to the specific uses to be made of it, the computer system it will be stored in, and the budget available for the project. For example, when cost is not a factor and the computer is large enough, the data may be in the form of actual manuscripts, word for word. However, if the user will need just samples or selected passages, there is really no need to store entire manuscripts. Simple descriptor terms, author's name, and/or title of the message may be all that needs to be stored. In general, it is better to store only those data which are thought to be relevant, and not complete manuscripts. The sample study included as a postscript to this chapter illustrates how data storage must be adapted to the particular project. It is important to remember that you can retrieve from an information retrieval system only what has been stored in it.

Basic Steps in Retrieval Operations

Once information has been collected and stored, several basic steps must be followed in order to perform information retrieval functions via a computerized system. The steps must be adapted to particular projects, and some may not be applicable in all instances. The key concept to remember in all information retrieval operations is that the system must be designed and operated to meet the needs of the user.[4]

---

[4] In this chapter it is assumed that the user of a retrieval system is not the person who operates the mechanical aspects of the system. By definition, the operator is the person who indexes the system, puts the information on cards, and performs mechanical operations in order to find the requested information. One person or several may perform the functions of an operator. It is also possible that the user of the system will be the operator-indexer. For purposes of discussion, however, the operator and the user will be considered separate entities. A user is the person who extracts needed information from data presented to him by the operator.

Many of the suggested steps which follow were adapted from Kent (1962, pp. 108–109):

> (1) A question or problem must exist and be recognized, and it must be verbalized or recorded for communication to the operator of a searching activity. (The operator of the search activity may in some cases be the individual who asks the question.)

This step is identical to the first step in any scientific research. It assumes that retrieval operations are not designed in a vacuum (for general use) but are stimulated by the need to answer a particular question. For example, a researcher may want to know how many times certain "emotional" words occur during a given speech. He has several options available. He can count them by reading through the speech himself, or he can instruct a computer to look for the key words and count them for him. Depending on the magnitude of the task, he probably would prefer to have the computer do the work. This type of problem would stimulate him to develop a retrieval system or adapt an existing one for his use.

To communicate the parameters of the problem to an operator of a computer system, the user should write down the question or problem. Writing it down will also help the user clarify and delineate the specifications of the desired system for himself.

> (2) The user must acquire a mechanical information retrieval system or arrange to use a computerized one.

If the investigator is at a large university, this step will most likely entail discussing his needs with the director of the data processing center, who can not only explain the machines available but also offer valuable advice about other aspects of the project. For example, he can help the investigator obtain the proper computer program and show him how to convert the raw data into usable form. If no such computing center is available, one of the many inexpensive mechanical retrieval systems, like the edge-punched card system, may be considered.

> (3) The operator of the information retrieval system must analyze the question for clues that will be useful in formulating a strategy of search.

This step involves meshing the needs and wants of the user with the capabilities of the system to be used and with the system operator's preconceived idea of the user's needs. An excellent example of analyzing the question before determining a strategy for search is presented in the sample study at the end of this chapter (pp. 492–502).

(4) The clues selected must be converted into a language and a strategy configuration that conforms to those of the information retrieval system used.

Two general information retrieval strategies are in common use. The first organizes data to anticipate questions which *will be* asked by users. The second searches data record by record when a question *is* asked by the user, with no prior organization or processing of data. The relative advantages and disadvantages of each strategy are apparent. The first should be used when needs can be carefully anticipated, when rapid retrieval is desired, or when the cost of storing and processing data is proportionally less than the cost of performing search operations. The second is used to best advantage when the user cannot anticipate specific needs, when the amount of time for the search operation is relatively unimportant, or when processing costs exceed those of the search operation.

Most retrieval systems combine both strategies. Which strategy will dominate is decided by often elusive economic considerations. Several investigations conducted to determine the relative costs and effectiveness of different retrieval strategies have produced conflicting results. Part of the problem has been defining effective retrieval operations. Some scholars have defined the effectiveness of the system in terms of ease of operation, others in terms of time to perform searching operation, and still others in terms of cost. Investigators are constantly attempting to produce the blend of processing and service activities which will yield best results for the user in a given research setting.

(5) The clues and search strategy selected must be formalized in terms of a language and program that will conform to those of the machine or computer used for information retrieval.

If the investigator decides to use one of the punched card systems, this step is obviously unnecessary; an information retrieval *program* may be used only in electronic computers. Though a system of classification and coding must be devised, no programming per se takes place. Encoding data for do-it-yourself retrieval systems like the edge-punched card involves a major problem. Several coding systems have been devised and are available,[5] but it is probably best to seek help from a retrieval expert in establishing the most effective coding system for a given project. Simple codes are easy to initiate, but they often prove inadequate in the long run. Several references at the end of the chapter explain the process of coding and encoding data to be stored in mechanical retrieval systems (*e.g.,* Kent, 1962).

---

[5] For further information, write The Director, SLA Classification Center, School of Library Science, Case Western Reserve University, Cleveland, Ohio, 44106.

When using electronic computers (such as IBM 1620, 1401, 7090, 360, etc.), programs are necessary. If the investigator is not a programming expert, he must depend on someone else to write the program. Most large computer centers have a staff of programmers who are willing to cooperate. Many of them are familiar with retrieval programs and may even have some available in their computer library. If not, they may order one from several sources. The *Share* Distribution Agency, a department of the IBM Corporation (590 Madison Avenue, New York, New York 10001), has several retrieval programs for rental or loan. Other retrieval programs available (along with code name and source) may be found in Bourne (1963), *Computers and The Humanities*,[6] Hays, Heinsz-Dostert, and Rapp (1966), and the *ACLS Newsletter* (1966) special supplement.

The researcher may participate in using a computer to a greater or lesser degree. If he knows nothing at all about computers, programs, or processing systems, he depends on a computer programmer (or the existence of a standard program) and a data processing staff. If he is a little more sophisticated in using computers, he may help design new programs or devise "flow charts" for the programmer; he may or may not process the data through the computer himself. If he is a qualified programmer, he writes his own program, validates it, and processes his own data.

When the investigator does not write his own program, he must be prepared to explain fully to the programmer the type of raw data he will have and the end results he requires. It is helpful to outline the step-by-step processes the data must go through before they are in usable form. For example:

(a) Sort out unwanted words from the document (speech), including *and, but, or, for, the, he, she, it, they, when, who, a, we, us, uh,* etc.

(b) Find all words which are the same in the text and list them in the order in which they occur by line, paragraph, and page of text.

(c) Alphabetize all entries when they have been compiled.

(d) Print out the resultant information.

With only these basic instructions, the experienced programmer can devise a suitable program. If the investigator must write his own program, considerable study (from weeks to months) may be necessary before he will be able to undertake such a project. It is the opinion of this writer (though not of some other researchers) that in this era of specialization it is generally

---

[6] See Volume I, No. 2, pp. 39–54 and Vol. I, No. 3, p. 108. *Computers and the Humanities* publishes an annual listing of projects in progress as well as computer programs available from individual scholars.

best for the user to leave the programming to experts and focus on the primary task of investigating the process of communication.

(6) The searching machinery of the information retrieval system must be set in motion.

After the program is completed and the data are in proper input form, the next step is to run the data through the computer. Again, whether the investigator actually "pushes the buttons" depends on his individual situation. Many computer laboratories require users to operate the machines themselves. Other centers do not permit users to operate the machines and have a complete staff to run all programs. If the investigator finds that he must run the computer himself, he should either ask an experienced operator to instruct him, or, better yet, have the operator accompany him when he runs his data through the computer.

The investigator should make sure that he has all data ready to go when he is assigned time on the machine. The computer time lost by having to correct errors on mispunched cards or eliminate the "bugs" in a carelessly written program can be extremely costly.

If the investigator is using one of the punched card systems, his searching operation is simple: he will run the needle or tumbler through a hole in the cards, and the cards notched at that spot will fall out of the deck. By using several different notches, he may obtain combined categories of information.

(7) A response must be obtained and the results analyzed.

If the investigator uses an electronic computer, his initial results may be a deck of cards with the coded information he seeks punched on them. He will have to refer to the original code and run the cards through the reader to find out the information he requested before he will be able to analyze his data.

The results provided by the computer or other machine systems are of little value until they are interpreted, organized, and applied to some hypothesis. Whether the investigator ends up with a computer print-out or a batch of notched cards as the final product of his information search, he must analyze his results — the final and most important step in information retrieval. If the investigator's goal is the development of a topical concordance, he will have to edit out many of the unnecessary words in the index and cross-reference related topics; if his data compare the percentage of proper nouns in a passage with the percentage of reflexive pronouns, he will need to interpret that information. It is important to remember that the information retrieval system is simply a research tool — a device for making research easier and more accurate. If it can achieve that end, it may be considered for use in a proposed project.

LANGUAGE PROBLEMS IN INFORMATION RETRIEVAL

The potential user of a retrieval system must be familiar with the language and organization of the particular system he wants to use. Operators of information retrieval machines are rarely scholars in the particular subject area compiled and stored in the machine. The user must be able to phrase his problem in terms the operator of the machine will understand. Until the problem is translated into usable language, the system cannot be put into operation. A practical illustration may help clarify this point.

Suppose an investigator wants to locate the titles of articles about voice published in speech journals. A retrieval system at his university library contains titles of all articles in the three national speech journals and the four regional journals. When discussing his problem with the operator of the information retrieval system, the investigator says only that he wants articles on voice; he does not specify further. When he obtains the response from the machine, he receives only article titles actually containing the word *voice*. Had he understood that the library's particular system was based on individual words which were not cross-referenced, he would have known to supply the operator with a list of key words related to voice, perhaps including *anatomy, organs, instruments, phonation, pitch, rate, resonance, respiration, teaching,* and so on. With this complete list at his disposal, the operator could have compiled a much larger body of literature pertaining to voice.

This illustration reinforces an important point about retrieving stored information: the investigator can get out of the system only what was initially stored in it. Though some mechanical and computerized information retrieval systems can provide cross-references of related terms, many others cannot. Computers cannot recognize that "pitch" and "vocal quality" are similar concepts. The user must make this relationship clear to the operator, who, in turn, will relay the information to the computer.

POSTSCRIPT: A SAMPLE STUDY

This postscript is provided so that interested readers may see how an actual investigation developed and set into operation computerized information retrieval techniques. The sample study was conducted by Barhydt (1964) under a grant from the United States Office of Education, Department of Health, Education, and Welfare, to search systematically for literature regarding information problems in educational research.

When reading the excerpt from Barhydt's investigation, the reader should keep in mind the admonition given earlier in the chapter — that each researcher must adapt the suggested steps for performing information retrieval operations to his own anticipated needs, the computer system used, and the budget for the project. Note that although Barhydt follows many of the steps listed earlier in the chapter, he modifies them slightly and adds some when necessary to meet his specific needs. For example, the steps labeled "Acquisitions and selection" and "Analysis and terminological control" in Barhydt's investigation would follow the first step suggested on p. 488 — "A question or problem must exist. . . ." Since the problem was evident to Barhydt, he felt no need to report it in his paper. The second step, ". . . arrange to use a computerized one [system]," was completed before Barhydt began his study. The major steps — adapting the raw data for computer storage, conducting the search, analyzing the results — are identical in all computerized information retrieval operations.

Barhydt stated the following objectives for his information retrieval project:

a. Analysis of subject content significantly deeper, more detailed, and more flexible than provided by existing systems (content was literature regarding information problems in educational research).

b. Control, or cross-referencing, of terminology more flexible and more interdisciplinary in nature than that provided by existing systems.

c. A mechanism for exploiting the body of literature indexed in the manner described above which would permit the system to function on both a centralized and decentralized basis.

With these objectives in mind, Barhydt initiated a workable computerized information retrieval system. The following section is quoted directly from Barhydt's paper reporting the results of his project.[7]

(1) *Acquisition and Selection.* The base point for acquiring media and media-related research was William Allen's bibliography for his summary of audio-visual communication in the *Encyclopedia of Educational Research.* A "citation index" search was conducted, restricting selection where the material did not appear to be within the loosely defined limits specified by Title VII of the NDEA. Preliminary criteria for inclusion were then developed. Since this area is one of direct concern to educational researchers and possibly one of only peripheral concern to this group, a complete discussion may be found in the Center's final report to the USOE for Title VII Project B–170a. Basically the criteria are as follows: "Research," as we have defined it, means controlled experiment, the reporting of which is accompanied by quantified data. Included are research reviews if they make a contribution to the analysis or synthesis of a particular area. The file of "research" includes studies of and related

---

[7] From G. C. Barhydt, Western Reserve Unversity computer index of educational research. In *Proceedings of the 1964 clinic on library applications of data processing,* pp. 59–72. Copyright © 1965 by the University of Illinois Board of Trustees. Reprinted by permission of the author and the University of Illinois Graduate School of Library Science.

to the utilization of the newer educational media: ETV, motion pictures, tape recorders, teaching machines, etc.

In selecting material to be included in the file we are in the role of judge; a judge, as defined by H. L. Mencken, is a law student who marks his own examination papers. We do have what can be considered preliminary criteria for inclusion: a base for extension or reduction of the contents of the file.

(2) and (3) *Analysis and Terminological Control.* The Western Reserve University semantic-coded telegraphic abstract approach has been applied to the research studies in the file. In view of our present and past work in other fields and our current work in other techniques, the Center feels that this approach is a reasonable one. It offers the capability of providing specific, generic and other relationships necessary in dealing with educational research literature. We are prepared to modify the system if it seems advisable, and to incorporate, where appropriate, the results of our own research and the research of others.

The first step in analysis is to prepare a telegraphic abstract (TA: Figure 1). The TA provides a detailed machine-readable index to a research study and is constructed as follows. Index terms (descriptors) are selected from the text of the document and written in the right-hand column of the TA form. Although any indexable word may be selected, *i.e.,* no authorized list of descriptors must be consulted, well-defined rules govern the categories of information to be included for a particular kind of study.

Several kinds of relationships among index terms are then established by the use of role indicators (roles, Figure 2). Role indicators specify:

a. Logical relationships, —

KEJ	=	population,
KAM	=	process,
KQJ	=	agent of process,
KWJ	=	device or material prepared;

b. Facets of the study, —

KEC	=	subject matter taught,
KAP	=	dependent variable(s),
KAL	=	independent variable(s); and

c. Descriptive information, —

KAB	=	type of material or study,
KIT	=	date of study.

Level indicators (links, Figure 3) are also incorporated into the TA. These symbols, (..), (.), (,), are signals of the closeness of association between the elements of a TA.

In the example below, the level indicator (..) marks the beginning of that portion of the TA dealing with the experimental group variables (A).

FIGURE 1

Do not write in this space

M–3803

Col. 6–8	Role Indicator (Col. 28–80)	Col. 6–8	Description (Col. 9–27)
1	. . KAB,	2	Research
3	. KIT,	4	1962
5		6	
7	. . KEJ,	8	Experimental Group
9		10	
11	. . KEJ,	12	Control Group
13		14	
15	. . KAM,	16	Matching
17	. KQJ,	18	Mathematics
19		20	Aptitude
21		22	
23	. . KEC,	24	Electronics
25	. KQJ,	26	Filmed
27		28	Programmed
29		30	Instruction
31	. KQJ,	32	Lecture
33		34	Demonstration
35	. KQJ,	36	Textbook
37		38	
39	. . KAM,	40	Testing
41	. KQJ,	42	Psych Corp EPSAT
43	. KQJ,	44	Achievement
45		46	Test
47	. KQJ,	48	Mathematics
49		50	Test

Col. 6–8	Role Indicator (Col. 28–80)	Col. 6–8	Description (Col. 9–27)
51	.. KAM,	52	Data
53		54	Analysis
55	. KQJ,	56	F Ratio
57		58	Variance
59		60	T Test
61		62	
63	.. KAP,	64	Experimental Group
65		66	Electronics
67		68	Achievement
69	. KAL,	70	Filmed
71		72	Programmed
73		74	Instruction
75		76	
77	.. KAP,	78	Control Group
79		80	Electronics
81		82	Achievement
83		84	
85	. KAL,	86	Lecture
87		88	Demonstration
89		90	
91	. KAL,	92	Textbook
93		94	
95		96	
97		98	
99		100	

Abstracter _____

_____

FIGURE 2

Role Indicators

Role Indicator	Functional Meaning
KAB	Type of study
KIT	Date of study
KIS	Geographical or environmental location
KEJ	Population acted upon or studied
KAM	Process carried out on, by, or in relation to KEJ
KEC	Subject taught
KQJ	Agent of process (of KAM or KEC)
KWV	Attribute given
KAH	Condition of process
KUP	Attribute or behavior determined
KAP	Dependent variable; attribute or behavior influenced
KAL	Independent variable; influencing factor
KEW	Person interviewed or answering questionnaire
KWC	That toward which an attitude is noted
KWJ	Device or material prepared

This list comprises all the role indicators used in the TA. Their sequence and use in a TA are dependent on the characteristics of the individual document.

FIGURE 3

Level Indicators

Symbol	Use
Space ( )	To separate two or more role indicators on a single line of the TA.
(,)	To separate a role indicator from the word or words to which it applies.
(.)	To separate one role indicator-word(s) combination from the next.
(..)	To separate one group of related role indicator-word(s) combination from the next.
(□ . . .)	To separate groups of unrelated role indicator-word(s) combinations from each other.*

* In instances where a document contains or discusses two or more unrelated or loosely related experiments or surveys.

Similarly marked are the control group variables (B). By separating the role-term combinations into groups or levels such as these, false associations can be avoided during the searching operation.

A	.. KAP, (dependent variable)	Experimental Group Reading Listening
	. KAL, (independent variable)	Language Laboratory I.Q.
B	.. KAP,	Control Group Reading Listening
	. KAL,	Lecture Demonstration I.Q.

The next step is the encoding of the TA by the application of the semantic code to each word listed. If the word has previously appeared in a TA and been coded, this may be accomplished by mechanical means. If not, the process is as follows.

The semantic code is comprised of: three letter combinations called semantic factors, which represent concepts; alphabetical infixes, which show the relationship of the factor to the word being coded; numerical infixes, which delimit a concept; and numerical suffixes, which establish the uniqueness of each code. For example, the code for the Minnesota Multiphasic Personality Inventory (MMPI) is:

DACM MUSR MYMT 1017 3102

Breaking this down we have the semantic factors

D__CM	=	printed document,
M__SR	=	measurement,
M__MT	=	emotion,

and adding the alphabetical infixes appropriate for each factor,

A	=	categorical infix,
U	=	productive infix,
Y	=	attributive infix,

the code tells us that the MMPI

is a document — D*A*CM,

is *used for* measurement — M*U*SR, and that

the concept emotion is an important characteristic of the word(s) coded — M*Y*MT

Since there are many aspects of the concept emotion, a numerical infix has been assigned to the factor M__MT to designate, in this instance, the concept of personality.

MYMT 1017 — Personality

Thus far we have **DACM MUSR MYMT 1017.** Since other closely related tests may be coded in the same way, *e.g.,* The Rorschach Inkblot Test (RIT), a numerical suffix is added to establish a unique code for each word(s).

$$\text{MMPI} = \text{DACM MUSR MYMT 1017 } \textit{3102}$$
$$\text{RIT} = \text{DACM MUSR MYMT 1017 } \textit{3304}$$

A search therefore can be made on any generic-specific level retrieving all tests of this type (by programming for DACM, MUSR, MYMT 1017) or by specifying the unique code for a specific test. By the additional specification of the relationship established by the roles and levels, a very powerful searching tool can be constructed.

Concurrently with the preparation of the TA, a conventional abstract of the original document is prepared (Figure 4) [p. 500].

(4) *Recording of Results on a Searchable Medium.* Each role indicator along with its punctuation, and each word on the TA are punched on separate Hollerith cards. The words are matched with a card reproduction of the code dictionary and where a word has previously been encoded the proper code is gang-punched from the dictionary card onto the word card. Codes are assigned by an individual to new words entering the system, and these new words and their codes are added to the code dictionary. All cards for role indicators and coded words are then sorted in the order in which they appear in the TA. Abstracts are processed in blocks of 100 and the detailed index (TA) is transferred from the cards to storage on magnetic tape.

(5) *Storage of Records or Source Documents.* The original document is shelved by accession number. It is hoped that hard-to-get documents will be available on demand, although the cost is somewhat prohibitive. Conventional abstracts are filed according to accession number and await the results of a search.

(6) *Question-Analysis and Development of Search Strategy.* In a recent paper by two members of the Center's staff, some illuminating observations are made on the problems of question analysis in a real situation (Rees and Saracevic, 1963). It is pointed out that there is frequently a distinction between:

— what the questioner needs
— what he thinks he needs
— what he wants

FIGURE 4

M–3803. Kopstein, Felix F., Richard T. Cave and Virginia Zachert, "Preliminary Evaluation of a Prototype Automated Technical Training Course," *Technical Documentary Report,* no. MRL-TDR-62-78 (Wright-Patterson Air Force Base, Ohio: Behavioral Sciences Laboratory, 6570th Aerospace Medical Research Laboratories, Aerospace Medical Division, Air Force Systems Command, July, 1962), 26 pp.

The Keesler Mathematics Test and the Psychological Corporation Electronic and Physical Sciences Aptitude Test are used to match three groups of Air Force Trainees during six weeks of a course on the principles of electronic communication. The experimental group consists of a randomly selected set of 14 students with scores in the middle 60 percent of the distribution. The control group is a matched set of 14 students who are aware of their participation in a research project, but who are taught by lecture-demonstration. The blind control group, another matched set of 14 airmen, is also taught by lecture-demonstration, but is wholly unaware that its performance is under experimental consideration. The experimental group receives all of its instruction from 35mm film projected with the Auto Tutor Mark I. The film is organized along the principles of intrinsic programming. Three progress tests are administered at two week intervals and scores are analyzed by F ratio, analysis of variance and t-test. No significant differences are found between control and blind control groups. While examination scores for control groups are somewhat higher than scores for the experimental groups, the differences are not great. A replication of the original study produces results which are not significantly different.

— what he is prepared to read
— how much of what he gets he is prepared to read
— how much time he is willing to devote to it all
— in what sequence he would like to read what he gets

The best method for determining the answer to the questions raised above is as yet unknown; no research has been done relating to the nature of the question-asking process, although increasing attention is being devoted at the Center to precise identification of the areas of investigation. It is obvious though, in the light of our experience, that question analysis must be approached with a great deal of care (Rees and Saracevic, 1963).

The education project at the Center asks each questioner to:

1. State his question on three levels.
   — Specific
   — More generic
   — Most generic
2. Define the terms in the question.
3. List those terms he associates with the question terms.
4. Describe the purpose of his research.

In instances where this outline is followed rigorously and completely, the Center's question analysts have a good beginning. The real problem is whether the questioner can define his research needs so precisely. To provide more information for the question analyst telephone contact with the questioner is very desirable, and frequently used.

Once the analyst has what appears to be a complete statement of the question, the question is analyzed for searchable concepts; these are translated into the indexing language of the system and are organized so that they correspond to the logic of the question. Searchable concepts are those which match the indexing concepts used by the system. Generic, specific and associated concepts not specified by the question, but derived from the analyst's knowledge of the file or from conversations with specialists are then added to the search program. One of the computer listings of the semantic code dictionary is arranged alphabetically by code so that the thesaural relationships established by the code are apparent.

In formulating the logical structure of the question program the following connectives can be used.

$$A \cdot B = A \text{ and } B$$
$$A + B = A \text{ or } B$$
$$A - B = A \text{ but not } B$$

Any question therefore can be expressed as an algebraic polynomial of logical sums, products and differences, of semantic codes.

Let me briefly illustrate the search structuring with an example. The question submitted by a researcher is "Give me abstracts of all studies dealing with the use of educational media in teaching biology at the below college level." The concepts identified as "searchable" are media, biology, educational institution and college.

$$\text{Let } A = \text{media}$$
$$B = \text{biology}$$
$$C = \text{educational institution}$$
$$C^1 = \text{college}$$

Using the logical connectives we have

$$A \cdot B \cdot (C - C^1)$$

Applying the appropriate role indicators

$$
\begin{array}{lcl}
\text{KQJ} & = & \text{agent of process} \\
\text{KEC} & = & \text{subject taught} \\
\text{KIS} & = & \text{location of population}
\end{array}
$$

the program becomes

$$\text{KQJ} \cdot \text{A} \cdot \text{KEC} \cdot \text{B} \cdot \text{KIS} \cdot (\text{C} - \text{C}^1)$$

Since KQJ . A must be associated with KEC . B and not with any other word of the telegraphic abstract, the level indicators must be added. Additional level indicators are then included to designate the precise grouping of all the terms to be searched.

4 level — a role indicator and the word to which it applies
5 level — a group of terms closely associated within the study
6 level — all words relating to the same study

Our complete program is as follows:

$$
6 \left\{ 5 \left[\begin{array}{c} 4 \qquad\qquad 4\ 4 \qquad\qquad 4 \\ (\text{KQJ} \cdot \text{A}) \quad\bullet\quad (\text{KEC} \cdot \text{B}) \end{array} \right] 5 \; 4\left[\begin{array}{c} \quad\quad 4 \\ \text{KIS} \cdot (\text{C} - \text{C}^1) \end{array} \right] 6 \right\}
$$

(7) *Conducting of Search.* The question program is keypunched and the question transferred to computer memory. The computer, a GE-225, compares the analytics of each document on tape with the analytics of the question and where they match, prints out the document accession number.

(8) *Delivery of Search Results.* Conventional abstracts corresponding to the accession numbers identified by the computer are pulled manually from the file and mailed to the questioner. The above is intended as an elementary summary of the structure of the system.

References and Selected Readings

American Council of Learned Societies Newsletter, June 1966 (special supplement). Published by The American Council of Learned Societies, New York, New York.

Arnovick, G. N. *A computer-processed information recording and association system.* Paper presented at the Symposium on statistical association methods for mechanized documentation, Smithsonian Institution, Washington, March 1964. Los Angeles: Planning Research Corporation, 1964.

Arnovick, G. N. *An information storage and retrieval file organization based on a second order of term inversion.* Los Angeles: Planning Research Corporation, 1964.

Barhydt, G. C. Western Reserve University computer index of educational research. In *Proceedings of the 1964 clinic on library applications of data processing.* Urbana: University of Illinois Graduate School of Library Science, 1965. Pp. 6–14.

Becker, J., and Hayes, R. M. *Introduction to information storage and retrieval: Tools, elements, theories.* New York: John Wiley (Wiley Information Science Series, Vol. 1), 1963.

Bourne, C. P. *Methods of information handling.* New York: John Wiley, 1963.

Clevenger, T., Jr., and Bowman, N. A. Research notes. *Journal of Communication,* 1964, **14,** 190–195.

Computers and the Humanities. (All issues.) Published by Queens College of The City University of New York, Flushing, New York.

Computers for the humanities? A record of the conference sponsored by Yale University on a grant from IBM, New Haven, Conn., January 1965. New Haven, Conn.: Yale University Press, 1965.

Conference on the use of computers in humanistic research. Sponsored and published by Rutgers, The State University, and the International Business Machines Corporation, New Brunswick, N.J., December 1964.

Danielson, W. A., and Bryan, S. D. Computer automation of two readability formulas. *Journalism Quarterly,* 1963, **40,** 201–206. (a)

Danielson, W. A., and Bryan, S. D. A readability analysis for card data using the Danielson-Bryan and the Farr-Jenkins-Patterson formulas. *Programming Note No. 103.* Chapel Hill: Computation Center, University of North Carolina, 1963. (b)

Danielson, W. A., and Bryan, S. D. Readability analysis program for magnetic tape data using the Danielson-Bryan formula. *Programming Note No. 104.* Chapel Hill: Computation Center, University of North Carolina, 1963. (c)

Educom. Bulletin of the Interuniversity Communications Council, 1966, **1** (8). (Entire issue devoted to computers for humanists.)

Fang, I. E. Flesch's reading ease score and a syllable counter. *Behavioral Science,* in press.

Frandsen, K. Information retrieval of communication research: Some proposals for action. *Business Communication,* 1966, **3,** 1–9.

Green, B. F., *et al.* Baseball: An automatic question-answerer. *Proceedings of the 1961 Western Joint Computer Conference.* San Francisco: New York Institute of Radio Engineers, 1961. Pp. 219–224.

Gross, B. M. Operation basic: The retrieval of wasted knowledge. *Journal of Communication,* 1962, **12,** 67–83.

Hays, D. G., Henisz-Dostert, B., and Rapp, M. L. *Computational linguistics: Bibliography, 1965.* Santa Monica, Cal.: RAND Corporation, 1966.

Hillman, D. J. *An empirical testing program for models of information storage and retrieval systems,* Final Report. Published by the Center for the Information Sciences, Lehigh University, Bethlehem, Pa., 1964.

Hillman, D. J. *Study of theories and models of information storage and retrieval,* Report No. 9. Published by the Center for the Information Sciences, Lehigh University, Bethlehem, Pa., 1964.

Holsti, O. R. A computer content analysis program for analyzing attitudes: The measurement of qualities and performance. Paper presented at the National

Conference on Content Analysis, University of Pennsylvania, Philadelphia, November 1967.

Information on scientific documentation. Supplement 2. U. S. Department of Commerce, National Bureau of Standards, Clearing House for Federal Scientific and Technical Information, January 1967.

Information systems research. Tempo, 1965, Final Report. Published by the Deacon Project, General Electric Company, Santa Barbara, Cal.

Kent, A. *Textbook on mechanized information retrieval.* New York: Interscience Publishers, 1962.

Kopstein, F. F., Gave, R. T., and Zachert, V. Preliminary evaluation of a prototype automated technical training course. *Technical Documentary Report,* No. MRL-TDR-62-78. Wright-Patterson Air Force Base, Ohio: Behavioral Sciences Laboratory, 6570th Aerospace Medical Research Laboratories, Aerospace Medical Division, Air Force Systems Command, July 1962.

Lamb, S. M. What computers may do with the printed word. *Computers for the humanities?* A record of the conference sponsored by Yale University on a grant from IBM, New Haven, Conn., January 1965. New Haven, Conn.: Yale University Press, 1965. Pp. 30–40.

Leed, J., and Vincent, H. P. (Eds.) The computer and literary style. *Kent Studies in English,* 1966, No. 2. Published by the Kent State [Ohio] University Press.

Lipete, Ben-Ami. Information storage and retrieval. In G. Piel *et al.* (Eds.), *Information.* San Francisco: W. H. Freeman, 1966. Pp. 175–192.

Luhn, H. P. The automatic creation of literature abstracts. *IBM Journal of Research and Development,* 1958, **2,** 159–165.

Nonconventional scientific and technical information systems in current use, 1966, No. 4. Published by the National Science Foundation, Washington, D.C.

Paisley, W. J., and Parker, E. B. Information retrieval as a receiver-controlled communication system. *Education for Information Science,* 1965, **1,** 23–31.

Phrase-structure oriented targeting query language. Tempo, 1965, No. 1. Published by the Deacon Project, General Electric Company, Santa Barbara, Cal.

Piel, G., *et al.* (Eds.) *Information.* San Francisco: W. H. Freeman, 1966.

Rees, A. M., and Saracevic, T. Conceptual analysis of questions in information retrieval systems. *Automation and Scientific Communication,* Part 2. Short papers, American Documentation Institute Meeting, 1963.

Sharp, H. S. Pitfalls of information retrieval. *Industrial Research,* 1961, **3,** 1–9.

The Contributors

EDMUND J. AMIDON (Ph. D. University of Minnesota, 1959), Professor of Educational Psychology at Temple University, is a staff associate of the National Training Laboratories and Chief Coordinator and Advisor for the Association for Productive Teaching. In addition to numerous articles, he has written or co-written four books. He is also coauthor and developer of several multimedia kits, tape series, and courses designed to teach Interaction Analysis and observation.

LARRY L. BARKER (Ph. D. Ohio University, 1965) is Associate Professor of Speech at The Florida State University. He has designed, directed, and taught in two USOE-NDEA Institutes. He is the coauthor of *Speech: Interpersonal communication* and coeditor of *Conceptual frontiers in speech-communication* and *Behavioral objectives and instruction*. In addition, he has contributed numerous articles to journals in speech and psychology.

SAMUEL L. BECKER (Ph. D. The University of Iowa, 1953) is Chairman of the Department of Speech and Dramatic Art at The University of Iowa. He has published numerous journal articles and is coauthor of two books, *Television: Techniques for planning and performance* and *A bibliographical guide to research in speech and dramatic art*. His major research interests include mass media, visual communication, and speech pedagogy.

RALPH R. BEHNKE (Ph. D. University of Kansas, 1966) is Assistant Professor of Speech at The Florida State University. His research in psychophysiological behaviors and their relationship to communication variables has established him as one of the leading developers of psychophysiological measuring instruments.

JOHN WAITE BOWERS (Ph. D. The University of Iowa, 1962) is Associate Professor in the Department of Speech and Dramatic Art at The University of Iowa. He has published prolifically in the journals and has contributed to Miller and Nilsen (Eds.), *Perspectives on argumentation,* and Nilsen (Ed.), *Essays on rhetorical criticism*. His *Designing the communication experiment* is forthcoming.

WILLIAM D. BROOKS (Ph. D. Ohio University, 1965) is Associate Professor of Communication at Purdue University. He has published more than 20 journal articles and been a consultant or an adviser to several educational, fund-raising, and political campaign groups, including the U.S. Office of Education and the Educational Testing Service. His research interests center on speech education and teaching communication to culturally deprived children.

THEODORE CLEVENGER, JR. (Ph. D. The Florida State University, 1958) is Chairman of the Department of Speech at The Florida State University. He has written or co-written numerous journal articles and several books, including *A strategy of oral communication and audience analysis.* He has been editor of the *Journal of Communication* and has held several offices in the Speech Association of America and the National Society for the Study of Communication.

NANCY BOYLAND COLLINS (M. A. Purdue University, 1968) was formerly an instructor at Queens College of the City University of New York. Her research has focused on nonverbal communication.

DONALD K. DARNELL (Ph. D. Michigan State University, 1964) is Associate Professor in the Department of Speech and Drama at the University of Colorado. He has published articles in the *Quarterly Journal of Speech* and the *Journal of Communication* and is currently developing an English language proficiency test for foreign students that uses a clozentropy procedure.

PHILIP EMMERT (Ph. D. Ohio University, 1965) is Assistant Professor of Speech Communication at Case Western Reserve University. He has presented papers at regional and national speech conferences and been a consultant to the City of Cleveland and the Cleveland Foundation. His current research is in attitude formation and modification, with special attention to racial attitudes and prejudices.

FRANCIS J. KELLY (Ph. D. University of Texas, 1963) is Professor of Educational Psychology at Southern Illinois University. Among his major publications are *Educational psychology: A behavioral science view* and *Research design in the behavioral sciences: Multiple regression approach.*

ROBERT J. KIBLER (Ph. D. Ohio State University, 1962), Professor of Speech at The Florida State University, is the author of numerous journal articles and coeditor of two books, *Behavioral objectives and instruction* and *Conceptual frontiers in speech-communication.* His research interests center on the relationships among cognitive, affective, and behavioral measures of speech behavior.

MERVIN D. LYNCH (Ph. D. University of Wisconsin, 1963) is Associate Professor of Educational Statistics at Northeastern University. He has recently published articles in *Journalism Quarterly, Journal of Broadcasting,* and *Journal of Communication.* Professor Lynch's research interests currently center on the quantitative analysis of language.

GERALD R. MILLER (Ph. D. University of Iowa, 1961) is Professor and Director of Graduate Studies in the Department of Communication at Michigan State University. He edited *Perspective on argumentation* and is the author of *Speech communication: A behavioral approach.* In 1967 he received an award from the Speech Association of America for outstanding scholarly publication. His major research interests are in the areas of persuasion and communication education.

W. CHARLES REDDING (Ph. D. University of Southern California, 1957) is Professor of Speech and Director of the Communication Research

Center at Purdue University. He has written numerous articles and is recognized nationally as a scholar and consultant in the area of organizational communication. He is the author of the widely used text *Business and industrial communication.*

FREDERICK WILLIAMS (Ph. D. University of Southern California, 1962) is Chairman of the Center for Communication Research in the School of Communication at the University of Texas. Dr. Williams has recently published two books: *Reasoning with statistics* and *Language and poverty: Perspectives on a theme.* His current research interests focus on psycholinguistic and sociolinguistic models of language behavior.

Index[1]

[1] This is an unorthodox index. It seemed to the editors that the purpose of an index for a book of this kind — 16 chapters by 16 authors, all using their own pet terms and approaches for the same concepts — would be tying together loose ends. Hence, for the most part, the main entries represent the basic ideas of each chapter, and the subentries show where they appear throughout the book. Extensive references and cross-references guide the user to synonymous or related concepts and terms.

Several concepts proved too global to be useful as main entries: "data," "relationships," and "selection," to name a few. However, they are included in the index as subentries where pertinent.